"This pioneering volume is the first collection of em
ies of populism at the elite and mass level, which is t
dominant ideational approach. It should be required re:
many new scholars of populism."

Cas Mudde, *Sta*

University of Georgia, USA

"This volume is sure to be a landmark in the comparative study of populism. It brings together a team of scholars who share an ideational approach to the study of populism, and it demonstrates how this approach lends itself to a wide range of methodological tools – both quantitative and qualitative – to empirically analyze populist ideas in elite political discourse and mass beliefs. In so doing, it brings much-needed analytical coherence to a field of study where scholars too often disagree on fundamental concepts and speak past one another."

Kenneth M. Roberts, *Richard J. Schwartz Professor, Cornell University, USA*

"*The Ideational Approach to Populism* is a timely and compelling book that takes seriously the ideology and appeals of populist movements. Its rigorous and compelling analyses of populism range from Latin American party manifestoes, to episodes of historical populist mobilization in Europe, to experimental evidence regarding the role of corruption as a catalyst for populist support. The result is a rich and multi-faceted volume that is a must-read for scholars of populism – and for others intrigued by the phenomenon."

Anna Grzymala-Busse, *Michelle and Kevin Douglass Professor, Political Science, Stanford, USA*

The Ideational Approach to Populism

Populism is on the rise in Europe and the Americas. Scholars increasingly understand populist forces in terms of their ideas or discourse, one that envisions a cosmic struggle between the will of the common people and a conspiring elite. In this volume, we advance populism scholarship by proposing a causal theory and methodological guidelines – a research program – based on this ideational approach. This program argues that populism exists as a set of widespread attitudes among ordinary citizens, and that these attitudes lie dormant until activated by weak democratic governance and policy failure. It offers methodological guidelines for scholars seeking to measure populist ideas and test their effects. And, to ground the program empirically, it tests this theory at multiple levels of analysis using original data on populist discourse across European and US party systems; case studies of populist forces in Europe, Latin America, and the US; survey data from Europe and Latin America; and experiments in Chile, the US, and the UK. The result is a truly systematic, comparative approach that helps answer questions about the causes and effects of populism.

Kirk A. Hawkins, Brigham Young University, USA.

Ryan E. Carlin, Georgia State University, USA.

Levente Littvay, Central European University, Hungary.

Cristóbal Rovira Kaltwasser, Universidad Diego Portales, Chile.

Routledge Studies in Extremism and Democracy

Series Editors: **Roger Eatwell**, *University of Bath*, and
Matthew Goodwin, *University of Kent.*
Founding Series Editors: Roger Eatwell, *University of Bath*, and
Cas Mudde, *University of Antwerp-UFSIA.*

www.routledge.com/politics/series/ED

This new series encompasses academic studies within the broad fields of 'extremism' and 'democracy'. These topics have traditionally been considered largely in isolation by academics. A key focus of the series, therefore, is the (inter-)*relation* between extremism and democracy. Works will seek to answer questions such as to what extent 'extremist' groups pose a major threat to democratic parties, or how democracy can respond to extremism without undermining its own democratic credentials.

The books encompass two strands:

Routledge Studies in Extremism and Democracy includes books with an introductory and broad focus which are aimed at students and teachers. These books will be available in hardback and paperback. Titles include:

Radical Right-Wing Populist Parties in Western Europe
Into the Mainstream?
Edited by Tjitske Akkerman, Sarah L. de Lange and Matthijs Rooduijn

The Populist Radical Reader
A Reader
Edited by Cas Mudde

The Far Right in America
Cas Mudde

Routledge Research in Extremism and Democracy offers a forum for innovative new research intended for a more specialist readership. These books will be in hardback only. Titles include:

42. **The Ideational Approach to Populism**
Concept, Theory and Analysis
Edited by Kirk A. Hawkins, Ryan E. Carlin, Levente Littvay, and Cristóbal Rovira Kaltwasser

43. **Fascism, Populism and American Democracy**
Leonard Weinberg

44. **Militant Democracy**
The Limits of Democratic Tolerance
Bastiaan R. Rijpkema

The Ideational Approach to Populism

Concept, Theory, and Analysis

Edited by Kirk A. Hawkins, Ryan E. Carlin, Levente Littvay, and Cristóbal Rovira Kaltwasser

Routledge
Taylor & Francis Group
LONDON AND NEW YORK

First published 2019
by Routledge
2 Park Square, Milton Park, Abingdon, Oxon OX14 4RN

and by Routledge
711 Third Avenue, New York, NY 10017

Routledge is an imprint of the Taylor & Francis Group, an informa business

British Library Cataloguing in Publication Data
A catalogue record for this book is available from the British Library

Library of Congress Cataloging in Publication Data
A catalog record has been requested for this book

ISBN: 978-1-138-71651-3 (hbk)
ISBN: 978-1-138-71653-7 (pbk)
ISBN: 978-1-315-19692-3 (ebk)

Typeset in Bembo
by Swales & Willis Ltd, Exeter, Devon, UK

To those who strive for democracy and resist polarization

Contents

Figures

Tables

Contributor biographies

Sahar Abi-Hassan is a PhD candidate at the Department of Political Science at Boston University. She holds a master's in Government and International Affairs from Virginia Tech. Her research includes the impact of political attitudes and discursive interactions on political institutional behavior. Her publications include the gender and populism chapter in the *Oxford Handbook of Populism.*

Koen Abts is a lecturer at the sociology department of Tilburg University and research fellow at the Institute of Social and Political Opinion Research (KU Leuven). He is the research coordinator of the Belgian National Election Study (BNES) and the Belgian Ethnic Minorities Election Study (BEMES). His research focuses on resentment, welfare attitudes, prejudice, populism, and Euroscepticism.

Rosario Aguilar is associate professor in political science at the Centro de Investigación y Docencia Económicas (CIDE). She specializes in political psychology and political behavior in comparative perspective. Her work has appeared in *Comparative Political Studies*, *Electoral Studies*, *Swiss Political Science Review*, and *Latin American Research Review.*

Ioannis Andreadis is an associate professor of quantitative methods in social sciences at the School of Political Sciences, Aristotle University of Thessaloniki. He is a web survey expert, designer and programmer of HelpMeVote.eu, and a member of the steering committee of the Comparative Candidate Survey. For a more detailed CV, please see: www.polres.gr/en/andreadis/.

Eva Anduiza is a professor of political science at Universitat Autònoma de Barcelona.

Flavio Azevedo is a Fulbright fellow at New York University and a PhD candidate at the Center for Comparative Politics at Cologne University. He is interested in psychological and comparative approaches investigating dispositional processes underlying ideological subscription, as well as in evaluating current practices in the measurement of ideology.

Hans-Georg Betz is currently an adjunct professor of political science, University of Zurich. He is the author of several books on radical right-wing populism in Western Europe and numerous articles and book chapters on the radical right, populism, and nativism, both past and contemporary.

Simon Bornschier directs the Research Area Political Sociology at the Institute for Political Science at the University of Zurich. His research focuses on the transformation of West European party systems, as well as on democratization, representation, and political protest in Latin America

Nebojša Blanuša teaches social and political psychology and theories of nationalism at the Faculty of Political Science, University of Zagreb, Croatia, where he is currently chair of the Department of Croatian politics. He is interested in areas and topics such as: theoretical and political psychoanalysis, discourse theory, research methods in social sciences, conspiracy theories, populism, nationalism, cultural trauma, political cynicism, historical and political cleavages, Euroscepticism, etc. He is the author of *Conspiracy Theories and Croatian Political Reality 1980–2007* (Plejada, 2011, in Croatian) and co-editor of *EU, Europe Unfinished: Mediating Europe and the Balkans in a Time of Crisis* (Rowman and Littlefield International, 2016).

Ethan C. Busby is an assistant professor at Clemson University. He specializes in political psychology, experimental methods, and the politics of extremism.

Ryan E. Carlin is an associate professor of political science and director of the Center for Human Rights and Democracy at Georgia State University. His research interests are comparative political behavior and public opinion, with a regional emphasis on Latin America. His work has been funded by the National Science Foundation, USAID, the Mellon and Ford Foundations, and the Latin American Studies Association. He is co-editor of *The Latin American Voter* (University of Michigan Press, forthcoming) and his work has appeared in many academic journals.

Gisela Delfino has a psychology PhD (University of Buenos Aires) and is a professor and associate researcher at the Psychology and Psychopedagogy Research Center (CIPP), Argentine Catholic University (UCA) – National Scientific and Technical Research Council (CONICET), Buenos Aires, Argentina.

David Doyle is an associate professor of politics at the University of Oxford and a Fellow of St Hugh's College. His work is primarily concerned with the political economy of Latin America. Currently, he is focusing on two large projects: the first on tax compliance and the social contract and the second on the political effects of remittances and migration.

Margarita Gómez-Reino is an associate professor of political science at the Department of Política Science and Administration at Universidad Nacional de Educación a Distancia (Spain). She is the author of *Nationalisms in the European Arena. Trajectories of Transnational Party Coordination* (Palgrave Macmillan, 2017).

Marijana Grbeša is an associate professor at the Faculty of Political Science, University of Zagreb. She teaches courses in political marketing, media research methods, media and the public and pop politics. She has published a number of articles and book chapters dealing with political communication and the media. She was the head of the Journalism Department and the Vice-Dean for Science and International Relations at the Faculty of Political Science, University of Zagreb.

Kirk A. Hawkins is an associate professor in the Department of Political Science at Brigham Young University in Provo, Utah. He studies Latin American politics and political organization. He was first drawn to populism by his studies of Hugo Chávez's movement in Venezuela.

Thierry Kochuyt holds a PhD in social sciences from the KULeuven and has been lecturing as a freelance academic in Lebanon (USJ, ESA), Belgium (KUB, KULeuven), the UAE (Leicester University, Nottingham Trent University, HCT), and Bulgaria (NBU, AUB, ESFAM). He has published in *Sociological Review*, *Revue Tiers Monde*,

Social Compass, and *Journal of Ethnic and Migration Studies*. Recently, with Koen Abts he released "Ongehoord Populisme" on which his chapter is partly based.

Levente Littvay researches survey and quantitative methodology, behavior genetics and socialization using twin and family studies, and the psychology of radicalism and populism. He has secured close to a million dollars in grants for his research and is an award-winning teacher of graduate courses in research design, applied statistics, electoral politics, voting behavior, political psychology, and American politics. He is an academic co-convener of ECPR's Methods Schools, Team Populism's head of Team Survey and an associate editor of *Twin Research and Human Genetics*.

Iván Llamazares is a professor of political science at the University of Salamanca. He coordinates the research project Economic Crisis and New Parties funded by the Spanish Ministry for the Economy and Competitiveness (Research Grant CSO2013-47667-P).

Luke March is a professor of post-soviet and comparative politics at the University of Edinburgh. His main research interests include the politics of the European (radical) Left, Russian politics, populism, radicalism and extremism in Europe and the former Soviet Union. He has published in a range of journals including *Party Politics*, *Comparative European Politics*, *Europe–Asia Studies* and *East European Politics*. His books include *Radical Left Parties in Europe* (Routledge, 2011), and *Europe's Radical Left: From Marginality to the Mainstream?* (edited with Daniel Keith, Rowman and Littlefield 2016).

Jennifer McCoy is distinguished university professor of political science at Georgia State University and author of *International Mediation in Venezuela*. She is a specialist in polarization and democratic erosion, mediation and conflict, and electoral processes and election observation

Yazmin Morlet Corti is a PhD candidate in politics. Her focus is on comparing online user privacy behaviors between cultures from an interdisciplinary perspective through game simulation She holds a MA in Political Science from CEU in Budapest and a BA in Communication Sciences and Political Communication from UNAM in Mexico.

Wendy Rahn is a professor of political science at the University of Minnesota. Among other things, she has served during her career as co-editor of the journal *Political Psychology*, and as a member of the Board of Overseers of the American National Election Studies. Her research interests include political attitudes and behavior, food and health politics, and American political history.

Guillem Rico is 'Ramón y Cajal' research fellow at the Department of Political Science, Universitat Autònoma de Barcelona. His research interests include political attitudes and behavior, public opinion, political socialization, political leadership, and populism. He has published in journals such as *Political Behavior*, *Political Psychology*, and *Electoral Studies*.

Cristóbal Rovira Kaltwasser (PhD, Humboldt University of Berlin) is a professor of political science at Diego Portales University in Santiago de Chile. Before joining Diego Portales University, he was a Marie-Curie Research Fellow at the University of Sussex in the UK and a postdoctoral fellow at the Social Science Research Center Berlin (WZB) in Germany. He is the author (together with Cas Mudde) of *Populism: A Very Short Introduction* (Oxford University Press, 2017) and the editor (together with Paul Taggart, Paulina Ochoa Espejo, and Pierre Ostiguy) of *The Oxford Handbook of Populism* (Oxford University Press, 2017). He has published articles in *Comparative*

European Politics, *Democratization*, *Government & Opposition*, *Latin American Research Review*, and *Party Politics and Political Studies* among others.

Saskia P. Ruth-Lovell is a research fellow at the German Institute of Global and Area Studies (GIGA). Her research interest lies in comparative politics, clientelism, populism and Latin American studies. More specifically, she focuses on the consequences of different political mobilization strategies on the quality of democratic governance in Latin America. She has published articles in *The Journal of Politics*, *Latin American Politics*, and *Society and Political Studies*.

Berto Šalaj is an associate professor at the Faculty of Political Science, Zagreb University. He has a BA, MA, and PhD in political science. He is currently teaching courses in Political Socialization and Political Education, Democracy and Civil Society and Social Capital and Civil Society in Southeastern Europe. He has published a number of articles on political culture, social capital, democracy and populism.

Christian H. Schimpf is a PhD candidate in political science at the Graduate School of Economics and Social Sciences at the University of Mannheim. He is also a data processing specialist with the Comparative Study of Electoral Systems (CSES) Secretariat at the GESIS Leibniz Institute for the Social Sciences, Mannheim. His research interests include comparative political behavior, populism and public opinion. His research has been published in *Political Studies*, *Politics and Governance*, and the *Zeitschrift für Vergleichende Politikwissenschaft*.

Matthew M. Singer is an associate professor of political science at the University of Connecticut, his research focuses on Latin America. His research interests include public opinion and voting behavior, with an emphasis on how voters seek to hold politicians accountable for their actions. Singer is the co-editor of *The Latin American Voter: Pursuing Representation and Accountability in Challenging Contexts* and author of articles published in the *Journal of Politics*, *British Journal of Political Studies*, *Comparative Politics*, *Comparative Political Studies*, *European Journal of Political Research*, and *Electoral Studies*, among other journals. He holds a PhD from Duke University.

Bruno Castanho Silva is a postdoctoral researcher at the Cologne Center for Comparative Politics (CCCP), University of Cologne. His research interests are on quantitative methods, causal inference, and populism.

Bram Spruyt is associate professor of sociology at the Vrije Universiteit Brussel (Belgium) and member of the Research group TOR. His main research interests include the study of public opinion, cultural sociology, and the sociology of education.

Marco Steenbergen holds the Chair of Political Methodology at the University of Zurich and is an affiliated faculty member in the political psychology program of UC Irvine. His research interests include social statistics, the political psychology of electoral behavior and public opinion, political parties, and political representation.

Steven M. Van Hauwaert is an Alexander von Humboldt fellow at the University of Mainz and the principal investigator of the Global Public Opinions Project (GPOP). His primary research interests are in the field of comparative political behavior and public opinion, as well as populism and political extremism. Currently, his academic contributions have appeared, or are forthcoming, in a number of edited volumes and the journals *Acta Politica*, *Comparative European Politics*, *Electoral Studies*, *European Journal* *of Political Research, European Societies*, (GPOP). His primary research interests are in the field of comparative political behavior and public opinion, as well as populism and political extremism. Currently, his academic contributions have appeared, or are forthcoming, in a number of edited volumes and the journals *Acta Politica, Comparative European Politics, Electoral Studies, European Journal of Political Research, European Societies*, and *Journal of Public Integration*. He is also an associate editor of the ECPR journal *Political Research Exchange* (PRX).

Stijn van Kessel is a lecturer in European politics at Queen Mary University of London. His main research interests are populism, Euroscepticism, and the positions, voters, and electoral performance of populist parties in Europe. He authored the monograph *Populist Parties in Europe: Agents of Discontent* (Palgrave Macmillan, 2015) and published articles in journals including *European Journal of Political Research*, *Journal of European Integration*, *Journal of Political Ideologies*, *Acta Politica*, and *Government and Opposition*.

Nina Wiesehomeier is an assistant professor at IE University, School of International Relations. Her research interests revolve around executives, ideology and issues of political representation, political preferences, and political behavior.

Preface

Team Populism had its beginnings in spring 2014 when a few of us met at the Midwest Political Science Association conference to talk about collaborative research on populism. Interest in populism was growing, and better empirical and theoretical tools were now available. There also seemed to be greater conceptual clarity, with scholars gravitating towards a few, discrete definitions, many of which took populist ideas as their core feature. Yet the study of populism left much to be desired. Causal arguments were a relatively new focus, and the few available explanations were regionally specific and unpersuasive. Many supposedly empirical studies of populism were based on the impressions of the authors, with no independent measures of populism and few attempts at cross-regional comparison. Most scholars continued to work in their own regions, unaware of methodological and empirical developments elsewhere. We sensed an opportunity to do more than just write a few co-authored papers. Instead, we decided to create a multi-year, coordinated, scientific effort to identify the causes of populism.

Since our first official meeting later that year at the ECPR general conference in Glasgow, our mission has become clearer and our team larger. Team Populism now brings together scholars from across the globe to systematically study the causes (and consequences, a more recent addition) of populism. This means that we try to explain why populist leaders, movements and parties are more electorally successful in some countries than others. We do so by studying multiple levels of analysis, and we draw on different methodological tools, including experiments, surveys, comparative analysis, and case studies. Above all, we gain comparative perspective by coordinating our research across countries and regions.

Team Populism is organized as a large-scale scientific collaboration. We have a division of labor, with individual teams pursuing methodologically oriented tasks; we engage in small-scale analyses, but also create and analyze data across regions; we convene conferences and workshops; and we apply for funding. We are motivated by the belief that we can do more as a team, not just because of the economies of scale in collecting and analyzing data, but because of the cross-fertilization of ideas that happens when groups of people collaborate. We intend for our work to be scientific, in the best spirit of the term. We work honestly and openly, comparing others' theories and methods to our own, and sharing contradictory findings.

Team Populism is also distinguished by its policy emphasis. Although we are all social scientists by training and temperament, we want to make a difference with our work. Populism has an enormous impact on democracy, the content of government policy, and social unity; all of us decided to study it because of how it affected our lives. Wherever possible, we choose research questions that are more likely to produce answers for policy stakeholders, and we make these policy implications explicit (a sample of which is in the concluding chapter).

Over the past three years Team Populism has implemented these principles in a series of highly productive conferences, workshops and panels. These events have allowed us to outline a conceptual, theoretical and methodological framework that we term the *ideational approach* to the study of populism. Along the way we have accumulated a trove of research, including raw data, new methods, and findings. We needed a venue to showcase all these products, many of which would be better understood together. It became clear that the best way of communicating all of this was through a coordinated volume. This would be more than just another edited volume highlighting new frontiers in the study of populism, but a unified statement of Team Populism's vision for scholarship. This book is the product of that effort.

We thank many people and organizations that have helped us along the way. ECPR sponsored some of our most productive meetings, including conferences or workshops in Glasgow, Nijmegen, and Pisa. We thank the administrators, especially Marcia Taylor, for their assistance. The Wheatley Institution at Brigham Young University provided much of funding for the London and Provo conferences, as well as administrative assistance for the Provo conference; they were instrumental in creating this volume. We are especially grateful to Richard Williams, Emily Reynolds, and their staff for their help. At the London conference, the staff at the BYU London Centre were especially generous with their time, including Jim Faulconer and Alvaro Magalhães; we also give special thanks to the Institute of Latin American Studies at the University of London, which provided one of our venues. The joint University of Utah-BYU National Resource Center for Latin American Studies generously supported the Provo conference (as well as a few discussants); we especially thank Claudio Holzner, Sam Handlin, Kit Lund, and Jeff Shumway. The BYU David M. Kennedy Center for International Studies helped us fund and advertise the London and Provo conferences, and we particularly acknowledge Kirk Larsen and Lynn Elliott for their support. Central European University provided most of the support for our Summer University course in Budapest. We are especially grateful to Eva Barbara Bodogan, Eva Gedeon, Sarolta Szabo, and Kornelia Vargha for admin support, and Federico Vegetti, Martin Molder, Sara Kende, and Sharon Belli for academic support. The International Society for Political Psychology partially funded our Summer University course and allowed us to sponsor a panel at the Warsaw meetings; we are especially grateful to Severine Bennett and members of the selection committees. At Georgia State University, the Center for Latin American and Latino Studies provided research support and travel funding. We also acknowledge support from Universidad Diego Portales, the Chilean Fund for Scientific and Technological Development (FONDECYT project 1180020) and the Center for Social Conflict and Cohesion Studies (COES, CONICYT/FONDAP/15130009). Last but not least, the BYU College of Family, Home and Social Sciences and the BYU Department of Political Science funded many of the administrative costs of Team Populism and portions of the London and Provo conferences, as well as an authors' conference in Washington, DC. We especially thank the department chair, Sven Wilson, for his persistent support of our project.

Individual acknowledgments by authors appear in specific chapters. However, many other individuals helped directly in the preparation of this book. We thank Rebecca Dudley and McKinney Voss for being such able assistants: reaching out to authors, compiling the text, and generally helping us stay organized. We thank Eliza Tanner Hawkins for reading over significant portions of the manuscript. We are grateful to Craig Fowlie at Taylor and Francis for helping us see the volume through, and also to Emma Chappell, Richard Skipper, and Rebecca McPhee at Routledge for their editorial assistance. We are very glad that Roger Eatwell and Matthew Goodwin saw promise in the volume and were willing to include it in the *Extremism and Democracy* Series. Last but not least, we thank the anonymous reviewers of our prospectus and manuscript, whose generous but forthright comments greatly improved the text.

Chapters in the volume have benefitted from specific grants. Work on the introduction and conclusion by Rovira Kaltwasser was supported by the Chilean Fund for Scientific and Technological Development (FONDECYT project 1180020), the Chilean Millennium Science Initiative (project NS130008) and the Center for Social Conflict and Cohesion Studies (COES, CONICYT/FONDAP/15130009). In the chapter by March, the University of Edinburgh Strategic Research Support Fund helped finance the data collection. Grbeša and Šalaj's chapter was partly funded by the University of Zagreb and its Faculty of Political Science. The chapter by Castanho Silva et al. was supported by a small grant from Central European University under its Research Support Scheme. Bornschier's chapter benefited from funding by the Swiss National Science Foundation (Grant 100017_149531). The chapter by Andreadis et al. received funding from University of Connecticut's Research Excellence Program, Chilean Millennium Science Initiative (project NS130008), Chilean National Fund for Scientific and Technological Development (FONDECYT project 1140101) and Spanish Ministry for the Economy and Competitiveness (Research Grant CSO2013-47667-P). The chapter by Gómez-Reino and Llamazares also benefitted from Spanish Ministry for the Economy and Competitiveness (Research Grant CSO2013-47667-P). The chapter by Busby et al. was supported by a grant from the John Fell Fund at Oxford University (Project 133/012) and internal research funding from Swansea University. And the chapter by Aguilar and Carlin was supported by a Professional Development Grant from the Center for Latin American and Latino Studies at Georgia State University.

No chapter in this book is an entire reprint of material elsewhere, but portions of some chapters draw on previously published materials. An early version of the Introduction can be found in the Hawkins, K., Read, M. and Pauwels, T. (forthcoming) "Populism and its Causes," *Oxford Handbook on Populism*, eds. Cristóbal Rovira Kaltwasser, Paul Taggart, Paulina Ochoa-Espejo, and Pierre Ostiguy (Oxford: Oxford University Press). Chapter 2 draws heavily on Luke March, "Left and right populism compared: The British case," *The British Journal of Politics and International Relations*, Vol 19, Issue 2, pp. 282–303. Some research results reported in Grbeša and Šalaj's chapter appear in the article by Grbeša, M. and Šalaj, B. (2016) "Textual Analysis of Populist Discourse in 2014/2015 Presidential Election in Croatia." *Contemporary Southeastern Europe* 3(1): 106–127. In the chapter by Andreadis and Ruth-Lovell, earlier versions of the part of this chapter referring to Greek candidates are based on Stavrakakis, Y., Andreadis, I., and Katsambekis, G. (2016) "A new populism index at work: identifying populist candidates and parties in the contemporary Greek context." *European Politics and Society*. A short memo based on the findings of Castanho Silva et al. was published on the Team Populism website. Portions of the chapter by Abi-Hassan were published in Abi-Hassan, S. (2015). Some of the vote-choice analyses of Chile and Greece in Chapter 10 are forthcoming in Hawkins, K., Rovira Kaltwasser, C., and Andreadis, I. "The Activation of Populist Attitudes." *Government & Opposition*. "Populist Discourse and the Remarking of the Political Opposition in Venezuela." *Uruguayan Journal of Political Science* 24(2) 29–48. An extended version of the chapter by Abts, Kochuyt and van Kessel will be published in Dutch as a book entitled *Ongehoord Populisme. Gesprekken met Vlaams Belang-kiezers over stad, migranten, welvaartsstaat, integratie en politiek* (Brussels: Academic & Scientific Publishers). In the chapter by Carlin and Aguilar, a portion of the findings from the case selection section (the results of the polls from the Centro de Estudios Públicos (CEP) in Figure 17.1) appeared in an article by these authors in the 2017 special issue of *Swiss Political Science Review*.

The study of populism will continue to evolve. In Team Populism, we have already moved from our focus on methodological tools and a theoretical framework to applying these tools and testing the theory. Many of us are now exploring the consequences of populism, especially in terms of its psychology, and how societies polarized by populist forces can overcome their divisions. We expect that additional refinements in method and theory come along the way. We hope this volume serves as a touchstone for that research, not only as a source of conceptual, theoretical, and methodological tools, but also an example of what social scientists are capable of doing when they coordinate their best work.

Introduction

The ideational approach

Kirk A. Hawkins and Cristóbal Rovira Kaltwasser

Academics and pundits alike were shocked on the morning of June 24, 2016, when the result of the so-called Brexit referendum was announced: approximately 52% of the British electorate had voted in favor of leaving the European Union. A similar shock was felt on November 9, 2016, when media outlets around the world announced that Donald Trump had won the US presidential election. Part of the shock came because commentators had gotten the poll numbers wrong—most 11th-hour estimates showed Brexit losing and Hillary Clinton winning (Atanasov and Joseph 2016; Cillizza 2016; Hanretty 2016). But it also came because voters had endorsed radical options with potentially severe consequences. These included (depending on the country) doing away with free trade and the free movement of labor, the targeting of immigrants based on religion, and withdrawing from NATO. Why would voters in two of the wealthiest and most established democracies approve policies that could undermine key domestic institutions, not to mention the postwar global system upon which capitalism and democracy had flourished?

The answer from many commentators was that these movements were *populist*. The victory of the "leave" option in the Brexit referendum and of Donald Trump in the US election manifested a deep mistrust of the voting public against the establishment and an increasing demand to respect the will of the people at all cost. This outlook was reflected in the content of the candidates' messages as well as their form—Trump's impolite language and repetition of popular conspiracy theories, for example, or emotional arguments about immigration in both countries (Kazin 2016). Furthermore, these campaigns were connected to radical populist forces making headway in other regions in recent years, such as Chavismo in Venezuela, Viktor Orbán in Hungary, Podemos in Spain and the Front National in France (Calamur 2016; Carroll 2016; Wofford 2016). Although Trump or Brexit supporters had different issue positions from some of these other groups, they all used similar language claiming that democracy was being subverted by political and economic elites, a language that encouraged ordinary citizens to band together and reclaim control of the political system. By implication, supporters of these groups were motivated by similar causes.

Labeling these and similar movements "populist" feels satisfying, perhaps because in ordinary language the word is a pejorative to describe organizations and ideas that we think are demagogic. If used in some of the more technical ways we describe below, it is even accurate. But by itself the label doesn't answer the question of why people voted for these politicians and proposals. Indeed, commentators using the label offered a variety of explanations for the causes of Trump's victory or the Brexit vote. These included the fallout from the Eurozone crisis or the bailout in the US (Lee 2016; Whitehouse 2016); widespread anger over the negative impact of economic globalization (Sides and Tesler 2016); an authoritarian backlash against secular progressive values (Inglehart and Norris

2016); or a self-reinforcing cycle of party fragmentation (Friedman 2017). While each of these arguments contained important insights, most of them were highly specific, explaining populist forces in only certain countries or regions. After all, explanations based on the Great Recession or a cultural clash over secular progressive values could not explain the resurgence of left-populism in Latin America in the 2000s, let alone Gaitanismo in Colombia of the 1940s, or the People's Party in the US of the 1890s. None of these arguments were generalizable to populist forces across the globe, and most of them failed to speak to the actual populist content of these parties and movements, in the sense of a message about some cosmic struggle between the people and the elite.

The lack of a clear answer should not surprise us, until recently, scholars who studied populism could have not provided a good one either. Research on populism traces its roots to the 1960s, but these early accounts were not helpful at explaining populism's reemergence over succeeding decades. Scholars looked for explanations in highly specific historical and economic conditions, such as policies of import-substituting industrialization and the challenge of late modernization. But in the 1990s as populist forces reappeared in neoliberal versions in Latin America, it became evident that populism could not be limited to a particular set of economic policies (Roberts 1995; Weyland 1999). And when populist forces made headway in Western Europe in the 2000s, it no longer made sense to explain these as products of delayed industrialization and urbanization (Betz 1994; Kitschelt 1997). Populists came in a variety of ideological stripes and responded to diverse historical conditions, making it difficult to determine if they had some kind of common causality.

In response to these anomalies, and driven by the recent (re)emergence of populist forces, scholars have begun to study populism with a very different focus: populism's ideas. These scholars argue that the common discourse of populist parties and movements reveals a shared way of seeing the political world: as a Manichean struggle between the will of the common people and an evil, conspiring elite. They argue that these ideas, expressed in the rhetoric of leaders and supporters, have a real impact on politicians' behavior in office and the resultant policies. Moreover, these ideas are one of the main factors motivating people to mobilize and support populist forces. We call this the *ideational approach* to populism.

To be clear, early work on populism often talked about populist ideas. In fact, almost every scholarly approach to populism has in some way acknowledged the unique, anti-establishment, pro-people rhetoric of populist forces. This includes earlier studies by economists and sociologists (Di Tella 1965; Dornbusch and Edwards 1991; Germani 1978; Ionescu and Gellner 1969). But these early works gave little attention to the content and causal properties of these ideas, and they did not see these ideas as the key feature of populist forces. The new ideational approach distinguishes itself through its focus. According to this approach, populist ideas are the distinguishing feature of these parties and movements. While many of the material or organizations features we sometimes associate with populism—such as charismatic leadership or a certain profile of economic policies—are real and matter for the electoral success of populist forces, they are contingent on historical or regional context and may even be a product of these underlying ideas.

Putting ideas at the center of the definition is a crucial step towards understanding populism's causes. But it is only the first step. Some early studies that used the ideational approach provided unsatisfying causal arguments because, although they defined populist forces by their ideas, they continued to explain the emergence and electoral success of these forces largely in terms of material factors or other aspects of culture that were regionally or temporally specific (Hawkins 2003; Ivarsflaten 2008; Oesch 2008; Van der Brug, Fennema, and Tillie 2005). While these theories offered important pieces of the explanation for specific parties and movements, they were not fully ideational because they did not explain what makes populist ideas an important part of these politicians' appeal, or how these ideas might operate in the mind of voters. In fact, many studies that invoked an ideational approach did not actually measure the populist rhetoric of their politicians or the populist ideas of their voters, drawing instead on proxy measures such as issue stances or the outsider status of party leaders.

To move the field forward and better answer questions about the emergence of populist forces, this volume develops the ideational definition into a true approach. By this, we mean a full-blown research program that includes a causal framework and methodological prescriptions. Building an approach requires framing a causal argument that takes populist ideas as its starting point, one that develops causal mechanisms connecting citizens' cognition to politicians' rhetoric, and linking individual-level attributes to aggregate outcomes for party systems and countries. It also means specifying the implications of this argument for methodological issues, including the most appropriate tools for measuring populism and testing our hypotheses. And ideally, it is constructed in such a way that it provides policy recommendations for key stakeholders.

In the remainder of this introductory chapter we lay out the basic framework. We start by presenting the ideational definition of populism. After this, we elaborate our theoretical framework, which brings in the notion of populist attitudes and their activation. We follow by showing the implications of the theory for measurement and method. At the end of the chapter, we summarize the individual contributions in the rest of the volume.

The ideational definition

It is common wisdom that populism is a contested concept among scholars. Some definitions stress organizational features such as strong leadership and top-down mobilization (e.g., Weyland 2001); others emphasize economic aspects such as unsustainable policies in favor of wealth redistribution (e.g., Acemoglu, Egorov, and Sonin 2013) or discursive elements, such as a moral and Manichean language that pits the people against the elite (e.g., Mudde 2004). Although this conceptual battle is far from over, a growing number of academics use the ideational approach. In this view, populism is best conceived in minimal terms as a unique set of ideas, one that understands politics as a Manichean struggle between a reified will of the people and a conspiring elite (Hawkins 2009, 2010).

The ideational definition of populism has three main parts: a) a Manichean and moral cosmology; b) the proclamation of 'the people' as a homogenous and virtuous community; and c) the depiction of 'the elite' as a corrupt and self-serving entity. In other words, something is defined as "populist" if it has all three of these conditions. So, one cannot categorize a particular discourse as populist solely on the basis of anti-establishment rhetoric or purely on references to "the people" as a political body that is morally superior. The peculiarity of the populist set of ideas lies precisely in the combination of these elements (Mudde and Rovira Kaltwasser 2013). This means that populism is a moral discourse that not only exalts popular sovereignty, but understands the political field as a cosmic struggle between "the people" and "the elite."

The classic work of Sartori (1970) suggests that in order to understand the singularity of any phenomenon it is important to distinguish its opposites. When it comes to populism, the clearest two are elitism and pluralism. Elitism can be thought of as a discourse that inverts the morality of the terms 'the people' and 'the elite': it depicts the former as a dangerous mob that cannot think rationally, and portrays the latter as a minority that because of its intellectual and moral superiority should be in charge of the government. There is no better example of this set of ideas than technocratic thinking, which mistrusts the wisdom of the masses and has blind faith in the judgment of experts (Caramani 2017). On the other hand, pluralism views society as a complex ensemble of individuals and groups with different opinions. Therefore, it is skeptical about both the existence of a general will of "the people" and the alleged superiority of "the elite." Instead of advancing a Manichean language, it favors the presence of diversity within society and maintains that politics is about reaching agreements between different sectors. This is why pluralists are inclined to conceive of popular sovereignty as an open-ended process rather than the realization of a self-evident will of the people (Ochoa Espejo 2011).

Populism, elitism, and pluralism differ fundamentally from classical ideologies such as conservatism, liberalism, and socialism. The latter are complex, consciously articulated sets of ideas that offer a wide-ranging map of the political and social world. As Michael Freeden (2003, 78) indicated, ideologies should be thought of as inclusive networks of ideas offering solutions to all the important political issues confronting a society. In contrast, populism is a much simpler set of ideas that usually appears in combination with these other worldviews. Not surprisingly, populism has a chameleonic nature: depending on the context of its emergence, it adopts different ideological shapes (Taggart 2000). This is why one can identify varieties of populism from the left, right, and some would argue, center. The formation of these different ideological shapes is related to the social grievances that are most relevant in each society and subsequently politicized by populist forces, each of which provides particular understandings of who belongs to "the people" and "the elite" (Mudde and Rovira Kaltwasser 2017, 21–22).

Within the group of scholars who define populism as a set of ideas, there are some subtle, but often important, differences among those who see populism as a discourse or as an ideology.[1] The first option has been defended vigorously by Ernesto Laclau and his followers, who are prone to develop a *normative* theoretical framework. This perspective is based on a fundamental critique of the economic reductionism inherent to Marxism and the intent to develop a post-structuralist school of thought, according to which political identities are created through discursive practices. Therefore populism should be seen as an attempt to generate a new hegemonic order that pits "the people" against "the elite" (Laclau 2005). However, some scholars also use the notion of discourse in a more positivist fashion, seeking to empirically assess the presence of populist claims and the degree of populism in different discourses (Bonikowski and Gidron 2016; Deegan-Krause and Haughton 2009; Hawkins 2009). Seen in this light, populism is a rhetorical style or political frame predicated on the fundamental conflict between "the people" and "the elite" (Aslanidis 2016; Moffitt 2016). Moreover, this political style is not necessarily stable over time as there is important variation in the presence of populist claims in different settings; thus, political actors do not always exhibit the same levels of populism.[2]

The second option was championed by Cas Mudde, who defined populism as a "thin-centered ideology," one that "considers society to be ultimately separated into two homogenous and antagonistic groups, 'the pure people' and 'the corrupt elite', and which argues that politics should be an expression of the *volonté générale* (general will) of the people" (Mudde 2004, 543). The term "thin-centered ideology" was coined by Michael Freeden (1996) to analyze ideologies that rely on a limited number of core concepts and thus have limited programmatic scope. Because thin-centered ideologies are often attached to other worldviews, the term is a useful way of theorizing about populism's tendency to combine with other sets of ideas. In fact, scholars in this group identify subtypes of populism such as exclusionary populism, which usually combines populism with nativist interpretations of nationalism, and inclusionary populism, which links populism with some form of socialism (Mudde and Rovira Kaltwasser 2013).[3]

For most people, though, the differences between those who understand populism as a discourse or a thin-centered ideology are very slight. After all, both options assume that populism is a type of ideas that is distinct from a classical ideology, in that it is not the product of conscious elaboration and tends to have low programmatic scope. Likewise, scholars in both groups argue that populist forces can be found on all sides of the political spectrum, and that populism usually maintains a difficult relationship with liberal democracy. Given this, we use the notions of "discourse," "frame," "thin-centered ideology" and "worldview" somewhat interchangeably throughout the volume.

A question that sometimes emerges among ideational scholars, as well as their critics, is whether populism refers only to ideas in the abstract or if it refers to the people or groups that embody and act on them. This is an important theoretical distinction, one that we and others capture with terms such as "activation" and "mobilization"; we do not presume that populist ideas automatically translate into action (cf. Jansen 2011). In practice, though, ideational scholars use "populism" to refer to ideas, actions, and agents, with the understanding that the latter only count as populist if they come packaged in populist ideas. A related question is whether we should treat populism as a dichotomous, either–or affair, in which individuals and groups are either populist or not. While some scholars make strong arguments about populism's modality—that it requires a qualitative, wholesale shift in rhetoric preventing the coexistence of populist and non-populist ideas—the theory we adopt in the next section allows for multiple sets of competing ideas in an individual's thinking, and hence in what they express at any given moment. Populism in the ideational sense is better conceived as a continuous variable. That said, throughout this volume we frequently adopt the shorthand of referring to "populist parties" or "populist voters" without specifying hard and fast thresholds.

As a point of reference, there are several other alternative definitions of populism in the academic literature. Besides the ideational approach, there are three other prominent conceptualizations: structuralist, economic, and political–strategic. Because ideational studies often draw insights from these other conceptualizations, they are worth briefly mentioning.

Scholars initially advanced a structuralist understanding of populism to analyze the emergence of leaders such as Juan Domingo Perón in Argentina and Getúlio Vargas in Brazil. According to this approach, populism is a specific regime type controlled by strong leaders who build heterogeneous class alliances favoring excluded sectors through the implementation of a state-led economic model (Cardoso and Faletto 1979; Germani 1978). Defined this way, populism is the result of abrupt processes of modernization, which by generating societal dislocations, facilitate the formation of "orphaned masses" that can be easily mobilized by charismatic leaders (Oxhorn 1998). This conceptualization was useful for analyzing populism in Latin American during the 1940s and 1950s, but didn't work as well with later waves of populism in the region, or when faced with the emergence of populist forces in other places of the world. In addition, the structuralist approach puts too much emphasis on the existence of heterogeneous class alliances, overlooking the fact that this is a key characteristic of catch-all parties and social movements that are not necessarily populist. Finally, given that the structuralist approach defines populism as a type of political regime, it does not allow for the analysis of populist forces that are not in power.

Economic definitions of populism focus on the type of policies that populist forces seek to implement. The most influential work is the book by Dornbusch and Edwards, which conceptualizes populism as "an approach to economics that emphasizes growth and income distribution and deemphasizes the risks of inflation and deficit finance" (Dornbusch and Edwards 1991, 9). Daron Acemoglu and his colleagues offer an alternative economic definition that conceives of populism as "the implementation of policies receiving support from a significant fraction of the population, but ultimately hurting the economic interests of this majority" (Acemoglu, Egorov, and Sonin 2013, 2). Thus, populism is first and foremost a bundle of unsustainable—though popular—economic policies that might generate some benefits in the short run, but are damaging in the long run. Economic approaches have two main limitations. First, they emphasize consequences of populism without offering a clear conceptualization of the phenomenon. Second, they focus unduly on leftist versions of populism while overlooking rightist variants that promote neoliberal reforms, such as Ross Perot in the US or Alberto Fujimori in Peru.

The third conceptual camp is political–strategic. Kurt Weyland best articulates this approach by defining populism as "a political strategy through which a personalist leader seeks or exercises government power based on direct, unmediated, uninstitutionalized support from large numbers of mostly unorganized followers" (Weyland 2001, 14). The political–strategic conceptualization does not focus on the type of policies populist forces prefer or their outcomes; thus, it can accommodate both leftist and rightist subtypes of populism. However, the excessive focus on leadership renders this concept unsuitable for analyzing institutionalized political parties or grassroots social movements that employ populist ideas (Mudde and Rovira Kaltwasser 2017). Moreover, the political–strategic approach does not offer a set of reasons why ordinary people might, under certain circumstances, become fervent populists.

The ideational approach to populism offers a productive way to think about and study populism. It overcomes deficiencies seen in other conceptualizations, and allows scholars to analyze not only the supply- but also the demand-side of the populist phenomenon.

The ideational theory

Concepts are most useful when they are attached to a theory, in the sense of a causal argument. Good concepts repackage reality in ways that make causal connections clearer, thereby providing "theoretical utility" (Gerring 1999). If ideas are the core of populism, it follows that they have some independent causal power with measurable effects. These effects should be visible at different levels of analysis, and should operate across time periods and countries. They should also interact sensibly with other political ideas, such as traditional political ideologies.

Populist attitudes

We start our ideational theory at the individual level with the concept of populist attitudes. Survey research suggests that populist ideas at the mass level can be conceived as a set of beliefs that are widespread across citizens in Europe and the Americas (Akkerman, Mudde, and Zaslove 2014; Elchardus and Spruyt 2016; Hawkins, Riding, and Mudde

2012; Hawkins, Rovira Kaltwasser, and Andreadis forthcoming; Van Hauwaert and Van Kessel 2018). While there is predictable variation in these beliefs across different national populations (e.g., in terms of age, gender, and education), most citizens agree at least moderately with populist statements about the nature of the people, the elite, and the fundamental conflict between them. Furthermore, responses to these statements cohere sensibly and are distinct from responses associated with other political discourses, such as pluralism and elitism, as well as measures of traditional ideologies such as liberalism and conservatism.

However, these survey data also highlight a puzzle. Citizens in most countries do not generally view their traditional politicians as a conspiring elite, band together in broad coalitions that overlook their distinct interests, and vote for candidates propounding a populist message. Even in countries where populist forces are the most electorally successful, they only periodically win control of government (Hawkins and Rovira Kaltwasser 2017a; see also Chapter 1 by Hawkins and Silva). Thus, populist attitudes do not consistently track with support for populist forces.

The way to solve this puzzle is by rethinking the nature of populist ideas. In certain respects, populist ideas at the level of ordinary citizens are not a true attitude: they are not consciously held in the same way as, say, someone's views on abortion or pension reform. This is why we have insisted that they are not a full ideology in the classical sense. At the same time, populist ideas are not reducible to a personality trait. They are more consciously articulated and politically specific, invoking at least some programmatic content concerning the appropriate nature of democracy.

Thus, we argue that populist attitudes function as a latent demand or a *disposition*. This is a common concept from the attitudinal and trait literature in psychology, which recognizes that many attitudes captured in survey instruments are not always fully expressed. Instead, they must be activated by an appropriate context and by linguistic and emotional cues (e.g., Chanley 1994; Tett and Guterman 2000; Cesario et al. 2010). Populist ideas behave much the same way. While a subset of individuals in any population is likely to apply their populist attitudes to every circumstance around them, most people require a context that makes the activation of populist attitudes sensible, and interpretive help from other people who can catalyze this process. Thus, *populism at the level of individual citizens is a latent demand that must be activated through context and framing.*

Furthermore, because acting on these populist attitudes requires collective action, citizens take into account the availability of other activists and politicians who are capable of embodying this message and coordinating their efforts. These activists and politicians must not only share a populist discourse but have similar views on other ideologies and issues that combine with populism and fill it out. Thus, for citizens to become populist voters requires *a ready supply of like-minded populists*. Let us lay out each of these steps in detail.

Context

For populist attitudes to become active, they require a social context that makes the populist message sensible. Populism argues that political elites are conspiring against the people, acting knowingly in ways that benefit themselves at the public's expense. We argue that the type of context that produces a populist response is an *intentional failure of democratic representation*. By this, we mean much more than a government decision that somehow harms the interest of a set of constituents. Rather, it is a situation in which politicians' act knowingly against one set of constituents in order to benefit others. Furthermore, the action can be seen as unfair, or a violation of their constituents' rights as citizens to equality before the law. The result is a feeling of indignation or resentment (see Betz this volume, Chapter 8).

In general terms, there are two different contexts and two different types of these failures of representation, both of which reflect the set of linkages that undergirds their system of representation. First, in economically less-developed countries, intentional failures of democratic representation most often take the forms of widespread, systematic *corruption*. By this we mean a situation in which the political elite routinely and knowingly use their control of state resources to benefit their personal or partisan interests at the expense of the public, often in ways that are illegal. Representation in these countries is typically based on clientelistic linkages, or the conditional exchange of goods and services for political support (Hicken 2011; Kitschelt 2000; Luna 2014). While clientelism can be a stable basis for political representation, it is prone to illegal activity and undermines the capacity of institutions to uphold the rule of law. Too often, neither the voters nor the outsiders are fully aware of the kinds of institutional fixes that are required to eliminate corruption and reform the state, or they are unwilling to implement these changes because of how they would harm their own interests, and the cycle of clientelism and populism continues. Because these problems of corruption and state weakness are deep and persistent, populist forces are likely to be radical and electorally successful (Kenny 2017; see also Bornschier in this volume, Chapter 9).

Second, in economically developed countries, populism is more often a response to failures of programmatic representation. By this we mean that parties appeal to voters primarily on the basis of policy positions rather than clientelism (Kitschelt et al. 2010), but parties have become ideologically distant from their voters, missing or ignoring the issues that their voters would like to see on the public agenda. The problem is rarely one of outright corruption (although scandals happen in every government), but rather the growing tension between responsibility and responsiveness (Kriesi 2014; Mair 2009; Mudde and Rovira Kaltwasser 2017). Because of constraints or opportunities created by technological change or other global forces (think of economic liberalization and the increasing influence of international organizations), established political parties may progressively behave in a responsible way, adopting policy positions and supporting reforms that are allegedly required for economic and political development. However, this move towards responsibility implies that established political parties are losing their responsiveness function, i.e. they have serious problems at responding to the demands of voters. This is especially true if politicians appear to be collaborating with each other in keeping unwanted issues and constituencies out of government. These failures of representation are usually lesser than in the developing world, affecting narrower sets of citizens without threatening the integrity of the larger state, and so populist forces are often linked to smaller constituencies. Nevertheless, the more difficult it is to reconcile the roles of responsibility and responsiveness, the higher the odds that populist forces become entrenched in the political system.

Framing

A context of representational failure is necessary for populist attitudes to become sensible, but citizens may not immediately interpret their context in a populist way, i.e., as a reflection of elite conspiracies against the people. Making this interpretive move often requires political entrepreneurs who can frame the problem as more than a narrow policy failure requiring minor reform. Thus, populist actors are a catalyst in the activation of populist attitudes. Note that we are not arguing that populist entrepreneurs create populist attitudes out of nothing—the ideas are already there. But, to borrow a term from the framing literature in communications and political psychology, they must be made *salient*, or brought to the fore of citizens' thinking (Entman 1993).

At least three cognitive mechanisms seem to be involved in populist framing. First, populist rhetoric makes a *dispositional attribution of blame*. Attribution is a psychological term for the process by which people explain the causes of what they see around them. Psychologists have long noted the tendency of individuals to blame unwanted outcomes on the disposition, or intentional behavior, of external factors, while they instead focus on situational factors or impersonal events and circumstances if they blame themselves (Heider 1958; Hewstone 1990). Populism seems to play off of this bias by encouraging citizens to blame government failures on the intentional actions of knowing elites, i.e., on dispositional factors, rather than situational ones.

Second, populist frames invoke a specific set of in- and out-group identities (Meléndez and Rovira Kaltwasser 2017). The notion of in-group/out-group identities comes from social identity theory, which claims that people naturally place themselves and others in reified groups, adopt the norms associated with the identity, and construct exaggerated stereotypes of their own group and competing groups; these identities become valued for their own sake and are an important source of self-esteem (Tajfel et al. 1971; Tajfel and Turner 1979). Populism invokes two very specific identities: an in-group of the people (a democratic subject constituted by some sort of majority of ordinary citizens) and an out-group of the elite (the rulers, defined largely in opposition to the people). For populist attitudes to be activated, government failures must be framed as affecting the democratic community, specifically, the norms of citizenship that help define that community.

Third, populist frames rely heavily on emotional triggers, such as fear and anger (Hameleers, Bos, and de Vreese 2016; Rico, Guinjoan, and Anduiza 2017). Studies of human cognition increasingly recognize the importance of emotions as markers or triggers that facilitate decision-making and action. Strong emotions in specific behavioral contexts can activate beliefs and attitudes in unanticipated ways (Ajzen and Fishbein 2005). Anger in particular motivates individuals to identify a causal agent (Keltner, Ellsworth, and Edwards 1993) and seek to punish or scapegoat them (Abelson 1995). Moreover, populist frames are inclined to exploit negative emotions: they don't often say much about who 'the people' are, but rather emphasize the dishonest activities undertaken by 'the establishment'.

Organization

Populist politicians do more than provide populist rhetoric that frames the social context; they construct organizational vehicles that overcome the collective action problems inherent to populist mobilization (Hawkins and Rovira Kaltwasser 2017b). Citizens with active populist attitudes know they will have to work with other citizens in order to restore the political system to the people. This is especially true in light of their perception of a conspiring elite that is, by definition, powerful; confronting this elite alone is dangerous. Adding to this complication, it is not enough to challenge the elite; the people require a plan of action that can guide their efforts constructively. Without the capacity for concerted action towards a credible goal, citizens with active populist attitudes may slip into cynicism or despair rather than mobilize.

Citizens motivated by a populist discourse confront at least two types of collective action problem. First, there is a cooperation problem: populist forces must be large to win absolute control of government, but as support grows larger, members are increasingly unlikely to have common policy positions. Social heterogeneity makes cooperation more problematic (Olson 1971). Second, there is a coordination problem. Although populism implies that individual citizens should be actively involved in the cause, it also implies that these citizens should rule and govern directly, without entrusting their voices to professional politicians and bureaucrats. This belief means that supporters of populist forces will be wary of the permanent, hierarchical organizations that are generally required for coordinating election campaigns and policy positions in large communities.

Populist forces overcome these collective action problems using three organizational modes, each characterized by the employment of the populist set of ideas, but reflecting different tradeoffs in electoral success and the constraints of their material environment (Mudde and Rovira Kaltwasser 2017). These conform to roughly two of the three main types of political organization studied by social scientists: political parties and movements, with the latter appearing in two distinct subtypes.[4]

The first is an *institutionalized party*, or a political party that features a permanent, professionalized organization and an identity independent of any leader or external group (Levitsky 2003; Randall and Svåsand 2002). For instance, populist radical right parties in Europe typically develop permanent, professionalized, hierarchical organizations, which might be controlled by a strong leader during a period of time, but are normally not fully dependent on that specific leader (Mudde 2007). Often, these are niche parties, with narrowly focused issue positions and a relatively small share of the vote. By reducing the number of potential constituents and settling for a minority stake in government, politicians and their activists can more easily identify a set of common policy positions that satisfies their electorate. Furthermore, if the party is electorally small, it means that layers of bureaucracy can be eliminated, thus ensuring that members and activities feel close to party leaders and have opportunities to participate meaningfully in party activities, even as the party preserves a professionalized organization with a cadre of dedicated politicians.

Although it is not very common, it sometimes occurs that an established non-populist party transforms into a populist party. This can happen because of the pressure of certain factions of the party and/or because of the arrival of a new political leader. For instance, the Austrian Freedom Party (FPÖ) started as a non-populist party but adopted a populist discourse once Jörg Haider became its chairman. However, this feat is more difficult to manage in larger, catch-all parties, which have diverse interests and organized factions; they must either shed some of their Weberian apparatus in order to serve the wishes of the leader, or the leader and his populist faction must moderate their populism in order to placate their members' diverse interests. While it is still too early to examine the interaction between Donald Trump and the Republican Party in the US, this could be another example of how a non-populist catch-all party is at least partly transformed by a leader with a populist rhetoric.

The second pattern is for populist forces to appear as *social movements* that from below assemble large numbers of individuals, who for particular reasons (e.g. economic crisis or corruption scandals) are upset with the establishment. These are truly bottom-up forms of collective action, uncontrolled by either a professionalized, Weberian hierarchy or strong leaders. As with other social movements, populist ones struggle to coordinate their actions and are not well suited for electoral campaigning. In consequence, they are harder to identify in our analyses in this book, which focus heavily on populist forces that have successfully competed for control of government. However, populist social movements are probably more common than we think (see Aslanidis 2016), and they are politically relevant even if they do not directly capture public office. They not only affect the political agenda of existing parties, but may give rise to new leaders and parties that successfully adopt the issues being politicized by the movement. A clear recent example is the United States, where after the Great Recession *two* populist social movements appeared: the Tea Party and the Occupy Wall Street movement. One of these had an immediate impact on the Republican Party, helping reshape local electoral races and the party's agenda in Congress and state governments (Formisano 2012; Skocpol and Williamson 2013), and both of them fed into the movements that ultimately supported the candidacies of Donald Trump and Bernie Sanders.

That said, not all populist movements are *social* movements. There is a third pattern of organization—particularly common in Latin America but also more recently in Southern Europe (e.g. Beppe Grillo's Five Star Movement)—consisting in the emergence of a network style of organization united around a charismatic leader. Such personalistic or charismatic movements (we use the term interchangeably throughout this volume and our other work) rely on the populist set of ideas to construct a common identity that distinguishes the leader as the embodiment of the popular will. With the leader as an "empty signifier" (Laclau 2005) of their individual wills, citizens can hold their policy concerns in abeyance, trusting that the leader will eventually enact policies that benefit them personally. Charismatic or personalistic leaders are not a perfect solution to the collective action problems that populist forces confront—they struggle to resolve long-term problems of leadership succession (Panebianco 1988)—but they can transform movement-style organizations into something that is highly effective at winning elections. They enable followers to serve the leader and enact his decisions, including his directions about how to run the campaign or deliberate over policy, while still allowing them to feel directly, personally connected to the popular will. Hence, some of the most electorally dominant populist forces organize around personalistic leaders, even if they are often short-lived.

We can speculate about the material environments that make these three organizational modes more likely. Building on our earlier argument about the relevance of context, we think that institutionalized parties are more likely to appear in programmatic party systems with relatively moderate problems of representation related to the growing tension between responsiveness and responsibility. The programmatic basis of party competition in these countries means that ideological positions are generally more important to create and maintain, and the relatively lower demand for populism means that fewer citizens are willing to delegate power to a charismatic leader. Instead, populist parties emerge on the left or right side of the political spectrum to politicize specific issues that remain unaddressed by mainstream left or right parties. In contrast, populist forces controlled by charismatic leaders are more common in countries with deeper struggles with democratic governance. Citizens in these clientelistic systems are less concerned about the policy positions of parties and more focused on their ability to deliver tangible material benefits. Also, deeper and more frequent policy crises make citizens more willing to accept the risk of voting for a leader who promises to do away with institutional checks on the executive branch in order to deliver and fulfill a set of radical promises.

Unlike these other two forms of populist organization, populist social movements seem to exist in both contexts. While we have pointed to examples of these movements in economically developed countries such as the US, they can also be found in developing countries such as Ecuador and Bolivia, where important protest movements preceded and informed the rise of better-organized populist forces (De la Torre 2013; Roberts 2006). It would be tempting to argue that grassroots populist movements are simply the precursors of any organized populist phenomena, but we think the answer is more complex. Many instances of both institutionalized niche parties and charismatic movements have origins devoid of any grassroots effort. This is a form of populist organization that has gone largely understudied, and more research is needed to better understand its origins and its relationship to the more electorally engaged kinds of populism.

Alternative theories

In the previous section we outlined the ideational theory and its causal explanations. Although this ideational theory has growing support, other arguments have been used to explain the success or failure of populist forces. In this section we explain the points of overlap and contention between the ideational theory and three main competitors, focusing on the underlying causal mechanisms. Two of these mechanisms are cultural, founded in either a mass-society thesis that highlights the psychological importance of identity and norms, or a modernization-based perspective that asserts the significance of changing values. The other is a Downsian, political-economy perspective that centers on the ability of parties to address voters material interests. A discussion of these alternative theories allows us to clarify the contributions of the ideational approach while appreciating their points of intersection.

Cultural mechanisms: mass-society

The mass-society perspective is perhaps the oldest. It draws from Durkheim's classic theory that human beings require a social glue of norms and identity to provide meaning and direction to their lives, and that structural change can undermine this sense of identity. Earlier scholars using the mass-society thesis (Arendt 1973; Kornhauser 2013) claimed that modern industrialization and urbanization were uprooting citizens from a traditional milieu. These masses were easy prey for populist demagogues, who could offer a new political identity of "the people" built around the leader and his movement. Early social psychologists added to this argument by noting that the masses were often semi-literate and thus easily persuaded by emotional rhetoric and flashy imagery (Le Bon 1960).

More recent versions of this argument recognize that the processes of industrialization and urbanization are old news in most societies. Instead, they argue that in many countries, the shift to a knowledge or service-based economy has once again deprived individuals of the norms that they require to organize and make sense of life, creating a sense of normlessness and resentment that provide fertile ground for populist movements (Elchardus and Spruyt 2016). Additionally, some scholars of developing countries argue that the creation of a sustainable, modern identity has never occurred for large segments of the population, particularly for those who work in the informal sector. For those individuals, populism still provides meaning and identity (Chalmers et al. 1997; Oxhorn 1998).

An important variation on this argument comes from scholars in the radical tradition of Laclau. Although Laclau was not concerned with normlessness, he did see the creation of a popular identity as a solution to the age-old Marxist problem of fostering a unified working class identity. Historically, people in the working class had let competing identities, such as nationalism or religion, interfere with their objective class interests. Rather than struggle to persuade workers of their true, objectively based identity, Laclau and his co-author, Chantal Mouffe, argued that these cultural/psychological categories were an intrinsic part of politics and should be embraced (Laclau and Mouffe 2004).

In particular, a popular identity—an identification with "the people" in the populist sense—was a viable solution that provided a unifying identity in opposition to capitalist elite, especially when built around the figure of a charismatic leader (Laclau 2005).

Cultural mechanisms: modernization

The second cultural argument is based on modernization theory's emphasis on values as the key causal mechanisms driving human behavior. Classic modernization theory did not consider the problem of populism. But early modernization theorists, led by the work of Lipset (1959), argued that many people held an authoritarian set of values that predisposed them to political extremism. These values were authoritarian in the sense suggested by Adorno et al. (1950), in that individuals with these values craved moral clarity and order. For Lipset, these authoritarian values were common to people in the working class and originated in the lack of higher education and dysfunctional family relations common to poverty. Whether this extremism fell on the ideological left or right was a product of historical contingency; members of the working class were not really ideologically committed to the right or the left because of its economic prescriptions, but because of the extremists' promise of moral certainty.

This notion of authoritarian values has informed an important current of theorizing about the radical right in Europe, where it is asserted that authoritarian values help explain working class support (Betz 1994; Kriesi et al. 2012). Working class individuals are disturbed by the spread of secular, post-materialist values, which emphasize moral relativism and tolerance for minority cultural groups. They want politicians who not only take strong positions but defend conservative traditions as the source of that order. Thus, populism represents a backlash against cultural globalization (Inglehart and Norris 2016).

Rational choice mechanism

The third alternative is a Downsian one borrowing loosely from rational-choice, political–economy arguments about the basis of democratic representation and party competition. Although Downs (1957) did not discuss populism, scholars who apply this perspective argue that support for populist parties is driven less by any cultural mechanism than a basic need to maximize material self-interest. Voters seek policies that benefit themselves materially; hence, the most important axes of spatial competition are economic. Voters support populists when the traditional parties stop defending their constituents' material interests.

Current Downsian arguments are much like cultural arguments in that they see globalization as the main force driving support for populism; however, the mechanism is economic. In the advanced industrial democracies, globalization leaves behind unskilled blue-collar and white-collar laborers, while in the poorer countries it leaves behind skilled workers from the formal sector. Globalization is not just an impersonal force, but a product of policy decisions by traditional politicians in government; parties that promote policies of globalization such as free trade may position their economies for better international competition and increases in GDP, but they do so at the expense of previously protected constituencies. The "losers of globalization" vent their anger at the traditional parties by voting for populist outsiders who promise retrenchment and an end to austerity, as well as opposition to government bureaucrats (such as the EU or the US federal government) that implement this global order (Betz 1994; Kitschelt 1997; Kriesi et al. 2012). Thus, while the consequences are largely the same as in the values-based argument, their rationale for populism is different.

An important strain of this argument circulates among scholars who study populism in the developing world or in post-Soviet societies. Here, the concern is less about globalization, although globalization is seen as an important catalyst of recent movements. Instead, the more fundamental problem is state weakness and corruption. In most post-colonial societies of the developing world, deep economic inequalities are entrenched and defended by elites who inherited a system of extractive institutions. A similar problem prevails on post-Soviet societies, where inequality is much lower but state institutions remain less effective and have been captured by a segment of the political elite. In both sets of countries, populists succeed by making a credible offer to overturn this system and redirect state benefits towards underprivileged groups (Hanley and Sikk 2016). Although very similar to the ideational argument with its emphasis on corruption, these scholars see the main causal mechanism as economic, rather than normative.

Critique

The ideational argument is clearly not at odds with many of the general claims made by these theories. It agrees that culture and material interests both inform citizen preferences, helping determine which ideological flavor of populism appeal to each segment of voters. Voters with active populist attitudes are not just attracted to any populist forces, but to those that share their other ideological positions on the right or left. It also sees citizens as reasoning individuals that take into account the constraints imposed by their environment. But the ideational theory highlights an additional set of meanings than either of the classical arguments based on mass-society or modernization theory, and contra the Downsian perspective it argues that normative ideas are significant foundations of citizen preferences.

First, while the ideational approach recognizes the existence of a popular identity and its potential as a motivating force, it does not see the *absence* of this identity as a particularly serious contemporary problem. The creation of popular identities is a central feature of the historical incorporation of the middle- or lower-classes into democracy; during those critical junctures the ability of a party or leader to credibly articulate this identity often ensured enduring loyalty and electoral success (Collier and Collier 1991). But in most of the democracies that we study, the period of mass incorporation is a distant memory, and the notion of one's belonging to a popular democratic subject is now firmly rooted. The problem of populism in most countries is not the creation of a popular identity, but its mobilization. Regarding Laclau's version of this argument, we would simply add that the construction of populist identities is only one option among many for engaging in democratic reform—pluralism is another. Furthermore, given the tendency of populist discourse to undermine the institutions of democratic contestation (Hawkins and Ruth 2015; Houle and Kenny 2018; Huber and Schimpf 2016; Mudde and Rovira Kaltwasser 2012), it is not clear that every emergence of a populist identity is something positive.

Our critique of the modernization theory is more sympathetic and straightforward: while we think authoritarian values explain much of the support for radical right parties (or left-libertarian values for some of the radical left), we do not see them as strong explanations for populist parties per se. For example, even among populist radical right parties, these values can explain only the ideological—radical right—portion of their appeal, such as opposition to immigration and secularizing institutions. While we agree that this is a critical part of the explanation for contemporary populist forces, these values alone do not answer the question of why voters prefer that radicalism assume a populist form, framed as a struggle of the elite against the people. The fact that these ideational elements do not always coincide is demonstrated by extreme right-wing parties, such as Golden Dawn in Greece, which frame issues in nationalist terms that relegate the demos to a secondary position. Ultimately, the ideational approach argues that we must consider the interaction of ideological stances and discourse to fully explain support for particular populist forces.

The ideational approach also has an ambivalent relationship with Downsian arguments. On the one hand, the rational choice argument for ends–means calculation, i.e., thin rationality, is clearly compatible with the ideational approach. Both accept the impact of institutions and the competitive partisan space—quintessential Downsian tools—and agree that once we get to the aggregate level, we can treat citizens as actors who make calculating decisions about whether to join in populist mobilization. These calculations ultimately shape organizational choices and electoral success.

However, the ideational approach does not fully embrace the Downsian perspective at the individual level, steering clear of a thick-rationality that reduces the preferences of these individuals to their material self-interest. The Downsian emphasis on material self-interest helps explain the concern for economic inequality that animates many populist movements today, on the right and more especially on the left, but it leaves little room for the normative concerns that animate and, we argue, define populist forces. Populism is ultimately a complaint that inequalities are violations of democratic norms of equality before the law. To understand populists' appeal, we must incorporate an additional set of arguments about the normative foundations for democracy, the contexts that violate these norms, and the means by which they are framed and activated.

To be clear, few of the Downsian scholars we have cited here rely exclusively on claims that voters act on their interests (e.g., Betz 1994; Kriesi et al. 2012); most of them suggest that citizens consider a mix of material and non-material, values-based concerns when they decide to support populists. Our discussion has ignored these common sense arguments in an effort to focus more carefully on underlying causal mechanisms. But ultimately, neither modernization nor Downsian arguments are sufficient to explain the appeal of populist forces; they must incorporate the additional, ideational dimension to understand the range of concerns that motivate citizens and to better understand the cognitive pathways by which these ideas come into force.

Methods

An approach is more than a concept or even a concept-plus-theory, but includes epistemological claims. It is a way of studying something. At the most general level we can say that the ideational approach has an affinity with positivism because it seeks to measure and explain populism objectively. We embrace general theorizing and the use of data to test our arguments. But at a more specific level, the ideational approach speaks to two fundamental methodological tasks: measuring populist ideas, both quantitatively and qualitatively; and testing our causal arguments.

Quantitative measurement

Most of what we do in this volume is measure populism quantitatively—an essential task for describing populism at the level of politicians or citizens and, ultimately, testing our theory. Furthermore, given our stance about the continuous scaling of populist ideas, especially at the aggregate level, we would like these measures to be continuous and precise. But there is a large toolkit of methods for measuring ideas quantitatively, from traditional public opinion surveys to content analysis. Scholars using the ideational approach need to know when each method is appropriate.

Generally speaking, existing research adopts one of two modes of measuring populism: content analysis at the elite level, and surveys at the mass level. Content analysis, which ranges from human-coded analysis to automated content analysis, is common at the elite level because of the difficulty of getting politicians to participate in interviews and fill out lengthy questionnaires; hence, it draws from natural texts (those produced for an audience besides the researcher) such as speeches, party manifestos, and debates. In contrast, surveys are an obvious choice for analyzing mass level attitudes, because ordinary citizens are much more willing to take surveys, and because it is difficult to find consistent samples of texts containing mass discourse across countries.

We endorse both methods. The ideational approach requires measuring populist ideas at the level of both politicians and citizens, and each method has its advantages. Given the widespread availability of texts, we think that content analysis will continue to offer the most reliable measures of populist ideas at the elite level. We are especially excited about the possibilities it offers for analyzing populist ideas in the past, something that cannot be done with surveys (cf. Hawkins and Rovira Kaltwasser 2017a; Bonikowski and Gidron 2016). And given the lack of natural texts at the level of individual citizens, we think that public opinion surveys will remain an essential tool for measuring populist attitudes. Hence, we spend time in individual chapters developing content analysis techniques and survey attitude inventories with the goal of providing a set of guidelines for researchers.

However, current research has clearly not exhausted the possibilities for quantitative measurement, and in this volume we take these methods—textual analysis and surveys—in new directions. One of these directions is elite surveys. While difficult in some locations, such as at the federal level in the United States, elite surveys have been successfully conducted for Latin American legislatures for over two decades now (the University of Salamanca's Parliamentary Elites in Latin America survey), and more recently among parliamentary candidates in European countries (the Cooperative Candidate Study). Elite surveys suffer the same problems as public opinion surveys (e.g., no retroactive analysis) but like other surveys they let us connect populist attitudes to other attitudes and experiences at the individual level, and they offer the possibility of measuring the congruence of citizens' attitudes with those of their representatives.

Another possibility is textual analysis of mass-level texts. While analyzing natural texts is very difficult to do systematically at this level, it is possible to include open-ended questions in surveys and analyze the responses. As we show in this volume (see the chapter by Busby, Doyle, Hawkins and Wiesehomeier), this can provide additional outcome measures for experiments that are more truly behavioral, in that they let subjects speak for themselves rather than in ways that the researcher imposes. They may also be used to validate responses to closed-ended survey questions.

A final possibility standing outside the modalities of surveys and content analysis is expert surveys, that is, surveys of journalists and academics who are asked to qualify the cases they know well. While expert surveys have their own flaws, they enjoy most of the same advantages as regular surveys, especially the ability to gauge multiple ideological dimensions simultaneously, and can be much less expensive. However, these are probably only accurate at gauging attitudes of parties and prominent politicians.

Qualitative measurement

Qualitative measurement—the attempt to spell out the substance of ideas, especially how their elements are interrelated—is an essential step in coming up with quantitative measurement (we can't say how much of an idea is present until we specify its content). Qualitative measurement in the form of textual analysis informed much of the work that went into defining populism over the past decade or two (c.f. de la Torre 2000; Hawkins 2003; Mudde 2007). Even within the current ideational framework, qualitative techniques are needed to flesh out the substance of populism in specific contexts: who constitutes the people, who makes up the elite, and what policy reforms are needed to restore the people as sovereign.

Although this volume is less focused on qualitative measurement, it points out two areas for improved research. First, qualitative techniques should be applied more often at the mass level. Qualitative techniques are usually applied to elite texts, especially speeches, and in a few cases they are also applied through elite interviews; there are several examples of these qualitative techniques in this volume. However, open-ended interviews and qualitative textual analysis can and should be done at the mass level. The chapter by Abts, Kochuyt, and van Kessel (Chapter 14) is an important example of this application, consisting almost entirely of semi-structured interviews of populist voters. Their data allow us to show how populist ideas are developed in the minds of ordinary citizens. Their findings not only verify the populist logic of self-righteous popular sovereignty, but offer evidence of how populist ideas are repeated at the mass level, evidence that is possibly more vivid and persuasive than tables of mean populist attitudes in a survey.

A second area where qualitative analysis could be further developed is in measuring the conversational dynamics implicit in the discursive approaches of Laclau's Essex school. While the ideational approach asserts that populist ideas already exist in the minds of citizens, waiting to be activated, this has yet to be fully demonstrated. Laclau's discursive approach argues instead that populist ideas are only rough notions that needed be given shape and content through a political dialogue, and that there are typical ways this dialogue proceeds. The chapters by Abi-Hassan (Chapter 13) and Abts, Kochuyt, and van Kessel (Chapter 14) develop these points by showing how populist discourse is echoed by the supporters and opponents of populist forces. We hope that others scholars will follow up on their efforts.

Testing theories

The other meaning of "method" refers to the testing of causal arguments, or theories. Social scientists generally talk about three of these methods: experimental, quantitative (multivariate modeling), and qualitative (process tracing). In recent years there has been a methodological convergence, with scholars increasingly drawing on all of these methods in order to make stronger causal inferences. We argue that scholars using the ideational approach also need to apply multiple methods. This reflects more than just scholarly ecumenicalism, but the individual-level focus of the ideational theory.

The ideational approach tries to build up to the aggregate level: it seeks to explain why whole parties systems and countries are sometimes dominated by populist forces. Explanations at this aggregate level are relevant to important sets of policymakers and citizens who are concerned about the national-level context that makes populism attractive. These stakeholders are concerned about the conditions that make particular countries prone to populism, but also the conditions that make other countries and whole regions susceptible. This analytical focus—at the general, aggregate level—makes statistical modeling, or quantitative analysis, useful.

But the ideational approach is also concerned about explaining populism at the level of individual human beings, in terms of their psychology, and it seeks to connect the aggregate to the individual level through a series of causal mechanisms. Answers to these causal questions appeal to different sets of stakeholders, such as local politicians or NGOs that work in conflict resolution. Testing these types of theoretical arguments requires a different set of methodological tools, including process tracing through case studies (qualitative research) because of the ability of this method to get at causal sequencing; and public opinion surveys and experiments, because of their capacity to capture causality in the minds of individuals.

Not every piece of ideationally oriented research has to use all of these methods at once—no single chapter in this book does. But taken together, the ideational approach has multiple observable implications that require multiple methods. In this volume, we explore all of these in an attempt to show that, at first cut, the theoretical framework seems to work, but also to highlight the potential for future analyses at all levels of analysis. In the conclusion to this book, we outline these findings and methodological recommendations.

Book outline

The aim of this introduction has been to lay out the rough contours of the ideational approach. This means providing not only a clear conceptualization of populism, but a theoretical framework that takes the role of ideas seriously, together with a set of methodological guidelines for measuring populist ideas and testing our theory. The rest of this book shows this ideational approach in action. All the chapters of this book rely on the ideational definition, but they look at the populist phenomenon from different angles. Specifically, the chapters in Part I focus on measurement, while chapters in Part II test theory.

The chapters in Part I focus primarily on quantitative measurement, starting with populism at the elite level and working down to the mass level. We open with a chapter by Hawkins and Castanho Silva (Chapter 1) comparing two techniques of textual analysis: holistic grading (a human-based approach) and automated textual analysis. The purpose of these chapters is to identify which technique performs better at analyzing large numbers of texts across multiple countries, an essential tool for generating large comparative datasets. Luke March and Berto Šalaj and Marijana Grbeša are the authors of the next two chapters, both of which show the capacity of more traditional forms of textual analysis to decompose populist discourse and provide more fine-grained studies of populist content. March measures the level of populist ideas in electoral manifestos in the United Kingdom, while Šalaj and Grbeša analyze news interviews of Croatian politicians.

The next two chapters stay at the level of elites but test less common techniques for measuring populist ideas. The chapter by Nina Wiesehomeier (Chapter 4) develops expert surveys to measure the populist ideas of political parties, and she presents preliminary findings coming from two rounds of expert surveys applied in Latin America. Another path is followed by Ioannis Andreadis and Saskia Ruth-Lovell, whose chapter (Chapter 5) focuses on elite surveys in Greece and Bolivia. These surveys measure the level of populist ideas among politicians by using the same items developed for mass surveys.

The last two contributions of this part move to the mass level with public opinion surveys. In one chapter (Chapter 6), Steven M. van Hauwert, Christian Schimpf and Flavio Azevedo use Item Response Theory to test existing survey inventories (including some used in this book!), showing that they tend to have compressed scales. Partially in response, the following chapter (by Castanho Silva and a host of co-authors) develops a new inventory of populist attitudes. Using a psychometric approach, the authors test over 150 items to create a more balanced scale capable of working across multiple countries. We consider this new inventory a gold standard for future attitudinal research.

Part II is centered on testing different elements of the theoretical framework. It includes contributions employing all of the major methodologies (quantitative/comparative, qualitative/process tracing, and experiments) and covering different countries and world regions, as well as different types of populism.

The part starts with several chapters using quantitative/comparative methods across time and countries. Hans-Georg Betz's contribution (Chapter 8) makes a broad historical comparison of five populist experiences and identifies some of the key elements that explain success at political mobilization across time; it is one of the first comparative historical analyses using the ideational approach. After this, Simon Bornschier combines ideational and party-system explanations to offer a novel twist on the ideational theory, which he applies to a comparative analysis of two European case studies (France and Germany) and two Latin American case studies (Uruguay and Venezuela); it is one of the first spatial analyses of populism. The next chapter is written by Ioannis Andreadis, Kirk A. Hawkins, Iván Llazamares and Matthew Singer, who rely on survey items applied in contemporary Bolivia, Chile, Greece and Spain to examine vote preference in different contexts, thus combining individual- and country-level analysis for parties of the left and right. Finally, Castanho Silva (Chapter 11) uses fuzzy-set Qualitative Comparative Analysis to test the ideational theory against other theories at the country level—the only large-N, country-level study in our volume.

The next four chapters in this part are case studies emphasizing process-tracing; these cover a broad range of ideological subtypes and regions. Margarita Gómez-Reino and Iván Llamazares make an in-depth analysis of the case of the left populist Podemos in Spain to show an often forgotten aspect in the study of populism, namely, the role that intellectuals can play in the diffusion and adaptation of the populist set of ideas. Sahar Abi-Hassan examines the extent to which the opposition to Chavismo in Venezuela has been one of the main drivers of the polarization that the country has experienced since the coming into power of Hugo Chávez in 1998. Her study highlights the interplay of ideas that populist discourse elicits and how this conversation becomes antagonistic. A different angle is explored by Koen Abts, Thierry Kochuyt and Stijn van Kessel, who undertake a detailed analysis of interviews with supporters of the populist radical right party Vlaams Block/Belang in Belgium. They show that the populist set of ideas is part and parcel of how constituents, and not just political elites, observe political reality. Finally, the chapter by Wendy Rahn (Chapter 15) uses survey data from the US to describe the evolution of Trump's populist constituency; it is one of the first efforts to show the impact of populist attitudes in the United States, and especially across time.

The last two chapters in this part use experimental methods to evaluate the causal mechanisms of the ideational approach at the individual level. The chapter by Ethan Busby, David Doyle, Kirk Hawkins, and Nina Wiesehomeier (Chapter 16) shows the results of two cross-national laboratory experiments on the nature of populist threat.

They are especially interested in the impact of information about corruption. The other chapter, by Rosario Aguilar and Ryan Carlin (Chapter 17) presents an online experiment in Chile. They use the study to gauge the interaction of authoritarian attitudes with populism.

The book finishes with a conclusion that not only summarizes the substantive findings of the volume and directions for future study, but provides something that we hope will be a hallmark of future populism research: a discussion of the policy implications of the ideational approach generally and the specific results of this volume. It also delves briefly into a discussion of the consequences of populism, a topic we intentionally omitted from this volume, but that can also be understood using the ideational approach.

Note: The volume has an online appendix with supplementary analyses for several chapters, as well as replication datasets and instruments. These files are available at the Team Populism website, https://populism.byu.edu/.

Notes

1 For a more detailed analysis of the differences within the ideational approach, see (Poblete 2015).

2 At this stage, it is important to note that some scholars define populism as a political style, but this definition usually overlaps with the conceptualization of populism as a discourse, since the populist political style is characterized by the development of the Manichean distinction between "the people" and "the elite." Those who conceptualize populism as a political style are inclined to focus not only on the words of populist actors, but their behavior and/or performative repertories, such as bad manners and transgressive language (Moffitt and Tormey 2014; Ostiguy 2017). This has implications for measurement, suggesting the need to sample additional types of text.

3 Freeden (2017) recently argued that applying "thin-centered ideology" to populism stretches the concept, because even thin-centered ideologies are consciously articulated while populism is not. We agree this is an important caution but also argue that in substance this is how ideational scholars already understand populism.

4 The third type of political organization, interest groups, does not usually appear in a populist form. We think this has to do with interest groups' emphasis on lobbying, rather than direct political action, together with their reliance on fundraising and paid professionals.

References

Abelson, Robert P. 1995. 'Attitude Extremity'. In *Attitude Strength: Antecedents and Consequences*, 25–41. Mahwah, NJ: Lawrence Erlbaum Associates.

Acemoglu, Daron, Georgy Egorov, and Konstantin Sonin. 2013. 'A Political Theory of Populism'. *The Quarterly Journal of Economics* 128 (2):771–805.

Adorno, Theodor W., Else Frenkel-Brunswik, Daniel J. Levinson, and R. Nevitt Sanford. 1950. *The Authoritarian Personality*. New York: Harper & Row.

Ajzen, Icek, and Martin Fishbein. 2005. 'The Influence of Attitudes on Behavior'. In *The Handbook of Attitudes*, edited by B.T. Johnson, M.P. Zanna, and D. Albarracín, 173–221. Mahwah, NJ: Lawrence Erlbaum Associates.

Akkerman, Agnes, Cas Mudde, and Andrej Zaslove. 2014. 'How Populist Are the People? Measuring Populist Attitudes in Voters'. *Comparative Political Studies* 47 (9):1324–1353.

Arendt, Hannah. 1973. *The Origins of Totalitarianism*. New York: Houghton Mifflin Harcourt.

Aslanidis, Paris. 2016. 'Is Populism an Ideology? A Refutation and a New Perspective'. *Political Studies* 64 (1):88–104.

Atanasov, Pavel, and Regina Joseph. 2016. 'Analysis | Which Election Forecast Was the Most Accurate? Or Rather: The Least Wrong?' *Washington Post*: The Monkey Cage. 30 November 2016. www.washingtonpost.com/news/monkey-cage/wp/2016/11/30/which-election-forecast-was-the-most-accurate-or-rather-the-least-wrong/.

Betz, Hans-Georg. 1994. *Radical Right-Wing Populism in Western Europe.* New York: St. Martins Press.

Bonikowski, Bart, and Noam Gidron. 2016. 'The Populist Style in American Politics: Presidential Campaign Discourse, 1952–1996'. *Social Forces* 94 (4):1593–1621.

Calamur, Krishnadev. 2016. 'What Europe's Far Right Sees in Trump's Win'. *The Atlantic*, 10 November 2016. www.theatlantic.com/international/archive/2016/11/trump-far-right-europe/507314/.

Caramani, Daniele. 2017. "Will vs. Reason: The Populist and Technocratic Forms of Political Representation and Their Critique to Party Government." *American Political Science Review* 111 (1): 54–67.

Cardoso, Fernando Henrique, and Enzo Faletto. 1979. *Dependency and Development in Latin America.* Berkeley, CA: University of California Press.

Carroll, Rory. 2016. 'Insult, Provoke, Repeat: How Donald Trump Became America's Hugo Chávez'. *The Guardian*, 22 June 2016, sec. US news. www.theguardian.com/us-news/2016/jun/22/donald-trump-hugo-chavez-political-similarities.

Cesario, Joseph, Jason E. Plaks, Nao Hagiwara, Carlos David Navarrete, and E. Tory Higgins. 2010. 'The Ecology of Automaticity How Situational Contingencies Shape Action Semantics and Social Behavior'. *Psychological Science* 21 (9):1311–17.

Chalmers, Douglas A., Carlos M. Vilas, Katherine Hite, Scott B. Martin, Kerianne Piester, and Monique Segarra, eds. 1997. *The New Politics of Inequality in Latin America: Rethinking Participation and Representation.* New York: Oxford University Press.

Chanley, Virginia. 1994. 'Commitment to Political Tolerance: Situational and Activity-Based Differences'. *Political Behavior* 16 (3):343–363.

Cillizza, Chris. 2016. 'How Did Polls Miss the Presidential Election Result so Badly?' *Washington Post.* 9 November 2016. www.washingtonpost.com/news/the-fix/wp/2016/11/09/why-polling-faces-a-moment-of-reckoning-after-the-2016-election/.

Collier, Ruth Berins, and David Collier. 1991. *Shaping the Political Arena: Critical Junctures, the Labor Movement, and Regime Dynamics in Latin America.* Princeton, NJ: Princeton University Press.

Deegan-Krause, Kevin, and Tim Haughton. 2009. 'Toward a More Useful Conceptualization of Populism: Types and Degrees of Populist Appeals in the Case of Slovakia'. *Politics & Policy* 37 (4):821–841.

De la Torre, Carlos. 2000. *Populist Seduction in Latin America: The Ecuadorian Experience.* Athens, OH: Ohio University Press.

De la Torre, Carlos. 2013. 'In the Name of the People: Democratization, Popular Organizations, and Populism in Venezuela, Bolivia, and Ecuador'. *European Review of Latin American and Caribbean Studies* 95:27–48.

Di Tella, Torcuato S. 1965. 'Populism and Reform in Latin America'. In *Obstacles to Change in Latin America*, edited by Claudio Véliz, 47–74. London: Oxford University Press.

Dornbusch, Rudiger, and Sebastian Edwards, eds. 1991. *The Macroeconomics of Populism in Latin America.* Chicago, IL: University of Chicago Press.

Downs, Anthony. 1957. *An Economic Theory of Democracy.* New York: HarperCollins Publishers.

Elchardus, Mark, and Bram Spruyt. 2016. 'Populism, Persistent Republicanism and Declinism: An Empirical Analysis of Populism as a Thin Ideology'. *Government and Opposition* 51 (1):111–133.

Entman, Robert M. 1993. 'Framing: Toward Clarification of a Fractured Paradigm'. *Journal of Communication* 43 (4):51–58.

Formisano, Ronald P. 2012. *The Tea Party: A Brief History.* Baltimore, MD: Johns Hopkins University Press.

Freeden, Michael. 1996. *Ideologies and Political Theory: A Conceptual Approach.* Oxford: Oxford University Press.

———. 2003. *Ideology: A Very Short Introduction*. New York: Oxford University Press.

———. 2017. 'After the Brexit Referendum: Revisiting Populism as an Ideology'. *Journal of Political Ideologies* 22 (1):1–11.

Friedman, Uri. 2017. 'What If the "Populist Wave" Is Just Political Fragmentation?' *The Atlantic*, 17 March 2017. www.theatlantic.com/international/archive/2017/03/dutch-election-wilders-populism/519813/.

Germani, Gino. 1978. *Authoritarianism, Fascism, and National Populism*. New Brunswick, NJ: Transaction Publishers.

Gerring, John. 1999. 'What Makes a Concept Good? A Criteria Framework for Understanding Concept Formation in the Social Sciences'. *Polity* 31(3):357–393.

Hameleers, Michael, Linda Bos, and Claes H. de Vreese. 2016. '"They Did It" The Effects of Emotionalized Blame Attribution in Populist Communication'. *Communication Research* 44 (6):870–900.

Hanley, Seán, and Allan Sikk. 2016. 'Economy, Corruption or Floating Voters? Explaining the Breakthroughs of Anti-Establishment Reform Parties in Eastern Europe'. *Party Politics* 22 (4):522–533.

Hanretty, Chris. 2016. 'Here's Why Pollsters and Pundits Got Brexit Wrong'. *Washington Post: The Monkey Cage*. 24 June 2016. www.washingtonpost.com/news/monkey-cage/wp/2016/06/24/heres-why-pollsters-and-pundits-got-brexit-wrong/.

Hawkins, Kirk A. 2003. 'Populism in Venezuela: The Rise of Chavismo'. *Third World Quarterly* 24 (6):1137–1160.

———. 2009. 'Is Chávez Populist? Measuring Populist Discourse in Comparative Perspective'. *Comparative Political Studies* 42 (8):1040–1067.

———. 2010. *Venezuela's Chavismo and Populism in Comparative Perspective*. Cambridge: Cambridge University Press.

Hawkins, Kirk A., Scott Riding, and Cas Mudde. 2012. 'Measuring Populist Attitudes'. *Working Paper Series on Political Concepts, ECPR Committee on Concepts and Methods*.

Hawkins, Kirk A., and Saskia Ruth. 2015. 'The Impact of Populism on Liberal Democracy'. In *8o Congreso de La Asociación Latinoamericana de Ciencia Política*. Lima.

Hawkins, Kirk A. and Cristóbal Rovira Kaltwasser. 2017a. 'The Ideational Approach to Populism'. *Latin American Research Review* 52(4): 513–528.

Hawkins, Kirk A. and Cristóbal Rovira Kaltwasser. 2017b. 'What the (Ideational) Study of Populism Can Teach Us, and What It Can't'. *Swiss Political Science Review* 23 (4), 526–542.

Hawkins, Kirk A., Cristóbal Rovira Kaltwasser, and Ioannis Andreadis. Forthcoming. 'The Activation of Populist Attitudes.' *Government and Opposition*.

Heider, Fritz. 1958. *The Psychology of Interpersonal Relations*. Hillsdale, NJ: Lawrence Erlbaum Associates, Publishers.

Hewstone, Miles. 1990. 'The "Ultimate Attribution Error"? A Review of the Literature on Intergroup Causal Attribution'. *European Journal of Social Psychology* 20 (4):311–335.

Hicken, Allen. 2011. 'Clientelism'. *Annual Review of Political Science* 14 (1):289–310.

Houle, Christian, and Paul Kenny. 2018. 'The Political and Economic Consequences of Populist Rule in Latin America'. *Government and Opposition* 53 (2):256–287.

Huber, Robert A., and Christian H. Schimpf. 2016a. 'Friend or Foe? Testing the Influence of Populism on Democratic Quality in Latin America'. *Political Studies* 64 (4):872–889.

Inglehart, Ronald, and Pippa Norris. 2016. 'Trump, Brexit, and the Rise of Populism: Economic Have-Nots and Cultural Backlash'. *HKS Faculty Research Working Paper Series RWP16-026*.

Ionescu, Ghiţa, and Ernest Gellner, eds. 1969. *Populism: Its Meanings and National Characteristics*. London: Weidenfeld and Nicolson.

Ivarsflaten, Elisabeth. 2008. 'What Unites Right-Wing Populists in Western Europe? Re-Examining Grievance Mobilization Models in Seven Successful Cases'. *Comparative Political Studies* 41 (1):3–23.

Jansen, Robert S. 2011. 'Populist Mobilization: A New Theoretical Approach to Populism'. *Sociological Theory* 29 (2):75–96.

Kazin, Michael. 2016. 'How Can Donald Trump and Bernie Sanders Both Be "Populist"?' *The New York Times*, 22 March 2016. www.nytimes.com/2016/03/27/magazine/how-can-donald-trump-and-bernie-sanders-both-be-populist.html.

Keltner, D., P. C. Ellsworth, and K. Edwards. 1993. 'Beyond Simple Pessimism: Effects of Sadness and Anger on Social Perception'. *Journal of Personality and Social Psychology* 64 (5):740–752.

Kenny, Paul. 2017. *Populism and Patronage: Why Populists Win Elections in India, Asia, and Beyond*. Oxford: Oxford University Press.

Kitschelt, Herbert. 1997. *The Radical Right in Western Europe: A Comparative Analysis*. Ann Arbor, MI: University of Michigan Press.

———. 2000. 'Linkages between Citizens and Politicians in Democratic Polities'. *Comparative Political Studies* 33 (6–7):845–879.

Kitschelt, Herbert, Kirk A. Hawkins, Juan Pablo Luna, Guillermo Rosas, and Elizabeth J. Zechmeister. 2010. *Latin American Party Systems*. Cambridge: Cambridge University Press.

Kornhauser, William. 2013. *Politics of Mass Society*. New York: Routledge.

Kriesi, Hanspeter. 2014. 'The Populist Challenge'. *West European Politics* 37 (2): 361–378.

Kriesi, Hanspeter, Edgar Grande, Martin Dolezal, Marc Helbling, Dominic Höglinger, Swen Hutter, and Bruno Wüest. 2012. *Political Conflict in Western Europe*. Cambridge; New York: Cambridge University Press.

Laclau, Ernesto. 2005. *On Populist Reason*. London: Verso Books.

Laclau, Ernesto, and Chantal Mouffe. 2004. *Hegemonía Y Estrategia Socialista: Hacia Una Radicalización de La Democracia*. Buenos Aires: Fondo de Cultura Económica.

Le Bon, Gustave. 1960. *The Crowd: A Study of the Popular Mind*. New York: The Viking Press.

Lee, Timonthy B. 2016. 'Brexit: The 7 Most Important Arguments for Britain to Leave the EU'. Vox. 22 June 2016. www.vox.com/2016/6/22/11992106/brexit-arguments.

Levitsky, Steven. 2003. *Transforming Labor-Based Parties in Latin America: Argentine Peronism in Comparative Perspective*. Cambridge, UK: Cambridge University Press.

Lipset, Seymour Martin. 1959. 'Democracy and Working-Class Authoritarianism'. *American Sociological Review* 24 (4):482–501.

Luna, Juan Pablo. 2014. *Segmented Representation: Political Party Strategies in Unequal Democracies*. Oxford: Oxford University Press.

Mair, Peter. 2009. 'Representative versus Responsible Government'. *MPIfG Working Paper* 9 (8): 1–19.

Meléndez, Carlos and Rovira Kaltwasser, Cristóbal. 2017. 'Political Identities: The Missing Link in the Study of Populism'. *Party Politics*, DOI: 10.1177/1354068817741287

Moffitt, Benjamin. 2016. *The Global Rise of Populism: Performance, Political Style, and Representation*. Palo Alto, CA: Stanford University Press.

Moffitt, Benjamin, and Simon Tormey. 2014. 'Rethinking Populism: Politics, Mediatisation and Political Style.' *Political Studies* 62 (2): 381–397.

Mudde, Cas. 2004. 'The Populist Zeitgeist'. *Government and Opposition* 39 (4):542–563.

———. 2007. *Populist Radical Right Parties in Europe*. Cambridge: Cambridge University Press.

Mudde, Cas, and Cristobal Rovira Kaltwasser, eds. 2012. *Populism in Europe and the Americas: Threat or Corrective to Democracy?* Cambridge: Cambridge University Press.

———. 2013. 'Populism'. In *The Oxford Handbook of Political Ideologies*, edited by Michael Freeden, Marc Stears, and Lyman Tower Sargent, 493–512. Oxford: Oxford University Press.

Mudde, Cas, and Cristóbal Rovira Kaltwasser. 2017. *Populism: A Very Short Introduction*. Oxford: Oxford University Press.

Ochoa Espejo, Paulina. 2011. *The Time of Popular Sovereignty: Process and the Democratic State*. University Park, PA: Penn State Press.

Oesch, Daniel. 2008. 'Explaining Workers' Support for Right-Wing Populist Parties in Western Europe: Evidence from Austria, Belgium, France, Norway, and Switzerland'. *International Political Science Review / Revue Internationale de Science Politique* 29 (3):349–373.

Olson, Mancur. 1971. *The Logic of Collective Action: Public Goods and the Theory of Groups*. Cambridge, MA: Harvard University Press.

Ostiguy, Pierre. 2017. 'Populism: A Socio-Cultural Approach', in *The Oxford Handbook of Populism*, edited by C. Rovira Kaltwasser, P. Taggart, P. Ochoa Espejo, and P. Ostiguy, 73–97. New York: Oxford University Press.

Oxhorn, Philip. 1998. 'The Social Foundations of Latin America's Recurrent Populism: Problems of Popular Sector Class Formation and Collective Action'. *Journal of Historical Sociology* 11 (2):212–246.

Panebianco, Angelo. 1988. *Political Parties: Organization and Power*. Translated by Marc Silver. New York: Cambridge University Press.

Poblete, Mario. 2015. 'How to Assess Populist Discourse through Three Current Approaches'. *Journal of Political Ideologies* 20 (2):201–218.

Randall, Vicky, and Lars Svåsand. 2002. 'Party Institutionalization in New Democracies'. *Party Politics* 8 (1):5–29.

Rico, Guillem, Marc Guinjoan, and Eva Anduiza. 2017. 'The Emotional Underpinnings of Populism: How Anger and Fear Affect Populist Attitudes.' *Swiss Political Science Review* 23 (4):444–461.

Roberts, Kenneth M. 1995. 'Neoliberalism and the Transformation of Populism in Latin America: The Peruvian Case'. *World Politics* 48 (01):82–116.

———. 2006. 'Populism, Political Conflict, and Grass-Roots Organization in Latin America'. *Comparative Politics* 38 (2):127–148.

Sartori, Giovanni. 1970. 'Concept Misformation in Comparative Politics'. *American Political Science Review* 64 (4):1033–1053.

Sides, John, and Michael Tesler. 2016. 'How Political Science Helps Explain the Rise of Trump (Part 3): It's the Economy, Stupid'. *Washington Post*. May 4, 2016. www.washingtonpost.com/news/monkey-cage/wp/2016/03/04/how-political-science-helps-explain-the-rise-of-trump-part-3-its-the-economy-stupid/.

Skocpol, Theda, and Vanessa Williamson. 2013. *The Tea Party and the Remaking of Republican Conservatism*. Reprint edition. New York: Oxford University Press.

Taggart, Paul A. 2000. *Populism*. Philadelphia, PA: Open University Press.

Tajfel, Henri, M.G. Billig, R.P. Bundy, and Claude Flament. 1971. 'Social Categorization and Intergroup Behaviour'. *European Journal of Social Psychology* 1 (2):149–178.

Tajfel, Henri, and John Turner. 1979. 'An Integrative Theory of Intergroup Conflict'. In *The Social Psychology of Intergroup Relations*, edited by W.G. Austin and S. Worchel, 33–47. Monterey, CA: Brooks/Cole.

Tett, Robert P., and Hal A. Guterman. 2000. 'Situation Trait Relevance, Trait Expression, and Cross-Situational Consistency: Testing a Principle of Trait Activation'. *Journal of Research in Personality* 34 (4):397–423.

Van der Brug, Wouter, Meindert Fennema, and Jean Tillie. 2005. 'Why Some Anti-Immigrant Parties Fail and Others Succeed: A Two-Step Model of Aggregate Electoral Support'. *Comparative Political Studies* 38 (5):537–573.

Van Hauwaert, Steven, and Van Kessel, Stijn. 2018. 'Beyond Protest and Discontent: A Cross-National Analysis of the Effect of Populist Attitudes and Issue Positions on Populist Party Support'. *European Journal of Political Research* 57 (1): 68–92.

Weyland, Kurt. 1999. 'Neoliberal Populism in Latin America and Eastern Europe'. *Comparative Politics* 31 (4):379–401.

———. 2001. 'Clarifying a Contested Concept: Populism in the Study of Latin American Politics'. *Comparative Politics* 34 (1):1–22.

Whitehouse, Mark. 2016. 'Thank 2008 Financial Crisis for Trump's Rise'. Charlotte Observer. 24 November 2016. www.charlotteobserver.com/opinion/op-ed/article116796648.html.

Wofford, Ben. 2016. 'Pinochet. Chavez. Trump?' POLITICO Magazine. Accessed August 16, 2016. www.politico.com/magazine/story/2016/03/bienvenido-el-presidente-trump-213764.

Part I

Measuring populist ideas

1 Textual analysis

Big data approaches

Kirk A. Hawkins and Bruno Castanho Silva

One of the main challenges in studying populism in comparative perspective is finding ways of measuring it across a large number of cases, including not just multiple countries but multiple parties within countries. Most large-N studies classify cases by fiat, based on literature reviews or the judgments of country specialists (see, for example, Doyle 2011; Levitsky and Loxton 2013; Bustikova 2014; Mudde 2007; Mudde 2014). The problem with the first approach is that it often relies on second-hand literature instead of primary sources, and has little room for testing reliability. The problem with the second is that it depends on experts' different conceptions of populism, which frequently diverge from the ideational approach adopted in this volume. Ultimately, these approaches struggle to provide an objective basis for comparing cases across different contexts.

While other chapters overcome this challenge by implementing techniques such as surveys of political elite attitudes or systematic expert surveys, here we provide a head-to-head comparison between two techniques of textual analysis: holistic grading and computer assisted textual analysis through supervised learning. Generally speaking, textual analysis is useful for anyone using the ideational approach to populism because it is focused on ideas, and because the ideas of political elites can be hard to measure through anything except texts, such as speeches or manifestos, that the politician produces for other audiences besides the researcher. Most of the earliest efforts at measuring populism objectively were, in fact, textual analyses by scholars favoring some kind of ideational definition (Armony and Armony 2005; Jagers and Walgrave 2007; Hawkins 2009). Here we explore a particularly difficult version of this challenge by adapting textual analysis to the measurement of populism across party systems in large numbers of countries. Much of the current methodological literature on textual analysis promotes automated textual analysis as an ideal means of dealing with "big data" issues (Quinn et al. 2010; Hopkins and King 2010; Laver, Benoit, and Garry 2003; Lucas et al. 2015). However, populism is a different sort of idea than the themes being measured in much of that literature, and human techniques might be more appropriate.

To help resolve this issue, and to provide data that we use in other chapters, we test a validated human-based approach to measuring populism—holistic grading (Hawkins 2009)—and apply it to 144 parties from 27 countries in Europe and the Americas. Specifically, we look at campaign documents—electoral manifestos and speeches by party leaders—from all main parties in each political system to observe how populist each actor is, and compare that to a range of international cases. In the process we create the first cross-regional dataset classifying entire party systems. With these data in hand, we first observe how populism is distributed across the regions in this study, and how specific parties are classified. Next, we compare these results to supervised learning methods that can, theoretically, also confront the challenge of categorizing large numbers of texts across multiple languages. We find promising results for both.

Holistic grading

We approach the challenge of measuring populism with a very specific definition in mind, the ideational one. This defines populism as a discourse dividing the political world into two camps: the good, identified with the virtuous will of the common people; and the evil, embodied in a conspiring elite. Because populism sees the political system as having been subverted, it calls for a "systemic change," or liberation of the people from the grip of the elites. It also tolerates undemocratic means to achieve this goal since, in this framing, the elites are thieves who do not deserve a fair treatment, and the enforcement of the people's will should not be blocked by formalities and institutions.

The ideational definition lends itself to operationalization and measurement, because it identifies elements that should be present in a discourse for it to be populist. Following it, researchers have used different content analysis methods to measure populism in recent years. Jagers and Walgrave (2007) test a dictionary-based approach to classify populist parties in Flanders, which is extended to three more countries in Rooduijn and Pauwels (2011). This technique consists in defining a dictionary of "populist" terms and classifying documents based on their frequency. In contrast, Rooduijn, de Lange, and van der Brug (2014) use human-based content analysis of party manifestos from five European countries. This approach has paragraphs as units of analysis, and uses trained coders to classify each one as populist or not, with the aggregated proportion of populist paragraphs being the party score. A third comparative approach has been put forward in Hawkins (2009), and consists of holistic grading. There, chief executives' speeches are coded as a whole, without breaking them down into words or paragraphs.[1]

From these alternatives, this paper uses the third. Although the Introduction to the volume raises methodological concerns regarding the accuracy of other techniques, our reasons here are more practical. The dictionary-based technique demands a high knowledge of each specific country and time period for the selection of relevant terms. It is feasible in single case studies or small-n comparisons, as in the chapters by March (Chapter 2) and Šalaj and Grbeša (Chapter 3), but becomes less so when a larger number of countries are included. Of the other two techniques, both depart from a similar definition of populism and could potentially be used for the purposes of this study. Hawkins' approach has the upper hand, however, for having been tested and validated across a large number of countries and time-periods. The original study (Hawkins 2009) included 40 contemporary and historical presidents and prime-ministers from Latin America, Europe, and Asia, while a second round was done with chief executives from Eastern Europe and Central Asia (Hawkins 2013). Furthermore, because it works at the level of whole texts, it can be used to generate data relatively quickly, at least for human-coded analysis. The technique by Rooduijn et al. (2014) has not yet been applied outside of France, Italy, Germany, the Netherlands, and the United Kingdom, and while it has the clear advantage of generating more fine-grained data, it is much more time consuming.

Holistic grading was developed in educational psychology for assessing students' writing (White 1985; Sudweeks, Reeve, and Bradshaw 2004). It is a human-based approach that evaluates the text as a whole. Coders are trained to assign scores based on the elements of the concept and a set of anchor texts defined as examples for the each score in the scale. In our case, coders were trained in English on the concept of populism, and the set of training documents and anchor texts were also in English. In order to ensure the validity of our measure, the anchor texts were drawn from a variety of regions and capture different ideological flavors of left and right.[2] The training emphasized that the most important dimension of populism is the notion of a reified will of the common people, and that this reified people has to be defined in opposition to an "elite," which is powerful and oppressive. Therefore, even if there was a great deal of anti-elitism in the text, coders could not assign a score of 1 unless there was also a reified will of the people. As in Hawkins (2009, 1062), scores come from a 0–1–2 scale defined as follows:

0 A speech in this category uses few if any populist elements. Note that even if a manifesto expresses a Manichaean worldview, it is not considered populist if it lacks some notion of a popular will.
1 A speech in this category includes strong, clearly populist elements but either does not use them consistently or tempers them by including non-populist elements. Thus, the discourse may have a romanticized notion of the people and the idea of a unified popular will (indeed, it must in order to be considered populist), but it avoids bellicose language or references to cosmic proportions or any particular enemy.
2 A speech in this category is extremely populist and comes very close to the ideal populist discourse. Specifically, the speech expresses all or nearly all of the elements of ideal populist discourse, and has few elements that would be considered non-populist.

Because coders in earlier studies reported that it was often difficult to choose between these blunt categories, this time we instructed them to give decimal scores, and said that 0.5 rounded up to a categorical 1, and 1.5 rounded up to a categorical 2, and that they should consider these qualitative differences when assigning decimal points. After the training, coders received the texts, whether speeches or manifestos, and coded them in their original language (most coders were native speakers). For each text, the coder filled out a rubric that included a score, representative quotes, and a qualitative summary of their judgment. Each coder worked independently and filled out one rubric per document; afterwards, final scores were discussed with the other coders and the coordinator to clarify questions and check for possible misunderstandings.

Sampling

Two innovations were introduced to this sample relative to previous studies using holistic grading. First, because our goal was to capture the level of populism in the party system, the sample was expanded from chief executives to all major parties (usually all those receiving more than 1% of the vote). Second, in order to capture as many parties as possible, we focused on coding party manifestos rather than speeches. Manifestos are a common choice in analyses of partisan ideology but also in the populism literature (Rooduijn and Akkerman 2017; Rooduijn and Pauwels 2011; see also March's chapter in this volume). The main reason is that these documents explore a party's discourse as an institution, which may be distinct from that of its top candidates. Also, together with speeches, manifestos are the documents most comparable across countries: almost everywhere parties produce some kind of election program. This means we are looking for populist discourse in documents that are produced and made public with similar purposes across cases. Moreover, as a practical note, manifestos are more accessible than speeches across time and space. It is very difficult to find speeches for defeated candidates (and sometimes even for winning ones) more than one or two election cycles back, while manifestos are usually available for longer periods. We think this makes manifestos an essential text for studies of whole party systems.

Some might question the relevance of party manifestos in certain contexts. In many countries, especially in Latin America, few voters actually bother to read them, and people are often unaware that parties even have them. There are a few standard answers to this objection. First, there is the empirical observation that parties actually do implement a fair share of what they promise in their electoral manifestos (e.g. Bara 2005; Budge and Hofferbert 1990; Naurin 2014). Therefore, even if no one is reading them, manifestos provide insights into what political parties are thinking and what they will do once in power. Second, even if parties do not see their manifesto as their highest priority, writing it still requires effort by people involved in the communication side of the campaign who are usually party members; odds are that they approximate the average party discourse.

In terms of coverage, the total sample includes 144 parties from 27 countries in the Americas and Western Europe.[3] The selection of countries was partly dictated by convenience: we had to include those for which there were coders who spoke the language. This was less of a problem in the Americas, where most of South America plus the whole North America were included. In Western Europe the sample was more limited, but we could not identify any evident biases: the sample includes countries where populism is often said to be high, and others where it is usually off the radar. Also, it includes both Southern and Northern European countries. What are completely absent, though, are post-socialist Central and Eastern European cases.

Our target was to include every party that received more than 1% of the valid national votes. This was met for half the countries in our sample. In the other half, either manifestos were unavailable for smaller parties (as, for example, in Bolivia, Ecuador, or Argentina), or party system fragmentation imposed a higher limit: with too many parties, our resources for hiring coders became scarce, and we sensed the diminishing marginal utility of coding the eleventh party in a country just to meet the quota (such as the Party for the Animals in the Netherlands).[4] All documents are from the most recent national elections up to March 2015 in which the chief executive was defined.[5]

Validation with speeches

To test the validity and reliability of results obtained with manifestos, we also collected and coded party leaders' speeches in 18 of our countries.[6] We focused on the two campaign speeches most likely to be similar in format across the two countries: the opening speech where the candidate announced his or her candidacy, and the final or closing speech of the campaign. If we find that manifestos give widely different results when classifying parties, it is an indication that coding the two kinds of documents actually measures two different things, and that reliable measures for individual parties require more than just the one text.

We use speeches by the party main candidate (leader, in case of parliamentary systems, or presidential candidate, for presidential systems) from national election campaigns. While for the manifesto we effectively use a census sample, as there is usually only one manifesto, for speeches we use a quota sample (the beginning and ending speeches of the campaign).

The beginning speech is ideally the one where the candidate is announced by the party, or confirms her candidacy, frequently done in a large party event with significant media coverage. The second speech comes from the end of the race, a few days before the election (first round, in cases where there is a runoff), often given in the context of a large rally closing the campaign that also has significant media coverage. The reasoning behind this choice is to, first, capture the discourse in distinct moments in the race. Also, if it is possible to have speeches from events that received large coverage, we are looking at those that have the most potential to be heard by the largest number of voters; if a politician is to use a populist discourse, these are the moments when she is most likely to have been heard. Finally, limiting the number of speeches to two is dictated by a practical reason: it is very difficult to find more than two campaign speeches for some candidates.[7]

Results

Manifestos versus speeches

This is the first time that holistic grading has been applied on such a large scale to party manifestos, and some issues of adapting it to this kind of document emerged. First, as coders began reporting results, many indicated that there were two very different tones in some manifestos, where the preamble, or introduction, contained high levels of populism, while the rest (always a list of policy proposals) had a more pragmatic or technical feel. We decided to ask coders to give separate scores for the preamble/introduction, where it existed, and the list of policy positions. In the end, we found that the mean level of populism in preambles is slightly higher than on the list of positions: 0.29 compared to 0.23. The difference, however, is not statistically significant.[8] The scores for all parties coded are found in the Appendix, in Table 1A.1. In it, the manifesto column is a simple mean of the preamble and the list of issues scores, the same practice adopted by Rooduijn et al. (2014). Because the preamble is always shorter than the list of positions, the net result is to weight the preamble more heavily.[9]

The results confirm an intuitive expectation: manifestos are less populist than speeches. Given their nature as formal party documents for elite consumption, it is not surprising that the tone is more sober. The mean grade for manifestos is 0.30, while that of speeches is 0.46. This difference is statistically significant on a paired-sample t-test ($t = 2.40$, $p < .05$). Speeches from the beginning and end of the campaign have no difference on levels of populism (means of 0.47 and 0.46, respectively). In categorical terms, this means the average campaign speech is almost at the 0.5 threshold that indicates the presence of necessary elements of populism. This shows that populism in political campaigns might not be dominant, but still has a non-negligible presence.

The correlation between speeches' and manifestos' final scores is presented in Figure 1.1. It is 0.56, and there are only two cases of parties where one kind of document received a categorical 2 (a decimal score equal or above 1.5) and the other a categorical 0 (a decimal below 0.5). These are the *Rivoluzione Civile* (RCI), in Italy, with an average for speeches of its leader, Antonio Ingroia, of 1.5, while the manifesto scored 0.4, and the *Solidaridad Nacional* (SN), from Peru, whose manifesto received a 0.0 and the candidate's speech 1.6.[10] These results indicate that, when possible, it is ideal to have both manifestos and speeches to give a more complete picture of how populist individual parties are, but in the absence of speeches, manifestos still give a reasonable approximation.

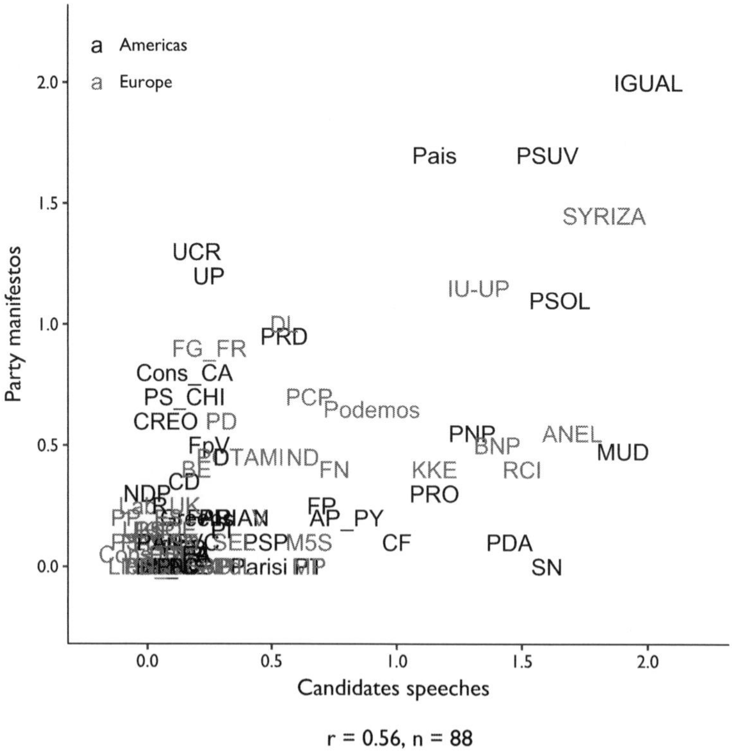

Figure 1.1 Candidates' speeches and party manifestos

Figure 1.1 shows a few parties close to the top, some more or less scattered in the middle, and many in the lower-left corner. Focusing on the specific parties, we see that those on the top are PSUV, Hugo Chávez's party in Venezuela; two other Latin American ones that closely follow his discourse, Alianza PAIS in Ecuador and Partido Igualdad in Chile; and the Greek SYRIZA. These are the only parties where it is possible to find the use of very strong populism consistently across different kinds of texts. This also gives an informal validation check to the results, since most scholars who study these parties (including those in this volume) seem to agree that they are highly populist in their discourse.

Intercoder reliability

After the coding efforts in Hawkins (2009; 2013) showed high intercoder reliability, it seemed possible to have only one coder doing some cases, in order to increase the number of countries and parties covered. Part of this sample, therefore, is based on the grades assigned by only one coder. For the other part (103 documents out of 308), two were kept, and the results of intercoder reliability checks confirm that the method is reliable. Krippendorff's alpha is high: 0.85 for manifestos, 0.87 for speeches. Using only one coder for part of the sample should not bring major measurement errors. Figure 1.2 shows the correlations between scores assigned by two coders to each document.

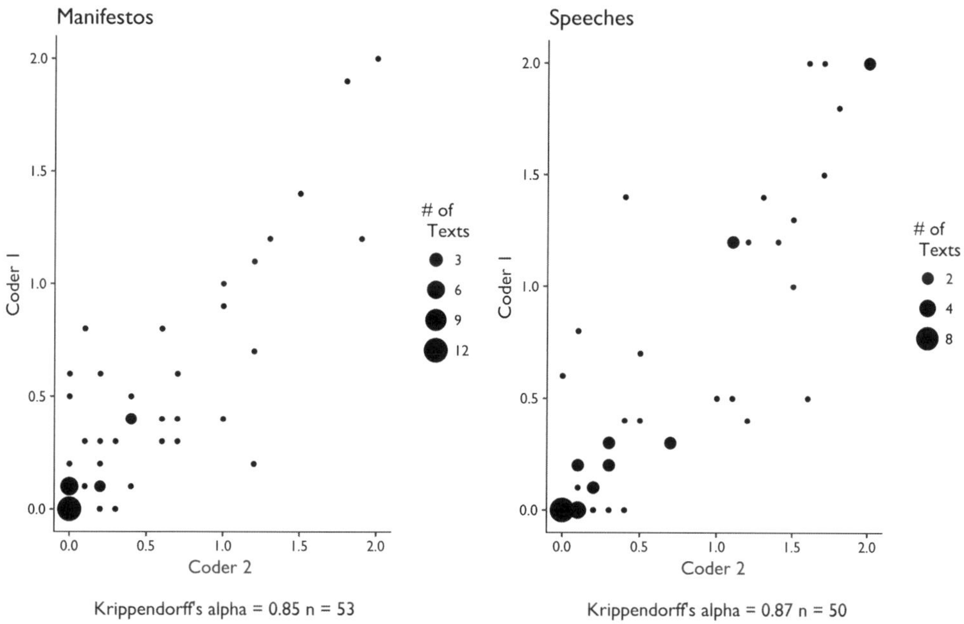

Figure 1.2 Intercoder score correlations

Document format

Eighty-three speeches in our sample were available only on video format, while 91 were coded from transcripts. One might hypothesize that speeches graded from videos, where the coder can see the emotions and receive all the non-verbal communication from the speaker, might be perceived as more populist than those coded from transcripts. A comparison of these two groups, however, does not indicate such a difference. Indeed, speeches coded from video have a higher average grade (0.50) than those from text (0.41). However, the reason we used video is because they were not available in another format, and that is often caused by the simple fact that no one bothered to transcribe them. In fact, video-speeches came mostly from smaller parties, with an average vote share of 16.7%, compared to 22.6% for transcribed speeches. Most importantly, we also observe that manifestos of parties for which we coded video-speeches are more populist (0.38) than those for which speech transcripts were available (0.30). It seems, therefore, that speeches for which there are no transcripts are simply from smaller and more populist parties.

Regional differences

Having shown that manifestos can provide a reasonably accurate dataset for large-N analyses of populism, we focus on them for the remainder of our analysis. Table 1.1 indicates all parties whose manifestos surpassed the categorical threshold of 0.5, indicating there is a non-negligible component of populism in their discourse, even if it is not consistently used. Four of the five most populist parties identified, all of which received a grade above 1.5, are from Latin America. They are the Partido Socialista Unido de

Table 1.1 Populist manifestos in Europe and Americas

Score	*Americas*	*Europe*
≥ 1.5	Partido Igualdad, Chile (2.0)	Coalition of the Radical Left (SYRIZA), Greece (1.5)
	Partido Socialista Unido de Venezuela, Venezuela (1.9)	
	Alianza Pais, Ecuador (1.7)	
	Movimiento al Socialismo, Bolivia (1.6)	
≥ 1.0	Unión Cívica Radical, Argentina (1.3)	Nationaldemokratische Partei Deutschlands, Germany (1.4)
	Unidad Popular, Uruguay (1.2)	Die Linke, Germany (1.3)
	Partido Socialismo e Liberdade, Brazil (1.1)	Partij voor de Vrijheid, Netherlands (1.3)
	Partido de la Revolución Democrática, Mexico (1.0)	Izquierda Unida-Unidad Popular, Spain (1.2)
		Schweizerische Volkspartei, Switzerland (1.0)
		Freiheitliche Partei Österreichs, Austria (1.0)
		Democràcia i Llibertat, Spain (1.0)
≥ 0.5	Mesa de la Unidad Democratica, Venezuela (0.8)	Front de Gauche, France (0.9)
	Conservative Party, Canada (0.8)	Esquerra Republicana de Catalunya, Spain (0.8)
	Bloc Québécois, Canada (0.8)	Partido Comunista Português, Portugal (0.7)
	Partido Socialista, Chile (0.7)	Podemos, Spain (0.7)
	Creando Oportunidades, Ecuador (0.6)	Partito Democratico, Italy (0.6)
	Partido Nacionalista Peruano, Peru (0.6)	Independent Greeks (ANEL), Greece (0.6)
	Frente para la Victória, Argentina (0.5)	Parti Populaire, Belgium-WAL (0.6)
		British National Party, UK (0.5)

Venezuela (PSUV), founded by Chávez; the Movimiento al Socialismo, Evo Morales' party in Bolivia; Alianza Pais, from president Rafael Correa of Ecuador; and a small party from Chile, Partido Igualdad, whose leader in the 2013 presidential campaign, Roxana Miranda, closely followed the radical-left ideology of the previous three. High levels of populism are also found in one European party in our dataset: SYRIZA in Greece. All of these except Partido Igualdad are familiar cases of populism from the media and the scholarly literature.

Interestingly, all of these cases of high populism are leftist in their "thick" ideology. Indeed, Bolivarianism, in particular, is also found to be strongly associated with the next-highest levels of populism: of the four Latin American parties that have scores between 1.0 and 1.5, two are connected to this movement, while another, the *Partido de la Revolución Democrática*, is the main leftist party in Mexico. The one exception is the *Unión Cívica Radical*, a center-left Argentinean party, not usually associated with populism. That said, among the European parties in this middle rank, over half could be considered right-leaning, and when we reach the lower ranks of populist parties (those with scores between 0.5 and 1.0), we even see one or more rightist parties in the Americas. Thus, the dataset identifies populism on both sides of the ideological spectrum, even if leftist versions are more strongly populist.

As the near absence of cases in the top-right box hints, populism is stronger in Latin America than in Europe. While we identified 13 parties with a score higher than 0.5 in Latin America, meaning 28.9% of the regional sample, there were only 16 European ones in this range out of 92, or 17.4%. Therefore, not only are the highest levels of populism found in Latin America, but the proportion of populist parties to the total in the region is substantively larger than in Europe. This point is made in Figure 1.3, which compares the means of populism in party manifestos across the two regions. The gray bars are unweighted mean scores of populism, while black ones present scores weighted by parties' vote-share. Latin American averages are higher than European ones. More than that, populism in Latin America is used by electorally stronger parties: when we factor in the vote-shares, the level of populism in manifestos goes up. In other words, populism is a more mainstream discourse in Latin America.

This pattern is an important finding in itself. While this has not been openly expressed or argued for, the common assumption in studies comparing populist parties in both regions is that they are populist to the same extent. Mudde and Rovira Kaltwasser (2012), for

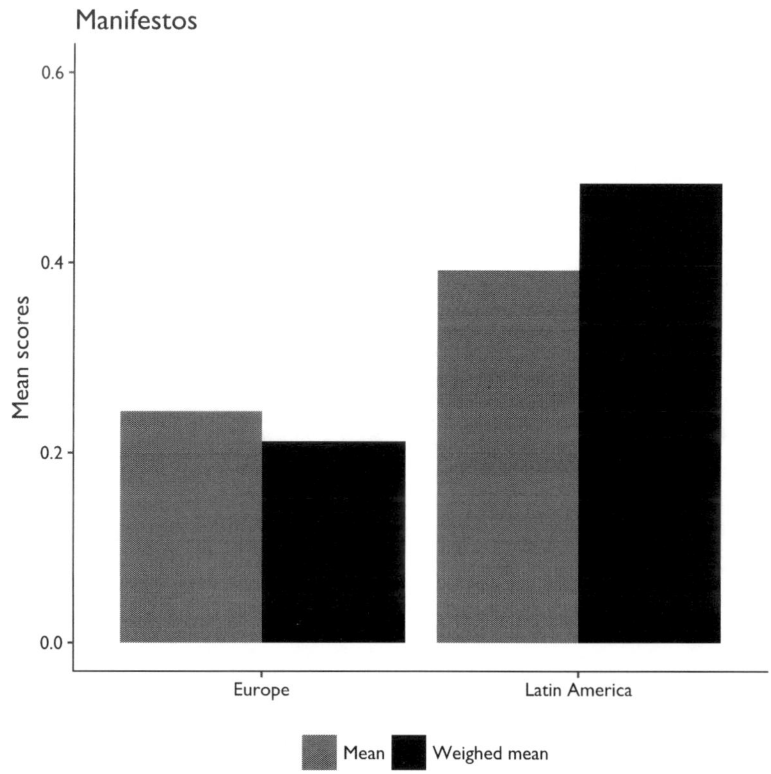

Figure 1.3 Populism means across regions

example, study the difference between left and right populism, concluding that one is inclusionary (left) while the other is exclusionary (right). They select typical cases of each: the French National Front and the Freedom Party of Austria for right-wing populism, and Evo Morales and Hugo Chávez for left-wing. The underlying assumption is that the only thing that differentiates these movements, at least in terms of their ideas, is their "thick" ideology—populism is treated as a constant. What we see here, however, is that the National Front, with a score for its manifesto of 0.4, is not nearly as populist as Morales' MAS (1.55) or Chávez's PSUV (1.85). And while the Freedom Party of Austria might come closer (1.0), it is still one category below the two Latin American ones. Thus, while populism is clearly not absent in Western Europe (our sample confirms this), there is a significant regional disparity in strength.

Thus, we find that holistic grading can be effectively deployed across large numbers of documents and across different textual genres, including both speeches and manifestos. However, human-coded textual analysis can still be slow (a typical analysis of a speech took our coders an hour, while that of a manifesto could be two hours), making it more expensive to produce data, especially large, cross-country datasets. Also, training coders is not easy, and other scholars might be reluctant to attempt a technique that requires specialized knowledge and experience, not to mention additional time. Many of these challenges could be resolved through automated textual analysis. In the next section we explore the potential for this technique.

Automated textual analysis

Automated textual analysis has been gaining traction in the social sciences as a way of measuring ideas reliably in large bodies of texts. Considering that what we present in this paper is, to date, the largest classification of political documents in terms of their level of populism, it seemed appropriate to test whether it is possible to develop a statistical model that can automatically classify manifestos, one that can reproduce the results obtained with human coding. If so, it would be a suitable replacement for human-coded techniques for large, quantitative datasets of populist discourse. We apply our efforts to the entire sample of manifestos coded, including those used for training coders, so that we have 154 documents in total.

To do this, we use machine learning techniques to perform *supervised classification* of documents.[11] This means that we develop a statistical model for analyzing texts based on a comparison of word frequencies, one that weights words that predict whether a document should be classified as populist or not. If you will, it is a kind of dictionary analysis that generates the dictionary automatically. This kind of approach involves three steps: first, splitting the sample into a training set and a test set; second, using the training set to develop a model that predicts classification scores in this subsample; and third, applying the model to the test set and computing the error rate, to see if the results are acceptable. There are different ways of calculating error, but all of the ones we use here assume that the closest we can get to the "true scores" of a text is the human classification. Therefore, each time the computer classifies a document with a different grade than human coders, it counts as an error.

There are multiple algorithms that can be used in the second step, training the model. No one outperforms the other absolutely, and each has its strengths and weaknesses depending on the data and the classification task at hand (James et al. 2013).

Our first choice is an elastic-net regression (Zou and Hastie 2005), which combines two kinds of regularized regression: the ridge (Hoerl and Kennard 1970) and the lasso (Tibshirani 1996). Besides predicting documents' classification, it also effectively selects those words (or stems) with the highest predictive power to classify documents as (non-)populist. In addition, we tested other commonly used algorithms to train the model, but none presented results that came close to those obtained with the elastic net, our best performer.[12]

Procedure

The corpus was prepared in the following way. First, texts were translated into English with Google Translator; an inspection of the output showed satisfactory results.[13] After that, they were pre-processed to make computerized analysis more practical. The procedures applied were standard: we turned all words to lower case, removed punctuation, numbers, and stop words (such as prepositions and articles), stemmed the words, and removed unnecessary space (meaning, everything besides a single space between each word). Our units of analysis are *unigrams*, i.e., single words or stems. Sparse terms—those that were present in fewer than 30% of the documents—were removed, as well as common terms that were present in more than 75% of documents. This reduces the demand for computational power and reduces noise, by removing information that is unlikely to help in classifying.[14] For the purposes of classification, we use manifestos' categorical scores instead of decimal grades. In total, there are 8 categorical 2 manifestos, 27 categorical 1s, and the remaining 119 are zeros. Because 8 is too small a number of manifestos for classifiers to work properly, we also do one sub-optimal test combining the 1s and 2s into a single group, forming a binary distinction of populist/not-populist.

Since the number of documents is not very large, we use a leave-one-out cross-validation (LOOCV) approach when training the model. In this technique, we first create a test-set with only one document, use all the n-1 remaining texts to train the model, and then predict the classification of that one manifesto in the test set. The procedure is repeated n times, until every text is in the test-set once and only once. This has the advantage of giving the most unbiased estimates of error rates, and is to be preferred over other validation approaches (larger test sets) whenever the number of texts to be classified does not make the method too time-consuming (James et al. 2013).

Results

Table 1.2 Accuracy of elastic-net regression classification

		Classifier		
		0	*1*	*2*
	0	119	0	0
Manual	*1*	18	9	0
	2	2	0	6
Lowest cross-validation error rate		0.14		
Krippendorff's alpha		0.55		

Notes: $\alpha = 0.9$, N = 154, with leave-one-out cross-validation.

Table 1.3 Accuracy of elastic-net regression classification on binary outcomes

		Classifier	
		0	*1*
Manual	*0*	119	0
	1	10	25
Krippendorff's alpha		0.79	

Notes: α = 0.5, N = 154, with leave-one-out cross-validation.

Table 1.2 shows the results of elastic net regression classification. Krippendorff's alpha, our measure of reliability between the training and test sets, is 0.55, much below the desired minimum of 0.75 or 0.8. While the classifier performs better than a coin toss (in which case Krippendorff's alpha would be 0), we see it has a significant problem when classifying documents originally coded with a 1. In 18 out of 27 cases it scored them with a 0, getting only 9 right. For very populist manifestos, however, the performance was not bad: six correctly classified out of eight. The same might be said for very non-populist manifestos: none of the 119 zeros was classified as populist. These results suggest that the automatic classifier is able to correctly classify very populist and very not-populist documents, but has problems with "in-between" cases. Those are manifestos that, following the description, "include strong, clearly populist elements but [. . .] not consistently."

Table 1.3 shows the results of testing these models with a binary classification of the manifestos (with 1 and 2 scores changed to 1). These are superior and give cause for optimism. The model correctly classified all 119 zeros, and 25 out of 35 1s. This is an acceptable accuracy, as exemplified by a 0.79 Krippendorff's alpha, which indicates that this method is as reliable as what we strive for with human coders. While the binary classification of populism does lose much of the information available when using decimals or the three-point category, these results suggest that a better performance of such models with more nuanced classifications might be a matter of more training data—i.e., more hand-coded manifestos for it to practice on.

The elastic-net regression also attributes a regression coefficient to each stem in the data. Larger coefficients mean that the stem is better at predicting populism, while larger negative coefficients mean the stem is important for predicting non-populism. The elastic-net model for the binary classification identified 104 stems that are predictive of populism or not-populism. Figure 1.4 plots all of them, aligned according to the size of their coefficient. Those below zero are predictive for non-populism (0), while those above zero are predictive for populism (1). The models seem to have face validity in capturing this concept: we can identify among the largest coefficients, for instance, *elit, domin, injust, fortun, lie, privileg, monopoli* and others that might indicate a belligerent discourse against an elite. Also, there are some that may be seen as references to "the people" and its general will, such as *mass, referendum, street, sovereignti, popular, movement,* and *struggle.* Another interesting point is the presence of *IMF*, referring to one of the most common targets of left populists in Latin America. On the non-populist side, there seem to be more stems referring to material issues, such as *countrysid, bureaucraci, recess, viabl, poorest, percentag, fossil, tuition, prescript, or brand.* These do not seem to reference any particular discourse, but combine terms we might associate with pluralism as well with pragmatic or technical discourse.

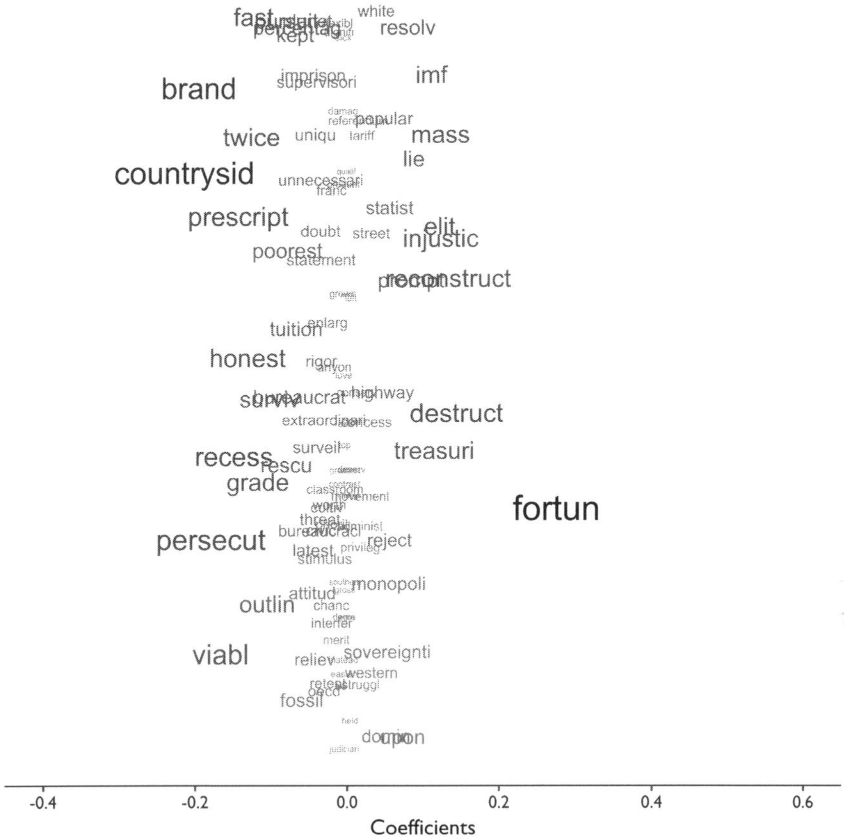

Figure 1.4 Predictive stems for (non-)populism

Discussion

This chapter started by introducing what is, up to date, the most comprehensive dataset of political parties classified by how populist their discourses are. We applied a technique of holistic grading to party manifestos and to candidate speeches from Western Europe and the Americas, to see how much populism was displayed in these texts. From the methodological perspective, we showed that holistic grading can transition to manifestos—a novelty in its application—and that it is possible to use only one coder if resources are scarce and the focus is on producing a large dataset rather than diagnosing particular parties. We also presented results on automated classification of these documents, and showed that computerized text analysis could potentially be successful in identifying populism if there is enough data for training models.

The classification data on their own are a relevant contribution that may be used for a wide array of future research. Models trying to explain support for populist parties, for instance, have up to now mostly relied on dichotomous divisions based on literature reviews or experts' classifications of parties (see, for instance, Bustikova 2014; Doyle 2011; Remmer 2011). It is now possible to model these preferences based on data on parties' levels of populism in comparative perspective, across different regions, derived directly from party communication and coded using a single definition of the term (see Castanho Silva later in this volume). This reduces measurement error, increases precision (by using a continuous measurement instead of a dichotomous one), and increases the comparability of results. If country experts overestimate the level of populism in parties they know well, this may now be corrected by having a scale that puts parties into fully comparative perspective.

A clear regional cut stands out from the results. While there are populists in both regions, the level of populist discourse found among Latin American parties and politicians is much higher than that found among their European counterparts. A prototypical European populist, the National Front, had a score of 0.4 for their manifesto, and Marine Le Pen's 2012 campaign speeches received an average of 0.75 out of 2. Other typical European populists did not fare much higher: Beppe Grillo's speeches averaged 0.65, Berlusconi's 0.35, and Nigel Farage's a round zero (bearing in mind that his speeches come a few years before the Brexit campaign). The Sweden Democrats' score, whose recent electoral success has spurred much debate in Europe about the rise of yet another radical right populist party, shows that it might be radical right, but it is definitely not populist—it is not even the most populist party in Sweden. This does not mean populism is not found in all cases expected. Nick Griffin and the British National Party get moderately high scores, as does the German extreme-right NPD, and Geert Wilders' PVV in the Netherlands. However, if we isolate only the populist portion of their discourse, they are still not as radically populist as a couple of Latin American examples.

A skeptical reader might say that low scores for some parties are the result of a bad measurement or a poor selection of texts, rather than parties' lack of populism. It is possible to find quotes by Farage, for example, which sound very populist. We admit that relying on a single text such as a manifesto is risky for making judgments about particular parties and advise other scholars to use larger samples when this is the objective. But especially where we *are* relying on larger samples of texts, there are two counterarguments that should be offered. First, while three documents might not be ideal, and there may be large variation in a politician's discourse, the odds of all three being the few non-populist exceptions from a very populist candidate are quite small. As we have seen, strongly populist actors have this discourse even in the list of policy proposals of their party manifestos. Second, our selection of speeches has a partial bias for high profile speeches: the opening and closing of campaigns. The simple fact that speeches were available online often indicates that they received at least some attention, and were not obscure talks to small audiences. Therefore, we are capturing political discourse in moments when it has a better chance of being heard by the public. If populism is to matter in a politician's discourse, those are the right times. It might be that a politician's tone is more populist to her partisans than to the general public, but then the question goes to another level: is intra-party populism more relevant than the party's discourse made for mass consumption? If our larger concern is with the causes of support for populism in the society where it is embedded, the answer is probably negative.

We should also describe what our coders used to justify giving low grades to supposedly very populist European parties. In general, student coders have identified these parties as being "very nationalist, but not populist," in that "people are not portrayed as an oppressed majority with a unified will" (in comments to the Sweden Democrats' manifesto), or that there is "no notion of a reified will [of the people]" (comments to the Vlaams Belang). According to the coding of the National Front, "The manifesto is nationalist, but it lacks enough references to the general will or to a reified people to be considered populist." Given that a notion of the "general will" of a homogeneous people is central and necessary to the existence of populism, its absence in these manifestos is the main reason why they do not receive higher scores.

These findings have important consequences for future research comparing populist experiences in the two regions, a topic which is currently flourishing. Knowing that Latin American populists are more radical in their populism than Europeans may have implications for explaining their support, as well as for the parties' and politicians' actions in office. For example, this might be one of the keys to explaining the openly anti-democratic actions taken by some Latin American populists in recent years (see Levitsky and Loxton 2013; Huber and Schimpf 2015). Such a high degree of populism comes together, by definition, with a high level of demonization of the opposition, which is used to justify their persecution as illegitimate actors. At the same time, it reinforces the argument made by Mudde and others (Mudde 2013; 2014) that public fears about the rise of radical right populism in Europe may be exaggerated. Not only have they not been as successful as one might think from reading the news but, in general, they are not as populist as generally thought. While concerns may be raised over their right-wing ideology, their populism may not be as important an issue.

If these findings call for a change in how we see populism in Europe, they are also of practical concern for the state of Latin American politics. While for some readers it may be sobering to see that Marine Le Pen is far from the populism of Evo Morales or Nicolas Maduro, the fact that her score is similar to that of moderate Latin American leaders, who are not usually associated with populism, may show just how deeply ingrained this discourse is in the region's political culture. In this chapter, the European "surprises" were mostly cases that were expected to be very populist and turned out not to be. In Latin America, the "surprises" were rather parties that unexpectedly had moderate or high levels of populism (even rising above prime European examples) and are commonly not thought of as such, for example, Peruvian president Ollanta Humala, who is usually seen as having dramatically moderated his tone during his successful electoral bid in 2011; or Henrique Capriles, the leader of the opposition to Chavismo in Venezuela who, our findings indicate, adopted much of his opponent's populist discourse. This observation, coupled with the finding that populism in Latin America is the language of stronger parties, gives cause for concerns over how its democracies will continue dealing with the divisive aspects of this discourse.

Regarding results observed with machine learning classifiers, there is reason for moderate optimism over the possibility of automating the coding of manifestos. The sample at hand is not one where classifiers would be expected to excel: there are relatively few documents, they were long (sometimes a few hundred pages), they come from a variety of countries and languages, and all of them were converted automatically into English. Moreover, the concept we try to capture is known to be elusive and subtle. To make matters more complicated, when applying holistic grading to manifestos, it is often the case that populism can be found only in a few important paragraphs. For an algorithm looking for words to do the classification, this is a small fraction of the total amount of information and may easily go unnoticed.

Given these difficulties, elastic net regression might be said to have gone beyond expectations, showing an ability to reliably classify manifestos on a binary populist/not-populist division. Where it does not perform well are in texts where the elements of populism are clearly present, but used inconsistently and not so strongly. At this point, there are two ways of explaining the inaccuracy. First, it may be that this is the limit of automated classification: populism in these texts is such a subtle topic that it requires human interpretation and contextual information to be identified, and there is no counting of words that can replace that. Or second, it might just be a matter of adding more data. With a large enough sample of manifestos, the training models would be able to capture the small differences that make for a score of 1. However, knowing which one of the two is correct depends on a larger amount of data and further study.

Notes

1 For a review of content analysis methods measuring populism, see Poblete (2015).
2 For the speeches training, we use speeches by Robert Mugabe of Zimbabwe (scored a 2), Evo Morales of Bolivia (a 2), Sarah Palin of the United States (1), Stephen Harper of Canada (1), Barack Obama of the United States (0), and Tony Blair of the UK (0). Because the manifesto training comes after the speech training and coding, we rely on a more narrow set of anchor texts from the US, including the Populist Party platform of 1892 (scored a 2), the Progressive Party platform of 1912 (1), the Progressive Party platform of 1924 (1), the Libertarian Party platform of 1972 (0), the US Democratic Party platform of 2000 (0), and the American Independent Party platform of 2008 (0). We also use a manifesto from Australia, the Australian National Party manifesto of 2010, which provides a contemporary example of strong populism (scored a 2). The rubric and the anchor texts are available in the online data appendix for this volume at the Team Populism website, https://populism.byu.edu/.
3 Greek parties did not produce proper electoral manifestos for the January 2015 elections. However, they all had editorials that outlined party policies, and these documents were used as the most comparable to manifestos.
4 Countries where the 1% rule applied: Belgium (vote shares considered for each electoral college), Brazil, Canada, Colombia, Germany (Pirate Party Germany, with 2% of list votes, were not included), Mexico, Peru, Spain, United Kingdom, Uruguay, United States, and Venezuela. Countries with a 5% cutoff: Argentina, Austria, Bolivia, Chile, Ecuador, France, Greece, Italy, Netherlands, Paraguay, Portugal, Sweden, and Switzerland. In some of these, one or more smaller parties were still included, when sources were available. From Norway, only the three largest parties are present in the sample.
5 Exceptions are Canada, where documents from 2006 were used; Austria, where we coded the 2008 legislative election; and Spain, where we included the December 2015 election.
6 Countries in which we did not include speeches: Austria, Belgium, Bolivia, Canada, Germany, Ireland, Netherlands, Norway, and Switzerland.
7 In Hawkins (2009) it was suggested that three to four speeches were enough for a reliable grade. However, in that study each politician's discourse was studied for all her time in office. Because we are limiting the sample to political campaigns—shorter in time, and with almost repeated speeches over several days—it may be expected that there is less variance, and fewer speeches may be needed.
8 Paired-sample t-test, $t = -0.86, p = 0.39$.
9 The length of manifestos ranged from four pages, from the German AfD, to 810, from the Walloon *Ecolo*. The length of preambles spans from two paragraphs to five pages.
10 Both might be explained by two shortcomings in the data available from these parties. The RCI manifesto was one of the few that had no preamble, only a list of policy positions, which may have contributed to its lower score. For the SN, only one speech from its presidential candidate, Luis "Lucho" Castañeda Lossio, was found and coded, and the version of the speech had been edited before it was made available. This score, therefore, is more sensitive to the possibility of a single non-representative speech or of non-representative fragments that have been kept.
11 Another popular alternative is *unsupervised* learning, which essentially produces a word distribution in graphical form that a human being must assess *a posteriori*. See Grimmer and Stewart (2013) for a comprehensive assessment of automated text analysis methods.
12 They are support vector machine (SVM, Karatzoglou, Meyer, and Hornik 2006), classification tree with random forests (Liaw and Wiener 2002; Ripley 2015), logistic boosting (Friedman, Hastie, and Tibshirani 2000), and scaled linear discriminant analysis (Läuter, Glimm, and Kropf 1998; Peters and Hothorn 2015). For these methods we used off-the-shelf software with default

settings from the R package "RTextTools" (Jurka et al., 2014). We applied leave-one-out-cross validation for each one to obtain the best predictive model for all classifiers, and used Krippendorff's alpha (Krippendorff 2004) between each individual classifier and the manual code to evaluate the quality of results.

13 We read a sample of passages from translations and compared to texts in the original languages. While syntax and nuances might be lost, words were translated accurately. These models use a "bag-of-words" assumption, meaning that the order in which words appear in a text does not matter; they only consider the frequency of terms in each document. Therefore, translating words accurately, even if losing syntax or nuances, is the most important goal. The choice of language is due to the fact that automatic translators are usually considered to work better with English as a target, one of the reasons being that for many pairs of languages the automatic translator does not do the translation directly, but through English. We have also run all the analyses on the subsample of documents in Spanish, the language with most documents in our sample (43 manifestos). However, the models' performance is very poor due to the small sample.

14 We tested different levels of ratios for sparsity and commonality—including no removal of sparse or common words—and the numbers used (30% and 75%, respectively) are the ones under which the algorithm presented its best classifying performance. All transformations were done using the "tm" package for R (Feinerer and Hornik 2015; Feinerer, Hornik, and Meyer 2008).

References

Armony, Ariel C., and Armony, Victor. 2005. "Indictments, myths, and citizen mobilization in Argentina: A discourse analysis." *Latin American Politics and Society* 47: 27–54.

Bara, Judith. 2005. "A question of trust: Implementing party manifestos." *Parliamentary Affairs* 58(3): 585–599.

Budge, Ian and Richard I. Hofferbert. 1990. "Mandates and policy outputs: U.S. Party platforms and federal expenditures." *American Political Science Review* 84(1): 111–131.

Bustikova, Lenka. 2014. "Revenge of the radical right." *Comparative Political Studies* 47(12): 1738–1765.

Doyle, David. 2011. "The legitimacy of political institutions: Explaining contemporary populism in Latin America." *Comparative Political Studies* 44(11): 1447–1473.

Feinerer, Ingo and Kurt Hornik. 2015. *tm: Text Mining Package*. R package version 0.6-2.

Feinerer, Ingo, Kurt Hornik, and David Meyer. 2008. "Text mining infrastructure in R." *Journal of Statistical Software* 25(5): 1–54.

Friedman, Jerome, Trevor Hastie, and Robert Tibshirani. 2000. "Additive logistic regression: A statistical view of boosting." *Annals of Statistics* 28(2): 337–407.

Grimmer, Justin and Brandon M. Stewart. 2013. "Text as data: The promise and pitfalls of automatic content analysis methods for political texts." *Political Analysis* 21(3): 267–297.

Hawkins, Kirk. 2009. "Is Chavez populist?: Measuring populist discourse in comparative perspective." *Comparative Political Studies* 42(8): 1040–1067.

Hawkins, Kirk. 2013. "Measuring populism in comparative perspective." In *XXXI International Congress of the Latin American Studies Association*, May 29 – June 1, Washington DC.

Hoerl, Arthur E. and Robert W. Kennard. 1970. "Ridge regression: Biased estimation for nonorthogonal problems." *Technometrics* 12(1): 55–67.

Hopkins, Daniel J. and Gary King. 2010. "A method of automated nonparametric content analysis for social science." *American Journal of Political Science* 54(1): 229–247.

Huber, Robert A. and Christian H. Schimpf. 2015. "Friend or foe? Testing the influence of populism on democratic quality in Latin America." *Political Studies* 64(4): 872–889.

Jagers, Jan and Stefaan Walgrave. 2007. "Populism as political communication style: An empirical study of political parties' discourse in Belgium." *European Journal of Political Research* 46(3): 319–345.

James, Gareth, Daniela Witten, Trevor Hastie, and Robert Tibshirani. 2013. *An Introduction to Statistical Learning: With Applications in R*. New York, NY: Springer.

Jurka, Timothy P., Loren Collingwood, Amber E. Boydstun, Emiliano Grossman, and Wouter van Atteveldt. 2014. *RTextTools: Automatic Text Classification via Supervised Learning*. R package version 1.4.2.

Karatzoglou, Alexandros, David Meyer, and Kurt Hornik. 2006. "Support vector algorithm in R." *Journal of Statistical Software* 15(9): 1–28.

Krippendorff, Klaus. 2004. *Content Analysis: An Introduction to Its Methodology*, 2nd ed. Thousand Oaks, CA: Sage.

Läuter, Jurgen, Ekkehard Glimm, and Siegfried Kropf. 1998. "Multivariate tests based on left-spherically distributed linear scores." *The Annals of Statistics* 26(5): 1972–1988.

Laver, Michael, Kenneth Benoit, and John Garry. 2003. "Extracting policy positions from political texts using words as data." *American Political Science Review* 97(2): 311–331.

Levitsky, Steven and James Loxton. 2013. "Populism and competitive authoritarianism in the Andes." *Democratization* 20(1): 107–136.

Liaw, A. and Wiener, M. 2002. "Classification and regression by randomForest." *R news* 2(3):18–22.

Lucas, Christopher, Richard A. Nielsen, Margaret E. Roberts, Brandon M .Stewart, Alex Storer, and Dustin Tingley. 2015. "Computer-assisted text analysis for comparative politics." *Political Analysis* 23: 254–277.

Mudde, Cas. 2007. *Populist Radical Right Parties in Europe*. Cambridge: Cambridge University Press.

Mudde, Cas. 2013. "Three decades of populist radical right parties in Western Europe: So what?" *European Journal of Political Research* 52(1): 1–19.

Mudde, Cas. 2014. "The far right and the European elections." *Current History* 113(761): 98–103.

Mudde, Cas and Cristóbal Rovira Kaltwasser. 2012. "Exclusionary vs. inclusionary populism: Comparing contemporary Europe and Latin America." *Government and Opposition* 48(2): 147–74.

Mudde, Cas and Cristóbal Rovira Kaltwasser. 2013. "Populism." In *Oxford Handbook of Political Ideologies*, edited by Michael Freeden and Marc Stears, 493–512. Oxford: Oxford University Press.

Naurin, Elin. 2014. "Is a promise a promise? Election pledge fulfilment in comparative perspective using Sweden as an example." *West European Politics* 37(5): 1046–1064.

Peters, Andrea and Torsten Hothorn. 2015. *ipred: Improved Predictors*. R package version 0.9-5.

Poblete, Mario E. 2015. "Review article: How to assess populist discourse through three current approaches." *Journal of Political Ideologies* 20(2): 201–218.

Quinn, Kevin M., Burt L. Monroe, Michael, Colaresi, Michael H. Crespin, and Dragomir R. Radev. 2010. "How to analyze political attention with minimal assumptions and costs." *American Journal of Political Science* 54: 209–228.

Remmer, Karen L. 2011. "The rise of leftist-populist governance in Latin America: The roots of electoral change." *Comparative Political Studies* 45(8): 947–972.

Ripley, Brian. 2015. *tree: Classification and Regression*. R Package version 1.0-36.

Rooduijn, Matthijs and Teun Pauwels. 2011. "Measuring populism: Comparing two methods of content analysis." *West European Politics* 34(6): 1272–1283.

Rooduijn, Matthijs, Sarah L. de Lange, and Wouter van der Brug. 2014. "A populist Zeitgeist? Programmatic contagion by populist parties in Western Europe." *Party Politics* 20(4): 563–575.

Rooduijn, Matthijs and Tjitske Akkerman. 2017. "Flank attacks: Populism and left-right radicalism in Western Europe." *Party Politics* 23(3): 193–204.

Sudweeks, Richard R., Suzanne Reeve, and William S. Bradshaw. 2004. "A comparison of generalizability theory and many-facet Rasch measurement in an analysis of college sophomore writing." *Assessing Writing* 9(3): 239–61.

Tibshirani, Robert. 1996. "Regression shrinkage and selection via the lasso." *Journal of the Royal Statistical Society. Series B (Methodological)* 58(1): 267–88.

White, Edward M. 1985. *Teaching and Assessing Writing: Recent Advances in Understanding, Evaluating, and Improving Student Performance*. San Francisco, CA: Jossey-Bass Publishers.

Zou, Hui and Trevor Hastie. 2005. "Regularization and variable selection via the elastic net." *Journal of the Royal Statistical Society, Series B (Methodological)* 67: 301–320.

Appendix

Complete list of party scores

Table 1.A1 Complete list of party scores

Country	*Year*	*Party*	*Manifesto Total*	*Speeches Total*	*Party Total*	*Electoral Result*
Argentina	2011	UCR	1.3	0.2	0.75	11.14
Argentina	2011	CF	0.1	1	0.55	7.96
Argentina	2011	FP	0.25	0.7	0.48	5.86
Argentina	2011	FpV	0.5	0.25	0.38	54.11
Argentina	2011	FAP	0.2	0.25	0.23	16.81
Austria	2008	SPO	0.1		0.1	29.26
Austria	2008	OVP	0		0	25.98
Austria	2008	FPO	1		1	17.54
Austria	2008	Gruenen	0.1		0.1	10.43
Austria	2008	BZO	0.2		0.2	10.7
Belgium-WL	2014	PP	0.55		0.55	4.1
Belgium-WL	2014	PS	0.15		0.15	31.43
Belgium-WL	2014	CDH	0.05		0.05	13.43
Belgium-WL	2014	Ecolo	0		0	8.89
Belgium-WL	2014	FDF	0		0	4.85
Belgium-WL	2014	MR	0		0	25.96
Belgium-FL	2014	CD-V	0		0	18.47
Belgium-FL	2014	Groen	0		0	8.46
Belgium-FL	2014	N-VA	0.1		0.1	32.22
Belgium-FL	2014	PvdA	0.1		0.1	3.24
Belgium-FL	2014	SP.A	0.05		0.05	14.04
Belgium-FL	2014	VB	0.2		0.2	5.84
Belgium-FL	2014	Open-VLD	0		0	15.55
Bolivia	2014	MAS	1.55		1.55	61.36
Bolivia	2014	PDC	0.3		0.3	9.04
Bolivia	2014	UD	0.25		0.25	24.23
Brazil	2014	PSOL	1.1	1.65	1.38	1.55
Brazil	2014	PT	0	0.65	0.33	41.59
Brazil	2014	PSB	0.08	0.15	0.11	21.32
Brazil	2014	PSDB	0	0.15	0.08	33.55
Canada	2006	Cons	0.8	0.15	0.48	36.27
Canada	2006	BQ	0.75		0.75	10.48

(*continued*)

Table 1.A1 (continued)

Country	*Year*	*Party*	*Manifesto Total*	*Speeches Total*	*Party Total*	*Electoral Result*
Canada	2006	NDP	0.3	0	0.15	17.48
Canada	2006	Greens	0.2	0.2	0.2	4.48
Canada	2006	Lib	0	0.05	0.03	30.23
Chile	2013	IGUAL	2	2	2	1.24
Chile	2013	PRO	0.3	1.15	0.73	10.99
Chile	2013	PS	0.7	0.15	0.43	46.7
Chile	2013	Parisi	0	0.45	0.23	10.11
Chile	2013	UDI	0	0.03	0.01	25.03
Colombia	2014	PDA	0.1	1.45	0.78	15.23
Colombia	2014	CD	0.35	0.15	0.25	29.25
Colombia	2014	PVC	0.1	0.2	0.15	8.28
Colombia	2014	PCC	0	0.1	0.05	15.52
Colombia	2014	U	0	0.1	0.05	25.69
Ecuador	2013	Pais	1.7	1.15	1.43	57.17
Ecuador	2013	PSP	0.1	0.48	0.29	6.73
Ecuador	2013	CREO	0.6	0.08	0.34	22.68
Ecuador	2013	PRIAN	0.2	0.35	0.28	3.72
France	2012	FN	0.4	0.75	0.58	17.9
France	2012	FG	0.9	0.25	0.58	11.1
France	2012	Verts	0.15		0.15	2.31
France	2012	UMP	0	0.25	0.13	27.18
France	2012	PS	0.1	0	0.05	28.63
France	2012	MoDem	0		0	9.13
Germany	2013	NPD	1.4		1.4	1.3
Germany	2013	Linke	1.3		1.3	8.6
Germany	2013	Gruene	0.2		0.2	8.4
Germany	2013	CDU	0		0	34.1
Germany	2013	FDP	0		0	4.8
Germany	2013	SPD	0		0	25.7
Germany	2013	AfD	0		0	4.7
Germany	2013	CSU	0		0	7.4
Greece	2015	ANEL	0.55	1.7	1.13	4.75
Greece	2015	ND	0.45	0.63	0.54	27.81
Greece	2015	PASOK	0.1	0.05	0.08	4.68
Greece	2015	GD	0	0.28	0.14	6.28
Greece	2015	SYRIZA	1.45	1.83	1.64	36.34
Greece	2015	KKE	0.4	1.15	0.78	5.47
Greece	2015	POTAMI	0.45	0.38	0.41	6.05
Ireland	2011	SF	0.33		0.33	9.9
Ireland	2011	Lab	0.3		0.3	19.5
Ireland	2011	FG	0.25		0.25	36.1
Ireland	2011	FF	0.03		0.03	17.5
Italy	2013	RCI	0.4	1.5	0.95	2.25
Italy	2013	PD	0.6	0.3	0.45	25.42
Italy	2013	M5S	0.1	0.65	0.38	25.55

Italy	2013	SEL	0.1	0.35	0.23	3.2
Italy	2013	PdL	0	0.35	0.18	21.56
Italy	2013	LN	0.1	0	0.05	4.08
Italy	2013	SC	0	0	0	8.3
Mexico	2012	PRD	0.95	0.55	0.75	31.59
Mexico	2012	PRI	0.05	0.18	0.11	38.21
Mexico	2012	PAN	0.1	0.05	0.08	25.41
Mexico	2012	PNA	0.05		0.05	2.29
Netherlands	2012	CDA	0.05		0.05	8.5
Netherlands	2012	D66	0		0	8
Netherlands	2012	PvdA	0		0	24.8
Netherlands	2012	PVV	1.25		1.25	10.1
Netherlands	2012	SP	0.2		0.2	9.7
Netherlands	2012	VVD	0		0	26.6
Norway	2013	A	0		0	30.8
Norway	2013	FrP	0		0	16.3
Norway	2013	H	0		0	26.8
Paraguay	2013	APA	0	0.1	0.05	37.11
Paraguay	2013	AP	0.2	0.8	0.5	5.88
Paraguay	2013	PC		0.05	0.05	45.83
Peru	2011	PNP	0.55	1.3	0.93	31.7
Peru	2011	AGC	0	0.1	0.05	18.51
Peru	2011	F11	0	0.05	0.03	23.55
Peru	2011	PP	0	0.1	0.05	15.63
Peru	2011	SN	0	1.6	0.8	9.83
Portugal	2011	PCP	0.7	0.65	0.68	7.9
Portugal	2011	BE	0.4	0.2	0.3	5.17
Portugal	2011	PSD	0.05	0.1	0.08	38.66
Portugal	2011	CDS-PP	0.05		0.05	11.71
Portugal	2011	PS	0	0.05	0.03	28.05
Spain	2015	ERC	0.7		0.7	2.39
Spain	2015	PNV	0	0	0	1.2
Spain	2015	DL	1	0.55	0.78	2.25
Spain	2015	PP	0.2	0	0.1	28.71
Spain	2015	IU-UP	1.15	1.33	1.24	3.68
Spain	2015	Cs	0.15	0	0.08	13.94
Spain	2015	Podemos	0.65	0.9	0.78	20.68
Spain	2015	PSOE	0.15	0.08	0.11	28.76
Sweden	2014	MP	0	0.65	0.33	6.89
Sweden	2014	V	0.2	0.45	0.33	5.72
Sweden	2014	SD	0.1	0.15	0.13	12.86
Sweden	2014	SAP	0	0.25	0.13	31.01
Sweden	2014	FP	0.05	0.1	0.08	5.42
Sweden	2014	C	0	0.1	0.05	6.11
Sweden	2014	KD	0	0.1	0.05	4.57
Sweden	2014	M	0	0.1	0.05	23.33

(continued)

Table 1.A1 (continued)

Country	*Year*	*Party*	*Manifesto Total*	*Speeches Total*	*Party Total*	*Electoral Result*
Switzerland	2011	SVP	1		1	26.6
Switzerland	2011	SPS	0.3		0.3	18.7
Switzerland	2011	CVP	0.1		0.1	12.3
Switzerland	2011	FDP	0.1		0.1	15.1
Switzerland	2011	BDP	0.05		0.05	5.4
Switzerland	2011	GP	0		0	8.4
UK	2010	BNP	0.5	1.4	0.95	1.9
UK	2010	SNP		0.65	0.65	1.7
UK	2010	Lab	0.25	0.05	0.15	29
UK	2010	UKIP	0.15	0.01	0.08	3.1
UK	2010	Cons	0.05	0	0.03	36.1
UK	2010	LibDem	0	0	0	23
Uruguay	2014	UP	1.2	0.25	0.73	1.13
Uruguay	2014	PI	0.15	0.3	0.23	3.09
Uruguay	2014	FA	0.05	0.2	0.13	47.81
Uruguay	2014	PC	0	0.15	0.08	12.89
Uruguay	2014	PN	0	0.1	0.05	30.88
US	2012	D	0.45	0.3	0.38	51.1
US	2012	R	0.25	0.05	0.15	47.2
Venezuela	2013	PSUV	1.7	1.6	1.65	50.6
Venezuela	2013	MUD	0.48	1.9	1.19	49.1

Notes: **Party Total:** average between manifesto and speech score; **Electoral Result:** electoral result in the election coded. First round of presidential if presidentialist country, legislative if parliamentary. Presidential results used for France. For Germany, which has a mixed electoral system, we include only votes for the party list.

2 Textual analysis

The UK party system

Luke March

The UK has been seen as a cardinal example of the (contested) theory of the European populist Zeitgeist: the thesis that populism is on the increase and has been enthusiastically adopted even by mainstream parties (Mudde 2004; Rooduijn et al. 2014). The mainstream UK parties – Labour, Conservatives and the Liberal Democrats – have been regarded as demonstrating high propensity to populism. Moreover, in addition to the right-wing populist British National Party (BNP) and UK Independence Party (UKIP), Britain has allegedly seen a rise in left-wing populism, first indicated by minor radical left parties such as Respect and the Scottish Socialist Party (March 2011), latterly by the rhetoric of politicians such as Ed Miliband and Jeremy Corbyn (the former and current Labour leaders) (e.g. Freedland 2013). Overall, the term "populism" is prevalent in mainstream British political discourse, even if its precise meaning is controversial (Mair 2002; Bale et al. 2011).

Accordingly, there are good reasons for focusing on the UK, as a study both of the populist Zeitgeist and of the related question of the relationship between the alleged populism of the mainstream parties and those of more radical parties of right and left. This is a particularly interesting area of analysis in view of recent advances in measuring populism. Reacting against the tendency of previous comparative analysis to declare certain parties populist "by fiat" without clear or consistent criteria (Hawkins 2009), a number of analysts have developed sophisticated techniques for providing more consistent temporal and spatial comparative measurement of populism (e.g. Reungoat 2010; Jagers and Walgrave 2007; Vossen 2010; Rooduijn and Pauwels 2011). However, these have been criticised for "degreeism" (their assumption that all parties are more-or-less populist) and hence their inability to distinguish between populist and non-populist parties (Pappas 2016).

Accordingly, this chapter develops a novel two-stage technique to compare the populism of different political parties. The first stage is a classical content analysis of party manifestos adapted from Rooduijn and Pauwels (2011). The revisions help more clearly distinguish between populist and non-populist parties and to refute the charge of degreeism. The second stage is a qualitative analysis of respective party manifestos, which provides a more holistic overview and thereby allows us to focus more clearly on how respective parties' populisms differ.

The chapter applies this technique to a comprehensive analysis of key UK party actors, both populist and allegedly so. It focuses on three *mainstream parties* (the Conservative Party, Labour Party and Liberal Democratic Party); two *non-mainstream parties* that are sometimes regarded as populist (the regionalist/separatist party Scottish National Party (SNP) and the Green Party of England and Wales); two *populist radical right parties* (the BNP and UKIP); and one *populist radical left party* (Respect).

The main questions of this chapter are the following:

- Is there a populist Zeitgeist in the UK? Have "mainstream" parties become more populist over the period of study?
- To what extent do non-mainstream and populist parties differ from them?
- To what degree do the measurement techniques utilised adequately explain the principal differences among UK populist parties, and the reasons for them?

This chapter makes four main substantive contributions. First, it provides empirical richness to the study of UK parties and thereby shows that a) the populist Zeitgeist in the UK barely exists either among the mainstream and non-mainstream parties, since such parties have not become more populist over time; b) genuine populism is confined to parties of the radical left and radical right, especially the latter.

Second, it makes the methodological point that there are advantages and disadvantages to disaggregated measures of populism. If the focus is simply on providing numerical categories that can be summed, they can be misleading, and attention is needed on how the components interrelate; the second stage of qualitative analysis is essential to fully understanding this inter-relation. Therefore, the chapter reinforces that the ideational approach demands we pay careful attention to the contextual operationalisation of populism, especially in textual analysis.

This inter-relationship of components is key. The chapter makes two important and linked theoretical arguments about the ideational approach. One of these – its third main point – is that *all* populism's core claims need to be substantially present to justify calling an actor populist. This volume's introduction noted that the peculiarity of the populist set of ideas lies precisely in the combination its core elements, i.e. that *all* core components of the definition are jointly necessary. The methodology here reinforces that a cosmology of people-centrism and anti-elitism are core to populism, which is politicised through invocations to popular sovereignty.

Fourth and finally, it follows that what is often called the "thin", "mainstream" or "soft" populism, which underpins the Zeitgeist concept, isn't really populism at all but *demoticism* (closeness to the common people), which is necessary but by no means sufficient for populism. Therefore analysts should not call parties "somewhat populist" just because their rhetoric is demotic. Indeed, mainstream political actors regularly invoke people-centrism and popular sovereignty (especially) and anti-elitism (more rarely), but this does not make them populist.

The chapter proceeds as follows: the first section briefly sets out the definition of populism then discusses the theory of the populist Zeitgeist; the second describes the methodology; the third section presents the content analysis of party populism; the fourth section provides the holistic qualitative analysis; the fifth section discusses the findings; the final section concludes.

A populist Zeitgeist?

This chapter's approach to the ideational definition of populism (see the Introduction to this volume) utilises Cas Mudde's view of populism as a thin-centred ideology "that considers society to be ultimately separated into two homogeneous and antagonistic groups, "the pure people" versus "the corrupt elite," and which argues that politics should be an expression of the volonté générale (general will) of the people" (Mudde 2004, 543). The main elements of Mudde's definition will define the methodological variables (see below).

It is populism's "thin" nature and "empty-heartedness" that explain how it easily combines with other "full" host ideologies (Stanley 2008; Taggart 2004). From this ensues the contagiousness at the heart of the alleged Zeitgeist. Mudde (2004) argued that the Zeitgeist was explained not merely by the rise of genuine populist parties, but by the mainstreaming of populism. "Mainstream populism", or what Mudde later (2013, 9) calls "soft populism" has become routinised among various non-radical political actors, not least in the UK. Many other authors have seconded this thesis (e.g. Albertazzi and McDonnell 2007; Zaslove 2008).

However, the concept has received strong critique. Rooduijn et al. (2014; cf. Rooduijn 2013) argue that there is no evidence for any escalating "spiral" of populism. Mainstream parties are not becoming more populist, nor are they becoming "contaminated" under the influence of successful populist parties. Moreover, since some populist parties become *less* populist with increased electoral success, the thesis is weakened still further.

Because such analysis is more systematic than the ad hoc cases comprising Mudde's argument, it appears a robust rebuttal of the Zeitgeist thesis. However, others have argued that the thesis may still have validity in less-known cases such as Latvia (Balcere 2014). More pertinently for this chapter, the UK is regarded as a partial exception. According to Rooduijn et al. (2014), the UK has the highest average populism score for mainstream parties, as well as the highest single average for a mainstream party (the Liberal Democrats). Moreover, whereas for some, former Labour PM Tony Blair was the UK politician most prone to populism (Mudde 2004; Mair 2002), others suggest this is also true of the Conservatives and Liberal Democrats (Rooduijn and Pauwels 2011). Indeed, the Conservatives have allegedly long had a "love affair with populism" (Bale 2013, 29).

There are several reasons for this apparent prevalence of British populism. Above all, the majoritarian electoral system encourages adversarial politics and the salience of wholesale attacks on the political elite (van Kessel 2015, 147). Although majoritarianism simultaneously marginalises genuine populist parties, partisan dealignment combined with centralised party machines has contributed to the mainstreaming of populist discourse (Mair 2002). Latterly, devolution in Scotland and Wales has contributed to populist insurgency by regionalist/separatist parties (such as the SNP) against the "Westminster elite" (Dommett 2016).

Overall then, the existing literature leads us to expect that the UK is still a good example of the populist Zeitgeist, where "mainstream populism" is dominant and even increasing.

Operationalising populism

Recent years have seen a growth in "methodological populism": attempts to measure party populism systematically and comparatively. They have emerged out of disappointment with older comparative approaches, several of which either do not have clear definitional criteria for examining populism, or apply such criteria unevenly or non-transparently, sometimes without even specifying the sources of their information (Hawkins 2009; Pauwels 2011; Sikk 2009).

The most sophisticated analyses have developed systematic coding to provide temporal and spatial consistency to the examination of populism in political statements (e.g. Reungoat 2010; Pauwels 2011; Pauwels 2014; Hawkins 2009; Jagers and Walgrave 2007). The preferred method used here is an adaptation of the classical content analysis technique developed by Rooduijn and Pauwels (2011; Rooduijn et al. 2014). While not suitable for large-n studies (for which they advocate quantitative computer analysis), this approach provides ample detail for an in-depth analysis of populism where the emphasis is not just quantitative (counting the instances and proportion of populism) but qualitative (understanding how populism is constructed, what is meant by it and how it differs between parties). This approach focuses on ideational factors analysed via party manifestos. Several other approaches prefer to analyse party broadcasts, leaders' speeches or a panoply of party statements (e.g. Hawkins 2009; Jagers and Walgrave 2007). Whereas these give valuable and rounded insights, they are less suitable in programmatic party systems such as the UK's. Whereas party manifestos are seldom widely read, they are the documents that most succinctly summarise party stances for the benefit of a wider audience, and are an accessible source for tracing the evolution of party ideas *comparatively over time*. In sum, this approach provides consistent, valid and reliable temporal and spatial comparative measurement of party populism. There is nothing intrinsic to the methodology that prevents it being used to examine other types of textual source.

It is argued that the main disadvantage of measuring populism is "degreeism" (Pappas 2016). Many measurements assume that populism is a continuous/ordinal (*more-or-less*) rather than a dichotomous/nominal (*either-or*) concept (e.g. Jagers and Walgrave 2007; Rooduijn and Akkerman 2015, 3; Pauwels 2011; Hawkins 2009). Whereas this makes *prima facie* sense given the aforementioned "empty-hearted" or "chameleonic" nature of populism (Taggart 2000), it potentially becomes difficult to separate populism from non-populism. For instance, methods that provide an aggregated populism "score" on an explicitly ordinal scale can look confusing, because some "populist" actors turn out to have scores little higher than the mainstream, whereas conversely some mainstream actors demonstrate higher scores than populists (Hawkins 2009; Pauwels 2011; Rooduijn et al. 2014). At the extreme, this can lead to vague statements, such as "allegedly populist parties turn out to be rather populist indeed" and "there are also some mainstream parties that turn out to be rather populist" (Rooduijn and Pauwels 2011, 1277).

In truth, the allegations of degreeism are much overstated. Sartori allows for degreeism, *provided that* concept formation occurs before quantification (Sartori 1970, 1038). Moreover, even full ideologies are to some extent degreeist, with fluid and diachronically flexible morphological cores (Freeden 1996, 83–84). This is still more so with thin-centred ideologies: since they do not represent rigid world-views, actors can emphasise them to different degrees for strategic reasons (Stanley 2008, 108).

Stijn van Kessel (2014) offers a useful approach to distinguish between degrees of populism. At a higher level of abstraction, populism is a "discourse", used potentially by *any* political actor. As such, populism is a "descriptor", and a continuous concept: actors become more or less populist over time. At a lower level of abstraction, populism is an ideology. As such it is a "classifier" and dichotomous variable. The line will in practice be difficult to draw but primarily involves temporal consistency: whereas populist discourse is fleeting, populist ideology is routinised within actors' public appeals. However, van Kessel's use of the term "discourse" is problematic, since it is more commonly used in the Laclauian tradition with very different implications. As outlined below, I prefer the terms "demotic/demoticism" to denote quasi-populist rhetoric falling short of ideological populism. Demoticism clearly overlaps with "populist style" as used in the chapter by Marijana Grbeša and Berto Šalaj (Chapter 3), who also seek to distinguish ideational populism from more frequent uses with an "inclusive" methodology, although the term is broader.[1]

The redesign of the Rooduijn/Pauwels content analysis used here aims a) to allow more fine-grained qualitative analysis; b) precisely to distinguish more clearly between populism and non-populism; and c) to disaggregate parties' specific ideological components. As with their approach, extensively trained coders used a codebook to analyse party manifestos using indices of populism.[2] The three indices were *people-centrism, anti-elitism* and *popular sovereignty*. People-centrism was operationalised by asking coders to identify positive references to a homogeneous people. Apart from "the/our people", such references could include notions such as "the/our country", "we/us", "everyone" and *partes-pro-toto* references (subgroups meaning the whole, e.g. "working people", "every family"). Anti-elitism was measured by negative references to homogeneous elites. The critique had to be expressed towards the elite in general rather than sub-categories of that elite (e.g. "the Establishment" rather than "the Tories") although *partes-pro-toto* categories were again coded (e.g. "establishment parties"). Finally, popular sovereignty was operationalised by coding invocations to "power to the people". These could be general ("popular control") or specific (e.g. "referenda"). To distinguish clearly from people-centrism, sentences were coded only once and as popular sovereignty when they had specific action-oriented or normative emphases (e.g. "people need . . ."). For each index, coders were provided with an exhaustive list of populist and non-populist words and phrases, but also required to interpret the context during coding. Following analysis, I calculated the percentage of quasi-sentences referring to the three indices, and made an initial assessment of the degree of populism in each party.

The first major change from the Roouduin/Pauwels design was to match the indices more closely to Mudde's ideological definition. Rooduijn and Pauwels used a two-fold populism index (people-centrism vs. anti-elitism), whereas I added the third (popular sovereignty), which satisfies the last clause of Mudde's definition (politics as expression of the *volonté générale*). Populism has both descriptive and proscriptive elements, i.e. it "arises from a dissatisfaction with existing politics but also is an attempt to fix its representational failures" (Beasley-Murray 2010, 27). Therefore this last element is essentially about the operationalisation of the first two: the specific mechanisms and policies whereby people can be empowered and the elite dispossessed.

Most existing approaches concur that people-centrism and anti-elitism are *the* core concepts, but add a different range of supplementary ones. For example, some focus on exclusionism or "claims for democracy" (Vossen 2010). Others focus on Manicheanism or "sense of crisis" (Hawkins 2009; Rooduijn 2014). Most such supplementary elements can be incorporated in my three indices. Exclusionism is the most problematic, because some analysts argue that an "exclusion strategy" is intrinsic to populism, i.e. the antagonistic relationship between the people and elite, the emphasis on homogeneity of these terms, and populism's Manicheanism mean that certain "outsider" groups that do not fit into the "true people" are denigrated (Jagers and Walgrave 2007; Albertazzi and McDonnell 2007, cf. the Grbeša and Šalaj, this volume, Chapter 3). Mény and Surel (2002) further add that this exclusion works in two dimensions, a *horizontal* relationship between people and "dangerous others" and a *vertical* one between people and the elite. However, whereas the latter is undoubtedly intrinsic to populism, there is nothing necessarily exclusivist about the concept of people, and the nature of this concept may differ markedly, for instance between right and left populists, who are generally regarded as more inclusionary (March 2011). Accordingly, including exclusionism within the core definition of populism would *a priori* bias the definition towards right wing-populism (Rooduijn et al. 2014). "Claims for democracy" or direct democracy are not espoused by all populists, and are part of general demands for popular sovereignty. Manicheanism is implied by the central dichotomy between the pure people and turpitudinous elite.

Finally, the notion of "crisis" is undoubtedly important but is also integral to the central people–elite dichotomy: for the populist, any grave crisis will be elite-generated, will dramatically impinge on the people, and will be resolved by a return to true popular power (Taggart 2000, 93–94; Betz 2002, 198).

The second difference was to use "quasi-sentences" rather than paragraphs as the main unit of analysis. As in the Comparative Manifestos Project, a quasi-sentence is a sentence or clause that encapsulates a discrete relevant and meaningful statement (Werner et al. 2011). I considered paragraph coding too broad-brush to allow meaningful qualitative analysis, whereas conversely, using just words as the unit of analysis was likely to miss crucial nuances of meaning. The third difference was to have a two-stage analysis, following the content analysis with a more detailed qualitative analysis of the party manifestos (below). The qualitative analysis aimed to provide a more fine-grained comparative approach, and more specifically to typologise the similarities and differences between forms of populism, while avoiding over-relying on percentages for questions of interpretation.

For the content analysis, the *mainstream parties* (the Conservative Party, Labour Party, and Liberal Democratic Party) are all parties that have recently participated in UK national governments. The *populist parties* have all been described as such in the literature (e.g. Goodwin 2011; Ford and Goodwin 2014; March 2011). The *non-mainstream parties* are of more uncertain populist nature. Whereas the SNP is often described as such, the Green Party of England and Wales is little studied, although it has been seen as becoming a left-populist "UKIP of the Left" (*The Economist* 2014). Consequently, the eight parties chosen are the main relevant UK party actors during the period of analysis. The elections chosen are UK-wide (Westminster) elections in 2001, 2005, 2010 and 2015, which gives a comparably sized dataset to existing studies.

Content analysis results

Table 2.1 shows the *overall* populism scores per party. These demonstrate similar strengths and weaknesses to the original Rooduijn/Pauwels data. On one hand, the scores have *face validity*, showing that allegedly populist parties are indeed more populist (Rooduijn and Pauwels 2011, 1276). The average score for populist parties is higher than both the mainstream and non-mainstream parties in every election (albeit not always by much). On the other hand, some individual non-populist party manifestos have higher scores than some individual populist party manifestos.

At first glance, these results seem to suggest that there is mixed evidence for the populist Zeitgeist. There is a generally moderate level of party populism, with modest differences between mainstream, non-mainstream and populist parties. As such, it appears that all parties are more-or-less populist. Certainly, the mean scores for the mainstream parties do rise (from 9.2 in 2001 to 14.8 in 2015), albeit peaking at 15.4 in 2010. Conversely, the average for the non-mainstream and populist parties is stable, with even slight declines in 2010–2015. Moreover, the overall mean populism score for all parties increases only marginally from 14.6 (2001) to 16.0 (2015).

Tables 2.2 and 2.3 show the utility of having a *disaggregated* three-fold index, breaking the overall populism score into components. *Prima facie* the parties' overall populism scores look problematic. For instance, while in Table 2.1 the overall average for the Conservatives (16.69) and the SNP (16.31) is only marginally below the mean for the lowest-scoring populist party, Respect (17.05), closer attention to the individual components makes significant differences apparent. Both the mainstream parties and the non-mainstream

Table 2.1 Parties' overall populism score 2001–2015

Party	*Election*			
	2001	*2005*	*2010*	*2015*
Mainstream parties				
Conservative	11.8	18.3	22.1	14.0
Labour	10.4	12.3	16.0	19.4
Liberal Democrats	5.3	5.6	8.2	11.1
Average: mainstream parties	*9.2*	*12.1*	*15.4*	*14.8*
Non-mainstream parties				
Green Party	10.3	14.9	11.5	13.1
SNP	8.7	19 .7	25.3	15.7
Average: non-mainstream parties	*9.5*	*17.3*	*18.4*	*14.4*
Populist parties				
BNP	34.5	28	20.7	N/A
UKIP	21.3	34.4	20.1	22.8
Respect	N/A	16.3	21.7	N/A
Average: populist parties	27.9	26.2	20.8	22.8
Average: all parties	*14.6*	*18.7*	*18.2*	*16.0*

Source: Author's calculations from party manifestos. The populism score represents the percentage of populist quasi-sentences per manifesto.

parties have scores that are very heavily loaded on the people-centrism index (averages of 9.86 and 11.13 respectively), with much less on the popular sovereignty score (2.57 and 2.42 respectively) and, crucially, very low anti-elitism scores (0.42 and 0.84 respectively, with some manifestos having barely any anti-elitism at all). In contrast, the populist parties score more evenly across all three indices. The average populist people-centrism score is barely different from the other parties (10.53), but the popular sovereignty score is over twice as high (5.09) and the anti-elitism score is over seven times higher than that of the other classes of parties (5.88).

This is the crucial element of the revised indices that allows us to distinguish definitively between populism and non-populism. The populist parties display each of the core elements of populist ideology, even when (as with Respect), their *overall* score is not substantially different from some non-populist parties. In contrast, the near-negligible anti-elitism of the mainstream and non-mainstream parties means that while they look populist, they do not contain all the necessary constitutive criteria to satisfy a "classical" ideological definition of populism. It is the *combination* of the core criteria that makes them populist, and classifying them as such without even one such criterion is concept-stretching (van Kessel 2014, 104). Indeed, the Manichean people-elite dichotomy is absolutely fundamental to populism (Laclau 2007).

As noted above, the appeal for popular sovereignty is a mechanism for politicising populism. But it is by no means unique to populism – after all, the Rousseauian *volonté générale* is highly influential on modern republican and democratic thought. Perhaps support for popular sovereignty is a "motherhood and apple pie" issue – i.e. it represents little more

Table 2.2 Disaggregated populism scores: mainstream parties

	People-centrism	*Anti-elitism*	*Popular sovereignty*	*Overall populism score*
Conservatives				
2001	9.15	1.07	1.62	11.84
2005	13.76	0.0	4.51	18.28
2010	15.83	0.56	5.73	22.12
2015	12.93	0.27	0.82	14.01
Average	**13.24**	**0.49**	**2.96**	**16.69**
Labour				
2001	8.15	0.18	2.05	10.38
2005	9.88	0.17	2.25	12.31
2010	13.09	0.30	2.57	15.96
2015	16.63	0.43	2.28	19.35
Average	**11.35**	**0.26**	**2.27**	**13.88**
Liberal Democrats				
2001	2.30	0.26	2.73	5.29
2005	2.40	0.80	2.40	5.61
2010	4.14	1.34	2.68	8.15
2015	8.79	0.08	2.20	11.06
Average	**5.0**	**0.50**	**2.49**	**7.94**
Overall average	**9.86**	**0.42**	**2.57**	**12.83**

Source: As Table 2.1. Each score represents the percentage of total quasi-sentences per manifesto.

than a euphemistic and superficial reference to the concept's social desirability, without amounting to a substantive ideological commitment (cf. Diamond 2010, 103). Academic use of terms such as "thin populism" and "soft/mainstream" populism has tended to obscure this. For example, the concept of "thin populism" is simply defined as "closeness to the people" (Jagers and Walgrave 2007). But which office-seeking party would not appeal directly to people? Indeed, "closeness to the people" by itself, without any attempt at articulating a popular, antagonistic identity, is not populism (Laclau 2007).

This is why I use *demotic/demoticism* to denote invocation of the common people and/or popular sovereignty without this fundamental antagonism. Such demoticism may lead to populism but is not itself populism. Arguably, much of the populist Zeitgeist is actually a demotic Zeitgeist. Indicatively, Mudde has qualified his earlier view of the populist Zeitgeist as indicating a "mainstream populism" where mainstream politicians "voice some of the most pure examples of contemporary populism" (Mudde 2004, 551). His more recent concept of "soft populism" indicates "not that all political parties . . . have become essentially populist parties, but that most parties use populist themes in their political discourse" (Mudde 2013, 9). If so, then this is clearly "populism" not as ideology, but only in van Kessel's fleeting "discursive" sense. But it could be demoticism, not populism at all.

There is also evidence in Tables 2.2 and 2.3 that mainstream and non-mainstream parties used this demoticism more situationally than ideologically. For instance, the highest

Table 2.3 Disaggregated populism scores: non-mainstream and populist parties

	People-centrism	*Anti-elitism*	*Popular sovereignty*	*Overall populism score*
Non-mainstream parties				
Green Party				
2001	7.4	1.19	1.69	10.33
2005	11.09	0.64	3.20	14.92
2010	9.20	0.33	2.00	11.53
2015	9.87	0.46	2.79	13.12
Total	**9.47**	**0.57**	**2.47**	**12.51**
SNP				
2001	5.76	0.22	2.66	8.65
2005	17.42	0.0	2.25	19.66
2010	19.68	2.96	2.69	25.33
2015	12.52	0.95	2.18	15.65
Total	**12.80**	**1.10**	**2.42**	**16.31**
Average non-mainstream parties	**11.13**	**0.84**	**2.45**	**14.41**
Populist parties				
BNP				
2001	21.81	3.63	9.09	34.54
2005	10.64	10.53	6.83	28.00
2010	9.13	6.57	5.03	20.73
Total	**10.04**	**8.08**	**5.85**	**23.96**
UKIP				
2001	13.68	4.40	3.26	21.34
2005	20.83	4.69	7.03	34.38
2010	6.86	5.28	7.92	20.05
2015	17.87	2.37	2.53	22.77
Total	**15.75**	**3.60**	**4.13**	**23.47**
Respect				
2005	5.21	6.16	4.89	16.27
2010	9.43	4.71	7.55	21.70
Total	**5.82**	**5.95**	**5.28**	**17.05**
Average populist parties	**10.53**	**5.88**	**5.09**	**21.49**

Source: As Table 2.2.

average score for both mainstream parties and non-mainstream parties (15.4 and 18.4 respectively), as well as the highest mean anti-elitism scores (for all except Labour and the Greens) and highest mean popular sovereignty scores (for all except the Greens) occurred in 2010. This was the election in the immediate wake of the financial crisis and Westminster expenses scandal when there were ample incentives for parties to dabble in anti-elite rhetoric (except for Labour, the incumbent government at the time).

Certainly, this was the occasion of the Conservatives' most ostensibly populist sentiments, such as "our social fabric is frayed and our political system has betrayed the people" (Conservatives 2010). With the exception of UKIP, the genuinely populist parties do not have this 2010 spike in anti-elitism and popular sovereignty, indicating that it is a less tactical, more sustained part of their appeal.

Overall, these results endorse the populist Zeitgeist only as regards a high general propensity to demoticism; outside the genuinely populist parties, populism appears neither as a core ideological feature, nor much more than a fleeting and marginal component. Analysis now moves to the second stage (the qualitative analysis), focussing briefly on the people-centrism, anti-elitism and popular sovereignty elements of each party type in turn. This section reinforces the distinction between the demoticism of the mainstream and non-mainstream parties and the distinct and varied populism of the genuine populists.

The mainstream parties

Substantiating the previous points, the mainstream parties (above all the Conservatives and Labour) are highly demotic, but have only occasional and ambiguous traces of genuine populism. Certainly, a handful of the mainstream parties' statements look on face value to be populist invocations of the people, using terms little different from those in populist parties' manifestos, e.g. "we can change direction, begin to return power to people" (Labour 2015). However, generally the "people" plays second fiddle to other preferred terms (e.g. "citizens", "our country", "our community", "the public"). People-centrism is generally used implicitly, with frequent use of "we" or "our" as mainstream parties highlight their identification with popular aspirations (the Conservatives' 2010 claim that "we are all in this together" is typical). The Conservatives and Labour, in particular, are prone to using "our" to denote shared ownership of the country and its resources ("our borders", "our NHS", "our society", etc.). Although this could in principle reflect a populist homogeneous people and its "imagined community", it more likely indicates these parties' roles as catch-all organisations aiming to attract the median voter (and also, by implication, to show that they are governments-in-waiting, responsible enough to protect national attainments). This is also perhaps a reason why the Liberal Democrats have the lowest average people-centrism score of any party examined (5.0), since they had little prospect of entering government until 2010. This score also reflects the party's libertarian host ideology, which emphasises individual (and minority) rights as much as those of community, nation or people: "[w]e want to build a society which gives individual[s] . . . opportunities to pursue their aims, develop their talents and shape their successes" (Liberal Democrats 2005).

Reflecting the above discussion, where anti-elitism exists at all, it is rarely either counterposed to a "good people" or focused on specific nefarious elites. Rather, it is nebulously expressed ("remote politicians", "the privileged few"). The highest anti-elite scores are for the Conservatives (2001) and Liberal Democrats (2010). In the former manifesto, anti-elitism is largely "anti-intermediaries" populism (de Raadt et al. 2004), i.e. not focused on specific elites but rather the elitist intermediary mechanisms that limit the accountability of the elite before the people, in this case "remote bureaucracy" and "political correctness". In the latter manifesto, there is a quasi-populist anti-elitism: "[A]t the root of Britain's problems today is the failure to distribute power fairly between people. Political power has been hoarded by politicians and civil servants; economic power has been hoarded by big businesses." As noted above, this indicates a direct response to the financial crisis and recent scandals. Even in this manifesto, the Liberal Democrats' overall anti-elitism score (1.34) is comparatively low. Moreover, the 2015 manifesto contained just a single anti-elitist reference.

It is also symptomatic that the mainstream parties' invocations to popular sovereignty are generally banal ("the ability to govern ourselves", "opportunity for all"). More specific policies are present, and these are on occasion similar to those of the populist parties, e.g. the Liberal Democrats, Labour (2010), UKIP and Respect have called for a more proportional electoral system, while both the Liberal Democrats (2010) and BNP have called for the automatic recall of MPs. Generally though, for the mainstream parties, enhanced popular sovereignty involves greater public access to services and nebulous, non-specific statements about enhancing popular control.

The non-mainstream parties

As implied by the content analysis, the non-mainstream parties differ from the mainstream parties largely only by degree: their people-centrism and popular sovereignty scores are similar, and they are only mildly more anti-elitist. Again, both parties do utilise quasi-populist statements, e.g. "Bringing government to the people" (Green Party, 2010), or "The people can give real power to Scotland" (SNP, 2010). Sometimes the accent on popular homogeneity is still stronger, as with the Greens' 2015 manifesto "For the Common Good", which focuses on an inclusive "humane, caring society" (Green Party 2015). Mostly, however, both parties use similar demotic phrases to the mainstream parties (e.g. "our society", "our country", "our environment", "our oil wealth", "our streets"). Moreover, whether they are truly invoking a homogeneous "pure people" is ambiguous. For example, of all the parties examined, the SNP most regularly employs the phrase "the people" (usually as "the Scottish people" or "People of Scotland"). But it implies internal diversity, not homogeneity (e.g. "the people of our nation", "people across Scotland"). Moreover, both parties share with the mainstream parties a visible emphasis on specific national subgroups (e.g. transport users, the mentally ill for the Greens, expectant mothers and hospital patients for the SNP). This bespeaks an underlying liberalism and individualism that is not populist.

Both parties express infrequent anti-elite sentiments that are usually as vague as those of the mainstream parties. For example, the Greens' 2010 manifesto contrasts itself with the "main political parties" and their "out-of-touch" politicians. Reflecting its separatism, the SNP sees the London/Westminster parties ("the Westminster system") as being inimical to Scottish interests. However, unlike the mainstream parties, the non-mainstream parties occasionally express more vehement anti-elitism. For the Greens, this was most apparent in 2001 and 2015: "[m]illions of people face routine discrimination . . . while a powerful elite manipulate the system" (Green Party 2001); "the rich and powerful have forced us to live in their fantasy world – a world that suits the minority not the majority" (Green Party 2015). Yet this still does not comprise a detailed anti-elite critique, being a handful of phrases focussed on a catch-all constituency (the rich, powerful, corporate interests). The SNP's anti-elitism peaked in 2010 (with a score of 2.96, higher than UKIP in 2015). However, virtually all these anti-elite quasi-sentences refer to "the London/UK parties" and their "cuts agenda". There is only one example of a fuller anti-elite critique: "[t]he London parties are part of the same metropolitan political machine– a machine that leaves the ordinary men and women of our country on the outside" (SNP 2010). All in all, the non-mainstream parties' anti-elitism occasionally indicates borderline populism, but is neither consistent nor developed enough to count as a core ideological trait.

Similarly, the non-mainstream parties' references to popular sovereignty are as generalistic as those of the mainstream parties, amounting to vague messages of empowerment. The Greens, for instance, focus on "provid[ing] decent public services and quality of life for all" (Green Party 2001), while the SNP will "equip . . . the Scottish people with the same powers as every other normal country in the world" (SNP 2001). Of the two, only the Greens develop more specific policies: not just constitutional reform but direct democracy including citizen's initiatives, referenda on local government decisions, recall of elected politicians, and a People's Bank. In contrast, the SNP's popular sovereignty revolves entirely around an Independence referendum, which "will allow us to take decisions on all the major issues" (SNP 2010). No other specific proposals to augment popular power are outlined *ad interim*.

The populists

Only the populist parties actually present a critique sustained enough to be regarded as a populist thin-centred ideology. In each case, the ideology cleaves closely to the "host ideology", which provides most of its content, and explains each party's divergent policy preferences. We will take the two right-wing populists (the BNP and UKIP) in turn, before examining the rather different case of Respect.

Ideologically, the BNP was an "extreme right" party with a propensity to xenophobic authoritarianism, which has gradually become more moderate and populist, moving from biological to cultural racism and broadening its anti-establishment critique (Goodwin 2011). In contrast, UKIP has developed from a single-issue Euro-rejectionist pressure group into a more genuine populist radical right party, while maintaining a neoliberal and anti-EU ideological core (Ford and Goodwin 2014).

Each party's populism clearly reflects this ideological core. For the BNP, its people-centrism reflects nativism (exclusivist ethnic nationalism). It usually qualifies "people" with ethnic nationalist terms ("native/indigenous British people"), while speaking in overtly nationalist as often as populist terms (e.g. "once proud nation"). In contrast, UKIP deliberately distinguishes itself from the "blood and soil" ethnic nationalism of extremist parties by espousing open, inclusive civic nationalism (UKIP 2010). However, UKIP's people is still culturally defined, as it opposes "multiculturalism and . . . promotes uniculturalism – aiming to create a single British culture embracing all races and religions" (UKIP 2010).

Alone of the parties here, the BNP expounds in detail an archetypal populist "heartland" (Taggart 2000): a clean, beautiful country, respectful of historical traditions and symbols, such as Christianity, old crafts, the traditional pub and the red telephone box (BNP 2010; BNP 2003). The ethnic nature of the BNP's world-view is reinforced by its manifestos' concern with existential challenges to this idyllic heartland: mass immigration, multiculturalism, the black population's alleged propensity to crime, and the threat of Islamism. In contrast, UKIP's "heartland" is referred to only implicitly: a "free, democratic" and crime-free Britain run by Westminster not Brussels, respecting family and other British values. In other respects, UKIP's people are rational market agents, usually "taxpayers", otherwise "citizens", "the electorate" and "the public".

Contrary to Mudde's definition, even the populist parties' "people" is not *entirely* homogeneous: all (especially Respect) refer repeatedly to several sub-groups (e.g. students, farmers, NHS patients). Nevertheless, the BNP comes closest to the ideal-type. Although UKIP's people resembles the BNP's in key respects, e.g. emphasis on law and order and (albeit less draconian) anti-immigrant sentiment, its high people-centrism score reflects that much is little different from the mainstream Conservative Party. This was particularly evident in 2015. UKIP's rising support allowed it to become more office-oriented, arguing for "opportunity for real change in our politics" (UKIP 2015). The manifesto was replete with similarly demotic invocations to protect "our borders", "our NHS", etc., blending the catch-all intentions of the mainstream parties and the party's more authentically populist aims to put "power . . . back into the hands of the people".

Compared with the aforementioned parties, the populists' anti-elitism is far more developed. Both the BNP and UKIP attack three sets of targets: corrupt national politicians and political parties; foreign (principally EU) elites; and intermediaries (such as bureaucratism and political correctness) whereby these elites allegedly control their populations. The BNP's anti-elitism is far more vehement, sustained and detailed: the "regime" is quasi-totalitarian, employing "Orwellian methods of intellectual terrorism" (BNP 2010), the EU aims at "the eventual liquidation of Britain as a nation and a people" (BNP 2005), while among the vexatious intermediaries are left-liberal ideologies like the "cult of global warming" and egalitarianism.

In contrast, UKIP's anti-elitism score is relatively low (3.57). This reflects a neo-liberal, conservative world-view that, unlike the BNP, essentially accepts UK political institutions (e.g. monarchy and parliamentary sovereignty). Therefore, UKIP barely concerns itself with national political elites, except when they are the "regional agents" of its main enemy, Brussels. True, UKIP inveighs against the "old political parties" and "the LibLabCon-sensus" and like the BNP, excoriates political correctness and multiculturalism, but its *raison d'être* remains ending participation in the "undemocratic and autocratic European Union" with "its unelected bureaucrats, commissioners, multiple presidents and judges" (UKIP 2010).

Each party's emphasis on popular sovereignty replicates the mainstream and non-mainstream parties' vague invocations to popular involvement. But both the BNP and UKIP buttress this with emphases on national sovereignty, border control and freeing the populace from the EU's tutelage. Each has relatively developed direct democratic proposals, especially the BNP, with its emphasis on non-bureaucratic government that is "closer to the people", "Citizens' Initiative Referenda", recall mechanisms for MPs and local devolution (BNP 2005; BNP 2003). UKIP is consistently vaguer and less anti-establishment, but has a similar policy agenda to "give meaningful power back to the British people and not just talk of localism" (UKIP 2005). Each shows "welfare chauvinism" (i.e. enhanced welfare rights that exclude foreigners) and demonstrably talks of the National Health Service, not "the International Health Service" (UKIP 2015; BNP 2010). Consistent with their relative authoritarianism, UKIP proposes restricting migration via border controls, the BNP via deportation of illegal immigrants and repatriation of legal immigrants and their descendants (BNP 2010).

At first glance, Respect could not be more different, being an explicitly left-wing, internationalist party. Reflecting its specific origins in the anti-Iraq war movement in 2004, Respect also has a strong communalist element, with its best electoral performances in Muslim constituencies (March 2011). Respect is certainly *less* populist than either the BNP or UKIP, not just in overall score (Table 2.3: 17.05 vs. 23.96 and 23.47), but in people-centrism (5.82 vs. 10.04 and 15.75). It's easy to see why. First, its internationalist and anti-conflict emphasis means that it actually spends relatively little time addressing the British people, rather than those of Venezuela, Palestine or Kashmir. However, there are still numerous references to "ordinary people" and "working people", especially "the millions who, through the betrayals of New Labour, have lost their political voice" (Respect 2005).

Second, although we have noted that the right-wing populists also refer to sub-groups, Respect is more so inclined, and therefore devotes much attention to particularist constituencies such as pensioners, LGBT groups, immigrants, and religious (especially Muslim) minorities. Moreover, although Respect's core ideology is downplayed (there is no mention of socialism or anti-capitalism), the party still has strong class-based elements: a "vote for Respect is a vote . . . to help create a clear, radical, working-class voice" (Respect 2005).

Relative to the right-wing populists, Respect's anti-elitism is much more focused on economic issues. Although it refers to the establishment's "tyranny, prejudice . . . abuse of power" and "shallowness and cynicism", particularly towards immigrants, the vast bulk of its critique is directed towards "big business and the mainstream politicians who do its bidding" (Respect 2005). It attacks "big corporations and the wealthy", "the rich elite" and the "cutthroat privateers". Unlike the right-wing populists, the foreign elites it excoriates are explicitly economic ones in the multinationals, the World Trade Organisation (WTO), the International Monetary Fund (IMF) and the World Bank. Unlike the BNP and UKIP, it is not Euro-rejectionist, claiming to support Europe while opposing the current EU, which is "dominated by big business interests", and which transfers power from elected parliaments to unelected bureaucracies (Respect 2005). Another stark contrast is that, this mention apart, Respect has little to say about bureaucratic or other intermediaries.

As regards popular sovereignty, Respect maintains this greater focus on economic than political sovereignty. This latter accent is vague (e.g. "encouraging the full participation of all communities in the political process") (Respect 2010), although there are commitments to local democratic control and electoral reform. The overall aim is economic democracy, the ideal that "public services should be publicly owned and democratically controlled by those who use them and those who work in them" (Respect 2005). This means greater public ownership of "key sectors of the economy" including transport, water, gas and electricity services and a commitment to a "fully-funded, publicly-owned NHS, delivering care free at the point of use". These are classical socialist themes, albeit in a slightly more populist idiom.

Conclusion

Britain is often seen both as having a high propensity to populism and being a cardinal example of the populist Zeitgeist. The empirical contribution of this chapter was a holistic focus on key mainstream, non-mainstream and populist parties that interrogated this question. It showed that there was very questionable evidence for this Zeitgeist. There is little evidence of sustained increase in populism among the mainstream or the non-mainstream parties. The only genuinely populist parties occupy the radical left and right of the political spectrum, with distinct populisms emerging from their different ideological cores.

In particular, the chapter showed that the populist parties were distinguished by much higher anti-elitism scores and higher popular sovereignty scores than the other party categories. It argued that only the populist parties demonstrated populism as a consistent, core (thin-centred) ideology, not just demonstrating closeness to the people but creating popular identities in juxtaposition to nefarious elites. In the UK context, it is the right-wing populists that are more populist than the left, both in overall score and with their greater emphasis on people-centrism. Whereas Pauwels (2014, 25–26) argues that populism is fully compatible equally with both the right and left's core ideological concepts, because the people can be constructed as either nation or class, the UK examples appear to show more "elective affinity" between populism and the right, i.e. the right's core ideological concepts (nationalism, collectivism) accommodate better to the homogeneous "pure people" than do the left's (working people, diversity). Certainly, Respect remains too internationalist, too class-based and too focussed on minority rights to make the homogeneous pure people its sole category. Although both the BNP and UKIP also appeal to sub-groups, their focus on the nation, country and monoculturalism against nefarious "others" (immigrants) makes their homogenising emphasis stronger and clearer.

The second main contribution of this chapter is its methodology. The two-stage analysis combines quantitative (content) and qualitative approaches to provide a holistic view of party populism. There are some weaknesses but many strengths to this approach. Initially, the content analysis proved misleading, when the focus was on providing summative numerical categories: all parties seemed indistinguishably populist. However, the disaggregated content analysis much more clearly distinguished between non-populist and populist parties, while demonstrating a clear variation in the extent of populism among the latter. To this degree, the methodology manages to combine both dichotomous and continuous concepts and measurements of populism: i.e. it proved possible both to tell who is populist and who is not, *and* how populist they are. Nevertheless, given that fleeting elements of populism appeared in the quantitative analysis of the non-populist parties, the qualitative analysis proved invaluable in providing more detailed and nuanced judgements as to what is populism and when, and how its elements interrelate. Overall, the technique used here strengthens the ideational approach's ability both to "meet the 'either-or' criterion of conceptualization", as well as to clarify "distinctions of a 'more-less' nature" (Mudde 2017, 35).

The chapter makes two further important theoretical points. First, it reinforces that all the core ideational components of populism need to be present to label an actor populist. People-centrism, anti-elitism and appeals to popular sovereignty are abundant in British politics, as undoubtedly elsewhere. However, as Mudde has recently noted, implicitly revising his earlier Zeitgeist concept, "it makes little sense to label political actors who have a clear pluralist ideology but occasionally use a few populist frames in their campaigns a 'weak populist'" (Mudde 2017, 36).

Second, and finally, the methodology helped distinguish clearly between genuine populism and demoticism. This latter is ubiquitous in the UK, as demonstrated by parties' high people-centrism and popular sovereignty scores, even when their anti-elitism is virtually absent. Since "thin", "mainstream" or "soft" populism make up the core of the populist Zeitgeist, and are far closer to demoticism than genuine populism, we may cast further doubt on this Zeitgeist.

There are two main questions that emerge from this analysis. First is whether such observations apply beyond Britain. Because the UK is regarded as so populism-prone, the lack of a genuine Zeitgeist even here arguably demonstrates that the pan-European populist spectre is much less all-encompassing than often assumed (cf. the chapter by Hawkins and Silva, this volume). Second is the relationship between demoticism and populism. Demoticism appears a necessary but not sufficient component of populism, but how and why the former can become the latter is less clear. At the very least, the ubiquity of demoticism indicates that populism potentially has a fertile "breeding ground". Whereas this chapter's analysis demonstrates little sign of non-populist parties becoming more populist despite propitious socio-economic conditions, the centrality of demotic slogans (e.g. "Take Back Control") to the successful Leave campaign in the UK's 2016 Brexit referendum has shown that, in certain circumstances, demoticism becomes the most visible, and perhaps potent, accompaniment to populism.

Notes

1 "Demoticism" can conceivably be ideational (ideas that reinforce claims to represent the people') *and* stylistic ('everyday' or 'low' discourse implying that the speaker is 'one of the people'). Generally, demoticism is an all-pervasive feature of the contemporary media landscape that reinforces populism but is generally less coherent and apolitical. See Turner (2010).

2 The codebook and indices are available from the author. The author wishes to thank Carl Truedsson and Sofia Widen for research assistance.

References

Albertazzi, Daniele, and Duncan McDonnell. 2007. "Introduction: The Sceptre and the Spectre." In *Twenty-First Century Populism: The Spectre of Western European Democracy*, edited by Daniele Albertazzi and Duncan McDonnell, 1–11. Basingstoke: Palgrave.

Balcere, Ilze. 2014. "Populism in the Manifestos of Latvian Political Parties: Increasingly Used but Ineffective?" *Journal of Baltic Studies* 45(4): 477–497.

Bale, Tim. 2013. "More and More Restrictive—But Not Always Populist: Explaining Variation in the British Conservative Party's Stance on Immigration and Asylum." *Journal of Contemporary European Studies* 21(1): 25–37.

Bale, Tim, Stijn van Kessel, and Bryan T. McGraw. 2011. "Thrown around with Abandon? Popular Understandings of Populism as Conveyed by the Print Media: A UK Case Study." *Acta Politica* 46(2): 111–131.

Beasley-Murray, Jon. 2010. *Posthegemony: Political Theory and Latin America*. Minneapolis, MN: University of Minnesota Press.

Betz, Hans-Georg. 2002. "Conditions Favouring the Success and Failure of Radical Right-Wing Populist Parties in Contemporary Democracies." In *Democracies and the Populist Challenge*, edited by Y. Mény and Y. Surel, 197–213. Basingstoke: Palgrave.

BNP. 2003. *BNP Scotland Manifesto. Freedom: The Manifesto of the British National Party*. Glasgow: BNP Scotland.

———. 2005. *Rebuilding British Democracy. British National Party General Election 2005 Manifesto*. Welshpool: BNP.

———. 2010. *Democracy, Freedom, Culture and Identity. British National Party General Elections Manifesto 2010*. Welshpool: BNP.

Conservatives. 2010. *Invitation to Join the Government of Britain. The Conservative Manifesto 2010*. London: The Conservative Party.

Diamond, Larry. 2010. "Introduction." *Journal of Democracy* 21(4): 102–5.

Dommett, Katharine. 2016. "Post-Democratic Party Politics." *Political Quarterly* 87(1): 86–90.

Ford, Robert and Matthew Goodwin. 2014. *Revolt on the Right: Explaining Support for the Radical Right in Britain*. Abingdon: Routledge.

Freeden, Michael. 1996. *Ideologies and Political Theory a Conceptual Approach*. Oxford: Clarendon.

Freedland, Jonathan. 2013. "Behold, Ed Miliband's New Populism of the Left." *The Guardian*. September 24. www.theguardian.com/commentisfree/2013/sep/24/ed-miliband-leftwing-positions-brighton-speech.

Goodwin, Matthew. 2011. *New British Fascism: Rise of the British National Party*. Abingdon: Routledge.

Green Party. 2001. *Green Party Manifesto. Reach for the Future*. London: Green Party.

———. 2010. *Fair is Worth Fighting for. General Election Manifesto 2010.* London: Green Party of England and Wales.

———. 2015. *For the Common Good. General Election Manifesto 2015.* London: Green Party of England and Wales.

Hawkins, Kirk A. 2009. "Is Chávez Populist? Measuring Populist Discourse in Comparative Perspective." *Comparative Political Studies* 42(8): 1040–67.

Jagers, J., and S. Walgrave. 2007. "Populism as Political Communication Style: An Empirical Study of Political Parties' Discourse in Belgium." *European Journal of Political Research* 46(3): 319–45.

Kessel, Stijn van. 2014. "The Populist Cat-Dog: Applying the Concept of Populism to Contemporary European Party Systems." *Journal of Political Ideologies* 19(4): 99–118.

Kessel, Stijn van. 2015. *Populist Parties in Europe.* Basingstoke: Palgrave.

Labour. 2015. *Britain Can Be Better. The Labour Party Manifesto 2015.* London: The Labour Party.

Laclau, Ernesto. 2007. *On Populist Reason.* Reprint. London: Verso.

Liberal Democrats. 2005. *Liberal Democrats: The Real Alternative.* London: Liberal Democrats.

———. 2010. *Change That Works for You. Liberal Democrat Manifesto 2010.* London: Liberal Democrats.

Mair, Peter. 2002. "Populist Democracy vs. Party Democracy." In *Democracies and the Populist Challenge*, edited by Y. Mény and Y. Surel, 81–98. Basingstoke: Palgrave.

March, Luke. 2011. *Radical Left Parties in Contemporary Europe.* Abingdon: Routledge.

Mény, Y., and Y. Surel. 2002. "The Constitutive Ambiguity of Populism." In *Democracies and the Populist Challenge*, edited by Y. Mény and Y. Surel, 1–21. Basingstoke: Palgrave.

Mudde, Cas. 2004. "The Populist Zeitgeist." *Government and Opposition* 39(4): 542–63.

———. 2013. "Three Decades of Populist Radical Right Parties in Western Europe: So What?" *European Journal of Political Research* 52(1): 1–19.

———. 2017. "An Ideational Approach." In *The Oxford Handbook of Populism*, edited by Cristobal Rovira Kaltwasser, Paul Taggart, Paulina Ochoa Espejo, and Pierre Ostiguy, 27–47. Oxford: Oxford University Press.

Pappas, Takis S. 2016. "Modern Populism: Research Advances, Conceptual and Methodological Pitfalls, and the Minimal Definition." Politics: Oxford Research Encyclopedias. http://politics.oxfordre.com/view/10.1093/acrefore/9780190228637.001.0001/acrefore-9780190228637-e-17.

Pauwels, Teun. 2011. "Measuring Populism: A Quantitative Text Analysis of Party Literature in Belgium." *Journal of Elections, Public Opinion & Parties* 21(1): 97–119.

———. 2014. *Populism in Western Europe: Comparing Belgium, Germany and the Netherlands.*, Abingdon: Routledge.

Raadt, Jasper de, David Hollanders, and André Krouwel. 2004. "Varieties of Populism: An Analysis of the Programmatic Character of Six European Parties." 2004/04. Working Papers Political Science. Amsterdam: Vrije Universiteit.

Respect. 2005. *Peace, Justice, Equality. The Respect Manifesto for the May 2005 Election.* London: Respect.

———. 2010. *Homes, Jobs and Peace: Manifesto for a Hung Parliament.* Manchester: Respect.

Reungoat, Emmanuelle. 2010. "Anti-EU Parties and the People: An Analysis of Populism in French Euromanifestos." *Perspectives on European Politics and Society* 11(3): 292–312.

Rooduijn, M. 2013. "A Populist Zeitgeist? The Impact of Populism on Parties, Media and the Public in Western Europe." PhD thesis. Amsterdam: Amsterdam Institute for Social Science Research.

Rooduijn, Matthijs. 2014. "The Nucleus of Populism: In Search of the Lowest Common Denominator." *Government and Opposition* 49(4): 573–599.

Rooduijn, Matthijs, and Teun Pauwels. 2011. "Measuring Populism: Comparing Two Methods of Content Analysis." *West European Politics* 34(6): 1272–1283.

Rooduijn, Matthijs, and Tjitske Akkerman. 2015. "Flank Attacks Populism and Left-Right Radicalism in Western Europe." *Party Politics*, July, doi:10.1177/1354068815596514.

Rooduijn, Matthijs, Sarah L. De Lange, and Wouter Van Der Brug. 2014. "A Populist Zeitgeist? Programmatic Contagion by Populist Parties in Western Europe." *Party Politics* 20(4): 563–575.

Sartori, Giovanni. 1970. "Concept Misformation in Comparative Politics." *The American Political Science Review* 64(4): 1033–1053.

Sikk, Alan. 2009. "Parties and Populism." 2009–02. Working Paper. UCL School of Slavonic and East European Studies. CEPSI, Centre for European Politics, Security & Integration.

SNP. 2001. *We Stand for Scotland*. Edinburgh: Scottish National Party.

———. 2010. *Elect a Local Champion. Manifesto 2010*. Edinburgh: SNP.

Stanley, Ben. 2008. "The Thin Ideology of Populism." *Journal of Political Ideologies* 13(1): 95–110.

Taggart, Paul. 2000. *Populism*. 1st ed. Buckingham: Open University Press.

———. 2004. "Populism and Representative Politics in Contemporary Europe." *Journal of Political Ideologies* 9(3): 269–88.

The Economist. 2014. "A UKIP of the Left." September 13. www.economist.com/news/britain/21616997-green-party-embraces-left-wing-populism-ukip-left.

Turner, Graeme. 2010. *Ordinary People and the Media: The Demotic Turn*. London: Sage.

UKIP. 2005. *UK Independence Party Manifesto 2005. WE WANT OUR COUNTRY BACK*. Birmingham: UKIP.

———. 2010. *UKIP Manifesto April 2010. Empowering the People*. Newton Abbot: UKIP.

———. 2015. *Believe in Britain. UKIP Manifesto 2015*. Newton Abbot: UKIP.

Vossen, Koen. 2010. "Populism in the Netherlands after Fortuyn: Rita Verdonk and Geert Wilders Compared." *Perspectives on European Politics and Society* 11(1): 22–38.

Werner, Annika, Onawa Lacewell, and Andrea Volkens. 2011. "Manifesto Coding Instructions (4th Fully Revised Edition)." In *The Manifesto Data Collection. Manifesto Project* by Andrea Volkens, Onawa Lacewell, Pola Lehmann, Sven Regel, Henrike Schultze, and Annika Werner. Berlin: Wissenschaftszentrum Berlin für Sozialforschung (WZB). https://manifesto-project.wzb.eu/.

Zaslove, Andrej. 2008. "Here to Stay? Populism as a New Party Type." *European Review* 16(3): 319–336.

3 Textual analysis

An inclusive approach in Croatia

Marijana Grbeša and Berto Šalaj

The dilemma that has marked a large amount of research on the topic – is populism an ideology or a style – has led scholars to overwhelmingly side with one of the predominant understandings. In this chapter we go beyond the constricting "either-or" paradigm. We reconcile these two understandings through a methodological design that simultaneously measures populism in an ideational sense and as a style. The utility of such a combined approach is that it can identify *true* populists and distinguish them from politicians who resort to a populist style only for the sake of gaining public sympathy but whose understanding of politics is not essentially populist in an ideational sense.

In the first part of the chapter, we look at the distinction between populism in an *ideational sense* and populism as a *political communication style*. Conceptualized as a set of ideas, populism is here understood as a thin-centered ideology that has a central core, but lacks additional values and content present in other "true" ideologies. At the core of any populist doctrine is the idea that society is divided into two homogenous and mutually conflicted groups: honest people and corrupt elites. People are also often believed to be endangered by "dangerous others" commonly identified among minorities, financial institutions or the media. We argue that the presence of a Manichean discourse, which is reflected in the simultaneous presence of people-centeredness and anti-elitism, is a necessary and sufficient condition for someone to be labeled "true" populist, while the presence of "dangerous" groups (other than political elites) is not considered central to populism, but is quite common and may be useful in defining different subtypes of populism.

Contrary to ideational conceptualization of populism, populism as a political communication style is here understood as a communication tactic used by a variety of political actors (populist and mainstream) to get in with the people in order to gain their support. It is operationalized through three categories: politicians' positive mentioning of the people, their use of language that typically belongs to the private sphere, and their use of "empty signifiers." We argue that populist communication style must be present among populist politicians, at least in terms of their people-centredness, but it can also be identified in communication of mainstream politicians. However, mainstream politicians never share populists' resentment towards elites or their Manichaean understanding of politics as a conflict between "us" (the people) and "them" (political elites).

In the second part of the chapter we present our method of textual analysis and apply it in two studies of populist discourse of Croatian politicians. The first, benchmark study analyzes newspaper interviews of 11 Croatian politicians (both suspected populists and mainstream politicians) in the period between two local elections, in 2009 and 2013. The second study analyzes interviews of the four presidential candidates in the 2015 Croatian presidential election. The findings of these studies suggest that Croatia represents a relevant and comparatively curious case for several reasons. First, in the last couple of years populist candidates and parties have started to successfully dissolve the country's solid two-party political system; second, there is an interesting variance in subtypes of populism traced in the country; and last, right-wing populism has not been detected in the discourse of the investigated political actors, which is surprising given the recent outburst of right-wing populism across Europe, as well as Croatia's own traumatic political history, which left a permanent imprint on the relationship towards ethnical minorities.

In the concluding part of the chapter we discuss the potentials and the shortcomings of our method.

Conceptualization: moving beyond the "ideology or style" dilemma

Contemporary accounts on populism suggest that there are two main approaches. The first one sees populism primarily as a communication style that is based on politicians' references to the people. Advocates of this approach (c.f. Jansen 2011; Moffitt and Tormey 2014; Taguieff 1995; Tarchi 2002) argue that populism should be treated as a type of political rhetoric or style available to different social and political groups rather than an ideology. They insist that populism is a "tactical device" (Jagers and Walgrave 2007) for attracting public support, which is built around a rhetoric of simplicity and directness. Proponents of this approach argue that populism cannot be viewed as a set of ideas i.e. political ideology, because populist movements do not have clearly and coherently expressed attitudes on the majority of important contemporary political issues and above all, they lack core values – such as freedom, equality or social justice.

Conversely, the second, larger, group of scholars (c.f. Kaltwasser 2014; Mudde 2004; Stanley 2008; Van Kessel 2015) argues that there are reasons to treat populism as a coherent political ideology. They seek to identify common features of different populist movements, which would allow for populism to be treated as a political ideology. Although people-centeredness and antagonistic relationship towards elites represent the central core of populism, it needs additional values and substance to make sense of the political world in which it acts. Since these values and substances vary significantly depending on the context, populism may be considered a "thin-centered ideology" (Freeden 1996, 2003) but still an ideology that is built on a common set of specific ideas. This approach to understanding populism has become increasingly associated with what is referred to in this volume as "the ideational approach" (e.g. Hawkins 2009; Mudde and Kaltwasser 2013).

One possibility to reconcile stylistic and ideational approach is to suggest that populism is a "matter of degree" rather than to understand it exclusively as a style or as an ideology (see Pauwels 2011; Rooduijn and Pauwels 2011). The grading approach is by no means a new one and it typically revolves around a set of indicators that enable identification of different levels of populism, ranging usually from "light populism," which pretty much regards populism as communication style to "heavy populism" which embodies populism as ideology. The criteria that must be met by a politician, party or a movement to be labeled as either a "light" or a "heavy" populist vary across studies.[1]

Despite differences in the selection of the defining criteria, one of the biggest benefits of the grading approach that examines populism on an ideology-style scale is that it can encompass a variety of actors, ranging from mainstream politicians to suspected populists. In this respect, Akkerman (2003) argues that "populist style" should be differentiated from populism as a "model of politics" pointing out that even established political parties and leaders gladly adopt a populist style. However, what distinguishes these *populist-style* politicians from *true populists* in an ideational sense is the fact that they do not advocate a dual, but rather a pluralist view of politics.

We build on the idea that populism may be graded but we move beyond the practice of investigating populism either as an ideology or as a populist style. We develop a research design that includes investigation of populism both in an ideational and stylistic sense; we include both "usual suspects" of populism and mainstream politicians. The value of such an inclusive approach is that it enables differentiation between *true ideational populists* and *populist-style* politicians and thus contributes to resolving one of the usual conceptual dilemmas.

We follow Mudde's definition of populism as

> an ideology that considers society to be ultimately separated into two homogeneous and antagonistic groups, "the pure people" versus the "corrupt elite," and which argues that politics should be an expression of the volonte generale (general will) of the people.
>
> (2004, 543)

Hence, for someone to be labeled populist, positive evaluation of the people and negative evaluation of political elites should be present. In other words, using Goertz's (2008) notion about constructing concepts, we argue that the simultaneous presence of both features is a necessary and sufficient condition to identify someone as populist in an ideational sense. Therefore, if people-centeredness is present, but without clearly expressed resentment towards elites, we cannot talk about populism in an ideational sense but merely about populist style.[2] Almost all parties and politicians may occasionally resort to populist style, primarily to attract voters. The use of populist style by mainstream political parties or candidates will vary, depending on specific social and political circumstances. Studies of populism as a style usually complement investigation of references to the people with examination of other forms of familiarization with the people, such as the use of specific language figures that tend to make a bond between politician and the people (see Jagers and Walgrave 2007).

Although we argue that people-centeredness and anti-elitism are jointly necessary conditions for someone to be labeled populist, these variables alone don't tell us much about the content of populism in question. The concept of "dangerous others" may be helpful in that respect. "Dangerous others" are social groups who are perceived to threaten the unity and homogeneity of the average people because they promote certain interests. Although political elites represent dangerous others by definition, they are not embraced by our concept of the "dangerous others." We use this label to refer to social groups other than political elites who are perceived to threaten the efforts to bring power and government back to the people. In some circumstances, immigrants are identified as a threat because they are thought to take away jobs from the domestic populace; likewise, ethnic and religious minorities can threaten the way of life and culture of the majority. In these circumstances right-wing populism arises, which is intolerant of the rights of minorities and immigrants. On the other hand, if big foreign businesses and entrepreneurs are perceived as a threat, then populism reaches for left-wing political messages and policies, such as the nationalization of the property of foreign companies. In other words, populism varies from left to right depending on the identity of the out-groups and the values and characteristics of the ruling elites it opposes. If these elites are predominantly liberal, then populism will be reactionary, as has largely been the case in Europe over the last two decades. If, on the other hand, dominant elites are conservative, populism will be based on leftist political values and will advocate the rights of workers against the interests of rich entrepreneurs, as exemplified by the cases of Hugo Chávez in Venezuela, Evo Morales in Bolivia and Rafael Correa in Ecuador. Populism, therefore, can be left-wing and right-wing, both authoritarian and libertarian, both progressive and reactionary, depending on the values of the elites and the 'dangerous others' that it opposes.

Some authors argue that the presence of "dangerous others" should be considered the third defining feature of populism (see Albertazzi and McDonnell 2008). Nevertheless, such a conceptualization has not been broadly embraced, mostly because it is excluding and instantly eliminates certain cases that most researches have categorized as populism, and we do not recommend incorporating it into the ideational approach. There are several examples of the so-called "centrist populism" (Ucen 2007) such as Miro Cerar in Slovenia (Havlik 2015) or Ivan Grubišić in Croatia (Grbeša and Šalaj 2014) whose populism lacks "dangerous others." Therefore, we find it reasonable to dismiss "dangerous others" as a necessary condition for someone to be labeled populist, but we find it very useful as a tool for defining different subtypes of populism. Moreover, such an approach seems both broad and precise enough to encompass most of the well-known cases of populism but still does not undermine the diversity of all specific cases. The strength of the proposed concept is that it can address broad range of cases, from Syriza in Greece, to Beppe Grillo in Italy or the Front National in France.

In sum, our inclusive approach is essentially based on an ideational understanding of populism but combines it with stylistic understanding to make a clear distinction between *true* populist politicians and mainstream politicians who resort to populist style but who are essentially not populists. People-centeredness and attachment with "ordinary people" is what these two understandings have in common. What fundamentally differentiates them is antagonism towards political elites that is always present with true populist but is missing from the discourse of populist-style mainstream politicians. "Dangerous others" in our conceptualization serve the task of identifying different subtypes of detected populism.

Research design and methodology

Although most empirical research on populism still resorts to qualitative analysis of cases, studies that use some form of quantitative measurement have been gaining prominence in the last decade (c.f. Hawkins 2009; Pauwels 2011; Rooduijn and Pauwels 2011). In this chapter we align with authors who favor measuring populism quantitatively with techniques that can be easily replicated and used across different times, countries and cases. However, we develop a more traditional method of content analysis that decomposes the text and measures populism's components, much the same as the method used by March in his chapter (Chapter 2). This differs from both the holistic approach and the computer automated approach employed in the chapter by Hawkins and Castanho Silva (Chapter 1), both of which gauge populist ideas as a totality. We base our research on this traditional approach to content analysis because carefully tailored categories enable differentiation between populists in an ideational sense and populist style politicians. Moreover, they allow inferences about the nature of detected populism. It is not possible to measure these components accurately unless a traditional form of content analysis is used.

We operationalize populism on two levels – on an ideational and stylistic level. On an ideational level, populism is examined through the presence of its two defining features: references to the people and an anti-elite sentiment. Although we do not regard references to "dangerous others" as a necessary feature of true populism, we also measure the presence and identity of "dangerous others" in politicians' public discourse because we find it useful in determining the subtype of detected populism. Conceived as a political communication style, populism is examined through three categories: politicians' explicit referencing to the people, their attempts of displaying proximity to the people by using private and informal language (cf. Jagers and Walgrave 2007) and their use of "empty signifiers" that are typical of populist discourse (cf. Kumar 2014).

The context and the relevance of the Croatian case

After declaring independence in 1991 and abandoning its status of a constitutive republic in the socialist Yugoslavia, Croatia found itself at the beginning of a brutal war. The rebellion of the Serbian nationalists, backed by the federal army and the regime of Slobodan Milošević, escalated into open aggression, which lasted for almost five years. The consequences of the conflict are still present in the political life of Croatia and are reflected in a number of issues – the economy, the status of Croatian war veterans, the trauma of the war victims, the protection of the Serbian minority rights, etc. Croatia joined the EU in 2013, becoming the youngest member of the Union. It is a parliamentary democracy with a unicameral parliament whose 151 representatives are elected through a proportional electoral system. Croatia has a president too; although the president's role is mostly ceremonial, he/she has certain authorities, primarily in the domains of foreign policy and defense. The president is directly elected to a five-year term through a majority-runoff system, with the whole country serving as a single constituency.

Parliamentary and local elections are held every four years. The conservative Croatian Democratic Union (*Hrvatska demokratska zajednica*, HDZ) ruled the country from 1990 until 2000. It was replaced by a leftist coalition led by the Social Democratic Party (*Socijaldemokratska partija Hrvatske*, SDP) that governed until 2003. HDZ then took over again and governed until 2011, when it was again replaced by SDP and a leftist coalition that governed until 2015. The government was then formed by HDZ and a newly established populist party, Bridge (*Most*). However, their internal conflicts led to the rapid fall of the government. An early election was held in 2016 that resulted in victory of HDZ which, again, was unable to establish a government on its own but had to come to an agreement with its disobedient populist partner, Bridge.

In the last couple of years, Croatia's solid two-party system has been challenged by a number of populist options, with Bridge and Human Wall (*Živi zid*) being the most prominent. In the 2016 parliamentary election, Bridge won 13 seats and Human Wall 8. The studies we present in this chapter were conducted before the rise of these two options. Nonetheless, they include politicians whose populist discourse carved the way for these newcomers. The rise of populist discourse in the last couple of years is one of the reasons why we consider Croatia a relevant case. The interesting variance in subtypes of populism adds to the relevance of the case, as does the fact that none of the populist options or candidates covered by our studies fit the definition of "right-wing" populists, which is intriguing given the recent tendencies in Western democracies, as well as Croatia's traumatic war history which is still reflected in an ambiguous relationship towards Serbian minority.

Sample, categories and coding

Building on the premise that populist discourse is reflected in communication practices of politicians, parties and movements, our two content analyses of populism were conducted on the interviews of Croatian politicians, published in the country's major newspapers and magazines.

Since most studies of populist discourse are conducted on party manifestos or some other form of official party material (party election broadcasts, etc.) our choice of investigated corpus may seem unusual. However, this decision was carefully considered. First, it was made for the reasons of consistency and availability: interviews were the only communication platform that was common to all analyzed actors in our first study, given their diverse backgrounds, positions and roles (mayors, MPs, state officials, party members, independent). The same type of material was used in the second study in order to test the replicability of our method. Second, we would argue that mediatized discourse is more revealing than the official one, because it reflects statements that are spontaneous and less guarded. Hence, it is reasonable to assume that interviews will capture the fundamentals of politicians' discourse. On the other hand, the limitation of interviews as a research material is the immanent presence of the media filter. Although it is less pertinent than in the news articles, it needs to be acknowledged and properly addressed by researchers.

The first study – the benchmark study – includes all interviews of 11 Croatian politicians that appeared in the country's main newspapers in the period between two local elections (May 2009 and June 2013).[3] Contrary to the bulk of empirical studies that focus exclusively on alleged populist politicians (e.g. Ivarsflaten 2007), it involves mainstream politicians as well, which stems from the logic of our approach. The final sample includes 192 interviews of 11 prominent politicians, both suspected populists (Milan Bandić, Nikica Gabrić, Ivan Grubišić, Željko Kerum, Dragutin Lesar, Ruža Tomašić) and the mainstream politicians (Tomislav Karamarko, Jadranka Kosor, Ivo Josipović, Zoran Milanović, Vesna Pusić) (see Table 3.1).

The second study is an analysis of the populist discourse of the four presidential candidates in the 2015 presidential election (Kolinda Grabar-Kitarović, Milan Kujundžić, Ivo Josipović and Ivan Vilibor Sinčić). We examined the entire population of 39 interviews,[4] which is the total number of interviews that these four candidates gave in the country's leading newspapers and magazines between 1 November 2014 and Election Day (11 January 2015).[5]

The unit of analysis in both studies is a single interview (excluding the words of the journalists and coding only politicians' answers/statements). The presence of investigated components was traced on the level of a whole interview that was treated as a single unit of measurement. For instance, coders were asked to register if the "dangerous others" are mentioned in the interview. If even one single reference was present, the whole interview was coded as positive for this variable. Coders were asked to write down all such references, which were later decoded and qualitatively interpreted by the leading researchers. Although each occurrence of a reference was registered, the total number of references was counted only when it was necessary to gauge their valence (positive, negative or neutral). This was the case with two main components – references to the people and references to political elites. The modal valence of all references was recorded as the overall sentiment of the interview towards the people or political elite. Given a relatively low overall frequency of supporting components (the presence of "dangerous others," privatization strategies and empty signifiers), reporting their prominence within a single interview would not have contributed to the relevance of results. However, in principle,

Table 3.1 Politicians included in the benchmark study (study 1)

Suspected populists			
Politician	*Position / Occupation*	*Description*	*Number of analyzed interviews*
Milan Bandić	Currently serving his sixth term as a mayor of Zagreb.	Until 2010 a prominent member of the Social Democratic Party of Croatia (SDP), but fell out with them during the 2009/2010 presidential election when he decided to run against SDP's Ivo Josipović; confronted Josipović as an independent but later established his own party – Milan Bandić – Party of Labour and Solidarity (*MB-Stranka rada i solidarnosti*).	11
Nikica Gabrić	Physician.	At the time of our analysis, the president of a newly established political party National Forum (*Nacionalni forum*); his party never made it to the Parliament and was subsequently shut down.	5
Ivan Grubišić	Catholic priest.	An independent MP from 2011 to 2015; ran as leader of the independent list 'Alliance for civic and ethic Croatia' (*Savez za građansku i etičku Hrvatsku*)	13
Željko Kerum	Entrepreneur.	At the time of analysis, an MP representing his own party, Croatian Citizens' Party (*Hrvatska građanska stranka*); between 2009 and 2013, the mayor of Split, the second biggest town in Croatia; failed to qualify for a second term.	11
Dragutin Lesar	Retired.	At the time of analysis, an MP and leader of the left-wing political party Croatian Labourists – Labour Party (*HL – Stranka rada*).	18
Ruža Tomašić	Member of the European Parliament.	A member of Croatian parliament from 2011 to 2013; until recently the leader of the right-wing Croatian Party of Rights dr. Ante Starčević (HSP AS).	6

(continued)

Table 3.1 (continued)

MAINSTREAM POLITICIANS			
Politician	*Position / Occupation*	*Description*	*Number of analyzed interviews*
Ivo Josipović	University professor of law, former president of Croatia.	Became the third president of Croatia after winning the 2010 presidential election as the candidate of the Social Democratic Party (SDP); in 2015 lost the presidential election to Kolinda Grabar-Kitarović, candidate of the Croatian Democratic Union (HDZ).	47
Tomislav Karamarko	Member of Croatian Democratic Union (HDZ).	At the time of analysis, an MP and president of the Croatian Democratic Union (HDZ), the strongest opposition party.	22
Jadranka Kosor	Retired. Former Prime Minister of Croatia.	Prime minister and president of Croatian Democratic Union (HDZ) from 2009 to 2011; after being expelled from the party in 2013, became an independent MP and remained in the Parliament until 2015.	17
Zoran Milanović	Social Democratic Party (SDP), former prime minister of Croatia	Prime minister from 2011 to 2015; also former leader of the Social Democratic Party (SDP).	22
Vesna Pusić	MP, Croatian People's Party – Liberal Democrats (HNS – LD).	Longstanding leader of the liberal Croatian People's Party – Liberal Democrats (HNS – LD); Croatian minister of foreign affairs from 2011 to 2015.	20

measuring both the presence and prominence of established components could be done in future studies and would be helpful in longer texts.

We conducted a human-coded content analysis because we found it better suited for the method proposed in this chapter. Certain categories that are part of our research design involve complex qualitative reading that is better achieved with human coders (such as understanding underlying political values of the interviewees). The coding was conducted by two extensively trained human coders, both graduate students at the Faculty of Political Science in Zagreb. For both studies the agreement between coders was strong across all categories. In the first study it ranged from Cohen's kappa = .79 to 1.00 and in the second from Cohen's kappa = .74 to 1.00.[6]

Both analyses are based on a codebook originally devised for the 2009–2013 benchmark study. The complete codebook and detailed coding instructions are available in the appendix. The codebook is structured around three analytical dimensions – people-centeredness, anti-elitism and the presence of "dangerous others." Within **the first dimension**, the interviews are first coded for the presence of references to the people as a homogenous collectivity (explicitly, "the people" or by using other words that were treated as its synonyms such as "the citizens," "voters," etc.). References to certain segments of the population, such as youth, pensioners or women were not treated as a reference to the people as a collectivity and were not included in the analysis. The references were then coded for the presence of politicians' explicit identification with the people (e.g. "we the people," "me and my fellow citizens"), which implied greater familiarization with the people than referencing alone.

Aside from explicit references to the people, politicians may seek to connect with the people in other, more refined ways. Therefore, the decision was made to devise an additional category that measures efforts of politicians to appear close to ordinary people by introducing certain private cues into the public discourse. This process is commonly known as "privatization of politics" (e.g. Grbeša 2010; Holtz-Bacha 2004; Langer 2012). Privatization techniques may be explicit, such as the politicians' use of references to his/her family; or subtle, such as the use of informal, colloquial or humorous language that brings politicians closer to "common people" (e.g. "I mean, it is wonderful to be in Rijeka, back home. I try to come as often as possible (. . .) I go to see my friends and family, I come here very often," (Kolinda Grabar-Kitarović, *Novi list*, 11-12-2014)). The coders were instructed to omit references that were prompted by journalists, instead of being spontaneously introduced by politicians.

Finally, building on Kumar's (2014) analysis of Obama's 2008 campaign, we introduce the concept of "empty signifiers" as another indicator of "reaching out to the people" (next to the use of explicit, positive references to the people and strategies of privatization). The notion of "empty signifiers" was originally coined by Laclau (2005) and refers to a word, an idea, a phrase that is elusive and to which people with different ideologies may assign different meanings. Words like *justice, equality* or *freedom* illustrate the case quite well.[7] Kumar (2014) demonstrates how Obama in his speeches successfully fostered empty signifiers such as "change" or "change we can believe in" and "hope" that were later uncritically reinforced by journalists.

The second dimension examines politicians' attitudes towards political elites and is first examined through the presence of references to political elites ("politicians," "politics") and the valence of those references. References to specific politicians were registered only if a certain politician was mentioned as an example of politics or political elites as a whole. Two supporting indicators were also introduced to measure the attitude of Croatian politicians towards elites: their intention to identify with political elites and conversely, their efforts to be perceived as non-professional politicians. The identification with elites was introduced to examine the tendency of mainstream politicians to appear close to elites, rather than to the people. On the other hand, the second indicator was used to additionally examine politicians' efforts to reinforce the gap between "us" and "them" by suggesting that politics is not their core profession and that they should not be perceived as professional politicians, which is something that, according to Heywood and Fieschi (2004, 302), all populists strive for (e.g. "MPs should act as MPs for the reasons of honor, and they should be paid where they actually work (. . .), instead of being professional politicians" (Ivan Grubišić, *Novi list*, 19-03-2011)). Finally, we introduced a control category that records politicians' view of the relations between different groups in society (e.g. pluralist vs. dualistic vs. a technocratic view of the political system and processes). If the defining features of populism are present in a politician's communication discourse, his/her view of the political system is expected to be dualistic.

The third dimension looks at the presence of references to "dangerous others." The interviews were coded for the presence of references to "dangerous others" in general and specifically to the presence of references to "dangerous media," "dangerous financial elites," "dangerous minorities" (sexual, ethnic or other) and the "dangerous EU."

Results

The benchmark study, 2009–2013 (study 1)

The benchmark study was conducted for the period between two local elections, with one presidential election and one parliamentary election in-between (in 2009/2010 and 2011 respectively). The results establish the presence of ideational populists in Croatia. Furthermore, they empirically underline the difference between these true populists and populist-style politicians, i.e., mainstream politicians who occasionally or systematically resort to populist style as a part of their communication strategy.

The presence of populism in an ideational sense was established in four cases (Milan Bandić, Ivan Grubišić, Željko Kerum and Dragutin Lesar), all of whom we identified earlier as the "usual suspects" (see Figure 3.1).

The presence of populism in an ideational sense was not established in the remaining seven cases. Five of them are politicians who are commonly recognized as *mainstream* politicians (Ivo Josipović, Tomislav Karamarko, Jadranka Kosor, Zoran Milanović and Vesna Pusić) and who advocate one of the classic political ideologies (social democracy,

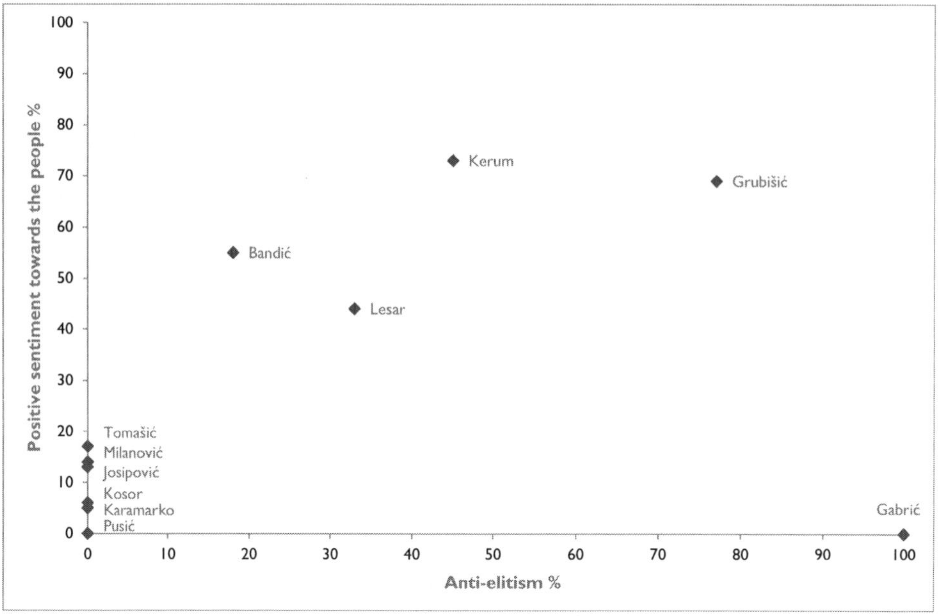

Figure 3.1 Positive references to the people and anti-elitism, study 1

Christian democracy, liberalism etc.). Two of them – Ruža Tomašić and Nikica Gabrić – are commonly labeled as "populists" in the public discourse, but their interviews did not contain content that would actually substantiate this impression. Ruža Tomašić is commonly perceived as a right-wing populist; however, the findings dismiss such a perception because she doesn't make a single negative reference to political elites and makes positive comments about the people in only 17 percent of her interviews. Nikica Gabrić is also commonly recognized as "populist" by the media, but the findings do not support this assumption either. His consistent criticism of political elites without a single reference to the people may be labeled "technocratic" but not "populist." The second finding is related to those politicians who were identified as populists. The strength of the two fundamental populist cues suggests that it is possible to talk about "strong" populists (Ivan Grubišić and Željko Kerum) and "weak" populists (Milan Bandić and Dragutin Lesar). As shown in Figure 3.1, Grubišić and Kerum often referred to the people and demonstrated a strong resentment towards elites. In addition, in all their interviews they strongly rejected the image of political professionals and in the vast majority of their interviews they cherished the "dual" conception of politics (Grubišić in 85 percent of his interviews and Kerum in 64 percent). On the other hand, Milan Bandić's, interviews are abundant in his attempts to appear close to the people (e.g., "My true and only coalition partners are my fellow citizens" (Večernji list, 11-05-2013)), but they are modest in all other elements that point to "true" populism. Anti-elitism is present in only 18 percent of his interviews and he regards himself as a professional politician in 9 out of 11 examined interviews. Most importantly, the populist view of politics does not categorically permeate his interviews, as is the case with other populists. Therefore, he should be regarded as a borderline case between a populist politician and a populist-style politician. Finally, positive references to the people and negative references to elites were found in the interviews of the former president of the Croatian Labour Party, Dragutin Lesar, although to a lesser degree than in the interviews of "strong" populists. His "weak" position is, however, truly rooted in his understanding of himself as a professional politician (expressed in all his interviews), which departs from typical populist self-identification, but also in his consistent recognition of pluralism as a proper political order (recognized in 11 out of 18 interviews). To the degree that he can be considered populist, Lesar's systematic negative referencing to financial elites allows us to label him a true representative of left-wing populism, similar to what has been dominant in Latin America in the last two decades, but which has, in recent years, emerged in a number of European countries. Interestingly, "dangerous others" were generally very vaguely present in politicians' public discourse – in only 14 percent of all examined interviews. The only relevant result in this category (besides Lesar's) was for Kerum, who condemned media, economic elites or the EU in 54 percent of his interviews (see Table 3.2).

Right-wing populism, commonly characterized by hostility towards ethnical, religious or sexual minorities was not detected in the interviews. This type of populism has been dominant in many European countries during the last two decades. Thus, it is interesting that Croatia's most prominent politicians were not reinforcing this discourse.

The analysis of populism as political communication style was primarily set to determine tendencies of politicians to relate with the people. It focused on the use of explicit positive references to the people, the use of privatization strategies (references to family, use of humor, colloquial language and similar) and the use of "empty signifiers." Expectedly, the strongest presence of populist style was detected among populist politicians. Besides reported frequent references to the people, Kerum, Bandić and to a lesser

Table 3.2 Presence of the "dangerous others", study 1

Politician	*Number of interviews*	*Presence of the "dangerous others"* (*% out of total number of interviews*)	*Who are the "dangerous others"?*
Milan Bandić	11	0	–
Nikica Gabrić	5	0	–
Ivan Grubišić	13	1 (8%)	Media elites
Ivo Josipović	47	0	–
Tomislav Karamarko	22	8 (36%)	Communists Media elites Economic elites
Željko Kerum	11	6 (54%)	Media elites Economic elites European union
Jadranka Kosor	17	1 (6%)	Media elites
Dragutin Lesar	18	14 (78%)	Economic elites
Zoran Milanović	22	2 (9%)	Populists
Vesna Pusić	20	0	–
Ruža Tomašić	6	2 (33%)	Enemies of Croatia
Total	**192**	**34 (14%)**	–

degree Grubišić, gladly used every-day language or references from their private life: "Every day we run, me and my dog Rudi. He takes shower with me every morning . . . my golden retriever. He is five and a half years old. My faithful friend" (Milan Bandić, Jutarnji list, 11-05-2013). Mainstream politicians, who generally made very few positive references about the people (see Figure 3.1), occasionally resorted to privatization techniques. Private cues were most willingly used by Ruža Tomašić and Jadranka Kosor, although almost all examined politicians at some point resorted to the use of more informal language (see Figure 3.2).

Ivan Grubišić was the heaviest user of empty signifiers of all examined politicians (see Figure 3.3). Considering his frequent "empty" referencing to "moral" and "common good," he may be conditionally labeled a "moralizing populist": "I entered politics to prove that a person can deal with social problems and be moral and just at the same time" (*Slobodna Dalmacija*, 12-05-2012).

Interestingly, as presented in Figure 3.3, the use of empty signifiers was not common to the remaining three identified populists who used them in less than 10 percent of their interviews.

As for the use of empty signifiers by mainstream politicians, the two most important men in the country at the time of analysis used them the most – Prime Minister Zoran Milanović in 23 percent of his interviews (e.g. "developing consensus") and President Ivo Josipović in 26 percent (e.g. "new justice"). It has to be noted that Josipović's increased use of empty signifiers coincided with his winning presidential campaign. However, although some mainstream politicians occasionally resorted to the use of privatization techniques and empty signifiers, they were all very reluctant to make positive references about the people. Therefore, it would be far-fetched to make confident claims about the presence of populist style with any of the examined mainstream politicians. Yet, to the

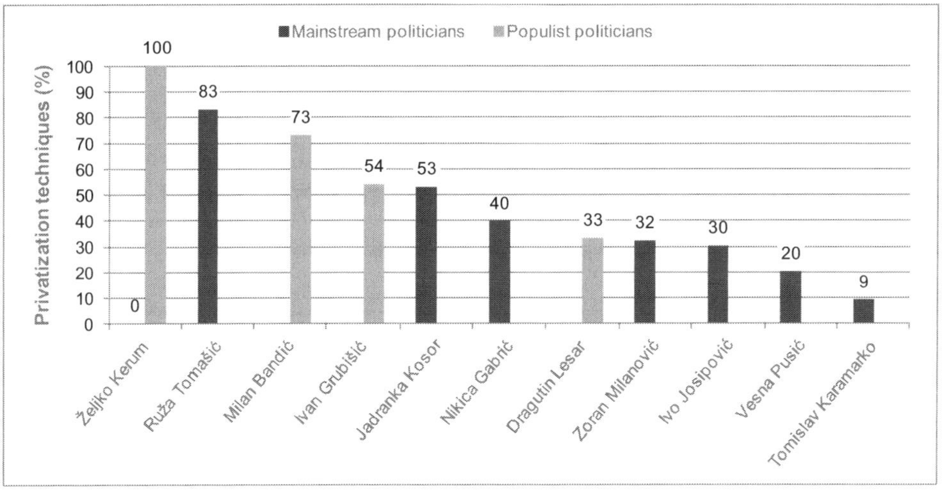

Figure 3.2 The use of "privatization" techniques

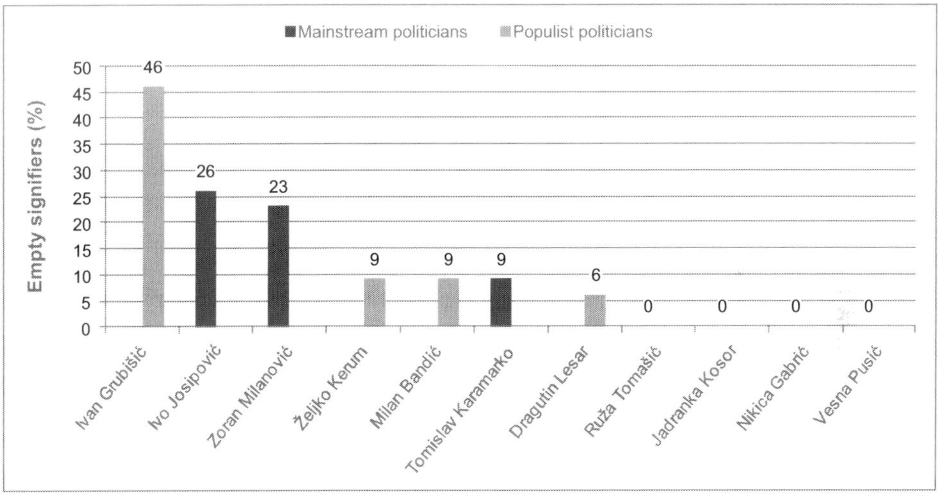

Figure 3.3 The use of empty signifiers, study 1

extent to which populist style was present among mainstream politicians, it was mainly exercised through the use of empty signifiers and privatization techniques rather than the explicit positive mentioning of the people.

In summary, this study empirically confirmed the presence of populism in Croatian political discourse. We identified four populist politicians and two subtypes of populism: left-wing populism and what we conditionally labeled "moralizing populism." Contrary to our initial assumption and the predominant trends in Europe, right-wing populism was not detected. Populist style was always present with politicians who were in this study identified as true populists but it was not decisively identified in the discourse of mainstream politicians.[8]

Populism in the 2014/2015 presidential election (study 2)

The 2014/2015 presidential election in Croatia was primarily a contest between incumbent Ivo Josipović, the candidate of the governing Social Democratic Party (SDP) and another 16 parties of the left and center; and Kolinda Grabar-Kitarović, the candidate of the right-wing Croatian Democratic Union (HDZ) and another seven right-wing parties. The election was narrowly won by the challenger Grabar-Kitarović, making her the first Croatian female president.

The two front-runners were challenged by two underdogs, Ivan Vilibor Sinčić, the young leader of Human Wall *(Živi zid)*, a non-governmental organization (later transformed into a party) whose main objective was to obstruct the evictions from people's homes; and Milan Kujundžić, the candidate of the rigid right-wing coalition led by Croatian Dawn – The Party of the People (*Hrvatska zora – stranka naroda*). Although neither of them made it to the second round, Sinčić, who was completely unknown until few weeks before the election, achieved a remarkable result by winning 16.4 percent of the vote.

The results of our analysis point to three important findings. First, the analysis of the two dimensions that are central to populism – positive references to the people and anti-elitism – allow us to identify Ivan Vilibor Sinčić and Milan Kujundžić as true populists (see Figure 3.4).

Their position of "strong populist" is reinforced by their dualistic understanding of political system (Sinčić in eight out of nine interviews and Kujundžić in three out of five) as well as their refusal to be recognized as political professionals, an element that was moderately present with Kujundžić (in three out of five interviews) and strongly with Sinčić (in all his interviews). Second, analysis of the "dangerous others" revealed Sinčić's extreme resentment towards economic elites, which allow us to conditionally label his populism as "left-wing": "We need to dismiss corrupt political and bankers' oligarchy

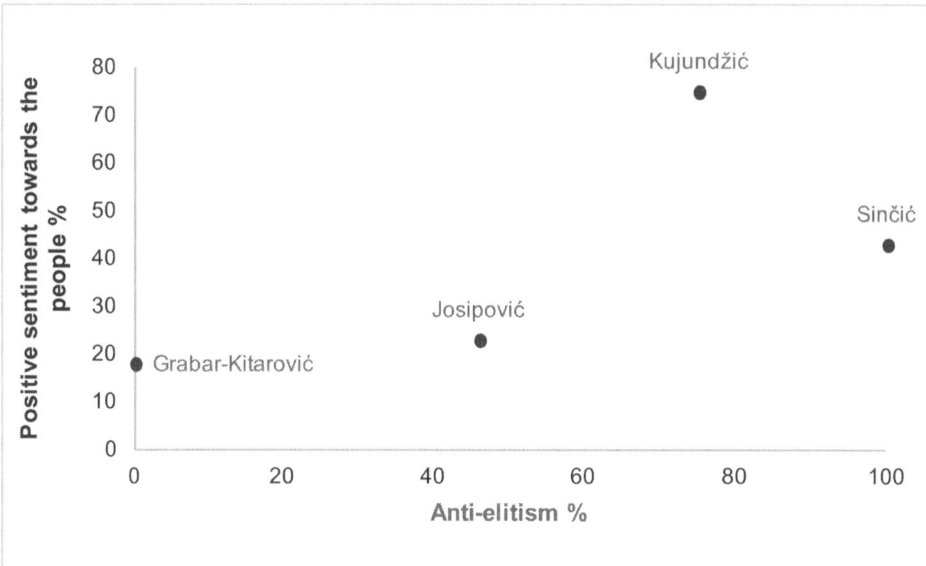

Figure 3.4 Positive references to the people and anti-elitism, study 2

who has not done anything for this country in 25 years," (*Jutarnji list*, 06-12-2014). His well-articulated criticism of political and economic elites that was registered in six out of nine interviews, apparently struck a chord with the voters and translated into remarkable electoral results (see Table 3.3).

On the other hand, Kujundžić's strong national appeals were most obviously expressed in his specific references to "Croatian people": "We are going to disturb political elites because the light that will be turned on in new Croatia is great; it is the light I am going to turn on as a president with Croatian people," (*Večernji list*, 29-11-2014). His nationalist pleads were reinforced in the empty signifiers he used, such as "New Croatia" and "national strategic consensus". However, those appeals were completely devoid of aversion towards minority groups or any other "dangerous others," and therefore did not translate into a true right-wing populism. Therefore, his populism could be conditionally labeled "national populism." Ultimately, the absence of any clear signs of right-wing populism seems to confirm the results reported in the benchmark study.

Finally, analysis of the two frontrunners showed that Kolinda Grabar-Kitarović maintained her mainstream position. She showed no signs of anti-elitism and resorted to what could be understood as populist style on rare occasions by positively addressing the people and using empty signifiers such as "new unity" or "Croatian unity" (Figure 3.5).

Table 3.3 Presence of the "dangerous others", study 2

Candidate	*Number of interviews*	*Presence of the "dangerous others"*	*Who are the "dangerous others"?*
Kolinda Grabar-Kitarović	12	0	–
Ivo Josipović	13	0	–
Milan Kujundžić	5	0	–
Ivan Vilibor Sinčić	9	6 (67%)	Economic elites (6)
TOTAL	**39**	**6 (15%)**	–

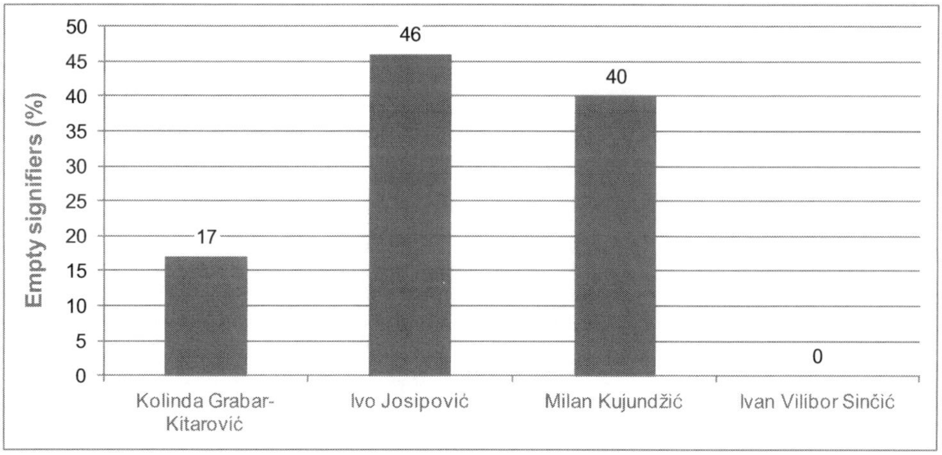

Figure 3.5 The use of empty signifiers, study 2

She resorted to private language in two of her interviews, which are, interestingly, the only two cases in the whole study where the private language was used. Other candidates in the presidential election did not resort to privatization techniques whatsoever, and hence we have not reported them in a graph.

In contrast to her predominantly mainstream position, Ivo Josipović transformed himself in the course of the campaign from a mainstream politician into an "almost true populist." This was mostly visible in his criticism of political elites (see Figure 3.4) and his use of empty signifiers ("second Republic", "guardian of civic Croatia"). This is probably due to his attempts to win the game he felt he was losing. Nevertheless, the race was won by the politician who mainly stuck with the mainstream political discourse. The only candidate who seems to have benefited from populism is the political outsider Sinčić, who leveraged his newly acquired visibility to win one seat for his party Human Wall in the 2015 parliamentary election, and eight seats in the 2016 parliamentary election.

The utility of an inclusive approach

In order for populism to be treated as a political ideology, a simultaneous presence of the two *sine qua non* criteria is required: people-centeredness and anti-elitism. Such a conceptualization that inspires this volume seems precise enough to exclude irrelevant cases but broad enough to include a range of populist movements. However, if only one of the two necessary features is present, we cannot talk about populism in an ideational sense. In this chapter we argue that if only references to the people are present, without clearly expressed resentment towards elites, we can talk about populism as a communication style. To measure it we supplement the examination of the use of the word "the people" and its synonyms with the detection of certain language that points to "familiarization" with the people, as well as the measurement of empty signifiers. Although we lean on a grading approach that examines populism on a continuum between style and ideology, we move beyond the "ideology or style" divide towards a more comprehensive approach that incorporates both levels of analysis. We create a measurement design that elucidates the relationship between these two understandings and points to easy ways of measuring both of them simultaneously. We call it an "inclusive approach" and base it on a classical textual analysis. The results of the two Croatian studies in this chapter suggest that the proposed method is able to: a) establish the presence of "true" (ideational) populism; b) differentiate between populism in an ideational sense and a stylistic sense; and c) make inferences about different subtypes of populism in terms of more specific content.

Populism in an ideational sense was detected in the discourse of six investigated Croatian politicians, all of whom entered the analyses as suspected populists. Populist style was inevitably present with all six of them, yet it was distinctly present in the discourse of only one mainstream politician, Ivo Josipović. This can be at least partly attributed to the fact that in both analyzed periods he was involved in his presidential campaign (in 2009/2010 as a challenger and in 2014/2015 as in incumbent). This speaks in favor of the argument that mainstream politicians are keen to resort to populist cues during election periods in order to win over the voters, but that obtaining a fully populist discourse is not so easily manipulated. This argument should be dealt with more closely in future studies.

Populism, similarly to pluralism, may be considered as a meta-ideology that contains different subcategories or different subtypes. Operationalization of different subtypes of populism remains one of the most demanding tasks of populism research. Based on the lessons learned from the studies presented here, we propose three devices that may be helpful in that respect. First, identification of the "dangerous others" in a politician's discourse may be useful in differentiating left and right-wing populists. Second, analysis of the kind of "empty signifiers" that politicians use may tell us more about the nature of their populism (e.g. "moralizing populism"). Finally, analysis of the actual terms politicians use to refer to the people may also prove useful in defining various subtypes of populism (e.g. "national populism").

We believe that the method presented in this chapter represents a stimulating contribution to studying and measuring populism for all aforementioned reasons. However, the lessons learned from empirical assessment show that it can be improved. First of all, in order for results to be more convincing, the analysis should be conducted on a larger sample of texts for each leader. This could be achieved by expanding the type of material to similar formats, such as television debates or political talk shows, or by drawing on entirely different genres, such as official party material or social media. Second, the analysis would benefit from measuring the frequency or prominence of investigated categories within a single unit of analysis, instead of just registering their overall absence or presence, as was the case with some categories (privatization strategies, empty signifiers and the "dangerous others"). Finally, future research of populism in Croatia should include the discourse of Bridge and Human Wall, both of which represent intriguing cases in a comparative European perspective.

Notes

1 For instance, Jagers and Walgrave (2007) argue that appealing to the people is a minimal and sufficient condition for someone to be labeled "thin" populist while "thick" populism includes also anti-establishment and exclusion of certain population categories.

2 It is also possible to talk about anti-elitism that is not accompanied by positive references to the people or which is all the more so, complemented by negative references to the people. It is possible to categorize these cases as "technocracy" or politics of *anti-establishment* but it is not possible to categorize them as populism.

3 The newspapers included in this study are *Jutarnji list, Večernji list, Novi list, Slobodna Dalmacija, Glas Slavonije, Globus* and *Forum*. We call this the benchmark study because it is the first quantitative study of populism in Croatia. Populism has been vastly present in Croatian media discourse as a common point of reference but only in recent years has it become the object of scientific inquiry.

4 Number of interviews per candidate: Kolinda Grabar-Kitarović 12, Ivo Josipović 13, Milan Kujundžić 5, Ivan Vilibor Sinčić 9.

5 *Jutarnji list, Večernji list, Novi list, Slobodna Dalmacija, Globus, Gloria* and *24Express*.

6 For a complete list of categories see the appendix. The codebook can also be found at the Team Populism website.

7 The notion of "empty signifiers" is originally developed by Ernesto Laclau in his seminal study *On Populist Reason* (2005). Although we borrow his idea of "empty signifiers," our understanding of populism is significantly different from the one developed by Laclau. Our understanding of populism is based on its two defining features – resentment towards elites and positive assessment of the people. Laclau, on the other hand, believes that any other term (and not exclusively the people) can serve as the nodal point of populist mobilization. This means that populist discourse may be equated with political discourse which terminates any possibility of clear and precise operationalization of the term. Yannis Stavrakakis and Giorgos Katsambekis criticize Laclau arguing that in this way "populism becomes synonymous with politics and any signifier can potentially become the nodal point of a populist discourse. If, however, this is the case, then how can we conceptually account for the difference between an antagonistic discourse articulated around "the people" and any other such discourse? In other words, the risk here is to lose the conceptual particularity and operationality of "populism" as a tool for concrete political analysis and thus to weaken the empirical applicability of this approach" (2014, 139).

8 For detailed results of the study see Grbeša and Šalaj (2014).

References

Akkerman, Tjitske. 2003. "Populism and Democracy: Challenge or Pathology?" *Acta Politica* 38(1): 147–159.

Albertazzi, Daniele and Duncan McDonnell. 2008. "The Sceptre and the Spectre." In *Twenty-First Century Populism: The Spectre of Western European Democracy*, edited by Daniele Albertazzi and Duncan McDonnell, 1–11. New York: Palgrave.

Freeden, Michael. 1996. *Ideologies and Political Theory: A Conceptual Approach*. Oxford: Clarendon Press.

———. 2003. *Ideology*. Oxford: Oxford University Press.

Goertz, Gary. 2008. "Concepts, Theories and Numbers: A Checklist for Constructing, Evaluating and Using Concepts or Quantitative Measures." In *The Oxford Handbook of Political Methodology*, edited by Janet Box-Steffensmeier, Henry Brady and David Collier, 87–119. Oxford: Oxford University Press.

Grbeša, Marijana. 2010. "Privatisation of Politics in Croatia: Analysis of the 2003 and 2007 Parliamentary Elections." *Medijska istraživanja* 16(2): 57–79.

Grbeša, Marijana and Berto Šalaj. 2014. "Faces of Populism in Croatia." Paper presented at the IPSA Conference, Montreal, July 2014.

Havlik, Vlastimil. 2015. "Centrist Populism on the Rise: The Czech Republic and Beyond." Paper presented at the conference, "Solving the Puzzles of Populism," London, May 2015.

Hawkins, Kirk A. 2009. "Is Chavez Populist? Measuring Populist Discourse in Comparative Perspective." *Comparative Political Studies* 42(8): 1040–1067.

Heywood, Paul M. and Catherine Fieschi. 2004. "Trust, Cynicism and Populist Anti-politics." *Journal of Political Ideologies* 9(3): 289–309.

Holtz-Bacha, Christina. 2004. "Germany: How the Private Life of Politicians Got into the Media." *Parliamentary Affairs* 57(1): 41–52.

Ivarsflaten, Elisabeth. 2007. "What Unites Right-Wing Populists in Western Europe?: Re-Examining Grievance Mobilization Models in Seven Successful Cases." *Comparative Political Studies* 41(1): 3–23.

Jagers, Jan and Stefaan Walgrave. 2007. "Populism as Political Communication Style: An Empirical Study of Political Parties Discourse in Belgium." *European Journal of Political Research* 46(3): 31–45.

Jansen, Robert S. 2011. "Populist Mobilization: A New Theoretical Approach to Populism." *Sociological Theory* 29(2): 75–96.

Kaltwasser, Rovira Cristóbal. 2014. "The Responses of Populism to Dahl's Democratic Dilemmas." *Political Studies* 62(4): 470–87.

Kumar, Anup. 2014. "Looking back at Obama's campaign in 2008: 'True Blue Populist' and Social Production of Empty Signifiers in Political Reporting." *Journal of Communication Inquiry* 38(1): 5–24.

Laclau, Ernesto. 2005. *On Populist Reason*. London: Verso.

Langer, Ana I. 2012. *The Personalisation of Politics in the UK. Mediated Leadership from Attlee to Cameron*. Manchester: Manchester University Press.

Moffitt, Benjamin and Simon Tormey. 2014. "Rethinking Populism: Mediatisation and Political Style. " *Political Studies* 62(2): 381–397.

Mudde, Cas. 2004. "The Populist Zeitgeist." *Government and Opposition* 39(4): 541–563.

Mudde, Cas and Cristóbal Rovira Kaltwasser. 2013. "Populism." In *The Oxford Handbook of Political Ideologies*, edited by Michael Freeden, Marc Stears and Lyman Tower Sargent, 493–512. Oxford: Oxford University Press.

Pauwels, Teun. 2011. "Measuring Populism: A Quantitative Text Analysis of Party Literature in Belgium." *Journal of Elections, Public Opinion and Parties* 21(1): 97–119.

Rooduijn, Matthijs and Teun Pauwels. 2011. "Measuring Populism. A Comparison of Two Methods of Content Analysis." *West European Politics* 34(6): 1272–1283.

Stanley, Ben. 2008. "The Thin Ideology of Populism." *Journal of Political Ideologies* 13(1): 95–110.

Stavrakakis, Yannis and Giorgos Katsambekis. 2014. "Left-wing Populism in the European Periphery: The Case of SYRIZA." *Journal of Political Ideologies* 19(2): 119–142.

Taguieff, Pierre-Andre. 1995. "Political Science Confronts Populism: From a Conceptual Mirage to a Real Problem." *Telos* 103: 9–44.

Tarchi, Marco. 2002. "Populism Italian Style." In *Democracies and the Populist Challenge*, edited by Yves Meny and Yves Surel, 120–138. Basingstoke: Palgrave.

Ucen, Peter. 2007. "Parties, Populism and Anti-Establishment Politics." *SAIS Review* 27(1): 49–62.

Van Kessel, Stijn. 2015. *Populist Parties in Europe: Agent of Discontent?*. London: Palgrave Macmillan.

Appendix

Codebook

Interview ID ____

1 Newspaper / magazine (1st study):

1 *Jutarnji list*
2 *Večernji list*
3 *Novi list*
4 *Slobodna Dalmacija*
5 *Glas Slavonije*
6 *Globus*
7 *Forum*

1a Newspaper / magazine (2nd study):

1 *Jutarnji list*
2 *Večernji list*
3 *Novi list*
4 *Slobodna Dalmacija*
5 *Globus*
6 *Gloria*
7 *24sata Express*

2 Politician:
3 Publishing date: insert the date

References to the people

4 What is the predominant sentiment of the interview towards *the people?*

0. There is no reference to the people
1. Positive
2. Negative
3. Neutral

Note 1: Include and code all collective terms such as *citizens*, *inhabitants*, *community*, *Croatian society*, *Croats*, *public*, *voters* etc. Do not include references to particular segments of population (e.g. youth, women, pensioners).

Note 2: Enter all references pertaining to the people into provided column. Assign valence to each reference (neutral, positive or negative). Count the references and their valence and record prevailing valance as the overall sentiment of the interview. If you need to use a separate document for additional notes/comments, make sure to assign it an interview ID.

5 **Does the politician explicitly identify with the people (e.g. "me and my fellow citizens")?**

1 Yes
2 No

6 **Does the politician spontaneously use references that make him appear closer to the people (such as the references to the members of the family, humor, colloquial language etc.)?**

1 Yes
2 No

Note 1: Code **1. Yes** if at least one such reference is present in the interview. You do not need to count the references. Do not code if the reference was prompted by journalist instead of being spontaneously introduced (e.g. 'Your mother was sick during election campaign' or similar).

Note 2: Enter all such references into provided column. If you need to use a separate document for additional notes/comments, make sure to assign it an interview ID.

7 **Does the actor use "empty signifiers" (e.g. justice, new justice, change, common good)?**

1 Yes (which ones?)
2 No

Note 1: The notion of "empty signifiers" refers to a word, an idea, a phrase that is elusive and to which people with different ideologies may assign different meanings. Code **1. Yes** if at least one such reference is present in the interview. You do not need to count the references.

Note 2: Write down all detected empty signifiers into provided column. If you need to use a separate document for additional notes/comments, make sure to assign it an interview ID.

Anti-elitism

8 **What is the predominant sentiment of the interview towards *political elites?***

0 There is no reference to political elites
1 Positive
2 Negative
3 Neutral

Note 1: Include and code only if the reference pertains to elites as collectivity (politicians in general or "politics"). References to actual parties, politicians or government should be included only if a certain party, politician or a group of politicians (government for instance) is used as a proxy for political elites.

Note 2: Enter all reference pertaining to political elites into provided column. Assign valence to each reference (neutral, positive or negative). Count the references and their valence and record prevailing valance as the overall sentiment of the interview. If you need to use a separate document for additional notes/comments, make sure to assign it an interview ID.

9 Does the politician explicitly identify with political elites (e.g. "We politicians should fight for the common good"; 'I am a member of a political party and I believe that politicians should . . . ')?

1 Yes
2 No

10 Does the politician see himself/herself as a "political professional"?

1 Yes
2 No

Note: "Political professionals" are politicians who see their political activities as central to their professional life. "Political non-professionals" are politicians who see their political activities as something occasional, something which is not their core business and something that they will do for a limited period of time (because their core profession is something else, business or similar).

"Dangerous others"

11 Does the politician refer to "dangerous others"?

1 Yes
2 No

Note: "Dangerous others" are individuals or groups who do not belong to the people and who represent the threat to prosperity of the people. Make a note if "dangerous others" are other than those mentioned in categories 12 to 15 (e.g. "communists" etc.).

12 Does the politician identify media elites as the "dangerous others" (e.g. media in general, editors, journalists, media corporations etc. but not an actual journalist, editor, media owner, publishing company etc.)?

1 Yes
2 No

13 Does the politician identify economic elites as the "dangerous others" (e.g. business in general, banks, bank owners, foreign companies, corporations but not an actual businessman, banker, bank etc.)?

1 Yes
2 No

14 Does the politician identify minorities as the "dangerous others" (e.g. sexual, religious, ethnical etc.)?

1 Yes
2 No

15 Does the politician identify EU and its institutions as the "dangerous others"?

1 Yes
2 No

16 Which of the following descriptions best represents the attitudes expressed in the interview?

1 All political elites are the same. There are no real differences between them. Differences between political elites and political parties are only fictional. The real political differences are present only between political elites and the people.
2 There are real, substantial differences between political elites. These are the most important differences in our society. These differences do not allow us to treat political elites as a unique and homogenous group.
3 All political elites are incompetent and inapt and therefore politics should be in the hands of a strong leader who would be guided by his own competence and not by the will of the people.
4 None of the above / it cannot be established.

4 Expert surveys

Nina Wiesehomeier

Recent discussions on conceptualization appear to coalesce around definitions of populism as a set of ideas and a discourse, facilitating empirical measurement and thus comparative studies. This consolidation has led to advancements in quantitative research applying various techniques of text analysis to measuring populism in selected countries (e.g. Hawkins 2009; March (this volume); Rooduijn and Pauwels 2011). Uncovering degrees of populism by being more attentive to nuances among political actors, be they political parties or leaders, and moving beyond the commonly used populist/non-populist dichotomy prevalent in more qualitative research, these studies have greatly improved our understanding of this political phenomenon.[1] However, we are left with important limitations.

By concentrating only on measuring the degree of populism in isolation from other ideological features, such techniques have so far not advanced our understanding of populism in terms of, for instance, programmatic appeal, nor have they advanced our larger comparative understanding as large scale cross-national approaches to the measurement of this political phenomenon are mostly lacking.[2] Furthermore, depending on the region in question, textual analysis may be hampered by problems of data availability (see for instance Hawkins and Rovira Kaltwasser forthcoming). In addition, studies using text analysis necessarily have to rely on different textual sources across different units of analysis that may have been devised for different audiences serving a very different purpose. In other words, the data-generating process of party manifestos vs. speeches by party leaders are likely to be quite dissimilar, which means that comparisons between leaders and parties based on this data may be difficult, although such comparisons may be very pertinent, particularly in presidential systems. And finally, a more directed comparison of the most common definitions used in such approaches and their capacity of capturing populism is still missing.

To help to overcome such limitations, this chapter uses expert surveys to measure populism in the context of Latin American presidential systems. In political science, expert surveys are most commonly used as a method to estimate empirical policy spaces and the positions of political actors within those spaces. The best-known examples have applied expert surveys to estimate party positions on a dimension of left-right political ideology (Castles and Mair 1984; Huber and Inglehart 1995), party locations on numerous policy dimensions and their importance to parties (e.g. Laver and Hunt 1992; Benoit and Laver 2006; Wiesehomeier and Benoit 2009), and party positioning on European integration (Marks and Steenbergen 2004; Rohrschneider and Whitefield 2007). Moreover, expert surveys provide us not only with the means of simultaneously measuring the degree of populism of political actors as well as their location on various positional issues; they also allow us to simultaneously measure, and thus compare, placements of political actors such as presidents *and* political parties on the same metric (Wiesehomeier and Benoit 2009).

The use of expert surveys, the results of which are typically aggregated into a mean, along with assessments of uncertainty associated with these estimates, is especially useful to provide information on complex phenomena (for more details on expert surveys as a research instrument see Benoit and Laver 2006; Wiesehomeier and Benoit 2009). Expert surveys are an explicit *a priori* approach to measuring political phenomena of interest, and as such they give the researcher complete flexibility of perceiving the phenomena in question, in our case populism, either as a package of attributes from different domains, or rather as being composed of features that are potentially separable into different dimensions.[3]

As the following discussion will show, the characteristics of expert surveys may be particularly advantageous for navigating the complexities of a phenomenon such as populism. Seeking to clarify overlaps and differences among the most prominent definitions of populism as a set of ideas, an informal style, or as a strategy, this chapter reports results of two waves fielded in 2011/2012 and 2015 in Argentina, Brazil, Bolivia, and Chile that used different approaches to measuring the degree of populism of up to 47 political parties and four presidents. While the earlier study exploits the overlap of these definitions and conceives of populism as a bundle of attributes combined in a single metric, the second study disaggregates these attributes, leaving it to empirical tests to explore how they, and thus the different conceptualizations of populism, relate to each other. Contrasting both approaches, the discussion underlines that having disaggregated dimensions not only allows for a more fine-grained approach to studying political actors, but already points towards important differences among definitions.

Using the disaggregated measures of the second wave of the expert survey only, the chapter subsequently proceeds to examine if and how ten separately measured policy dimensions and the general left-right scale are associated with the degree of populism. This analysis is performed on a more comprehensive sample of 165 political parties and 18 presidents in 18 Latin American countries. The results indicate that across Latin America, populism is not related to social policy (interpreted as policies on matters such as abortion, gay rights, and euthanasia) or minority rights. Rather, populist actors are distinguished by their views on economic redistribution, a preference for tough measures to fight crime, and a rejection of a closer relationship with the United States. Although, all in all, the results indicate a left-wing variant of populism across Latin America (see also Levitsky and Roberts 2011; Mudde and Rovira Kaltwasser 2011; 2013), they strongly suggest shortcomings of understanding populism as a narrow discursive approach or as informality in relating to people, as both of these measures are only able to capture specific subtypes of populism.

Operationalizing populism

The underlying assumption of expert surveys is that the key substantive issues on which judgments are sought can be identified in advance. Respondents, in our case experts with a high degree of specialized knowledge about party politics in their own national contexts, are then presented with these predefined questions or scales and asked to use their best judgments in placing given actors on this metric we describe. Hence, using expert surveys successfully requires that each scale we ask experts to assess is given a clear title and is anchored at each end with two precise substantive definitions of the scale endpoints based on a theoretical understanding of the issue we are interested in.

In recent years, conceptual discussions have centered on populism as a political strategy (i.e. the political-institutional approach), as an informal style, or as a set of ideas (i.e. the ideational approach or discourse). While populist discourse is the underlying logic that unites these different conceptualizations (see Hawkins and Rovira Kaltwasser this volume, Introduction, but also Hawkins and Riding 2009), there are some important, albeit at times subtle differences. Weyland (2001), for instance, defines populism as a *political strategy* used by leaders to appeal to a heterogeneous electorate, emphasizing a personalistic relationship (see also Levitsky and Roberts 2011; Taggart 1995; 2000). Although specifying populism as a strategy does not ignore the content of the populist appeal, populism in this sense is linked to a particular form of political mobilization and therefore to a particular form of political organization with a focus on the rather unmediated relationship between a personalistic leader and his followers.

Populism as a *set of ideas* on the other hand, emphasizes the antagonistic, Manichaean nature of populism, "a discourse which sees politics as divided in moral terms" (Hawkins and Silva 2016, 3). Politics is presented as a conflict between the two opposing poles of "the people" vs. "the elite." Understood as a discourse, populism is consequently a mode of political expression that allows "[redefining] the people and their adversaries" (Panizza 2005, 8; see also Laclau 2005) and for which therefore the central form of identification of the struggle over power comes in the form of antagonism, in the form of anti-establishment, anti-elite and anti-status-quo rhetoric. Although related to the purely discursive approach, the ideational definition (Hawkins and Rovira Kaltwasser in this volume, Introduction; Mudde 2004; Mudde and Rovira Kaltwasser 2011; 2013), stresses that this binary morality is the essential part of the populist tenet. Populist ideas represent "the people" as a homogenous, uniform majority with an identifiably unified will that should be the basis of all governing and "the elite" as a corrupt ruling class, as the exploitative minority that has hijacked the political process. Yet, while "populist ideas are the main driving force" (Hawkins and Rovira Kaltwasser forthcoming, 7), the precise implications of these ideas for how populist actors understand the wider democratic system and the decision-making process is seen as context dependent and open to empirical investigation.

In partial contrast to both of these, conceptualizations of populism as an *informal style* give greater priority to the status markers or identities of the elite and people, and less attention to the antagonism between them and the idea of democratic betrayal that animates this. However, like the other definitions, it sees the elements of populism as orthogonal to the general left-right dimension. For example, Ostiguy (2009) treats populism in spatial terms as a separate quantifiable dimension of political competition with clearly defined opposites of a "high" and "low" identity. This identity dimension in turn consists of two sub-dimensions: socio-cultural and political-cultural, which both relate to "ways of *being* and *acting* in politics" (Ostiguy 2009, 5, emphasis in the original). On the social-cultural sub-dimension, politicians at the high end tend to be well-mannered, with a rational and ethically oriented discourse, while at the low end politicians tend to use slang and demonstrate overall a more unmediated demeanor. The political-cultural sub-dimension refers to modes of leadership, with more formal and institutionally mediated procedures on the high end of the scale, and personalistic authority on the low end. Overall then, the high-low axis contrasts more abstract political appeals emphasizing properness in manners and procedures on the "high" with appeals on the "low" that have a quality of immediacy for both decision-making and relating to the people.[4]

Understanding populism as a continuum is helpful as it allows us to move away from simple categorizations of parties and leaders as being either populist or not, depending on whether they espouse a necessary combination of populist characteristics. However, although the advances in empirical measurement discussed above provide us with a sliding scale of populism, the degrees uncovered in these studies are merely indicating a "more or less" of populism. This is unsatisfactory as it remains unclear what the absence of populism means. Locating political actors on a scale to capture degrees of populism thus raises the question of how to define its opposing pole. Defining this opposite may improve our understanding of what parties and leaders actually do.[5]

Mudde and Rovira Kaltwasser (2013) argue that populism, in fact, has two opposites in elitism and pluralism (see also Hawkins 2009; Plattner 2010). While elitism effectively reverses the morality attached to "the people" and "the elite," thereby maintaining a dualistic outlook on social order, pluralism acknowledges the inherent diversity in society. Thus, pluralist actors consider the different groups that constitute the social fabric of a country as legitimate, and favor the diffusion of power, emphasizing deliberation and consensus to overcome any emerging conflicts. Mudde and Rovira Kaltwasser (2013, 153) highlight that in the context of political competition most parties adhere to the pluralist worldview as part and parcel of liberal democracy. Thus, to anchor the endpoints of the predefined scale on which experts were asked to locate given actors, populism was treated as a continuum with two opposing endpoints of populism vs. pluralism. This is akin to Ostiguy's (2009) definition of his scale endpoint of "high," which appears to be rooted in a pluralistic understanding of political appeals.

A bundled approach

The considerable overlap among conceptualizations of populism highlighted above forms the point of departure for the first approach to measuring populism. The first wave of expert surveys aimed at capturing the complexity of populism as a *bundle of attributes* combined in a single metric with two well-defined endpoints.[6] In such an operationalization political appeals are thus understood as taking place on a single scale, on a continuum of populist to pluralist appeals, and experts were consequently asked to locate political parties and presidents in Argentina, Brazil, Bolivia, and Chile on this single dimension entitled "political communication."[7] The substantive definitions of the scale endpoints asked country experts to locate political parties and presidents along a 20-point scale, where 1 indicated the populist end defined as:[8]

- "Highlights the interest of the people, with reference to the sovereign will of the majority. Condemns the ruling class and interest groups. Emphasizes personal authority, capable of leadership and a decisive resolution of problems. Uses an informal style and slang." (1)

and 20 indicated the pluralist endpoint as:

- "Highlights the interests of citizens, with references to civic or republican values. Recognizes the ruling class and interest groups as legitimate. Emphasizes impersonal authority, the formality of procedures and separation of powers. Uses a "well-educated" style and more formal language." (20)

The wordings of the opposing poles thus combine different elements present in the conceptualizations discussed above and contrast them with their corresponding opposites of pluralism. Reference to the people is fundamental to all approaches, although the antagonistic nature of the discourse is of less importance to the informal style. The emphasis on leadership is pertinent to populism understood as a strategy and the "low" end of the political-cultural dimension, while the last element refers to the socio-cultural dimension in the style approach.

A disaggregated approach

By design, this bundle only provides the possibility of measuring positions on these elements together. It may be argued that this masks important differences among the definitions, but also among actors to be located on such a scale: it may be possible for a political actor to score high for populism on one of those attributes, e.g. engaging in the use of informal language, but to exhibit pluralist tendencies on others. Measuring these elements on separate dimensions, therefore, allows exploring potential variability and how the dimensions, and thus different conceptualizations, relate to each other. Consequently, the second expert survey disaggregated the bundle into separate dimensions with concise and straightforward wordings of the endpoints.

The goal of focusing more closely on the areas of overlap among the different definitions meant parting with the most distinguishing feature of populism as a strategy and the political-cultural element of the "low." Excluding this feature also opens the possibility of exploring empirically the relation between populism and organizational characteristics (see also Mudde and Kaltwasser 2013). At the same time the aim was to strengthen differences among conceptualizations. As a result, the wording of the remaining elements was revised in several rounds of discussions and feedback obtained from selected focus groups.[9] Regarding the ideational approach, for instance, the wording needed to avoid ambiguities while making sure that it captured the essence of the two opposing camps of "the pure people" and the "corrupt elite." As both function as empty signifiers (Laclau 1977; see also Mudde and Rovira Kaltwasser 2013), for the sake of parsimony and in order to avoid compromising scale comparability across countries, the wording was kept general so that experts could then interpret the endpoints as befitted their own country's context.

Expressions such as "the will of the majority" or "the unified will of the common people" triggered confusion and were not interpreted by focus group participants in an unequivocal way as signaling populism. Rather it was argued that in political competition politicians would in general defend acting in the name of "the will of the people" and that the distinction would emerge from how this group would be conceived of. In its final version, therefore, the wording aimed at capturing the degree to which the pure people, the heartland of the nation (Taggart 2000), are emphasized opposite to a pluralist understanding of society.

People-centrism:[10]

- Identifies with the common people and celebrates their authenticity. (1)
- Refers more generally to citizens and their unique interests. (20)

In a similar vein, the expression "treating opponents as legitimate" appeared difficult to match to non-populist conduct, and a reference to a "corrupt elite" proved equally ambiguous regarding both the question of who constitutes the elite and what would be considered as corrupt. Hence, the element aiming at measuring the degree of anti-elitism in moral terms vis-à-vis the acceptance of the political elite as the legitimate representatives of divergent and dissenting opinions in society was adapted accordingly.

Anti-elite: morality

- Demonizes and vilifies opponents. (1)
- Treats opponents with respect. (20)

As an embodiment of the purely discursive approach, the Chapel Hill expert survey (CHES) item was used that measures populism as the saliency of antagonism in terms of anti-status-quo-rhetoric (Polk et al. 2017).[11] Thus, respondents were asked to judge whether for a political actor "anti-establishment and anti-elite rhetoric" was salient.

Anti-elite: rhetoric

- Not important at all. (1)
- Extremely important. (20)

Finally, the socio-cultural dimension of the high-low axis in politics was maintained as capturing informality in style.

Informal style:

- Uses an informal style and popular language. (1)
- Uses a "well-educated" style and more formal language. (20)

In addition, country experts were asked to judge positions of political actors on up to 14 distinct policy dimensions and the general left-right ideological axis. Results of some of these items are analyzed later in the chapter, once the results of the different approaches to measuring populism are discussed, and help us analyze the question of what particular issue dimensions are attached to populism across Latin America.

Bundled versus disaggregated

The operationalization of populism as a single bundled dimension was deployed in 2011/2012 in Argentina and Bolivia, two countries in which populism could be expected to be salient in political competition, and in Brazil and Chile, two countries in which it was not. The disaggregated approach, on the other hand, was implemented in a survey fielded in 2015 in all 18 Latin American countries. For a contrast of these different approaches to measuring populism, in total we can thus compare experts' placements of 3 presidents and 34 political parties across both surveys.[12] It has to be pointed out that the response rate in 2015 was lower than in 2011/2012. In the latter instance, the survey yielded about 91 valid responses across all four countries, a figure that dropped to 62 in 2015.

As both waves also asked respondents to locate parties and presidents on the general left-right dimension, in a first step we can compare these sets of measures that are trying to capture the exact same underlying quantity across the two surveys as a way of cross-validating our results. Figure 4.1 plots the association between the experts' mean left–right placements of parties and presidents in the first and the second waves along with a linear fit and 95% confidence interval and shows that with an $r = 0.97$ the left–right scores between the two waves match up almost perfectly.

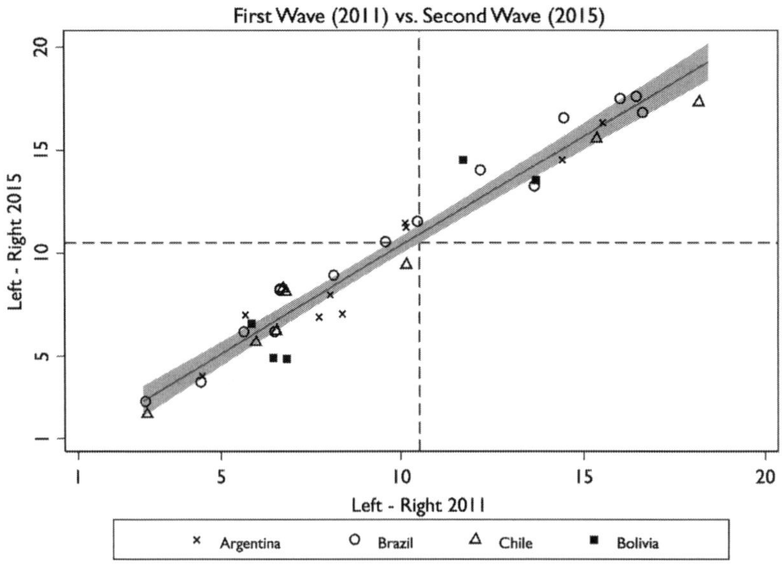

Figure 4.1 The general left–right ideological dimension

Similar to political actors' left–right placements, our measures of populism across the two waves try to capture the same underlying quantity, albeit, of course, using different approaches – whereas in the first wave we place political actors on one single metric, in the second wave the elements combined should capture the degree of populism of political parties and presidents. Table 4.1 provides evidence that the latter is indeed the case. As the second column indicates, the results from the principal component analysis including the four different dimensions measured at the respondent level show that a single factor emerges, explaining 54% of the variance on an underlying common dimension.[13] We can thus proceed and create an additive populism index created from the four individual

Table 4.1 Factor analysis results

	4 countries	
	Factor 1	*Uniqueness*
Principal components results		
Eigenvalue	2.18	
Adjusted eigenvalue	1.11	
Cumulative variance explained	0.54	
Variable and rotated factor loadings		
People-centrism	**0.87**	0.25
Anti-elite (morality)	**0.83**	0.31
Anti-elite (rhetoric)	**0.72**	0.49
Informal style	**0.47**	0.78
N	494, 4 parameters	

Note: Eigenvalues are adjusted based on Horn's Test of principal components (using Stata library paran)

dimensions of people-centrism, anti-elite sentiments (as morality and as importance of rhetoric) and the informality of style of the second wave, and compare the results to the scores on the bundle obtained from the first wave.

Figure 4.2 contrasts these experts' mean placement of parties and presidents, again providing a linear fit and 95% confidence interval. Although with a correlation of 0.81 the agreement between the two different measures is still quite high, the figure hints at the problematic nature of the bundled measure.[14] The strongest connection among placements for political actors on the single metric of the first wave and the populism index based on the disaggregated dimensions from the second wave can be found for the two countries in which populism is a salient feature of political competition, namely, Argentina and Bolivia. The association is mainly driven by both the respective presidents and the presidential parties which can be found in the southwest corner of the figure.

In other words, in political systems in which populism is an important part of political competition, the "usual suspects" who score high on populism as a bundle of attributes also score high for populism on each of the disaggregated dimensions. For instance, former Argentine president Cristina Kirchner receives a mean placement of 4.63 on the populism item in 2011/2012 and 4.60 on the populism index in 2015, while her party *PJ-Frente para la Victoria* both times receives a score of 4.54. The same can be said for the "obvious" pluralist contenders, such as the Argentine *Partido Socialista* with a mean placement of 14.87 in the first and of 14.28 in the second wave; we find only a few moderate cases in these countries. In Brazil and Chile the picture is reversed and we almost exclusively find moderate political actors on the aggregate measure from the first wave. Given that populism is less salient in competition in these countries, overall this appears to make sense. Yet, witness the dispersion of Brazilian and Chilean political actors along the horizontal cross-lines indicating the mid-point of the populism measure as a bundle. Put differently, these results suggest that in political systems in which populism is less salient, using a bundle of attributes may not allow experts to be more nuanced; most actors end up as being scored as moderately populist.

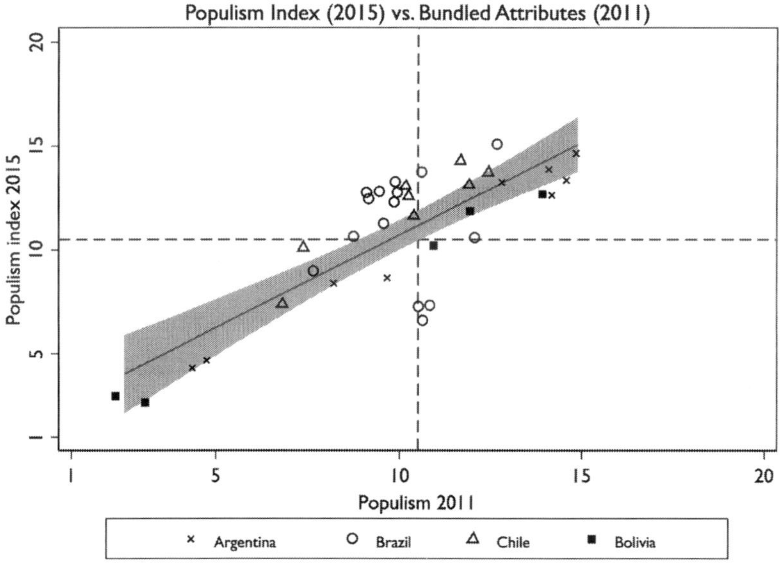

Figure 4.2 Contrasting measurement approaches

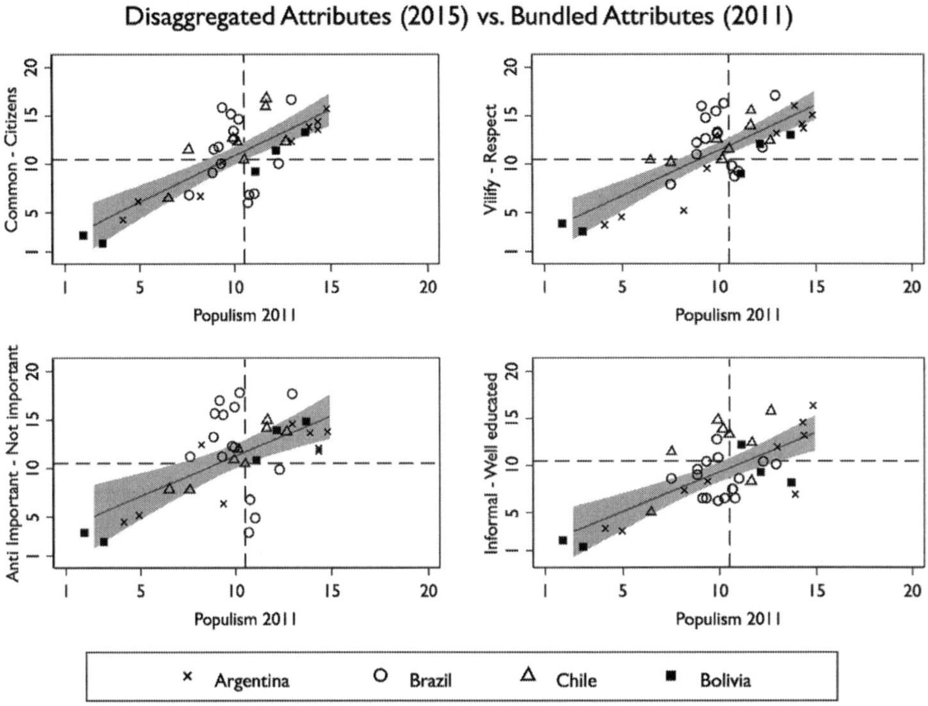

Figure 4.3 Contrasting measurement approaches II

To shed further light on this, Figure 4.3 contrasts experts' mean placement of parties and presidents on the single metric of the first wave with each of the individual attributes of the second wave, providing a linear fit and 95% confidence interval.[15] All four panes highlight a remarkable variance on the individual dimensions, leading to even more dispersion around the mid-point of the bundled measure, a variation that becomes more glaring when excluding the Argentine and Bolivian presidents and presidential parties typically located in the south-west corner. This is particularly pertinent in the lower-left hand pane, contrasting populism as a bundle with the saliency of anti-establishment rhetoric, but is also pronounced in the upper left-hand pane contrasting people-centrism with the single populism metric. The sub-dimensions may thus play an important role in political competition in countries such as Brazil and Chile, which is, however, masked by forcing experts to judge political actors on a single metric combining different attributes. It appears that experts average out variation we may find on individual dimensions, leading to a loss of valuable information on individual actors and party systems.[16]

Ultimately, however, we cannot know for certain whether experts confronted with the task of classifying parties and presidents on a bundled measure indeed consider all of the attributes in conjunction or whether some particular element stands out in their minds. This is important, as from a conceptual point of view only the combination of the individual components of the ideational approach would render an actor populist. Given these complications, it is preferable to mirror potential conceptual complexities of populism in its measurement approach and to exploit the availability of disaggregated components. Disaggregation, for instance, offers the possibility of probing into the question of how the individual attribute relate to each other, which, given current discussions on conceptualization and measurement, is a desirable property. Figures 4.4 and 4.5 contrast experts' mean placements of parties and presidents on the individual dimensions of people-centrism, anti-elitism as morality and rhetoric, and populism understood as informal style. Although the disaggregated measures in this second wave have been deployed in all 18 Latin American countries, for the ease of visual inspection these contrasts are only displayed for the four countries in the focus of this section.[17]

The first thing to notice is that the individual dimensions allow for much more variation of actors' placements across both, the countries in which populist appeals are salient and those in which it is not a central part of political competition. The disaggregated information also reveals how the individual elements relate to each. As the south-west pane of Figure 4.4 shows, with an r = 0.89, the closest fit can be found between the two dimensions aiming at measuring the ideational definition of populism as people-centrism and the moral treatment of the elite as vilifying the political opponent.

In contrast, as the left-hand pane of Figure 4.5 shows, the connection between people-centrism and the CHES measure of anti-elitism is less pronounced and we observe off-quadrant cases across all party systems. For instance, *Peronismo Federal* and *Frente Renovador* in Argentina and the *Partido Republicano da Ordem Social*, the *Partido Trabalhista Brasileiro* and the *Partido Democrático Trabalhista* in Brazil espouse people-centrism, but without necessarily expressing anti-elite rhetoric. The *Frente de Izquierda y de los Trabajadores* in Argentina and the *Partido Humanista* in Chile, on the other hand,

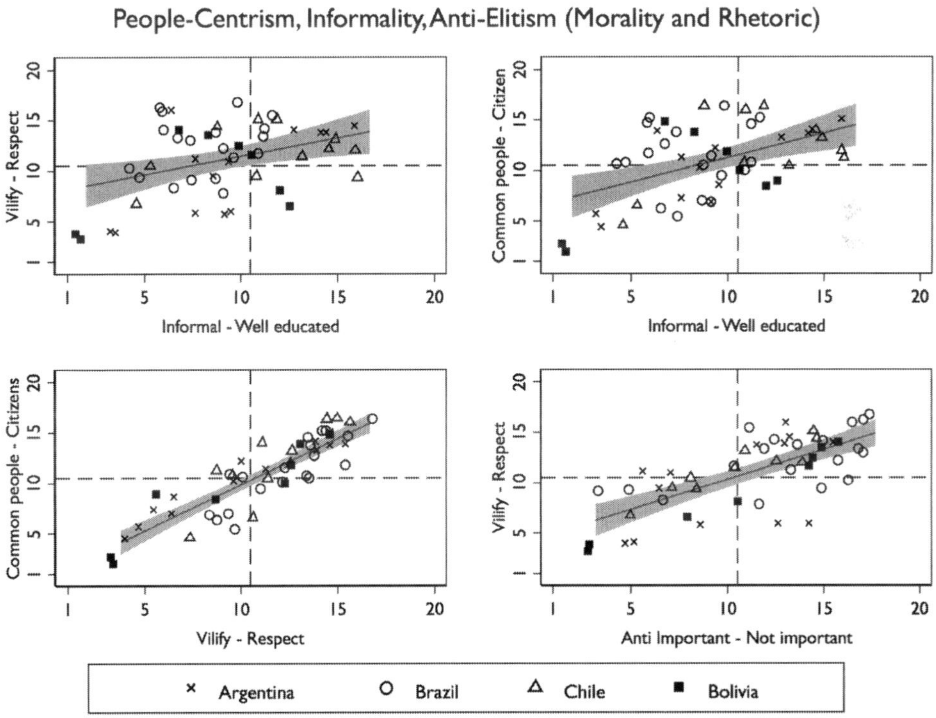

Figure 4.4 Contrasting disaggregated dimensions

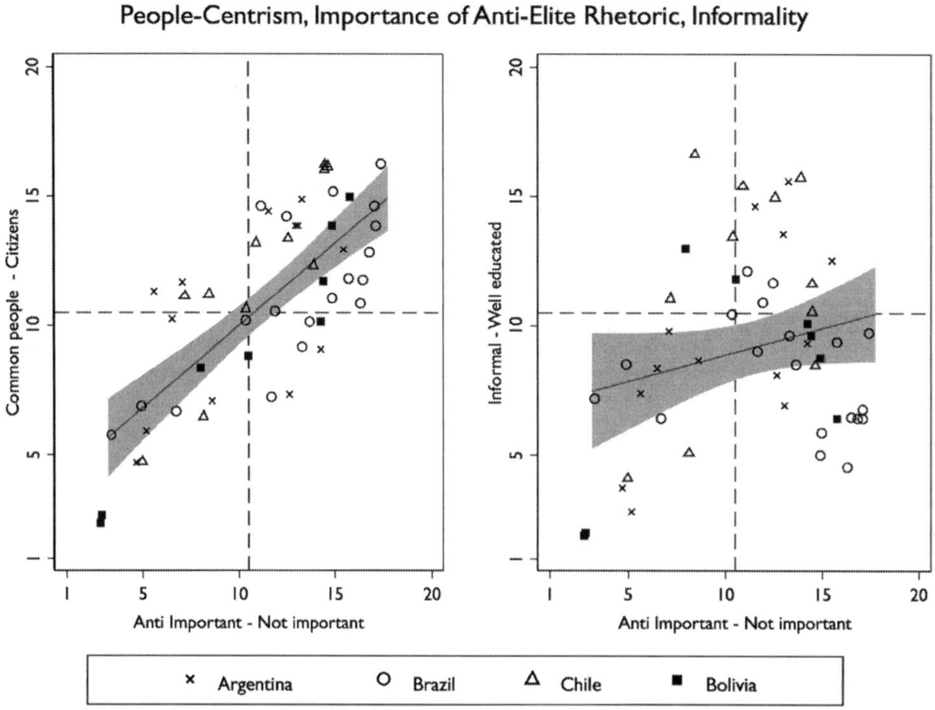

Figure 4.5 Contrasting disaggregated dimensions II

do appeal to the citizenry as a diverse body, but do so with an emphasis on anti-elite rhetoric. Similarly, the south-east pane of Figure 4.4 indicates that *Peronismo Federal* and *Frente Renovador* from Argentina, the *Partido Democrático Trabalhista* and to a lesser extent the party *Solidariedade* from Brazil, and the *Movimiento Sin Miedo* from Bolivia all discredit and vilify their opponents, but without stressing antagonistic rhetoric.

Thus, contrary to combining several attributes into a bundled dimension, disaggregated measures allow for a more fine-grained differentiation among types of political actors. We may find political parties emphasizing people-centrism without pushing anti-elite sentiments, while we also can find clear cases of anti-elite parties which refrain from populist appeals to a homogeneous group of "the people," but rather appeal to a broader citizenry, an assessment facilitated by clearly defining the opposing pole of populism. In addition, we can gain a better understanding of if and how actors differ from each other. Such a contrast may be of particular interest in presidential systems as presidents and their own parties may be subject to different incentives when it comes to political competition (see for instance Arnold, Doyle, and Wiesehomeier 2017; Wiesehomeier and Benoit 2009).

A look at the scores of former Argentine president Cristina Kirchner and her party's on the disaggregated measures, for instance, highlight interesting differences. While on their level of anti-elitism both actors are quite similar (anti-elite rhetoric 4.95 vs. 5.10 for her party; vilifying the opponent 4.43 vs. 4.33 for her party), the ex-president is judged to be slightly more informal (2.96 vs. 3.87 for her party), but to appeal much less to a homogenous people (6.04 vs. 4.87 for her party). As presidents have to appeal to the entire nation, such moderation highlights the different constraints under which presidents and their parties operate. Since expert surveys allow us to measure presidents and their parties on the same metric, they offer us the possibility to examine such differences.

Overall, the results highlight that people-centrism and the moral treatment of the elite are – in line with the conceptualization of the ideational approach – closely related, a relationship that, as the figures show, is least influenced by the presence of actors deemed highly populist such as the Argentine and Bolivian presidents and presidential parties. Simple anti-elite rhetoric, on the other hand, seems to be far less connected to painting the opponent in moral terms, a feature that lies at heart of any definition of populism, or to the emphasis on "the people." Informality shows an even weaker relationship with both people-centrism and anti-elite stances, using either two measures of the latter. In other words, respecting the opponent and championing the citizens can be accomplished in a quite colloquial way, as is the case of for instance the *Partido Demócrata Cristiano* in Bolivia, but it is certainly possible to espouse anti-elite sentiments in a well-mannered form, as can be observed with the *Partido Verde* in Bolivia.

Thus, disaggregated measures do not only shed a much needed light onto conceptual discussions, but also open up the possibility to explore those differences in empirical research further. One of these questions that the results in this section give rise to is whether the variation observed on individual attributes also relates to different policy content. The following section probes into this question, expanding the sample to all 18 countries and thus a total of 165 political parties and 18 presidents.

Populism and policy appeals in Latin America

When moving to the full sample of 18 countries, the patterns highlighted in the previous section are confirmed (see Wiesehomeier 2017). Just as with the reduced sample, the data indicate a substantial overlap among the different conceptualizations of populism and a particular close fit between the two dimensions aiming at measuring the ideational approach. But it also shows a significant amount of dispersion, marking potentially different types of political actors across Latin America. As the expert survey also asked respondents to judge the placements of parties and presidents in their countries on a number of policy issues independently from the populism items, we can explore the question of whether we can identify a common type of populism across the region in terms of policy appeals irrespective of the conceptualization used.

Table 4.2 shows the results of a series of linear regressions of positioning on people-centrism, anti-elitism as morality, a combined index for the ideational approach, anti-elite rhetoric, and populism as informal style, pooling the countries and using as explanatory variables positioning on ten issue dimensions.[18] These issues include the three dimensions concerning economic policy, social policy, and environmental policy that form part of Benoit and Laver's (2006, Chapter 4) "hard core" and the dimensions of regional economic cooperation (understood as a preference for the trading bloc ALBA, the Bolivarian Alliance for the Peoples of Our America (*Alianza Bolivariana para los Pueblos de Nuestra América*)), privatization, and religious principles in politics. Positioning on these policy dimensions has been found to describe policy competition across Latin America well, forming an underlying left-right dimension (see Wiesehomeier and Benoit 2009). Furthermore, policy dimensions that have been deemed to be related to populism in Latin America, such as anti-Americanism, and to be related to its rather inclusive nature compared to a more exclusionary variant of populism in Europe (Mudde and Rovira Kaltwasser 2013), such as redistribution and minority rights, are included. Because the survey in addition asked experts to place parties and presidents on the general left-right dimension, "taking all aspects of party policy into account," Table 4.2 also shows the results for linear regressions of populism and its subcomponents on positioning on the left-right ideological axis.

How do policy appeals compare across the individual attributes? In other words, can we observe differences or can we rather identify common issues across the individual dimensions rooted in different conceptualizations? As Table 4.2 indicates, comparing the results across people-centrism, anti-elitism as morality and rhetoric, and populism as informal style, reveals interesting areas of common ground, but also highlights important differences.

As the first column of Table 4.2 indicates, people-centrism, the first attribute of the ideational approach, is strongly connected to rejecting closer ties to the United States, the only substantive issue that is, in fact, related to all four attributes. A one unit change on the scale ranging from 1 (rejecting closer ties) to 20 (favoring closer ties) amounts to a change of 0.33 on the people-centrism dimension. In addition people-centrism is connected to the trade-off between the respect for individual liberties and security. Political actors at the populist end of this scale support tough measures to fight delinquency, violence and organized crime, which fits the strong-men image some Latin American populists espouse. While the appeal to a homogeneous people is also weakly related to a preference for religious principles, redistribution just misses the 10% significance level.

Positioning on anti-elitism in its moral version (column 3), the second attribute of the ideational approach, is also connected to anti-Americanism, albeit to a lesser extent. It is more strongly related to pertinent domestic issues such as a preference for lowering taxes, favoring religious principles in politics, supporting tough measures to fight crime, and most importantly to a preference of redistribution of wealth from the rich to the poor. A one unit change on the scale ranging from 1 (strongly favors redistribution) to 20 (strongly opposes redistribution) amounts to a change of 0.38 on the anti-elite (morality) dimension. The combination of the dimensions of people-centrism and anti-elite morality into a single populism index based on the ideational approach (column 5) confirms that populism across the region is linked to a weak preference for religious principles in politics, the support of crime fighting measures, a strong rejection of close ties with the United States and a clear preference for redistribution.

Anti-elitism, understood as the importance of antagonistic rhetoric (column 7), on the other hand, captures mostly anti-neoliberal and anti-American stances. A one unit change on the dimension of the relationship to the United States amounts to a shift of almost half a unit (0.43) on the anti-elite rhetoric scale ranging from 1 (important) to 20 (not important at all). Anti-elite rhetoric is equally strongly connected to a preference for the trading bloc ALBA – indeed, anti-establishment rhetoric is the only dimension related to regional cooperation embodied by this left-wing alliance.

These substantive differences point to important differences in measurement. The item measuring anti-elite sentiment in moral terms avoided the use of the word "elite," instead referring to an opponent, while the CHES measure aiming at capturing populism via one single item based on the discursive approach incorporated it. It appears that at least in the case of Latin America, in experts' minds anti-elite rhetoric is predominantly associated with international actors, while anti-elite sentiment in terms of vilifying an opponent appears to be linked to internal actors. In this sense the relationship between

Table 4.2 Populism and policy appeals in Latin America

Policy dimension	*People-centrism*		*Anti-elite (morality)*		*The ideational approach*		*Anti-elite (rhetoric)*		*Informal style*	
	(1)	*(2)*	*(3)*	*(4)*	*(5)*	*(6)*	*(7)*	*(8)*	*(9)*	*(10)*
Taxes vs. spending	–0.18	–	–0.26**	–	–0.31	–	–0.18	–	–0.37**	–
	(0.17)		(0.13)		(0.22)		(0.12)		(0.16)	
Social policy	–0.08	–	0.05	–	–0.06	–	0.08	–	–0.07	–
	(0.12)		(0.11)		(0.16)		(0.11)		(0.12)	
Environment	–0.12	–	–0.06	–	–0.15	–	0.14*	–	–0.30**	–
	(0.11)		(0.10)		(0.15)		(0.08)		(0.12)	
Religion	–0.16*	–	–0.13	–	–0.22**	–	–0.19**	–	–0.04	–
	(0.09)		(0.08)		(0.11)		(0.08)		(0.09)	
Privatization / deregulation	0.18	–	0.27	–	0.32	–	–0.15	–	0.19	–
	(0.19)		(0.20)		(0.28)		(0.13)		(0.16)	
Regional cooperation	0.12	–	0.04	–	0.14	–	0.44***	–	0.10	–
	(0.11)		(0.11)		(0.15)		(0.08)		(0.10)	
Minorities	0.10	–	0.05	–	0.12	–	0.07	–	-0.05	–
	(0.06)		(0.07)		(0.08)		(0.05)		(0.07)	
Individual liberties / security	–0.18*	–	–0.23***	–	–0.29**	–	–0.02	–	–0.25**	–
	(0.10)		(0.09)		(0.13)		(0.09)		(0.10)	
Relationship with the USA	0.33***	–	0.17*	–	0.42***	–	0.43***	–	0.46***	–
	(0.11)		(0.10)		(0.14)		(0.10)		(0.11)	
Redistribution	0.25	–	0.38**	–	0.44**	–	0.24**	–	–0.03	–
	(0.15)		(0.15)		(0.22)		(0.10)		(0.13)	
The general left–right	–	0.35***	–	0.42***	–	0.56***	–	0.71***	–	0.08
		(0.05)		(0.05)		(0.07)		(0.04)		(0.06)
Constant	6.69***	6.17***	7.02***	5.72***	10.20***	9.03***	0.35	3.65***	12.29***	8.27***
	(1.36)	(0.66)	(1.51)	(0.55)	(1.87)	(0.90)	(1.03)	(0.52)	(1.52)	(0.77)
N	172	172	172	172	172	172	172	172	172	172
R-squared	0.48	0.19	0.51	0.34	0.53	0.26	0.79	0.60	0.49	0.01

Note: robust standard errors in parentheses. Standard errors are clustered on parties and presidents

*** $p<0.01$, ** $p<0.05$ * $p<0.1$

the preference for redistribution of wealth and anti-elite rhetoric as measured by the CHES item is also much weaker.

Aggressive rhetoric in the form of criticism of neoliberal politics, verbal confrontations with the United States, and a rejection of the Free Trade Area of the Americas (FTAA) is, of course, best epitomized by prototypical left populist presidents such as Néstor and Cristina Kirchner in Argentina, the late Hugo Chávez in Venezuela, who established ALBA as an alternative to the FTAA, and Evo Morales in Bolivia, who due to his background as a coca peasant unionist entered politics with a clearly developed anti-neoliberal and anti-American stance. The CHES item then captures a substantive part of populism in the region; however, it only captures a very specific subtype. With its emphasis on the antagonistic nature of populism, the CHES item misses an important part of the conceptualization of populism as a set of ideas, while the term "elite" may simply carry strong ideological connotations.

This is confirmed by the measures' strong relationship to positioning on the general left-right ideological axis, as highlighted in column 6 of Table 4.2. A one unit change on the left–right scale ranging from 1 (left) to 20 (right) amounts to a 0.71 change on the CHES item of antagonistic rhetoric ranging from 1 (important) to 20 (not important at all). As columns (2), (4) and (6) show, both dimensions aiming at measuring the ideational approach and their combination also reveal a left variant of populism in Latin America. Yet, their relationship with the general left–right ideological axis is much weaker compared to the saliency of anti-establishment rhetoric, with people-centrism showing the weakest relationship. In other words while people-centrism and anti-elitism in its moral form capture a left tendency, they also detect pertinent domestic issues that go beyond a simplistic left-right distinction. The dimensions rooted in the idealistic approach therefore provide us with an insight into policy issues without confounding populism with ideology as is the case with a narrow discursive approach focusing on antagonism.[19]

Using the immediacy in demeanor and relating to people as a proxy for populism (column 9), also raises questions. Informal style shows its strongest connection to the rejection of closer ties with the United States, suggesting a clear left tendency. It is, however, also strongly connected to right tendencies in the form of a preference for economic growth even at the cost of damage to the environment, a relationship that none of the other populism items seems to capture. In addition it relates to the promotion of cutting public services to cut taxes and shows its weakest link to the preference for tough measures against delinquency. Given this policy mix it is not surprising that the last column of Table 4.2 indicates that this dimension is clearly orthogonal to left–right, as envisioned by Ostiguy (2009). Yet, as the factor analysis has shown, whether informality can be understood as a distinguishing element of populism seems less clear. Combined with the striking lack of a connection to redistribution, a policy issue that consistently has been linked to contemporary populism across the region, informal style may thus rather capture a performative element of politics that may very well be shared by populist and pluralist actors rather than identifying populism across the region.

Conclusion

The challenges of measuring populism are, of course, manifold, and the resulting quantities have important implications on our capacity to answer outstanding questions. Contrasting two different approaches to measuring populism, this chapter has not only highlighted the advantages of expert surveys as a tool, but has also shed light on potential problems of one approach over another. Although it may be tempting to have only one single item in a survey to capture populism – after all we want to ease the burden on respondents by avoiding unnecessary long surveys – the discussion has shown that a bundled solution has important drawbacks. Disaggregating populism into different attributes, on the other hand, allows us to uncover interesting variation along the individual dimensions, which facilitates a more fine-grained assessment of political actors and systems. This is of particular interest for presidential systems where institutional incentives may play out differently for presidents and parties, actors that can be measured on the same metric using expert surveys, and thus compared. A disaggregated approach, however, may also help to highlight differences among populist actors in parliamentary systems that currently may be muted.

More importantly, however, this chapter has also shed light on pertinent conceptual issues by exploring these individual dimensions rooted in different conceptualizations of populism and their relationship to policy appeals. What we want – and need – is a "jack of all trades device," a measure that is firmly rooted in a sound conceptualization, able to capture the diversity and complexity inherent to populism's capacity of attaching itself to different ideologies (aka policy appeals), while at the same time able to provide a comparative perspective indicating a broader tendency (aka the ideological left–right).

The analysis suggests that definitions of populism in terms of a narrow discursive approach focusing on anti-elite rhetoric, and a definition based on identity focusing on the informality in demeanor and relating to people, may only capture parts of populism. Even though these may be substantive parts, they rather tap into a very reductionist understanding of populism. Isolated features, as important elements as they may be, do not constitute full manifestations of populism, and consequently these measures seem to be missing important domestic appeals populist in the region have in common. The stark relationship of both, anti-elite rhetoric and informal style, with a rejection of closer ties with the United States in addition begs the question whether anti-elite rhetoric also captures a performative element. While I explore the implications of this in more detail elsewhere (Wiesehomeier 2017), the results in this chapter underline that relying on a single item such as anti-elite rhetoric may be misleading for a more comprehensive understanding of populism.

At least for the Latin American region, an operationalization of populism as a set of ideas in the form of the ideational approach that takes into consideration its components of people-centrism and anti-elitism in its moral version, as well as their combination into an overall index, captures populism best. Not only do these measures highlight the fluidity of and shifts across political systems, but they also mirror the essence of populism – that the programmatic content of populist appeals may change depending on context. While anti-Americanism is the clearest left contender, it is increasingly difficult to extrapolate clear left-right ideological positions on the policy dimension of redistribution across all Latin American countries. In some instances right-leaning candidates successfully contested elections promising to keep redistributive policies previously introduced by left governments (see Montero 2010; Wiesehomeier and Doyle 2013). Similarly, promises to fight crime have been made on the left and on the right.[20] Religion may be a predominantly conservative domain, yet we find a considerable number of leftist actors with preferences for religious principles in politics across the region (see Wiesehomeier 2010). And although lowering taxes can carry effects of poverty reduction by providing incentives for people to leave the informal sector (see Tumen 2016), as a trade-off with public service reduction it is an economic policy mostly related to the right. Thus, combining measures operationalizing full instances of populism grounded in the ideational approach may be our "jack of all trades," highlighting diversity in appeals, pinpointing to policy issues exploited by populist actors, and providing us with a broad tendency across countries without confounding populism with ideology.

Notes

1 For a discussion of "degreeism" and the conceptualization of populism see Aslanidis (2016, 92–93).
2 One major exception is Hawkins and Castanho Silva (Chapter 1).
3 This a priori nature also detaches the researcher from any posterior interpretation of the dimensions, an interpretation that is not unambiguous as it risks being influenced by the researcher's own interests and perspectives.
4 For a similar performative approach, see Moffitt (2014) and Moffitt and Tormey (2014).
5 It would be equally unsatisfactory to simply measure the degree of leftism of political actors instead of either locating them on a continuous axis of left–right or providing a measure for their degree of rightism at the same time. However, nothing prevents researchers using text analysis from measuring a separate scale of for instance pluralism and to then combine these measures into one metric, similar to the Comparative Manifesto's approach to measuring left-right party placements.
6 This is the approach taken by the Chapel Hill expert survey (CHES) project on party positioning on European integration for their "GAL/TAN" dimension (Hooghe et al. 2002). Respondents are asked to locate political parties on a scale with the endpoints Green/Alternative/Libertarian combining attitudes to democratic participation, libertarianism (e.g. attitudes to abortion, homosexuality), and ecology and the opposing pole of Traditional/Authoritarian/Nationalism, combining traditional values, defense, opposition to immigration.
7 As it is a loaded term, the use of the word "populism" was avoided in the survey.
8 I would like to thank Cristóbal Rovira Kaltwasser, Kirk Hawkins, and Pierre Ostiguy for feedback and fruitful discussions when devising these definitions.
9 I would like to thank Cristóbal Rovira Kaltwasser, Kirk Hawkins and the participants of focus groups with students and staff at Brigham Young University and Swansea University in February/March 2015 for discussions and feedback.
10 The titles given to the different attributes in this section were not used in the survey itself. To avoid bias, the title indicated to respondents that the survey was eliciting judgments on political communication of political parties and presidents.
11 I would like to thank Gary Marks and Ryan Bakker from the CHES for early access to this question wording and allowing its usage in my survey.
12 In the case of Chile the presidents changed between two waves, from Sebastián Piñera to Michelle Bachelet, and so these had to be omitted.
13 Yet, the varimax rotated factor loadings indicate that populism as informal style shows by far the weakest loading.
14 Excluding informal style from the index drops the result for the coefficient of the pop-index to 0.62, with an r-squared of 0.56.
15 For ease of interpretation, the anti-establishment and anti-elite dimension has been flipped so that 1 indicates now the populist endpoint.
16 The construction of the index obviously also results in attenuation. Yet, given that the individual measures allow for more variance, this effect is less pronounced. Note that the uncertainty of the placement scores on the single metric are not larger vis-à-vis individual dimensions.
17 As these results are taken from the 2015 expert survey wave only, the number of cases increases and the results show the locations of four presidents and 47 parties.
18 For the exact wording of these dimensions see Appendix.
19 Testing for a curvilinear relationship between the different conceptualizations of populism and ideology to detect extreme right and extreme left populists confirms the patterns detected here. Anti-elite rhetoric shows a strong left bias and a quasilinear relationship (for a similar

problematic pattern in the European case see Polk et al. 2017), while the relationship between the items measuring the ideational approach rather uncovers a left tendency. Informality, on the other hand, confirms its presence on both, the left and the right. These results are available upon request.

20 Interestingly, recent discussions of public security on the left and the right ideological spectrum are increasingly linked to immigration. The 2017 Chilean presidential campaign is a prominent example.

References

Arnold, Christian, David Doyle, and Nina Wiesehomeier. "Presidents, Policy Compromise, and Legislative Success." *The Journal of Politics* 79(2): 380–395.

Aslanidis, Paris. 2016. "Is Populism an Ideology? A Refutation and a New Perspective." *Political Studies* 64: 88–104.

Benoit, Kenneth and Michael Laver. 2006. *Party Policy in Modern Democracies*. London: Routledge.

Castles, Francis and Peter Mair. 1984. "Left–Right Political Scales: Some 'Expert' Judgments." *European Journal of Political Research* 12(1): 73–88.

Hawkins, Kirk. 2009. "Is Chávez Populist? Measuring Populist Discourse in Comparative Perspective." *Comparative Political Studies* 42(8): 1040–1067.

Hawkins, Kirk and Scott Riding. 2009. "Populism in Latin America: The AmericasBarometer 2008." Paper presented at the Annual Meeting of the Midwest Political Science Association, Chicago, April 1–5.

Hawkins, Kirk and Bruno Castanho e Silva. 2016. "Mapping Populist Parties in Europe and the Americas." Paper presented at "Explaining Populism: Team Populism January Conference," Provo-UT, January 28-30.

Hawkins, Kirk and Cristóbal Rovira Kaltwasser. "The ideational approach to populism." Forthcoming in *Latin American Research Review*.

Huber, John and Ronald Inglehart. 1995. "Expert Interpretations of Party Space and Party Locations in 42 Societies." *Party Politics* 1(1): 73–112.

Hooghe, Lisbeet, Gary Marks, and Carole Wilson. 2002. "Does Left/Right Structure Party Positions on European Integration?" *Comparative Political Studies* 35(8): 965–989.

Laclau, Ernesto. 1997. *Politics and Ideology in Marxist Theory: Capitalism, Facism, Populism*. London: New Left Books.

Laclau, Ernesto. 2005. *On Populist Reason*. London: Verso Books.

Laver, Michael, and W. Ben Hunt. 1992. *Policy and Party Competition*. New York: Routledge.

Levitsky, Steven and Kenneth Roberts 2011. *The Resurgence of the Latin American Left*. Baltimore: The Johns Hopkins University Press.

March, Luke (this volume). "Populist Ideology in the UK Party System: Measurement and Practice."

Marks, Gary and Steenbergen, Marco. 2004. 2004: Marks/Steenbergen Party Dataset. Available from www.unc.edu/~gwmarks/data.htm.

Moffitt, Benjamin. 2014. "How to Perform Crisis: A Model for Understanding the Key Role of Crisis in Contemporary Populism. " *Government and Opposition* 50(2): 189–217.

Moffitt, Benjamin and Simon Tormey. 2014. "Rethinking Populism: Politics, Mediatisation and Political Style." *Political Studies* 62(2): 381–397.

Montero, Alfred. 2010. "Their Separate Ways: Leftist Mobilization and Clientelist Continuity in Brazilian Subnational Politics." Paper presented at the workshop on *Political Consequences of Declining Inequality in Brazil*, Oxford University, December 3.

Mudde, Cas. 2004. "The Populist Zeitgeist." *Government and Opposition* 39(4): 542–563.

Mudde, Cas and Cristóbal Rovira Kaltwasser. 2011. "Voices of the Peoples: Populism in Europe and Latin America Compared." *Kellogg Institute Working Paper No. 378*.

Mudde, Cas and Cristóbal Rovira Kaltwasser. 2013. "Exclusionary vs. Inclusionary Populism: Comparing Contemporary Europe and Latin America." *Government and Opposition* 48(2): 147–173.

Ostiguy, Pierre. 2009. "The High and the Low in Politics: A Two-Dimensional Political Space for Comparative Analysis and Electoral Studies." *Kellogg Institute Working Paper No. 360.*

Panizza, Francisco. 2005. *Populism and the Mirror of Democracy*. London: Verso Books.

Plattner, Marc F. 2010. "Populism, Pluralism, and Liberal Democracy." *Journal of Democracy* 21(1): 81–92.

Polk, Jonathan, Jan Rovny, Ryan Bakker, Erica Edwards, Liesbet Hooghe, Seth Jolly, Jelle Koedam, Filip Kostelka, Gary Marks, Gijs Schumacher, Marco Steenbergen, Milada Vachudova, and Marko Zilovic. 2017. "Explaining the Salience of Anti-Elitism and Reducing Political Corruption for Political Parties in Europe with the 2014 Chapel Hill Expert Survey Data." *Research & Politics* 4(1): 1–9.

Rohrschneider, Robert/Whitefield, Stephen. 2007. "Representation in New Democracies: Party Stances on European Integration in Post-Communist Eastern Europe." *Journal of Politics* 69(4): 1133–1146.

Rooduijn, Matthijs and Teun Pauwels. 2011. "Measuring Populism: Comparing Two Methods of Content Analysis." *West European Politics* 34(6):1272–1283.

Taggart, Paul. 1995. "New Populist Parties in Western Europe." *West European Politics* 18(1): 34–51.

Taggart, Paul. 2000. *Populism*. Buckingham: Open University Press.

Tumen, Semih. 2016. "Entrepreneurship in the Shadows." *Economics of Transition*: n/a-n/a.

Weyland, Kurt. 2001. "Clarifying a Contested Concept: Populism in the Study of Latin American Politics." *Comparative Politics* 34(1): 1–22.

Wiesehomeier, Nina. 2010. "The Meaning of left-Right in Latin America. A Comparative View." *Kellogg Working Paper 370.*

Wiesehomeier, Nina. 2017. "Populism vs. Anti-Elite Rhetoric. A Comparison Based on Expert Survey Results." Paper presented at the XIII Congreso de AECPA, Santiago de Compostela, September 22.

Wiesehomeier, Nina and Kenneth Benoit. 2009. "Presidents, Parties and Policy Competition." *Journal of Politics* 71(4): 1435–1447

Wiesehomeier, Nina and David Doyle. 2013. "Discontent and the Left Turn in Latin America." *Political Science Research and Methods* 1(2): 201–221.

Appendix

Questionnaire expert survey

Taxes v. spending

Promotes raising taxes to increase public services. (1)

Promotes cutting public services to cut taxes. (20)

Social policy

Favors liberal policies on matters such as abortion, homosexuality, divorce and euthanasia. (1)

Opposes liberal policies on matters such as abortion, homosexuality, divorce and euthanasia. (20)

Privatization (Bolivia, Brazil, Colombia, Mexico, Paraguay, Uruguay)

Promotes maximum state ownership of business and industry, such as gas, oil, electricity and telecommunications. (1)

Opposes all state ownership of business and industry, such as gas, oil, electricity and telecommunications. (20)

Deregulation (all that did not have privatization)

Favors high levels of state regulation and control of the market. (1)

Favors deregulation of markets at every opportunity. (20)

Environment

Supports protection of the environment, even at the cost of economic growth. (1)

Supports economic growth, even at the cost of damage to the environment. (20)

Relation with United States

Rejects a closer relationship of ____________ with the United States.

Supports a closer relationship of ___________ with the United States

Regional cooperation

Favors closer ties to ALBA (Bolivarian Alliance for the Peoples of Our America). (1)

Rejects closer ties to ALBA (Bolivarian Alliance for the Peoples of Our America). (20)

Individual liberties/ security

Promotes protection of civil liberties, even when this hampers efforts to fight crime/ delinquency, violence and organized crime. (1)

Supports tough measures to fight crime/delinquency, violence and organized crime, even when this means curtailing civil liberties. (20)

Indigenous people/minorities

Supports the assimilation of minorities and their abidance by the laws of the majority. (1)

Supports the right of minorities to live their own lifestyle even if this renders necessary special laws. (20)

Religion

Supports religious principles in politics. (1)

Supports secular principles in politics. (20)

Redistribution

Position on redistribution of wealth from the rich to the poor.

Strongly favors redistribution (1)

Strongly opposes redistribution (20)

The general left–right dimension

Please locate each party on a general left-right dimension, taking all aspects of party policy into account.

Left (1) Right (20)

Political communication 2011

Highlights the interest of the people, with reference to the sovereign will of the majority. Condemns the ruling class and interest groups. Emphasizes personal authority, capable of leadership and a decisive resolution of problems. Uses an informal style and slang. (1)

Highlights the interests of citizens, with references to civic or republican values. Recognizes the ruling class and interest groups as legitimate. Emphasizes impersonal authority, the formality of procedures and separation of powers. Uses a "well-educated" style and more formal language. (20)

Political communication 2015

Question 1

Identifies with the common people and celebrates their authenticity (1)

Refers more generally to citizens and their unique interests (20)

Question 2

Demonizes and vilifies opponents. (1)

Treats opponents with respect. (20)

Question 3

How important is the following for the party:

The salience of anti-establishment and anti-elite rhetoric

Not important at all (1)

Extremely important (20)

Question 4

Uses an informal style and popular language (1)

Uses a "well-educated" style and more formal language (20)

5 Elite surveys[1]

Ioannis Andreadis and Saskia P. Ruth-Lovell

The phenomenon of populism poses many challenges to comparativists around the world, as outlined in the introduction to this volume. Due to different perspectives on the topic, researchers have especially struggled with conceptual clarity. In recent years, however, they have come to more agreement on how to define populism (e.g. Akkerman, Mudde and Zaslove 2014; Hawkins and Rovira Kaltwasser forthcoming; Mudde and Rovira Kaltwasser 2012a; Panizza 2005). The emergence and success of populist parties is associated with some sort of crisis of democratic representation, which comes along with the dealignment of partisan attachments. This allows populist contenders to attract discontented voters with an anti-establishment appeal (Barr 2009). It is this kind of rhetoric – usually articulated around a discursive claim to represent "the people" against a hostile establishment frustrating their demands – that seems to unite populist parties (Laclau 2005).

In this chapter, we present the findings of two research projects designed to test if and how populist attitudes among political elites can be measured. Studying populist attitudes at the elite level may enhance our ability to assess the position of each political candidate within the political system. To do so, we define populism – in line with the ideational approach to the study of populism described in the introduction to this volume – as a formal discursive articulation dividing society into two relatively homogeneous and antagonistic groups: the people versus the elite (Hawkins and Rovira Kaltwasser 2017), often resulting in the construction of a "thin-centred ideology" (Freeden 1998, 750). The exact content of this ideology depends on secondary elements that may be combined with such an appeal. From this perspective, populism may be related to many contents, structures, and strategies and can thus acquire antithetical political connotations.

One major advantage of such an approach is that it lends itself well to analysing the populist phenomenon in a comparative way. Based on this approach, empirical research has recently advanced in the task of measuring the complexities of populism, e.g. through textual analysis of political speeches or public opinion surveys to measure populist attitudes of voters (Akkerman, Mudde and Zaslove 2014; Hawkins, Riding and Mudde 2012; Hawkins 2009). However, with the exception of key political figures like presidents, prime ministers, and political parties in general (Wiesehomeier 2015), the inclination of parliamentary elites towards populist attitudes has yet to be substantively explored, especially from a comparative perspective.

But why is it worth studying elites and what is the added value of this approach, given that existing analyses of manifestos and other discursive material seem to cover the supply side? Similar to studies on citizens' attitudes – i.e. the demand side – which have been the subject of sustained research, it is important to analyse the supply side of populist attitudes below the party level. While parties function as the intermediaries between citizens and the state, they are far from being unitary actors, and much has been written about the degree of ideological cohesion and party discipline of individual legislators, candidates or party activists (on Greece see Andreadis 2015; on Denmark see Hansen and Rasmussen 2013; on Latin America see Ruiz Rodríguez 2006). Hence, measuring populist attitudes on the individual (legislator or candidate) level enables us to gain insight into the within-party variation of the phenomenon, something that measures aimed at analysing populism at the meso-level, based on manifesto data or through expert surveys, fail to capture. Moreover, political elite surveys have the advantage to capture the discursive crystallizations of populist attitudes across different types of party functionaries – i.e. rank-and-file and party leaders – while measures based on individual political speech data – which measure populism on the individual level as well – usually include only the most visible party representatives, like presidents, prime ministers, or party leaders. It is astonishing how little we know about political elites' populist attitudes given that their study could offer a more accurate picture of how abstract ideological principles and formal electoral pledges (to be found in manifestos) shape the attitudes of real subjects who, by embodying the positions of their party in their everyday interaction with voters, act as its privileged interpreters, its influential agents and in-betweens.

This chapter sets out to close this gap by presenting and discussing two new datasets measuring populist attitudes through candidate and parliamentary elite surveys: the Greek Candidate Survey from 2015 and the Parliamentary Elites in Latin America (PELA) Survey from the University of Salamanca in Bolivia in 2015. Both datasets asked respondents (candidates and elected parliamentarians) to indicate their level of agreement with a series of statements on a five-point Likert scale, which we use to create an index of populist attitudes as detailed below. In what follows we first provide preliminary descriptive evidence on the distribution of this index of populism and its components among different political parties in these countries and its relationship with the ideological left-right divide. In analysing the data, this chapter also seeks to investigate populist attitude patterns and link them to other relevant political aspects. Our central aim is to determine whether we can use a theoretically informed battery of survey items and the resulting populism index to discriminate between populist and non-populist parties.

The chapter is structured as follows: in the next section, we elaborate on the definition of populism. In the third section, we discuss our measurement followed by a description of the two datasets. We provide first descriptive empirical evidence on Greece and Bolivia in section four. Section five concludes.

What is populism?

As mentioned above, for decades populism posed a conceptual challenge to comparative researchers. It has been largely defined along the lines of phenomenological typologies based on feature lists or core characteristics (e.g. organizational structure, social base), which led to many versions of populism distinguished by a series of adjectives or prefixes (Schedler 1996, 292) and finally to different case selections (see especially Weyland 2001). In recent years, however, researchers aiming at cross-regional comparisons have come to more agreement on how to define populism (Hawkins and Rovira Kaltwasser 2017; Mudde and Rovira Kaltwasser 2012b, and the introduction of this volume). Instead of focusing on narrow and region-specific definitions of populism, they follow a broader conceptualization based on an ideational approach. In line with the common reference to an anti-elite, anti-party, or anti-establishment discourse, and with an orientation charted by earlier definitions put forward by Canovan (1999) and Laclau (1980), populism is defined as "*an ideology that considers society to be ultimately separated into two homogeneous and antagonistic groups, 'the pure people' versus 'the corrupt elite,' and which argues that politics should be an expression of the* volonté générale *(general will) of the people*" (Mudde 2004, 543, italics in the original). This approach, nevertheless, is open to using narrower definitions of the concept to distinguish subtypes of the phenomenon. For example, the contents of such an, often, vague discourse do not form part of its conceptual core to the extent that they are determined through its articulation with other ideological, programmatic or personalistic elements (e.g. socialism, neo-liberalism, or charisma). Only the combination of a populist discourse with other ideological contents can determine the exact nature of the antagonism between "the people" and "the elite" in a particular political setting and historical conjuncture. Thus, the recurrence of an anti-elite rhetoric and the central location of claims to be the party or the leader truly representing "the good people" seem indeed to unite all populist orientations. At the same time, other ideological elements articulated around this formal framework help to distinguish different forms of populism – such as left- or right-wing populism, neo-populism, or indigenous populism (Abts and Rummens 2007; Mudde 2004).

Such a definition of populism lends itself very well to a systematic measurement of populist phenomena. Based on this definition populism has been measured using several techniques of content analysis, e.g. holistic grading of speeches, sentence coding of party manifestos, or computerized content analysis of media texts (e.g. Hawkins 2009; Hawkins and Castanho Silva in this volume, Chapter 1; Rooduijn and Pauwels 2011, and March in this volume, Chapter 2). While these studies focused mainly on the supply side of populism – political parties and party leaders – other studies use the ideational approach to measure populist attitudes within the citizenry as a means to explain the rise and mobilization potential of populist parties in different regions of the world (see Akkerman, Mudde and Zaslove 2014; Hawkins, Riding and Mudde 2012; Hawkins, Rovira Kaltwasser and Andreadis 2018). We combine the insights from these latter studies that measure populist attitudes on the individual level with the focus of the former studies on the supply side of populism to measure populist attitudes among political elites.

Only recently have researchers begun to transfer the items from public opinion surveys on populism to political elite surveys (Andreadis and Stavrakakis 2017; Stavrakakis, Andreadis, and Katsambekis 2017; Ruth and Ramírez Baracaldo 2015). This approach has significant potential advantages over existing measures on the supply side, namely, that it captures the within-party variation of the populist phenomenon and that it is not confined to the study of very prominent, and thereby visible party figures. Moreover, if we use comparable items to inquire after populist attitudes within the political elite, we will be able to compare them with survey data measuring populist attitudes within the citizenry. The comparison of elite and public opinion surveys would enable us to test if elites engage in relations of *polarizing trusteeship* or *moderating trusteeship* with their constituents (see Kitschelt et al. 1999, 309–310), thereby either increasing or decreasing the importance of populism within political representation.

Research design

State of the art: measuring populist attitudes with surveys

Survey items to measure populist attitudes within the public have been developed and tested recently by Hawkins, Riding and Mudde (2012) to analyse populism in the United States. These authors developed a set of survey items that incorporate both the ideas and the language in which statements of the core ideas of populism are expressed. The first battery of these populist attitude items was included in the 2008 AmericasBarometer surveys conducted by the Latin American Public Opinion Project (LAPOP) at Vanderbilt University. Additionally, Hawkins, Riding and Mudde (2012) used a similar battery of items in a subsample of 1,000 respondents from the 2008 Cooperative Congressional Elections Studies (CCES), an Internet survey conducted by Yougov/Polimetrix; and the 2008 Utah Colleges Exit Poll (UCEP), a sample of 950 respondents that was collected during the November 2008 general elections.

Building on the aforementioned studies, Akkerman, Mudde and Zaslove (2014) have tested a battery of items to measure populist attitudes and to investigate whether these attitudes can be linked with party preferences on a representative data set of 586 Dutch respondents. This battery consists of three types of questions with a target to measure (1) populist attitudes, (2) pluralist attitudes, and (3) elitist attitudes. Based on the findings of this paper, populist attitudes can be measured by the six items presented in Table 5.1. The same items were deployed in both the 2015 Greek Candidate Survey (CCS) and the 2015 Bolivian sample of the Parliamentary Elites in Latin America (PELA) survey managed by the University of Salamanca (USAL).[2]

The 2015 Greek Candidate Study

The Greek Candidate Study is part of the Comparative Candidate Survey (CCS), a joint multi-national project with the goal of collecting data on candidates running for national parliamentary elections in different countries using a common core questionnaire in a post-election candidate survey conducted in each country. CCS is conducted after the elections in order to collect data at the same period that data on voters are collected as part of national election studies. This means that in order to understand the findings presented in the following sections of this chapter, we should take into account that the candidates give their answer when they already know the electoral outcome and whether their political parties are in government or not.

In Greece, the Candidate Survey is usually run as a mixed-mode survey and the first mode is always a web-survey (Andreadis 2010) followed by face-to-face or telephone interviews. The data of these studies is available from the website of the Hellenic National Election Studies (www.elnes.gr) and has been used in many national and international publications (e.g. Andreadis 2012; Freire et al. 2014; Teperoglou, Chadjipadelis and Andreadis 2010; Teperoglou et al. 2014).

Table 5.1 Populist attitude items

POP1	The politicians in Congress/Parliament need to follow the will of the people
POP2	The people, and not politicians, should make our most important policy decisions
POP3	The political differences between the elite and the people are larger than the differences among the people.
POP4	I would rather be represented by a citizen than by a specialized politician
POP5	Elected officials talk too much and take too little action
POP6	What people call "compromise" in politics is really just selling out on one's principles

Sources: Hawkins, Riding and Mudde (2012: 8–9) and Akkerman, Mudde and Zaslove (2014:1331)

Parliamentary Elites in Latin America (PELA 2015)

Since the late 1990s the PELA team conducts representative surveys of parliamentary elites in 18 countries in the region at the beginning of each legislative period. The surveys include questions about the values of legislators, their behaviour, as well as their opinion on concrete issues of the region and the socio-political panorama of the respective countries. They include questions on issues related to the quality of democracy, the ideological orientation of lawmakers and the position of their political parties and party leaders, their attitudes towards representation, democracy, and the economy. Moreover, the surveys include items on the organization of legislative parties and their social base.

The dataset has been used to study a wide range of topics like the ideological structuration of party systems and political competition along the left-right divide (Alcántara Sáez and Rivas 2007; Alcántara Sáez 2008; Kitschelt et al. 2010; Wiesehomeier 2010), the congruence between political elites and their constituents with respect to political issues or political values (Hawkins, Kitschelt and Llamazares 2010; Ruiz Rodríguez and García 2003; Saiegh 2009), the quality and structure of political representation (Carnes and Lupu 2015; Luna and Zechmeister 2010; Marenghi 2011), the nature of the executive-legislative relationship (García 2009), as well as legislative career paths and intra-party behaviour (Alcántara Sáez 2012; Carnes and Lupu 2015; Inácio and Magalhães Araújo 2011; Martínez Rosón 2012).

The survey is conducted based on structured, face-to-face interviews with parliamentarians. The PELA database, as of now, consists of five waves with a set of continuously asked core questions as well as changing question batteries on specific topics. The data is available through the project website of the Observatorio de Élites Parlamentarias en América Latina (http://americo.usal.es/oir/elites/bases_de_datos.htm). Among the first countries that included the six populist attitude items was Bolivia in winter 2015. Hence, the PELA surveys provide a valuable dataset with which we can explore the relationship between populist attitudes and several other aspects of interest.

Preliminary descriptive evidence from Greece and Bolivia

The Greek CCS was conducted from mid-February to the end of July 2015 and its initial target was to collect data from candidates of the seven parliamentary parties. Unfortunately, the Communist Party of Greece (KKE) has never agreed to participate in the Greek Candidate Study. Likewise, Golden Dawn (GD) usually replies that all candidates share the same opinion, that of its leader, along the lines of the *Führerprinzip*. As a result, our target population is the group of all candidates running with the five following parties: Coalition of the Radical Left (SYRIZA), New Democracy (ND), The River (RIVER), Panhellenic Socialist Movement (PASOK), Independent Greeks (ANEL).

At this point, we want to highlight that the Greek dataset is based on responses by candidates. All major Greek political parties have the same number of candidates. Thus, a representative sample of candidates should include approximately the same number of candidates from each party. Elsewhere (Andreadis 2016), we estimate the response rate of the Greek CCS 2015 as between 35.2% and 37.6% (depending on how the cases of unknown eligibility are used in the formula). We also demonstrate that the distribution of the candidates in the sample is very similar to the corresponding distribution in the population with regard to i) gender and ii) their electoral districts. The elected MPs are slightly under-represented in the sample, but the gap is not very large (8.1% of the sample and 12.5% of the population). This difference is not important: for instance, if we study only the non-elected MPs, all parties will appear slightly more populist, but the difference of the populism index will be very small (less than 1.5%). The distribution per party is presented in Table 5.2.

Turning to Latin America, as mentioned before, Bolivia figures among the first countries within the PELA survey that included the six items on populist attitudes. Moreover, Bolivia has been frequently associated with the phenomenon of populism, especially since the rise of Evo Morales to the presidency in 2005 (Madrid 2008, Madrid 2011). Hence, we take the advantage here to provide a first analysis of the populist attitudes of legislators in the most recent legislative terms in Bolivia from 2015–2020.

The 2014 presidential and legislative elections in Bolivia was the second election under the new constitution from 2009 and the third consecutive election of Evo Morales for the presidency (Alpert, Centellas and Singer 2010; Centellas 2015). Morales, one of the most prominent populist presidents in Latin America, rose to power in 2005 with his party *Movimiento al Socialismo* (MAS) (de la Torre 2013; Madrid 2008). His initial campaign in 2005 capitalized on the deeply rooted discontent with traditional political elites, and his rise to power resulted in a complete restructuring of the party system (Crabtree 2013; Mayorga 2006). Throughout his previous terms, the political climate polarized and the MAS clashed with regional opposition parties, especially on issues of the nationalization of natural resources and political decentralization (Gray Molina 2010). Nevertheless, the MAS managed to win both the presidential and parliamentary election in 2014 with a comfortable majority of more than 60% of the vote. The main competitor of the MAS in the 2014 race (winning nearly 25% of the seats in the lower chamber) was the newly formed alliance *Unidad Demócrata* (UD) between the *Unidad Nacional* (UN), with its presidential candidate Samuel Doria Medina, and several regional opposition governors (Centellas 2015). The third party that won nearly 8% of the seats in the lower chamber in 2014 was the *Partido Demócrata Cristiano* (PDC) with its presidential candidate Jorge Quiroga.

The PELA survey has been conducted in Bolivia in the end of 2015 and covers the legislators who serve in the legislative period from 2015–2020. Legislators have been randomly sampled and stratified by political party (see Table 5.3). For Bolivia, the sample

Table 5.2 Distribution of respondents per party, Greek CCS 2015

Party	*Frequency*	*Candidates (%)*
SYRIZA	115	21.9
ND	102	19.4
RIVER	108	20.6
PASOK	98	18.7
ANEL	102	19.4
Total	525	100.0

Table 5.3 Distribution of respondents per party, PELA survey 2015

Party	*Frequency*	*Respondents (%)*	*Seats (%)*
MAS	57	61.3	67.6
UD	28	30.1	24.6
PDC	8	8.6	7.7
Total	93	100	100

Source: PELA 2015.

includes 93 legislators, which equal 72% of the lower legislative chamber. The PELA surveys are based on face-to-face interviews. Nonresponse with respect to our items of interest is below 1% in our samples.

Although the two datasets discussed in this chapter follow a similar approach in measuring populist attitudes in political elites, the survey designs differ in two aspects. Since the Greek data is based on a candidate survey the sample includes both successful (i.e. elected) and unsuccessful (non-elected) candidates, while the PELA data is based on interviews with elected parliamentarians only. Nevertheless, according to Stavrakakis, Andreadis and Katsambekis (2017) the differences between elected and non-elected candidates are not large. Replicating the calculation of the populism index using only the sub-group of the 2015 Greek candidate sample that is created after the removal of the elected MPs, they get very similar results (all parties appear slightly more populist, but the differences are very small).

Constructing a populism index for political elites

Before we continue with the analysis of the results we need to verify that the six items we have used are closely related to each other in the two country samples. We need to test the internal consistency of the items mainly because the items have been tested so far only on voters. Indeed, this is the first time these items are used on candidates or parliamentarians, thus we need to check if the reliability of the scale when applied on voters remains intact when the scale is applied on candidates (Greek sample) or parliamentarians (Bolivian sample). Cronbach's alpha for the six items included in the Greek Candidate Study gets the value of 0.75, suggesting that the items have relatively high internal consistency. This value is similar to the value that Akkerman, Mudde and Zaslove (2014) have found in their study (0.82). Cronbach's alpha for the six items in the Bolivian sample, however, only reaches a value of 0.47 suggesting that the six items have a rather low internal consistency.

In order to decide which items we should include in our populist attitudes index in the two country samples, we run Mokken Scale Analysis using the R package Mokken (van der Ark 2012; van Schuur 2003).[3] In the remainder of this section, we discuss the results from these analyses separately for the two countries. Therefore, Table 5.4 includes the output for the Greek case and Table 5.5 for the Bolivian case.

The first column of Table 5.4 reports the item scalability coefficients Hi after running Mokken scale analysis on all items. As can be seen, the coefficient of POP5 is lower than the usual rule of thumb for single items (0.3) and the overall H coefficient of the scale is 0.372, which is lower than the usual rule of thumb for H scales (0.4). This is why we re-ran the analysis excluding item POP5 (see the second column). As can be

Table 5.4 Output of Mokken scale analysis – Greece

	Mokken scale analysis	
	Item coefficients Hi	
	6 items	*5 items*
POP1	0.421	0.491
POP2	0.426	0.495
POP3	0.351	0.399
POP4	0.362	0.364
POP5	0.203	
POP6	0.443	0.462
H	0.372	0.442

seen, the H scale improves when POP5 is dropped from the calculation, which is why we calculate the populism index for the Greek data based on the remaining five populist attitude items. For more details on the application of the method, see Stavrakakis, Andreadis and Katsambekis (2017).

We proceed in a similar way for the Bolivian case. The Mokken scale analysis, this time however, identifies two scales, with three items consistently loading on the first scale and two items loading on a second scale. Following the same rule of thumb as before, we reach an H coefficient above 0.4 in both of these scales. The only item that does not consistently load on either of these two scales is POP6 "What people call 'compromise' in politics is really just selling out on one's principles." Hence, for the Bolivian data, we use two separate sets of items to calculate two sub-dimensions of populist attitudes. The first dimension taps into the component of *people-centrism* common among populist attitudes, with POP1 "The politicians in Congress need to follow the will of the people", POP2 "The people, and not politicians, should make our most important policy decisions", and POP4 "I would rather be represented by a citizen than by a specialized politician." The second dimension, on the other hand, taps into the component of *anti-elitism* common in

Table 5.5 Output of Mokken scale analysis – Bolivia

	Mokken scale analysis	
	Item coefficients Hi	
	People-centrism *3 items*	*Anti-elite* *2 items*
POP1	0.345	–
POP2	0.434	–
POP3	–	0.413
POP4	0.431	–
POP5	–	0.413
POP6	–	–
H	0.411	0.413

populist attitudes, with POP3 "The political differences between the elite and the people are larger than the differences among the people" and POP5 "Elected officials talk too much and take too little action." For a detailed discussion of the different substantive dimensions that have been subsumed under the concept of populism see the chapter by Castanho Silva et al. in this volume as well as Hawkins and Rovira Kaltwasser (2017) and Mudde (2004). We will come back to these patterns in our discussion below.

Comparing political parties' degree of populism in Greece and Bolivia

As a result, from the analyses in the previous section, we construct an index of populism as the mean value of the five populist attitude items in Greece and two indices of populist attitudes in Bolivia (using the mean values of the items that belong in each scale). As Figure 5.1 indicates, according to the Greek populism index the candidates of PASOK, ND and RIVER – parties generally assumed to be non-populist – score below 3.5 while the candidates of both SYRIZA and ANEL – parties generally assumed to be populist – score over 3.5. ANEL candidates score higher than SYRIZA candidates on the populism index but the difference between these two parties is not significant. PASOK, ND and RIVER candidates do not differ significantly on the same index and form a common group. But this group (the candidates of PASOK, ND and RIVER) scores significantly lower on this scale and is significantly different from the group of SYRIZA and ANEL candidates.

While Figure 5.1 shows that the five-item additive index works very well in Greece, we still have not explained why POP5 does not. In Table 5.6 we compare the major partner in the current coalition government of populist parties (SYRIZA) with the major party of the opposition (ND), which is considered as non-populist. Except POP5, all

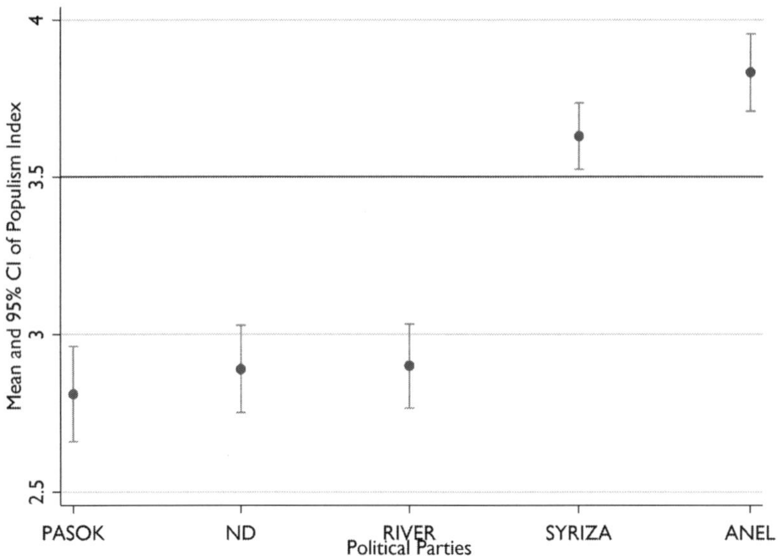

Figure 5.1 Populism index by political party – Greece

other comparisons presented in Table 5.6 are significant at the 0.001 level, indicating that for all five items that were used to create the populist attitudes index, SYRIZA candidates score significantly higher than ND candidates. Again here, POP5 "Elected officials talk too much and take too little action" is an exception. It seems that it has been interpreted in a way that equates "elected officials" with members of the current government. Such an interpretation could explain the lower scores of SYRIZA candidates and the higher scores of ND candidates. It may be that SYRIZA candidates wanted to protect the ministers of their coalition government (data were collected in a period when the Finance Minister Varoufakis was accused of spending most of his time giving interviews). At the same time, the interpretation could also explain the higher scores of ND candidates, because through their responses to this item they find a way to criticize the members of the current government.

Figure 5.2 shows the party differences with respect to the two sub-dimensions of populism in Bolivia. We find substantive party differences between MAS and UD legislators; legislators of the PDC, however, appear to be less consistent with respect to their populist attitudes on both the people-centrism as well as the anti-elite dimensions of populism. As expected, MAS legislators score consistently higher on populist attitudes highlighting the importance of "the people" (see left panel) – with a mean of 4.5 and a very low standard deviation of 0.52. The UD, on the other hand, scores consistently lower on people-centrism attitudes with a mean of 3.4 and a standard deviation of 0.75. Surprisingly, on average, MAS legislators have consistently lower populist attitudes with respect to the anti-elite dimension of populism compared to both the party system mean of 3.3 (sd = 1.17) as well as the average legislator of the UD (mean = 3.75, sd = 0.91). Since these findings go against most of the current literature with respect to the degree of populism in Bolivia, we need to inspect these party differences in more detail (de la Torre 2013; Madrid 2011; Webber 2010).

In order to explain the results for Bolivia, we may also inspect the differences on the item level (including all six items) for the president's party MAS and the main opposition party UD (see Table 5.7). We find that MAS legislators are significantly more populist with respect to how much politicians need to follow the will of the people (POP1), if people should make the most important policy decisions (POP2), and if people can be better represented by a citizen than by a specialized politician (POP4). They are less so

Table 5.6 SYRIZA/ND differences

Item	*SYRIZA*			*ND*			*t*	*p*
	N	*Mean*	*S.D.*	*N*	*Mean*	*S.D.*		
POP1	107	4.18	.627	95	3.65	.998	4.41	<0.001
POP2	106	3.95	.832	96	2.81	1.059	8.45	<0.001
POP3	106	4.08	.825	86	3.13	1.003	7.04	<0.001
POP4	109	3.08	.862	96	2.64	.985	3.44	0.001
POP5	101	3.39	.883	96	3.72	.914	–2.60	0.010
POP6	102	2.84	1.002	96	2.36	.964	3.42	0.001

Source: The Greek Candidate Study 2015

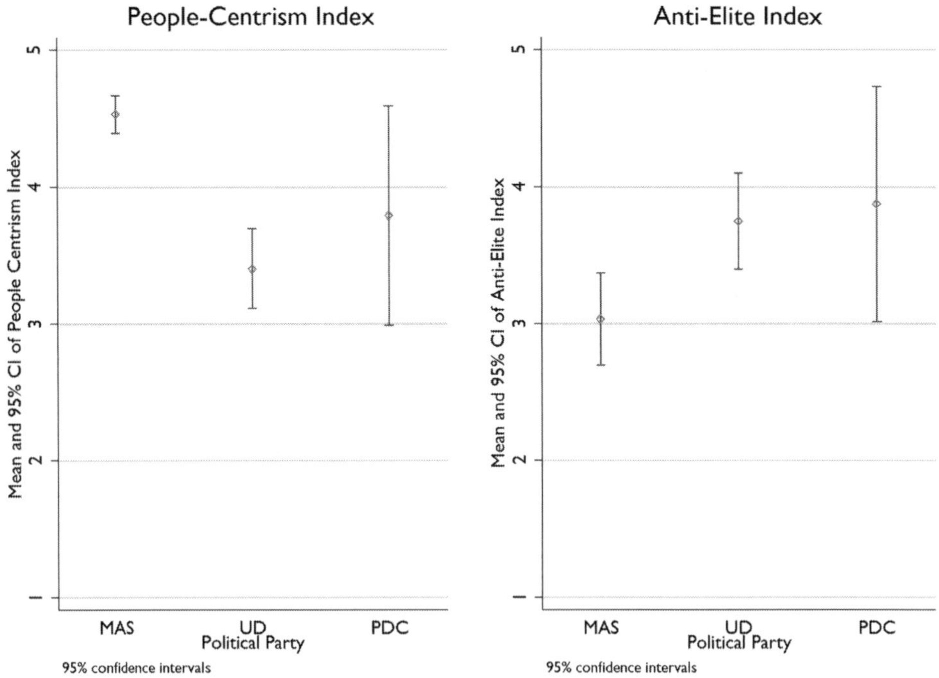

Figure 5.2 People-centrism and anti-elite index by political party – Bolivia

with respect to the differences between the elite and the people (POP3) and concerning the attitude that elected officials talk too much and take too little action (POP5), which is where UD legislators reach consistently higher scores compared to MAS legislators. Consequently, while the reference to "the people" as well as "the will of the people" seems to be at the core of MAS legislator's populist appeal, ten years of experience in government may have tamed the anti-elite and anti-government elements of the populist ideology of these legislators. Hence, the findings highlight the bottom-up character and strong focus on "the people" of the MAS that started out as a heterogeneous social movement in the 1990s and early 2000s (Crabtree 2013; de la Torre 2013). The findings of the low anti-elite stance of MAS legislators also resonate with data from populist discourse analysis showing that the intensity of the populist discourse of Evo Morales decreased considerably from his first to his second term (Hawkins and Kocijan 2013; Hawkins 2009) and hints to a moderating pull that experience in power may have on populist actors (Abts and Rummens 2007; Schedler 1996). It also falls in line with the findings from the chapter by Andreadis, Hawkins, Llamazares and Singer in this volume (Chapter 10), which show a weakening connection over time between the populist attitudes of Bolivian voters and their preference for MAS. Hence, our findings point to an important intervening variable that has been discussed in the populism literature for quite some time and needs to be taken into account, especially with respect to the viability of the populist discourse: the government or opposition status of political actors (Heinisch 2003; Mudde and Rovira Kaltwasser 2012b).

Table 5.7 MAS/UD differences

Item	*MAS*			*UD*			*t*	*p*
	N	*Mean*	*S.D.*	*N*	*Mean*	*S.D.*		
POP1	57	4.84	0.05	28	4.32	0.17	3.65	0.0005
POP2	57	4.51	0.12	28	2.96	0.25	6.38	0.0000
POP3	55	3.2	0.21	28	3.79	0.23	−1.78	0.0795
POP4	57	4.25	0.11	28	2.93	0.25	5.66	0.0000
POP5	57	2.77	0.18	28	3.71	0.22	−3.19	0.0020
POP6	57	2.68	0.18	28	2.46	0.29	0.66	0.5135

Source: PELA 2015.

Conclusion

In this chapter, we explore if the measurement of populist attitudes in citizens may travel to political elites as well. We find that they do but that they show different patterns both across countries and across parties. Drawing from earlier studies on populist, elitist and pluralist attitudes in voters (Akkerman, Mudde and Zaslove 2014; Hawkins, Riding and Mudde 2012) we adapted a set of survey statements and deployed them in the Greek module of the CCS and the Bolivian sample of the Parliamentary Elites in Latin America surveys (PELA). Our exploratory analyses show that most of the six populist attitude items proposed in the literature consistently construct a single scale in the Greek case, while we identified two sub-dimensions of populist attitudes in the case of Bolivia, where we find differences with respect to *people-centrism* (POP1, POP2, and POP4) as well as *anti-elite* elements (POP3 and POP5) in the populist discourse to be the most consistent aspects across parties.

These different patterns across countries led us to compare political elites on the level of political parties in more detail. Here again, we found that legislators from different political parties show a clear pattern in the Greek case but a more diverse pattern in Bolivia. As expected, SYRIZA and ANEL consistently score higher on populism than their traditional counterparts (PASOK, ND and RIVER) do. In Bolivia, however, we find legislators from the party of President Evo Morales – MAS – to be the least populist with respect to anti-elite attitudes, while legislators of the two opposition parties UD and PDC score consistently higher on this dimension. On the contrary, we find that MAS legislators score considerably higher on those items that focus on the populist subcomponent of people-centrism (POP1, POP2, and POP4) compared to the two opposition parties. Both patterns resonate with MAS history that is grounded in its bottom-up development from a social movement to a long-term government party (Crabtree 2013).

Our findings highlight several interesting insights and new avenues for future research: First, while we find consistent populist attitudes among the elite, these do not necessarily consist of the same populist items identified in other contexts for citizens. More research is necessary to identify both regional specific patterns of the populist discourse and patterns that distinguish the elite from the citizenry in their attitudes towards populism. Second, and related to the latter point, our analysis across both cases highlights the importance of government status and its relation to the "anti-elite" component of populist discourse. Our results indicate in both cases that anti-elite attitudes are considerably higher in opposition legislators than in government legislators. Even the short experience of SYRIZA in Greece already highlights that items like POP5 (elected officials talk too much and take too little action) undermine the function of a governing party in supporting the government. A finding that arises even more so in the Bolivian case, where the MAS has been in government for three consecutive presidential terms. Several studies on populism have shown that a populist appeal may be well suited to compete (successfully) in elections but less suited for the time consuming and compromise prone day to day business of governing. Hence, future research needs to address the possibility that populist attitudes in political elites may vary over time conditional on either political campaign logic or government status.

This chapter presented a first glimpse at these emerging datasets on populist attitudes in Europe and Latin America. With the completion of more datasets, more substantive comparisons will become possible and more conclusive support for what seems like a promising avenue for future research will hopefully be established.

Notes

1 Many thanks are due to Yannis Stavrakakis for his comments on earlier drafts of this chapter.
2 The only item that had to be changed because it was not suitable for candidates or parliamentary elites was item POP4: "I would rather be represented by a citizen than by a specialized politician" that was changed to "People can be better represented by a citizen than by a specialized politician."
3 According to van Schuur (2003), for ordinal items, it is better to use Mokken scale analysis instead of factor analysis.

References

Abts, Koen and Stefan Rummens. 2007. "Populism Versus Democracy." *Political Studies* 55(2): 405–424.

Akkerman, Agnes, Cas Mudde and Andrej Zaslove. 2014. "How Populist Are the People? Measuring Populist Attitudes in Voters." *Comparative Political Studies* 47(9): 1324–1353.

Alcántara Sáez, Manuel and Cristina Rivas. 2007. "Las Dimensiones De La Polarización En Los Parlamentos Latinoamericanos." *Política y gobierno* 14(2): 349–390.

Alcántara Sáez, Manuel. 2008. "La Escala De La Izquierda: La Ubicación Ideológica De Presidentes Y Partidos De Izquierda En América Latina." *Nueva Sociedad* 217: 72–85.

Alcántara Sáez, Manuel. 2012. *El Oficio De Politico*. Madrid: TECNOS.

Alpert, Alexandra, Miguel Centellas and Matthew M. Singer. 2010. "The 2009 Presidential and Legislative Elections in Bolivia." *Electoral Studies* 29(4): 757–761.

Andreadis, Ioannis. 2010. "Web-Based Political Surveys (Greek)." In *Proceedings of the 23rd Panhellenic Statistics Conference: Statistics and Internet*, 44–51. Athens: Greek Statistical Institute.

Andreadis, Ioannis. 2012. "Measuring Satisfaction with Democracy among Candidates: What Is the Effect of the Electoral Outcome?" Paper presented at the 2nd Plenary Conference of the CCS, Mannheim, January 27–29.

Andreadis, Ioannis. 2015. "Estimating the Position of Political Parties: Comparison between an Expert Survey and a Candidate Survey." Paper presented at the Using Expert Judgements Workshop, Malta, October 7–9.

Andreadis, Ioannis. 2016. "The Greek Candidate Study 2015. Web Based Surveys Greek Election 2015." Ann Arbor, MI: Inter-University Consortium of Political and Social Research http://doi.org/10.3886/E62191V1

Andreadis, Ioannis and Yannis Stavrakakis. 2017. "European Populist Parties in Government: How Well are Voters Represented? Evidence from Greece." *Swiss Political Science Review*, 23(4), 485–508 http://doi.org/10.1111/spsr.12255

Barr, Robert R. 2009. "Populists, Outsiders and Anti-Establishment Politics." *Party Politics* 15(1): 29–48.

Canovan, Margaret. 1999. "Trust the People! Populism and the Two Faces of Democracy." *Political Studies* 47(1): 2–16.

Carnes, Nicholas and Noam Lupu. 2015. "Rethinking the Comparative Perspective on Class and Representation: Evidence from Latin America." *American Journal of Political Science* 59(1): 1–18.

Centellas, Miguel. 2015. "The 2014 Presidential and Legislative Elections in Bolivia." *Electoral Studies* 38: 94–97.

Crabtree, John. 2013. "From Mnr to the Mas: Populism, Parties, the State, and Social Movements in Bolivia since 1952." In *Populism of the Twenty First Century*, edited by Carlos de la Torre and C. Arnson, 269–295. Baltimore and Washington: The Johns Hopkins University Press and the Woodrow Wilson Center Press.

de la Torre, Carlos. 2013. "In the Name of the People: Democratization, Popular Organizations, and Populism in Venezuela, Bolivia, and Ecuador." *European Review of Latin American and Caribbean Studies* 95: 27–48.

Freeden, Michael. 1998. "Is Nationalism a Distinct Ideology?" *Political Studies* 46(4): 748–765.

Freire, André, Marco Lisi, Ioannis Andreadis and José Manuel Leite Viegas. 2014. "Political Representation in Bailed-out Southern Europe: Greece and Portugal Compared." *South European Society and Politics* 19(4): 413–433.

García, Mercedes. 2009. *Presidentes Y Parlamentos: ¿Quién Controla La Actividad Legislative En América Latina?* Madrid: Centro de Investigaciones Sociológicas.

Gray Molina, George. 2010. "The Challenge of Progressive Change under Evo Morales." In *Leftist Governments in Latin America. Successes and Shortcomings*, edited by K. Weyland, R. Madird and W. Hunter, 57–76. Cambridge: Cambridge University Press.

Hansen, Martin Ejnar and Niels Erik Kaaber Rasmussen. 2013. "Does Running for the Same Party Imply Similar Policy Preferences? Evidence from Voting Advice Applications." *Representation* 49(2): 189–205.

Hawkins, Kirk A. 2009. "Is Chávez Populist? Measuring Populist Discourse in Comparative Perspective." *Comparative Political Studies* 42(8): 1040–1067.

Hawkins, Kirk, Scott Riding, and Cas Mudde. 2012. "Measuring Populist Attitudes." Working Paper Series on Political Concepts #55. ECPR Committee on Concepts and Methods. www.concepts-methods.org/Files/WorkingPaper/PC_55_Hawkins_Riding_Mudde.pdf.

Hawkins, Kirk and Bojana Kocijan. 2013. "Codebook for Measuring Populist Discourse among chief executives in CEE and Central Asia." https://populism.byu.edu/Pages/Data.

Hawkins, Kirk A., Herbert Kitschelt and Iván Llamazares. 2010. "Programmatic Structuration around Religion and Political Regime." In *Latin American Party Systems*, edited by Herbert Kitschelt, Kirk A. Hawkins, J. P. Luna, G. Rosas and E. Zechmeister, 236–278. Cambridge: Cambridge University Press.

Hawkins, Kirk A. and Cristóbal Rovira Kaltwasser. 2017. "The Ideational Approach to Populism." *Latin American Research Review*, 52(4): 513–528.

Hawkins, Kirk A., Cristóbal Rovira Kaltwasser and Ioannis Andreadis. 2018. "The Activation of Populist Attitudes." Government and Opposition Online first. doi: 10.1017/ 846 gov.2018.23.

Heinisch, Reinhard. 2003. "Success in Opposition – Failure in Government: Explaining the Performance of Right-Wing Populist Parties in Public Office." *West European Politics* 26(3): 91–130.

Inácio, Magna and Paulo Magalhães Araújo. 2011. "Dinámica Intercameral Y Coordinación Partidista En Brasil." In *Algo Más Que Presidentes: El Papel Del Poder Legislativo En América Latina*, edited by M. Alcántara Sáez and M. García, 361–389. Zaragoza: Fundación Manuel Giménez Abad de Estudios Parlamentarios y del Estado Autonómico.

Kitschelt, Herbert, Zdenka Mansfeldova, Radoslaw Markowski and Gábor Tóka. 1999. *Post-Communist Party Systems. Competition, Representation, and Inter-Party Cooperation.* Cambridge: Cambridge University Press.

Kitschelt, Herbert, Kirk A. Hawkins, Juan Pablo Luna, Guillermo Rosas and Elizabeth J. Zechmeister. 2010. *Latin American Party Systems*. Cambridge: Cambridge University Press.

Laclau, Ernesto. 1980. "Populist Rupture and Discourse." *Screen Education* 34: 87–93.

Laclau, Ernesto. 2005. *On Populist Reason*. London: Verso.

Luna, Juan Pablo and Elisabeth J. Zechmeister. 2010. "Political Representation in Latin America." In *Latin American Party Systems*, edited by H. Kitschelt, K. A. Hawkins, J. P. Luna, G. Rosas and E. J. Zechmeister, 118–144. Cambridge: Cambridge University Press.

Madrid, Raúl. 2008. "The Rise of Ethnopopulism in Latin America." *World Politics* 60(3): 475–508.

Madrid, Raúl. 2011. "Bolivia: Origins and Policies of the Movimiento Al Socialismo." In *The Resurgence of the Latin American Left*, edited by S. Levitsky and K. M. Roberts, 239–259. Baltimore, MD: The Johns Hopkins University Press.

March, Luke. 2018. Textual analysis: the UK party system, this volume.

Marenghi, Patricia. 2011. "Resolver Los Problemas De La Provincia: La Representación Territorial En Las Actitudes De Los Legisladores Latinoamericanos." In *Algo Más Que Presidentes: El Papel Del Poder Legislativo En América Latina*, edited by M. Alcántara Sáez and M. García, 271–302. Zaragoza: Fundación Manuel Giménez Abad de Estudios Parlamentarios y del Estado Autonómico.

Martínez Rosón, María del Mar. 2012. "La Carrera Parlamentaria: ¿La Calidad Importa?" In *Políticos Y Política En América Latina*, edited by M. Alcántara Sáez, 174–212. Madrid: Siglo XXI.

Mayorga, René Antonio. 2006. "Outsiders and Neopopulism: The Road to Plebiscitarian Authoritarianism." In *The Crisis of Democratic Representation in the Andes*, edited by S. Mainwaring, A. M. Bejarano and E. Pizarro Leongómez, 132–167. Stanford: Stanford University Press.

Mudde, Cas. 2004. "The Populist Zeitgeist." *Government and Opposition* 39(4): 541–563.

Mudde, Cas and Cristóbal Rovira Kaltwasser, eds. 2012a. *Populism in Europe and the Americas. Threat or Corrective for Democracy?* Cambridge: Cambridge University Press.

Mudde, Cas and Cristóbal Rovira Kaltwasser. 2012b. "Populism and (Liberal) Democracy: A Framework for Analysis." In *Populism in Europe and the Americas. Threat or Corrective for Democracy?*, edited by Cas Mudde and Cristóbal Rovira Kaltwasser. Cambridge: Cambridge University Press.

Panizza, Francisco. 2005. *Populism and the Mirror of Democracy*. London: Verso Books.

PELA. 2015. Manuel Alcántara (ed.). *Proyecto de Elites Parlamentarias Latinoamericanas (PELA)*. Universidad de Salamanca (1994–2018).

Rooduijn, Matthijs and Teun Pauwels. 2011. "Measuring Populism: Comparing Two Methods of Content Analysis." *West European Politics* 34: 1272–83.

Ruiz Rodríguez, Leticia M. 2006. "Coherencia Partidista: La Estructuración Interna De Los Partidos Políticos En América Latina." *Revista Espanola de Cienca Política* 14: 87–114.

Ruiz Rodríguez, Leticia M. and Mercedes García. 2003. "Coherencia Partidista En Las Élites Parlamentarias Latinoamericanas." *Revista Espanola de Cienca Política* 8: 78–102.

Ruth, Saskia P. and Adriana M. Ramírez Baracaldo. 2015. "Measuring Populist Attitudes in Latin America's Parliamentary Elites." Paper presented at the ALACIP Annual Congress, Lima (Peru).

Saiegh, Sebastian M. 2009. "Recovering a Basic Space from Elite Surveys: Evidence from Latin America." *Legislative Studies Quarterly* 34(1): 117–145.

Schedler, Andreas. 1996. "Anti-Political-Establishment Parties." *Party Politics* 2(3): 291–312.

Stavrakakis, Yannis, Ioannis Andreadis and Giorgos Katsambekis. 2017. "A New Populism Index at Work: Identifying Populist Candidates and Parties in the Contemporary Greek Context." *European Politics and Society*: 18(4), 446–464 doi: 10.1080/23745118.2016.1261434.

Teperoglou, E., T. Chadjipadelis and Ioannis Andreadis. 2010. "Cleavages of Voters and Candidates in the National and the European Dimension: Convergences and Divergences (Greek)." *Science and Society – Journal of Political and Moral Theory* 25: 37–63.

Teperoglou, E., André Freire, Ioannis Andreadis and J.M.L. Viegas. 2014. "Elites' and Voters' Attitudes Towards Austerity Policies and Their Consequences in Greece and Portugal." *South European Society and Politics* 19(4): 457–476.

van der Ark, L. Andries. 2012. "New Developments in Mokken Scale Analysis in R." *2012* 48(5): 27. doi: 10.18637/jss.v048.i05.

van Schuur, Wijbrandt H. 2003. "Mokken Scale Analysis: Between the Guttman Scale and Parametric Item Response Theory." *Political Analysis* 11(2): 139–163. doi: 10.1093/pan/mpg002.

Webber, Jeffery R. 2010. "Carlos Mesa, Evo Morales, and a Divided Bolivia (2003–2005)." *Latin American Perspectives* 37(3): 51–70. doi: 10.1177/0094582x10364033.

Weyland, Kurt. 2001. "Clarifying a Contested Concept. Populism in the Study of Latin American Politics." *Comparative Politics* 34(1): 1–22.

Wiesehomeier, Nina. 2010. "The Meaning of Left-Right in Latin America: A Comparative View." In *Working Paper #370*, edited by K. Institute.

Wiesehomeier, Nina. 2015. "Presidents, Parties and Populism: Preliminary Results from Expert Surveys." Paper presented at the ALACIP Congreso Latinoamericano de Ciencia Política, Lima, July 22–24.

6 Public opinion surveys

Evaluating existing measures[1]

Steven M. Van Hauwaert, Christian H. Schimpf, and Flavio Azevedo

Over the last three decades, populist actors have established themselves as influential political forces around the world (de la Torre 2015). To grasp the phenomenon, the discipline puts a particular focus on populism's conceptualisation (e.g., Albertazzi and McDonnell 2008; Canovan 2005; Mudde 2004; Weyland 2001), as well as the identification of its underlying causes (e.g. Kriesi and Pappas 2015; Mudde 2007) and the evaluation of its consequences (e.g. Mudde and Rovira Kaltwasser 2012; Rooduijn, de Lange, and van der Brug 2014). Until recently, however, most of these studies almost exclusively focused on populism as a supply-side phenomenon.

In contrast, the study of populism as a demand-side phenomenon, particularly in the form of *populist potential amongst individuals*, has received much less attention. Yet, it represents an important component in understanding the rise and fall of populist forces (cf. Hawkins and Rovira Kaltwasser in the Introductory chapter of this book). At this time, we do not (yet) have a comprehensive understanding of its measurement, its empirical evaluation and its implications. Yet, a series of recent studies is making gradual intakes into this field. Most commonly, populism is theorised as an ideational construct, which – as a set of ideas – can manifest itself at the individual level and, therefore, can be measured (Akkerman, Mudde, and Zaslove 2014; Hawkins and Riding 2010; Hawkins, Riding, and Mudde 2012; Stanley 2011).[2] Either implicitly or explicitly, the majority of these studies interpret populism as an attitudinal construct that influences political behaviour. At the same time, comprehensive theoretical and/or measurement studies in support of this rationale remain largely absent. This chapter provides some initial empirical insights into the potential interpretation of populism as an attitudinal construct.[3]

To capture populism at the individual level, scholars have gradually, yet systematically, converged around a battery of survey items (or at least parts of it) that was originally designed by Hawkins and Riding (2010). Even in light of this convergence, scholars have yet to reach a common standard to measure what some refer to as *populist attitudes* (e.g. Akkerman, Mudde, and Zaslove 2014). Oftentimes, the lack of coherent results in the measurement of populist demand by means of different items and different combinations of items, which in turn makes both within- and between-country comparisons of populism complex, if not impossible. An additional concern that arises pertains to the cross-national validity and reliability of survey items and batteries as a whole, which often remain assumed, rather than empirically tested. In this chapter, we seek to remedy this empirical caveat by (i) providing an initial comparison and overview of instruments to measure populist attitudes in different contexts, and (ii) evaluating the items that measure populist attitudes through psychometric assessment. We test items from different data sets across the Americas (LAPOP, CCES, UCEP and UDP) and Europe (LIVEWHAT, SNES, WoPo) and use item response theory (IRT) models for our empirical analysis.

In this chapter, we proceed as follows. We introduce the reader to the growing literature of individual-level interpretations of populism (such as populist latent attitudes), as well as to the items and scales that scholars have developed. Following this, we discuss why additional empirical tests of the scales and items are essential. We then introduce the data sets and our methodological approach, followed by the results section in which we present our findings for each of the data sets separately. We conclude with a more comparative discussion of our results, which indicate (i) current measures of populist attitudes often fail to provide information about respondents at either extreme (low and high level) of the populism scale, and (ii) we identify instances in which certain items might be redundant because they fail to provide any additional information about a respondent's level of populism. Based on these findings, we discuss the implications for further research in the broader area of populist attitudes. These are the foundation for the ensuing scale development chapter by Silva et al. (Chapter 7 in this book).

Populist attitudes: conceptualisation and importance

The idea to conceive populism not only as a supply side but also as a demand side phenomenon arguably dates back to Axelrod (1967) who discovers what he refers to as a "weak cleavage" in American public opinion that runs along the lines of "1890s populism" (Axelrod 1967, 51).[4] Few others, however, continued to pursue that path of research in the immediate aftermath (see Dryzek and Berejikian (1993) and Farrell and Laughlin (1976)), despite a diverse set of populist expressions in the twentieth century (ideologies, leaders, parties, movements, policies, etc.). Yet, with an ever more extensive amount of research covering populism over the last two to three decades now, it does not come as a surprise that ultimately, interest in populism as an individual-level phenomenon would be rediscovered. Starting with Hawkins and Riding (2010), Stanley (2011) and Hawkins, Riding, and Mudde (2012), scholars of populism and public opinion began to invest in understanding what they commonly refer to as *populist attitudes*.

In line with one of this book's central premises, most of the studies that examine populist attitudes typically share the conception that there is a set of ideas that underlie the larger notion of populist proclivities. These populist attitudes cannot be observed and measured directly as they are said to be latent (cf. Introductory chapter by Hawkins and Rovira Kaltwasser in this book). Populist attitudes can then be described as a "tendency that is expressed by evaluating a particular entity with some degree of favor or disfavor" (Eagly and Chaiken 1993, 1), where the so-called "entity" is congruent with the ideas of populism. Specifically, these ideas include anti-elitism, the inherent belief in a general or popular will (a *volonté générale*), and a Manichean worldview (Hawkins 2009; Rooduijn 2014).

Measuring populist attitudes

Based on this common theoretical understanding, initial empirical studies examined the question of how populist attitudes can be measured in the first place. In the process, researchers developed a series of items and scales now available to the wider research community. Hawkins and Riding (2010) were among the first to develop a set of Likert-scale items specifically developed to capture populist attitudes. They developed six of these items based on populism as an ideational construct.[5] Originally, these items were included in the 2008 AmericasBarometer (LAPOP 2008) and fielded in 24 American countries. The authors further refined this measurement by (i) putting the principal focus on capturing the Manichean view of politics, and (ii) limiting the scale to four items they eventually fielded in the 2008 CCES and UCEP surveys (cf. also Hawkins, Riding, and Mudde 2012).[6] At about the same time, Stanley (2011) designed eight Likert-scale items to measure populism in Slovakia. These accounted for the homogeneity of the people and the elite (two items), the antagonistic nature of political life (two items), attitudes towards democracy (two items), and the moral dimension of politics (two items). After this, Akkerman, Mudde, and Zaslove (2014) proposed eight items that served as a supposed direct measurement of populist attitudes. To advance the scale, they built on the original set of items by Hawkins and Riding (2010), but added further items aimed at measuring the Manichean dimension of populism as well as some of its antipodes, such as pluralism (three items) and elitism (three items). They applied their proposed measure of populist attitudes to the Netherlands to also examine whether the demand for populism was met by the supply (Melendez and Rovira Kaltwasser 2017).

Empirical inferences based on populist attitudes

Beyond developing a valid measure to capture populist attitudes, scholars drew on their scales to examine how widespread these attitudes actually are. Most of the previously discussed studies conclude that populist attitudes are prevalent and pervasive among the public (e.g. Akkerman, Mudde, and Zaslove 2014; Hawkins and Riding 2010; Hawkins, Riding, and Mudde 2012; Stanley 2011). Nonetheless, without questioning the general spread of populist attitudes, other studies conclude that there is a fair amount of variance between individuals with regards to their levels of populist attitudes. For instance, in trying to explain the individual differences, Elchardus and Spruyt (2016) find correlations between feelings of relative deprivation and populist attitudes, which – according to them – "is in the first place a consequence of declinism" (p. 15). Further disagreement exists regarding the role and impact of populism. Various scholars have looked at the (potential) influence of populist attitudes on individual voting behaviour. Stanley (2011) finds that populist attitudes are common among the Slovakian electorate but their influence on vote choice is rather limited, in particular in comparison to other factors, such as nationalism or economic preferences. Additional empirical results suggest differently and, in fact, reveal that populist attitudes closely interact with more substantive policy concerns, both for left- and right-wing populist party supporters (Van Hauwaert and van Kessel 2018).

What unites these studies is their objective to complement research on populism as a party-level phenomenon and to understand whether and how demand-side populism has contributed to the pervasiveness of contemporary populism. Based on our review, we can make three central observations. First, one of the more general indications from the studies populist attitudes is the "widespread hypothesis", that is, the claim that populist attitudes are considerably common among the public. Second, scholars have started to conduct inferential research (particularly regarding vote choice), but until this point, they still draw different conclusions. These differences particularly relate to the role populism plays on the individual level. We suspect, however, that rather than being substantial, these differences may arise from the potential lack of a unified and well-rounded populism measurement. Third, and related to the previous point, we observe that many items used to measure populist attitudes are similar in some respect and have followed Hawkins and Riding (2010) in their formulations. Yet, there exist considerable differences across the items developed and the scales constructed (see also Table 6.1). Given the cross-continental context in which these items now have been used, it becomes increasingly important to pay particular attention to issues of scale construction, scale development and overall measurement evaluation.

With a wide range of options available to researchers in terms of items and scales (to measure both single ideas of populism, such as anti-elitism, as well as the overall concept), none of these items and scales have thus far been held accountable to (i) whether or not they actually measure populist attitudes, and (ii) if so, to what extent they measure such attitudes (for an exception, see Van Hauwaert, Schimpf, and Azevedo 2017). It is only such an analysis that would allow us to identify the populist items that work best in the field and form the most complete and parsimonious measurement of populist attitudes. A comprehensive assessment of the accuracy and validity of the measurement of populist attitudes, however, is essential to any empirical study that uses these populist items to draw inferences and/or parallels with other political phenomena. An initial test of eight such populist items across nine countries in Europe, for instance, suggests that existing scales can be limited in the extent to which they measure populist attitudes (Van Hauwaert, Schimpf, and Azevedo 2017). Particularly, they can struggle to capture extreme values of populist attitudes, both at the upper and the lower levels of the construct. Additionally, the results of this initial study also suggest that existing populist scales contain several superfluous items that measure almost identical components of populism, while other components are left unmeasured. We argue these results make the critical assessment of the available measures even more necessary.

Table 6.1 provides an extensive overview of the most important survey items scholars have used to measure populism. From this, we can make four important observations. First, almost all measurements include some form of the "good vs. evil" and the "will of the people" questions. These provide an indication of a Manichean worldview and the belief in a general will, respectively. Second, researchers commonly include some kind of reference to the distance between the people and the elite(s), which serves as an indicator of (anti) elitism. Third, many of the questions strike us as context specific, referring to unique institutions or practices. Since we can observe similar formulations across the Americas, but different ones in Europe, we should interpret context as continental (world regions), not national (countries). Last, the majority of items that refer to elites operationalize them as "politicians" or some form of "the legislature" – this despite the fact that theoretical accounts do not typically restrict the meaning of elites to politicians, but also include economic or cultural elites.

Altogether, while populist attitudes and their measurement have gained more attention as of late, most studies limit their attention to substantial rather than measurement concerns. In the absence of proper measurement studies, (i) most existing studies suffer from limited external validity, (ii) most proposed populist measurements remain largely unproven, and (iii) most substantive conclusions drawn from these studies are at risk of being unsubstantiated or even misinformed. This is unfortunate, particularly seeing how the number of different items that propose to measure populist attitudes is increasing, despite a general trend toward the use of some form of the original Hawkins and Riding (2010) items (see Table 6.1). With that in mind, we set out to answer some important questions, namely (i) which items work "best" or are most informative to comprehensively and parsimoniously capture populist attitudes in certain contexts, and (ii) whether different items work equally well independent of context. While we are not able to provide conclusive evidence for both of these questions, we do provide a number of initial insights that will not only contribute to the broader populist measurement debate, but will also lay the foundation for the scale development approach proposed in the following chapter.

Table 6.1 Question wordings throughout the existing literature

	CCES 2008	*CCES 2012*	*UCEP 2008*	*LAPOP 2008*	*LAPOP 2010*	*UDNP 2013*	*UDP 2015*	*SNES 2010*	*WoPo 2011*	*LIVEWHAT*
Distance between people and elite/s (anti-elitism)										
The people should govern directly and not through elected representatives. How much do you agree or disagree?				pop107	pop107					
The biggest obstacle to progress in our country is the dominant class or oligarchy that takes advantage of the people. How much do you agree or disagree with that view?				**pop112** (1) (2)						
The political differences between the people and the elite are larger than the differences among the people.		bya415				P69c	P41_C		POP3	populism_3
Politicians (elected officials) talk too much and take too little action.	byu324	bya414				P69e	P41_E		POP5	populism_5
Our country would run better if decisions were left up to successful business people.	byu326	bya410								
Our country would run better if decisions were left up to non-elected, independent experts	byu327	bya411				P70a	P42_B			
Ordinary people can't be trusted to make the right choices about our nation's problems.		bya404				P69g	P41_G	a11g		
Politicians should lead the people, not follow them.		bya412				P70b	P42_A			
The particular interests of the political class negatively affect the welfare of the people										populism_7
Politicians always end up agreeing when it comes to protecting their privileges.										populism_8
Most politicians are basically honest people.								a11a		
Ordinary people are divided by very different values.								a11b		
Improvement of ordinary people's life is prevented by elite which is not controlled.								a11c		
Not all the politicians are the same, some really do care what people want.								a11d		
People who belong to political elite are divided by different values.								a11f		
Best government is which decides about everything alone and guarantees order and stability.								a11i		

A Manichean wordview										
Politics is ultimately a struggle between good and evil.	byu320	bya401	pop_good					a11h	POP6	
In today's world there is a struggle between good and evil, and people must choose between one of the two.				pop109 (2)						
What people call "compromise" in politics is really just selling out on one's principles.	byu325					P69f	P41_F		POP7	populism_6
The inherent belief in a general or popular will (volonté générale)										
The politicians in Congress need to follow the will of the people.	byu321	bya403	pop_foll			P69a	P41_A		POP1	populism_1
Our presidents/prime ministers must follow the will of the people because what the people want is always right.				**pop106** (1) (2)						
Politicians in Congress have to follow the will of society							P41_H			
The power of a few special interests prevents our country from making progress.	byu322	bya405	pop_spec							
The people, not the politicians, should make our most important policy decisions.	byu323	bya407	pop_peop			P69b	P41_B		POP2	populism_2
Once the people decide what is right, we must prevent opposition from a minority.				pop110 (2)						
Those who disagree with the majority represent a threat to the interests of the country.				pop113	pop113					
I would rather be represented by an ordinary citizen than an experienced politician.		bya408				P69d	P41_D		POP4	populism_4
Democracy is about achieving compromise among differing viewpoints.		bya402	pop_comp			P70c	P42_C	a11e		
Diversity limits my freedom.		bya409								
Freedom depends on diversity.			pop_div							
It is important to listen to groups with different opinions.		bya413								
In a democracy it is important to hear from all groups						P70d	P41_D			

(continued)

Table 6.1 (continued)

	CCES 2008	*CCES 2012*	*UCEP 2008*	*LAPOP 2008*	*LAPOP 2010*	*UDNP 2013*	*UDP 2015*	*SNES 2010*	*WoPo 2011*	*LIVEWHAT*
When our opposition presents new and challenging positions, there is something we can learn by listening.			pop_list							
Interest groups have too much influence over political decisions.									POP8	
It is necessary for the progress of this country that our presidents/prime ministers limit the voice and vote of opposition parties. How much do you agree or disagree with that view?				pop101 (2)	pop101					
When the Congress hinders the work of our government, our presidents/prime ministers should govern without the Congress. How much do you agree or disagree with that view?				pop102	pop102					
When the Supreme Court/Constitutional Tribunal hinders the work of our government, it should not be paid attention to by our presidents/prime ministers. How much do you agree or disagree with that view?				pop103	pop103					

* Items to measure populism as a style: pop101, pop102, pop103 (all from LAPOP 2008)

* Items to measure pluralism: pop_comp, pop_div, pop_list (all from UCEP 2008)

* Items to measure stealth democracy: byu324, byu325, byu326, byu327 (CCES 2008); bya402, bya404, bya408, bya409, bya410, bya411, bya412, bya413, bya414, bya415 (CCES 2012)

* Bold text indicates the items used for a populist scale in the literature

(1) Not asked in the USA

Previous tests, results, and methods

In light of these unanswered questions, we examine and discuss how some of the scales of populist attitudes have been constructed and developed. In a first step, we focus on the methods that have been applied in the studies cited above. We then propose an alternative, and in our opinion more suitable, method to comprehensively analyse the characteristics of both survey items and item batteries that supposedly measure populist attitudes. The majority of studies of populist attitudes rely on Principal Component Analysis (PCA) or – to a lesser extent – Confirmatory Factor Analysis (CFA). However, we propose to use Item Response Theory (IRT) and particularly a Graded Response Model (GRM).[7] In what follows, we briefly discuss why IRT can be helpful when evaluating and developing particular items and scales.

Most studies that examine populist attitudes rely on PCA to determine whether their item batteries, or a subset, measure the same underlying concept (cf. Akkerman, Mudde, and Zaslove 2012; Hawkins 2010; Hawkins, Riding, and Mudde 2012). However, this particular technique serves the purpose of data reduction for subsequent analyses but cannot display how well the individual items and their sum, the scale, capture the latent construct (Bartholomew and Knott 1999). Formulated differently, PCA conceptualises constructs as causally determined by the items, as opposed to the other way around (Comrey 1988; Edwards and Bagozzi 2000). Elchardus and Spruyt (2016), however, apply CFA to their four items. In contrast to PCA, CFA is a commonly applied method for scale development that identifies the underlying dimensions of an instrument (Brown 2006).

In this chapter, however, we propose an IRT framework to comprehensively analyse the item and scale characteristics of proposed populist measurements. (For an empirical application, see Van Hauwaert and van Kessel 2018). In general, IRT evaluates the relationship between the responses individuals give to specific items and the underlying latent construct. Particularly, IRT allows us to model the probability of endorsement of a particular response to a survey item, and further assumes this probability is contingent on an individual's level of the latent variable (Hambleton and Jones 1993; Sibley and Houkamau 2013). Compared to CFA (and PCA), IRT has a number of notable advantages. Perhaps most importantly, IRT allows both the precision of measurement (what is typically called, the *information*) and the measurement error to differ across different levels of a latent construct. This means IRT models can specify at which point or range of a latent variable a particular scale provides an accurate measurement and at which point or range it does not. Differently put, IRT has the possibility to capture the scale's accuracy at each level of the latent construct.[8] And while CFA and IRT model techniques can, in fact, be very similar, IRT models provide the additional benefit to determine the contribution of each item in terms of the information that they provide about the latent construct. Thus, the application of IRT models can be particularly useful to maximise the internal validity of a scale, while simultaneously allowing researchers to formulate parsimonious scales. In sum, considering that two important ambitions of this chapter are to identify the usefulness of the plethora of individual items that are currently being proposed as populist measurement and to make strides towards a unified measurement of populist attitudes (cf. also the following chapter), we refer to use IRT over CFA for our analyses.

Data and methods

One of our principal goals throughout this chapter is to assess different items and instruments used across different contexts with IRT. We use a number of existing data sets that all include some proposed measurement of populist attitudes. This has two specific advantages. First, such a harmonized approach allows us to cross-validate our results and increase the generalizability of our findings. Second, since our included data sets cover such a broad range of countries across both Europe and the Americas (North and South), it also gives us the opportunity to empirically analyse some of the patterns of variance between and within countries and regions.

We include analyses for the 2012 Cooperative Congressional Election Study (CCES), the 2010 Slovakian National Election Study (SNES), the 2011 Work and Politics (WoPo) survey, the 2014 LIVEWHAT survey and the 2015 *Encuesta Nacional* by the Universidad Diego Portales (UDP).[9] Together, these data sets allow us to cover a broad geographical scope, including Western Europe (LIVEWHAT, WoPo), Eastern Europe (LIVEWHAT, SNES), North America (CCES) and South America (UDP). We take a theory-driven approach and only perform our IRT analyses on the items that have been used as indicators of ideational populism. This means we exclude items that indicate pluralism, stealth democracy or even populism *as a style* from these analyses. For some background and contextual characteristics of the data sets and their data collection, we refer to Table 6.A1 in the Appendix.

Empirical results

An important drawback from harmonising the analysis of such a large number of data sets is that comparisons can become challenging. Particularly, considering the same survey items do not always measure the theorised concepts of *populism* or *populist attitudes*, it becomes difficult to use more integrated methods (for example, Differential Item Functioning (DIF) analysis). Thus, we restrict our analyses to single data sets, providing a more reflective rather than empirically driven discussion about the comparisons of items in the concluding section.[10]

In what follows, we provide readers with a condensed IRT analysis and discussion for each data set. More specifically, as part of each separate analysis, we display two key parts of information that are generally part of the IRT paradigm side-by-side: a test information curve (scale-level) and a set of item information trace lines (item-level). The former allows us to gain insights in the overall informative qualities of a proposed populism scale from a specific data set. The latter provides – for each survey item– an indication of its contribution to the overall information of the populist instrument. Together, these provide detailed and unique insights into different populism scales and indicators.[11]

Measuring populist attitudes in the USA: 2012 CCES

The 2012 CCES survey includes a core set of four items that are typically used as indicators for populist attitudes. These items refer to the Manichean worldview (1) and to the so-called *volonté générale* (3). From Table 6.1, we see that the 2012 populist indicators are repeated from the 2008 CCES wave and the 2008 UCEP survey.[12] Using this 2008 data, Hawkins and Riding (2010) find a clear populism construct; yet, they also show sizeable correlations between populism and stealth democracy. Even though both CCES waves include various stealth democracy indicators, we are solely interested in how a latent populism variable and its items perform.

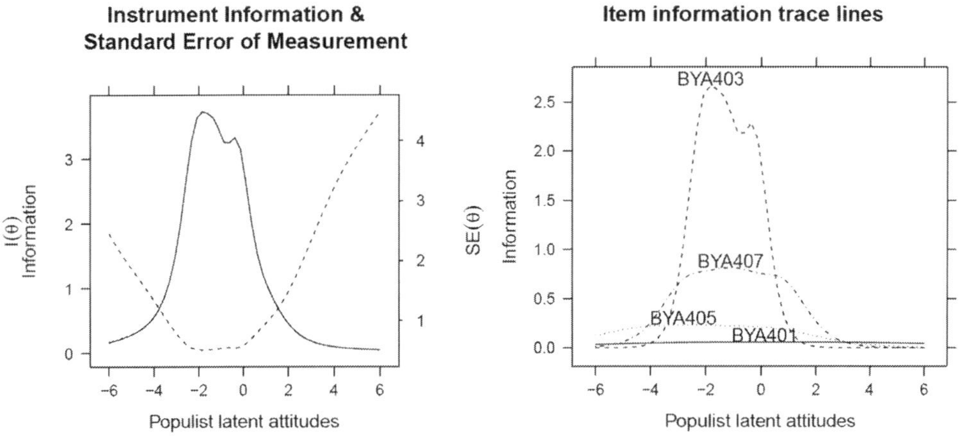

Figure 6.1 CCES test information curve and item information trace lines

Figure 6.1 shows the results of the IRT analysis for the four items that are included in the 2012 CCES wave. The left-side panel of Figure 6.2 indicates that the aggregate scale is only really informative alongside the [–2 ; 0] interval, meaning the scale only appropriately discriminates those who are moderately averse to populism. Furthermore, the scale is clearly not able to discriminate individuals with more extreme populist attitudes, at either extreme of the scale. When we examine the individual item contributions, we must conclude that three out of four items are limited in the information they provide. Only item "BYA403" (will of the people) is informative. Even more, the similarity between the information curve on the left and the individual trace line of item "BYA403" stands out. While this is not conclusive evidence, it raises questions about the necessity of the other CCES items. Put more extremely, perhaps rather than using these four items as a scale, scholars could just rely on the single item as a proxy of populism – at least in this specific context.

Measuring populist attitudes in Slovakia: 2010 SNES

The 2010 SNES survey includes eight items that are designed to measure populism, and are loosely based on Hawkins and Riding's (2010) operationalisation of populism. Unlike other studies, Stanley (2011) does not generate a scale but individually models the items and argues that each item serves as a proxy for a specific component of populism. But, would a scale using these items provide a good measurement of populist attitudes? A number of items are unique, yet three items find overlap with other surveys, namely a11h (good vs. evil), a11e (democracy) and a11g (trust people).

Figure 6.2 shows a relatively wide test information curve, providing high levels of information in the [–1; 3] interval, i.e. the items capture a relatively broad range of the latent variable. Furthermore, we can also observe that the SNES scale would have difficulties accurately measuring those at the lower end of the scale (i.e. low levels of populist

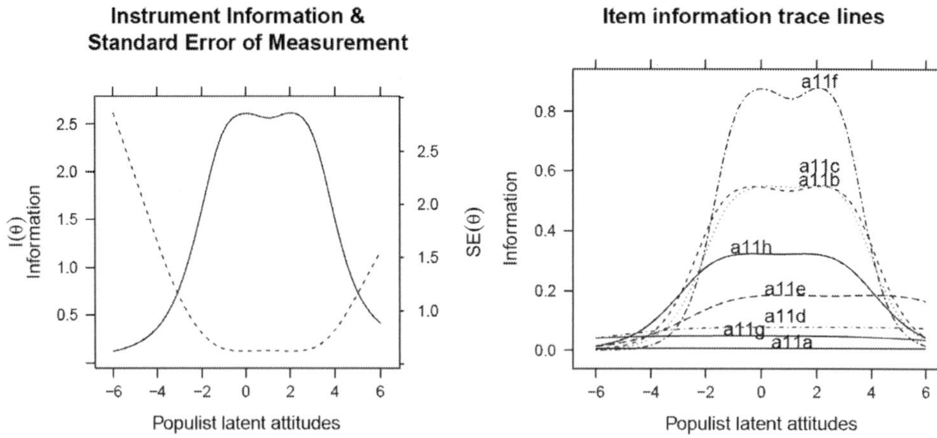

Figure 6.2 2010 SNES test information curve and item information trace lines

attitudes), as indicated by the left tail of the error measurement curve. At the higher end of the scale, the measurement does not appear to have such a problem, or at least not to the same extent.

To some extent, this observation is also reflected in the individual item information lines. Seeing how they are all located right of the middle, the items in the Slovakian sample appear better suited to measure higher values of populism than they do lower values. When we compare the curves with one another, we can divide them in three arbitrary groups. A first group provides little to no information in the measurement of populism (five items). A second group provides good levels of information and measure a relatively broad scope of our construct. This includes the variables a11h (good vs. evil), a11b (ordinary people) and a11c (ordinary people). Third, item a11f (elite values) clearly stands out in that it provides – by far – most information out of all items. From a theoretical IRT perspective, we would expect some items to have a higher peak than others; however, lower peaked items should then cover a broader scope of the latent construct in order to be equally valuable (i.e. provide the same information). As we can observe, this is clearly not the case for the less informative SNES items.

Furthermore, our empirical analysis allows for an important theoretical and more substantive insight. That is, the items that are generally most informative also broadly capture the three key attributes of populism, namely anti-elitism, a Manichean divide and an affinity to the common will. While we remain cautious in drawing any comparative conclusions, it indicates this scale allows for a particularly well-matched connection between theory and empirics – at least in this particular context. As we will reflect on other data sets, it will become clear this is certainly not always the case.

Measuring populist attitudes in the Netherlands: 2011 WoPo

The items, used by Akkerman, Mudde, and Zaslove (2014), were part of an online survey that was fielded in the Netherlands in November 2011. Regarding the populism items, this survey relies directly on the original work by Hawkins and Riding (2010), but it also adds to it. Namely, it includes two fully novel items (POP3 and POP4) and two items suggested by Hawkins and Riding (2010) for the purposes of future research (POP5 and POP7). Akkerman, Mudde, and Zaslove (2014) identify six relevant items for their proposed populism scale (POP1-5, POP7).[13] Together, these six items operationalise the three central aspects of populism [see Table 6.1] and the scale has quickly developed into an important reference point for subsequent attempts to measure populism.

Figure 6.3 shows that the 6-item scale that was used in Akkerman, Mudde, and Zaslove (2014) covers a relatively broad range of the information of the latent populism scale [–3: 2]. While it is not perfect as to the information it provides, we can argue the scale is at least informative in the Dutch context, and perhaps even more informative than some of its counterparts discussed below. Much like other scales evaluated in this chapter, the left-hand panel of Figure 6.3 indicates the scale measures respondents better at the lower end of the scale, compared to the upper end of the scale. Furthermore, there is a subset of items that works better in comparison to the others. The right-hand panel of Figure 6.3 indicates that items 3, 5, and 7 stand out as the most informative. Interestingly, whereas item 5 is the most informative, it captures slightly less of the range of the latent populism scale with all other items better equipped to measure high levels of populism. Out of all the items, Item 1, which aims at measuring the extent to which respondents agree with the statement that the politicians should follow the will of people, is the least informative. Interestingly, similar items turned out to be more informative relative to all other items in other country contexts (e.g. UCEP 2008 and UDP 2015). This result could indicate that, after all, populism varies in its meaning by context, which would have important consequences for its measurement and some of the generalisations drawn from this survey.

Measuring populist attitudes across Europe: LIVEWHAT

The LIVEWHAT survey provides a cross-national measurement of populist attitudes across nine European countries (France, Germany, Greece, Italy, Poland, Spain, Sweden, Switzerland, and the UK). Its populist items are largely drawn from previous studies by Hawkins and Riding (2010) and Akkerman, Mudde, and Zaslove (2014) and have been used in comparative empirical studies such as Van Hauwaert and van Kessel (2018). They data set also offers two unique items that arguably measure European populist attitudes (populism_7 and populism_8).

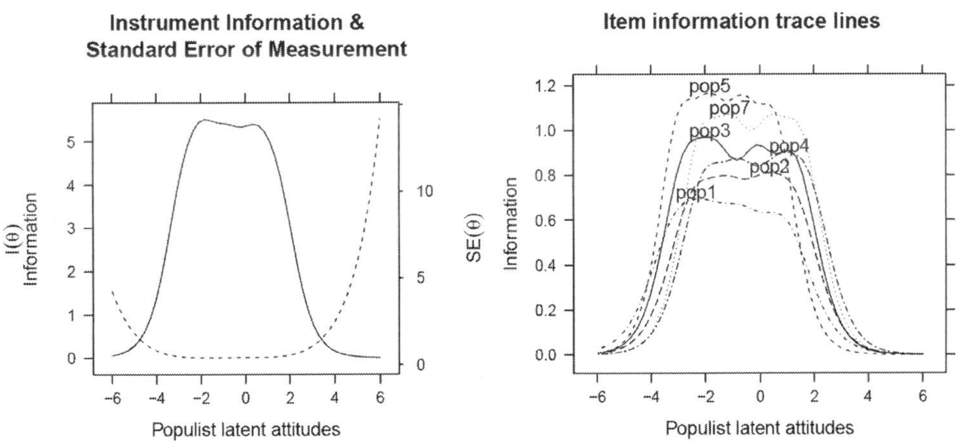

Figure 6.3 2011 WoPo test information curve and item information trace lines

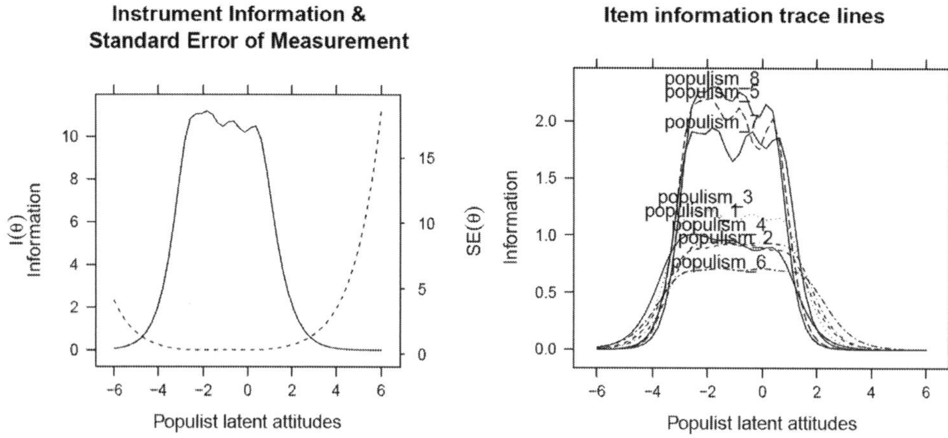

Figure 6.4 LIVEWHAT test information curve and item information trace lines

The LIVEWHAT test information curve indicates a [–3; 1] interval that can be considered to have high information. This means that within this particular interval of our latent construct, the proposed populism scale from these eight items is most reliable to measure populism. The steep increase of the measurement error curve on the right side of the graph indicates the LIVEWHAT scale has particular problems measuring high levels of populist attitudes, or capturing those with a high affinity towards populism. While this problem also appears to be somewhat present when levels of populist attitudes are very low, this is true to a lesser extent.

Much like the IRT-estimated populism scale in 2010 SNES survey, there are three populist items that stand out when it comes to providing information, namely populism_8 (elite action), populism_5 (elite interests) and populism_7 (elite privileges). Two of those are unique items, while populism_5 is a recurring item from the CCES and UDP surveys [cf. supra]. Contrary to – for example – the SNES scale, we observe that our three most informative items are most successful in measuring a particular theoretical component of populism, namely anti-elitism. The informative contributions of the other items remain both moderate and nearly identical. Not only do all items cover a similar scope of the latent construct (i.e. they all cover the same range of populist attitudes), but a number of them provide similar amounts of information as well. This could be a first indicator of a number of superfluous items in the proposed scale and a lack of parsimony in this particular eight-item scale. Interestingly, populism_6 and populism_3 are not that informative in a broader European context, whereas the same items proved to be quite informative in the Dutch context (2011 WoPo – POP3 and POP7, respectively). The item "politicians (or elected officials) talk too much and take too little action", however, does appear to be quite informative both across Europe (populism_5) and in the Netherlands (POP5).

Measuring populist attitudes in Chile: 2015 UDP

The 2015 UDP data set includes six items that are theorised to tap into the notion of populist attitudes (see e.g. Hawkins et al. 2016; Mélendez and Rovira Kaltwasser 2017). Looking at the items, we observe that the designed measurement of populist attitudes includes one of the most common anchors, namely the "will of the people" item. Additionally, we find important overlap between the UDP items and the LIVEWHAT (five items), as well as the 2012 CCES (two items). For researchers interested in populism and populist attitudes, Chile provides an interesting case because it has now fielded three different surveys waves that include these items.

As a whole, Figure 6.5 illustrates that an IRT estimated populism scale in Chile is most informative in the [−1; 3] interval. While comparisons across data sets are difficult, this would constitute the broadest "informative range" of our included data sets. However, the high-peaked information curve indicates this particular scale has difficulty measuring extreme values of populist attitudes. Likewise, we do observe our test information curve is left-skewed, meaning it does better (albeit slightly) at measuring an affinity toward populism than an aversion to populism.

Figure 6.5 further illustrates that the individual information levels amongst the six different items differ considerably. Again, comparison across data sets is difficult, but this particular scale does not include completely uninformative items and the overlap between items appears more limited, indicating different items capture unique parts of the latent construct. Based on the amount of information provided by each item, item P41_A (will of the people) is the most informative item. This is perhaps not surprising, considering it is typically one of the core indicators of populist attitudes. Furthermore, a number of items, particularly those with lower levels of information (P41_F and P41_D), cover a larger scope of the populist construct (i.e. they have wider tails). This contributes to their uniqueness and thereby also usefulness as part of the scale.

Conclusions and comparative reflections

Over the past years, populism research has grown exponentially and its scope continues to broaden. Yet, at the same time, several aspects of the study of populism remain

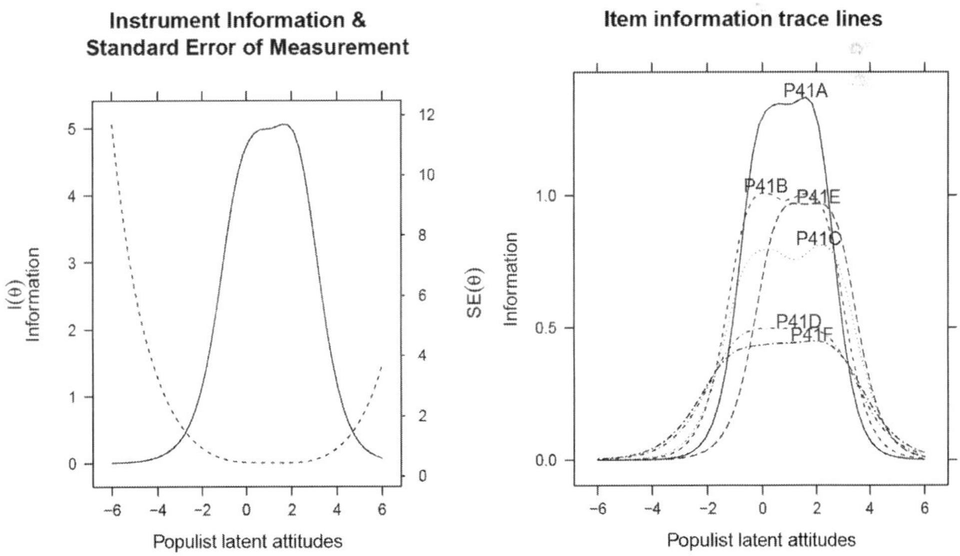

Figure 6.5 2015 UDP test information curve and item information trace lines

underdeveloped, most notably the study of its demand-side and its translation as a latent attitudinal construct. While scholars primarily explore how widespread populist attitudes are and what consequences these attitudes have for political behaviour, we know very little about the intrinsic characteristics of populist attitudes. While measurement studies should precede more substantive research questions, the accurate, parsimonious and comprehensive measurement of populist attitudes is currently still in its infancy. Consequently, much of the research using populist attitudes draw conclusions from a relatively unexplored measurement tool.

With that in mind, this chapter sought to shed some light on several of the measurements (instruments) of populist attitudes the literature uses or proposes, exactly to avoid any misinformed or incorrect conclusions. In an effort to offer a comprehensive empirical analysis of existing populist scales, we use multiple data sets from different contexts in Europe and across the Americas and we propose a methodological paradigm (IRT) that provides us with a number of unique possibilities. We examined how scales as a whole faired in these different contexts, but we also examined single items within these scales to assess the levels of information each survey item contributes to the overall populism scale. Particularly this latter aspect is something current literature often foregoes, but can be extremely informative for scale development, item repetition and general survey design.

On the basis of our results, we can draw several preliminary conclusions and provide an initial comparative reflection on the interpretation of populism as an attitude.[14] First, a notable majority of the populism scales are limited in their ability to measure populist attitudes at the extremes, and this both for very low and very high levels of populism. Concretely, this means that regardless of the scale or the context, most proposed populist measurements have difficulty to accurately capture or discriminate against those individuals who are either quite averse to populism or quite prone to it. There are, however, some exceptions to this observation, particularly the items used by Stanley (2011) as part of the 2010 SNES data set. His scale differs from others in that it provides higher levels of information for those respondents who are located at the higher end of the latent populism construct. In its specific context (Slovakia), we thus suggest this particular set of items fares better in comparison to other scales in different contexts. That being said, without further empirical analyses and more in-depth scale comparisons based on anchor items (so-called *equating*), this conclusion is preliminary and must remain subject to further empirical scrutiny.

Second, we also observed that across most scales, there exists great heterogeneity with regard to the information provided by individual items. Even though item inclusion and formulation should be a theoretical process, careful empirical analysis teaches us there is certainly some kind of disconnect between theory and empirics. This may result from two possibilities that, again, have to be considered within the specific context in which the respective surveys have been fielded. On the one hand, it is quite possible that items with low levels of information are not formulated well enough to properly measure the latent construct. Upon analysis, one must question the contribution of such items throughout the scale development process. Considering there are quite a few items like this included in the proposed populism scales, we would urge future scale development efforts to account for this. On the other hand, even though there is currently little evidence that populism is a context-specific construct, the role of specific dimensions of populist attitudes (e.g. the will of the people) differs or can even depend on the context (e.g. country) certain items are fielded in. A brief cross-country measurement invariance test confirms this (see Van Hauwaert and van Kessel 2018), which in itself hints at some heterogeneity in the measurement of populist attitudes. Combined, these two preliminary observations indicate that certain items can be considered a better fit than others.

Much in line with this last point, we must also consider how well a proposed measurement scale covers the concept of populism. Perhaps the most striking similarity between the graphs throughout this chapter is the relative inability of proposed populism scales to measure the populist construct from one extreme to the other. Part of this can be attributed to what we have referred to as low-information and identical items being included in scales [cf. infra]. However, a more theoretically driven explanation of this could be the construct's primary focus on certain aspects of populism, rather than on all (or at least multiple) of its dimensions. While our IRT analysis provides more detailed insights into this argument, this is already clear from Table 6.1. Most items indicate anti-elitism and the *volonté générale*, while only few items (often with relatively limited information) gauge the Manichean component of populism.

These observations have ample implications for researchers who intend to use any of the data sets for their own analyses or for those who seek to field their own survey and are looking for existing scales or individual items to draw from. For empirical analyses, researchers should take into account that their populist scale can be contextually limited and is unlikely to measure the full range of the latent construct within the context of analysis. While this is – by itself – not necessarily problematic, it does limit the inferences one can draw from the analyses, particularly when looking to generalise findings beyond the specific context. It is something we encounter all too often, particularly with studies that take the USA or the Netherlands as their primary focus.

For those who initiate their own research, different pitfalls must be carefully considered. The verbatim duplication of certain scales into different context does not necessarily guarantee accurate measurement of populist attitudes and thus, ideally, should be preceded by extensive pre-tests if possible. Furthermore, even when relying on only the most informative items, it may result in identical information across respondents. In other words, since we indicated most populist items (and really all populist scales) have difficulties measuring extremes, it is likely that even "good" (highly informative) items provide similar information levels across a similar, yet limited range of the latent construct. Therefore, when developing items or scales, one might consider adjusting the (number of) items based on their informative contributions.

Finally, we repeat that the research on populist attitudes is still in its infancy. As such, we need additional (exploratory) studies that test new (sets of) items or new item formation to find items and scales that are more informative and cover a larger scope of the latent construct than those we have tested here. Further, this would allow us to test for items that can be used in more than one context. For these types of studies, we encourage researchers to also include at least two (preferably even more) of the items that have been used in the above-cited studies as anchor items. In other words, we would recommend future studies with "new" (and better) items to measure populism should include a number of "old" items. This makes newly developed and tested scales comparable (in terms of validity) to existing ones and allows for a better evaluation of scales and their often contextual insights. In line with this suggestion, Silva et al. (Chapter 7 in this book) take such an explorative approach as they set out to analyse how a wide variety of potential populist items measures the phenomenon across different contexts.

Notes

1 An earlier version of this chapter has been presented at the 2016 ECPR General Conference in Prague. We would like to thank Joost van Spanje and Robert Huber for their feedback on previous versions of this chapter. We recognize all those who have generously contributed data to this chapter: Ben Stanley, Olga Gyarfasova, Agnes Akkerman, Cristóbal Rovira Kaltwasser, and Kirk Hawkins. Christian H. Schimpf acknowledges the support by the University of Mannheim's Graduate School of Economic and Social Sciences funded by the German Research Foundation. Flavio Azevedo acknowledges the support by the University of Cologne's Center for Comparative Politics and the Cologne Graduate School. We would also like to thank the editors of this book for their combined efforts to continuously improve this chapter.

2 For a more detailed account of the ideational interpretation of populism, as well as its implications for the study of populism, we refer to Hawkins (2009; 2010), Mudde and Rovira Kaltwasser (2013) and Rovira Kaltwasser (2014).

3 We recognize that the interpretation of populism as an attitudinal construct, rather than just an opinion, remains contested in the recent literature. We argue, however that (i) this (theoretical) debate does not fall within the scope of this chapter, and (ii) the different terminology – while one might agree or disagree – does not make a difference for the substantial conclusions we intend to draw in this chapter. For a more detailed discussion of this contentious formulation, we refer to some of our work elsewhere (e.g. Van Hauwaert, Schimpf, and Azevedo 2017). For a more general discussion of the distinction between attitudes and opinions, we refer to Bergman (1998) and Oskamp and Schultz (2014).

4 The literature has also advanced some less complete measurements of populism. Elchardus and Spruyt (2016) used only four items that measure the people-centrist component (two items) and to some extent, the anti-elitist view of populism (two items). Ford, Goodwin, and Cutts (2012) limit the scope of their populism measurement to popular hostilities and discontent with major parties.

5 The other three items were constructed differently in order to capture populism as a "political-institutional style" (cf. also Barr 2009; Roberts 2003; Weyland 2001).

6 While reducing their populism measurement, the authors also complement the populism scale in two particular ways. In the 2008 UCEP survey they include three items that serve as indicators of pluralism, a concept closely related to populism. In the 2008 CCES survey, they include four items that serve as indicators of stealth democracy, a concept that has been found to encompass populism (cf. Hibbing and Theiss-Morse 2002).

7 For a more detailed discussion of IRT in the field of political science, we refer to Jackman (2008). For a more detailed analysis of the GRM, we refer to Samejima (1997). We rely on a GRM because of the ordered polytomous data structure of most populist items (cf. Samejima 1997).

8 Whereas most of the political science literature refers to reliability, the IRT literature uses the concept of information to refer to the measurement precision of an instrument. Altogether, reliability can be thought of as a simplified version of IRT's information (Wainer and Thissen 1996).

9 In the appendix (Figures 6.A1 to 6.A5), we also include empirical analyses of the 2013 UDNP survey in Chile, the 2008 LAPOP survey in both Latin America and the USA, the 2008 UCEP survey in Utah and the 2008 CCES survey in the USA.

10 As part of the IRT paradigm, a more comparative approach or so-called *equating*, that is the comparison of scales based on similar items, may be possible in some instances, but certainly not for all data sets here. In order to apply equating correctly, the different data sets would require a number of stable anchor items between them.

11 Table 6.A1 in the Appendix provides information about the scale-level information of the populist measurements from the different data sources included in this chapter.

12 The primary difference between the populist items in the UCEP and the CCES surveys is that the UCEP survey relies on 4-point answer scales, whereas the UCEP survey gives respondents 5-point Likert-type scales with labels at the extremes. See also Table 6.1.

13 In their survey, Akkerman, Mudde, and Zaslove (2014) added two additional items. The wordings of the items were a) "Politics is ultimately a struggle between good and evil" and b) "Interest groups have too much influence over political decisions." However, the first item was found to

relate to a separate elitism scale, rather than the populism scale. The second item was found not to be related to any of the proposed theoretical constructs and thus, Akkerman, Mudde, and Zaslove (2014, 1334) eliminated it from their analyses. For reasons of comparability, we therefore focus our analyses on the six items that were used to construct the final populism scale in the original paper.

14 Note that all comparative insights should be taken with the appropriate grain of salt. As a consequence of the large variety of populism items and the subsequent absence of an appropriate set of anchor items, we were not able to compare all scales in a single harmonized analysis. In other words, our conclusions are based on the assumption that despite operational differences, all scales essentially measure the same construct.

References

Akkerman, Agnes, Cas Mudde, and Andrej Zaslove. 2014. "How Populist Are the People? Measuring Populist Attitudes in Voters." *Comparative Political Studies* 47(9): 1324–1353.

Albertazzi, Daniele, and Duncan McDonnell, eds. 2008. *Twenty-First Century Populism: The Spectre of Western European Democracy*. Houndmills and Basingstoke and Hampshire [England] and New York: Palgrave Macmillan.

Axelrod, Robert. 1967. "The Structure of Public Opinion on Policy Issues." *Public Opinion Quarterly* 31(1): 51–60.

Barr, Robert R. 2009. "Populists, Outsiders and Anti-Establishment Politics." *Party Politics* 15(1): 29–48.

Bartholomew, David J., and Martin Knott. 1999. *Latent Variable Models and Factor Analysis*. 3rd edn. (Wiley series in probability and statistics). London: Arnold. Available at: http://site.ebrary.com/lib/academiccompletetitles/home.action.

Bergman, Manfred Max. 1998. "A Theoretical Note on the Differences between Attitudes, Opinion, and Values", *Revue Suisse de Science Politique*, 4(2): 81–93

Brown, T.A. 2006. *Confirmatory Factor Analysis for Applied Research*. New York: Guilford Press.

Canovan, Margaret. 2005. *The People*. (Key concepts). Cambridge: Polity.

Comrey, Andrew L. 1988. "Factor-Analytic Methods of Scale Development in Personality and Clinical Psychology." *Journal of Consulting and Clinical Psychology* 56(5): 754–61.

De La Torre, Carlos, ed. 2015. *The Promise and Perils of Populism: Global Perspectives*. Lexington, KY: Univ. Press of Kentucky.

Dryzek, John S., and Jeffrey Berejikian. 1993. "Reconstructive Democratic Theory." *The American Political Science Review*, 87(1): 48–60.

Eagly, Alice H., and Shelly Chaiken. 1993. *The Psychology of Attitudes*. Fort Worth and TX: Harcourt Brace Jovanovich College Publishers.

Edwards, Jeffrey E., and Richard P. Bagozzi. 2000. "On the Nature and Direction of Relationships between Constructs and Measures." *Psychological Methods* 5(2): 155–174.

Elchardus, Mark, and Bram Spruyt, B. 2016. "Populism, Persistent Republicanism and Declinism: An Empirical Analysis of Populism as a Thin Ideology." *Government and Opposition* 51(01): 111–33.

Farrell, James J., and Patrick R. Laughlin. 1976. "A Scale to Measure Populist Attitudes." *The Journal of Psychology*, 94(1): 33–38.

Ford, Robert, Matthew J. Goodwin, and David Cutts. 2012. "Strategic Eurosceptics and polite xenophobes: Support for the United Kingdom Independence Party (UKIP) in the 2009 European Parliament elections." *European Journal of Political Research*, 51(2): 204–34.

Hambleton, Ronald K., and Russell W. Jones. 1993. "An NCME Instructional Module on: Comparison of Classical Test Theory and Item Response Theory and Their Applications to Test Development." *Educational Measurement: Issues and Practice* 12(3): 38–47.

Hawkins, Kirk A., Scott Riding, and Cas Mudde. 2012. "Measuring Populist Attitudes." *IPSA Committee on Concepts and Methods Working Paper Series*. Accessed December 15, 2014. Available at: www.concepts-method.org/.

Hawkins, Kirk A. 2009. "Is Chavez Populist? Measuring Populist Discourse in Comparative Perspective." *Comparative Political Studies* 42(8): 1040–67.

Hawkins, Kirk A. 2010. *Venezuela's Chavismo and Populism in Comparative Perspective*. Cambridge: Cambridge University Press.

Hawkins, Kirk A., and Scott Riding. 2010. Populist Attitudes and their Correlates among Citizens: Survey Evidence from the Americas. Paper prepared for the ECPR Workshop "Disassembling Populism (and Putting It Back Together Again): Collaborative Empirical Research on Interactions among Populism's Attributes," March 22–25, 2010, Muenster, Germany.

Hibbing, John R., and Elizabeth Theiss-Morse. 2002. *Stealth Democracy. Americans' Beliefs About How Government Should Work*. Cambridge, UK: Cambridge University Press.

Jackman, Simon. 2008. "Measurement." In *The Oxford Handbook of Political Methodology*, edited by Janet M. Box-Steffensmeier, Henry E. Brady, and David Collier, 119–151. Oxford: Oxford University Press (The Oxford handbooks of political science).

Kriesi, Hans-Peter, and Takis Pappas eds. 2015. *European Populism in the Shadow of the Great Recession*. Colchester: ECPR Press (Studies in European political science).

Latin American Public Opinion Project (LAPOP). 2008. *The AmericasBarometer 2008*. Accessed October 10, 2015. Available at: http://vanderbilt.edu/lapop/raw-data.php.

Mudde, Cas. 2004. "The Populist Zeitgeist." *Government and Opposition* 39(4): 542–63.

———. 2007. *Populist Radical Right Parties in Europe*. Cambridge and UK and New York: Cambridge University Press.

Mudde, Cas, and Cristóbal Rovira Kaltwasser. 2013. "Exclusionary vs. Inclusionary Populism: Comparing Contemporary Europe and Latin America." *Government and Opposition* 48(2): 147–74.

——— eds. 2012. *Populism in Europe and the Americas: Threat or corrective for democracy?* Cambridge: Cambridge University Press.

Oskamp, Stuart, and P. Wesley Schultz. 2014. Attitudes and Opinions (3rd edition). New York, NY: Psychology Press

Roberts, Kenneth M. 2003. "Social Correlates of Party System Demise and Populist Resurgence in Venezuela." *Latin American Politics and Society* 45(3): 35–57.

Rooduijn, Matthijs. 2014. "The Nucleus of Populism: In Search of the Lowest Common Denominator." *Government and Opposition* 49(04): 573–599.

Rooduijn, Matthijs, Sarah de Lange, and Wouter van der Brug. 2014. "A Populist Zeitgeist? Programmatic Contagion by Populist Parties in Western Europe." *Party Politics* 20(4): 563–575.

Rovira Kaltwasser, Cristóbal. 2014. "The Responses of Populism to Dahl's Democratic Dilemmas." *Political Studies* 62(3): 470–487.

Samejima, Fumiko. 1997. "Graded Response Model." In *Handbook of Modern Item Response Theory*, edited by Wim J. Van der Linden and Ronald K. Hambleton, 85–100. New York: Springer.

Sibley, Chris G., and Carla Houkamau. 2013. "The Multi-Dimensional Model of Maori Identity and Cultural Engagement: Item Response Theory Analysis of Scale Properties." *Cultural Diversity & Ethnic Minority Psychology* 19(1): 97–110.

Stanley, Ben. 2011. "Populism, nationalism, or national populism? An analysis of Slovak voting behaviour at the 2010 parliamentary election." *Communist and Post-Communist Studies* 44(4): 257–270.

Van Hauwaert, Steven M., and Stijn van Kessel. 2018. "Beyond Protest and Discontent: A Cross-National Analysis of the Effect of Populist Attitudes and Issue Positions on Populist Party Support." *European Journal of Political Research* 57 (1): 68–92.

Van Hauwaert, Steven M., Christian H. Schimpf, and Flavio Azevedo. 2017. "Measuring Populism as a Demand-Side Phenomenon: A Psychometric Evaluation of Populist Attitudes across Europe." Working Paper.

Wainer, Howard, and David Thissen. 1996. "How Is Reliability Related to the Quality of Test Scores? What Is the Effect of Local Dependence on Reliability?." *Educational Measurement: Issues and Practice* 15(1): 22–29.

Weyland, Kurt. 2001. "Clarifying a Contested Concept: Populism in the Study of Latin American Politics." *Comparative Politics* 34(1): 1–22.

Appendix

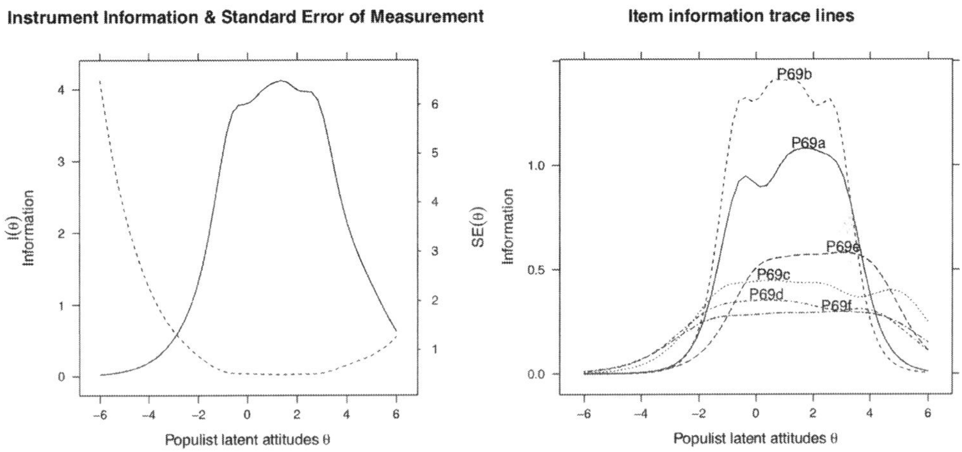

Figure 6.A1 2013 UDNP test information curve and item information trace lines

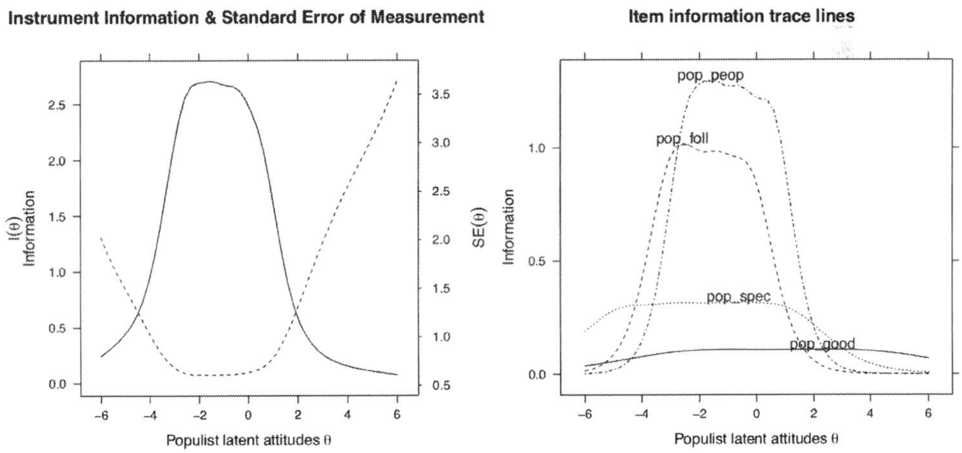

Figure 6.A2 2008 UCEP test information curve and item information trace lines

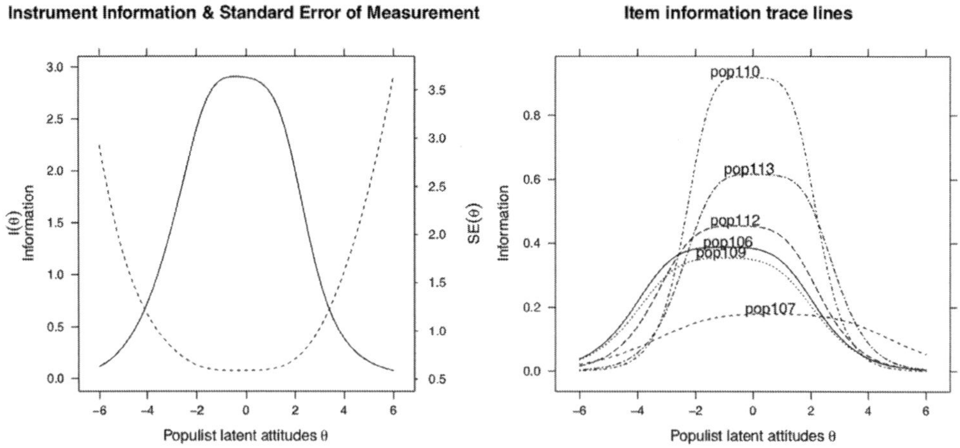

Figure 6.A3 2008 LAPOP (Latin America) test information curve and item information trace lines

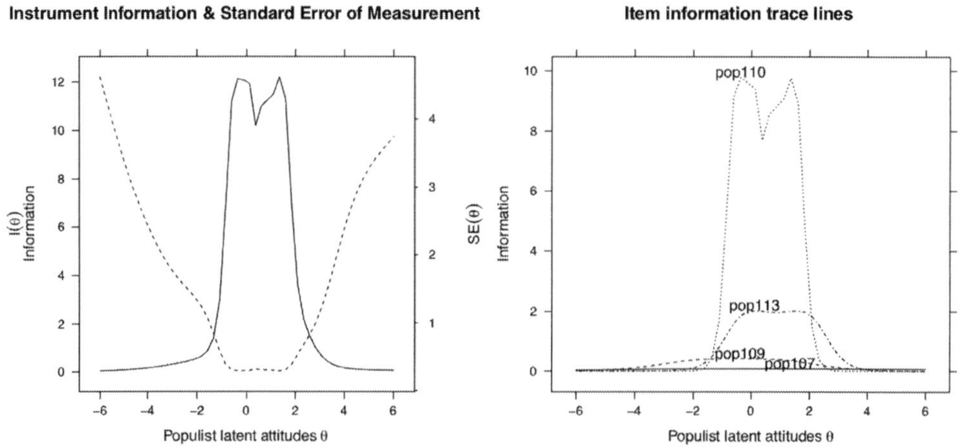

Figure 6.A4 2008 LAPOP (USA) test information curve and item information trace lines

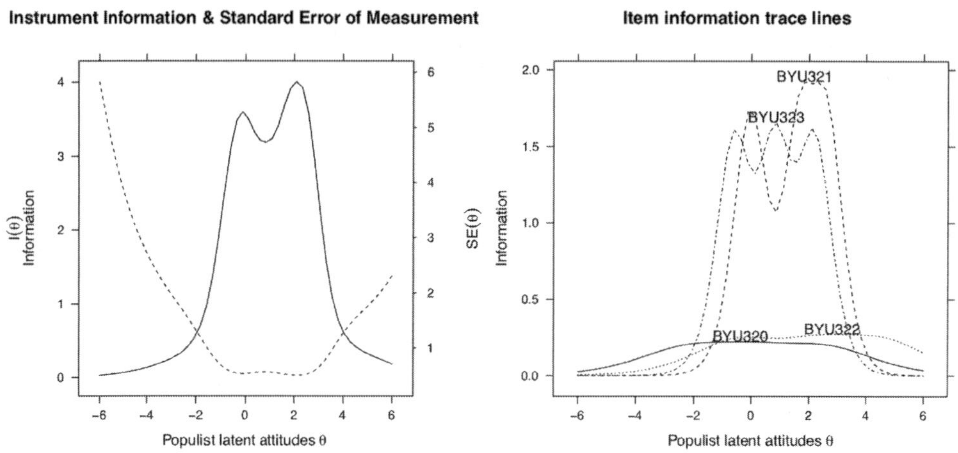

Figure 6.A5 2008 CCES test information curve and item information trace lines

Table 6.A1 Background and contextual characteristics of the data sets

Survey	*Year*	*Region*	*Countries*	*N*	*Valid cases**	*# Items*	*Answer categories*	*Labelled answer categories*	*Omega*	*Cronbach's alpha*
UCEP	2008	North America	USA (Utah)	6.697	882	7	5	Quartiles	0,72	0,67
CCES	2008	North America	USA	1.000	949	8	4	All (6)	0,76	0,73
CCES	2012	North America	USA	1.000	835	15	5	All (7)	0,70	0,64
LAPOP	2008	Americas	22 Latin American countries (1)	37.035	28.714	9	7	Extremes only	0,77	0,72
LAPOP	2008	Americas	USA	1.500	1.492	7	7	Extremes only	0,84	0,80
LAPOP	2008	Americas	Canada	2.032	1.911	4	7	Extremes only	0,64	0,60
LAPOP	2010	Americas	18 Latin American countries (2)	30.064	24.128	5	7	Extremes only	0,79	0,76
SNES	2010	Eastern Europe	Slovakia	1.203	879	9	7	Extremes only	0,61	0,55
UDP	2013	South America	Chile	1.805	1.423	11	5	All (4)	0,71	0,64
UDP	2015	South America	Chile	1.302	1.038	12	5	Extremes only	0.85	0,83
WoPo	2014	Western Europe	the Netherlands	631	582	6	5	Extremes only	0,85	0,81
LIVEWHAT	2015	Europe	9 countries (3)	18.368	18.368	8	5	All (5)	0,89	0,88

Note: All data sets are stripped of missing values via complete cases. This means, if an observation contained a missing value for one of the populist indicators in the data set, we excluded it from analysis. The survey in the Netherlands was completed by 631 respondents, but following Akkerman et al. (2014) we also delete all respondents who completed the survey in less than 10mins. Hence, the number of cases and valid cases differs.

(1) This includes 22 countries, namely Mexico, Guatemala, El Salvador, Honduras, Nicaragua, Costa Rica, Panama, Colombia, Ecuador, Bolivia, Peru, Paraguay, Chile, Uruguay, Brazil, Venezuela, Argentina, Dominican Republic, Haiti, Jamaica, Guyana (2009) and Belize. It does not include the USA and Canada.

(2) This includes 18 countries, namely Mexico, Guatemala, El Salvadr, Honduras, Nicaragua, Costa Rica, Panama, Colombia, Ecuador, Peru, Paraguay, Uruguay, Brazil, Dominican Republic, Haiti, Jamaica, Guyana and Belize. It does not include the USA and Canada.

(3) This includes 9 countries, namely France, Germany, Greece, Italy, Poland, Spain, Sweden, Switzerland and the UK

(4) muy de acuerdo, de acuerdo, ni de acuerdo ni en desacuerdo, en desacuerdo, muy en desacuerdo

(5) disagree strongly, disagree, neither, agree, agree strongly

(6) strongly agree, agree, disagree, strongly disagree

(7) strongly disagree, somewhat disagree, neutral, somewhat agree, strongly agree

7 Public opinion surveys

A new scale

Bruno Castanho Silva,[1] *Ioannis Andreadis, Eva Anduiza, Nebojša Blanuša, Yazmin Morlet Corti, Gisela Delfino, Guillem Rico, Saskia P. Ruth-Lovell, Bram Spruyt, Marco Steenbergen, and Levente Littvay*

With the ideational turn in populism studies (Mudde and Rovira Kaltwasser 2013), researchers have started to conceptualize and measure populism as a set of attitudes individuals hold about politics and society (e.g. Akkerman et al. 2014; Elchardus and Spruyt 2016; Hawkins et al. 2012; Rooduijn 2014b; Spruyt 2014; Stanley 2011). As proposed in the introduction to this volume, such attitudes are ordinarily dormant, but may be activated given a favorable context for populist discourse and its articulation by political actors. The measurement of these attitudes, however, has been far from uniform, as the review by Van Hauwaert, Schimpf, and Azevedo in Chapter 6 shows. The basis of the most commonly used scale today was set in Hawkins et al. (2012). It was extended into the popularized six-item version by Akkerman et al. (2014), and used by Spruyt et al. 2016, and in the chapters by Andreadis and Ruth-Lovell (Chapter 5); Andreadis et al. (Chapter 10); and Busby et al. (Chapter 16) in this volume.

However, as Van Hauwaert, Schimpf, and Azevedo have shown in Chapter 6, there is room for improvement in scale development. From a survey methodology perspective, the items fail to identify strong levels of populism and anti-populism and can only discriminate among moderate forms of it. They are not polarizing enough, as there seems to be a general trend of agreement: for all countries and items, the item averages are above the scales' middle point. A further limitation of the existing measures is that in most scales all items are positively worded – meaning that more agreement indicates more populism. For this reason it is impossible to discriminate between actual agreement with the content and acquiescence bias.

Our purpose with this study is to tackle the issue of scale development following practices common in psychology but that have yet to make their way into political science. We start with a large number of items, and use various techniques to select the few ones that work better at capturing populist attitudes. Next we test which items are *invariant* across countries – i.e., whether they measure the same thing, the same way, in different countries. Recent research has shown that several scales, some of which have been around for decades in social sciences, should not be used for cross-country comparisons because the measure is not invariant across cultures (Alemán and Woods 2016; Ariely and Davidov 2010; Piurko et al. 2011). Our analyses result in a short questionnaire of six or nine items, which has high cross-cultural validity, and captures a relatively wide range of information for this construct.

Dimensions of populism

We start with the definition of populism adopted in this volume: it should be seen as a set of ideas (whether a discourse, discursive frame, or thin-centered ideology, see Mudde

2004; Hawkins 2009; and Aslanidis 2016 for further debate), which opposes the good people against an evil elite, in a Manichaean division of politics where the voice of the good people should prevail (Mudde 2004; Mudde and Rovira Kaltwasser 2013; Hawkins 2009). From it we derive three elements, which we call the "core components" of populist attitudes: a) the notion of a good, homogeneous people as a political actor; b) anti-elitism; and c) the view of politics as a moral struggle, where one side is clearly good and the other evil – the Manichaean outlook. These are somewhat different from those proposed by Mudde (2004) and Mudde and Rovira Kaltwasser (2017): for them, people-centrism and popular sovereignty are distinct constructs. However, as the items and analyses below show, these two are hardly distinguishable from one another empirically, reason why we put them together.

These constructs can exist independently from one another. For example, not all Manichaean discourses are populist. It is possible to see politics as a struggle between good and evil and not fill these positions with "people" and "elites." Measuring the Manichaean element in its "pure" form (i.e., not applied to any ideology) enables us to assess its empirical relationship with other constituting elements of populism. The same applies for having a romanticized view of common people, or despising political elites.[2] Considering that all three are necessary components of the definition adopted here, we suggest that populism sits at the intersection of these three broader kinds of discourse, as depicted by the shaded area in Figure 7.1.

This conceptual map is of absolute importance in scale development because if populism indeed sits at the intersection of three kinds of discourse, its measurement should incorporate the different facets separately. Previous research rarely acknowledges this (for notable exceptions see Schulz et al. 2017 and Stanley 2011), and most often proposes unidimensional measurements, eliminating any items that fail to load together with the others. However, if populism has distinct subcomponents, one should expect that not all items will behave as if they are measuring a single construct.

Core constructs of populism and their measurement

Proceeding from this conceptual discussion, we now move to identifying measures for the core components of ideational populism. The first is praise of "the people," common to

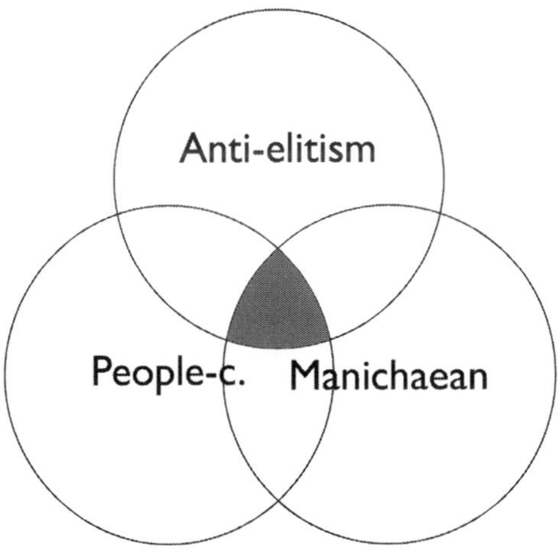

Figure 7.1 The three core components of populism

virtually any definition of populism (Ionescu and Gellner 1969; Canovan 1981). Second, anti-elitist, or anti-establishment ideas, which claim that a powerful and corrupt minority has taken over politics. And, third, a Manichaean, or good-versus-evil, view of politics (Hawkins 2009), in that populism only exists when the two sides – people and elites – are seen as in *moral* opposition to one another, instead of merely having programmatic disagreements.

Praise of the people/people's values

Praise of "the people" is the first identified characteristic of populism, no matter what specific definition one uses (see, for instance, Ionescu and Gellner 1969; Canovan 1981). The definition of who belongs to this people is one of the essential points in distinguishing between different kinds of populism,[3] and changes according to the time and context (Panizza 2005), making it an "empty signifier" (Laclau 2005). This variously and indeterminately defined people is glorified as a virtuous entity which embodies ideals of hard-work and honesty (Taggart 2000). There is a strong sense of the "common" or "ordinary" man, whose values and behavior are morally superior to those of other groups in society.

Populist discourse not only praises the people and its values, it also understands that *a)* the people is a homogeneous entity who *b)* has an identifiable "general will" that should be the basis of all politics (Mudde 2004).[4] There is no space for disagreements within the people – it is seen as having a single set of values, preferences, and interests, without room for legitimate differences (Müller 2016). Populism has a strong emphasis on popular sovereignty and the idea that the people's voice is not being heard by those in power (Canovan 1999; Mudde and Rovira Kaltwasser 2013). This results in calls, by populist actors, to "return the power to the people."

To capture this dimension, we have designed or collected 29 survey items from existing sources. Twelve items focus on the dimension of praising common people, while the other 17 tap into the idea of the people's general will as the basis of politics, or the homogeneity of the people (as defined in Schulz et al. 2017). Examples of the former include "generally speaking, average people are hard-working," and "I take pride in being an ordinary person." For the latter, some examples are "The politicians in Congress need to follow the will of the people," and "The will of the people should be the highest principle in this country's politics." We have also included several negative-worded items, such as "There is no such a thing as 'the will of the people" and "The worst politicians are those who come from the common people." The full list of items is in the Appendix.

Anti-establishment/anti-elite feelings

Populists always see an elite in opposition to that good people. The elite is a minority of corrupt forces who have subverted the political system to work for their benefit (Mudde and Rovira Kaltwasser 2013, 502). It may be found, depending on the context, dominating politics, the economy, culture, media, and/or the judiciary (Rooduijn 2014a, 577). The elite exploits the people in its pursuit for more power and profit, meaning that liberation from this domination is needed (Hawkins 2009). Who is categorized as elite (or as the people) varies according to time and place. Usual elite targets may be governments in general and its officials, the rich, supranational organizations, international financial bodies, or foreign countries and their leaders. What is essential is that this elite is represented in domestic politics as well – for example, the "lackeys of imperialism" in Latin America.

Items were designed to capture the idea of anti-elite feelings without going into detail of who the establishment[5] is – this is done at the sections that try to differentiate left- and right-wing populisms. Otherwise, ideology would certainly be a confounder. Therefore, it is often restrained to the political establishment and the idea of elites in abstract. Examples of items include "Elected politicians sell out to big business," "Politicians do not want to improve the lives of ordinary people," and "The government is pretty much run by a few big interests looking out for themselves." Some of the reverse-worded items are "Politicians are actually interested in what people like me think" and "Most politicians seek power to serve others."

Manichaean outlook on politics

As the description in previous sections already indicates, the division between the people and the elite is primarily moral (Mudde and Rovira Kaltwasser 2013), with one side being the monopolist of virtue, and the other of vice. In the existing measures (e.g. Hawkins et al. 2012; Akkerman et al. 2014) this element was incorporated in the wording of anti-establishment items. The Manichaean outlook was expressed by statements that accused established politicians of having betrayed the people. In this way the Manichaean outlook was not considered an essential element of politics per se but rather of the current state of democracy.[6] We follow a different track. No measurement attempt up to date has tried to gauge Manichaean attitudes of politics directly and individually (with the partial exception of Hawkins et al. 2012 and Stanley 2011), even though this is theoretically plausible. Keeping with the idea of measuring these dimensions separately, we developed questions on whether the respondent perceives politics as a moral struggle, without referring to people or elite. Our aim is to measure the Manichaean outlook of politics in its pure form and subsequently assess how this dimension relates to other dimensions of populist attitudes. Examples of items are "You can tell if a person is good or bad if you know their politics" or "People I disagree with politically are driven solely by greed." Reverse items include "The people I disagree with politically are not evil" and "In politics, everyone wants what they think is the best for the country." It is important to note that because we see this dimension as a kind of political cosmology or worldview (Hawkins and Rovira Kaltwasser, 2017) the items do not exclusively refer to the differences between "the people" and "the elite." On the contrary, the first three items refer to differences among the people themselves.

Potential populism dimensions

Any attempt would be incomplete if we ignored the plurality of views on what constitutes populism. We have conducted a literature review to find other constructs that have been considered part of the concept and, afterwards, used the mailing list of *Team Populism*[7] to ask for further inputs on what dimensions and questions might be considered. We have settled with the potential dimensions listed in the following sections, and collected or designed a number of survey items for each one individually as well.

Strong leader

Populism is sometimes associated with preference for a strong leader, along the lines of "delegative democracy" (O'Donnell 1994). Populist leaders, especially in Latin America, have claimed that being directly elected gives them a popular mandate to override other institutions if that is necessary for implementing the "general will" (Levitsky and

Loxton 2013). For some, populism would necessarily involve a preference for a personalist authority over institutions of representative democracy (Pappas 2014). To tap into this idea, we propose items such as "What our country needs is a leader who will be admired" or "Our presidents should do what the people want even when the laws prohibit him from doing it."

Simple, direct style

Much work on populism sees it not so much as a discourse, but as a style of dress, language, and performance (Moffitt 2016; Ostiguy 2017). Populism is said to have a direct and unmediated connection between leader and followers (Weyland 2001), based on charismatic appeal (Pappas 2016). To achieve this, the usage of a colloquial language, popular mannerisms and informal clothing are some of the tools employed by populist leaders who want to "look like the people" (see, e.g., de la Torre 2013, 37). We suggest a scale that taps into this preference for a "politician like me," and has negative attitudes towards what may be seen as complex political dealings or trade-offs. Examples of items in it are "I prefer politicians who tell it how it is," and "It's important for a political leader to be like the people he or she represents."[8]

Perception of crisis

In populist discourse, traditional parties are charged with having created an oligarchical system where there is no difference among them, thus hollowing the meaning of real democracy (Mouffe 2005, 64). This makes it necessary that a new, truly popular, kind of party appears (Mudde 2004, 546), in a call for liberation (Hawkins 2009). Proclaiming that there is a crisis of representation and in the functioning of democracy may be seen, therefore, as an essential aspect of populism (Rooduijn 2014a; Moffitt 2015). We tap into this dimension with items such as "The rights of individuals have been systematically curtailed in this country" (Dryzek and Berejikian 1993).

Anything-goes attitude

Hawkins (2010, 36) argues that a consequence of populist discourse is an "anything-goes" attitude, where formal procedures and liberal rights are seen as a hindrance to the realization of the will of the people. In short, because this general will is the highest principle in politics, anything and anyone setting limits to it is naturally seen as illegitimate. As such, this obstacle deserves to be removed, even if by illegal means, in the name of the greater good. This idea is very close to authoritarianism, or that populism essentially is *democratic illiberalism* (Pappas 2014). We have items that tap into a willingness to limit checks and balances institutions, as well as the rights of some groups that may be seen as enemies of the people (Seligson 2007). Namely, we use items from the Latin American Public Opinion Project's questionnaires,[9] from several waves, which read, for example, "It is necessary for the progress of the country that our presidents limit the voice and vote of the opposition parties."

Left and right populisms

What makes populism left or right is how "the people" and "the elite" are defined, based on the ideology with which it is associated in each case. Populists on the left, on one hand, see this division as one rooted in economic inequality (March 2007), where the people are seen as a majority of economically and socially disadvantaged groups, oppressed by a minority who, because of their resources, controls politics. The elite are the rich, financial institutions (both internal and external), and whoever may be associated with and subordinated to those actors. Right-wing populism, on the other hand, has a more nationalist understanding of "the people," which does not emphasize how it is dominated economically, but how the nation and its symbols are threatened by a minority (the "nativism" dimension in Mudde 2007). In economic terms, it frequently sees the people as middle class, hard-working individuals oppressed by the government, who want to take their money and give to privileged minorities. The elites are politicians, local and international, who use their control of the state to harm the national majority, benefiting themselves and their allies.

To complement the more neutral items from the batteries on core constructs, we have developed specific statements to reflect right- and left-wing versions of populism, associating actors to the roles of "people" and "elite" accordingly. For right-wing populism, we include items such as "People who pay no taxes should have no say in how this country is run," and "In this country, liberal intellectuals are the real enemy of the people." On the left, examples include "Big corporations accumulate wealth by exploiting the people" and "The unemployed, underemployed, marginalized groups – these are the real people who should have more voice in politics."

Data

Altogether, there are 145 survey items proposed for the ten dimensions outlined above. For our first two studies, we collected data in eight countries. In the United States, we used an online survey through Amazon's Mechanical Turk (MTurk), with 234 respondents, in May 2015. In Argentina, Croatia, Greece, Mexico, Spain, and Switzerland, we relied on samples of undergraduate and graduate students.[10] The sample sizes are 257 in Argentina, 193 in Croatia, 172 in Spain, 262 in Greece, 163 in Mexico, and 247 in Switzerland. In Belgium, we complemented a sample with students from the Free University in Brussels with respondents recruited through social media and university mailing lists. The survey was administered only in Dutch (N = 153). None of the samples approaches nationally representative, in line with the general practice of scale development in psychology. The main goal of this exercise is to explore dimensionality and questionnaire reduction, by getting a first glimpse into what items of the full list tap into populism constructs, and which ones work across different cultures. Therefore, the seven countries with student samples, plus the American online sample, offer enough variation to permit us, first, to reduce the long list into a shorter one with items that load together in the relevant dimensions, and second, to test which items are invariant across groups.

For our third study, we use a new round of data collected online in nine countries. For the United States we once again used Amazon's MTurk, while for the other eight (Brazil, France, Greece, Ireland, Italy, Mexico, Spain, and the United Kingdom) we used the crowdsourcing platform CrowdFlower. Because of its international pool of contributors, scholars have begun using it for scientific surveys. Results of testing show that respondents give answers with similar levels of quality to other online providers such as MTurk (Peer et al. 2017). Our sample sizes vary between 200 and 300 respondents for each country, except for a larger American sample of 505; all samples were collected between November 2016 and March 2017.[11]

Despite distortions in CrowdFlower samples relative to national populations, they are still more diverse than student and other convenience samples. Median ages for countries are around 27–30, with most respondents between 20 and 40. This is a bias towards younger respondents less pronounced than that observed with students. Education and income distributions are also more varied, as is geographic location. There are important gender imbalances – one of our samples is 80% male. However, ideological balance is more closely achieved than with undergraduate students. In sum, the imbalances in CrowdFlower samples (the largest being gender) are different from those in student samples (location, age, occupation, and ideology), in relation to their representativeness. Therefore, we do not expect biases to be correlated across the two.

Scale development, step by step

We proceed with reducing our initial 145 items into a manageable scale in three steps. First, all of them are included in factor analysis models, to identify the latent dimensions underlying all of these questions. We seek to find what constructs, of those theorized, can be retrieved from the data. This step gives us the coherent sub-dimensions to be measured, and a smaller list of items measuring each one. Second, we perform a test of measurement invariance on the student samples. This test tells us which items have high cross-cultural validity, and which ones should be dropped from the scale due to not working well across different cultures. Last, with a new round of cross-national data, we validate those findings about the cross-national validity of the remaining short scale.

Step 1: the factor structure of populism dimensions

The first study we conduct aims at identifying the underlying dimensions across the 145 survey items. We use exploratory factor analysis (EFA)[12] to uncover the number of latent variables (dimensions, or factors) that can explain the largest amount of variation in the items. EFA helps us observe whether our proposed items load on the proposed constructs, and which constructs grant the most explanatory leverage within these data. We apply the model to the pooled data with student samples and the first Amazon MTurk sample.

We run 11 EFA models, having from 2 to 12 factors. There is no consensus on how to choose the appropriate number of factors (m) to retain after EFA. We have tried several existing alternatives, as described in the online Appendix B. They fail to converge on a single solution, and we choose to follow an approach of using absolute indicators of model fit. This works by selecting the solution with the smallest number of factors that gives acceptable fit (Preacher et al. 2013). We pick the solution with four factors, as the first one in which both SRMR (Standardized Root Mean Square Residual) and RMSEA (Root Mean Square Error of Approximation) indicate good fit (meaning they are below 0.05).[13] We also follow a substantive interpretation: inspecting the items in each factor for solutions with a larger m, there are four stable and clearly identifiable factors, with more or less the same indicators across solutions; the others that show up tend to have few indicators or fail to present a meaningful theoretical construct. The solution with three factors does not discriminate indicators which seem to belong to different constructs.[14]

Conceptually, the four factors identified are interpreted as *people-centrism, anti-elitism, Manichaean outlook*, and *authoritarianism*. The first three are core constructs of populism, while the fourth is a construct whose connection to populism is debated conceptually

(Mudde and Rovira Kaltwasser 2017; Müller 2016) and empirically (see Aguilar and Carlin in this volume, Chapter 17). For each dimension we look at items with an absolute factor loading greater than 0.35. There are 19 for people-centrism, 37 for anti-elitism, 15 for Manichaean outlook, and 20 for authoritarianism. Table 7.1 presents the factor correlations from the EFA. While people-centrism and anti-elitism have a moderate correlation with one another ($r = 0.28$), the other factor correlations are rather small. This evidence suggests we are indeed capturing different dimensions that can be seen as separate constructs and should, accordingly, be measured separately.

Step 2: first test of measurement invariance

Given our large number of items, we could expect that EFA would return several ones for each possible dimension. While EFA completes the dimensionality reduction, questionnaire reduction continues with our first test of measurement invariance. This test tells us which items, for each dimension, should be retained as they work in similar ways across different countries. After this part, our goal of creating a more manageable scale, with few statements per dimension, can be obtained.

The most common way of testing the equivalence of measurement instruments is with Multiple Group Confirmatory Factor Analysis (MGCFA, Jöreskog 1971). In this strategy, three CFA models are fit to the data: the first where all estimated parameters are allowed to vary across groups (configural model), the second where factor loadings are constrained to be the same across groups (metric invariance), and the third where loadings and intercepts are held constant (scalar invariance). In other words, the configural one is equivalent to fitting separate CFA models in each country. In the metric invariance model, the factor loading of each single indicator on its latent variable (say, the loading of *"Quite a few of the people running the government are crooked"* on *Anti-elitism*) is forced to be the same in all countries. If the indicator measures that dimension similarly across countries, the factor loadings in the configural model would be similar anyway, and forcing equality is not expected to make the model worse. This evaluation is done with model fit information: if the more constrained models do not fit significantly worse than the less constrained, it means there is measurement invariance. Substantively, what the second model means is that an increase in one unit of the latent construct has the same impact on the observed indicators across all groups. The third model, scalar invariance, tests not only whether variation in the latent construct means the same for respondents in all groups, but also that respondents with the same level of the latent construct would give the same answer in all groups.[15]

Table 7.1 Correlation matrix after EFA

	Praise people	*Anti-elitism*	*Manichaean outlook*	*Authoritarianism*
Praise people	1.00			
Anti-elitism	.278	1.00		
Manichaean outlook	.073	.095	1.00	
Authoritarianism	.034	.006	.108	1.00

Multigroup CFA has been criticized for being too strict (see, for instance, a comparison with alternatives in Davidov et al. 2015). In cross-national surveys, items rarely work perfectly the same way in all countries, and the invariant models tend to be rejected. Alternative approaches that allow for slight noninvariance have been proposed. In this step we use the alignment method (Asparouhov and Muthén 2014). It modifies the configural model to align factors and intercepts, similar to a rotation in EFA, taking into account actual factor means and factor variances. Not only is this method more practical than MGCFA, and not demanding exact invariance, it also lists which indicators are (non) invariant in each group. MGCFA is used in our last validation test, in step 3.

For our model, we select all constructs we retain from EFA, and include twelve items with the highest absolute factor loadings as indicators of the predicted latent variables in the CFA alignment model.[16] We strive to include at least three negative-worded statements in each dimension, even if these would not be on the list of highest absolute loadings, because of their value in questionnaire design. Table 7.2 shows information for the five to seven best working items in each dimension at this stage. Items are chosen based on invariance, average loadings, and distributional characteristics, and we sought to include at least one negative-worded item in each category. It is possible to find at least four items with invariant factor loadings across all eight samples for each construct, and a few even have invariant intercepts across all countries. Those that violate invariance do so in only one or two samples. Moreover, we observe items with both higher and lower than average means, indicating it is possible to get indicators that people disagree with. Factor loadings are high for most of the indicators, with a few exceptions in the *people-centrism* dimension.

Broadly, items have face-validity in capturing the proposed concepts. A few points must be noticed at this stage: first, we observe a clear and distinctive Manichaean outlook element in populist attitudes. This is the first time such a construct has been tested, and it contributes to our empirical and conceptual understanding of how populist attitudes are structured. Second, exploratory factor analysis results show one cannot clearly distinguish between three theoretical constructs: "praise of the people,“ "homogeneous people/general will" and "simple, direct style." The six items in the people-centrism part of Table 7.2 are an amalgam with contributions from all three theorized constructs, amounting to a coherent idea of glorifying common people in politics. This is contrary to previous findings by Schulz et al. (2017), who distinguish between people homogeneity and popular sovereignty. While scholars go through great lengths to theoretically distinguish between these concepts, we find that individuals make less fine-grained distinctions when thinking about politics.

Third, the *anti-elitism* dimension has items not only from the original scale proposed for it, but also from those for left- and right-wing populism. Item *Ant4* in Table 7.3 was originally drafted for the left-wing populism scale, as it clearly frames corporations as the elite against whom to fight. *Ant2*, on the other hand, is a reverse-worded item from the right-wing populism scale. Nevertheless, both load together with more generic anti-establishment statements. The fourth point to highlight is that noninvariance is most egregious in two samples: Croatia (four loadings and five intercepts) and Switzerland (one loading and five intercepts). That might be caused by specificities of these student samples, or by different characteristics of populism in both countries in relation to the rest. For this reason it is essential to conduct an independent validation as we do in the next step.

Table 7.2 Invariance test with the CFA alignment method

Order	*Item*	*NI Load.*	*NI Int.*	*Mean int.*	*Mean load.*
People-centrism					
Ppl1.	Politicians should always listen closely to the problems of the people.	–	GR	6.29	0.50
Ppl2.	Politicians don't have to spend time among ordinary people to do a good job.*	–	–	2.87	–0.82
Ppl3.	The will of the people should be the highest principle in this country's politics.	–	–	5.15	0.90
Ppl4.	In a democracy, the will of the majority should prevail.	–	–	5.46	0.57
Ppl5.	It's important for a political leader to be like the people he or she represents.	–	–	4.86	0.92
Ppl6.	I prefer politicians who tell it how it is.	–	HR	6.00	0.50
Anti-elitism					
Ant1.	The government is pretty much run by a few big interests looking out for themselves.	–	–	5.23	1.18
Ant2.	Government officials use their power to try to improve people's lives.*	HR, CH	MX	3.66	–0.92
Ant3.	Quite a few of the people running the government are crooked.	–	HR, CH	5.48	1.10
Ant4.	Big corporations accumulate wealth by exploiting the people.	HR	–	5.11	1.22
Ant5.	Politicians are not really interested in what people like me think.	–	ES, CH	4.76	1.21
Ant6.	Politicians are actually interested in what people like me think.*	–	BE, CH	3.00	–1.01
Ant7.	The government is currently run for the benefit of all the people.*	HR	HR, AR	2.70	–0.87
Manichaean outlook					
Man1.	You can tell if a person is good or bad if you know their politics.	–	–	3.69	0.81
Man2.	I would never stop talking to a friend because of their political opinions.*	–	BE, CH	5.37	–0.88
Man3.	The people I disagree with politically are just misinformed.	–	HR	2.73	0.92
Man4.	Politics is a struggle between good and evil.	–	US, ES, BE, CH	3.94	0.60
Man5.	The difference between me and those who support other parties is that I care about what's good for everyone.	HR, MX	HR	4.13	0.80
Authoritarianism					
Aut1.	People who only say bad things about [country] should not be allowed to conduct even peaceful demonstrations. (any4)	–	–	1.85	1.12
Aut2.	People who only say bad things about this country have the same right as anyone else to appear on television to make speeches.* (any8)	–	CH	5.81	–1.20
Aut3.	People who only say bad things about our form of government, not just the current administration but the system of government, should not have the right to vote. (any3)	–	AR	1.84	0.94
Aut4.	People who only say bad things about [country] should have the same right as anyone else to conduct peaceful demonstrations.* (any5)	–	–	5.95	–1.16
Aut5.	People who only say bad things about this country should not be allowed to appear on television to make speeches. (any7)	–	–	2.06	1.20

Step 3: cross-national validation

In our final step, the items in Table 7.2 were fielded in new surveys in nine countries. To that we added three more negative-worded items for the Manichaean outlook battery since the best performing items there are all (but one) positively worded. Moreover, we do not include authoritarianism; this is a well defined distinct construct with over a half a century of scale development and its relation to populism is conceptually controversial. While the EFA identified an authoritarianism dimension from all those items, and several were invariant across student samples, it is distinct from the construct we are trying to measure. For this reason, items were selected only for *people-centrism, anti-elitism*, and *Manichaean outlook.*

The model tested is a multigroup CFA with three latent variables, and three indicators for each latent variable, as depicted in Figure 7.2. The results in it are those for the model with factor loadings constrained to be the same across countries (the loadings invariant model). Model fit is acceptable, with RMSEA and SRMR below 0.07, and TLI above 0.90. CFI is a bit below the recommended minimum of 0.95, and the chi-square test is significant (however, this test is known to be sensitive to large samples, as noted in Kline 2016). We have included a method factor to take into account the fact that some items are worded negatively, and because research shows that individuals respond differently to positive- and negative-worded statements (DiStefano and Motl 2006).[17] Factor loadings reported for individual items are unstandardized.[18]

Items work well for both the *anti-elitism* and *people-centrism* scales, with high absolute loadings. For Manichaean outlook, the first two work better, while the last (*"The people I disagree with politically are just misinformed"*) has a somewhat lower loading. This is an interesting finding because in terms of stereotype content (Fiske et al. 2002) the first two items differ from the third. Specifically, while the first two refer to "warmth" (i.e., people's intentions), the items that attribute political disagreement to misinformation taps into a "competence" related claim. It is clear that the Manichaean view on politics is basically a view that refers to people's intentions, so it is perhaps not surprising to find that exactly the items that refer to that element turn out to work best. From the top three suggestions for each dimension in Table 7.2, *Man2* had a low factor loading and decreased model fit substantively in this test.[19] We replaced it with another option of a negative worded item that had been present in the original questionnaire: "The people I disagree with politically are not evil." The final, nine-item scale tested is:

Box 7.1. Final item suggestions

People-centrism:

Ppl1. Politicians should always listen closely to the problems of the people.

Ppl2. Politicians don't have to spend time among ordinary people to do a good job.*

PPl3. The will of the people should be the highest principle in this country's politics.

Anti-elitism:

Ant1. The government is pretty much run by a few big interests looking out for themselves.

Ant2. Government officials use their power to try to improve people's lives.*

Ant3. Quite a few of the people running the government are crooked.

Manichaean outlook:

Man1. You can tell if a person is good or bad if you know their politics.

Man2. The people I disagree with politically are not evil.*

Man3. The people I disagree with politically are just misinformed.

A measurement invariance test with multigroup CFA shows that this model does not fit significantly worse than the configural model, i.e., one where factor loadings are allowed to vary across countries (meaning, in practice, one CFA is fit in each country), as seen in Table 7.3. These indicators capture the latent variables across all nine countries included in this sample in a similar manner. In other words, this survey instrument has a high degree of cross-national validity, at least for the countries tested. Note that the countries were selected to represent several regions, with variation in left and right-wing populism and varying degrees of populism overall. Model comparison is done with a chi-square test of model difference using the Satorra-Bentler (Satorra and Bentler 2001) correction. It works the following way: each model has a chi-square statistic indicating fit, where lower

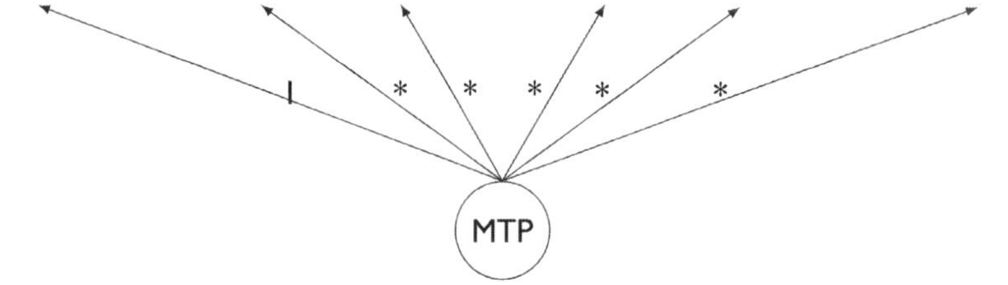

Figure 7.2 Multigroup confirmatory factor analysis with equality constraints on factor loadings

Notes: Unstandardized factor loadings, constrained to be the same across nine groups (countries). Estimation: maximum likelihood robust. Items measured on a 1–7 Likert scale. N = 2510. Model fit: chi-square = 514.884, df = 254, p<.001, RMSEA = .061 (90% CI: .054–.068), SRMR = .063, CFI = .924, TLI = .903. Factor loading of the method factor (*) = .97.

Table 7.3 Multigroup CFA invariance test

Model	*Chi-square*	*Chi-sq. Diff.*	df	p
New scale				
Configural	440.58			
Loadings	599.12	102.20	88	.14
Intercepts	912.57	322.17	40	<.001
Akkerman et al. (2014)				
Configural	230.76			
Loadings	297.15	59.935	40	.02
Intercepts	553.11	253.283	40	<.001

values indicate better fit. If we compare the difference in chi-squares between two nested models and there is a significant difference, it means that the second (more restricted) has a significantly worse fit than the first. If the model with constrained loadings is not significantly worse, the next step is constraining intercepts to be the same across groups, and once again testing whether the chi-square difference is significant. Measurement invariance, therefore, is achieved when we do not observe significant differences between models (i.e., $p > 0.05$). As a comparison, we have also tested the invariance of the six-item scale proposed by Akkerman et al. (2014) in the same data, which is currently the most used for measuring populist attitudes. Results in the lower part of Table 7.3 show that factor loadings are not invariant across countries: the model with constrained loadings fits significantly worse than the configural ($p = 0.02$).

While these results may seem a bit dark for the Akkerman et al. (2014) scale, we emphasize that a multigroup CFA is a conservative test of invariance. A p-value of .02 does not indicate a strongly non-invariant instrument. This means that researchers who have already collected data with the scale suggested by Akkerman et al. (2014) should conduct the appropriate measurement invariance tests on their own data before analyzing substantive results, but it does not *a priori* invalidate any analyses using their scales, including those in this book. However, if one plans to include a battery in cross-national surveys with multiple countries, non-invariance in the Akkerman et al. (2014) instrument would likely become an issue.[20]

Scale and item information

Following the analyses by Van Hauwaert, Schimpf, and Azevedo in Chapter 6, we conclude the assessment of this scale with a model to test the amount of information it contains, and how much of the latent construct it is able to capture. We have pooled the data for all nine countries and run a graded ratings scale model (Muraki 1992) to identify, first, the amount of information of this scale along the construct, and second the amount of information that each item contributes. This analysis was done in two ways: first, each dimension separately; and second, with the two top items of each construct pooled to form a short, unidimensional scale for populism.

Figures 7.3–7.5 have the information curves for each dimension on the left-hand side of each panel (solid lines). As can be seen, each set of items captures a different area of their respective dimensions, with the first two mostly on the negative side (on the [–3:1] interval) while the last (Manichaean outlook) performs better on individuals higher on

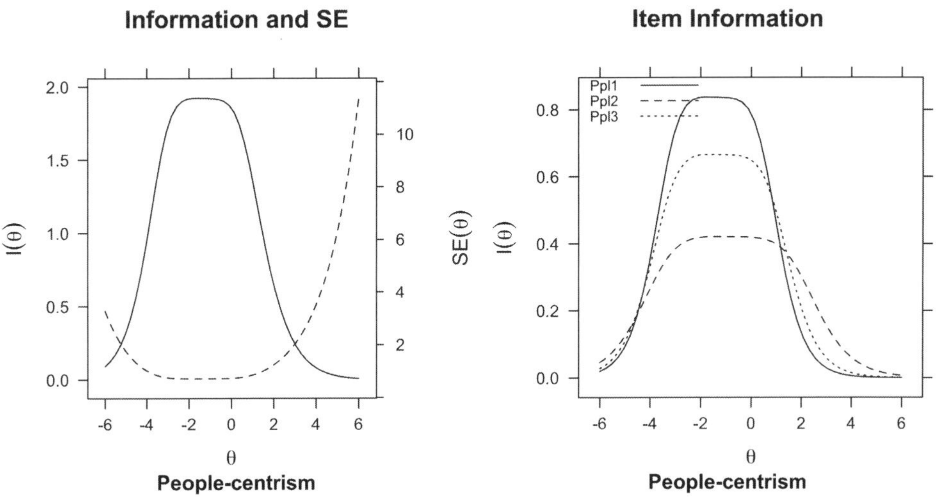

Figure 7.3 Information curves – people-centrism

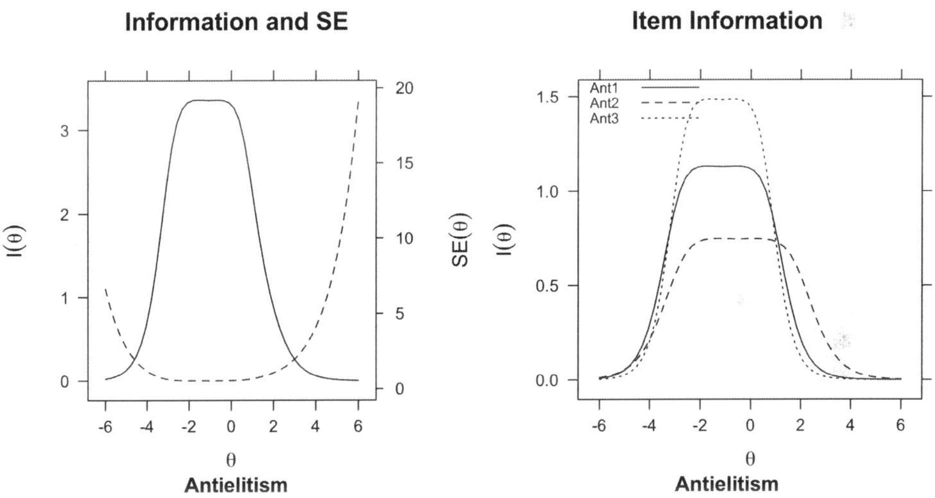

Figure 7.4 Information curves – anti-elitism

this trait (those in the [–1:3] range). At the extremes the dashed error curves become higher, indicating that the measure is less apt to capture individuals positioned on those levels of the construct. Item information curves show that for each scale there is one most informative item (Ant3, Ppl1, and Man1), and that the negative-worded items (Ant2, Ppl2, Man2) contribute by capturing information further away from the center in all three, even if it is not the highest level of information.

Information curves also suggest that the two positive-worded items in each scale capture a similar range of their constructs. Therefore, we test an aggregate short version of our scale with six items – the first positive and the negative-worded for each dimension

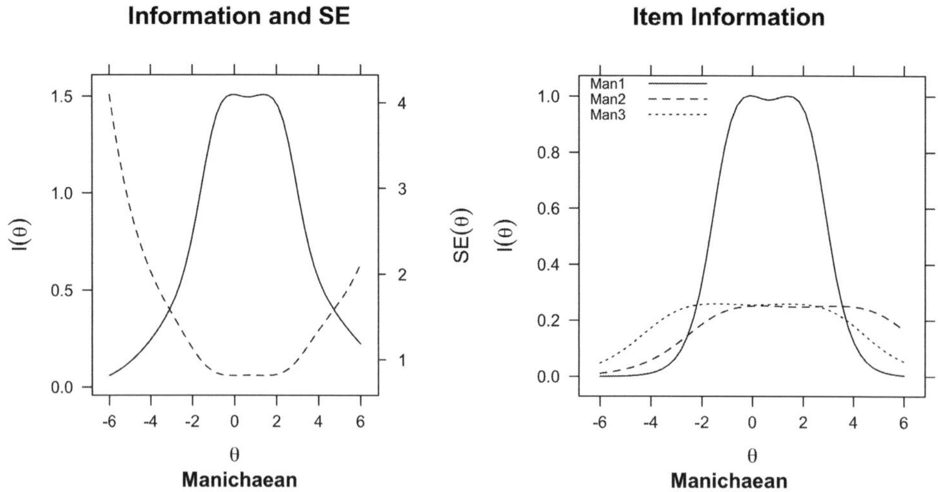

Figure 7.5 Information curves – manichaean outlook

(Ant1, Ant2, Ppl1, Pp2, Man1, Man2) – loading on a single construct.[21] The information curve for this short scale is in Figure 7.6, with a comparison to the information curve obtained with the Akkerman et al. (2014) six-item scale, which Van Hauwaert,

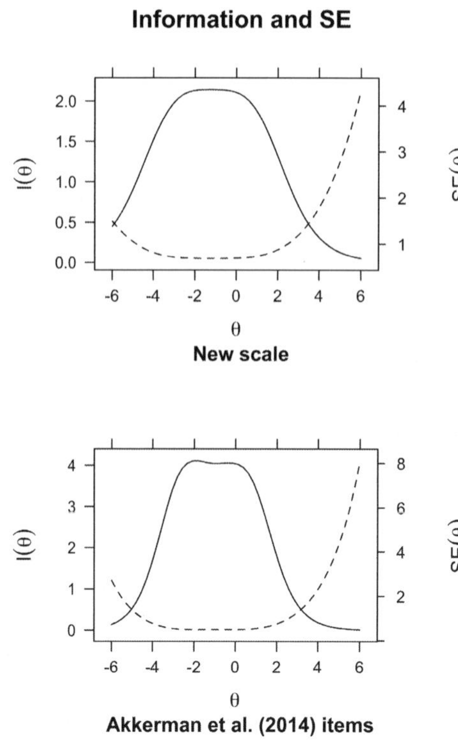

Figure 7.6 Scale information comparison

Schimpf, and Azevedo found to have a broad range in Chapter 6. Here, we see that the short version of the new scale captures a somewhat broader range than Akkerman et al. (2014), primarily on the low end of the scales, but both still fall short when discriminating extremely high levels of populism.

Conclusion

The first goal of this project is to suggest a psychometrically validated scale to measure populism as an attitude. We start with the core dimensions that compose the concept, develop batteries of questions to tap into them, and conduct exploratory analyses to identify those dimensions which can be found among the public. Confirming the ideational theory, we find three stable constructs that are clearly part of populism among our original 145: *people-centrism, anti-elitism*, and *Manichaean outlook*. We use two rounds of cross-national validation in order to reduce the original number of items for each into a short scale, and reach a final battery that can be used either with nine or six statements. Confirmatory factor analysis and Item Response Theory models show that the scale captures a broad range of the construct and has high cross-national validity.

This new scale has several advantages over existing alternatives: first, it has been developed with the concern for cross-cultural validity from its inception. Few, if any, of the existing scales have had their invariance tested to know whether they do work in a similar way to capture the phenomenon of populism in different countries. Until such an exercise is done, they should not be used to compare levels of populism, or even correlates, across large numbers of countries. The scale proposed here is a reliable instrument across 17 samples from 13 different countries, including both convenience (student) samples and more diverse, online ones. Moreover, in this process we have also mitigated potential translator effects for the languages we tested. Researchers who wish to apply this battery have a pool of languages into which these items have already been translated and in which their validity has been tested, available in the online Appendix C. While it is not possible to assure that the scale would be invariant in other countries than those included here, we sought for large regional coverage, as well as examples of cases with distinct kinds of populist parties (including no successful populists at all), to maximize the possibility that the scale would work well in countries we did not include.

A second advantage of this scale is dividing populism into its subcomponents and measuring each one separately. While some other scales have done that (e.g. Schulz et al. 2017; Stanley 2011; Oliver and Rahn 2016), ours is the first to depart inductively from a range of potential conceptual constructs and narrow the scale down into those that appear to be the most stable on the data, as well as conceptually sound following an ideational definition. Researchers now have the flexibility of investigating not only correlates of populist attitudes writ large, but how each one of its subcomponents might be related to a different set of social and psychological characteristics. Additionally, our analysis highlighted the importance of authoritarianism in relation to the other facets of populist attitudes. The structure of relationships between these concepts warrant additional work. And we encourage scholars to work with these dimensions in a flexible and theory-based way when they do their own research.

A concern can be raised regarding the data we used. Student samples are much more homogeneous than national populations, and so it is natural that sometimes findings from studies with them do not generalize. We attempted to minimize this problem by relying on a different kind of convenience sample for the validation exercise: those recruited through CrowdFlower. Nevertheless, they are still not representative of any population, and formed by individuals who chose to take the survey. As we argue earlier, the imbalances in CrowdFlower samples are different from those in student samples. Therefore, biases should not be correlated between the two. For instance, if an item works very well only among well-educated young people, it would perform poorly in the CrowdFlower samples, which are more diverse in this respect. Our samples, therefore, offer enough variation that these shortcomings are minimized. Moreover, much of the causes behind measurement non-invariance include translation effects, and terms or concepts that do not make sense in different contexts. These can be captured with cross-national samples even if they are not diverse. Finally, from a practical perspective, including the full batteries into representative cross-national surveys would have been prohibitively expensive – even the shorter questionnaires in CrowdFlower were 10-minute surveys. For the scale reduction exercise, we must rely on sub-optimal samples. However, now that we arrived at a short version, this can be included in surveys with representative samples, and their properties then reassessed.

From a theoretical perspective, we have two main findings. First, that a general Manichaean outlook of politics, dissociated from *people* and *elites*, is a component of populist attitudes. This had not been tested before, and in general only incorporated into how populists frame elites and the people. Second, we fail to statistically differentiate between praising common people and the idea of popular sovereignty in politics. These two are treated as conceptually distinct (e.g. in Mudde and Rovira Kaltwasser 2017), but at the attitudinal level are too close to be distinguished from one another. These findings call for a theoretical reevaluation of these dimensions' status within the concept of populism, at lease when seen in its psychological dimension.

Further, while the measurement divides populism into its components, we offer a short version of the scale. It has six items that can be used to measure a single underlying dimension, for those researchers who have stricter limitations on the amount of survey space they can use. Another contribution is offering negative-worded items in each of the dimensions, making sure that we are indeed measuring populist attitudes and not acquiescence bias. This is a shortcoming in several scales (an exception is Stanley 2011), and explains at least in part why populist attitudes are found to be so widespread almost everywhere they are measured.

Finally, another shortcoming of existing scales found by Van Hauwaert, Schimpf, and Azevedo was that they fail to capture the full breadth of populist attitudes: all scales either discriminate only moderate populism/non-populism, or work better on one end (full populists or full non-populists). The best performing one in this regard was found to be that proposed by Akkerman et al. (2014). The scale proposed here captures a somewhat broader range of the concept, offering information about full non-populists, and moderates on both sides of zero. Its advantage, however, lies in the cross-national validity of its application.

The benefit from this effort is not only the development of a more refined, psychometrically tested scale of populist attitudes. The division into dimensions also allows researchers to 1) use the dimensions that best fit their definition when doing future studies, creating more precise measurements; 2) study the relations between dimensions of populism that were previously unexplored or only hypothesized, and 3) study the impact of each dimension of populism individually over other outcomes of interest. It opens the possibility of analyzing the varieties of populist discourse and attitudes, and how different aspects of populism might predict, or be predicted by, other attitudes and behavior. Moreover, the high cross-national validity will be an essential tool for the blossoming comparative research on populism across countries and regions. Researchers in several areas have much to gain from this improved measurement.

Notes

1 Contact author: BCS. BCS wrote the paper with substantial support from BS; BCS, IA, LL ran the analyses; BCS and LL designed the study; IA, EA, NB, YMC, GD, GR, SR, MS collected data, provided valuable comments and edits, and are listed in alphabetical order; LL led the project. The authors would like to thank Andreea Nicutar, Daniel Kovarec, Elisa Totino, Federico Vegetti, Selina Kurer, and Sharon Belli for their help with questionnaire translation and survey implementation, and Sebastian Jungkunz and Nemanja Stankov for assistance with data cleaning and writing the codebooks.

2 Our measurement approach is very close to the elite-level ones conducted by Hawkins and Castanho Silva in this volume (based on Hawkins 2009), and by Rooduijn, de Lange, and van der Brug (2014): they also consider that all dimensions of populism must exist simultaneously, in the same text, for it to be considered populist. For example, texts that are anti-elitist but do not praise the people are not classified as populists in those scales. Seeing populism as a configural concept where all aspects have to be present for it to be characterized is, therefore, at the core of an ideational understanding.

3 We come back to this under the discussion of left- and right- varieties of populism.

4 These are two of the three separate dimensions proposed and measured in the scale by Schulz et al. (2017).

5 In this chapter we treat "elite" and "establishment" as equivalents. Within the concept of populism, they are both referring to the same group.

6 Indeed, one of the items that presented the Manichaean outlook of politics in essentialist language (i.e., "Politics is ultimately a battle between 'good' and 'evil'") failed to load on the populism dimension in the Netherlands (Akkerman et al., 2014). Because there was only one such item, it is was impossible to determine whether this item was part of a separate latent dimension that could not be tapped with all other items (which all were applied to populism).

7 See more at http://teampopulism.com and in the Preface.

8 Both conceptually and empirically (as we see in the analysis) this construct is eerily similar to the idea of glorifying the people.

9 Source: The AmericasBarometer by the Latin American Public Opinion Project (LAPOP), available at: www.lapopsurveys.org.

10 At the following institutes and dates: Argentine Catholic University (Argentina), June-August 2016, University of Zagreb (Croatia), Fall 2015; Aristotle University Thessaloniki (Greece), June 2015 and February/March 2016; Autonomous University of Barcelona (Spain), Fall 2015, National Autonomous University of Mexico, February/March 2016, and University of Zurich (Switzerland), September 2016.

11 The Irish sample was completed with 100 respondents from Qualtrics panels, due to there being too few CrowdFlower users in this country to reach our target of 250. While we also collected data through CrowdFlower and Qualtrics for Hungary, we have left it out of the analyses reported here due to concerns about response quality. While there is a sizeable useful sample, diagnostics show that many respondents there powered through the questionnaire without giving faithful answers, and several were able to reach the validation code at the end without actually taking the survey. Including the Hungarian sample in the analysis, however, does not change results either for invariance tests or information curves.

12 With an oblique rotation, since the dimensions are expected to correlate with one another (see Browne 2001).

13 The full table with model fit indicators for all solutions between 2 and 12 factors is in the online Appendix B.

14 Table 7.A1, in the online Appendix A, includes all items that have a factor loading above 0.3 in each of the constructs. Further, it indicates which items load into single dimensions on a Mokken scale analysis (Mokken 1971; Van Der Ark 2012). As we can see, there is broad agreement

regarding the composition of dimensions between MSA and EFA for anti-elitism and on the items with higher loadings in authoritarianism and Manichaean outlook. MSA produces a larger number of dimensions for the people-centrism dimension than EFA.

15 Metric invariance is usually accepted as sufficient, because for regression purposes it is enough that a change of one unit in the indicator means the same across groups.

16 We limit to 12 per scale (eleven for Manichaean outlook), leading to 47, so that the model is identified. With this number, the model has 147 free parameters, and our limit is 152: the number of observations in the smallest sample (153, Flanders), minus 1.

17 Four models were fit, following the suggestions by DiStefano and Motl (2006): model (a), reported, with a method-factor for positive-worded items; model (b) with a method factor for negative-worded items; model (c) with correlations among residuals of all positive-worded items, and model (d) with correlations among residuals of all negative-worded items. In the main text we present model (a), which has the best model fit. Fit indices for the others are: (b): Chi-square = 760.487, $df = 254$, $p < .001$, RMSEA = .085 (90% CI: .078-.091), SRMR = .088, TLI = .812, CFI = 853. Model (c): Chi-square = 357.662, $df = 129$, $p < .001$, RMSEA = .080 (90% CI: .071-.089), SRMR = .054, TLI = .838, CFI = .935. Model (d): Chi-square = 703.797, $df = 237$, $p < .001$, RMSEA = .084 (90% CI: .077-.091), SRMR = .086, TLI = .814, CFI = .864.

18 Items measured in Likert scales from 1 (Strongly disagree) to 7 (Strongly agree).

19 This item has a very positively skewed distribution in all samples, meaning that it was invariant on step 2, since most respondents agree with it in all countries, but does not provide much information since answers are clustered on the upper end.

20 The problematic item in this battery, for invariance, is "I would rather be represented by a citizen than by a specialized politician". If the factor loading for only this indicator is allowed to vary across groups, the constrained model does not fit significantly worse than the configural ($p = .18$). Doing the same for each of the other indicators still result in models with significantly worse fit.

21 Model fit: Chi-square = 53.873, df = 3, $p < .001$, RMSEA = .079, SRMR = .03, CFI = .959, applied on the pooled data (n = 2708). The lowest standardized loading is .331, for *Ppl2*. All residuals of negative-worded items are correlated to one another, as are those of positive-worded ones, to correct for method bias.

References

Agger, Robert. E., Marshall N. Goldstein, and Stanley A. Pearl. (1961). "Political Cynicism: Measurement and Meaning." *The Journal of Politics* 23(3): 477–506.

Akaike, Hirotogu. (1973). "Information Theory and an Extension of the Maximum Likelihood Principle." In *Second International Symposium on Information Theory*, edited by Boris N. Petrov, and Frigyes Csaki, 267–281. Budapest: Akademia Kiado.

Akkerman, Agnes, Cas Mudde, and Andrej Zaslove. (2014). "How Populist Are the People? Measuring Populist Attitudes in Voters." *Comparative Political Studies* 47(9): 1324–1353.

Alemán, José, and Dwayne Woods. (2016). "Value Orientations from the World Values Survey: How Comparable Are They Cross-Nationally?" *Comparative Political Studies* 49(8): 1039–1067.

Andreadis, Ioannis, and Yannis Stavrakakis. (2017) "European Populist Parties in Government: How Well are Voters Represented? Evidence from Greece." *Swiss Political Science Review*, 23(4), 485–508. doi: 10.1111/spsr.12255.

Ariely, Gal, and Eldad Davidov. (2010). "Can we Rate Public Support for Democracy in a Comparable Way? Cross-National Equivalence of Democratic Attitudes in the World Value Survey." *Social Indicators Research* 104(2): 271–286.

Aslanidis, Paris. (2016). "Is Populism an Ideology? A Refutation and a New Perspective." *Political Studies* 64(15): 88–104.

Asparouhov, Tihomir, and Bengt Muthén. (2014). "Multiple-group Factor Analysis Alignment." *Structural Equation Modeling: A Multidisciplinary Journal* 21(4): 495–508.

Browne, Michael W. (2001). "An Overview of Analytic Rotation in Exploratory Factor Analysis." *Multivariate Behavioral Research* 36(1): 111–150.

Cacioppo, John T., and Richard E. Petty. (1982). "The Need for Cognition." *Journal of Personality and Social Psychology* 42(1): 116–131.

Canovan, Margaret. (1981). *Populism*. London: Junction Books.

Canovan, Margaret. (1999). "Trust the People! Populism and the Two Faces of Democracy." *Political Studies* 47: 2–16.

Cattell, Raymond. B. (1966). "The Scree Test for the Number of Factors." *Multivariate Behavioral Research* 1(2): 245–276.

Davidov, Eldad, Jan Cieciuch, Bart Meuleman, Peter Schmidt, René Algesheimer, and Mirjam Hausherr. (2015). "The Comparability of Measurements of Attitudes toward Immigration in the European Social Survey: Exact versus Approximate Measurement Equivalence." *Public Opinion Quarterly* 79(SI): 244–266.

de la Torre, Carlos. (2013). "Technocratic Populism in Ecuador." *Journal of Democracy* 24(3): 33–46.

DiStefano, Christine, and Robert W. Motl. (2006). "Further Investigating Method Effects Associated With Negatively Worded Items on Self-Report Surveys." *Structural Equation Modeling: A Multidisciplinary Journal* 13: 440–464.

Dryzek, John S., and Joffrey Berejikian. (1993). "Reconstructive Democratic Theory." *The American Political Science Review* 87(1): 48–60.

Elchardus, Marc, and Bram Spruyt. (2016). "Populism, Persistent Republicanism and Declinism: An Empirical Analysis of Populism as a Thin Ideology." *Government & Opposition* 51: 111–33.

Fiske, Susan. T., Amy J. Cuddy, Peter Glick, and Jun Xu. (2002). "A Model of (Often Mixed) Stereotype Content: Competence and Warmth Respectively Follow From Perceived Status and Competition." *Journal of Personality and Social Psychology* 82(6): 878–902.

Funke, Friedrich. (2005). "The Dimensionality of Right-Wing Authoritarianism: Lessons from the Dilemma between Theory and Measurement." *Political Psychology* 26(2): 195–218.

Hawkins, Kirk. (2009). "Is Chavez Populist?: Measuring Populist Discourse in Comparative Perspective." *Comparative Political Studies* 42(8): 1040–1067.

Hawkins, Kirk A., Scott Riding, and Cas Mudde. 2012. "Measuring Populist Attitudes." *Working Paper Series on Political Concepts, ECPR Committee on Concepts and Methods.*

Hawkins, Kirk A., and Cristóbal Rovira Kaltwasser. (2017). "The Ideational Approach to Populism." *Latin American Research Review* 52(4): 513–528.

Horn, John L. (1965). "A Rationale and Test for the Number of Factors in Factor Analysis." *Psychometrika* 30(2): 179–185.

Ionescu, Ghita, and Ernest Gellner, editors. (1969). *Populism: Its Meanings and National Characteristics*. London: Weidenfeld and Nicholson.

Jöreskog, Karl G. (1971). "Simultaneous Factor Analysis in Several Populations." *Psychometrika* 36: 409–26.

Kline, Rex B. (2016). *Principles and Practice of Structural Equation Modeling*. The New York: Guilford Press, 4th. edition.

Laclau, Ernesto. (2005). *On Populist Reason*. London: Verso.

Levitsky, Steven, and James Loxton. (2013). "Populism and Competitive Authoritarianism in the Andes." *Democratization* 20(1): 107–136.

March, Luke. (2007). "From Vanguard of the Proletariat to Vox Populi: Left-Populism as a 'Shadow' of Contemporary Socialism." *SAIS Review* 27(1): 63–77.

Moffitt, Benjamin. (2015). "How to Perform Crisis: A Model for Understanding the Key Role of Crisis in Contemporary Populism." *Government and Opposition* 50(2): 189–217.

Moffitt, Benjamin. (2016). *The Global Rise of Populism*. Stanford: Stanford University Press.

Mokken, Rob J. (1971). *A Theory and Procedure of Scale Analysis*. The Hague: Mouton & Co.

Mouffe, Chantal. (2005). "The 'End of Politics' and the Challenge of Right-Wing Populism." In *Populism and the Mirror of Democracy*, edited by F. Panizza, 32–49. London: Verso.

Mudde, Cas. (2004). “The Populist Zeitgeist.” *Government and Opposition* 39(4): 542–563.
Mudde, Cas. (2007). *Populist Radical Right Parties in Europe*. Cambridge: Cambridge University Press.
Mudde, Cas, and Cristóbal Rovira Kaltwasser. (2013). “Populism.” In *Oxford Handbook of Political Ideologies*, edited by M. Freeden, L. T. Sargent, and M. Stears, 493–512. Oxford: Oxford University Press.
Mudde, Cas, and Cristóbal Rovira Kaltwasser. (2017). *Populism: A Very Short Introduction*. New York: Oxford University Press.
Müller, Jan-Werner. (2016). *What Is Populism?*. Philadelphia, PA: University of Pennsylvania Press.
Muraki, Eiji. (1992). “A Generalized Partial Credit Model: Application of an EM Algorithm.”, *Applied Psychological Measurement* 16(2): 159–176.
O’Donnell, Guillermo. (1994). “Delegative Democracy.” *Journal of Democracy* 5(1): 55–69.
Oliver, J. Eric, and Wendy M. Rahn (2016) “Rise of the Trumpenvolk: Populism in the 2016 Election.” *Annals of the American Academic of Political and Social Science* 667:189–206.
Ostiguy, Pierre. (2017). “Populism: A Socio-cultural Approach.” In *The Oxford Handbook of Populism*, edited by C. Rovira Kaltwasser, P. A. Taggart, P. Ochoa Espejo, and P. Ostiguy, 73–97. Oxford: Oxford University Press.
Panizza, Francisco. (2005). *Populism and the Mirror of Democracy*. London: Verso.
Pappas, Takis. S. (2014). “Populist Democracies: Post-authoritarian Greece and Post-communist Hungary.” *Government and Opposition* 49(1): 1–23.
Pappas, Takis. S. (2016). “Are Populist Leaders ‘Charismatic’? The Evidence from Europe”. *Constellations* 23(3): 378–390.
Peer, Eyal, Sonam Samat, Laura Brandimarte, and Alessandro Acquisti. (2017). “Beyond the Turk: Alternative Platforms for Crowdsourcing Behavioral Research.” *Journal of Experimental Social Psychology* 70: 153–163.
Piurko, Yuval, Shalom H. Schwartz, and Eidad Davidov. (2011). “Basic Personal Values and the Meaning of Left-Right Political Orientations in 20 Countries.” *Political Psychology* 32(4): 537–561.
Preacher, Kristopher J., Guangjian Zhang, Cheongtag Kim, and Gerhard Mels. (2013). “Choosing the Optimal Number of Factors in Exploratory Factor Analysis: A Model Selection Perspective.” *Multivariate Behavioral Research* 48(1): 28–56.
Rooduijn, Matthijs. (2014a). “The Nucleus of Populism: In Search of the Lowest Common Denominator.” *Government and Opposition* 49(4): 573–99.
Rooduijn, Matthijs. (2014b). “Vox Populismus: A Populist Radical Right Attitude among the Public?” *Nations and Nationalism* 20(1): 80–92.
Rooduijn, Matthijs, Sarah L. de Lange, and Wouter van der Brug. (2014). “A Populist Zeitgeist? Programmatic Contagion by Populist Parties in Western Europe.” *Party Politics* 20(4): 563–575.
Satorra, Alberto and Peter M. Bentler. (2001). “A Scaled Difference Chi-square Test Statistic for Moment Structure Analysis.” *Psychometrika* 66: 507–514.
Schulz, Anne, Philipp Müller, Christian Schemer, Dominique S. Wirz, Martin Wettstein, and Werner Wirth. (2017). “Measuring Populist Attitudes on Three Dimensions.” *International Journal of Public Opinion Research*. Online first. doi: https://doi.org/10.1093/ijpor/edw037.
Schwarz, Gideon. (1978). “Estimating the Dimension of a Model.” *The Annals of Statistics* 6(2): 461–464.
Seligson, Michael A. (2007). “The Democracy Barometers: The Rise of Populism and the Left in Latin America.” *Journal of Democracy* 18(3): 81–95.
Spruyt, Bram. (2014). “An Asymmetric Group Relation? An Investigation into Public Perceptions of Education-based Groups and the Support for Populism.” *Acta Politica* 49: 123–143.
Spruyt, Bram, Gil Keppens, and Filip Van Droogenbroeck. (2016). “Who Supports Populism and What Attracts People to It?” *Political Research Quarterly* 69(2): 335–346.
Stanley, Ben. (2011). “Populism, Nationalism, or National Populism? An Analysis of Slovak Voting Behaviour at the 2010 Parliamentary Election.” *Communist and Post-Communist Studies* 44(4): 257–270.

Stavrakakis, Yannis, Ioannis Andreadis, and Giorgos Katsambekis. (2017). "A New Populism Index at Work: Identifying Populist Candidates and Parties in the Contemporary Greek Context." *European Politics and Society*, 18(4), 446–464. http://dx.doi.org/10.1080/23745118.2016.1261434.

Taggart, Paul A. (2000). *Populism*. Buckingham: Open University Press.

Van Der Ark, L. Andries. (2012). "New Developments in Mokken Scale Analysis in R." *Journal of Statistical Software*, 48(5): 1–27.

Weyland, Kurt. (2001). "Clarifying a Contested Concept: Populism in the Study of Latin American Politics." *Comparative Politics* 34(1): 1–22.

Appendix

Complete list of items

Praise of the people

Generally speaking, average people are hard-working.

Generally speaking, average people are lazy.*

There is a silent majority who is too busy making an honest living to get involved in politics.

I take pride in being an ordinary person.

I take no pride in being an ordinary person.*

There's no such thing as "Real Americans."*

The opinion of ordinary people is worth more than that of experts and politicians (Elchardus and Spruyt 2016).

The opinion of experts and politicians is worth more than that of ordinary people.*

Ordinary people's opinions are more honest than that of experts and politicians.

Common sense is worth more than a formal education.

The best politicians are those who come from the common people.

The worst politicians are those who come from the common people.*

Homogeneous people and general will

The politicians in Congress need to follow the will of the people (Hawkins, Riding, and Mudde 2012).

We don't need politicians in Congress to follow the will of the people.*

The will of the people should be the highest principle in this country's politics.

The people, and not the politicians, should make our most important policy decisions (Akkerman, Mudde, and Zaslove 2014).

Politicians, and not the people, should make our most important policy decisions.*

The ordinary people are divided by many different values* (Stanley 2011).

Politicians might argue but ordinary people agree with each other (Schulz et al. 2017).

Political institutions that block the people's will should have no place in politics.

Political institutions should be there to block the people's will.*

Referendums are the ultimate measure of the will of the people.

There's no such a thing as "the will of the people."*

We cannot know what "the people" wants, even with elections.*

Only the people can make our country strong again.

Ordinary people can't be trusted to make the right choices about our nation's problems.*

In a democracy, the will of the majority should prevail.

In a democracy, minority rights need to be protected even if those views are unpopular.*

Politicians should always listen closely to the problems of the people (Elchardus and Spruyt 2016).

Anti-elitism

All governments, and the elites that live off them, want to control public opinion (Dryzek and Berejikian 1993).

The power of a few special interests prevents our country from making progress (Hawkins, Riding, and Mudde 2012).

Elected politicians sell out to various interest groups.

Elected politicians sell out to big business.

We shouldn't tolerate all these elected politicians selling out to big business.

Elected politicians should always remain loyal to their voters.

Politicians seek power for its own sake.

Most politicians seek power to serve others.*

Politicians do not want to improve the lives of ordinary people.

Regardless of the party in power, all governments just favor the bigwigs.

Politicians spend all of their time getting re-elected or reappointed – (rephrased from Agger, Goldstein, and Pearl 1961).

Politicians should spend less time thinking of reelection and more working for the people.

Not all politicians are the same; some genuinely care about what the people want* (Stanley 2011).

The people's demands are ignored in favor of what benefits the establishment (Stavrakakis, Andreadis, and Katsambekis 2017, Andreadis and Stavrakakis 2017).

People are often manipulated by politicians, and it is wrong (Agger, Goldstein, and Pearl 1961).

Politicians should never manipulate the people*.

Members of Congress quickly lose touch with ordinary people (Schulz et al. 2017).

Politicians are not really interested in what people like me think (Schulz et al. 2017).

Politicians are actually interested in what people like me think.*

People should stop reelecting politicians who don't care about what we think.

Quite a few of the people running the government are crooked (adapted from the American National Election Study – ANES).

Hardly any of the people running the government are crooked.* (adapted from ANES).

The government is pretty much run by a few big interests looking out for themselves (adapted ANES).

The government is run for the benefit of all the people (adapted from ANES).*

Manichaean outlook

Politics is a struggle between good and evil (Hawkins, Riding, and Mudde 2012).

What people call "compromise" in politics is really just selling out on one's principles (Akkerman, Mudde, and Zaslove 2014).

Sometimes it is necessary to make compromises in politics.*

Our country is at a crossroad, and there is only one correct way to go.

[Country]'s survival depends on us making the right choice in the next elections.

[Country]'s survival is not at stake in the next elections.*

Political decisions made in this country will change the lives of people all around the world.

Political decisions made in this country have little impact on the lives of people around the world.*

People I disagree with politically are driven solely by greed.

The ideals of the people I disagree with politically are devastating for society.

I do not consider the people whom I disagree with my political enemies.*

In politics, you have to keep your guard up when dealing with people you disagree with.

The people I disagree with politically are not evil.*

The people I disagree with politically are just misinformed.*

You can tell if a person is good or bad if you know their politics.

You can't tell if a person is good or bad just by knowing their politics.*

In politics, everyone wants what they think is best for the country.*

I would stop talking to a friend who had unacceptable political opinions.

I would never stop talking to a friend because of their political opinions.*

The difference between me and those who support other parties is that I care about what's good for everyone.

There is only one relevant division in politics: those who care for the people and those who care only for themselves.

Strong leader

Politicians should lead rather than follow the people (Akkerman, Mudde, and Zaslove 2014).

Politicians should follow rather than lead the people.*

What our country needs is a leader who will be respected by other governments.

What our country needs is a leader who will be admired.

What our country needs is a strong, determined President who will crush evil and set us on the right path again (Funke 2005).

I would not object if our country was temporarily ruled by an unelected official to solve difficult problems (Spruyt 2014).

The Congress slows down the work of our presidents, and should be ignored (LAPOP 2006).

Our presidents cannot ignore the Congress, even when it delays the work of the president* (LAPOP 2006).

Judges frequently hinder the work of presidents, and they should be ignored (LAPOP 2006).

Even when judges hinder the work of presidents, their decisions should be obeyed* (LAPOP 2006).

Our presidents should have the necessary power so that they can act in favor of the national interest (LAPOP 2006).

The power of the president should be limited so that they do not endanger our liberties* (LAPOP 2006).

Our presidents should do what the people want even when the laws prohibit him from doing it. (LAPOP)

Our presidents should obey the laws even when the people don't like it* (LAPOP).

Simple, direct style

Elected officials talk too much and take too little action (Akkerman, Mudde, and Zaslove 2014).

It is important that elected officials deeply discuss issues before taking action.*

I prefer politicians who tell it how it is.

The leading principle of political decision-making should be common-sense and not complicated political solutions.

Political solutions are usually complex, and there is little space for common-sense in decision making.*

"Liberal" and "Conservative" are not helpful categories for finding policy solutions.

Politicians should spend less time behind their desks, and more among ordinary people (Elchardus and Spruyt 2016).

Politicians don't have to spend time among ordinary people to do a good job.*

In politics, it's enough for me that someone gets the job done; I don't care how or why (adapted from "The Need for Cognition Scale," Cacioppo and Petty 1982).

In politics, the way something gets done is as important as the result.*

There are no easy or simple solutions in politics.*

I prefer a politician who I would like to sit down and grab a drink with.

It's important for a political leader be like the people he or she represents.

I prefer politicians who I feel like I could get to know as a person.

Right-wing populism

In this country, liberal intellectuals are the real enemy of the people.

In this country, liberal intellectuals are on the side of the people.*

The government and the elite it serves are the cause of the people's problems.

The government can solve people's problems.*

UN leaders want to strip our country of its sovereignty.

The United Nations is a conspiracy with the goal of destroying nation-states.

Government officials use their power only to mess with people's lives.

Government officials use their power to try to improve people's lives.*

People who pay no taxes should have no say in how this country is run.

People who pay no taxes still deserve a say in how this country is run.*

If I think of real Americans, I think mostly of the middle class.

Every citizen is part of the "American people."*

Left-wing populism

International financial institutions colonize our country and accumulate wealth by exploiting the people.

Big corporations are the ones really running this country.

Big corporations don't have a strong influence on how this country is run.*

Big corporations accumulate wealth by exploiting the people.

If big corporations accumulate wealth, that's because they produce useful things.*

We need to take the country back from the hands of Wall Street.

Our politics is hostage to the interests of a military-industrial complex.

Politics is divided between the haves and the have-nots.

The so-called division between the haves and the have-nots is really just an illusion.*

The unemployed, underemployed, marginalized groups – these are the real people who should have more voice in politics.

The unemployed, underemployed and marginalized groups already have enough voice in politics.*

The influence of big money in our politics is overstated.*

Part II

Testing the ideational theory

8 Populist mobilization across time and space

Hans-Georg Betz

In the Spanish municipal elections of May 2015, the incumbent mayors of Madrid and Barcelona, both from established parties, suffered a smarting defeat. Both were replaced by the candidates of a broad coalition of left-wing groups, which, in turn, crucially depended on the support of Podemos, a new radical left-leaning movement. Podemos was founded in January 2014 by a group of intellectuals and academics. Within a few months, Podemos developed into a formidable challenge to the Spanish political establishment. Between August and November 2014, support in the polls rose from 11 to 28 percent, way ahead of the two major established parties, the conservative People's Party (PP) and the Socialist Workers' Party (PSOE). The two parliamentary elections of December 2015 and June 2016 (both ending in a stalemate) confirmed Podemos' pivotal position in Spain's revamped party system, but also exposed the party's weaknesses and limited appeal. In the June election, Podemos failed both to surpass PSOE (albeit by a very narrow margin) and establish itself as the leader of the left-wing camp and to overcome widespread hostility inside PSOE to forge a coalition with Podemos. In the end, PSOE preferred tolerating a PP minority government to coming to terms with Podemos.

Podemos's dramatic rise in 2014 and 2015 and PSOE's growing hostility to the political newcomer both have a lot to do with Podemos' populist strategy. In fact, before engaging in politics, several prominent current and former members of the movement's top echelon had closely studied the most recent wave of populism in Latin America, and one even advised several left-wing populist governments in the region. Podemos's incursion into Spain's relatively stable party system is emblematic of the potential of populist mobilization in established liberal democracies. According to Robert Jansen, populist mobilization occurs when popular mobilization – the mobilization of "ordinarily marginalized social sectors into publicly visible and contentious political action" – gets infused with populist rhetoric – an anti-elitist discourse "that valorizes ordinary people" (Jansen 2011, 83). Jansen's analytical framework jibes well with the ideational approach informing this volume and its focus on the central position of ideas for the understanding of populism. It also throws light on the importance of discourse and framing. From this perspective, the success of populist mobilization depends to a large extent on the ability of populist movements to function both as "carriers and transmitters of mobilizing beliefs and ideas" and as "signifying agents" that are "actively engaged in the production of meaning for participants, antagonists, and observers" (Snow and Bedford 1988, 198).

In what follows, I apply this broad framework to the analysis of five cases of successful populist mobilization across time and space: late nineteenth-century American agrarian populism (the People's Party); the short-lived episode of *boulangisme* that occurred at roughly the same time in France; the Gaitanista movement in 1940s Colombia; and the upsurge of the Lega Nord in the early 1990s in northern Italy, and Podemos' irruption onto the Spanish political scene in 2014. In terms of their core constituency, these movements are highly diverse: Midwestern and Southern farmers in the United States; urban workers in France; the poor and marginal in Colombia; entrepreneurial producers in the affluent regions of Northern Italy; and a young and better educated urban population in Spain. Ideologically, the five movements arguably span the whole of the political spectrum.[1] Yet, all of these movements proved highly successful – at least for a short while – in mobilizing significant parts of the electorate on the basis of a common discourse centered on the notion of social justice. With this discourse, all of these movements not only managed to seriously challenge the political establishment but also to profoundly impact on the politics of their respective countries.

In the remainder of this chapter, I will explore the core points informing the populist discourse of each of these movements. I hope to demonstrate that successful populist mobilization crucially depends on populist actors' ability to invoke a distinct "discursive and stylistic repertoire" consisting of a limited "set of relatively standardized elements" that have historically evolved and "are well-known to, and available to be drawn on by, political actors" (Brubaker 2017, 4–5). The core elements of the repertoire of populist contestation are the appeal to, and arousal of, morally relevant emotions, such as anger, wrath, indignation and resentment (Haidt 2003; for their saliency for contemporary populism see Salmela and von Scheve 2017); and a morally based discourse that, in the name of ordinary, hard-working people, evokes notions of social justice and fairness, both directed against what is framed as a self-serving political establishment in collusion with parasitic economic and financial elites. Whether or not this repertoire of populist contestation gets activated is to a large extent contingent on favorable circumstances (what Hawkins and Rovira Kaltwasser in the Introduction call an "appropriate context"). I hope to show that the case studies that follow will allow us better to understand the conditions conducive to successful populist mobilization.[2]

Episode 1: the People's Party

The populist movement of the 1880s and 1890s emerged from the farms and rural communities in the South and Midwest of the United States. It grew out of the postbellum associations formed by farmers (the Alliance and the Grange) to promote cooperation and increase the farmers' bargaining power vis-à-vis banks, middlemen (such as grain elevator operators), and the railroads. In the late 1880s, farmers faced progressively worsening economic conditions. The reason was that agricultural goods bought "fewer and fewer industrial goods" (Verdier 1994, 116). Although falling shipping rates resulted in American grain flooding the European markets, American farmers (and particularly those in the Western frontier regions) saw small gains from the increased demand for their products. To make things worse, starting in early 1893, the United States entered the worst depression the country had hitherto experienced. It lasted for four years. Many farmers, already indebted and overburdened by mortgages, lost their farms in foreclosures (Steeples and Whitten 1998).

Confronted with a dramatic deterioration of their economic situation, the farmers' movement turned into an agrarian revolt, which quickly found political expression in the form of a political party, the People's Party. The new party's main political demand was for the government to relax its tight monetary policy and embark on a course of monetary inflation to redress the country's economic problems. This policy targeted primarily cash-strapped farmers, who hoped it would raise the price of their products and increase their income, but it also would have benefited the western mining states rich in silver deposits. The movement culminated in the 1896 presidential election, which saw the Democratic candidate, William Jennings Bryan, run on a populist "free-silver ticket." Bryan's defeat in the election marked the beginning of the end of the populist movement, with many leading populist politicians defecting to the Republicans and Democrats.

The agrarian revolt flared up at a time of profound socioeconomic transformation, which Mark Twain called the "Gilded Age." This was a time where the "traumas of technological innovation, expansion of corporate power, and commercial and cultural globalization" caused deep anxieties; where deflation and successive periods of deep recessions left many Americans fearing for their livelihood; where corporations "grew exponentially amid traumatic spasms of global capitalist development; where "a prosperous section of the middle class grew more comfortable and hard times pressed on most everyone else; and where government, largely subservient to business interests, did little to alleviate the anxieties of ordinary Americans" (Postel 2007, vii).

The fleeting success of agrarian populism was fanned by a deep-seated sense of injustice. As Mary Lease from Kansas put it in 1891, this was "no longer a government of the people, by the people, and for the people, but a government of Wall Street, by Wall Street, and for Wall Street." This was a country where the "common people are robbed to enrich their masters," where a few handful of men owned more wealth than all the paupers of the land together (Lease 1984, 106). An editorial in the Populist *Kansas Agitator* from the same year similarly charged that

> America (. . .) legislates for Wall street alone, creating conditions that take away from the poor the little that they have, and transferring it to the rich, and the "land of the free and the home of the brave" will soon be the "home of the rich and the land of the slave."[3]

The People's Party's "Omaha Platform" from 1892 expressed a profound disenchantment with a nation where "the fruits of the toil of millions [were] boldly stolen to build up colossal fortunes for a few" who "despise[d] the republic and endanger[ed] liberty;" where the "prolific womb of governmental injustice" was breeding "two great classes — tramps and millionaires."[4]

The populists' anger was directed primarily against corporate power. In the words of Tom Watson from Georgia, populism was foremost "the protest of the plundered against the plunderers – of the victim against the robbers" (Watson 1975, 23). At the same time, it was a protest against the State, the two major parties, and the political establishment in general. They were charged with having failed to protect ordinary people from the severe stresses caused by economic turmoil and dislocations while allowing themselves to become tools in the hands of big business and urban America. For Watson, populism was a creed that stood for "the doctrine that Government belongs to the governed and not to the governors," that government was created for the people and not "for the benefit of those in office." Populism was "antagonism to class legislation and to special privilege," its main objective "to check the tendency which concentrates political power and all material prosperity in the hands of the few" and "to restore the Government system of our fathers" (Watson 1905, 257, 259).

The populists considered themselves heirs and champions of Jeffersonian republican virtue against rampant political corruption and monopoly power (Cantrell 2010, 57). At the same time, they evoked a Jeffersonian "producerist" ethos:[5] Leading populists extolled the virtue of economic independence threatened by "bankers, speculators, and loan-sharking merchants – parasites who produced nothing but made money only by manipulating it, sucking the lifeblood from the honest labor of farmers, mechanics" and others engaged in productive labor (Lears 2009, 156). What the populists envisioned was the establishment of genuine economic democracy, "where opportunity was equal, where the distribution of the nation's wealth was equitable" (Nugent 1963, 236).

Despite their somewhat nostalgic vision, the populists were hardly antimodernist reactionaries. Their hostility to the railroads, for instance, was not inspired by Luddism, but by their objection to the abuse of economic power at the expense of farmers and workers. This led them to argue for new rules and regulations that would finally force the railroads to "deliver on their promise of faster, cheaper, and more equitable access to global markets." The same was true for industrialization. What the populists feared was that industrialization would lead to a massive transfer of economic – and ultimately political – power from erstwhile small, independent producers to a small group of plutocrats. In response, the populists advanced a range of radical solutions. Perhaps most radical of all was the notion that railroads and other monopolies should be owned and operated by the people via their government (Peffer 1899). This, of course, exposed them immediately to the charge of being socialists – or worse.

Yet, what the populists envisioned was a fundamental reform of the system, rather than its demise. This was a vision of an alternative way toward a modern, progressive industrial-capitalist America, more inclusive and cooperative, based on an educated, politically aware citizenry and an active government serving the people and controlled by them (via referenda and initiatives) rather than one that acted as an agency of a small "corporative and wealthy minority" (Postel 2007, 288). Dismissed as "wild-eyed, rattlebrained fanatics," cranks, and fools "who advocated communism" and to a large extent crushed by the defeat of 1896, the populists nevertheless scored a major and lasting victory.[6] In the decades that followed many of their central demands (e.g., the introduction of a graduated income tax, the regulation of the railroads, the direct election of senators by popular vote) were successively enacted by progressively-minded administrations. As Mary Lease noted in 1915, the seed that the populist movement had sown in the late nineteenth century, had fallen fertile ground (Jaycox 2005, 88).

Episode 2: the Boulangist crisis

The "Boulanger Affair" came to its final end in September 1891, when General Georges Boulanger, once an acclaimed war hero and Minister of War, committed suicide on the tomb of his mistress in Brussels, his chosen exile. This was an ignominious end for a man who just a few years earlier had been hailed as the "man of Providence" destined to fundamentally revolutionize the political landscape of the French Third Republic (1870–1940). Instead, the Boulangist movement fizzled out as quickly as it had risen to prominence, way before Boulanger's death. Yet, despite its ephemeral nature, *boulangisme* left a deep and lasting imprint on French politics.

The "Boulanger adventure" started in 1886, when the general was nominated Minister of War at the suggestion of the Radical deputy Georges Clemenceau who appreciated Boulanger's republican convictions, a rarity in a military still largely dominated by monarchist elements. A "charismatic hero on horseback" who understood how to appeal to Parisian crowds, Boulanger soon seemed to confirm all of the negative sentiments Jules Ferry, the former two-time prime minister, had expressed at the time of Boulanger's nomination (Conklin, Fishman and Zaretsky 2015, 84). For Ferry, Boulanger was nothing but an "audacious demagogue and seductive orator," a "dangerous actor" endued with an "immense vanity" and a gigantic sense of self-importance – and that was only half of the story. The other half, Ferry warned, was a "rare intelligence at the service of unlimited ambition," which informed a "well-conceived plan" that the general unrelentingly pursued (cited in Pisani-Ferry 1969, 55). Boulanger's ministerial colleagues soon came to share Ferry's judgment. In the spring of 1887, Boulanger was relieved of his duties and sent to the provinces. Soon thereafter he was forced to retire from the military and thus released into civilian life, which, ironically, allowed him to reenter political life.

Starting in 1888, Boulanger's allies put his name on a series of by-election ballots, all of which he easily won, to a large extent because of the support he garnered among royalist conservatives (Irvine 1988, 397). The Boulangist wave crested in January 1889, which saw Boulanger carry the day in a hotly contested by-election in Paris against an alliance of opponents united for the sole goal of his defeat. At this crucial point, Boulanger's entourage urged the general to act and dare a coup d'état against the parliamentary regime. Boulanger, however, was not convinced, believing instead that the upcoming general election to be held in the fall of 1889 would sweep him into power. A serious miscalculation. Aware of the danger posed by the Boulangist movement, all of the general's political adversaries banded together "using every means possible, legal and extra-legal, to liquidate *boulangisme* before the September–October election" (Winock 2004, 271). Boulanger was charged by the Minister of the Interior with conspiracy and treason, and issued a warrant of arrest. Instead of facing his detractors, the general chose to flee the country, seeking refuge in Brussels and London. Deprived of its icon, the Boulangist movement was soundly defeated in the fall election and soon disappeared from the political landscape of the Third Republic.

The Boulangist movement owed its dynamic to its ability to mobilize a panoply of disparate groups ranging from provincial peasants to Parisian workers, from staunch monarchists to far-left socialists (Passmore 2012, 45–72). What united all of these groups was their revulsion against "a ruling body monopolized by a corrupt oligarchy." As a populist movement it "sought to give vent to a *vox populi* that had been stifled by parliamentarism" while promoting its leader as the man of Providence who, "in the role of metaphorical Hercules, would clean the Augean stables" (Winock 2000, 14). Boulanger advertised himself as "the protest candidate of all democrats against this parliamentary regime, which debases France, disgraces the Republic, and assassinates *la patrie*."[7] The Boulangist populist mobilization derived its impetus from the confluence of several crises which compromised the legitimacy of the parliamentary regime. One was psychological: France's catastrophic defeat at the hand of the Prussians in the Franco–Prussian war and its loss of Alsace-Lorraine. The traumatism of the national disaster gave rise to wide-spread sentiments of revenge. Among its most prominent champions were Paul Déroulède, leader of the League of Patriots, and the journalist cum novelist Maurice Barrès, both of them prominent figures in the Boulangist movement (Sternhell 1972, ch. 2). What united these sentiments was both a profound sense of national humiliation and an obsession with retaking the two lost provinces from the Germans.

A second was socioeconomic: The 1880s were marked by a severe depression, which affected both agriculture and industry, with devastating social consequences. Under increasing pressure from new competitors in the international market, France suffered from a precipitous fall of its exports. At the same time, French agriculture experienced dramatic losses as a result of competition from cheap imports from overseas. French industry, in turn, faltered, partly because of protectionist barriers keeping French manufactures out of major markets (e.g. the United States), partly because French industrial productivity and technological innovation fell behind its main competitors (Levy-Leboyer and Bourguignon 1985, 43–53). Workers and peasants bore the brunt of the depression, with the threat of unemployment and poverty omnipresent. Paris alone, in 1883, counted more than 200,000 unemployed (Bonin 1987, 516; Garrigues 1992, 3–5). In response, social tensions significantly mounted, revealing the extent to which French society had become divided.

The anxieties and animosities engendered by these crises led to profound and widespread disenchantment with the governing Republican elite, which soon turned into a repudiation of the parliamentary regime. On the one hand, there was growing disgust with a government that seemed far too accommodating to Bismarck; on the other hand, there was deeply felt anger toward those in charge who appeared to be indifferent to the suffering of ordinary people and dragging their feet on the question of social reform. The Boulangist movement benefited from both. Boulanger not only promoted himself as the resolute defender of French national pride in the face of German provocation; he also marketed himself as a man of the people, who, as his 1888 program claimed, sided with those desperately looking for work. The resulting Boulangist synthesis of proto-socialism, populism, and nationalism greatly appealed to disadvantaged groups in society and helped to diffuse socialism in France (Sternhell 1978, 79). It mattered little that Boulanger's program was rather short on concrete measures to alleviate the socio-economic crisis (Sternhell 1971, 85–89; Garrigues 2012, 238–248). What there was, was primarily directed against competition from foreign labor – an issue, which would dominate the national populist agenda of left-wing Boulangists, such as Maurice Barrès, in the 1890s (Dornel 2014, 151–154).

This was hardly surprising. *Boulangisme* was rooted in traditional radical republicanism (the Boulangist deputies sat on the far left in parliament), yet largely dependent on the financial support of royalist sponsors. Therefore *boulangisme* could not but promote itself as ideologically amorphous – neither left nor right. What the various Boulangist tendencies had in common was their fundamental rejection of the existing parliamentary regime in the name of a radical republicanism (Garrigues 2013; Winock 2001, 135). Boulangist propaganda was relentless in attacking the parliamentary regime, characterized as a corrupt oligarchy; an assembly of irresponsible, ineffective "*tripoteurs*" (shady dealers), indifferent to the concerns of ordinary people; thieves and "vampires" (in collusion with "Israelite" circles – an association increasingly evoked by the Boulangist propaganda) accused of sucking out what was best in France and leading the country to ruin.[8] Corruption scandals did their part to lend credence to the charge that this was a "republic of thieves" desperately in need of a national savior who would sweep out the stable (the broom was the symbol of the Boulangist movement) and clean up the mess, thus bringing about national renewal and restoring honor to the republic (Angenot 1989, ch. 33). To accomplish this goal, *boulangisme* advanced a "heterodox democratic project" of a "plebiscitary and integrative democracy underpinning a strong state legitimized by universal suffrage" (Hermet 2001, 182).

Boulangisme represented the prototype of successful populist mobilization at a crucial period of transition from an elite-dominated politics to mass politics. Backed by financially potent royalist sponsors (notably the Duchess of Uzès), the Boulangists were in a position to far outspend their political rivals. The general's 1889 campaign was masterfully orchestrated by Georges Thiébaud, a leading Bonapartist figure who "employed all the techniques of modern mass politics – advertising, sloganeering, spectacle – to fasten the public attention on the General's personality" (Nord 2005, 303). The campaign employed dozens of billposters to plaster the walls of the city with millions of posters extolling the general (Angenot 1989, ch. 33). At the same time, peddlers were sent out into the countryside to distribute a whole slew of visual propaganda material, ranging from "brilliantly colored" portraits of the General on horseback to iconographic depictions of the General, "draped in the Tricolor, nailed to the cross" (Burns 1984, 70). The Boulangist press disseminated dozens of poems, commissioned by a close friend and financier of Boulanger, glorifying "*notre brav' général.*" And "an army of ambulant merchants" set out to hawk the text of popular songs eulogizing Boulanger (Angenot 2010, 11; Garrigues 2010, 17–19).

Boulanger's triumph in the election marked the height of a populist marketing campaign aimed at mobilizing widespread popular sentiments of socioeconomic malaise and channeling them against the political regime. The results revealed the extent of disenchantment among the popular classes – and particularly urban workers – who in large numbers defected from the established left parties to Boulanger: The Boulanger strongholds were predominantly located in the working-class areas of Paris and the industrial suburbs (Garrigues 2012, 245). Of the 44 seats the Boulangist movement won in 1889, a third was elected by the popular classes of Paris and its suburbs (Brunet 1998, 284).

Despite its rapid decline following Boulanger's flight into exile, the Boulangist movement left a significant mark on the subsequent history of French politics. As a popular movement that "took seriously the task of integrating the 'people' into the political process, *boulangisme* prefigured the mass movements of the twentieth century" (Hutton 1976, 86). By challenging traditional hierarchies, the Boulangist movement awakened the "political consciousness of parts of the working class and facilitated their orientation towards socialism" (Brunet 1998, 284). In the process, the Boulangist crisis contributed to the consolidation of the reviled parliamentary system by effecting the "assimilation of the republic and the parliamentary regime" (Winock 2004, 273). This, in turn, forced both the far left and the monarchist right to abandon their dreams of establishing direct democracy (radical left) or restoring the monarchy (royalist right). At the same time, however, the Boulangist ideological blend of populist socialism, virulent nationalism and anti-parliamentarism infected with antisemitism prepared the ground for a modern far right, which would continue to pose a fundamental challenge to the democratic order.[9]

Episode 3: the Gaitanista movement

On April 9, 1948, Jorge Eliécer Gaitán, at the time one of Colombia's most prominent political figures, was shot dead in the streets of Bogotá by an apparently mentally instable gunman, himself lynched by an enraged crowd shortly after the assassination. Gaitán's murder triggered a massive riot in the capital (*el Bogotazo*), which resulted in hundreds of deaths and left the center of Bogotá in ruins. Gaitán's assassination had a lasting impact on the country. It killed the chance for an open, inclusive, and democratic society, marking instead the beginning of decades of persistent violence (Braun 1986).

Daniel Pécaut has characterized the Gaitanista movement as "one of the most characteristic examples of a populist configuration" (Pécaut 2000, 51). Yet it has commanded considerably less academic attention than the populist mobilizations in Argentina, Brazil,

Mexico, and Peru.[10] The Gaitanista movement, unlike similar movements elsewhere in Latin America, never established an organizational form or managed to get institutionalized. During the period of intense violence following Gaitán's assassination many of the movement's leaders met a violent death. Others took up arms and went underground.

Unlike other prominent populist leaders, Gaitán was a political insider. A leading, albeit unconventional, figure of Colombia's Liberal Party, Gaitán held a number of high-level positions, among them short stints as mayor of Bogota and minister of education. Yet, because of his modest origins, mestizo background (which earnt him the derogatory epithet "*negro Gaitán*" from his detractors) and heterodox socialist convictions, Gaitán was very much of an outsider in the party. For much of his career, Gaitán sought to transcend the rigid bipolarization (i.e., Liberals versus Conservatives) that characterized Colombia's political system. He even founded an independent political movement with the intent "to push Liberalism left." After the Liberals appropriated much of his program, Gaitán returned to the Liberal fold (Green 1996, 289). In 1944, he started campaigning for the presidential election of 1946. However, his candidacy was largely undermined by the party leadership, which instead chose the mainstream Gabriel Turbay as its official candidate. In response, Gaitán launched a massive popular mobilization, promoting himself as the "people's candidate" who would bring about a moral and democratic restoration of the republic. With the Liberal vote divided between the two candidates, the party lost the election to the Conservatives. The following year, after finally gaining control of the party Gaitán launched a new mass mobilization supposed to win him the presidential election of 1950 – a campaign tragically cut short by his assassination.

Like other populist movements in Latin America, *gaitanismo* derived its impetus from its full frontal assault of the "oligarchy," defined primarily as the country's political class. In typically populist fashion, the Gaitanista discourse pitted the oligarchy, a small, corrupt, "unproductive and meritless elite" against the vast majority of ordinary people, whose "productive impulses" were stifled by the oligarchy (Braun 1986, 101; Pécaut 2000, 54). Gaitán defined the resulting antagonism in terms of a fundamental confrontation between the "political country" (*el país politico*), i.e., the oligarchy, and the "national country" (*el país nacional*), i.e., the people (*el pueblo*). In this way, Gaitán not only established the distinction between oligarchy and ordinary people, but also elevated the people in moral terms, reflected in the slogan "the people are superior to their leaders" (*el pueblo es superior a sus dirigentes*). At the same time, *gaitanismo* sought to transcend the political partisan divisions and unite the people behind the Gaitanista project. As Gaitán famously put it, there was no difference between "the malaria of the liberal peasants and the malaria of the conservatives" (Tahar Chaouch 2009, 256; Pécaut 2000, 53). Both shared misery and a common enemy – the oligarchy, which was only interested in enriching itself and couldn't care less about the plight of ordinary people.

Gaitanismo arose at a time of profound change throughout most of Latin America which, albeit to a lesser extent than other countries, also affected Colombia. Industrialization and urbanization engendered far-reaching socio-structural and socio-cultural transformations. These generated new pressures on the political system to which the political establishment was loath to respond. In addition, worsening economic conditions reflected in a dramatic rise in the cost of living increased popular disaffection with those in power.[11] Against that, *gaitanismo* offered a relatively comprehensive and coherent vision for the modernization of the country, which Gaitán promoted in numerous speeches. Central to this vision was a staunch belief in social justice as a precondition for democracy and social progress (Green 1996, 305). As the movement's political platform of 1947 put it, political democracy presupposed economic democracy (Sharpless 1978, 131). As long as the people lacked the basics in terms of health, education, and economic power, they lacked the fundamental capabilities necessary to participate in the political process.

In order to promote social and economic progress, *gaitanismo* advocated a strong, interventionist state that was in a position to promote industrial and agricultural development and implement major economic and social policies. Many of its proposals aimed at directing investments into productive enterprises that would create employment and contribute to economic growth. At the same time, the program called for the protection of domestic industry, the prohibition of monopolies, and the introduction of price controls on basic necessities, such as food staples, transportation, and rents (Dix 1978, 346; Sharpless 1978, 132). Although objectively, this mixture of regulation and intervention was hardly radical, it would have entailed a dramatic departure from the existing model and thus posed a far-reaching challenge to the political establishment (Molano Camargo 2008).

During the short span of its existence, the Gaitanista movement managed to mobilize a broad range of social groups, both urban and rural. Gaitán's appeal to the masses stemmed to a large extent from his ability to address ordinary people in their own words and in terms of their every-day experiences. An indefatigable orator, Gaitán had the ability to use "words as weapons," and create a "symbiotic relationship between himself and the crowd," reflected in his famous slogan, "*Yo no soy un hombre, yo soy un pueblo*" (Braun, 1986, 99–103). The appeal of the Gaitanista mobilization derived also from Gaitán's ability to accord his followers recognition and dignity. Thus he insisted that the "crowds on the streets," which the political establishment both despised and feared, constituted a vital part of true democracy. Social justice and the integration of the outsiders of Colombian society thus constituted the main tenets of *gaitanismo* (Braun 1986, 102; Green 1996, 305; de la Torre 2010, 17).

Episode 4: the Lega Nord

In April 2012, Umberto Bossi, until then the undisputed leader of the Italian Lega Nord, resigned his position as the Federal Secretary of the party in response to financial irregularities benefiting members of his own family. This was rather ironic, given the fact that the Lega Nord owed its dramatic rise in Italian politics in the early 1990s to a considerable degree to the corruption scandals that led to the collapse of the postwar party system and the disappearance of the major established parties. It took the party some time to recover from the fallout of the financial scandal and Bossi's resignation and reestablish itself as a major force in Italian politics. By 2015, the Lega Nord had not only regained much of its former strength in its traditional strongholds in northern Italy but made significant inroads in other parts of the country.

The Lega Nord is the result of the merger of various regional leagues that emerged in northern Italy at the end of the 1970s (Liga Veneta) and the early 1980s (Lega Lombarda). In late 1989, Umberto Bossi, who headed the Lega Lombarda, proposed to form a single organization, the Lega Nord. The merger was ratified at the new party's first federal congress in 1991, shortly after the Lega Lombarda's dramatic gains in the regional elections of 1990 in Lombardy and a significant upsurge of support for the other leagues in the rest of the north. Shortly after its foundation, the Lega Nord started its mobilization campaign for the upcoming parliamentary election of 1992. The campaign gained momentum from a series of revelations of massive political corruption (aka Tangentopoli), which led to the arrest of a growing number of local and national politicians, extensively covered on TV.

The scandals contributed to an "electoral earthquake," with the Lega Nord gaining a fifth of the vote in a number of northern regions, largely at the expense of the Christian Democrats and Socialists. The ensuing collapse of the political establishment and its replacement by new political movements, most prominently among them Silvio Berlusconi's Forza Italia, promised new opportunities for the Lega Nord for the new parliamentary elections to be held in 1994. Despite the fact, however, that as a result of the Lega Nord's alliance with Berlusconi, the party did well in the elections, Bossi soon came to realize that Berlusconi's popularity threatened to substantially erode the Lega Nord's support base. After a number of attempts to gain room to maneuver, Bossi decided that his best option was to throw in his lot with Berlusconi. The resulting alliance was short-lived. Within a few months, Bossi broke with Berlusconi and led the Lega Nord into splendid political isolation, a strategy that proved largely counterproductive. Self-imposed isolation not only made the Lega largely irrelevant as a potential coalition partner, it also reduced the party's appeal at the polls and provoked acrimonious splits among the party leadership (Albertazzi and McDonnell 2015, 35–36). By 2001, Bossi was ready to reverse his position and enter a political and personal alliance with Berlusconi, which would last until Bossi's resignation in 2012.

The Lega Nord's campaigns of the early 1990s combined virtually all elements of a typical populist mobilization: a charismatic leader, who instead of resorting to the aloof and purposefully obscure diction typical of the traditional Italian political class, used ordinary language, often interlaced with vulgarities to appeal to ordinary people; a discourse that clearly identified what had gone wrong in the country and who was to be blamed for it; and finally the presentation of a straightforward, easily understood remedy supposed to solve all the problems. As Bossi relentlessly maintained, the Lega had one central objective, the radical transformation of the Italian political system (Bossi with Vimercati 1993, 143). This meant the dissolution of the Italian centralized state to be replaced by a modern federalist one. Federalism was not only supposed to resolve the main problems plaguing the north, such as the transfer of resources via taxes from the productive north to the rest of the country; it was also supposed to break the political class's monopolistic hold on power, eliminate the existing system of clientelism and patronage (represented as "*Roma Ladrona*" in Lega propaganda) and replace the existing "partitocracy" with a genuine "democracy for the citizens" (Bossi 1998). The Lega program, Bossi maintained, aimed at bringing about a comprehensive revolution, involving all aspects of the Italian institutional, socioeconomic, sociocultural, and sociopolitical system. Its ultimate objective: to advance the cause of liberty, which, in Bossi's view, had replaced social justice as "the engine of history" (Bossi with Vimercati 1993, 15). In practical terms, the promotion of liberty meant above all freeing the productive forces in the advanced north from the burden inflicted on them by Italy's unproductive, protected, and subsidized sectors (Bossi with Vimercati 1993, 179–180). In case of failure, there was only one alternative – outright secession of the northern regions.

The electoral success of the Lega Nord during the early period of populist mobilization at the beginning of the 1990s depended to a large extent on Bossi's ability to articulate what Ilvo Diamanti has characterized as "*il male del nord*" (Diamanti 1996). With his aura of credibility and authenticity, Bossi managed to articulate the diffuse sentiments of disaffection and resentment that pervaded large parts of northern society – with respect to the established political parties, the shortcomings of the bureaucracy and infrastructure, widespread corruption, the Mezzogiorno, and, last but not least, the growing number of immigrants from outside the EU (*extracomunitari*) (Schmidtke and Ruzza 1993, 8;

Woods 1995, 197). In quintessentially populist fashion, Bossi constructed a narrative, which pitted "honest, hard-working and simple-living northern Italians attached to their local traditions" against a parasitic political establishment that by exploiting the North perpetuated its hold on power (Albertazzi and McDonnell 2015, 43).

The Lega adopted the question of immigration right early on and quickly established itself as the most intransigent advocate of highly restrictive immigration controls. For, as Bossi wrote in 1992, a country that was not in a position to provide enough resources for its own people, hardly was in a position to offer these resources "to millions of immigrants." If Italy had opened its doors to "a million of potential unemployed," it was because there was a lack of "political will" to stem the tide. There obviously was a plan to transform Italy into a "multiracial, multi-ethnic, and multi-religious society," which, Bossi charged, was "closer to hell than to paradise" (Bossi 1992, 147).

Immigration was already an issue for the Lega Nord in the early 1990s. At the time, however, the primary target of populist resentment were Southern Italians (particularly those who had come to settle in the north). As it became clear that the party's main objective, federalism, was not going to be attained and that there was not going to be a revolution, the party increasingly made immigration a central issue for mobilization in order to boost its electoral support. At the same time, the Lega Nord established itself firmly in the institutional structure of Berlusconi's republic, its organization getting increasingly dependent on public financial support. The party's newspaper, *La Padania*, alone, received more than 50 million euros between 1997 and 2013 from what once was denounced as "*Roma ladrona*" (Giurato and Pitoni 2015).

Episode 5: Podemos

As indicated above, Podemos was founded in 2014 by intellectuals and academics (most prominently Pablo Iglesias, Íñigo Errejón, and Juan Carlos Monedero), as a movement of the populist left. They drew their inspiration from three sources: first, the experience of Latin American neopopulist movements in Venezuela, Bolivia and Equador; second, from the organizational strategies of the *indignados* (aka Movimiento 15-M) movement, which, starting in spring 2011, launched a series of demonstrations against the austerity politics of the conservative Rajoy government; and third, from social theorists such as Antonio Gramsci and Ernesto Laclau, whose conceptual work on hegemony (Gramsci) and the "formation of an internal antagonistic frontier" (Laclau) provided central building blocks for a political strategy of populist insurgency.

The initial rise of Podemos has to be seen against the background of a profound post-2008 economic crisis, reflected in mass unemployment, particularly affecting the young, and levels of socioeconomic inequality that were higher than in any other country in Western Europe (Bolaños 2014).[12] The result was a deep political crisis, reflected in massive disaffection with the two major political parties, both marred by a series of major corruption scandals. As the country's leading newspaper put it in the summer of 2015, in Spain, corruption "is a characteristic of the system," pervading all major political parties as well as all major institutions (Álvarez Junco 2015). A survey taken at the time of the European elections showed that Spanish citizens ranked corruption and fraud second (36 percent) only to unemployment (81 percent) among the principal problems afflicting the country. Politicians and the political parties followed closely behind (26 percent) (CIS 2014a). In the course of the year, concern about corruption increased dramatically. In November, more than 60 percent ranked it among the most important problems (CIS 2014b). As a result, there was a massive increase in disenchantment with the political establishment, the political parties, and politics in general (Jurado 2014). Under these circumstances, Podemos's attack against the political class, which on the one hand relentlessly pursued a politics of austerity at the expense of ordinary citizens while lining its own pockets, fell on fertile ground. It was Podemos's self-declared goal to convert widespread public indignation into radical political change.[13]

The core of Podemos's strategy was to mobilize ordinary people, victimized by the economic crisis and government austerity policies, by bringing together disparate popular claims and demands and focusing them against a common enemy. In this way, the leaders of Podemos sought to provoke the establishment of Laclau's internal antagonistic frontier pitting ordinary people against the ruling class (to which Podemos referred as *la casta*), accused of governing "in the service of the economic elites" (Iglesias 2014a, 155; Errejón 2014a). The goal was to take over power from Spain's self-serving, corrupt elite, bring about a "post-neoliberal transformation via the state," make the country's institutions serve ordinary people and thus reestablish a measure of social justice (Iglesias 2015a, 15).

Crucial for the success of this strategy was, as Pablo Iglesias insisted, to break the dominant narrative (i.e., the cultural and political mechanisms used by the ruling class to justify the existing political and economic order), which secured *la casta* its hold on power and assured its political and cultural hegemony. For Podemos to win the struggle for hegemony and bring about real change, it would have to be able "to impose new interpretations of the situation and new possibilities of transformation" with the people (*el pueblo*) playing an active role (Iglesias 2015b). This strategy was informed by Podemos's "hypothesis," namely the notion that politics is essentially about the construction of meaning via discourse; that language and discourse represent fundamental battle grounds for contesting dominant narratives and constructing new collective identities; and that contestation had to be based on concrete claims and demands articulated by ordinary people (Errejón 2016; Errejón and Mouffe 2015).

At the time of its founding, the leaders of Podemos believed that there was a historical opportunity for political change because Spain was experiencing a "regime crisis." With movements such as the *indignados* challenging the dominant official narrative, there had opened up space for a populist discourse of the left. A political discourse, however, would only reach ordinary people, if it managed "to establish a certain identity between your analysis and what the majority feels," i.e., if it was inspired by common sense rather than dry, academic theory. The key to success lay in "making 'common sense' go in a direction of change" (Iglesias 2014b). This explains the central importance leadership has played in Podemos. In order to mobilize ordinary citizens for change, Podemos needed to translate "complex diagnostics" into easily understood narratives to be diffused via the media. This became the task of Pablo Iglesias, the telegenic leader of the party, whose prominent visibility in the media and ability to evoke "emotions and the symbolic" became the "most powerful communicative tool" for the party's populist campaigns (Errejón 2014b).

The party's results in the 2014 European elections – about 8 percent of the vote, which translated into five seats in the European Parliament – were a first indication that the strategy worked. In the months that followed, the party's mobilization generated a groundswell of support at the polls, which for a time elevated Podemos beyond the 25 percent mark. At the same time, some of its new narrative, such as the notion of *la casta*, entered the common vocabulary. Its analysis and demands provoked widespread debate in the mass media and forced the established parties to respond. The problems started with the parliamentary election of December 2015, which confirmed Podemos' strong position in the new Spanish party system, but also revealed its limitations. After a second disappointing result in the repeat election of 2016, open conflict erupted inside the party over the question of whether or not to maintain the party's populist strategic course. To be sure, the party had been instrumental in substantially challenging the logic and institutional arrangements of the post-Franco political system. In the process, however, it lost much of the impetus gained during the early period of populist mobilization.

The logic of populist mobilizations

In the remainder of this paper I will briefly explore what lessons can be drawn from the five cases outlined above with respect to the logic of populist mobilizations. Any analysis of instances of populist mobilization should start with an investigation of the contextual conditions and historical conjunctures that prepare their ground and allow them to flourish (Palacios 2011, 63). More often than not, populism is associated with socioeconomic crises, which quickly translate into political crises. As we have seen, late nineteenth-century agrarian populism in the United States and *boulangisme* in France occurred during a period of severe economic depressions; Podemos emerged in the wake of the Great Recession of 2008. In each of these cases, socioeconomic crisis quickly turned into a crisis of the established political parties and political representation in general. In the remaining two cases, populist mobilization was a direct response to a political crisis: Gaitanismo was part of a larger wave of populist mobilizations in Latin America, which was "intrinsically related to the crisis of these oligarchic regimes." A direct response to "a crisis of political incorporation" of newly emerging social groups, they represented "a democratizing reaction against the shortcomings of the liberal, representative regimes of the oligarchic order" (Peruzzotti 2013, 73). The rise of *leghismo* in northern Italy was intricately connected to the severe crisis of legitimacy of the postwar political system, which ultimate led to the collapse of the traditional party system. The electoral advances of the Lega Nord in the early 1990s coincided with monetary turbulences, following Italy's exist from the European Exchange Rate Mechanism (ERM) in the fall of 1992; a growing sovereign debt crisis (in 1992 national debt stood at over 100 percent of GDP and rapidly rising); and a progressive decline of Italy's competitiveness in the face of rising competition from Asia.

Populist mobilization relies to a large extent on the appeal to diffuse sentiments of resentment. In fact, the Canadian critical theorist Marc Angenot ranks populism, together with nationalism, among his "ideologies of *ressentiment*" the pernicious influence and impact of which he sets out to expose (Angenot 1996, 51–52). In Angenot's reading, resentment is nothing but vindictiveness and rancor and thus an entirely negative emotion, a pathetic weapon of the weak. This is a reading, grounded in Nietzsche, but which can also be found, at least in part, in Adam Smith, who classified resentment among the "unsocial" passions, together with hatred and spite (MacLachlan 2010). More recent interpretations of resentment present it in a more positive light.

The philosopher Jeffrey Murphy comes to the defense of resentment as an affirmation of "respect for self and respect for the moral order." In fact, Murphy goes on to charge that "lack of resentment reveals a servile personality – a personality lacking in respect for himself and respect for his rights and status as a free and equal moral agent" (Murphy 1999, 1359). What sustains resentment, the philosopher Amélie Rorty has noted, are "claims of rights, benefits, or privileges that seem unfairly distributed" – the result of "intentional malevolence or collusive intrigue" (Rorty 2000, 92–93). This suggests that resentment is intrinsically linked the questions of power and social justice. As such, as the philosopher

Robert Solomon maintains, it "involves a kind of blame and personal outrage, an outward projection, an overwhelming sense of injustice." From this it follows that justice "requires taking resentment seriously" (Solomon 1994, 103, 119). The rehabilitation of resentment has to a significant extent been prompted by John Rawls's influential *Theory of Justice*. What distinguishes resentment and its close cousin, indignation, from emotions such as anger is that resentment "always claims to rest on moral principle" for justification (Neu 2008, 34). For Rawls, resentment and indignation rank among what he calls "moral emotions" since they make "reference to an acknowledged right or wrong" and "invoke the concept of right." What distinguishes the two emotions is that resentment is "aroused by what we regard as wrongs done to ourselves;" indignation "is concerned with wrongs done to others" (Rawls 1999, 421–423).

Populist mobilizations derive much of their energy from the ability to tap into that overwhelming sense of injustice and powerlessness that characterizes both resentment and indignation. The populist revolt of the early 1890s in the United States is a case in point. It was fueled by moral outrage and "righteous indignation" in the face of an "industrial capitalism running rampant, growing callous, and becoming each year more antidemocratic," which left more and more citizens "impoverished, voiceless, and degraded," while a small minority, as the author of the Omaha Platform put it, appropriated the "fruits of the toil of millions" in order to "build up colossal fortunes (. . .) unprecedented in the history of mankind" (Creech 2006; Pollack 1967, xxvii). The same combination of moral outrage and righteous indignation in the face of rampant corruption and blatant social injustice has prepared the ground for Podemos's populist mobilization in Spain, which has ridden the wave of widespread disaffection with the established political class and traditional politics in general (Fernández-Albertos 2015, ch. 1). Similarly, in late nineteenth-century France, corruption scandals and the sentiment that the country has fallen into the hands of dark political-financial circles which with their "obscure machinations ruin the nation create a climate of widespread resentment, which proves fertile ground for Boulanger's populist campaign" (Angenot 1989, ch. 33, paragraph 25). And in Colombia, Gaitán's invectives against the corruption of the oligarchy had such an impact because they resonated strongly with widespread "resentment caused by the severe social differences" (Vázquez Piñeros 2007, 320). In the Italian case, the Lega Nord's populist mobilization profited from a variety of resentments bubbling underneath the relative affluence of the northern regions: against the political class, the *Mezzogiorno*; immigrants, big business the big unions, all of them charged with profiting from the hard work and enterprising spirit of northern producers while giving little in return (Biorcio 1997; Tomelleri 2015, ch.6).

The success of populist mobilization depends, very much in line with the ideational approach informing this volume, on favorable conditions and emotive predispositions outlined above; at the same time, it also depends on the availability of populist actors capable of putting diffuse sentiments of resentment and indignation into words, articulating unmet demands and thus evoking what the authors of the introduction call the "specific linguistic and emotional cues" that provide the fuel for populist mobilization. Their success, in turn, depends on their ability to clearly establish a new antagonistic "internal frontier" (Laclau) between "the people," constituted discursively as a political subject, and a discursively constructed and clearly defined unitary "enemy" (the elite, the political class, the oligarchy, the caste, etc.). The result is a particular style of political discourse, which, as the empirical evidence provided above clearly shows, is a common characteristic of all five cases. In each case, the populist leaders successfully translated sentiments of resentment and indignation into striking and memorable words and phrases (*la casta, Roma Ladrona, Wall Street owns this country, El pueblo es superior a sus dirigentes*). Yet, what about the questions of justice, equity and fairness associated with resentment and indignation? Evidence presented above suggests that in almost all cases, there is a strong appeal to social justice and fairness in order to gain legitimacy for the populist revolt. The demand for greater social justice and equality was central to the People's Party's "hayseed socialism" and resonates strongly among the *indignados* of Podemos (Clanton 1984, 144). It was a central tenet of Gaitán and his movement. As John W. Green has noted, it was the "Gaitanistas' shared moral sense of social justice and demands for more popularly based political representation" which "unified their multiclass mobilization and drew them to Gaitán, the symbol of their aspirations" (Green 1996, 310). Gaitanismo stood for social inclusion and "popular participation in the nation's political life" – an expression of "the popular will" (Green 2000, 180).

In the Boulangist movement, too, there was significant concern for social justice, promoted by the various dissident radical and socialist currents spearheaded by Maurice Barrès and Henri Rochefort (Sternhell 1972, 171). The General's program of 1888 explicitly evoked the social question using populist rhetoric designed to mobilize resentment. The program explicitly blamed "unemployment, ruin, and poverty" on those who passed "their needs, their appetites, and their unhealthy ambition before your need," and who cavalierly watched workers "suffer and die of hunger." Only with Boulanger, the workers' condition would change, for "Boulanger is work."[14] These were not idle words. During the legislative period 1889 to 1893, the majority of the Boulangist deputies in the National Assembly sided on social issues with the socialists and some radicals (Crapez 1998, 84). The only exception was the Lega Nord. This is perhaps not surprising given the strong spirit of ethnocentrism and individualist producerism informing the party's populist mobilization campaign. If there was an appeal to justice and equity it was made in support of demands for redressing the unfair treatment the north and its hardworking ordinary people had allegedly suffered for decades.[15] In short as Aldo Bonomi has argued, what was at the core of the Lega's mobilization was a claim to "distributive justice" (Bonomi 2008, 40–42).

The discussion of the logic behind populist mobilization would not be complete without a few words regarding the question of charisma. An exemplary case was Boulanger, who projected the image of the "providential man" and whose "charismatic power" of seduction mobilized the masses (Winock 2012, 81). In 1895, the French sociologist Gustave Le Bon observed that there "was not a village inn that did not possess a portrait" of General Boulanger. Boulanger was "attributed the power to remedy all injustices, all evils; and thousands of men would have given their lives for him" (Le Bon 1895, 64). In a similar vein, W. John Green has noted the quasi-religious devotion of many followers of Gorge Eliécer Gaitán, who saw in him the "savior" and "new messiah" who had come to redeem Colombia and deliver the oppressed, the "apostle of social justice" who had set out to defend the ordinary working people against the *oligarquías* (Green 1996, 308). Charisma played also a significant role in the success of the Lega Nord's populist campaign. As one early Lega supporter and activist put it, the Lega owed much to Bossi's "charismatic appeal," which led "the people to feel proud of who they are. For that they idolized him and followed him all the way" (Dematteo 2011, 57). Finally, in the case of Podemos, Pablo Iglesias consciously projected himself as a charismatic leader. In fact, charismatic leadership was an intricate part of Podemos' larger populist strategy (Errejón 2014a).[16]

The exceptional case is the American populists. The People's Party certainly had among its ranks a considerable number of politically savvy (e.g. William Peffer of Kansas and

James "Cyclone" Davis of Texas) and rhetorically seasoned (e.g., Mary Lease) local and regional leaders quite capable of keeping a large audience enthralled. Yet, none attained a predominant position in the party. The reason was, as Charles Postel has argued, that the People's Party represented a rather heterogeneous coalition of self-help and reform organizations, each one standing on its own merits. In addition, these organizations often "lacked trained or well-known political campaigners." As a result, the new party recruited professional politicians or prominent public figures from outside their ranks, who more often than not were "without the close connection to the new ideas or organizations from which Populism sprang." Moreover, some prominent "organic" leaders, such as Charles Macune, the leader of the Farmers' Alliance, never warmed to "third party politics" and thus were lost to the populist cause (Postel 2007, 12–13).

Conclusion

The five cases presented in this paper provide strong support for the ideational approach informing this volume by demonstrating that populist mobilizations follow a distinct logic, which seems to hold true across time and space. In general, populist mobilizations are triggered by a crisis of political representation, i.e., the inability, or lack of will, of the political establishment to respond to the anxiety and grievances of ordinary people during times of profound socioeconomic transformation. Crises of political representation, particularly if exacerbated by perceptions of entrenched, endemic corruption and fraud, are likely to engender diffuse sentiments of anger, resentment and indignation (Ziller and Schübel 2015). It depends on the availability of a populist actor and his or her ability to convert these sentiments into an internally consistent and coherent, yet emotionally charged discourse, whether or not a crisis of representation will eventually touch off a populist mobilization. Charisma certainly helps; but, as the American case clearly shows, it is not essential. What appears to be much more of essential importance, instead, is the ability of populist actors to translate vague emotions of disenchantment and resentment into a morally grounded discourse that evokes notions of social justice, equity, ethics and genuine participatory democracy into a coherent political doctrine promoting profound change while, at the same time, providing the forgotten and despised with a new sense of value.

Notes

1 Particularly the interpretation of *boulangisme* has been highly contentious, with some historians considering Boulangism to be a protofascist movement (Angenot 1989; Sternhell 2000). Recently, Grégoire Kauffmann has argued that in terms of ideas and political strategy, there is a direct line between *boulangisme* and the Front national under Marine Le Pen (Kauffmann 2016). Similar tendencies informed American interpretations of the populist movement. See Miller 1993.

2 For a similar approach with different case studies see Pappas 2012.

3 "Governments for the Strong." Kansas Agitator, April 21, 1891, p. 44. http://chroniclingamerica.loc.gov/lccn/sn83040052/1891-04-21/ed-1/seq-4/.

4 "Preamble to the 'Omaha Platform'," adopted by the People's Party, July 4, 1892. www.populist.com/populist.Omaha.platform.html.

5 Producerism originated in the late eighteenth century. Particularly noteworthy is William Manning's 1799 pamphlet, *The Key of Libberty*, which saw the main political conflict as deriving from a "Conceived Difference of Interest Between those that Labour for a Living and those that git a Living without Bodily Labour" and who tended to "associate together and look down with

two much contempt on those that labour." Manning quoted in Wood 1992, 279. For a discussion of Manning's political philosophy see Rana 2010, 126–129. For a prominent example of Populist producerism see Peffer 1890.

6 The first quote is from William Allen White's famous editorial "What's the Matter with Kansas," *The Emporia Gazette*, August 15, 1896: www.journalism.ku.edu/school/waw/writings/waw/newspaper/editorials/whatsthematter.html

The second refers to how eastern media viewed the Populists. See Edwards 1997, 107.

7 Aux Electeurs de la Banlieu, *L'Instransigeant*, January 14, 1889, p. 1.

8 According to Zeev Sternhell, anti-Semitism "was primarily a feature of the Boulangist left." Boulanger himself was not anti-Semitic and "refused any form of alliance with anti-Semitism" (Sternhell 1992, 464). On the anti-Semitism of the Blanquist left, see Hutton 1981, 158-159 and Joly 2007, 65.

9 Its most significant promoter was Maurice Barrès, whose "national socialist" ideological synthesis anticipated twentieth-century fascism (see Soucy 1967).

10 See, for instance, Freidenberg, 2007, which lists Gaitanismo among "other experiences" of Latin American populism.

11 In 1947, according to a contemporary observer, the cost of living index in Bogotá rose more than 30 points to an all-time high (Dozer 1949, 285)

12 Between 2002 and 2011, the ratio between the medium wealth of the top 10 and bottom 25 percent of Spanish households increased from 54 to 87, an increase of 60 percent (see Colectivo Ioé 2015). Surveys showed that the vast majority of the Spanish population not only were concerned about social inequality, but also believed that inequality was here to stay (Sanz Martín-Bustamante and Bravo 2015).

13 See the January 2014 manifesto Mover ficha: convertir la indignación en cambio politico, available online at www.cuartopoder.es/alsoldelacalle/files/2014/01/Mover-ficha-convertir-la-indignacio%CC%81n-en-cambio-poli%CC%81tico.pdf (accessed August 21, 2015).

14 "Programme du Général Boulanger." http://gallica.bnf.fr/ark:/12148/bpt6k1128115/f1.item.r=%22G%C3%A9n%C3%A9ral+Boulanger%22.langFR

15 In her study of the Lega Nord, Lynda Dematteo quotes an ex-militant of the Lega Nord who charges that in the early 1990s, northerners "felt more despised than even southerners (*meridionali*) did" (Dematteo 2011, 57).

16 A striking example of Iglesias' leadership pretension is the cover of a collected volume, edited by Iglesias, on the TV series *Game of Thrones*, which depicts a drawing of Iglesias (who identified himself with Daenerys Targaryen) comfortably seated on the Iron Throne (Iglesias 2014c).

References

Albertazzi, Daniele, and Duncan McDonnell. 2015. *Populists in Power*. Abingdon: Routledge.

Álvarez Junco, José. 2015. "Parábola de la corrupción." *El Pais*, July 15. http://elpais.com/elpais/2015/07/09/opinion/1436456462_170609.htm.

Angenot, Marc. 1989. *1889. Un état du discours social*. Quebec: Éditions Balzac. www.medias19.org/index.php?id=11003.

Angenot, Marc. 1996. *Les ideologies du ressentiment*. Montreal: XYZ éditeur.

Angenot, Marc. 2010. *La poésie socialiste au temps de la Deuxième Internationale. Discours social*. http://marcangenot.com/wp-content/uploads/2011/12/poesie_socialiste.pdf.

Biorcio, Roberto. 1997. *La Padania promessa*. Milan: il Saggiatore.

Bolaños, Alejandro. 2014. "España sufre la crisis más desigual." *El Pais*, June 19. http://economia.elpais.com/economia/2014/06/19/actualidad/1403175466_879515.htm.

Bonin, Hubert. 1987. "La Grande Dépression française à la fin du XIXème siècle: Réflexion sur sa datation et sur sa fonction. " *Histoire, économie et société* 6: 509–533.

Bonomi, Aldo. 2008. *Il rancore: Alle radici del malessere del nord*. Milan: Feltrinelli.

Bossi, Umberto. 1992. *Vento dal nord*. Milan: Sperling & Kupfer.

Bossi, Uberto. 1998. "Intervento del Segretario Federal, O. Umberto Bossi." October 25. www.leganord.org/phocadownload/ilmovimento/Presidente_Federale/discorsi_assemblee/1998_25ottobre_congresso.pdf.

Bossi, Umberto, with Daniele Vimercati. 1993. *La rivoluzione*. Milan: Sperling & Kupfer.

Braun, Herbert. 1986. *The Assassination of Gaitán: Public Life and Urban Violence in Colombia*. Madison: The University of Wisconsin Press.

Brubaker, Rogers. 2017. "Why Populism?" *Theory and Society* 46: 357–385.

Brunet, Jean-Paul. 1998. "Ouvriers et politique en banlieu parisienne." In *Ouvriers en banlieu, XIXe-XXe siècle*. Edited by Jacques Girault, 281–289. Paris: Les Éditions de l'Atelier/Éditions Ouvrières.

Burns, Michael. 1984. *Rural Society and French Politics: Boulangism and the Dreyfus Affair, 1886–1900*. Princeton, NJ: Princeton University Press.

Cantrell, Gregg. 2010. "'A Host of Sturdy Patriots': The Texas Populists." In *The Texas Left: The Root of Lone Star Liberalism*. Edited by David O'Donald Cullen and Kyle G. Wilkinson, 53–73. College Station: Texas A&M University Press.

Centro de Investigaciones Sociológicas (CIS). 2014a. "Barómetro de Mayo." Study n. 3024. May. http://datos.cis.es/pdf/Es3024mar_A.pdf.

Centro de Investigaciones Sociológicas (CIS). 2014b. "Barómetro de novembre." Study no. 3045, November. http://www.cis.es/cis/export/sites/default/-Archivos/Marginales/3040_3059/3045/es3045mar.pdf

Clanton, Gene. 1984. "'Hayseed Socialism' on the Hill, Congressional Populism, 1891–1895." *Western Historical Quarterly* 15: 139–162.

Colectivo Ioé. 2015. "La desigualdad se dispara un 60% en la primera década del s. XXI." *Diagonal*, March 7. www.diagonalperiodico.net/global/25983-la-desigualdad-la-riqueza-se-dispara-60-la-primera-decada-del-siglo-xxi.html.

Conklin, Alice L., Sarah Fishman, and Robert Zaretsky. 2015. *France and its Empire since 1870*, 2nd ed. Oxford: Oxford University Press.

Crapez, Marc. 1998. "Le socialism moins la gauche. Anticapitalisme, antisémitisme, national-populisme." *Mots* 55: 74–94.

Creech, Joe. 2006. *Righteous Indignation: Religion and the Populist Revolution*. Urbana, IL: University of Illinois Press.

de la Torre, Carlos. 2010. *Populist Seduction in Latin America*. Athens: Ohio University Press.

Dematteo, Lynda. 2011. *L'idiota in politica: Antropologia de la Lega Nord*. Milan: Feltrinelli.

Diamanti, Ilvo. 1996. *Il male del nord: Lega, localismo, secessione*. Rome: Donzelli.

Dix, Robert. 1978. "The Varieties of Populism: The Case of Colombia." *The Western Political Science Quarterly* 31: 334–51.

Dornel, Laurent. 2014. *La France hostile: Socio-histoire de la xénophobie (1870–1914)*. Paris: Fayard.

Dozer, Donald Marquard. 1949. "Roots of Revolution in Latin America." *Foreign Affairs* 27: 274–88.

Edwards, Rebecca. 1997. *Angels in the Machinery: Gender in American Party Politics from the Civil War to the Progressive Era*. New York: Oxford University Press.

Errejón, Íñigo. 2014a. "Muere Ernesto Laclau, teoretico de la hegemonía." *Público*, April 14. www.publico.es/actualidad/muere-ernesto-laclau-teorico-hegemonia.html.

Errejón, Íñigo. 2014b. "Qué es 'Podemos'?" *Le Monde diplomatique*. July 16. www.monde-diplomatique.es/?url=articulo/0000856412872168186811102294251000/?articulo=8c640f81-5ccc-4723-911e-71e45da1deca.

Errejón, Íñigo. 2016. "Podemos a mitad de camino." *Ctxt.es*, April 23. http://ctxt.es/es/20160420/Firmas/5562/Podemos-transformacion-identidad-poder-cambio.htm.

Errejón, Íñigo, and Chantal Mouffe. 2015. *Construir pueblo: Hegemonía y radicalización de la democracia*. Barcelona: Icaria editorial.

Fernández-Albertos, José. 2015. *Los votantes de Podemos: Del partido de los indignados al partido de los excluidos*. Madrid: Catarata.

Freidenberg, Flavia. 2007. *La tentación populista: Una vía al poder in America Latina*. Madrid: Editorial Słntesis.

Garrigues, Jean. 1992. *Le Boulangisme*. Paris: Presses universitaires de France.
Garrigues, Jean. 2010. "Boulanger, ou la fabrique de l'homme providentiel." *Parlement(s)* 13: 8–23.
Garrigues, Jean. 2012. "Le boulangisme comme mouvement social, ou les ambiguïtés d'un social-populisme." In *Histoires des mouvements sociaux en France de 1814 à nos jours*. Edited by Michel Pigenet and Danielle Tartakowsky, 238–248. Paris: La Découverte.
Garrigues, Jean. 2013. "Le boulangisme est-il antiparlementaire?" *Parlement(s)* Occasional Issue no. 9: 49–58.
Giurato, Francesco, and Atonio Pitoni. 2015. "Soldi ai partiti, 180 miliono di rimborsi: Così la Lega ha spremuto 'Roma ladrona'." *Il Fatto Quotidiano*, April 13. www.ilfattoquotidiano.it/2015/04/13/soldi-partiti-180-milioni-rimborsi-cosi-lega-spremuto-romaladrona/1583791/.
Green, John W. 1996. "'Vibrations of the Collective': The Popular Ideology of Colombia's Atlantic Coast, 1944–1948." *Hispanic American Historical Review* 76: 283–311.
Green, John W. 2000. "Guilt by Association: Jorge Eliécer Gaitán and the Legacy of His Studies in 'Fascist' Italy." In *Strange Pilgrimages, Exile, Travel, and National Identity in Latin America, 1800–1990s*. Edited by Ingrid Elizabeth Fey and Karen Racine, 179–192. Wilmington: Scholarly Resources.
Haidt, Jonathan. 2003. "The Moral Emotions." In *Handbook of Affective Sciences*. Edited by Richard J. Davidson and Klaus R. Scherer, and H. Hill Goldsmith, 852–870. Oxford: Oxford University Press.
Hermet, Guy. 2001. *Les populismes dals le monde: Une histoire sociologique. XIXe-XXe siècle*. Paris: Fayard.
Hutton, Patrick H. 1976. "Popular Boulangism and the Advent of Mass Politics in France, 1886–90." *Journal of Contemporary History* 11: 85–106.
Hutton, Patrick H. 1981. *The Cult of the Revolutionary Tradition: The Blanquists in French Politics, 1864–1893*. Berkeley, CA: University of California Press.
Iglesias, Pablo. 2014a. *Disputar la democracia: Política para tiempos de crisis*. Madrid: Ediciones Akal.
Iglesias, Pablo. 2014b. "The Left Can Win." *Jacobin Magazine*. September 12. www.jacobinmag.com/2014/12/pablo-iglesias-podemos-left-speech/
Iglesias, Pablo. 2014c. *Ganar o morir: Lecciones políticas en Juego de Tronos*. Madrid: Ediciones Akal.
Iglesias, Pablo. 2015a. "Understanding Podemos." *New Left Review* 93: 7–22.
Iglesias, Pablo. 2015b. "Guerra de trincheras y estrategia electoral." *Otra vuelta de tuerka Blog*. May 3. http://blogs.publico.es/pablo-iglesias/1025/guerra-de-trincheras-y-estrategia-electoral/
Irvine, William D. 1988. "French Royalists and Boulangism." *French Historical Studies* 16: 395–406.
Jansen, Robert S. 2011. "Populist Mobilization: A New Theoretical Approach to Populism." *Sociological Theory* 29: 75–96.
Jaycox, Faith. 2005. *The Progressive Era*. New York: Facts on File.
Joly, Laurent. 2007. "Antisémites et antisémitisme à la Chambre des députés sous la IIe République. " *Revue d'histoire moderne et contemporaine* 54(3): 63–90.
Jurado, Ignacio. 2014. "La insatisfacción con la democracia en España." *eldiario.es*, December 16. www.eldiario.es/piedrasdepapel/insatisfaccion-democracia-Espana_6_335676450.html.
Kauffmann, Grégoire. 2016. *Le nouveau FN: Les vieux habits de populisme*. Paris: Seuil.
Le Bon, Gustave. 1895. *Psychologie des foules*. Paris: Felix Alcan.
Lears, Jackson. 2009. *Rebirth of a Nation: The Making of Modern America, 1877–1920*. New York: HarperCollins Publishers.
Lease, Mary. 1984. "The Red Dragon of Wall Street vs. the Farmer." In *Outspoken Women: Speeches by American Women Reformers, 1635–1935*. Edited by Judith Anderson, 106–107. Dubuque: Kendall/Hunt Publishing Company.
Levy-Leboyer, Maurice, and François Bourguignon. 1985. *L'économie française au XIXème siècle. Analyse macro-économique*. Paris: Economica.
MacLachlan, Alice. 2010. "Resentment and Moral Judgment in Smith and Butler." *The Adam Smith Review* 5: 161–177.
Miller, Worth Robert. 1993. A Centennial Historiography of American Populism, *Kansas History* 16(1): 54–69.

Molano Camargo, Frank. 2008. "La coyuntura histórica del asesinato de Jorge Eliécer Gaitán Ayala." *Colombia Ciudad Paz-Ando* 1: 35–60. http://revistas.udistrital.edu.co/ojs/index.php/cpaz/article/viewFile/7413/9120

Murphy, Jeffrie G. 1999. "Forgiveness, Reconciliation and Responding to Evil: A Philosophical Overview." *Fordham Urban Law Journal* 27: 1353–1366.

Neu, Jerome. 2008. "Rehabilitating Resentment and Choosing What We Feel." *Criminal Justice Ethics* 27: 31–37.

Nord, Philip. 2005. The *Politics of Resentment: Shopkeeper Protest in Nineteenth-Century Paris*. New Brunswick: Transaction Publishers.

Nugent, Walter T. K. 1963. *The Tolerant Populists: Kansas Populism and Nativism*. Chicago, IL: The University of Chicago Press.

Palacios, Marco. 2011. *Populistas – el poder de las palabras: Estudios de políticas*. Bogotá: Universidad Nacional de Colombia.

Pappas, Takis. 2012. "Populism Emergent: A Framework for Analyzing its Contexts, Mechanics, and Outcomes." Florence. *EUI Working Papers*, RSCAS2012/01.

Passmore, Kevin. 2012. *The Right in France from the Third Republic to Vichy*. Oxford: Oxford University Press.

Pécaut, Daniel. 2000. "Populismo imposible: el caso colombiano." *Estudios politicos* 16: 45–70. https://dialnet.unirioja.es/descarga/articulo/5263861.pdf.

Peffer, William. 1899. "Populism; Its Rise and Fall: XII – Difference Between Democracy and Populism." *Chicago Daily Tribune*, July 7.

Peffer, William. 1890. *The Way Out*. Topeka: Kansas Farmer Company. www.kansasmemory.org/item/208179.

Peruzzotti, Enrique. 2013. "Populism in Democratic Times: Populism, Representative Democracy, and the Debate on Democratic Deepening." In *Latin American Populism in the Twenty-First Century*. Edited by Carlos de la Torre and Cynthia J. Arnson, 61–84. Baltimore, MD: The Johns Hopkins University Press.

Pisani-Ferry, Fresnette. 1969. *Le Général Boulanger*. Paris: Flammarion.

Pollack, Norman. 1967. Introduction to *The Populist Mind*. Edited by Norman Pollack, xix–xlviii. Indianapolis, IN: The Bobbs-Merrill Company.

Postel, Charles. 2007. *The Populist Vision*. New York: Oxford University Press.

Rana, Aziz. 2010. *The Two Faces of American Freedom*. Cambridge: Harvard University Press.

Rawls, John. 1999. *A Theory of Justice*. Revised edition. Cambridge: The Belknap Press of Harvard University Press.

Rorty, Amélie Oksenberg. 2000. "The Dramas of Resentment." *The Yale Review* 88: 89–100.

Salmela, Mikko, and Christian von Scheve. 2017. "Emotional Roots of Right-Wing Political Populism." *Social Science Information* 56: 567–595.

Sanz Martín-Bustamante, Marco, and Silvia Bravo. 2015. "La triple percepción de la desigualdad." *Metroscopia*, October 27. http://metroscopia.org/la-triple-percepcion-de-la-desigualdad/#_ftn1.

Schmidtke, Oliver, and Carlo E. Ruzza. 1993. "Regionalistischer Protest als 'Life Politics': Die Formierung einer sozialen Bewegung: die Lega Lombarda. *Soziale Welt* 44: 5–29.

Sharpless, Richard E. 1978. *Gaitán of Colombia: A Political Biography*. Pittsburgh, PA: University of Pittsburgh Press.

Snow, David A., and Robert D. Bedford. 1988. "Ideology, Frame Reference and Participant Mobilization." *International Social Movement Research* 1: 197–217.

Solomon, Robert C. 1994. "One Hundred Years of Ressentiment: Nietzsche's Genealogy of Morals." In *Nietzsche, Genealogy, Morality: Essays on Nitzsche's Genealogy of Morals*. Edited by Richard Schacht, 95–126. Berkeley, CA: University of California Press.

Soucy, Robert. 1967. "Barrès and Fascism." *French Historical Studies* 5: 67–97.

Steeples, Douglas W., and David O. Whitten. 1998. *Democracy in Desperation: The Depression of 1893*. Westport: Greenwood Press.

Sternhell, Zeev. 1971. "Barrès et la gauche: du boulangisme à 'la concard' (1889–1895). "*Le mouvement social* 75 : 77–130.

Sternhell, Zeev. 1972. *Maurice Barrès et le nationalisme français*. Paris: Presses de Sciences Po.

Sternhell, Zeev. 1978. *La droite révolutionnaire 1885–1914*. Paris: Seuil.

Sternhell, Zeev. 1992. "The Roots of Popular Anti-Semitism in the Third Republic." In *Hostages of Modernization: Studies on Modern Antisemitism 1870–1933/1939 Germany – Great Britain – France*. Edited by Herbert A. Strauss, 464–485. Berlin/New York: deGruyter.

Tahar Chaouch, Malik. 2009. "La presencia de una ausencia: Jorge Eliécer Gaitán y las desaventuras de populismo en Colombia." *Araucaria* 11: 251–262. www.redalyc.org/articulo.oa?id=28211598011.

Tomelleri, Stefano. 2015. *Ressentiment: Reflections on Mimetic Desire and Society*. East Lansing, MI: Michigan State University Press.

Vázquez Piñeros, María del Rosario. 2007. "La Iglesia y la violencia bipartidista en Colombia (1946-1953). Análisis historiográfico." *Anuario de Historia de la Iglesia* 16: 309–334. www.redalyc.org/articulo.oa?id=35516021.

Verdier, Daniel. 1994. *Democracy and International Trade: Britain, France and the United States 1860–1990*. Princeton, NJ: Princeton University Press.

Watson, Thomas E. 1905. "Populism." *Tom Watson's Magazine* 2: 257–260.

Watson, Thomas E. 1975. *The People's Campaign Book, 1892: American Farmers and the Rise of Agrobusiness*. Reprint, New York: Arno Press.

Winock, Michel. 2000. "Socialism and Boulangism, 1887–89." In *The Development of the Radical Right in France: From Boulanger to Le Pen*. Edited by Edward. J. Arnold, 3–15. Houndmills: Palgrave Macmillan.

Winock, Michel. 2001. *La fièvre hexagonale: Les grandes crises politiques 1871–1968*. Paris: Éditions du Seuil.

Winock, Michel. 2004. *Nationalisme, antisémitisme et fascisme en France*. Paris: Éditions du Seuil.

Winock, Michel. 2012. *La droite hier et aujourd'hui*. Paris: Perrin.

Wood, Gordon S. 1992. *The Radicalism of the American Revolution*. New York: Alfred Knopf.

Woods, Dwayne. 1995. "The Crisis of Center-Periphery Integration in Italy and the Rise of Regional Populism: The Lombard League. *Comparative Politics* 27: 187–203.

Ziller, Conrad, and Thomas Schübel. 2015. "'The Pure People' versus 'the Corrupt Elite'? Political Corruption, Political Trust and the Success of Radcial Right Parties in Europe." *Journal of Elections, Public Opinion and Parties* 25: 368–386.

9 Populist success in Latin America and Western Europe

Ideational and party-system-centered explanations[1]

Simon Bornschier

The idea that failures of democratic representation create populist potentials is central both to cleavage-based accounts of party system change, as well as to the ideational approach to populism. In the former framework, populists are seen as agents who re-establish congruence between party systems and specific segments of the electorate. The diagnosis of the ideational approach is one of a more generalized crisis of democratic representation. In both cases, however, representation failure is a necessary condition for populist success, and this is the first hypothesis that will be tested in this chapter. The remaining differences between the two approaches can be fleshed out by distinguishing majoritarian and what I call "segmented" populism. In the first type, presumably present in Venezuela, Ecuador, as well as Greece and Spain, the legitimacy gap is wide. The populist electoral coalition is therefore large and correspondingly diverse in ideological terms. The appeal of the second type is restricted to rather specific segments of the electorate that perceive a failure of democratic representation because their specific preferences are not represented in the party system. A prominent example is the electoral coalition rallied by the populist right in Western Europe, as I will show. Thus, while populism is likely to have a common cause across regions and time – namely, an unresponsive party system that erodes the legitimacy of the established parties – the choice of the thick ideology that segmented populists use in their mobilization is not a coincidence. Rather, it matters *which citizen preferences* lack representation. In the case of mainstream populism, voter preferences seem less decisive in determining the thick ideology that populists use, according to the evidence presented in this chapter.

These hypotheses are tested based on an in-depth analysis of two Latin American and two Western European cases. First, combining data on party positions with mass-level surveys, I show that a representation failure represents a necessary condition both for left-wing and right-wing populist success. Second, I show that left-wing populist voters in Latin America and right-wing populist voters in Europe differ in the degree to which they display homogenous outlooks in terms of "thick" ideologies their parties are associated with: Majoritarian populism in Latin America rallies ideologically diverse groups, while segmented populists in Western Europe find support almost exclusively among ideologically like-minded voters.

In Western Europe, where the populist right achieved its breakthrough from the 1980s onwards, I look at France as a case of populist success and Germany as one of failure until recently. While both countries' party systems were fairly responsive to voter preferences in terms of the traditional state-marked dimension of conflict in the 1970s, they differed in terms of their responsiveness along the libertarian-neo-conservatism divide, the second dimension of conflict prevalent in the 1970s. German parties were far more responsive along this "cultural" dimension than their counterparts in France, explaining the delayed manifestation of the populist right in Germany. In France, the Front National successfully redefined cultural conflicts and entrenched itself at one pole of a new cultural divide that encompasses all the elements we commonly use to define a cleavage (c.f. Bartolini and Mair 1990). The Front National's electorate is highly homogeneous in ideological terms, meaning that the party employed the segmented populist mobilization logic.

I compare these European cases to the breakthrough of new populist left parties in Latin America in the late 1990s and 2000s. Building on recent distinctions between the moderate and the populist left (Levitsky and Roberts 2011), I argue that the latter type was successful in countries where party systems lacked responsiveness along the classical economic dimension, pitting state intervention against market liberalism. The best example here is that of the Venezuelan party system, which had failed to offer voters contrasting economic policy propositions for several decades. The economic crisis of the 1980s and 1990s then provided a window of opportunity for populist actors. As we will see, the electoral coalition mobilized by the Movimiento V República is large and diverse, providing support for the hypothesis that Venezuela exhibits majoritarian populism. In Uruguay, on the other hand, a firmly entrenched center–left party contributed to high levels of congruence between party positions and voter preferences, strongly constricting the mobilization space for populist newcomers.

This chapter is structured as follows. I begin by presenting a theory of how established conflicts and alignments limit the space for populist actors, and then go on to present the distinction between majoritarian and segmented populism. In the fourth section, I justify the choice of cases to be included in the analysis along with a discussion of the political context in which populist actors were successful in Latin America and Western Europe, respectively. The ensuing section explains in detail the data and methods I use to measure representational congruence in my four cases. The empirical section presents the evidence for the two hypotheses tested in this paper, while the final section draws implications for the study of populism.

Representation failure and the populist challenge

Much of the literature has focused on proximate causes of the breakdown of parties or party systems, which often pave the way for the rise of populist challengers (e.g., Lupu 2014). Embedding these accounts in a more encompassing framework that includes proximate and more remote factors shows that short-term factors are often strongly shaped by long-term party system evolutions, and cannot be understood in isolation from them (c.f., Bornschier 2016). Adopting such a perspective allows us to take advantage of a vast literature that has studied the conditions shaping the fortunes of challenger parties that are not populist (see also Roberts 2015). My contention is that party systems under some certain conditions provide space for challengers – whether of a populist type or not – while the mobilization space for any kind of new actor is restricted under other conditions.

From a historical cleavage perspective, the capacity of new political actors to rally votes is limited by voters' existing partisan attachments (Lipset and Rokkan 1967; Rokkan 1999; Bartolini 2000). More generally, echoing Schattschneider (1975 [1960]), Kriesi and Duyvendak (1995) have postulated a zero-sum relationship between old and new divisions. To the degree that existing divisions remain salient and that new divides do not reinforce, but cut across them, the party system tends to "organize" new issues "out of politics," in Schattschneider's (1975 [1960], ch. 4) famous words. It is irrelevant in this respect whether existing alignments are strongly structured by social group membership – such as in the case of the traditional class and religious cleavages – or whether they are more strongly politically defined, as in the case of contemporary Western Europe's over-arching economic and cultural ideological alignments (Bornschier 2010, 57–60). As long as an individuals' group attachments and political identities related to the existing structure of conflict are stronger than his or her identification with a cause that draws a new group boundary – such as belonging to "the pure people" that is betrayed by the corrupt elite – the individuals' political alignment will remain stable. A change in political preference requires a prior transformation in an individuals' salience hierarchy of identities (Stryker 1980; 2000).

The degree to which new conflicts effectively remain latent depends on the strength of the collective identities entailed by the older divides, and on how strongly parties reinforce these collective identities by offering distinctive positions along the older divides (Bornschier 2010, ch. 3). If patterns of competition are segmented, social groups have strong loyalties and party preferences (Mair 1997, 162–171). As a consequence, the electoral market is tightly restrained and leaves little room for the emergence of new lines of opposition or new political parties.[2] The origin of every enduring structure of political alignments is thus a political conflict that has formed political group attachments.[3] Two factors shape whether the existing structure of conflict persists or is prone to being transformed. First, the degree to which the original conflict persists, or, put differently, the degree to which parties continue to present diverging policy propositions. Conflict reinforces the group attachments that underlie political divides, and thus perpetuates alignments (Sartori 1968; Bornschier 2010). It nurtures the ideological schemas, in Conover and Feldman's (1984) terms, that voters have in their minds and that help them understand politics and form preferences concerning the political issues of the day. There is now an impressive literature on party systems in the advanced democracies that underscores that conflict constitutes the reproductive mechanism underlying cleavages (e.g., van der Brug 2010; Evans and Tilley 2011; Adams et al. 2011; Evans and de Graaf 2013; Rennwald and Evans 2014). But there is also evidence from Latin America that polarization creates, while depolarization dilutes the links between social groups and parties that stabilize party systems (e.g., Torcal and Mainwaring 2003; Bornschier 2016).

There are two ways in which a lack of political options offered in the party system produces dealignment, thereby opening a window of opportunity for populist actors. In the first scenario, dealignment is triggered from above, by parties converging in their policy propositions. As a result, the links between voters and their preferred party are diluted, and voters become open for the appeals of new parties, movements, or charismatic leaders. In this scenario, voters continue to have diverging policy preferences, but these preferences are no longer represented by political parties. In the short term, catch-all strategies may be electorally rewarding, but in the medium term, parties that abandon their traditional program often lose significant vote shares (Karreth, Polk, and Allen 2012). In the longer run, if voters have nowhere else to go, party convergence will lead to a loss of confidence in the party system, and it may even result in a crisis of legitimacy of the entire political system. The established parties in such a situation are, of course, tempted to in some way or another inhibit the entry of competitors. Because they have abandoned the option of stipulating alternative policy proposals, which would help them to be responsive to voters' policy preferences, they are left with two principal options: The first is to form an outright cartel by outlawing fringe parties or by introducing hurdles to the registration of new parties that are difficult to overcome. The other option is to substitute programmatic partisan linkages with clientelistic efforts to maintain loyalties to the cartel.[4] Clientelism, in turn, requires financial resources that foster corrupt practices. Not only does this further erode legitimacy, thereby opening a window of opportunity for populists, who are known to thrive on crises of legitimacy (Hawkins 2010). The dependence on a constant flow of particularistic resources also makes clientelistic party systems vulnerable to populist challenges as soon as these resources dry up. In fact, this short-term factor plays an important role in explaining the timing of the breakdown of party systems if parties do not complement particularistic linkages with programmatic ones. Evidence is provided here by the Venezuelan case (Roberts 2003; Morgan 2011), as well as the PRI's loss of power in Mexico (Fox 1994; Magaloni 2006).

On the other hand, change can also come from below, as a result of the evolving preferences of voters. The potential for new political actors to redraw the dimensions of competition is thus determined by the degree to which established party system divisions resonate with the preferences and the concerns of the electorate. If parties represent a conflict between the working class and employers, then partisan attachments will fade as post-industrialization or the growth of the informal sector make the core constituencies along the divide shrink. Likewise, secularization has led to a declining share of churchgoers in the Western Europe, and to a declining importance of the religious cleavage. This is the second path to populism, where social structural change has weakened the roots that parties have in society. This situation differs from the one above in that no cartel of any kind is formed by the established parties. Thus, not only new political actors can take advantage of the process of dealignment by drawing up new conflicts, but established parties can also seek to exploit new issues. This occurred with respect to the issues promoted by the populist right in Germany and in Switzerland, for example. The two cases differ, however, in that the Swiss People's Party subsequently underwent a transformation into a full-fledged right-wing populist party, while the German Christian Democrats occupied the anti-universalistic terrain only temporarily and remained a center–right party (Lachat 2008; Dolezal 2008a; Bornschier 2010).

To summarize, populists will not be successful in a context where strong ideological divides are present and parties have strong links to like-minded constituencies. I argue that an erosion of a party system's roots in society – and the concomitant large number of floating voters that results from the process of dealignment – represents a necessary condition for populist success. Of course, dealignment must not be sufficient to trigger the electoral breakthrough of populists. Clientelism may for some time compensate for a lack of party system responsiveness and therefore obscure the fact that voters are dealigned. For another, non-populist forces may mobilize the electoral potentials that the established parties have neglected. The radical left in Western Europe may be considered such a force, to the degree that it does not make the way democracy works an integral part of its discourse. The verdict is open here, with some maintaining that all radical left parties in Europe are to some degree populist (Rooduijn and Akkerman 2017), while others distinguish Social-Populist parties from other sub-types of that are not to be considered populist (March and Mudde 2005). "Die Linke" in Germany is an ambiguous case in terms of classification, but as I will argue later on, it has to some degree come to occupy a left-wing space along the economic dimension that the Social Democrats have abandoned.

Comparing the ideational and the party system approach: how deep does the crisis of representation run?

Both the cleavage approach and the ideational approach to the study of populism insist that failures of democratic representation create potentials for anti-system populist mobilization. But the two approaches give different answers regarding the question how deep the crisis of representation runs. The cleavage-based explanation has focused on West European party systems that exhibit strong programmatic linkages between social groups and political parties, which are rooted in long-term ideological divisions. Contrary to early analyses that concluded that these linkages have eroded (Franklin et al. 1992), more recent research agrees that class-based linkages have evolved, but by no means disappeared (e.g., Kitschelt and McGann 1995; Evans 1999; Knutsen 2004; 2006; Kriesi et al. 2008). Thus, populism in this context is a phenomenon that accompanies the reconfiguration of voter-party linkages in mature party systems. As a consequence, the populist potential is made up of specific groups that lack representation due to top-down processes of party system change (meaning that parties have changed their ideological positions), or to evolving voter preferences (citizens have new concerns and demands). While these groups may voice distrust regarding the established parties and even the political system more generally, they also exhibit very similar outlooks in terms of the "thick" ideologies that in most cases accompany populists' Manichaean discourse.

The diagnosis of the ideational approach is one of a more deep-rooted democratic malaise, where large parts of the electorate have first lost trust in the existing parties, and then in the political system more generally (e.g., Hawkins 2010; Doyle 2011). Where parties have lacked responsiveness for a longer period of time, political support erodes, and populist messages will be successful. In several Latin American countries, policy differentiation was absent, and programmatic linkages between political elites and voters had become diluted (Luna and Zechmeister 2005; Kitschelt et al. 2010). To some degree, clientelism may compensate for the lack of programmatic responsiveness, but when this linkage weakens as well due to ebbing resources, party systems may rather suddenly collapse (Morgan 2011). In some of these contexts, left-wing populists successfully spearheaded a broad movement of discontent against the political system.

The cleavage-based and the ideational populism approach thus make differing predictions concerning the ideological homogeneity of the groups supporting populist challenger parties or movements. In the first case, populists' appeal is restricted to rather specific segments of the electorate whose preferences are not represented in the party system, and who as a consequence decry a failure of democratic representation. I call this "segmented" populism because it appeals to specific social groups, and show in the empirical part of this paper that this type of describes the way the populist right in Western Europe rallies its electoral coalition. Majoritarian populism, on the other hand, mobilizes a much more diverse coalition in ideological terms, which is held together by little more than the perception that elites are unresponsive to the preferences of the people. In those Latin American countries in which the populist left has emerged, it conforms more strongly to the encompassing type of populism.

Regional context and case selection

The theoretical predictions explaining the populist potential based on the intensity of existing party system divisions are tested drawing on two Latin American and two

Table 9.1 Cases, party system divides, and types of populist challengers

Country/case	*Crucial period prior to populist challenge*	*Dimensions of political space*	*Content of first dimension*	*Content of second dimension*	*Type of successful populist challenge*
Western Europe					
Germany	1970s–1980s	2	Economic	Cultural	Not successful
France	1970s	2	Economic	Cultural	Right-wing
Latin America					
Uruguay	1990s	1	Economic		None/not successful
Venezuela	1980s/1990s	1	Economic		Left-wing

Note: Evidence supporting the number of dimensions defining the political space and the substantive content of these dimensions is provided in the following section.

Western European cases. As shown in Table 9.1, these cases differ in terms of populist success within the time period covered by the data I use. Within each regional context, one case displays a successful populist party, while populists were not successful in the other country – or not until recently in Germany. The data I draw on in the latter case ends in the 2000s, and thus does not cover the breakthrough of the Alternative für Deutschland (Alternative for Germany, AfD) in 2017. However, the analysis presented in this chapter explains this delayed emergence of a populist right party in Germany very well, as compared to most other European countries. These diverging outcomes both within the European and the Latin American cases can be explained by the degree to which parties represented voter preferences prior to the period in which populist challengers arose, as the empirical section will seek to substantiate. The prior responsiveness of the party system also explains the type of populism – segmented or majoritarian – prevalent in the two contexts.

Furthermore, the two regions differ in that populism is associated with right-wing cultural ideologies in Western Europe, while left-wing populists drawing heavily on economic mobilization frames have triumphed in Latin America. This difference is due to the nature of the dimensions prevalent in the political space in the two regions and to the responsiveness of parties to voter preferences along these dimensions. In the following, I justify the case selection by discussing the context in which the populist right and the populist left emerged in Western Europe and Latin America, respectively.

Party systems in Western Europe have been marked by the conflicts triggered by the national and industrial revolutions (Rokkan 1999). As a result, political space has always been at least two-dimensional. The dimensions underlying party interactions have changed over time, however. While the state-market cleavage remains one of the two dimensions structuring party interactions (e.g., Kriesi et al. 2008), the traditional religious cleavage has been transformed into a new cultural dimension of conflict. A first restructuring of the political space occurred as a consequence of the mobilization of the New Social Movements of the left in the 1970s and 1980s (Kitschelt 1994). While the diffusion of universalistic values led the New Left to call for individual autonomy and the free choice of lifestyles, the diffuse anti-universalistic counter-potential present already in the 1970s (Sacchi 1998) remained largely untapped until the emergence of the radical populist right. The latter's innovation was a counter-ideologyto the New Left that meshes anti-universalism and strands of communitarian political thought (Bornschier 2010; see also Ignazi 1992; Rydgren 2005; Minkenberg 2000; Betz and Johnson 2004; Antonio 2000).[5] Because this background to right-wing populist mobilization is specific to Western Europe, this paper does not include any East-Central European cases. In Western Europe, empirical analyses of parties' issue positions in several countries in the 1990s reveal a two-dimensional political space constituted by the state-market divide and the opposition between universalistic values and a traditionalist-communitarian defense of the traditional national community (Kriesi et al. 2008; Bornschier 2010). Although these studies show the economic and cultural dimensions to be present in strikingly similar form in all Western European countries covered, the anti-universalistic potential gave rise to the emergence of powerful parties of the extreme populist right in France, while the corresponding potential was absorbed by the established right in Germany until the Christian Democrats abandoned the traditionalist-communitarian terrain under Chancellor Angela Merkel. Despite the challenge posed by the Republikaner (Republicans) in the 1980s, the populist right was thus unable to institutionalize in this period. I thus select the cases of France and Germany in the European context.

In Latin America, the most recent wave of populism is associated with the "left turn" of the late 1990s and 2000s, following an era of structural economic adjustment policies and austerity. While some of the left-wing parties that came to govern in the post-neoliberal era resemble classical mass parties and have taken decades to institutionalize, others represent new political movements that appeal to voters by mobilizing against the political establishment. Weyland, Madrid, and Hunter (2010) use the term "contestatory" left to distinguish the latter group – encompassing Venezuela's Bolivarian movement and Bolivia's Movement for Socialism – from the more moderate leftist parties that governed Uruguay, Chile, and Brazil. While the latter respect economic constraints and political opposition, the contestatory left presents a more profound challenge to the status quo both in terms of rhetoric and action. I will label the contestatory variant of the left as "populist," following the recent comparative literature (Mudde and Rovira Kaltwasser 2012; Roberts 2015; Rovira Kaltwasser 2015).[6]

Thus far, there are rather few attempts to explain why moderate left-wing mass parties have emerged in some countries and populist left parties in others (e.g., Weyland 2009). Remmer's (2012) analysis suggests that demand-side factors are not particularly relevant in explaining the choice of moderate or contestatory left-wing ideologies by parties in various countries. My hypothesis is that the lack of responsiveness of the party systems in the populist left countries explains why an anti-political establishment mobilization was successful in these cases. As outlined earlier, a persistent lack of parties to respond to the preferences of voters erodes partisan loyalties and the legitimacy of the political system, making voters open for appeals by new political actors. This is why Hawkins (2010) and Doyle (2011) have identified political distrust as a crucial factor driving support for populists such as Hugo Chávez in Venezuela. Venezuela is thus an obvious case to include in Latin America.[7] The moderate left in Chile, Uruguay, and Brazil emerged in a much more incremental process typical of classical mass parties. The ability of these parties to successfully compete and build a following tempered discontent and voters remained committed to a strategy of political change within existing institutions. Consequently, due to the relatively high degree of citizen support in these countries, the moderate left relies on economic policy appeals alone and does not adopt the anti-establishment rhetoric typical of the populist left. I chose Uruguay as a country featuring a moderate left: In comparison to the Chilean case, where the Socialists and Communists were established decades ago, the left-wing Frente Amplio was less entrenched prior to re-democratization in the 1980s. Brazil would also have constituted an interesting case, but its inclusion is ruled out by a lack of appropriate data to measure elite policy positions.

The analysis proceeds as follows: The next section now discusses the data used and the research design, while the following section presents aggregate evidence on the responsiveness of party systems in my four cases.

Measuring representational congruence prior to the populist phase in the four cases

One of the central junctures in the "chain of responsiveness" (Powell 2004) that runs from public preferences to political policies, is the congruence between voter preferences and party positions. According to the "responsible party model," first theorized by the APSA Committee on Political Parties (1950), and synthesized by Thomassen (1994, 251–2), congruence is achieved if, first, parties offer diverging programmatic offerings, and second, voters chose parties according to these offerings. Consequently, the quality of representation has frequently been assessed by looking at the correspondence between the political preferences of voters and their representatives (e.g., Dalton 1985; Powell 2000; Luna and Zechmeister 2005; see also Diamond and Morlino 2005).[8] This is the strategy I use here. To measure how responsive parties were to voter preferences prior to the populist phase in each context, I draw on data on party positions and voter preferences. Because there are no unique data sets that cover both regions, the data used differs in the two contexts. Employing the same analytical strategy, however, the results are nonetheless comparable between contexts. In Latin America, I compare the 1990s as the period preceding the "left turn," with the 2000s, after the Movimiento V República (MVR) gained power in Venezuela. In Western Europe, I focus on the period before and that after the extreme populist right emerged in the 1980s, analyzing the responsiveness of party systems in the 1970s and in the 1990s. Extending the analysis to the early 2000s allows me to demonstrate the persistent lack of political space for the populist right in Germany until recently, and to assess the impact of the populist right on representation in France.

To determine party positions in Western Europe, I rely on data based on the media coverage of election campaigns that is derived from a coding of party positions as reported in newspapers during election campaigns (Kriesi et al. 2008; see Dolezal 2008b for a detailed description of the data). The data predominantly captures statements that party exponents make at press conferences and on other occasions, and the campaign data therefore closely reflects what voters actually learn of the parties' positions. The data covers three electoral contests that took place between the late 1980s and the early 2000s and one election in the 1970s. Although it does not cover the 1980s in Germany, and will therefore be complemented by secondary evidence in the empirical part of this chapter, this data is rather unique in allowing for an analysis of the 1970s, which represents the crucial phase preceding the first challenge by the populist right in Western Europe. Furthermore, the issue categories used are tailor-made to specifically measure party positions along the two dimensions of political space prevalent since the 1970s.[9] The supply-side data is complemented with survey data from national election studies (the data sets used are specified in the Appendices). The combination of the information we have for party positions and voter preferences allows for an analysis of congruence for the 1978, 1988, 1995, and 2002 elections in France, and the 1976, 1994, 1998, and 2002 elections in Germany. While the data for Germany does not cover the period in which the AfD became a serious competitor, the analysis nonetheless explains the late breakthrough of a right-wing populist party in this country.

For the Latin American cases, I draw on unique data from the first wave of the University of Salamanca Surveys of Latin American Legislators (PELA), for which face-to-face interviews with legislators in Uruguay and Venezuela were conducted in 1995 (see Alcántara Sáez 2008). This point in time is very close to the fieldwork of the World Values Survey's (WVS) 1994–1999 wave, for which the interviews for these two countries were conducted in 1996. Combining these data sources, it is possible to assess the congruence of representation in Uruguay and Venezuela for the mid-1990s, prior to the election of Hugo Chávez in 1998.

In each context, I measure party system responsiveness along those dimensions of conflict that have been identified as the most salient ones in the literature. In Western Europe, a stable antagonism between support for the welfare state and economic liberalism forms the first dimension of political space throughout the period of study (Kriesi et al. 2008; Bornschier 2010). The second, cultural dimension is subject to change over time. In the 1970s, it strongly evolved around the universalistic convictions of the New Left, which put cultural liberalism, gender equality, human rights, and solidarity with the developing world on the political agenda. Mainstream left parties in France and Germany adopted many of the New Left issues initially put on the political agenda by the New Social Movements of the late 1960s and 1970s, and thereby underwent a transformation into so-called New Left parties. As in other West European countries, the political right in France and Germany initially responded by adopting a neoconservative position that is traditional in terms of values and critical of the state (Habermas 1985; Eatwell 1989). Universalism and anti-statism thus conceptually and empirically represent the two poles of the cultural divide in the 1970s, and I operationalize them using these categories from the media data discussed above.[10] In the 1980s or the 1990s, then, depending on the country, the cultural divide was transformed by a new response of the political right against the New Left pole. The new cultural conflict centers on the antagonism between universalistic values and a traditionalist–communitarian counter-conception of community, embodied above all in the opposition against immigration (Bornschier 2010).[11] In Germany, the established right was able to absorb the immigration issue roughly until very recently, while in countries with a populist right as in France it came to be owned by political outsiders. From the 1980s onwards, I thus use the categories measuring universalism and anti-immigration pledges to operationalize the cultural dimension.

For Latin America, analyses by Moreno (1999), Rosas (2010), and Bornschier (2013) converge in identifying the economic state-market divide as the most important ideological division. It is along this dimension that party system responsiveness in measured in this context, leaving aside secondary dimensions that differ from country to country, and center on regime (democracy vs. autocracy), the role of the military, and issues reminiscent of the religious cleavage (divorce and abortion).

I operationalize these dimensions at the party and voter levels by drawing on all available issue-specific items available in the surveys used. The way these items are aggregated differs in the Latin American and European contexts, however. My approach for Western Europe is to aggregate issues into dimensions using principal components factor analysis, following the procedure adopted by Kriesi et al. (2008) and Bornschier (2010). In these contexts, belief systems both at the elite and the mass level are highly structured, and responses to economic and cultural issue items invariably and clearly form two separate dimensions, with items belonging to each of these two dimensions being highly correlated. Uruguay is similar to Western Europe in this respect, where economic issues are related to an underlying dimension both at the elite and the mass level. This approach is highly problematic in Venezuela, however, where many of the items that theoretically should measure the same underlying dimension turn out to be unrelated in empirical terms. This is due to the lack of clear programmatic alternatives provided by the party system (Bornschier 2016), as well as to the overwhelming prevalence of clientelism (Coppedge 1994; Roberts 2003; Lyne 2008; Morgan 2011), which means that many voters are not accustomed to forming over-arching political preferences based on their specific issue preferences. For this reason, I have opted for additive indices to operationalize the state-market dimension both in Venezuela and in Uruguay, drawing on all available items in the PELA elite and WVS mass surveys.[12] The items used are listed in the Appendices.

The most important step in the analysis is to assess the correspondence between the positions of parties and those of their voters. Because the positions of parties and voters are not measured on the same scales, this correspondence can be judged only in *relative* terms. I thus measure congruence regressing the position of the party the respondent voted for on his/her individual preference along a given dimension.[13] Put differently, I use the ability of voter preferences to explain the ideological position of their preferred party as a measure of congruence. The most important information provided by this analysis is not the coefficient (which again is not independent of the differing scales on which parties and voters are placed), but whether individual preferences are a significant predictor of party choice. Consequently, I use the z-statistic of the ordered logit regression as a measure for the congruence of representation that can be compared across countries.[14]

Results: potentials for right-wing and left-wing mobilization in Europe and Latin America

We are now in a position to summarize the results of the analysis of responsiveness. In presenting the results, I complement responsiveness with the degree of polarization a divide entails at the voter level, because this is a key dimension to characterize the nature of competition between parties (Dalton 2008). Polarization impinges on the extent to which partisan camps differ strongly in terms of ideological outlook or whether different parties target the same groups of voters. To measure polarization, I calculate the standard deviation of party electorates' mean positions, weighted by party size.[15]

Latin America

Figure 9.1 shows the position of the two Latin American cases along the dimensions of polarization and congruence. Values of congruence below 2 do not reach statistical significance, thus this is a useful cut-off point to distinguish between responsive and unresponsive party systems. It is more difficult to define in absolute terms when polarization is high and when it is low, and the cross-regional comparison is therefore instructive: The vertical line that is drawn at 0.3 corresponds to an intermediate level of polarization in the European cases (see below). In comparison, party electorates in both Latin American countries are therefore far less polarized than their counterparts in Western Europe.

Despite similarly low levels of polarization, the results reveal that the mobilization space for populist left actors was much more tightly restrained in Uruguay in the 1990s, where the correspondence between voters' economic policy preferences and the economic policy position of the party they voted for is very high. The situation in Uruguay in the mid-2000s is similar, although both polarization and congruence have declined somewhat, reflecting the broader coalition rallied by the Frente Amplio in its

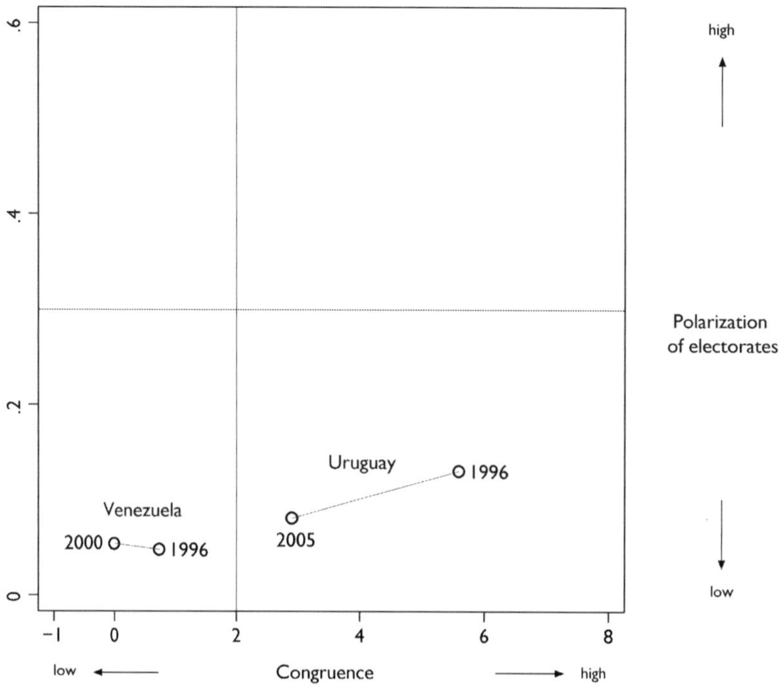

Figure 9.1 Congruence and polarization along the dominant party system divides in Latin America, mid-1990s

strategy to gain power by rallying a majority of voters. Nonetheless, the party system continues to mirror voters' economic policy preferences well (the relationship between voter preferences and party positions is significant at $p = 0.004$).

In Venezuela, on the other hand, the party system was not responsive of voter preferences prior to the rise of Chávez to power, providing a favorable populist breeding ground. Figure 9.2 shows the positions of parties and voters on which this assessment is based. We see that the two traditional parties, Acción Democrática (AD) and Comité de Organización Política Electoral Independiente (COPEI), both occupy a position to the right of the political center. Their voters are hardly distinguishable as well, and occupy a centrist position on average. Convergencia National (CONV), a spin-off from the long-established COPEI, is situated close to the traditional parties. The space to the left divide is occupied by Causa R and Movimiento al Socialismo (MAS). On the voter side, the overall differences between electorates are very small, and there is extensive ideological overlap (the bars below the mean positions show the standard deviation and thus the heterogeneity of party electorates). Only the electorate of MAS escapes the centrist dynamic and appears in touch with its party's ideological credentials.

The results of the ordered logit regression used to calculate the congruence between parties and voters indicate that voters preferences along the economic divide are unrelated to the positions of the parties they vote for. From this perspective, the implosion of the party system upon Hugo Chávez's appearance on the political

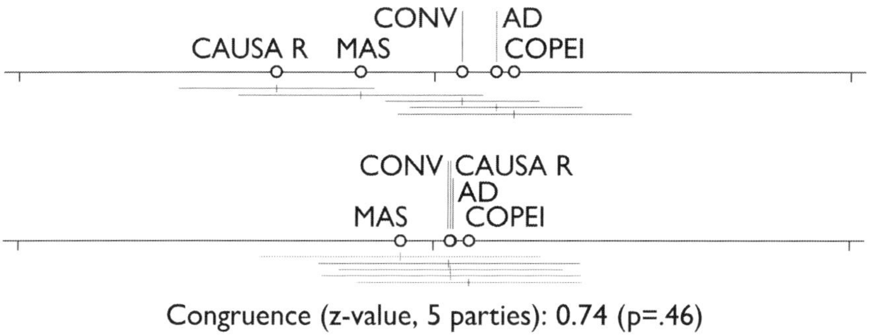

Legend: CAUSA R, La Causa Radical; MAS, Movimiento al Socialismo; CONV, Convergencia National; AD, Acción Democrática; COPEI, Comité de Organización Política Electoral Independiente.

Figure 9.2 Venezuela 1995–1996 – parties and voters on the state–market divide

scene is not that surprising. The party system progressively lost its roots in society due to the failure of the two major parties to offer differing policy packages to voters. Instead, as discussed earlier, they relied heavily on the cultivation of clientelistic linkages. Although new left-wing parties gained support in the 1980s, they seem to have been unable to present a viable alternative to AD and COPEI. MAS actually betrayed its electorate by joining a coalition to elect Rafael Caldera, a former COPEI politician, into the presidency under the banner of Convergencia National in 1993. In the 1996 World Values Survey used to determine voter preferences, a striking 59% of Venezuelan respondents declare that they would vote for none of the existing parties, or answer "don't know" when asked about their party preference. Thus, the institutionalized left was unable to re-establish confidence in party politics.

Although Hugo Chávez and his movement claimed to be the representatives of voters' true will, representation has not improved subsequent to the appearance of the Movimiento V República (MVR) in parliament, as the analysis of responsiveness in 2000 reveals. Voter preferences remain unrelated to parties' economic policy positions. As Figure 9.3 shows, this is partly due to the heterogeneous nature of the electoral coalition rallied by MVR. While MVR parliamentarians are clearly located on the left of the economic state-market dimension, their voters are on average situated slightly to the right of the political center. AD and COPEI voters actually express more left-wing credentials, which together with these parties' rather market-liberal position results in an overall negative relationship between voter preferences and party positions (the coefficient of the ordered logit regression is actually negative, as is the z-value indicated in Figure 9.3).[16] The extensive overlap between electorates indicates that the programmatic structuration of party choice is weak.

To summarize, the results so far confirm that differences in party system responsiveness explain why the populist left was successful in Venezuela, while a similar challenge did not occur in Uruguay, which featured a party system that clearly reflected voter preferences in the economic policy domain. While the low level of polarization in Uruguay's two-block system makes parties compete over similar groups of voters, the party system remained responsive in 2000s. The Frente Amplio and the parties of the right rally electorates whose preferences correspond to the parties they vote for. This is not the case in Venezuela, where party system responsiveness remains low even after the emergence of the Bolivarian Movement. The MVR clearly represents an instance of majoritarian

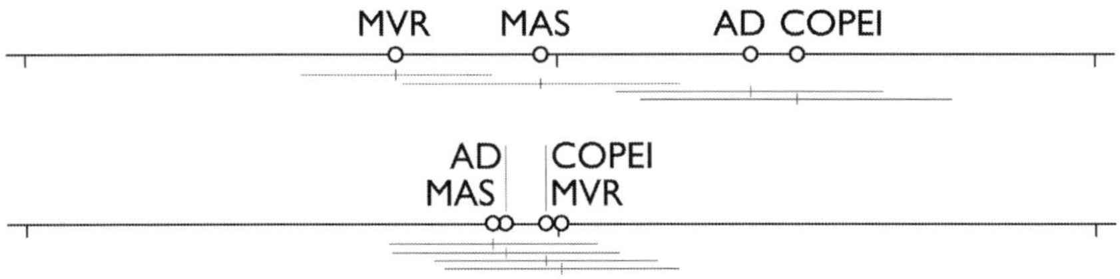

Congruence (z-value, 4 parties): -2.03 (p=.04)

Legend: MVR, Movimiento V República (Bolivarian Movement); MAS, Movimiento al Socialismo; AD, Acción Democrática; COPEI, Comité de Organización Política Electoral Independiente

Figure 9.3 Venezuela 2000 – parties and voters on the state–market divide

populism, whose supporters are not united by common policy preferences in the economic policy domain, despite the party displaying a staunchly left-wing position. This suggests that a mixture of charismatic and clientelistic linkages prevail in Venezuela.

Western Europe

In Western Europe, the French Front National spearheaded the rise of the populist right with its early breakthrough in the 1984 European parliament elections. The essential period defining the mobilization space for the populist right is therefore the 1970s, when the New Left had redefined the secular pole of the religious divide into the libertarian-universalistic pole of the nascent new cultural divide. The degree to which parties remained responsive to voter preferences amidst this shift strongly determined the appeal of the populist right, whose ideology meshed a traditionalist-communitarian counter-conception of community to that of the New Left with populist anti-establishment appeals. Figure 9.4 shows the degree of responsiveness of parties to voter preferences along the economic and cultural divides, along with the degree of polarization these divisions entailed at the voter level. As indicated before, I have drawn a line at a medium-level of polarization. In Europe, the relationship between partisans' policy preferences and parties' policy position is always significant, reflecting more coherent belief systems on the part of voters and the more strongly ideological nature of party competition when compared to Latin America. But the results show that there are important differences in degree. For this reason, I have – again arbitrarily – drawn a vertical line running halfway between the theoretical minimum in terms of congruence (no relationship between voter preferences and party positions) and the most congruent case in my sample.

We see two contrasts in Figure 9.4. The first is between the economic and the cultural divides. The economic cleavage in the 1970s was characterized by strong and fairly polarized alignments between voters and political parties both in Germany and in France. The potential for political newcomers along the economic divide, in other words, was limited. Along the cultural divide, on the other hand, we see a clear difference between Germany and France, the case of right-wing populist breakthrough. In Germany, congruence along the cultural divide was even stronger than in the economic domain, while the degree of polarization is similar. Germany witnessed a "renaissance of conservatism" in the 1970s as a reaction to the 1968 student movement and to the formation of a social-liberal government after the 1972 election, which performed a policy shift regarding the communist countries in the East. Confronted with the decline of

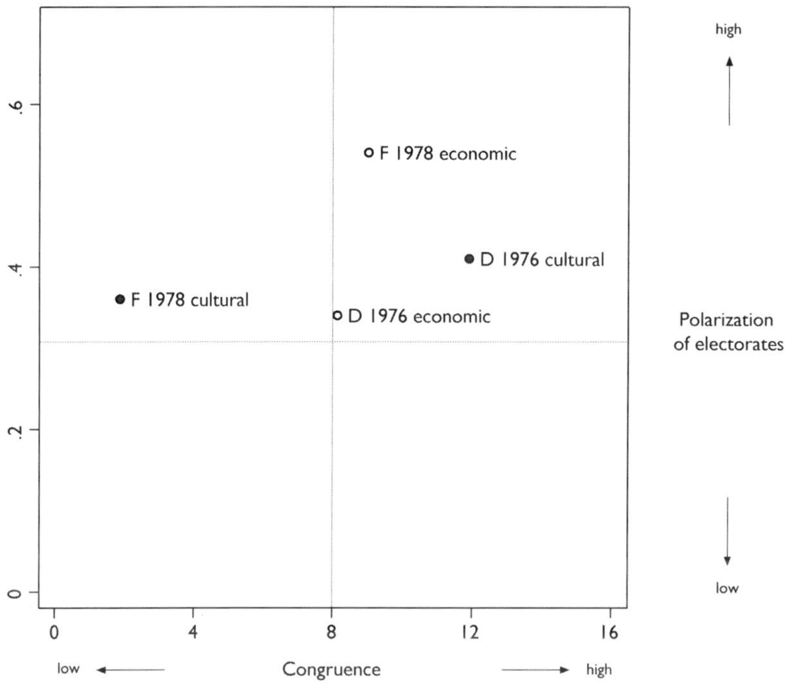

Figure 9.4 Congruence and polarization in the 1970s in France and Germany

religiosity and a programmatic vacuum, the Christian Democrats endorsed the Zeitgeist by stressing the importance of the family for moral guidance, and by propagating a new historical and national consciousness (Grande 1988).

Although the established right in Germany succeeded in rallying the anti-universalistic potential in the 1970s, the mobilization by far right parties was revived in the 1980s with the founding of the Republikaner party, which continued to challenge the political establishment into the 1990s. However, by taking a tough stance on immigration and by orchestrating German unification, the Christian Democrats won back the radical right potential (Thränhardt 1995; Schmidtke 2004; Stöss 2005, 38–40, 86; Bornschier 2012). At the same time, the new cultural conflict triggered a pluralization of the party system on the political left in the 1980s. The Social Democrats exhibited difficulties in maintaining their appeal both among traditional working class voters, as well as new support groups such as intellectuals and the 1968-generation, resulting in strong internal tensions (Kitschelt 1994, 39; Klingemann 1999; Niedermayer 2006, 115–116). Ultimately, they could not prevent the libertarian–universalistic electorate from defecting to the newly founded Green Party. Research on class voting suggests that this contributed to the formation of new links between social groups and political parties (Lachat 2007; Müller 1999). At the same time, the industrial workforce remains a stronghold of the Social Democrats (Oesch 2008a, 339–344), while it has become the core constituency of the populist right in countries where parties of this type are present (Bornschier and Kriesi 2013). Thus, the pluralization on the left ultimately contributed to the high levels of responsiveness exhibited by the German party system in later years, covered by the media data used in this chapter.

The data from the 1990s shown in Figure 9.5 suggest that the reconfiguration of the social structural bases of party support contributed to keeping the party system responsive to voters along the cultural dimension. Although congruence receded in 1994, it rose concomitantly to an increase in polarization in the 1998 campaign, and remained at that level in 2002. Not only the loyalties initially formed by the segmented cleavage of the 1970s and reinforced in the 1980s reduced the mobilization space for the far right, sporadically reappearing polarization in the 1990s and beyond did as well. Polarization along the cultural dimension is roughly comparable to the 1976 election in the 1990s and early 2000s, and reaches a peak in 1998, the election that ushered in the Red-Green government formed by Chancellor Schröder. In response to the government's reform of the nationality law, the mainstream right took an adversarial position and demanded that immigrants needed to adapt to what they dubbed Germany's "guiding (or mainstream) culture" (Schmidtke 2004, 171).

Turning to France, Figure 9.4 shows that the grip of the French party system along the cultural divide was far lower in the 1970s, in contrast to Germany. The relationship between voter preferences and party positions is significant even here, but in relative terms, it is clearly inferior both to that of Germany and to the strong ideological partisan alignments along the economic dimension in France. French electorates were fairly polarized even along the cultural dimension, possibly due to the strong role that religion still exerted on preferences with respect to cultural liberalism (see Bornschier 2008, 94). But these distinctive positions are not reflected in corresponding profiles on the part of political parties, as reflected in the low figure for congruence. Thus, the populist potential in France was clearly associated with the cultural dimension of competition.

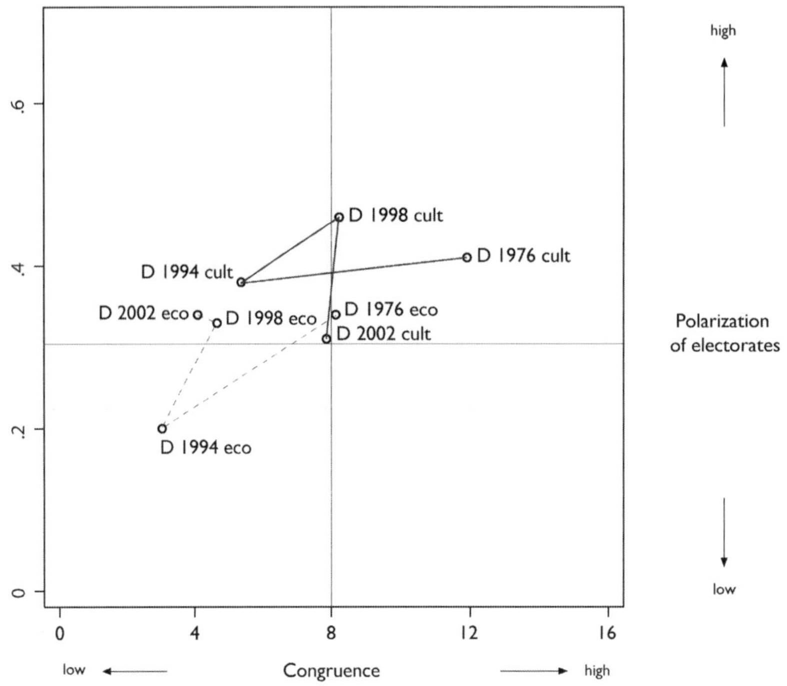

Figure 9.5 Congruence and polarization in Germany along the economic ("eco") and the cultural ("cult") dimensions, 1976–2002

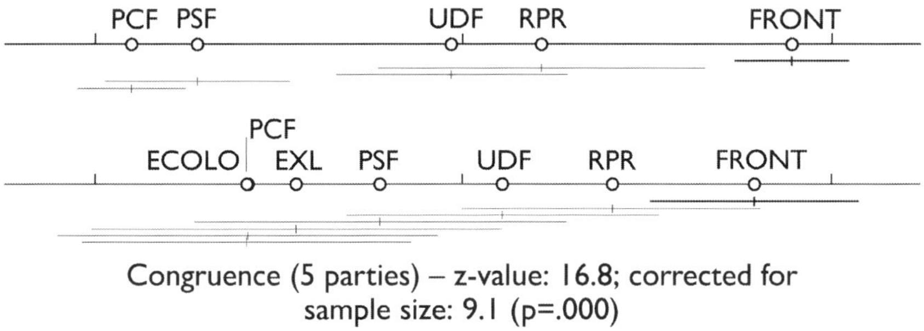

Legend: FRONT: Front National; RPR: Rassemblement pour la République (later UMP, Union pour und mouvement populaire); UDF: Union pour la Démocratie Française, small center parties; MRG: Mouvement des Radicaux de Gauche; PSF: Parti Socialiste Français; PCF: Parti Communiste Français; ECOLO: Greens, other ecologist parties; EXL: various extreme left parties.

Figure 9.6 France 1988 – parties and voters on the cultural divide

With the emergence of the Front National, the cultural dimension has become strongly segmented, as shown by Figure 9.6. Between 1978 and 1988, polarization has surged due to the Front National's staunchly traditionalist-communitarian position. There is a stark contrast between the New Left and its voters, encompassing the Socialists (PSF), the Communists (PCF) and the Greens (Ecolo) at the libertarian–universalistic pole of the cultural divide, and the Front National and its voters at the opposing pole. The mainstream right lies in between. The Front National rallies an electorate that clearly stands out for its ideological convictions in terms of the new cultural divide. Although there is some overlap with the voters of the Gaullists (RPR), the populist right's electorate is distinctively conservative, making the Front National a clear exponent of segmented populism.

As Figure 9.7 shows, the French party system continues to exhibit high levels of responsiveness after 1988. These results are in line with research that shows that the new cultural divide in Western Europe exhibits all three elements of Bartolini and Mair's (1990) classical definition of a cleavage (Oesch 2008a; 2008b; Stubager 2009; Oesch and Rennwald 2010; Minkenberg and Perrineau 2007). The populist right forms an integral part of this segmented cleavage: Not only the parties themselves, but also their voters are situated at the traditionalist–communitarian extreme of the new cultural dimension (see also Bornschier 2010, 106, 142). Thus, it is difficult to study the extreme populist right in isolation of the thick ideology it thrives upon. The traditionalist-communitarian ideology of the populist right is rooted in cultural transformations that have occurred since 1968, and that have profoundly reconfigured West European party systems.

Before we conclude, we may ask to which degree the results for Germany speak to the mounting radical left-wing and radical right-wing challenges to mainstream parties in this country. Although the data used does not cover the relevant period itself, the evidence assembled thus far does point to an untapped potential on the political left of the economic dimension. Returning to Figure 9.5, we see that in the elections covered by the data, the potential for realignment was actually higher along the economic than the cultural dimension. Since the 1970s, congruence along the economic cleavage has decreased, and is generally lower than in the cultural domain. These findings shed light on the rising success of the radical (populist) left represented by The Left ("Die Linke"). While the verdict concerning the question whether the latter is to be considered populist is out, this clearly

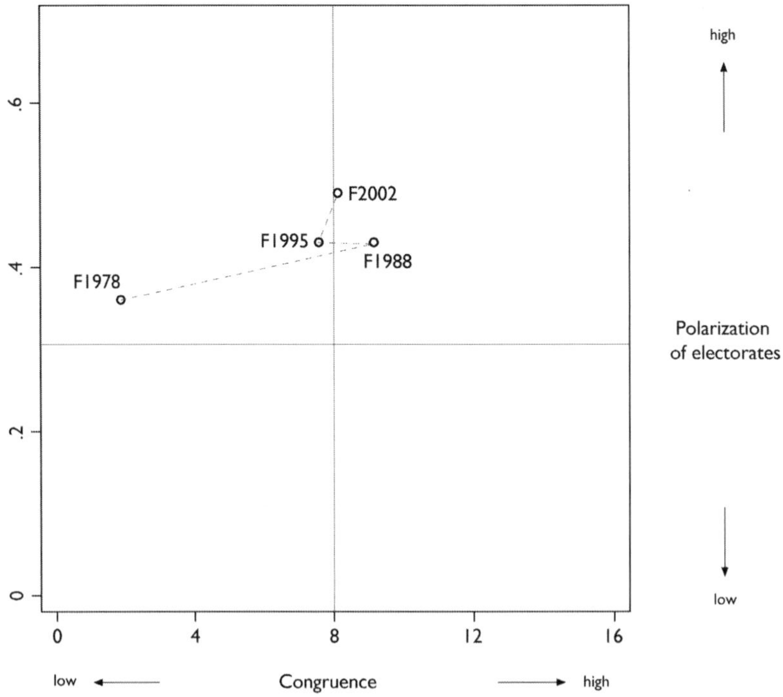

Figure 9.7 Congruence and polarization along the new cultural divide in France, 1970s–early 2000s

shows that the left-wing economic profile adopted by this party is not a coincidence, but results from the lack of other parties with clearly state interventionist profiles. A look at the detailed positions of parties and electorates in 2002 shown in Figure 9.8 reveal that the Social Democrats adopted a very centrist position in this campaign, in line with the preferences of its own electorate, but not with that of voters with more state interventionist inclinations.

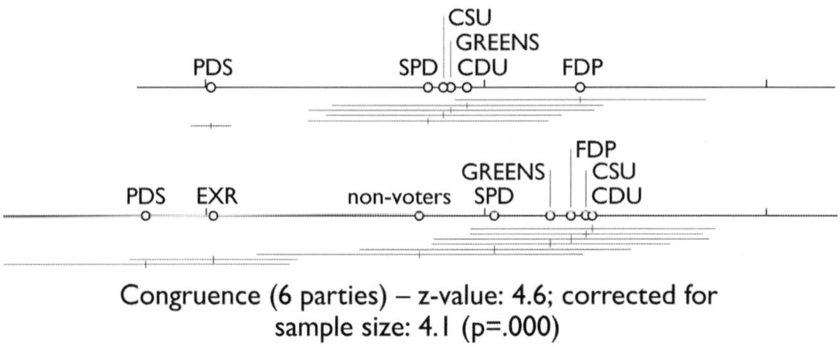

Legend: CDU, Christian Democratic Union; CSU, Christian Social Union (Christian Democrats in Bavaria); GREENS, Green Party; FDP, Free Democratic Party, liberals; EXR, extreme-right parties (National Democratic Party, German People's Union, and Republican Party combined); PDS, Party of Democratic Socialism (predecessor of The Left in Eastern Germany); SPD, Social Democratic Party; non-voters: respondents who declared that they had not voted in the past elections

Figure 9.8 Germany 2002 – parties and voters on the economic divide

Turning to competition on the political right, these findings presented here go a long way in explaining the lack of success of right-wing populist challengers in Germany until recently. It is highly plausible, however, that the more recent abandonment of the traditionalist-communitarian terrain by the Christian Democrats under Chancellor Merkel has contributed to the success of the Alternative for Germany (Alternative für Deutschland, AfD). As Schwarzbözl and Fatke (2016) show, this party rallies an electorate very similar in ideological terms to that of other right-wing populist parties in Western Europe.

Conclusion

Representation failure is a necessary condition to make populism successful. Populist entrepreneurs are able to capitalize on anti-elite sentiments only to the degree that the established parties have lost touch with voter preferences. A weakening of the programmatic alignments between parties and voters is a necessary, though not sufficient condition for populist success. Populist actors then promise to restore responsiveness. The ideational approach to populism points to a powerful ideology that political actors can use in situations of representation failure to activate certain attitudes among disillusioned voters and to give coherence to their beliefs.

But despite this common core emphasized by the ideational approach to populism, populist parties fall into at least two types. In one of them, which I have termed "segmented populism," a specific segment of the electorate lacks representation, and is therefore receptive to the anti-establishment mobilization of actors that denounce political elites for not addressing these concerns. This is the background of right-wing populist mobilization in Western Europe since the 1980s. The populist right in Europe rallies an electoral coalition that is highly homogeneous with respect to its position on the new cultural dimension, one of the two prime dimensions of ideological conflict on the continent. The "majoritarian" type of populism thrives in contexts where vast parts of the population have felt unrepresented long enough so as to result in a generalized erosion of legitimacy. This makes a majority electoral coalition open for radical political change. As the Venezuelan case demonstrates, the Bolivarian movement's state interventionist discourse is clearly of secondary importance, as it is not widely shared by its supporters. Populist voters in Venezuela either lack ideological understanding, or are rallied with the help of clientelistic inducements, perpetuating the traditional mode of linkage prevalent in the country. While majoritarian populism often makes party systems collapse, segmented populism can result in gradual realignment.

Interestingly, the Manichean element of the discourse of segmented and majoritarian populists is very similar – just as Chávez' Bolivarian movement, the Front National does not claim to represent manual working class voters, but "the people" as a whole. Yet, there is a profound difference in terms of the voters that are attracted by this discourse, and in the European cases, this has to do with the thick ideologies that populism is associated with. To understand the form that populism takes – majoritarian or segmented, as well as the thick ideologies it is associated with – we must take a party system perspective and look at the dividing lines and the positions of all relevant parties along these dividing lines. More specifically, the right-wing populist phenomenon in Western Europe cannot be understood without reference to the pacification of the religious cleavage and the emergence of the New Left. These dual processes provided populist entrepreneurs with an opportunity to mobilize voters holding a conception of community that is antagonistic to the universalistic convictions defended by the New

Left. Yet this potential was also amenable to mobilization by non-populist actors. Contrary to the French case, the established right in Germany remained responsive to its voters throughout the period studied in this chapter. The manifestation of the right-wing populist potential was therefore delayed in Germany, as compared to other countries. Where mainstream parties failed to absorb the right-wing populist potential, the populist right came to occupy the anti-universalistic pole of the new cultural divide, as the Front National's new culturalist ideology diffused among other right-wing populists in Western Europe (Rydgren 2005). By the same token, the analysis presented in this chapter tentatively suggests that The Left in Germany mobilizes an electorate that the Social Democrats no longer represent along the economic dimension.

The results also have implications for the study of the "Left turn" that swept Latin America after the late 1990s: Differences in the degree to which parties represented voter preferences in the 1990s shaped whether moderate left or populist left parties triumphed in this period. In Uruguay, the moderate left was already firmly entrenched at this point, and the mobilization space for new political actors was tightly constrained before the "left turn." The state-market divide thus remained the dominant political dimension in this country. The shape of ideological divisions and the prospects for representation that result from it in the countries with left-wing populist governments are less clear. On the one hand, the antagonism between the Bolivarian movement and a broad anti-populist coalition in Venezuela has the potential to evolve into a stable antagonism – more so than in Bolivia and Ecuador, where the majoritarian left-wing populism has also been successful. But during the time period covered by this analysis, the antagonism between populists and non-populists in Venezuela did not reflect differing underlying approaches to economic policy making capable of providing for programmatic representation. Contrary to what was the case with segmented populism in Europe, then, the majoritarian variant does not seem to restore the responsiveness of party systems.

Notes

1 Earlier versions of this paper were presented at the Team Populism London conference (2015), the 2015 Conference of Europeanists (CES) in Paris, APSA 2015 in San Francisco, and the ECPR Joint Sessions (Pisa, 2016). The author would like to thank Cristóbal Rovira Kaltwasser, Jan Rovny, Armin Schäfer, Chris Wlezien, as well as the participants of these workshops for their helpful and detailed comments. The usual disclaimer applies.

2 At the extreme, such a structure of opposition rules out any real competition between parties. Political systems characterized by pillarization, where the Netherlands used to be a prominent example, each party has its own constituency, and they do not really compete at all. The same is true of the pacts that were agreed upon in Colombia in 1958 (after the civil war known as La Violencia), and in the Punto Fijo pact in Venezuela in 1958. Whether loyalties persist in such a context depends on the continuing salience of the issues associated with the division in everyday politics, as I explain below.

3 Coser (1956) emphasizes the group-binding functions of political conflict. I use the terms party identification and political group identification interchangeably as partisanship can be viewed as a social identity (see Green, Palmquist, and Schickler 2002).

4 This is actually the ideal-typical case of Katz and Mair's (1995) cartel party thesis, a phenomenon that in this pure form is a more adequate description of Latin American countries such as Venezuela and Colombia, rather than in the Western European context, for which the theory was originally developed.

5 For a review of competing theories that see the rise of the populist right as a reaction against economic and cultural modernization or globalization, see Bornschier (2018).

6 The distinction between the moderate and the populist left can be further refined by taking into account organizational features of these parties or movements, namely, how concentrated or dispersed authority is (c.f., Levitsky and Roberts 2011; see also Weyland 2010). For the present purposes, it is not necessary to make these more fine-grained distinctions, as Roberts (2015, 142–144) points out that the concept of populism is compatible both with grass-roots/bottom-up and top-down/elite-directed modes of political mobilization.

7 This choice also has practical reasons, as Bolivia and Ecuador are not covered by the World Values Survey data I use. Peru, on the other hand, represents a prototypical case of populist mobilization, but the mid-1990s time point covered by the data is not ideal, as Alberto Fujimori came to power in 1991 already. A lack of data from the 1980s precludes an analysis of the Peruvian case.

8 A more sophisticated variant of this approach, the "thermostatic model" (Soroka and Wlezien 2010) takes a dynamic perspective and investigates how changes in public policy and voter preferences interact.

9 The specificity of the issue categories, as well as the fact that issue position and issue saliency are measured separately, represent clear advantages over the data collected by the Manifesto Project. The Chapel Hill Expert Surveys (CHES), the other main alternative to our data, reaches back only to 1999, and thus does not cover the phase prior to the emergence of right-wing populism in Western Europe.

10 More specifically, I use the categories "cultural liberalism," representing universalistic values, and "budgetary rigor." Although the latter category also has an economic component, it empirically forms part of the cultural dimension, indicating that it is employed by political actors in terms of an encompassing neo-conservative strategy, as analyses of the political space using Multidimensional Scaling (MDS) reveal (see Bornschier 2010, 73–76, 101–104, 180–184).

11 In empirical analyses of political space, immigration forms the counter-pole to cultural liberalism, which embody universalistic principles of justice and a multicultural conception of community. While it is at this pole that right-wing populist parties are situated, at least until the 2000s, the dimensionality of political space is the same even in those countries in which the populist right did not succeed in breaking into the party system due to the moderate right's efforts to politicize the immigration issue (Kriesi et al. 2008).

12 More specifically, I used only those items that exhibit meaningful variation, indicating that they are positional, rather than valence issues. I then standardized these issues and calculated legislators' and voters' mean position along them.

13 Technically, I attribute to each individual the policy position of his/her party, and then assess how well individual preferences explain the position of the party they voted for. Since the variance of the dependent variable is limited by the low number of parties competing, I use ordered logit instead of OLS regression. The approach is set out in more detail in Bornschier (2013).

14 The z-value is a measure for the significance of the predictions of these regressions, and thus depends also on sample size. Because the size of the sample varies strongly in the European cases, where I rely on national election studies, I weight the z-value by sample size to arrive at a measure that is comparable across contexts. For Latin America, the sample size hardly varies, and the results of the regressions are thus comparable between countries and over time. Direct comparisons across the Latin American and European contexts should be treated with caution, however.

15 Party strength is derived from the PELA elite surveys for the Latin American cases and from Kriesi et al. (2008) as well as a number of online-sources for the European cases.

16 In Figure 9.1, the value for representation for Venezuela is set to 0, the minimum of the scale.

References

Adams, James, Catherine E. de Vries, and Debra Leiter. 2011. Subconstituency Reactions to Elite Depolarization in the Netherlands: An Analysis of the Dutch Public's Policy Beliefs and Partisan Loyalties, 1986–98. *British Journal of Political Science* 42: 81–105.

Alcántara Sáez, Manuel, ed. 2008. *Politicians and Politics in Latin America*. Boulder, CO: Lynne Rienner.

Antonio, Robert J. 2000. After Postmodernism: Reactionary Tribalism. *American Journal of Sociology* 106 (2): 40–87.

APSA, Committee on Political Parties. 1950. Towards a more responsible two-party system. *American Political Science Review* September 1950 (supplement).

Bartolini, Stefano. 2000. *The Political Mobilization of the European Left, 1860–1980. The Class Cleavage*. Cambridge: Cambridge University Press.

Bartolini, Stefano, and Peter Mair. 1990. *Identity, Competition, and Electoral Availability. The Stabilization of European Electorates 1885–1985*. Cambridge, New York: Cambridge University Press.

Betz, Hans-Georg, and Carol Johnson. 2004. Against the Current – Stemming the Tide: The Nostalgic Ideology of the Contemporary Radical Populist Right. *Journal of Political Ideologies* 9 (3): 311–327.

Bornschier, Simon. 2008. France – the Model Case of Party System Transformation. In *West European Politics in the Age of Globalization*, edited by H. Kriesi, E. Grande, R. Lachat, M. Dolezal, S. Bornschier, and T. Frey. Cambridge: Cambridge University Press, 77–104.

———. 2010. *Cleavage Politics and the Populist Right. The New Cultural Conflict in Western Europe*. Philadelphia, PA: Temple University Press.

———. 2012. Why a Right-Wing Populist Party Emerged in France but Not Germany: Cleavages and Actors in the Formation of a New Cultural Divide. *European Political Science Review* 4 (1): 121–45.

———. 2013. Trayectorias históricas y responsiveness del sistema de partidos en siete países de América Latina. *América Latina Hoy* 65 (diciembre): 45–77.

———. 2016. Historical Polarization and Representation in South American Party Systems, 1900–1990. *British Journal of Political Science*. Published online ahead of print: https://doi.org/10.1017/S0007123416000387.

———. 2018. Globalization, Cleavages, and the Radical Right. In *Oxford Handbook of the Radical Right*, edited by Jens Rydgren. Oxford: Oxford University Press (forthcoming).

Bornschier, Simon, and Hanspeter Kriesi. 2013. The Populist Right, the Working Class, and the Changing Face of Class Politics. In *Class Politics and the Radical Right*, edited by Jens Rydgren. Abingdon and New York: Routledge, 10–29.

Conover, Pamela Johnston, and Stanley Feldman. 1984. How People Organize the Political World: A Schematic Model. *American Journal of Political Science* 28 (1): 95–126.

Coppedge, Michael. 1994. *Strong Parties and Lame Ducks. Presidential Partyarchy and Factionalism in Venezuela*. Stanford, CA: Stanford University Press.

Coser, Lewis A. 1956. *The Functions of Social Conflict. An Examination of the Concept of Social Conflict and Its Use in Empirical Sociological Research*. New York: The Free Press.

Dalton, Russell J. 1985. Political Parties and Political Representation. Party Supporters and Party Elites in Nine Nations. *Comparative Political Studies* 18 (3): 267–299.

———. 2008. The Quantity and the Quality of Party Systems: Party System Polarization, Its Measurement, and Its Consequences. *Comparative Political Studies* 41 (7): 899–920.

Diamond, Larry, and Leonardo Morlino. 2005. Introduction. In *Assessing the Quality of Democracy*, edited by L. Diamond and L. Morlino. Baltimore: Johns Hopkins University Press, ix–xliii.

Dolezal, Martin. 2008a. Germany: The Dog that Didn't Bark. In *Western European Politics in the Age of Globalization*, edited by H. Kriesi, E. Grande, R. Lachat, M. Dolezal, S. Bornschier, and T. Frey. Cambridge: Cambridge University Press, 208–233.

———. 2008b. The Design of the Study: The Distinguishing Characteristics of our Approach. In *West European Politics in the Age of Globalization*, edited by H. Kriesi, E. Grande, R. Lachat, M. Dolezal, S. Bornschier, and T. Frey. Cambridge: Cambridge University Press, 53–74.

Doyle, David. 2011. The Legitimacy of Political Institutions Explaining Contemporary Populism in Latin America. *Comparative Political Studies* 44 (11): 1447–73.

Eatwell, Roger. 1989. Right or Rights? The Rise of the "New Right." In *The Nature of the Right. American and European Politics and Political Thought since 1789*, edited by R. Eatwell and N. O'Sullivan. Boston, MA: Twayne Publishers, 3–17.

Evans, Geoffrey, ed. 1999. *The End of Class Politics? Class Voting in Comparative Context*. Oxford: Oxford University Press.

Evans, Geoffrey, and James Tilley. 2011. How Parties Shape Class Politics: Explaining the Decline of the Class Basis of Party Support. *British Journal of Political Science* 42: 137–161.

Evans, Geoffrey, and Nan Dirk de Graaf, eds. 2013. *Political Choice Matters: Explaining the Strength of Class and Religious Cleavages in Cross-National Perspective*. Oxford: Oxford University Press.

Fox, Jonathan. 1994. The Difficult Transition from Clientelism to Citizenship. Lessons from Mexico. *World Politics* 46: 151–84.

Franklin, Mark N., Tom Mackie, Henry Valen, and et al., eds. 1992. *Electoral Change. Responses to Evolving Social Und Attitudinal Structures in Western Countries*. Cambridge: Cambridge University Press.

Grande, Edgar. 1988. Neoconservatism without Neoconservatives? The Renaissance and Transformation of Contemporary German Conservatism. In *The Transformation of Contemporary Conservatism*, edited by B. Girvin. London: Sage, 55–77.

Green, Donald, Bradley Palmquist, and Eric Schickler. 2002. *Partisan Hearts and Minds. Political Parties and the Social Identities of Voters*. New Haven, CT: Yale University Press.

Habermas, Jürgen. 1985. *Die Neue Unübersichtlichkeit*. Frankfurt am Main: Suhrkamp.

Hawkins, Kirk A. 2010. *Venezuela's Chavismo and Populism in Comparative Perspective*. Cambridge: Cambridge University Press.

Ignazi, Piero. 1992. The Silent Counter-Revolution: Hypotheses on the Emergence of Extreme Right-Wing Parties in Europe. *European Journal of Political Research* 22: 3–33.

Karreth, Johannes, Polk, Jonathan T., and Allen, Christopher S. 2012. Catchall or Catch and Release? The Electoral Consequences of Social Democratic Parties' March to the Middle in Western Europe. *Comparative Political Studies* 46 (7): 791–822.

Katz, Richard S., and Peter Mair. 1995. Changing Models of Party Organization and Party Democracy. The Emergence of the Cartel Party. *Party Poltics* 1 (1): 5–28.

Kitschelt, Herbert. 1994. *The Transformation of European Social Democracy*. Cambridge: Cambridge University Press.

Kitschelt, Herbert, and Anthony J. McGann. 1995. *The Radical Right in Western Europe. A Comparative Analysis*. Ann Arbor, MI: University of Michigan Press.

Kitschelt, Herbert, Kirk A. Hawkins, Juan Pablo Luna, Guillermo Rosas, and Elizabeth J. Zechmeister. 2010. *Latin American Party Systems*. Cambridge: Cambridge University Press.

Klingemann, Hans-Dieter. 1999. Kontinuität Und Wandel Des Deutschen Parteiensystems, 1949–1998. In *Eine Lernende Demokratie. 50 Jahre Bundesrepublik Deutschland*, edited by Max Kaase and Günther Schmid. Berlin: Edition Sigma, 115–128.

Knutsen, Oddbjørn. 2004. *Social Structure and Party Choice in Western Europe. A Comparative Longitudinal Study*. Basingstoke: Palgrave-Macmillan.

Knutsen, Oddbjørn. 2006. *Class Voting in Western Europe. A Comparative Longitudinal Study*. Lanham, MD: Lexington.

Kriesi, Hanspeter, and Jan Willem Duyvendak. 1995. National Cleavage Structures. In *New Social Movements in Western Europe. A Comparative Analysis*, edited by H. Kriesi, R. Koopmans, J. W. Duyvendak, and M. G. Giugni. Minneapolis, MN: University of Minnesota Press, 3–25.

Kriesi, Hanspeter, Edgar Grande, Romain Lachat, Martin Dolezal, Simon Bornschier, and Timotheos Frey. 2008. *Western European Politics in the Age of Globalization*. Cambridge: Cambridge University Press.

Lachat, Romain. 2007. *A Heterogeneous Electorate: Political Sophistication, Predispositional Strength, and the Voting Decision Process*. Baden-Baden: Nomos.

———. 2008. Switzerland: Another Case of Transformation Driven by an Established Party. In *Western European Politics in the Age of Globalization*, edited by H. Kriesi, E. Grande, R. Lachat, M. Dolezal, S. Bornschier, and T. Frey. Cambridge: Cambridge University Press, 130–153.

Levitsky, Steven, and Kenneth M. Roberts. 2011. Latin America's "Left Turn": A Framework for Analysis. In *The Resurgence of the Latin American Left*, edited by S. Levitsky, and K. M. Roberts. Baltimore, MD: Johns Hopkins University Press, 1–28.

Lipset, Seymour Martin, and Stein Rokkan. 1967. Cleavage Structures, Party Systems, and Voter Alignments: An Introduction. In *Party Systems and Voter Alignments*, edited by S. M. Lipset and S. Rokkan. New York–London: The Free Press-Collier-Macmillan, 1–64.

Luna, Juan P., and Elizabeth J. Zechmeister. 2005. Political Representation in Latin America. A Study of Elite-Mass Congruence in Nine Countries. *Comparative Political Studies* 38 (4): 388–416.

Lupu, Noam. 2014. Brand Dilution and the Breakdown of Political Parties in Latin America. *World Politics* 66 (4): 561–602.

Lyne, Mona M. 2008. *The Voter's Dilemma and Democratic Accountability. Latin America and Beyond.* University Park: Pennsylvania State University Press.

Magaloni, Beatriz. 2006. *Voting for Autocracy. Hegemonic Party Survival and Its Demise in Mexico.* New York: Cambridge University Press.

Mair, Peter. 1997. *Party System Change. Approaches and Interpretations.* Oxford: Clarendon Press.

March, Luke, and Cas Mudde. 2005. What's Left of the Radical Left? The European Radical Left after 1989: Decline and Mutation. *Comparative European Politics* 3(1): 23–49.

Minkenberg, Michael. 2000. The Renewal of the Radical Right: Between Modernity and Anti-Modernity. *Government and Opposition* 35 (2): 170–188.

Minkenberg, Michael, and Pascal Perrineau. 2007. The Radical Right in the European Elections 2004. *International Political Science Review* 28 (1): 29–55.

Moreno, Alejandro. 1999. *Political Cleavages. Issues, Parties, and the Consolidation of Democracy.* Boulder, CO: Westview Press.

Morgan, Jana. 2011. *Bankrupt Representation and Party System Collapse.* University Park, PA: Pennsylvania State University Press.

Mudde, Cas, and Cristóbal Rovira Kaltwasser. 2012. Exclusionary vs. Inclusionary Populism: Comparing Contemporary Europe and Latin America. *Government and Opposition* 48 (2): 147–174.

Müller, Walter. 1999. Class Cleavages in Party Preferences in Germany – Old and New. In *The End of Class Politics? Class Voting in Comparative Context*, edited by Geoffrey Evans. Oxford: Oxford University Press, 137–80.

Niedermayer, Oskar. 2006. Das Parteiensystem Deutschlands. In *Die Parteiensysteme Westeuropas*, edited by Oskar Niedermayer, Richard Stöss, and Melanie Haas. Wiesbaden: VS Verlag, 109–133.

Oesch, Daniel. 2008a. The Changing Shape of Class Voting. An Individual-Level Analysis of Party Support in Britain, Germany Switzerland. *European Societies* 10 (3): 329–355.

———. 2008b. Explaining Workers' Support for Right-Wing Populist Parties in Western Europe: Evidence from Austria, Belgium, France, Norway, and Switzerland. *International Political Science Review* 29 (3): 349–373.

Oesch, Daniel, and Line Rennwald. 2010. The Class Basis of Switzerland's Cleavage between the New Left and the Populist Right. *Swiss Political Science Review* 16 (3): 343–371.

Powell, G. Bingham, Jr. 2000. *Elections as Instruments of Democracy. Majoritarian and Proportional Visions.* New Haven/London: Yale University Press.

Powell, G. Bingham, Jr. 2004. The Chain of Responsiveness. *Journal of Democracy* 15 (4): 91–104.

Remmer, Karen L. 2012. The Rise of Leftist-Populist Governance in Latin America: The Roots of Electoral Change. *Comparative Political Studies* 45 (8): 947–972.

Rennwald, Line, and Geoffrey Evans. 2014. When Supply Creates Demand: Social Democratic Party Strategies and the Evolution of Class Voting. *West European Politics* 37 (5): 1108–1135.

Roberts, Kenneth M. 2003. Social Correlates of Party System Demise and Populist Resurgence in Venezuela. *Latin American Politics and Society* 45 (3): 35–57.

———. 2015. Populism, Political Mobilizations, and Crises of Political Representation. In *The Promise and Perils of Populism: Global Perspectives*, edited by C. de la Torre. Lexington, Kentucky: The University Press of Kentucky, 140–158.

Rooduijn, Matthijs, and Tjitske Akkerman. 2017. "Flank Attacks Populism and Left-Right Radicalism in Western Europe." *Party Politics* 23 (3): 193–204.

Rokkan, Stein. 1999. *State Formation, Nation-Building, and Mass Politics in Europe: The Theory of Stein Rokkan, Based on His Collected Works*, edited by Peter Flora with Stein Kuhnle and Derek Urwin. Oxford: Oxford University Press.

Rosas, Guillermo. 2010. Issues, Ideologies, and Partisan Divides. Imprints of Programmatic Structure on Latin American Legislatures. In *Latin American Party Systems*, edited by H. Kitschelt, K. A. Hawkins, J. P. Luna, G. Rosas and E. J. Zechmeister. New York: Cambridge University Press, 70–95.

Rovira Kaltwasser, Cristóbal. 2015. Explaining the Emergence of Populism in Europe and the Americas. In *The Promise and Perils of Populism: Global Perspectives*, edited by C. de la Torre. Lexington, KY: The University Press of Kentucky, 189–227.

Rydgren, Jens. 2005. Is Extreme Right-Wing Populism Contagious? Explaining the Emergence of a New Party Family. *European Journal of Political Research* 44 (3): 413–437.

Sacchi, Stefan. 1998. *Politische Potenziale in modernen Gesellschaften. Zur Formierung links-grüner und neokonservativer Bewegungen in Europa und den USA*. Frankfurt/New York: Campus.

Sartori, Giovanni. 1968. The Sociology of Parties. A Critical Review. In *Party Systems, Party Organizations, and the Politics of New Masses, Beiträge zur 3. Internationalen Konferenz über Vergleichende Politische Soziologie, Berlin, 15.– 20. Januar 1968*, edited by O. Stammer. Berlin: Institut für politische Wissenschaft an der Freien Universität Berlin, 1–25.

Schattschneider, E. E. 1975 [1960]. *The Semisovereign People. A Realist's View of Democracy in America*. London: Wadsworth.

Schmidtke, Oliver. 2004. From Taboo to Strategic Tool in Politics: Immigrants and Immigration Policies in German Party Politics. In *Germany on the Road to "Normalcy": Policies and Politics of the Red-Green Federal Government (1998–2002)*, edited by Werner Reutter. New York/ Houndmills: Palgrave Macmillan, 161–181.

Schwarzbözl, Tobias, and Matthias Fatke. 2016. Außer Protesten nichts gewesen? Das politische Potenzial der AfD. *PVS Politische Vierteljahresschrift* 57 (2): 276–99.

Soroka, Stuart N., and Christopher Wlezien. 2010. *Degrees of Democracy: Politics, Public Opinion, and Policy*. Cambridge: Cambridge University Press.

Stöss, Richard. 2005. *Rechtsextremismus Im Wandel*. Berlin: Friedrich-Ebert-Stiftung.

Stryker, Sheldon. 1980. *Symbolic Interactionalism. A Social Structural Version*. Menlo Park, Readings: Benjamin/Cummings Publishing Country.

———. 2000. Identity Competition: Key to Differential Social Movement Participation? In *Self, Identity, and Social Movements*, edited by S. Stryker, T. J. Owens and R. W. White. Minneapolis, MN: University of Minnesota Press, 21–39.

Stubager, Rune. 2009. Education-Based Group Identity and Consciousness in the Authoritarian–Libertarian Value Conflict. *European Journal of Political Research* 48 (2): 204–33.

Thomassen, Jacques. 1994. Empirical Research into Political Representation: Failing Democracy or Failing Models. In *Elections at Home and Abroad. Essays in Honor of Warren Miller*, edited by M. K. Jennings and T. E. Mann. Ann Arbor, MI: University of Michigan Press, 237–264.

Thränhardt, Dietrich. 1995. "The Political Uses of Xenophobia in England, France and Germany." *Party Politics* 1 (1): 323–345.

Torcal, Mariano, and Scott Mainwaring. 2003. The Political Recrafting of Social Bases of Party Competition: Chile, 1973–95. *British Journal of Political Science* 33: 55–84.

van der Brug, Wouter. 2010. Structural and Ideological Voting in Age Cohorts. *West European Politics* 33 (3): 586–607.

Weyland, Kurt. 2009. The Rise of Latin America's Two Lefts. Insights from Rentier State Theory. *Comparative Politics* 41 (2): 145–164.

———. 2010. The Performance of Leftist Governments in Latin America. Conceptual and Theoretical Issues. In *Leftist Governments in Latin America: Successes and Shortcomings*, edited by K. Weyland, R. L. Madrid, and W. Hunter. Cambridge: Cambridge University Press, 1–27.

Weyland, Kurt, Raúl L. Madrid, and Wendy Hunter, eds. 2010. *Leftist Governments in Latin America: Successes and Shortcomings*. Cambridge: Cambridge University Press.

Appendix A

European cases

The analysis of party positions for the European cases is based on the data collected by Kriesi et al. (2008), and covers four elections in each country. It provides information on party positions in the parliamentary elections of 1975, 1994, 1998 and 2002 in Germany, and the presidential elections of 1988, 1995, and 2002 in France. Because no post-election voter survey is available for presidential elections in France in the 1970s, the analysis relies on the 1978 parliamentary elections for the time point in the 1970s. The following post-election surveys are used to measure voter positions:

France

Enquête post-électorale française, 1978 (Ref.: q0062)

Enquête post-électorale française, 1988 (Ref.: q0601)

Enquête post-électorale française, 1995 (Ref.: q0891)

Panel électoral français 2002 (Ref.: PEF 2002)

Surveys available at the Socio-Political Data Archive (http://cdsp.sciences-po.fr).

Germany

Wahlstudie 1976 (Ref.: ZA0823)

Nachwahlstudie 1994 (Ref.: ZA 2601)

Politische Einstellungen, politische Partizipation und Wählerverhalten im vereinigten Deutschland 1998 (Ref.: ZA 3066)

Bundestagswahlstudie 2002 (Ref.: ZA 3861).

Surveys available at the Central Archive for Empirical Social Research (ZA; www.gesis.org/).

Table 9.A1 Relevant issue-categories and available data on the demand side for each election, France and Germany

France

	Economic dimension		*Cultural dimension*	
	Welfare	Economic liberalism	Cultural liberalism	Budgetary rigor
1978	X	X	X	–

(continued)

Table 9.A1 (continued)

	Economic dimension		*Cultural dimension*	
	Welfare	Economic liberalism	Cultural liberalism	Immigration
1988	X	X	2 dimensions	X
1995	–	2 dimensions	X	X
2002	–	X	X	X

Germany

	Economic dimension		*Cultural dimension*	
	Welfare	Economic liberalism	Cultural liberalism	Budgetary rigor
1976	X	X	X	–
	Welfare	Economic liberalism	Cultural liberalism	Immigration
1994	X	X	X	X
1998	–	X	X	X
2002	–	X	X	X

Note: X denotes that the category can be operationalized and that a single dimension results from the factor analysis. Where one of the two relevant categories that form a dimension cannot be operationalized, only the other category is used. In two cases, the solution is two-dimensional ("2 dimensions"), and both underlying categories are used for the construction of the dimension.

Table 9.A2 Issue positions of parties: average direction of the coded sentences for the relevant categories of issues

France

	Welfare	*Budget*	*Economic liberalism*	*Cultural liberalism*	*Anti-immig.*
Extreme left					
1988	1.00	–1.00	–0.85	1.00	1.00
2002	1.00	0.25	–1.00		–1.00
PCF					
1978	0.94	–0.44	–0.94	0.46	
1988	0.91	–0.75	–1.00	1.00	–0.80
1995	0.75	–1.00	–0.94	0.83	–0.50
2002	1.00	0.33	–0.87	0.60	–1.00
PSF					
1978	0.71	–0.35	–0.86	0.76	
1988	0.72	0.21	–0.48	0.98	–0.46
1995	0.78	–0.10	–0.86	0.75	–0.44
2002	0.63	0.34	–0.67	0.46	–1.00
Ecologists					
2002	0.88	–0.25	–1.00	0.43	–1.00
MRG					
1978	0.77	0.17	–0.58	0.20	
1995	0.56	0.00	–1.00	1.00	–1.00
UDF					
1978	0.23	0.84	–0.37	0.07	

1988	0.16	0.87	0.30	0.82	0.78
1995	–0.33	1.00	–0.71	1.00	1.00
2002	–0.22	0.64	–0.28	0.40	–1.00
RPR					
1978	–0.05	0.85	–0.04	–0.72	
1988	0.20	1.00	0.32	0.12	0.56
1995	0.24	0.60	–0.47	0.26	0.76
2002	0.05	0.94	0.21	0.43	–0.85
FRONT					
1988	–0.05	0.88	–0.71	–0.79	1.00
1995	0.29	0.75	0.00	–0.69	0.68
2002	–0.13	1.00	0.41	–0.71	0.83

Germany

	Welfare	*Budget*	*Economic liberalism*	*Cultural liberalism*	*Anti-immig.*
PDS					
1994					
1998	0.85		0.06	0.80	
2002	1.00	0.00	–0.96	1.00	
Greens					
1994	0.86	–1.00	–0.70	0.71	–1.00
1998	0.58	1.00	–0.56	0.67	–1.00
2002	0.33	0.60	0.11	0.72	–1.00
SPD					
1976	0.27	–0.63	–0.29	0.66	
1994	0.34	0.87	–0.93	0.45	–1.00
1998	0.32	0.40	0.00	0.42	1.00
2002	0.59	–0.29	0.22	0.40	–0.44
FDP					
1976	0.07	–0.78	0.46	0.79	
1994	0.06	0.33	0.68	0.36	–0.75
1998	–0.52	0.92	0.96	0.87	–0.56
2002	–0.13	1.00	0.57	0.54	0.33
CDU 1976	0.48	0.59	0.55	–0.16	
1994	–0.02	0.57	0.32	0.49	0.85
1998	0.13	0.28	0.43	0.07	0.91
2002	0.30	0.56	0.20	0.44	0.56
CSU 1976	–0.10	0.00	0.67	–0.38	
1994	0.64	0.81	0.80	0.14	
1998	–0.07	0.96	1.00	–0.06	1.00
2002	0.63	0.63	0.38	0.23	0.67

Table 9.A3 Indicators used for the operationalization of issue-categories on the demand side

France

1978

Var	*Description*	*Category*
t26	supprimer avantages pour réduire inégalités sociales	welfare
t27	élargir le secteur nationalisé	ecolib
t29	limiter augmentation du niveau de vie pour lutter contre l'inflation	ecolib
t30	interdire les licenciements	ecolib
t71	supprimer le droit de grève ?	ecolib
t64	fier d'être français ?	cultlib
t73	pouvoir prendre la pilule avant la majorité ?	cultlib
t77	rôle de l'école : discipline ou esprit critique ?	cultlib
t87	envoyer les enfants au catéchisme	cultlib

1988

Var	*Description*	*Category*	*Dimension*
q1a6	Salaires égaux: n'encouragent pas à travailler	ecolib	Economic dimension
q4	Difficultés économiques: Etat doit-il contrôler entreprises ?	ecolib	
q31a2	Etat: devrait garantir revenu minimum	welfare	
q31a9	Rétablir impôt sur grandes fortunes	welfare	
q2a1	Couple non marié: condamnable ?	trad. values	Cultural dimension
q2a2	Avortement: condamnable ?	trad. values	
q2a3	Infidélité: condamnable ?	trad. values	
q2a4	Homosexualité: condamnable ?	trad. values	
q31a6	Femme: faite pour élever les enfants ?	trad. values	
q31a7	Société: il faut une hiérarchie	cultlib	
q10	Rôle de l'école: discipline ou esprit critique ?	cultlib	
q1a4	Fier d'être français	cultlib	
q31a5	Juifs ont trop de pouvoir en France	cultlib	
q31a8	Normal que les musulmans en France aient des mosquées	cultlib	
q1a9	Trop d'immigrés en France	immigration	
q31a3	On ne se sent plus chez soi comme avant	immigration	

1995

Var	*Description*	*category*	*dimension*
q36	priorité: compétitivité ou situation des salaries	ecolib	Economic dimension
q20a2	l'Etat intervient-il trop ou pas assez dans la vie économique	ecolib	

q7a1	trop d'immigrés en France	immigration	Cultural dimension
q7a6	on ne se sent plus chez soi comme avant	immigration	
q7a3	homosexualité est acceptable	cultlib	
q7a5	normal que les musulmans en France aient des mosquées	cultlib	
q7a7	normal qu'une femme puisse avorter	cultlib	
q22a1	rôle de l'école : discipline ou esprit critique	cultlib	
q20a1	rôle de la femme (à la maison ou même rôle que hommes)	cultlib	

Battery on positive/negative feelings

Var	*Description*	*Category*	*Dimension*
q21a4	compétition	ecolib	Economic dimension
q21a5	profit	ecolib	
q21a6	syndicat	ecolib	
q21a7	nationalisation	ecolib	
q21a12	privatisation	ecolib	
q21a2	féminisme	cultlib	Cultural dimension
q21a8	autorité	cultlib	
q21a13	islam	immigration	

2002, Wave 2

Var	*Description*	*Category*	*Dimension*
xq237	interdire les licenciements	ecolib	Economic dimension
xq239	Difficultés économiques: Etat doit-il contrôler entreprises ?	ecolib	
xq255	recherches sur le génôme humain	cultlib	Cultural dimension
xq58	rôle de l'école: discipline ou esprit critique	cultlib	
xq39p2_4	les juifs ont trop de pouvoir en France	cultlib	
xq39p2_1	trop d'immigrés en France	immigration	
xq39p2_3	immigrés: source d'enrichissement culturel	immigration	

Germany

1976

Var	*Description*	*Category*	*Dimension*
v503	Staatliche Kontrollen vs. wirtschaftliche Entscheidungen	ecolib	Economic dimension
v505	Wohlfahrtsstaat: Staat vs. Eigenverantwortung	welfare	

(continued)

Table 9.A3 (continued)

Var	*Description*	*Category*	*Dimension*
v504	Öffentliche Ordnung vs. persönliche Freiheit	cultlib	Cultural dimension
v518	Einstellung Scheidungsrecht	cultlib	
v519	Einstellung Abtreibungsrecht	cultlib	
v506	Politisches Mitspracherecht der Kirchen?	cultlib	

1994

Var	*Description*	*Category*	*Dimension*
v39	Skala zur staatlichen Wirtschaftsbelebung	ecolib	Economic dimension
v42	Skala zu staatlichem Wohnungsangebot	ecolib	
v104	Zustimmung, dass Gehorsam und Disziplin wichtig	cultlib	
v100	Mehr oder weniger Geld für Renten/Pensionen	welfare	
v27	Wichtigkeit, dass Staat für mehr Wohnungen sorgt	welfare	
v30	Wichtigkeit Zuzug von Ausländern zu regeln	immig	Cultural dimension
v41	Skala: Ausländerzuzug erleichtern/erschweren	immig	
v44	Müssen sich Ausländer anpassen?	immig	
v45	Ausländer zurückschicken?	immig	
v46	Politische Rechte für Ausländer	immig	
v47	Ausländer – Ehen mit Deutschen?	immig	

1998

Var	*Description*	*Category*	*Dimension*
v177a	Verantwortung Staat Arbeitsplatz für jeden	ecolib	Economic dimension
v350b	Einstellung Nationalisierung wichtiger Unternehmen	ecolib	
v176c	Wichtigkeit Gleichstellung	cultlib	Cultural dimension
v350a	Stolz Deutscher zu sein	cultlib	
v350c	Wieder Mut zu einem starken Nationalgefühl	cultlib	
v174b	Skala Immigration	immig	
v350l	Überfremdung durch Ausländer	immig	
v350n	Zustimmung Ausländer sollten Landsleute heiraten	immig	
v350r	Verständnis für Angriffe Asylbewerberheime	immig	

2002

Var	*Description*	*Category*	*Dimension*
v350b	Einstellung Nationalisierung wichtiger Unternehmen	ecolib	Economic dimension
v350a	Stolz Deutscher zu sein	cultlib	Cultural dimension
v350c	Wieder Mut zu einem starken Nationalgefühl	cultlib	
v174b	Skala Immigration	immig	
v350l	Überfremdung durch Ausländer	immig	
v350n	Zustimmung Ausländer sollten Landsleute heiraten	immig	
v350r	Verständnis für Angriffe Asylbewerberheime	immig	

Table 9.A4 Results of the ordered logit regressions to measure the congruence between voter preferences and party positions, Germany and France

Dimension	*Germany*			*France*		
	Year	*Cultural*	*Economic*	*Year*	*Cultural*	*Economic*
	1975			1978		
coef.		0.75	0.6		0.18	0.95
z		11.5	8.4		5.2	24.7
N		966	1033		2761	2740
	1994			1988		
coef.		0.46	0.25		0.78	0.24
z		5.9	3.8		16.8	6.5
N		1100	1252		1838	2492
	1998			1995		
coef.		0.73	0.44		0.70	0.78
z		9.8	5.7		17.1	20.3
N		1190	1225		2260	2529
	2002			2002		
coef.		0.73	0.36		0.74	0.39
z		8.0	4.6		17.7	11.2
N		1017	1125		2184	2693

Note: The results displayed in the figures in the main text show z-values corrected for sample size, while this table shows the raw results of the regressions. The sample size differs considerably between Germany and France, as this table shows, making it necessary to correct for sample size in order to compare responsiveness across the two contexts.

Appendix B

Latin American cases

The analysis of party positions in Uruguay and Venezuela is based on the PELA elite surveys conducted by the Elites project at the University of Salamanca (http://americo.usal.es/oir/elites/index.htm). The surveys used for Uruguay are Estudio 34 (legislative period 1995–2000) and Estudio 54 (legislative period 2005–2010), and for Venezuela Estudio 36 (legislative period 1993–1998) and studio 35 (legislative period 2000–2005). For both Uruguay and Venezuela, the most recent data set is used for the second time point. Because no survey was conducted in Venezuela subsequent to the one fielded in 2000, the second time point is earlier in this country.

For the first time point, face-to-face interviews with legislators were conducted in 1995, very close to the fieldwork of the World Values Survey's (WVS) Wave 3 (1994–1999) wave, where the interviews in Venezuela and Uruguay were conducted in 1996. For the second point in time, Wave 4 (1999–2004) was used for Venezuela (fielded in 2000) and Wave 5 (2005–2009) for Uruguay (fielded in 2006). Data and documentation are available under www.worldvaluessurvey.org.

Table 9.B1 Indicators used for the operationalization of issue-categories on the supply side (PELA elite surveys)

Uruguay

1995

Var	*Description*	*Category*	*Dimension*
p42	Opinion on privatization	ecolib	Economic dimension
p35a01	Opinion on responsibilities of the state: price control	ecolib	
p35a04	Opinion on responsibilities of the state: jobs for all	welfare	
p35a03	Opinion on responsibilities of the state: lodging	welfare	
p35a06	Opinion on responsibilities of the state: social insurance	welfare	
p35a08	Opinion on responsibilities of the state: unemployment insurance	welfare	
p35a10	Opinion on responsibilities of the state: look after the needs of all citizens	welfare	

2005

Var	*Description*	*Category*	*Dimension*
p35	Opinion on privatization	ecolib	Economic dimension
p28	Preference for regulated economy vs. market society	ecolib	
p2901	Opinion on responsibilities of the state: price control	ecolib	
p2904	Opinion on responsibilities of the state: guarantee employment	ecolob	
p2609	Opinion on responsibilities of the state: unemployment insurance	welfare	
p2910	Opinion on responsibilities of the state: cover the basic needs of citizens	welfare	

Venezuela

1995

Var	*Description*	*Category*	*Dimension*
p42	Opinion on privatization of state industries	ecolib	Economic dimension
p43	Opinion on privatization of public services	ecolob	
p35a04	Opinion on responsibilities of the state: jobs for all	welfare	
p35a03	Opinion on responsibilities of the state: lodging	welfare	
p35a06	Opinion on responsibilities of the state: social insurance	welfare	
p35a08	Opinion on responsibilities of the state: unemployment insurance	welfare	
p35a10	Opinion on responsibilities of the state: look after the needs of all citizens	welfare	

2000

Var	*Description*	*Category*	*Dimension*
p43	Opinion on privatization of state industries	ecolib	Economic dimension
p3501	Opinion on responsibilities of the state: price control	ecolib	
p3504	Opinion on responsibilities of the state: jobs for all	ecolib	
p3401	Opinion on statement: society is complex, the state cannot efficiently solve the problems of citizens	ecolib	
p3402	Opinion on statement: state intervention is the only way to reduce inequality	ecolib	
p3404	Opinion on statement: state should interfere as little as possible in society, private initiative is positive	ecolib	
p34a	Scale: neoliberalism vs. state intervention	ecolib	
p3503	Opinion on responsibilities of the state: lodging	welfare	
p3508	Opinion on responsibilities of the state: unemployment insurance	welfare	
p3510	Opinion on responsibilities of the state: look after the needs of all citizens	welfare	

Table 9.B2 Indicators used for the operationalization of issue-categories on the demand side (World Values Survey)

Uruguay

1996

Var	*Description*	*Category*	*Dimension*
v126	Public vs. private ownership	ecolib	Economic dimension
v128	Competition good or bad	ecolib	
v125	Incomes should be made more equal	welfare	
v127	Government responsibility that everybody is provided for	welfare	

2006

Var	*Description*	*Category*	*Dimension*
v117	Public vs. private ownership	ecolib	Economic dimension
v119	Competition good or bad	ecolib	
v116	Incomes should be made more equal	welfare	
v118	Government responsibility that everybody is provided for	welfare	

Venezuela

1996

Var	*Description*	*Category*	*Dimension*
v126	Public vs. private ownership	ecolib	Economic dimension
v128	Opinion on protectionism	ecolib	
v125	Incomes should be made more equal	welfare	
v127	Government responsibility that everybody is provided for	welfare	

2000

Var	*Description*	*Category*	*Dimension*
v142	Public vs. private ownership	ecolib	Economic dimension
v1440	Competition good or bad	ecolib	
v145f	Society aimed at: regulations vs. self-responsibility	ecolib	
v141	Incomes should be made more equal	welfare	
v143	Government responsibility that everybody is provided for	welfare	
v145d	Society aimed at: egalitarian vs. competitive	welfare	
v145e	Society aimed at: extensive welfare vs. low taxes	welfare	

Table 9.B3 Results of the ordered logit regressions to measure the congruence between voter preferences and party positions, Uruguay and Venezuela

Dimension	*Uruguay*		*Venezuela*	
	Year	*Economic*	*Year*	*Economic*
	1995/6		1995/6	
coef.		0.77		0.10
z		5.6		0.74
N		632		449
	2005		2000	
coef.		0.47		–0.49
z		2.9		–2.03
N		588		586

Note: The sample size does not differ considerably between Uruguay and Venezuela, and thus the z values are not corrected for sample size as in the European cases. The negative coefficient and z-value in Venezuela in 2000 is discussed in the main text.

10 Conditional populist voting in Chile, Greece, Spain, and Bolivia

Ioannis Andreadis, Kirk A. Hawkins, Iván Llamazares, and Matthew M. Singer

The ideational theory implies that support for populist parties stems from more than just their opposition to immigration or to globalization, their support for redistribution, or the charisma of their leaders; parties could potentially campaign based on these policies without using populist appeals. Instead, it argues that populist parties combine these issue positions with a model of representation whereby politics represents the conflict between the will of the people and a conspiring elite. The expectation is that voters who hold active populist attitudes are more likely to support populist parties. After all, populist parties' gambit is that such discourse will enable them to add support to whatever their policy positions might garner alone.

In this chapter, we test the individual-level implications of the ideational argument. We expect latent populist attitudes are widespread in many societies and that, when activated, they will lead people to support populist parties. Yet populist attitudes will not translate into political behavior without activation. We focus on three factors that should condition the linkage between populist attitudes and populist party support. As laid out in the introduction to this volume, electoral support for populist parties should be contingent on a context generating public demand for populist approaches and a party system supplying credible populist alternatives. Therefore, populist appeals will only win support from citizens to the extent that there is evidence that a conspiring elite exists and the system is not fully responsive to the popular will. This evidence could include party policies converging or corruption being (or perceived as) widespread. Moreover, as the crisis fades, those attitudes can become deactivated and stop being the basis of these parties' public support, even as populist parties continue evoking populist rhetoric. Finally, populist appeals alone are unlikely to win parties' support; voters might agree with a populist party about the state of political representation in their country but will not support that party if they reject its policy vision. If there is no crisis of representation or if populist party policies do not align with voter priorities, then we will not see voters convert their latent populist attitudes into support for populist parties.

We test these expectations using survey data from four cases where populist forces have emerged in the last decade: Chile, Greece, Spain, and Bolivia.[1] These four cases differ in the degree to which the party system has faced a crisis of representation, the availability of populist parties with different ideological positions, and the degree to which populists have become entrenched as the new ruling parties, allowing us to test predictions that flow from the ideational theory. Survey data confirm that latent populist attitudes are strong in all four cases. Yet, in two of the four cases (Chile and Bolivia), populist attitudes have minimal connection to voter choices, providing evidence that populist attitudes are less likely to be activated in a system where traditional parties are either perceived to provide strong representation (Chile) or in systems where the populist parties oversaw a robust economy and a meaningful expansion of public representation (Bolivia). In the other two cases (Greece and Spain), recent severe economic and political crises have activated populist attitudes and lead to populist votes, conditional on when voters agree with parties' ideological messages as well as their populist ones. Our study concludes that the relationship between populist attitudes and populist votes does not exist in a vacuum but emerges as voters respond to the populist parties' claims and overall policy vision.

Theory

Survey data collected in many societies shows that populist attitudes are widespread (see van Hauwaert et al. and Castanho e Silva et al. in this volume). Yet, the existence of populist attitudes does not mean that voters will automatically support a populist candidate or political party. Indeed, citizens hold a variety of policy views and political dispositions without automatically voting on them. Instead, three things must usually occur for an issue – any issue – to become salient. First, attitudes only become translated into votes as they are primed by candidates, parties, and the media (Iyengar and Kinder 1987; Druckman et al. 2004; Hart 2013). Second, issues only have an effect on the degree that voters identify those issues as personally important and relevant to the situation (Krosnick 1988; Young et al. 1991; Singer 2011). Third, a particular issue that has been primed and is deemed relevant can still have its impact fade if other issues are seen as more pressing (Edwards et al. 1995; Carlin et al. 2015).

The ideational theory developed in this volume speaks to each of these three conditions hypothesized by the general literature on issue salience. The first is satisfied by the presence of populist candidates who, by definition, are priming populist attitudes. But for these primes to have an electoral effect (the second condition), their credibility needs to be established and other issue considerations need to not trump these considerations.

The perceived relevance of populist primes is likely to be satisfied by the context in which they are made. Populist attitudes are unlikely to gain traction without a context that makes populist claims about the state of political representation in a country credible and important enough to consider. The ideational theory of populism stresses that populism emerges in the context of representational crises that allow voters to conclude that elite collusion is occurring. These democratic failures should make anti-elite sentiment more accessible and populism a more salient voting consideration. In the absence of these conditions, populist attitudes may exist but voters are unlikely to dwell on them when voting, focusing instead on parties' other programmatic and valence characteristics.

While the context can activate populist concerns, issue priming theories recognize that issues can also become deactivated if the underlying crisis fades (Edwards et al. 1995; Singer 2011). The implication is that populist ideals can become deactivated if the crisis of representation is resolved, either by institutional reforms or by improved economic and governance outcomes. If these good outcomes occur without populist parties ever gaining office, then the demand for populist parties may fade. If these improvements are overseen by populist parties, then voters may reward them for good performance. As a result, the connection between populist attitudes and support for populist parties may fade as valence replaces populist ideas as the main driver of their public support.

Finally, populist attitudes are unlikely to matter if populist ideas do not connect with issue positions that are meaningful to voters. Populism is a "thin-centered" ideology, as opposed to a "thick" or classical one (Mudde and Rovira Kaltwasser 2013; Stanley 2008) asserting that the will of the people is being blocked by a conspiring elite. Voters may accept that premise and be open to voting for a populist party, but they are unlikely to do so if they reject that party's articulation of what the will of the people is and the political and economic project it entails. Even in contexts where crises make populist appeals credible, voters will not support populist candidates whose policy programs they reject, because these policy aims are likely to be more salient than populist methods are. Populist attitudes, if activated, can explain why a left-leaning voter supports a populist leftist over a non-populist leftist, but should not lead that voter to support a populist conservative.

The ideational theory of populism suggests that voters support populist actors at least in part because they espouse populist ideals of representation. Yet, the effect of populist attitudes on vote choices will also likely be conditional, varying both across countries as the applicability of anti-elite sentiments vary and within them according to the policy positions those parties take and their resonance with the electorate across different contexts.

Four cases of potential populist mobilization

In this chapter, we explore four cases that differ sharply in terms of populist success: Chile, Spain, Greece, and Bolivia. Although these four cases all have parties that provide populist options for voters, the recent level of success of these parties varies widely. Not surprisingly, they also differ in the level of representation crises, the types of policy appeals that populist parties espouse, and the degree to which these populist forces have become political insiders. These differences allow us to look at some of the conditions under which populist attitudes translate into populist votes.

Table 10.1 summarizes the intensity of the populist appeals used by parties and political leaders in these four countries' party systems. We use the data provided by Hawkins and Castanho Silva in Chapter 1 in this volume, which uses holistic grading to measure discourse in the parties' platforms and campaign speeches. We also summarize the "thick" ideological appeals of parties as coded by expert surveys, and we summarize the parties' electoral strength in recent elections.

Table 10.1 Average populist discourse of presidential candidates and party leaders

	Populism score		*Left-right ideology*[1]	*Percentage in most recent election*
	Speeches	*Platform*		
Presidential candidate (Chile)				
Roxana Miranda (Equality Party)	2.0	2.0	2.47	1.24[2]
Marco Enriquez Ominami (PRO)	0.9	0.3	3.05	10.98
Michelle Bachelet (New Majority)	0.1	0.7	2.76	46.70
Franco Parisi (independent)	0.1	0.0	NA	10.11
Evelyn Matthei (Alliance)	0.0	0.0	9.00	25.03
Electorally weighted average	**0.2**	**0.4**		
Party (Spain)				
Unidad Popular	1.3	1.2	2.00[3]	3.68[4]
Democràcia i Llibertat	0.6	1.0		2.25
ERC		0.7	3.67	2.39
Podemos	0.9	0.6	1.67	20.68

Bildu		0.4	6.30	0.87
Ciudadanos	0.0	0.2	5.56	13.94
Partido Popular	0.0	0.2	7.30	28.71
Partido Socialista Obrero Español	0.1	0.2	3.80	22.00
Coalición Canaria		0.0	6.00	0.32
Partido Nacionalista Vasco	0.0	0.0	6.30	1.20
Electorally weighted average	**0.3**[5]	**0.4**		
Party leader (Greece)				
Tsipras (SYRIZA)	1.7		2.00	36.34[6]
Kammenos (ANEL)	1.3		8.78	4.75
Koutsoumbas (KKE)	1.2		0.67	5.47
Samaras (New Democracy)	0.5		7.22	27.81
Mihaloliakos (Golden Dawn)	0.5		9.89	6.28
Theodorakis (POTAMI)	0.4		4.89	6.05
Venizelos (PASOK)	0.1		4.78	4.68
Electorally weighted average	**1.0**			
Party (Bolivia)				
Movement for Socialism (MAS)	1.6	1.55	1.28	61.36[7]
Christian Democratic Party (PDC)		0.3	8.19	9.04
Democratic Unity (UD)		0.25	5.76	24.23
Electorally weighted average		**1.1**		

1 Taken from the Chapel Hill Expert Survey (Polk et al. 2017) for Spain and Greece and from Wiesehomeier and Benoit (2009) as compiled by Baker and Greene (2011) for Chile and Bolivia. Parties are coded by experts on their overall left-right placement on a 0–10 scale for the European parties and 1–20 for the Latin American ones; we have recoded the Latin American scores on the same 0–10 scale as the European ones.
2 Results of the 2013 Chilean presidential election, first round
3 Score for IU
4 Results for 2015 Spanish general elections
5 This weighted average is calculated being weighting each score by the percentage of the votes cast by parties for which speeches were scored.
6 Results of the January 2015 Greek general elections.
7 Results of the 2014 Bolivian presidential elections.

Voters in all four countries had the option of supporting a populist party. In the case of Chile, the most populist appeals came from radical candidates of the left such as Roxana Miranda of the Equality Party (see Aguilar and Carlin 2017, and in this volume, Chapter 17), whose speeches scored just as populist as those of Hugo Chávez and his successors. The center-left PRO coalition, an electoral vehicle for Marco Enriquez-Ominami, also espoused moderate levels of populist rhetoric. Yet the main parties—those that have dominated Chilean politics since the return to democracy—showed almost no reliance on populist appeals; a slight suggestion of populism appeared only in Bachelet's campaign platform and Parisi's closing campaign speech, and there were no traces of populism in any of Matthei's speeches or her platform. We see a significant difference in rhetoric between the non-populist traditional parties and the populist party upstarts that could have potentially mobilized electoral support.

Spain represents a case of somewhat greater populist success, although it is still one where populists have not come to power. Podemos ("We Can") emerged out of protest movements in the late 2010s to finish in third place in the recent 2015 and 2016 general elections.[2] Podemos combined strong demands for increased redistribution and a larger economic role for the state with populist rhetoric emphasizing the difference between the people and "the caste" (*la casta*), the political and economic elites that occupy a privileged social position and have dominated economic and political institutions in Spain. Podemos' speeches emerge in Table 10.1 as moderately populist, but not as strongly populist as many of the other cases in this volume due to its emphasis on discussions of class alongside its more general populist appeals, as well as a more subdued tone. Furthermore, Podemos is not the only populist alternative for Spanish voters. The established leftist party, the United Left (IU) competing under the Popular Unity banner, emerged as the most populist party in the 2015 elections. The IU strategically shifted to populism as it saw its position as the main leftist alternative to the traditional PP and PSOE being eroded by Podemos's rise. Likewise, Democracy and Liberty (DiL) and the Republican Left of Catalonia (ERC) stood out among the regional parties for their moderate to strong embrace of populist rhetoric. The other regional parties and the traditional national PP and PSOE, in contrast, used almost no populist rhetoric in their rhetoric or platforms.

In Greece, we find a strong case of recent populist success. A small slate of populist parties have competed in politics since the end of World War II, most notably the Greek Communist Party, or KKE, whose leader Dimitris Koutsoumbas' rhetoric makes frequent references to "the Greek people" and its capitalist enemies that match the definition of populism.[3] Yet, in the run up to the 2015 elections, a number of new major populist parties emerged on the left and the right that framed the crisis as an elite conspiracy against the Greek people. The two most prominent were SYRIZA, led by Alexis Tsipras; and Independent Greeks (ANEL) led by Panos Kammenos. Although these parties represented different views on other ideological dimensions, with SYRIZA seen as more consistently left and Independent Greeks as more socially right, both relied heavily on populist rhetoric.[4] The traditional governing parties were much less populist in their rhetoric, as the leaders of the outgoing coalition (Venizelos of PASOK and Samaras of New Democracy) both expressed little to no populism. The leader of POTAMI, a new centrist party formed by a political amateur, also registered a low level of populism.

Finally, Bolivia is also a case of populist success. The most populist party in Bolivia was its largest: the Movement for Socialism (MAS). The MAS differs somewhat from other cases of left-populism through its use of "ethnopopulist" appeals (Madrid 2012). The MAS has its origins in ethnic politics and has continued to mobilize traditionally disenfranchised ethnic groups behind Evo Morales personally (he is ethnically Aymara and speaks both Aymara and Quechua and worked as a coca farmer) and behind demands for ethnic and linguistic pluralism. Yet, the MAS reached out to non-ethnic voters through populist appeals that promised to use greater state intervention to generate economic development, all while denouncing corrupt and established elites. The political opposition to the MAS varied by election, as it has so far failed to consolidate or to articulate a programmatic alternative that resonates with voters (Centellas 2015). Yet, the opposition parties made fewer populist appeals in their platforms than the MAS in the most recent elections.[5]

The context for the activation of populist attitudes differs predictably across these four countries. Bolivia and Greece have had widespread – as opposed to punctuated – political and economic failures that should make populist appeals resonate with voters. In Bolivia, the traditional parties converged ideologically and enacted the neoliberal policies of the Washington Consensus (Kingstone 2011, 86–90), leaving few policy differences on which voters could distinguish them (Kitschelt et al. 2010; Singer 2016). A series of policy failures created dissatisfaction with existing parties and led to multiple populist parties emerging in the 1990s and 2000s in addition to the MAS. Large segments of the population were dissatisfied with neoliberal policies that failed to correct high levels of inequality and poverty. Corruption was very high; Bolivia consistently ranks in the bottom 30th percentile for control of corruption according to the World Bank's Governance Indicators. Finally, the major parties had all ideologically converged, as all three parties had ruled in coalition with each other and enacted the same basic neoliberal economic policies. This dissatisfaction culminated in the MAS winning the 2005 elections. While the MAS has been unable to make large strides in reducing corruption since taking office, the combination of a commodities boom and redistributive policies resulted in poverty being reduced by half since the MAS took office in 2005 (Vargas and Garriga 2015). Moreover, the MAS instituted a series of institutional reforms that their critics claim have weakened liberal democracy but which its supporters argue have empowered traditionally disempowered indigenous and impoverished groups (Pearce 2011; Farthing and Kohl 2014).

Corruption has also been a long-standing problem in Greece; the country ranks as the most corrupt country in Western Europe by Transparency International's Corruption Perceptions Index (CPI) and in the 54th percentile in the World Bank's control of corruption measure. The economic crisis also resulted in perceived failures of representation, as the European Commission, the European Central Bank, and the International Monetary Fund — the so-called Troika — compelled Greece to undergo a series of painful fiscal adjustments in exchange for a bailout loan despite popular opposition. Moreover, ND and PASOK were compelled to create a unity government that could manage the ongoing economic crisis, further blurring the differences between the major national parties. Finally, the traditional parties' reliance on patronage and corruption led to fiscal mismanagement that was seen as a key contributor to the crisis (Pappas 2013). These domestic and international factors created opportunities for populist parties to criticize the traditional parties as not only ineffective but as traitors of the Greek people.

Conditions for populist appeals were not quite as ripe in Spain. The main Spanish parties have generally provided clear programmatic differences along standard left-right dimensions (Dalton and Anderson 2011, 15) and in the mid-2000s Spain was in the 88th percentile of the World Bank's control of corruption index, 20 points higher than Greece. Yet, recent years brought challenges. The global economic crisis hit Spain particularly hard, and in 2010 the leftist PSOE government was compelled to enact austerity measures that it had previously rejected, policies that were maintained and deepened by the PP government after it won elections in 2011. This convergence in economic policies resulted in widespread social protests against the cuts to social programs. Spain was also rocked by several corruption scandals, which resulted in Spain falling to the 70th percentile in the World Bank's corruption control measures in 2015, which, while still higher than Greece's current ranking, was a large drop. All of these recent events should have created openings for populist parties.

Finally, of all four cases Chile has experienced the lowest degree of representational failure (Navia and Walker 2008). Kitschelt et al. (2010, 171) consider the Chilean party system the best approximation in Latin America of the programmatic ideal, i.e., a political system with parties that are internally consistent in their ideological message while consistently differentiating themselves from each other. Chile is also notable for a lack of corruption; in 2015 it ranked in the 87th percentile for the World Bank's control of corruption score, the second best score in Latin America. Yet, in recent years there have been signs of increasing political unresponsiveness that might create space for populist mobilization. Luna and Altman (2011) have shown that the party system is frozen at the elite level and increasingly disconnected from civil society. This disconnect has resulted in falling levels of partisanship (Lupu 2015, 235) and distrust in parties (Carlin 2014). Moreover, the traditional axes of party competition – class, religion, and attitude toward the Pinochet regime – have progressively weakened since the transition to democracy in 1989 (Bargsted and Somma 2013). The result has been massive waves of protests, the appearance of strong social movements (Donoso 2013), and the rise of the populist fringe parties highlighted in Table 10.1. Yet, these crises seem much smaller, in relative terms, than those facing the other three countries in this analysis.

These differences across the four cases suggest that populist parties should be best positioned to activate latent populist attitudes in Greece and Bolivia than in Spain or especially Chile. Yet, the context is not the only factor that should condition voter responses to populism. In three of these four cases (Chile, Spain, and Bolivia), populism is only attached to leftist policy positions, especially in economic terms. To the degree that populist attitudes are activated within these countries, their impact will be limited to voters sharing this policy vision. Greece, in contrast, provides latent populist voters with multiple policy alternatives. As described in Table 10.1, the Chapel Hill Expert Survey scores ANEL as strongly right and SYRIZA as strongly left. ANEL is less conservative on economic policies than on social issues, but its score on the markets question (5.6) still diverges from SYRIZA (1.44). This means that populist attitudes may split voters between these two parties depending on their ideological preferences (Andreadis, Stavrakakis and Demertzis 2018).

Finally, the electoral importance of populist attitudes in Bolivia may be limited by the success the MAS has had in improving economic and representation outcomes in the country since taking office. Corruption has remained widespread in Bolivia under MAS leadership, with some scandals implicating the friends and family of Morales, perhaps leading some Bolivians to view the MAS as now part of the conspiratorial elite against which they have traditionally railed. Yet, the strong economy, falling poverty, and increased outreach to impoverished and indigenous voters could send the message that the crisis of representation has passed. As a result, these policy successes may have deactivated the populist attitudes that were at the root of the party's rise. In this case, we are likely to observe a weak connection between voters' populist attitudes and their propensity to support the MAS or Morales.

How common are populist attitudes in our case?

To test these claims, we model vote choice in each country using a series of public opinion surveys conducted close to recent elections.[6] In each survey, we included the six-item battery for measuring populist attitudes developed by Akkerman et al. (2014) and discussed and critiqued elsewhere in this volume (Chapter 6) by van Hauwaert, Schimpf, and and Azevedo. While we acknowledge the weaknesses of this battery, it was the state of the art when we conducted these surveys and this chapter presents a first cross-regional attempt to systematically model the conditions under which these attitudes become politically activated.

One of the first findings to note is that all four cases also have substantial proportions of their electorates expressing agreement with populist attitudes. The data in Figure 10.1 confirm a generally high (although far from universal) agreement with the indicators of

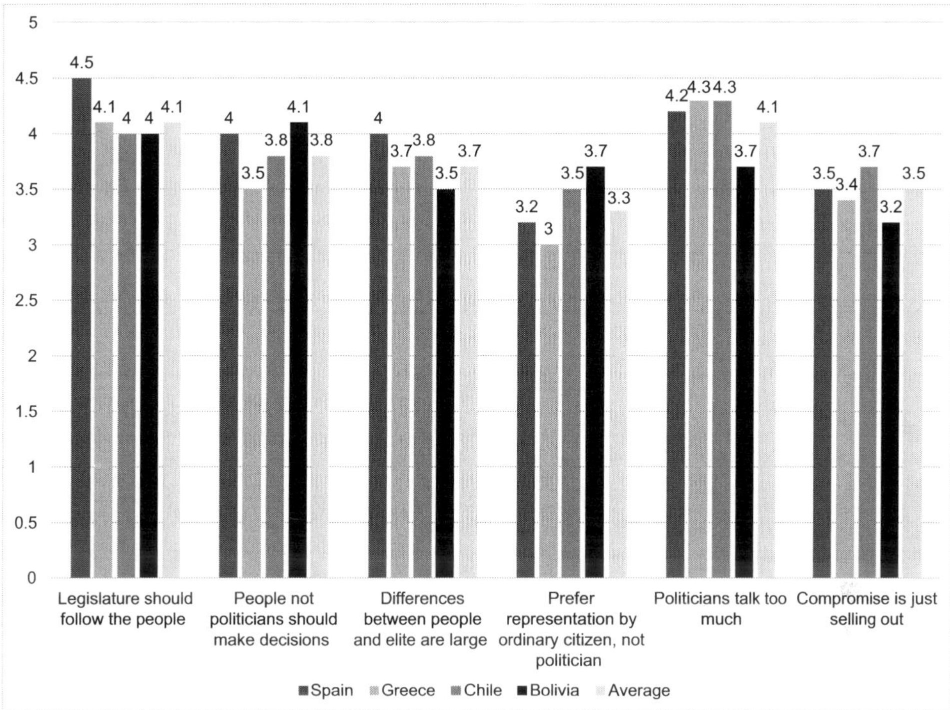

Figure 10.1 Levels of populist attitudes by country

populist attitudes in all four countries. Citizens are particularly likely to agree that politicians need to follow the will of the people and that politicians talk too much and take too little action. There is more moderate support for the statements that people and not politicians should make policy and that the differences between people and the elites are bigger than the differences between people. Finally, there was less support for the ideas that voters want to be represented by ordinary people or that compromise equates to selling out, but even in those cases, the average response in all countries was at least a 3 on the 5-point scale. Interestingly, general agreement with these ideas does not seem to vary according to the depth of recent political crises, as levels of agreement with these statements are just as high in any one country as in the others.

We further explore whether these questions measure a single, underlying, latent set of populist attitudes. In three of the four cases there is clear evidence. Specifically, in Spain, Greece, and Chile, separate factor analyses show the six populist items tap into a single strong factor (see Appendix 10.1 for details). Furthermore, Cronbach's alpha for the populist statements in Spain is 0.77, in Greece is 0.74, and in Chile is 0.70, suggesting that they scale reliably. In these cases, we can easily measure the extent to which individuals hold attitudes consistent with ideational populism. Results of the battery are less coherent in Bolivia. Specifically, the factor analysis shows that the questions load on two factors, although the second one has an eigenvalue just barely above the conventional threshold. The second factor is dominated by two questions that emphasize the role of the public in the policymaking process ("The people and not politicians should make our most important policy decisions," and "I would rather be represented by a citizen than by a specialized politician"). Yet, these two questions share enough commonalities with the other questions that if we do a factor analysis of the four questions that load on the first factor and either one or the other two questions, then a single factor emerges, although the question about preferring representation by a citizen instead of a specialized politician loads more weakly than the others. Not surprisingly, Cronbach's alpha (0.56) is also lower in Bolivia than it is in the other cases. Despite the weaker than expected coherence of the Bolivian data, the overall positive associations suggest these questions shed at least some light on how strongly different citizens hold populist attitudes and might be positioned to mobilize their support for populist candidates.

Association of populist attitudes with the vote

The data in Figure 10.1 suggest that the necessary attitudinal support for populist ideals exists in all four cases. Yet, the ideational theory argues that voters' populist attitudes, while widespread, require parties to activate them and a context in which they will resonate. Additionally, we argue that populist attitudes' effects on vote choice must also not be undermined by policy views that contradict the populists' policy vision. Our four cases vary on each of these dimensions and, therefore, permit a first-cut probe of these expectations.

Chile

In our first case, Chile, we expect that populist attitudes will not be fully activated within the electorate due to the lack of a deep representational crisis. To look at this, we model respondents' choice in the first round of the 2013 election as a multinomial logit, using vote for Matthei as the baseline since she represented the incumbent coalition. Our main independent variable is respondents' populist attitudes. We control for economic and social policy beliefs, evaluations of the economy, and partisanship, whose effects are consistent with expectations from previous work on Chile. But we see in Table 10.2 that populist attitudes are significant predictors of the vote for Enriquez-Ominami. In particular, while Bachelet voters were more likely to hold populist attitudes than Matthei voters, Enriquez-Ominami voters were significantly more likely to hold populist attitudes than voters for either traditional candidate. The predicted probability that a voter with high populist attitudes supports Bachelet is no different from the probability that a voter with low populist attitudes supports her (see Figure 10.2).[7]

Table 10.2 Unconditional model of candidate preferences in Chile, 2013 election

Variable	*Bachelet*		*MEO*		*Parisi*	
Populist attitudes index	0.42	*	0.89	**	0.09	
Social ideology	–0.18		–0.50	*	–0.18	
Economic ideology	–0.72		–0.27		–0.07	
Environmental protection	0.31	*	0.36		0.56	*
Constitutional change	0.28	*	0.38		0.08	
Sociotropic retrospective	-0.71	***	-0.71	**	–0.46	
Sociotropic prospective	0.02		-0.10		–0.01	
Pocketbook retrospective	0.05		0.36		–0.04	

Pocketbook prospective	0.26		0.87	**	−0.11			
Alianza	−3.72	***	−3.67	***	−3.52	***		
Nueva Mayoría	16.80		15.23		13.53			
Age	−0.02	*	−0.02	*	−0.05	***		
Sex	−0.08		−0.57		−0.41			
Education	−0.78	***	−0.39	*	−0.12			
Constant	3.42		−2.08		3.23			
Variable	*Other*		*None*		*Missing*		*Abstain*	
Populist attitudes index	0.61		0.52		0.35		0.31	
Social ideology	−0.98	***	−0.21		−0.17		−0.13	
Economic ideology	0.15		−0.12		−0.07		−0.22	
Environmental protection	0.08		0.10		0.17		0.06	
Constitutional change	0.54		0.32		0.20		0.50	***
Sociotropic retrospective	−0.60	*	−0.85	**	−0.54	**	−0.59	**
Sociotropic prospective	−0.09		0.08		0.12		−0.32	
Pocketbook retrospective	−0.37		−0.42		−0.14		0.01	
Pocketbook prospective	−0.19		0.07		0.31		0.04	
Alianza	−0.91		−22.05		−1.98	***	−3.75	***
Nueva Mayoría	14.17		13.24		15.59		14.81	
Age	−0.07	***	−0.02	*	−0.01		−0.07	***
Sex	−0.41		−0.43		−0.17		−0.41	
Education	0.58	**	−0.34	*	−0.35	***	−0.77	***
Constant	2.05		2.65		2.36		6.02	***
Model type	*Multinomial logit, Matthei is the baseline*							
N	1,456							
pseudo R2	0.16							

* $p<0.05$ ** $p<0.01$ *** $p<0.001$ (two tailed)

The results in Table 10.2 suggest that populist attitudes are becoming activated in Chile; however, the size of the effect is still small. If we consider a range of 2.5–5.0 on the scale of populist attitudes (about two standard deviations above and below the mean), the predicted shift in voting probability for Enriquez-Ominami is about 5 percentage points. Considering that he received 11.0 percent of the vote in the actual election, this is an important element of his overall political support. But these effects are sufficiently small that Enriquez-Ominami did not seriously challenge either of the main candidates in the first round despite the high levels of agreement with populist attitudes highlighted in Figure 10.1. Instead, many voters with populist attitudes turned to Bachelet despite her minimal use of populist rhetoric. This suggests that populist considerations were not activated in this election. Given the small size of these effects, to conserve space we omit any further test of the interaction between populist attitudes and ideology and move to our next country.

Spain

We expect populist attitudes to be slightly more activated in Spain than they are in Chile due to the recent convergence of the parties and corruption scandals. In Table 10.3 we

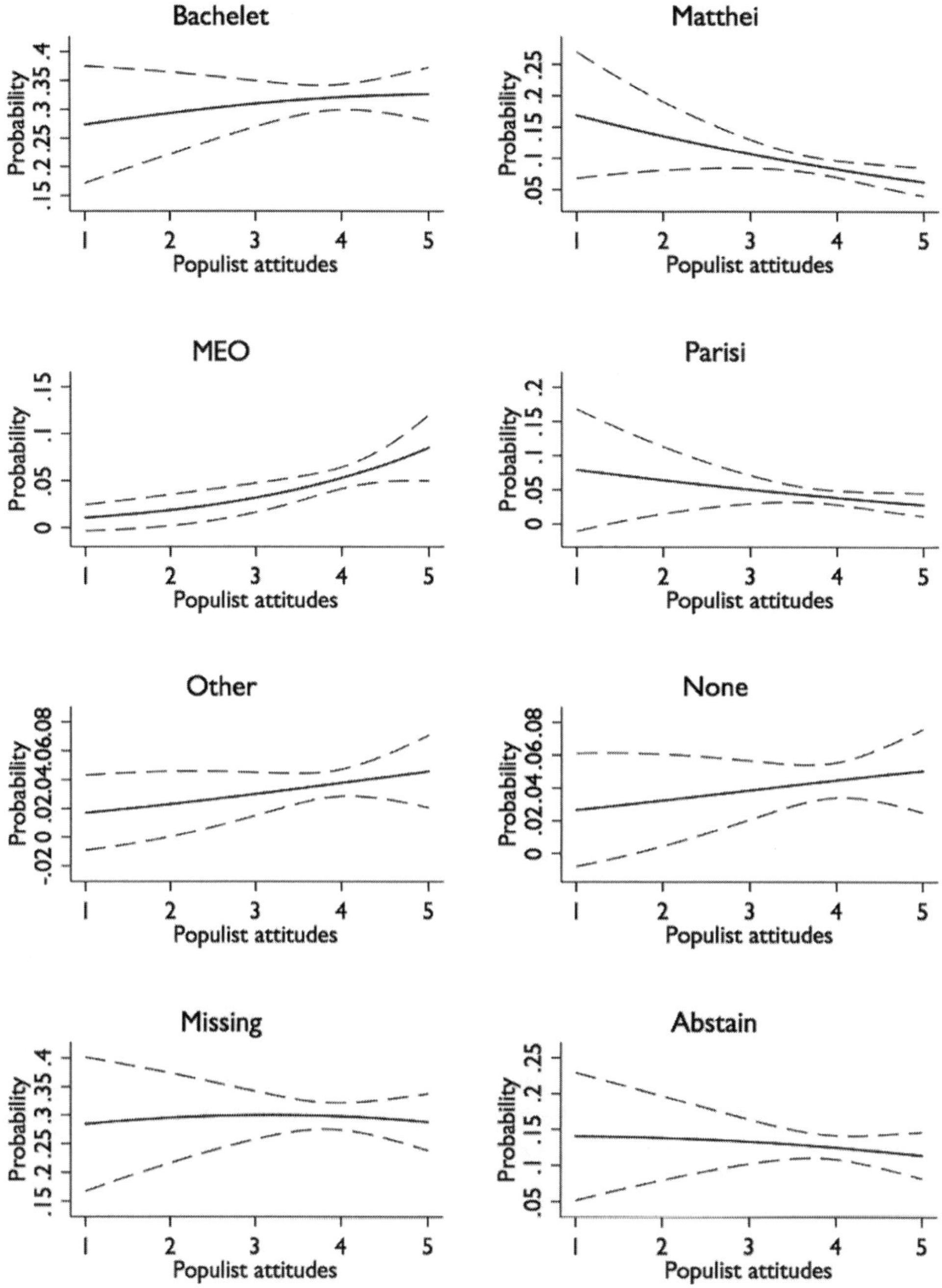

Figure 10.2 Predicted probabilities of Chilean voting, by populist attitudes (95% confidence interval)

model vote intention as a multinomial logit, with vote for the PP as the baseline category because this was the largest party in the 2015 general elections and also because this party's discourse did not include populist elements. For this analysis, we have merged into a single category the vote for Podemos and its regional alliances (En Marea in Galicia, En Comú Podem in Catalonia, and Compromís-Podemos-És el moment in Valencia). The model includes a fairly standard set of controls including preferences on economic policies and regional identities, retrospective economic measures, and demographic controls that are described in more detail in Appendix 10.2. While these results suggest a multitude of factors structuring voter choices in Spain, including ideology, regionalism, economic performance, and demographics, we focus our attention here on the role of populist attitudes.

The results in Table 10.3 confirm that populist attitudes have been politically activated in Spain. As one would expect, populist attitudes do not differentiate support for PSOE from support for the PP. Instead, holding populist attitudes leads voters to reject both traditional parties and vote for Podemos, Ciudadanos, the IU, or the ERC, or to abstain. Given the strong emphasis many of these parties gave to populist rhetoric in their campaigns and platforms, it is not surprising that voters who have a populist worldview were

Table 10.3 Unconditional model of party preference in Spain, 2015 election

Variable	*PSOE*		*Podemos*		*Ciudadanos*		*IU*	
Populist attitudes index	0.22		0.86	***	0.66	***	0.91	**
Left-right	−1.15	***	−1.07	***	−0.27	***	−1.31	***
Market	0.20		−0.27		0.03		−0.15	
Globalization	0.30		0.55	***	0.05		0.45	*
Peripheral identity	2.07	*	2.81	**	1.77		1.67	
Sociotropic retrospective	0.60	***	0.83	***	0.43	*	0.66	**
Sociotropic prospective	0.01		−0.09		0.04		0.24	
Primary education	0.11		−0.05		−0.65		−0.96	
College education	0.10		0.06		0.34		−0.08	
Age	−0.03	**	−0.05	***	−0.04	***	−0.03	*
Sex	0.22		0.59	*	0.49		−0.29	
Constant	4.14	**	3.14	**	0.61		−0.42	
Variable	*UPyD*		*DiL*		*ERC*		*Abstain*	
Populist attitudes index	0.85		0.86		0.55	*	0.84	***
Left-right	−0.53	**	−0.28		−1.00	***	−0.62	***
Market	−0.27		0.04		0.08		0.25	
Globalization	−0.10		0.18		0.15		−0.02	
Peripheral identity	1.93		7.23	***	7.14	***	3.15	**
Sociotropic retrospective	−0.05		0.98	*	0.47		0.21	
Sociotropic prospective	0.99	*	−0.07		−0.07		0.59	**
Primary education	1.42		−1.31		−0.78		−0.10	
College education	1.22		0.13		0.15		−0.06	
Age	−0.03		0.03		0.00		−0.04	***
Sex	0.32		−0.34		−0.10		0.17	
Constant	−5.21		−10.85	***	−2.83		−0.10	
Model type	*Multinomial logit, PP is the baseline category*							
N	1,208							
pseudo R2	0.22							

* p<0.05 ** p<0.01 *** p<0.001 (two tailed)

prone to support these parties instead of the traditional dominant parties. But populist values are also a significant predictor of vote for Ciudadanos, a party that did not include any populist elements in its campaign discourse but which, as a new party in the political scene, represented a break with the traditional party elite.

The sizes of these effects in Spain are larger than those observed in the Chilean case. If we again consider a range of 2.5–5.0 on the scale of populist attitudes, the predicted shift in voting probability for Podemos goes up by about 12 percentage points and for Ciudadanos goes up by about 5 percentage points. On the other hand, predicted support for the PP or PSOE falls by roughly 10 points (Figure 10.3).

Yet, the effects on average in Figure 10.3 are only for the average voter – they do not take into account how voters see the ideological program that populists are mobilizing. The data in Table 10.3 confirm that support for national parties in Spain is strongly shaped by left-right self-placement and, in the case of Podemos, by attitudes about globalization, while support for the Catalan parties (DiL, ERC) is shaped by attachment to a regional identity, as is support for Podemos due to its alliance with peripheral nationalist or regional forces and its defense of multinational federalism. We expect these two strong divides in Spanish politics to shape how populist attitudes get translated into votes, limiting the importance of populist attitudes for voters who reject the populist parties on ideological grounds.

We begin by looking at the effect of parties' ideological visions. Based on our unconditional analysis and our grading of party discourses, we expect populist attitudes to have opposite effects among leftist voters, making them less likely to vote for the traditional PSOE and more likely to support Podemos and IU. Yet, we expect populist attitudes will not lead conservative voters to support either of these parties because they are likely to disagree with Podemos and IU about what the will of the people is. Populist attitudes should be associated with a rejection of the PP, but we are less certain about how conservative populist individuals will vote because no party articulated a populist message with a conservative policy stance.

To test the conditioning role of ideology, we interact populist attitudes with left-right self-placements. The table of results is not presented here to preserve space (see Appendix 10.3) but in Figure 10.4 we plot the predicted marginal effect of populism on support for different parties conditional upon respondents' ideology. These results are generally consistent with our expectations. For example, the top row of Figure 10.4 shows that populism has no added effect on whether voters on the left support or reject the PP or on how voters from the right evaluate PSOE. Yet among those who are ideologically predisposed to support one of the traditional parties, attitudes about populism significantly structure reaction to those parties. Among left-oriented voters, populism has strong positive effects on voting for Podemos and negative effects on voting for the PSOE, as populists reject the traditional party and endorse its traditional alternative. The figure for IU voters is also consistent with our expectations, except that conditional effects do not reach statistical significance, perhaps due to the relatively small number of voters in this category. Similarly, among rightist voters populism has a negative effect on voting for the PP. Yet as conservative populists reject the PP, they generally do not cross the ideological divide to support Podemos or the IU despite their strong populist profiles. Instead, among voters on the right, populist attitudes led voters to support Ciudadanos, despite its relatively limited use of populist appeals in the speeches analyzed in Table 10.1. This suggests that a somewhat stronger populist discourse would have been more in line with the preferences of the voters of Ciudadanos and points to a possible opening in the political space in future elections for a right-leaning populist party.

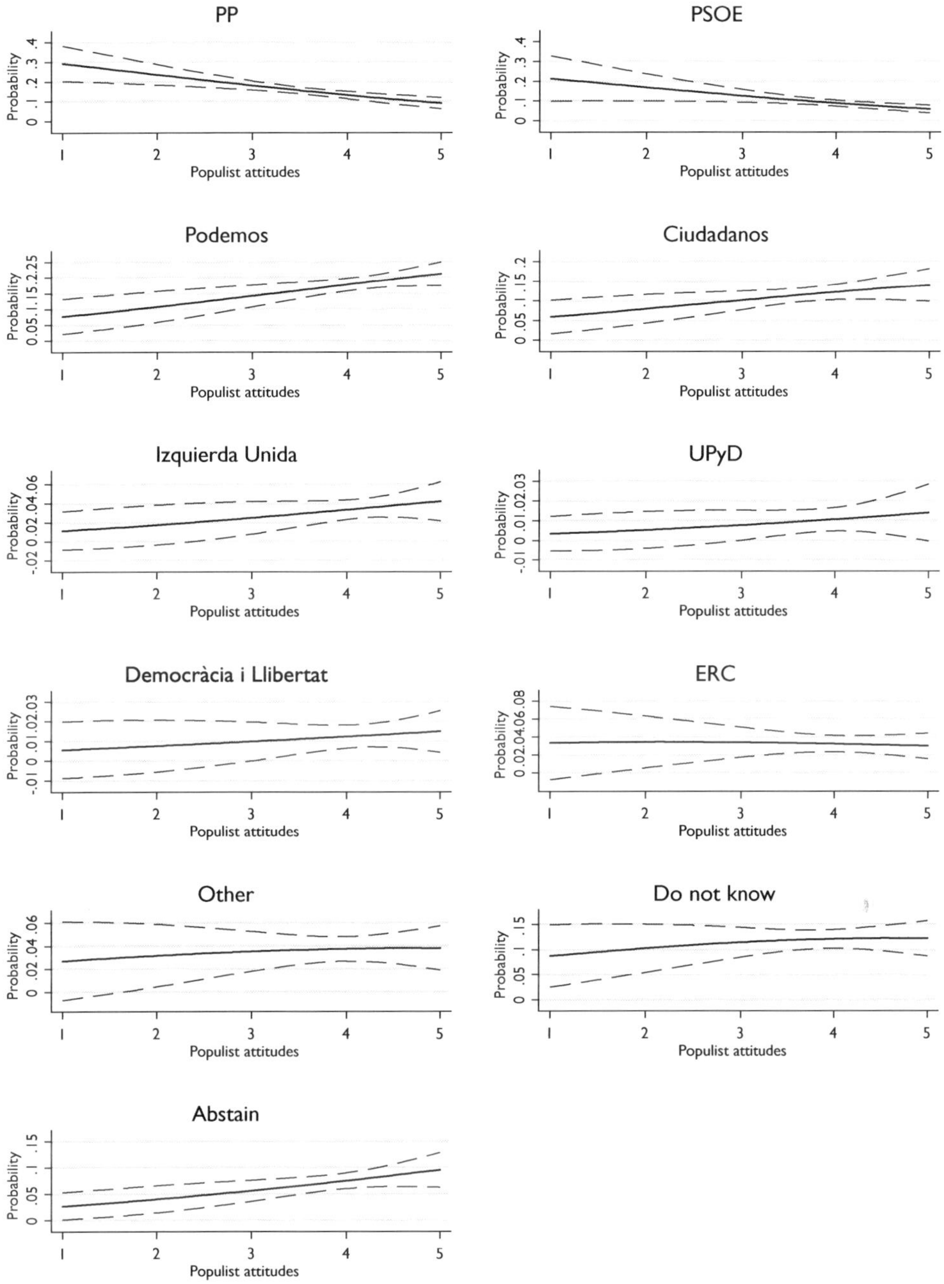

Figure 10.3 Predicted probabilities of Spanish voting, by populist attitudes (95% confidence interval)

While ideological divisions are important, center-periphery conflicts have also played a crucial role in the development of the Spanish party system and should shape how voters respond to populist appeals. More specifically, the electoral appeal of autonomist

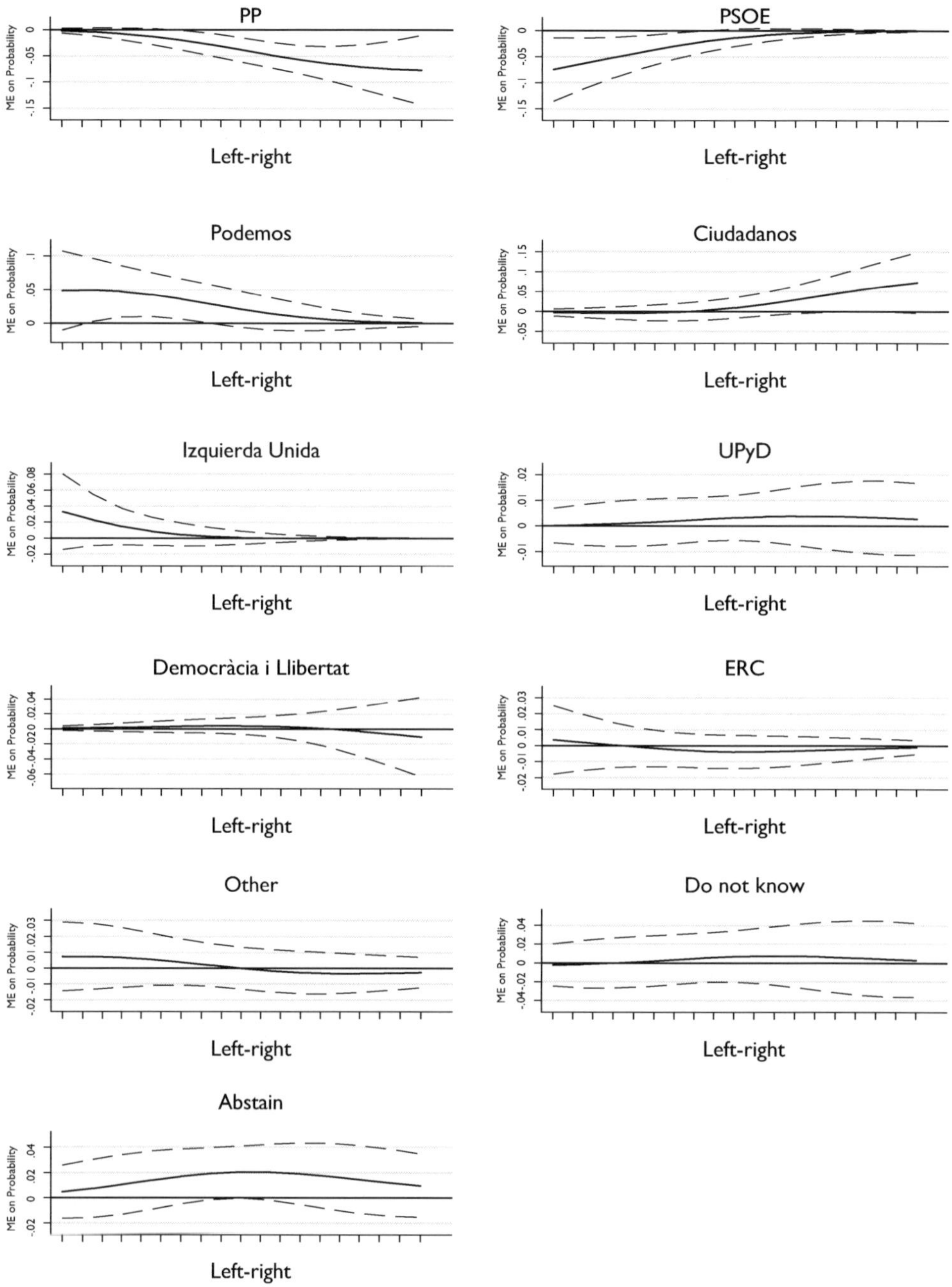

Figure 10.4 The predicted marginal effect of holding populist attitudes in Spain, conditional on left-right self-placement (95% confidence interval)

parties in the Basque country, Catalonia, and Galicia has been based on the strength of distinctive peripheral identifications in those territories (as shown by the very large coefficients for this variable in our unconditional voting models for ERC and DiL).

These regional attachments may also be more salient to voters than are populist appeals. In Appendix 10.3 we ran a model interacting the measure of peripheral identities with populist attitudes; the marginal effect of populism conditional on regional identities are graphed in Figure 10.5. These results show that populist attitudes significantly decrease the probability of voting for the PP and the PSOE while they increase the probability of voting for Podemos among voters who do not hold strong peripheral identifications. Yet among individuals for whom regional considerations are salient, populism has almost no added effect on how voters evaluate these latter parties. An analysis restricted to Catalan voters did not show any positive effects of populist attitudes on voting for DiL and ERC conditional on peripheral identifications, perhaps due to small sample sizes. There is some evidence that among the voters displaying strong peripheral identification, populism has significant positive effects on voting for Ciudadanos but the substantive significance of that effect is very small. These null results for populist attitudes among those with periphery identities suggest that, for the Spanish case at least, as regional identities become salient, the populism message becomes less important.

Greece

The Greek case has even more severe crisis characteristics than those that activated populist attitudes in Spain. Hence we expect to see populist attitudes translated more consistently into votes for populist parties. Yet, unlike in Spain, populists in Greece emerged on both the right and the left, espousing competing national projects as the will of the people (Andreadis and Stavrakakis 2017). The choice of populist party is likely to be conditional upon voters' additional policy views.

We model political support in Greece by using a two-part closed-ended question that asks whether respondents voted in the January 2015 election and, if so, which party they voted for. From this we model reported vote as a multinomial logit, using New Democracy as the baseline because it was the least populist of the major parties. The main predictor of interest is the populist attitude index, but the models include an array of controls for vote choice models, including measures of respondent ideology and issue concerns, assessments of economic performance, and demographics described in Appendix 10.2.

The results in Table 10.4 suggest that populist attitudes were strongly associated with voter choices in the January 2015 Greek elections. Individuals with strong populist attitudes are significantly more likely to vote SYRIZA and significantly less likely to vote for New Democracy, POTAMI, or PASOK. Voters for KKE and ANEL are also more likely to lean populist. The effects of populism for the first two parties are quite large. A shift from 2.5–5.0 in populist attitudes is associated with a 30 percentage point shift in the vote for SYRIZA and a (negative) shift of 25 percentage points for New Democracy.

As discussed, we do not necessarily expect populism to be the only issue on which voters choose, and that is what we see in Table 10.4: respondents' positions on economic ideology, socio-cultural preferences and the EU were correlated with political choices. The two major issues in the recent Greek elections were over relations with the EU and over social conservatism/nationalism, with populist parties on both sides of these divides. To test if voters take into account populist parties' positions on these salient issues, we interact populist attitudes with attitudes about European unification *and*, in a separate set of models, respondents' social ideology, nesting these terms in the basic models from Table 10.4.

The full models are available in Appendix 10.3; in the section below we jump to the conditional effects that emerge from that model. Figure 10.6 graphs the estimated effect

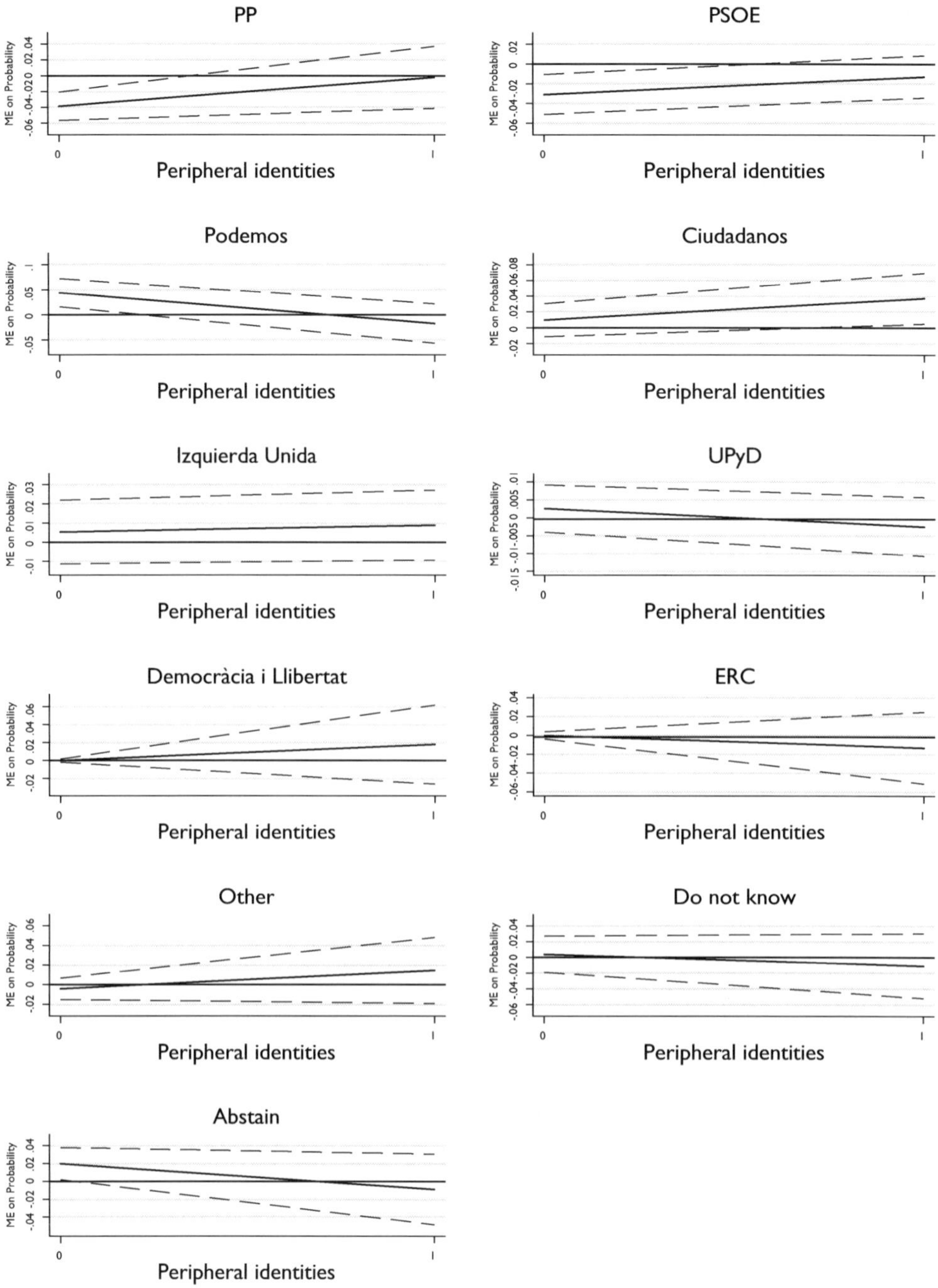

Figure 10.5 The predicted marginal effect of holding populist attitudes in Spain, conditional on self-identification with the national periphery (95% confidence interval)

of populist attitudes conditional only upon levels of EU support. The results confirm that populist attitudes correlate with a rejection of traditional parties. Populist attitudes are negatively associated with support for the incumbent and decidedly non-populist ND across the board. Non-populists who supported the EU were willing to support PASOK,

Table 10.4 Unconditional model of party preference in Greece

Variable	*SYRIZA*		*GD*		*POTAMI*		*KKE*		*ANEL*	
Populist attitudes index	1.56	***	1.09		0.24		1.61	**	1.24	**
Social ideology	−1.60	***	2.00	**	−1.15	***	−1.83	***	0.33	
Economic ideology	−6.30	***	−2.67		−0.15		−6.86	***	−5.58	***
European unification	−0.04		−0.14		0.10	*	−0.21	*	−0.17	**
Pocketbook retrospective	0.26		−0.15		0.07		1.39	**	0.51	
Pocketbook prospective	0.54	**	0.04		−0.08		−1.23	*	0.33	
Age	0.00		−0.03		−0.01		−0.03		0.02	
Sex	−0.10		−0.91		0.04		0.31		−0.52	
Education	−0.10		−0.31		0.11		−0.35		−0.20	
Constant	9.41	***	−3.87		1.41		11.67	**	2.11	
Variable	*PASOK*		*OTHER*		*NONE*		*MISSING*		*Abstention*	
Populist attitudes index	0.12		1.23	***	1.26	**	1.00	***	1.59	***
Social ideology	−1.47	***	−1.59	***	0.21		−1.01	***	−1.71	***
Economic ideology	−1.95		−4.26	***	−5.01	**	−3.31	***	−2.09	*
European unification	0.02		−0.04		−0.01		−0.01		−0.05	
Pocketbook retrospective	0.02		0.05		−0.57		0.09		0.25	
Pocketbook prospective	0.09		−0.82		0.03		−0.24		0.05	
Age	0.02		−0.00		0.01		0.01		−0.03	*
Sex	-0.09		−0.09		−0.89		−0.41		0.09	
Education	-0.19		−0.08		0.00		0.01		0.07	
Constant	5.81		7.84	*	2.01		5.31	*	2.82	
Model type	*Multinomial Logit, New Democracy is the baseline*									
N	910									
Pseudo R2	0.18									

* p<0.05 ** p<0.01 *** p<0.001 (two tailed)

but the impact of populism on voting for PASOK is not significant on the anti-EU side. This is probably related to the fact that PASOK has been the party with the strongest pro-EU policies since the beginning of the financial crisis; as a result, citizens with anti-EU attitudes would not vote for PASOK, no matter what their preferences are on other issues. Consequently, adding populism to anti-EU attitudes does not produce any additional damage for PASOK. Yet among those who supported the EU but were populist, support for SYRIZA emerges strongly. Populists who opposed the EU, in contrast, did not support SYRIZA but instead tended to vote for "other parties," a category primarily captures the vote for ANTARSYA and KKE-ML, communist parties which we were unable to include in our discourse analysis but which are generally regarded as extremist and anti-establishment; or populists abstained, which essentially represents a decision to vote against the highly popular but pro-EU SYRIZA.

However, there is a negative finding. The interaction is not significant or even in the expected direction for ANEL; not only does the confidence interval overlap the zero-effect line, but the trendline is basically flat. This finding is more dissatisfying, because the party is known for its anti-EU positions in the past; we expected it to emerge as an alternative for populist, anti-EU voters looking for an alternative to the pro-EU SYRIZA and the marginal communists.

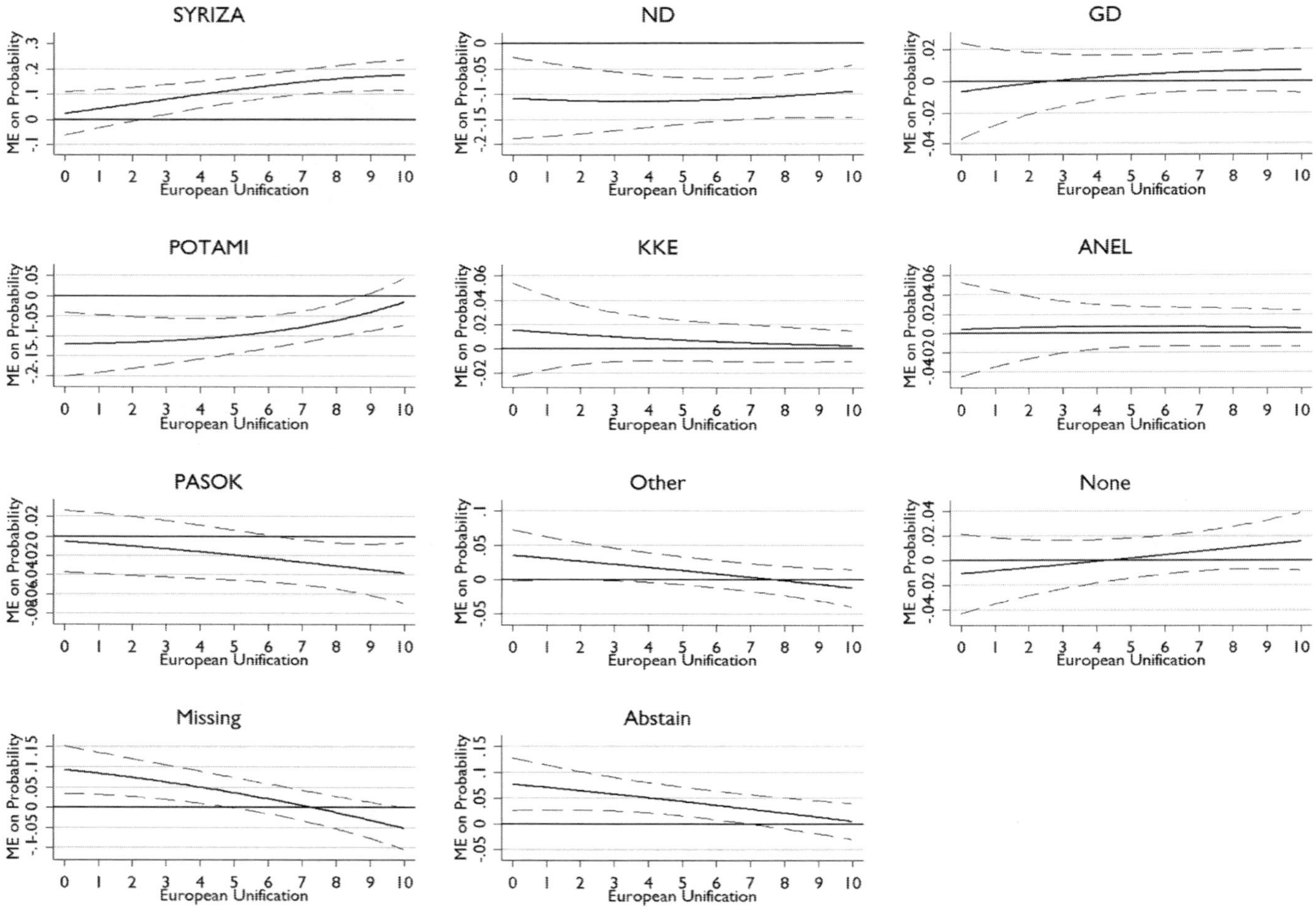

Figure 10.6 Marginal effects plots of Greek voting, populism x European unification (95% confidence interval)

The answer, we believe, requires taking into account a second ideological dimension: socio-cultural left-right self-placement. We do not use the overall left-right dimension because the right-wing populist parties in Greece a) tend to reject self-categorizations on the left-right dimensions and b) support many leftist economic policies, for example, strong intervention of the state in the economy and opposition to economic liberalism (Tsatsanis, Andreadis and Teperoglou, 2018). As a result, left-wing and right-wing populist parties do not have a significant distance on the economic left-right scale. On the other hand, they have very different preferences on most socio-cultural issues, such as law and order or immigration policy (Stavrakakis, Andreadis and Katsambekis, 2017). Thus, we interacted socio-cultural left-right self-placement with attitudes about the EU and populist attitudes.

The results of the model—a triple interaction—are difficult to depict even graphically. Thus, in Figure 10.7 we focus on just two parties, ANEL and, for a reference point, SYRIZA. Full results of the model, as well as graphs for other parties, are found in the online Appendix 3. The array of graphs describes the average marginal impact of populist attitudes at different levels of social ideology (vertically, across the rows of graphs) and European integration horizontally (across the x-axis). From this analysis we see that, for SYRIZA, there is no connection between populist attitudes and attitudes towards European integration among voters with left socio-cultural preferences, but there is a strong connection between populist attitudes and (positive) attitudes towards European integration among voters with a moderate/moderate-right ideology. The slope of the line is towards the upper right and is furthest from the zero reference line in these two middle graphs. However, we now also have a clear finding for ANEL. There is a strong connection between populist attitudes and (negative) attitudes towards European integration, but only among voters with a strong right socio-cultural ideology; the marginal effects line slopes downwards and left (low support for European integration) and clears the zero reference line only in the last row of graphs. Thus, the impact of populist attitudes for ANEL (and even SYRIZA) becomes much clearer once we take into account the multiple issues affecting this election. Populist attitudes have a stronger effect when paired with voter agreement with the party's policy positions.

Bolivia

We use a June 2016 survey of urban Bolivians to look at whether populist attitudes underlie individuals' ongoing support for Evo Morales' MAS party. The first dependent variable is how respondents would vote if an election were held today. Because of the divided and unsettled nature of the opposition to the MAS, with the main alternative party differing in each of the three national elections Morales won, we simply asked citizens to say if they would support the governing party, support a candidate from a party that is distinct from the current government, cast a null vote, or abstain. This measure asking for general support of the ruling party also allows for the uncertainty at the time of the survey about who Morales' successor will be. Voters were divided on the prospect of continuing MAS rule, with 34 percent of those who gave a valid response saying they would support the MAS, 39 saying they would support a different party, 24 percent saying they would cast a null or blank vote, and the remainder abstaining. The divided support for the MAS is not surprising as the survey came just a few months after voters voted against a referendum that would have allowed Morales to seek additional terms. Again, to avoid politicizing this issue, the question asked about voting for a representative of the current president's party without mentioning Morales by name. We model this dependent variable as a

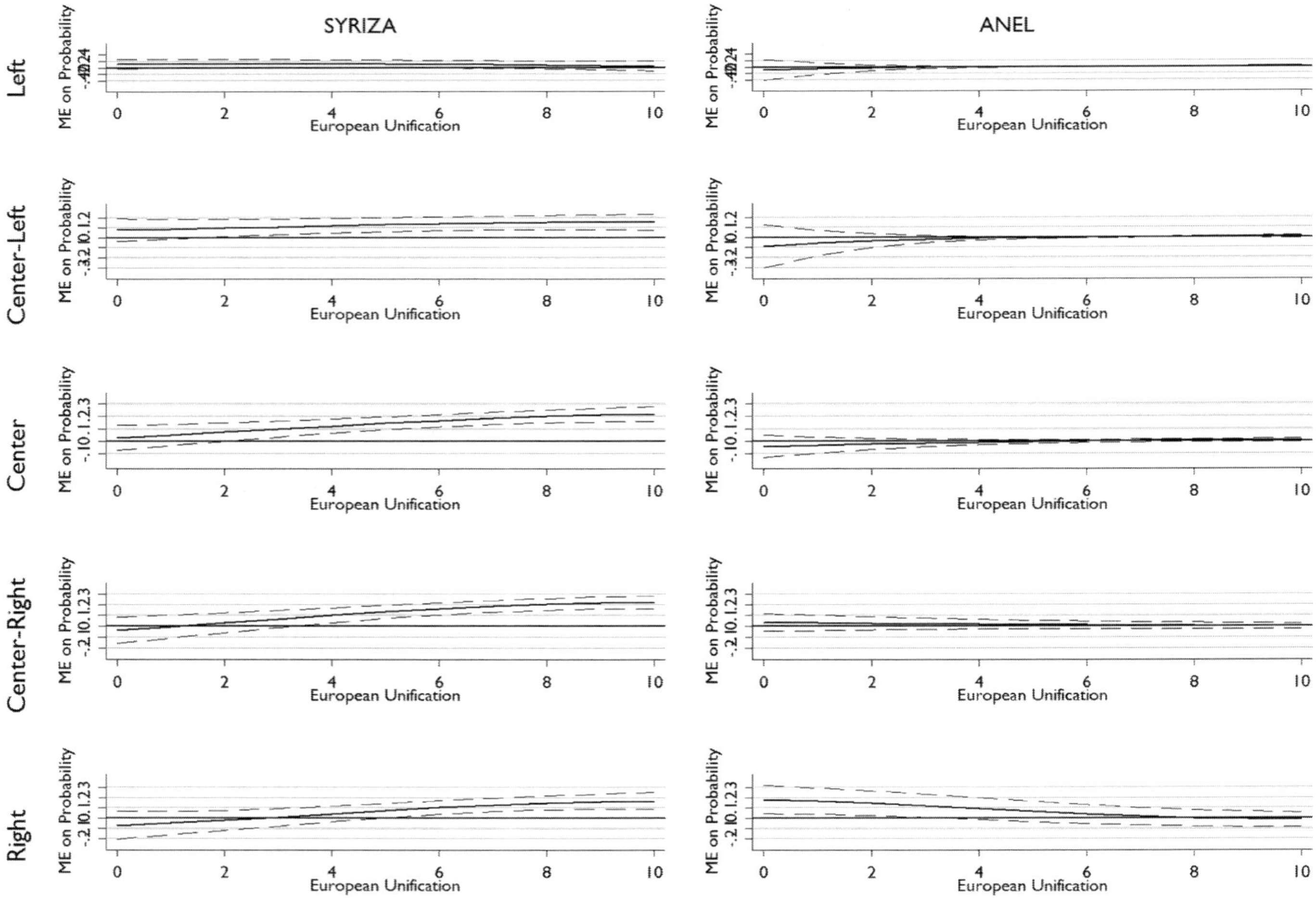

Figure 10.7 Marginal effects plots of Greek voting, populism x European unification x social ideology (SYRIZA and ANEL only)

multinomial logit, using support for the ruling MAS as the baseline category. We also model citizen approval of President Morales' job performance, in case attitudes about populism are more closely connected to the candidate than to his party. Approval of Evo Morales was higher than support for his party, with 55.8 percent of respondents expressing approval. We model this binary variable with a logit model.

Given the strong use of populism by the MAS's leadership, we would generally expect those who have a populist worldview to be most inclined to support the MAS and to approve of Morales. While the variables in Figure 10.1 do not load on a single dimension in Bolivia as well as they do in other contexts, we believe that they correlate strongly enough to explore whether they provide any insight into political dynamics. We created an additive scale of the six indicators of agreement with populist rhetoric.[8] The omnibus survey in which these questions were embedded does not provide any questions about policy preferences, but the model includes measures of how respondents perceived fluctuations in the national economy and their personal finances in the previous year as well as various demographic controls. The specific question wordings for the control variables are detailed in Appendix 10.2.

The key finding in Table 10.5 is that the level of agreement the respondent had with populist ideas is not significantly associated with either support for the ruling party or government approval in Bolivia in 2016. As one would expect given the extant literature on Bolivian politics, support for the ruling party is strongly connected to perceived fluctuations in the national economy and respondents' personal finances, is lower among wealthy and educated individuals, and is particularly strong among individuals who self-identify as either Quechua or Aymara compared to those who self-identify as Mestizo. Yet, populist attitudes have no independent effect on support for Morales. In results not presented here, we interacted the populist attitudes measure with levels of wealth, education, and ethnic self-identification to see if populist attitudes have a stronger effect on any subset of the electorate in a way similar to those observed in the other cases in this chapter, but the findings were still null.

The divergence of these correlations from the significant ones that emerge in Chile, Greece, and Spain is surprising given that the rhetoric employed by Morales and the MAS approximates the populist ideal. Yet, just as crises can provide contexts wherein politicians can prime and activate populist attitudes, this may be a case where strong performance has deactivated them. Bolivia's economy has averaged more than 4 percent annual growth for the 12 years Morales has been in office, poverty has been cut in half, and participatory institutional reforms have been enacted that have increased political representation of traditional marginalized indigenous communities. Thus, while the MAS could continue to employ populist rhetoric even after a decade in office, citizen support for the MAS may be less about its populism given its successes in reducing poverty and increasing political incorporation.

Survey data collected closer to Morales' ascension to power is consistent with the argument that populist attitudes were once activated and a key element of public support for Evo Morales. The full populist world-view battery developed by Akkerman et al. was not asked in any Bolivian surveys prior to the one we commissioned in 2016, but the 2008 AmericasBarometer conducted by the Latin American Public Opinion Project at Vanderbilt University[9] included two questions that tap into the key dimensions of populism: Manichean discourse and the conflict between the popular will and the conspiratorial elite.

Table 10.5 Vote intentions and presidential approval, Bolivia 2016

Variable	*Vote for the opposition*		*Blank vote*		*Abstain*		*Presidential approval*	
Populist attitudes	0.013		0.013		–0.051		–0.011	
Economy compared to previous year	–0.543	***	–0.344	**	–1.106	***	0.543	***
Personal finances compared to last year	–0.561	***	–0.488	***	–0.691	**	0.435	***
Education	0.120	*	0.111	*	0.010		–0.094	*
Female	–0.089		0.143		–0.269		0.025	
Age 16–25	0.457		0.287		1.628		–0.176	
Age 26–35	0.483		0.076		1.775		–0.093	
Age 36–45	0.396		0.045		1.174		–0.212	
Age 56–65	0.279		0.194		1.808		0.336	
Age 66+	0.254		–0.741		2.020		0.234	
Wealth	0.488	***	–0.063		0.602		–0.384	**
Quechua	–0.967	***	–0.775	*	-1.713	*	0.387	
Aymara	–0.893	***	–0.723	**	–0.252		0.511	**
White	1.217		1.358		–12.693	***	–1.018	
Other indigenous	–0.791		–0.017		–14.046	***	0.288	
Afro-Bolivian	0.543		1.027		–13.409	***	-0.594	
No ethnicity	–0.726		–0.338		0.724		0.147	
Constant	1.337	*	0.833		0.337		–0.914	
Model type	*Multinomial logit, vote for the President's party is the baseline*						*Binary logit*	
N	856						853	
χ^2	2411.29***						126.69***	

* p<0.05 ** p<0.01 *** p<0.001 (two tailed)

- Would you agree or disagree with the following statement: In the world today, there is a fight between good and evil and people need to choose between the two?
- Would you agree or disagree with the following statement: The largest obstacle for our country's progress is the dominant class or oligarchy that takes advantage of the people?

Respondents expressed their agreement/disagreement with these statements on a 7-point scale. Agreement with the second question was more common than the first, but in both cases more than 50 percent of respondents chose one of the three strongest levels of agreement while only 30 percent of respondents gave one of the three lowest responses to the first question and less than 20 percent disagreed with the second. We combine these two questions into an additive scale and use them to explore whether these two populist attitudes predict support for the ruling party over the opposition, abstaining, or casting a null vote if an election were held that day.[10] The multinomial logit in Table 10.6 shows that individuals who expressed general agreement with populist arguments in 2008 were indeed more likely to express support for Morales instead of either voting for an opposition candidate or casting a blank vote. While the difference between the results in Table 10.5

Table 10.6 Vote intentions, Bolivia 2008

Variable	*Vote for the opposition*		*Blank vote*		*Abstain*	
Populist attitudes	−0.101	**	−0.078	**	−0.058	
Economy compared to previous year	−1.243	***	−0.764	***	−0.809	**
Personal finances compared to last Year	−0.259		−0.422	**	−0.365	
Ideological self-identification on the right	0.492	***	0.330	***	0.333	***
Government should own more businesses	−0.258	***	−0.217	***	−0.147	*
State should reduce inequalities	−0.176	*	−0.149		−0.250	*
Income quintile	0.204	*	0.275	**	0.063	
Education	−0.006		0.016		0.034	
Age 16–25	0.175		0.376		0.094	
Age 26–35	−0.289		0.080		−0.675	
Age 36–45	0.201		0.173		−1.221	*
Age 56–65	0.029		0.244		−0.104	
Age 66+	0.654		0.439		0.311	
Female	0.099		0.063		0.280	
Ethnicity - mestizo	−0.560		−0.172		−0.473	
Ethnicity - indigenous	−1.971	***	−1.556	***	−1.942	*
Ethnicity - black	2.845	*	−12.419	***	−12.561	***
Ethnicity - mulato	14.112	***	14.765	***	−0.523	
Ethnicity - other	−1.170		−1.452		−13.469	***
Rural	-0.653		−0.478		−0.234	
Constant	1.954	**	1.140		0.284	
Model type	*Multinomial logit, vote for the President's party is the baseline*					
N	856					
F	44.95***					

* p<0.05 ** p<0.01 *** p<0.001 (two tailed)

and Table 10.6 could reflect the different samples and question wording, they also support the argument that the relationship between broad populist attitudes and support for populist governments in power can evolve with the quality of representation.

Conclusion

Populist parties win support because they tap into specific popular zeitgeists and by channelling discontent about the distribution of economic benefits, immigration, globalization, and other social problems that they hope to solve. Yet the question becomes whether these parties' emphasis on populist rhetoric gains them additional support in the way the ideational theory proposes. In particular, are voters drawn to these parties merely because of their traditional issue positions and appeals to interests, or also because they propose an alternative approach to political representation whereby the popular will can be made to overcome a hostile, conspiratorial elite? This chapter provides evidence that populist parties find strength in activating latent populist predispositions. In recent elections in Spain, Greece, and Chile, and in elections in the mid 2000s in Bolivia, populist parties drew predominantly on sectors of the population where populist attitudes were strongest. This confirms that to understand voter support for populist parties, we need to take seriously their populist ideas.

The results support two other aspects of the ideational argument. First, the broad existence of populist ideals in a population is not sufficient for populist parties to succeed. The data in Figure 10.1 suggest that Chileans should be just as predisposed to support populist politics as voters in Spain or Greece are. Yet, in countries such as Chile, where parties remain relatively ideologically distinct and where corruption is relatively uncommon, populist appeals are unlikely to be activated because there is no grave crisis of representation for populists to solve. Thus, in Chile we find widespread agreement with populist attitudes but relatively little connection of these attitudes to voter choices. The same should occur, we expect, in other cases where there is little context for populist action. In contrast, as the economic crisis reduced the economic policy space available for traditional parties and as perceived corruption became widespread in Greece and Spain (or earlier in Bolivia), populist attitudes became more politically salient, new populist parties emerged, and latent populist attitudes became active. The ideational theory of populism suggests that the same process could occur in practically any country following a similar set of representational failures.

Second, traditional ideologies and issue positions still matter for populist party voters. Even as populist attitudes in Spain and Greece became activated, voters with populist leanings did not automatically support populist parties. Instead, they looked also to the ideological visions those parties endorsed. Demand for populist representation does not trump other policy concerns. Instead, populist parties must find a mix of populist rhetoric and issue appeals that can win them electoral support. Moreover, if the crisis of representation that populist parties identify is not sufficiently strong, these populist attitudes will not be activated and voters may support a party who espouses those policies but is not populist, as will voters who hold those policy positions but who do not hold populist attitudes.

Finally, while the data from Greece and Spain show that crises can activate populist attitudes, the recent data from Bolivia suggest that populist attitudes become less politically salient when representation improves. In such a context, support for the ruling party again becomes based on its record in office. While some parties may keep activating populist attitudes in their ongoing battles against their political rivals or in an attempt to enact further institutional reforms, populists may see diminishing returns to explicit populist strategies if the country is not in crisis mode and populist attitudes are no longer active among the electorate.

Taken together, the individual-level results in this chapter confirm the central tenets of the ideational theory but also show how the ideational theory of populism can be compatible with, and perhaps fine-tuned by, a closer dialogue with canonical models of voting behavior by focusing on the specific processes by which attitudes get activated. In this respect, further work is needed to fully test the arguments outlined here about when populist attitudes become salient. In particular, survey data from a larger sample of countries than is currently available should be used to directly model how contextual variables like the level of policy convergence or perceived levels of corruption modify the impact of populist attitudes on populist-party support. We expect that cross-national data would confirm that latent populist attitudes are widespread but only become activated in contexts of deep representational failure.

Notes

1 The funding agencies for each of these surveys and details about the firms that carried them out are listed in the web appendices; we thank them for their support. All conclusions and errors are our own.
2 See Gomez-Reino and Llamazares in this volume (Chapter 12) for a more extensive discussion of the origins of Podemos.
3 Unfortunately, platforms were not available for all parties so we could not code them for this election.
4 Journalists often describe Golden Dawn as populist. Yet, our coders gave a low average score to party leader Mihaloliakos because he frequently celebrates the concept of the Greek nation (the land, its shared culture and history) with the Greek people in a subservient position. This coincides with the judgment of scholars (Mudde and Galanopoulos 2015; Stavrakakis and Katsambekis 2014). However, some speeches received a high score because they shifted their rhetoric and prioritized the Greek people and their struggle against external and internal enemies, thus showing that the party leader is capable of speaking populism.
5 Unfortunately, we were not able to find many published texts of speeches and so we were only able to code party platforms.
6 The specifics of the survey methodologies are described in the online appendix, but we summarize them here. The UNDP Survey in Chile is a nationally representative face-to-face survey conducted at the homes of respondents roughly at the time of the 2013 president election. The University of Salamanca survey in Spain is an online ISO 26362 certified panel survey carried out by the firm Netquest right before the December 2015 general elections. The Hellenic Voter Study for the Greek Parliamentary elections of January 2015 (Andreadis, Kartsounidou, and Chatzimallis 2015) is a mixed-mode survey conducted by the Laboratory of Applied Political Research at Aristotle University of Thessaloniki in June of that year, asking respondents to look back at the election. The Bolivia survey was the June 2016 Ipsos Omnibus survey, conducted face-to-face in the urban centers of La Paz, El Alto, Cochabamba, and Santa Cruz.
7 To save space we do not further explore the interaction between populist attitudes and policy concerns because these attitudes have generally not been activated within the electorate.
8 In other analyses, we dropped the indicator that measured preferences for having a citizen as a representative, but the same null results emerged across all indicators.
9 The survey is based on face-to-face interviews with a nationally representative complex stratified sample. See www.vanderbilt.edu/lapop/ for information and to download the data.
10 The model contains standard demographic controls and measures of government performance, respondent ideology, and preferences on economic management. The analysis uses survey weights to reflect the sample design. The specific variable measures are available in Appendix 10.2.

References

Aguilar, Rosario, and Ryan E. Carlin. 2017. Ideational Populism in Chile? A Case Study. *Swiss Political Science Review* 23(4):404–422.

Akkerman, Agnes, Cas Mudde, and Andrej Zaslove. 2014. How Populist are the People? Measuring Populist Attitudes in Voters. *Comparative Political Studies* 47: 1324–1353.

Andreadis, Ioannis, Evangelia Kartsounidou, and Charalampos Chatzimallis. 2015. Innovation, an Answer to Lack of Funding: The 2015 Hellenic National Election Voter Study www.polres.gr/en/sites/default/files/elnes2015a.pdf.

Andreadis, Ioannis, and Yannis Stavrakakis. 2017. European Populist Parties in Government: How Well are Voters Represented? Evidence from Greece. *Swiss Political Science Review*, *23*(4), 485–508.

Andreadis, Ioannis, Yannis Stavrakakis and Nicolas Demertzis. 2018. Populism, Ethnic Nationalism and Xenophobia. *Science and Society: Journal of Political and Moral Theory*, 37, 11–40.

Baker, Andy, and Kenneth F. Greene. 2011. The Latin American Left's Mandate: Free-Market Policies and Issue Voting in New Democracies. *World Politics* 63(1): 43–77.

Bargsted, Matias, and Nicolas Somma. 2013. Social Cleavages and Political Dealignment in Contemporary Chile, 1995–2009. *Party Politics* 22(1): 105–124.

Carlin, Ryan E. 2014. What's Not to Trust? Rubrics of Political Party Trustworthiness in Chile and Argentina. *Party Politics* 20(1):63–77.

Carlin, Ryan E., Greg J. Love, and Cecilia Martínez-Gallardo. 2015. Cushioning the Fall: Scandals, Economic Conditions, and Executive Approval. *Political Behavior* 37(1), 109–130.

Centellas, Miguel. 2015. The 2014 Presidential and Legislative Elections in Bolivia. *Electoral Studies* 37(June): 94–97.

Dalton, Russell J., and Christopher J. Anderson. 2011. *Citizens, Context, and Choice: How Context Shapes Citizens' Electoral Choices*. New York: Oxford University Press.

Donoso, Sofia. 2013. Dynamics of Change in Chile: Explaining the Emergence of the 2006 Pingüino Movement. *Latin American Politics and Society* 45(February): 1–29.

Druckman, James N., Lawrence R. Jacobs, and Eric Ostermeier. 2004. Candidate Strategies to Prime Issues and Image. *Journal of Politics* 66(Nov): 1180–1202.

Edwards III, George C., William Mitchell, and Reed Welch. 1995. Explaining Presidential Approval: The Significance of Issue Salience. *American Journal of Political Science* 39(Feb): 108–134.

Farthing, Linda C., and Benjamin H. Kohl. 2014. *Evo's Bolivia: Continuity and Change*. Austin, TX: University of Texas Press.

Hart, Austin. 2013. Can Candidates Activate or Deactivate the Economic Vote? Evidence from Two Mexican Elections. *Journal of Politics* 75(4): 1051–1063.

Iyengar, Shanto, and David R. Kinder. 1987. *News That Matters: Television and American Opinion*. Chicago, IL: University of Chicago Press

Kingstone, Peter. 2011. The Political Economy of Latin America: Reflections on Neoliberalism and Development. New York: Routledge Press.

Kitschelt, Herbert, Kirk A. Hawkins, Juan Pablo Luna, Guillermo Rosas, and Elizabeth J. Zechmeister. 2010. *Latin American Party Systems*. New York: Cambridge University Press.

Krosnick, J. (1988). The Role of Attitude Importance in Social Evaluations: A Study of Political Preferences, Presidential Candidate Evaluations, and Voting Behavior. *Journal of Personality and Social Psychology* 55(2), 196–210.

Luna, Juan Pablo, and David Altman. 2011. Uprooted but Stable: Chilean Parties and the Concept of Party System Institutionalization. *Latin American Politics and Society* 53(Summer): 1–28.

Lupu, Noam. 2015. Partisanship in Latin America. In *The Latin American Voter: Representation and Accountability in Challenging Contexts*. Ryan Carlin, Matthew Singer, and Elizabeth Zechmeister, eds. Ann Arbor, MI: University of Michigan Press, 226–245.

Madrid, Raul. 2012. *The Rise of Ethnic Politics in Latin America*. New York: Cambridge University Press.

Mudde, Cas and Cristóbal Rovira Kaltwasser. 2013. Exclusionary vs. Inclusionary Populism: Comparing Contemporary Europe and Latin America. *Government and Opposition* 48(April): 147–174.

Mudde, Cas and Antonis Galanopoulos. 2015. Populism and Liberal Democracy: Is Greece the Exception or the Future of Europe? *Open Democracy*. April 29. www.opendemocracy.net/can-europe-make-it/antonis-galanopoulos/interview-with-cas-mudde-populism-and-liberal-democracy-is-greece-exception-or-".

Navia, Patricio, and Ignacio Walker. 2008. Political Institutions, Populism and Democracy in Latin America. In *Democratic Governance in Latin America*. Scott Mainwaring and Timothy R. Scully, eds. Palo Alto, CA: Stanford University Press.

Pappas, Takis S. 2013. Why Greece Failed. *Journal of Democracy* 24(2): 31–45.

Pearce, Adrian J. 2011. *Evo Morales and the Movimiento Al Socialismo in Bolivia: The First Term in Context, 2006–2010*. London: Institute for the Study of the Americas, University of London.

Polk, Jonathan, Jan Rovny, Ryan Bakker, Erica Edwards, Liesbet Hooghe, Seth Jolly, Jelle Koedam, Filip Kostelka, Gary Marks, Gijs Schumacher, Marco Steenbergen, Milada Vachudova and Marko Zilovic. 2017. "Explaining the salience of anti-elitism and reducing political corruption for political parties in Europe with the 2014 Chapel Hill Expert Survey data." *Research & Politics* 4 (1): 1–9.

Singer, Matthew M. 2011 Who Says "It's the Economy"? Cross-National and Cross-Individual Variation in the Salience of Economic Performance. *Comparative Political Studies* 44(March): 284–312.

Singer, Matthew M. 2016. Elite Polarization and the Electoral Impact of Left-Right Placements: Evidence from Latin America, 1995–2009. *Latin American Research Review* 51(2):174–193.

Stanley, Ben. 2008. The Thin Ideology of Populism. *Journal of Political Ideologies*. 13(1): 95–110.

Stavrakakis, Yannis, and Giorgos Katsambekis. 2014. Left-wing Populism in the European Periphery: The Case of SYRIZA. *Journal of Political Ideologies* 19(2): 119–142.

Tsatsanis, Emmanouil, Ioannis Andreadis and Eftichia Teperoglou. 2018. Populism from Below: Socioeconomic and ideological correlates of populist attitudes in Greece. *South European Society and Politics*.

Vargas, Mauricio and Santiago Garriga. 2015. Explaining Inequality and Poverty Reduction in Bolivia. IMF Working Paper. Washington, DC: IMF. www.imf.org/external/pubs/ft/wp/2015/wp15265.pdf

Wiesehomeier, Nina, and Kenneth Benoit. 2009. Presidents, Parties, and Policy Competition. *The Journal of Politics* 71(4):1435–1447.

Young, Jason, Cynthia J Thomsen, Eugene Borgida, John L Sullivan, John H Aldrich. 1991. When Self-interest Makes a Difference: The Role of Construct Accessibility in Political Reasoning. *Journal of Experimental Social Psychology* 27(3): 271–296.

Appendix 10.1

Principal-component factors analyses

As discussed in the text, we performed factor analyses on the battery of populism indicators for each of our four samples. The factors (rotated in the case of Bolivia) are presented in the tables below.

Table 10.A1 Factor analysis of populist attitudes scale in Chile

Variable	*Factor 1*	*Uniqueness*
Congress follow people	0.70	0.52
People not politicians	0.73	0.47
Differences between people and elite	0.64	0.59
Ordinary citizen, not experienced politician	0.63	0.60
Politicians talk too much	0.62	0.62
"Compromise" is just selling out	0.57	0.67
Eigenvalue	2.98	
N=1,498		

Table 10.A2 Factor analysis of populist attitudes scale in Spain

Variable	*Factor 1*	*Uniqueness*
Congress follow people	0.66	0.56
People not politicians	0.76	0.42
Differences between people and elite	0.70	0.52
Ordinary citizen, not experienced politician	0.68	0.54
Politicians talk too much	0.73	0.46
"Compromise" is just selling out	0.61	0.63
Eigenvalue	2.87	
N=1,208		

Table 10.A3 Factor analysis of populist attitudes scale in Greece

Variable	*Factor 1*	*Uniqueness*
Congress follow people	0.75	0.44
People not politicians	0.72	0.49
Differences between people and elite	0.59	0.65
Ordinary citizen, not experienced politician	0.67	0.55
Politicians talk too much	0.55	0.69
"Compromise" is just selling out	0.73	0.47
Eigenvalue	2.73	
N = 982		

Table 10.A4 Factor analysis of populist attitudes scale in Bolivia

Variable	*Factor 1*	*Factor 2*	*Uniqueness*
Congress follow people	0.56	0.32	0.58
People not politicians	0.30	0.67	0.46
Differences between people and elite	0.66	–0.02	0.57
Ordinary citizen, not experienced politician	–0.08	0.82	0.33
Politicians talk too much	0.52	0.34	0.61
"Compromise" is just selling out	0.70	–0.04	0.51
Eigenvalue	1.94	1.00	
N=951			

Appendix 10.2

Survey details and question wording

Chile

The UNDP Survey in Chile is a nationally representative face-to-face survey conducted at the homes of respondents roughly at the time of the 2013 president election. 1,800 people were surveyed with probability proportional to population (ppt), using a sample that was stratified by region and zone (urban/rural); the resulting margin of error is 2.5 percent with 95 percent confidence, and the design effect is 1.15. The survey was in the field between August 17 and October 9, 2013 and was carried out by the firm STATCOM.

Table 10.A5 Variables and summary statistics, Chile

Variable	*Mean*	*s.d.*
Populist attitudes: Index of six populism items described in the text, averaged.	3.9	0.61
Economic ideology: For the following activities, would you say the following activities are better that the state be in charge (1), the private sector be in charge (2), or a mixture of the two/it is the same (1.5). Asked for health, education copper mining, public transportation, and pensions. Then we take the average for the questions.	1.4	0.32
Social ideology: How much do you agree or disagree with the following policies: Gay marriage, adoption by gay parents, euthanasia, abortion following rape, abortion under other circumstances, legalization of marijuana, constitutional recognition of indigenous peoples like the Mapuche, direct election of mayors. Strongly agree, agree, neither agree or disagree, disagree, strongly disagree. Coded so that 1 = strongly left and 5 = strongly right	3.1	0.91
Need for constitutional change: Some people think that Chile needs to make some reforms. Please tell me if the following areas need change: constitutional reform. 1 = change not needed 2 = undecided 3 = moderate change 4 = deep change needed.	3.5	0.88
Environmental protection: Which of the following phrases do you most strongly agree with? Protect the environment, even if it slows growth and results in the loss of some jobs (3), Economic growth and creating jobs should be the priority, even if the environment is affected in some way (1), don't know (2).	2.5	0.85

Sociotropic retrospective: How does the country's general situation compare to 10 years ago? (1) worse, (2) the same, (3) or better.	2.2	0.75
Sociotropic prospective: What will the country's general situation be in 10 years? (1) worse, (2) the same, (3) or better.	2.4	0.64
Egotropic retrospective: How does your family's general situation compare to 10 years ago? (1) worse, (2) the same, (3) or better.	2.4	0.67
Egotropic prospective: What will your family's situation be in 10 years? (1) worse, (2) the same, (3) or better.	2.5	0.61
With what party do you self-identify or sympathize? A series of 0/1 dummy variables that include:		
• Support for parties in the **Nueva Mayoría**	14.5% sympathize	
• Support for parties in the **Alianza**	6.8% sympathize	
• Support for **all other parties or no party at all** (baseline)	78.7% sympathize	
Sex: 1 = male 2 = female	1.60	0.48
Age in years	46.8	17.7
Education: What is the last year of education you completed. Incomplete elementary education (1), Complete education (2), secondary incomplete (3), secondary complete (4), incomplete professional institute or technical education (5), incomplete professional institute or technical education (6), incomplete university (7), complete university (8), postgraduate (9).	63.1% have complete secondary or higher	

Spain

For this analysis we use an online survey launched by an Universidad de Salamanca research team and carried out by the firm Netquest in December 2015, just before that year general elections. Our database contains 1,208 respondents sampled by age, gender, and region on the basis of census data (all 17 Spanish autonomous communities were included).

Table 10.A6 Variables and summary statistics, Spain

Variable	*Mean*	*s.d.*
Populist attitudes: Index of six populism items described in the text, averaged.	3.9	0.78
Left-right (0 left; 10 = right)	4.22	2.58
Globalization (see below)	–0.05	0.98
Market	0.03	0.96
The Globalization and Market variables were extracted through a factor analysis of preferences regarding the following policies (responses range from 0 to 10, where 0 indicates total agreement and 10 indicates total disagreement), which yielded these two factors (those in *italics* loaded most strongly on the globalization factor):		
-State economic intervention		
-Economic redistribution from the rich to the poor		
-Raising taxes to improve public services		
-Same-sex marriage		

(continued)

Table 10.A6 (continued)

Variable	*Mean*	*s.d.*
-Right to privacy even if it hinders fight against crime *-Restrictive immigration policy* *-Expanding EU authority over the economic policies of member-states* -Environmental protection prevailing over economic growth		
Peripheral identity: This variable is based on the recodification of the following question on regional/Spanish identities: Which of the following sentences would you say better reflect your feelings? (1) I feel only Spanish (2) I feel more Spanish than Basque, Catalan, Andalusian (identifier for each autonomous community) (3) I feel as Spanish as Basque, Catalan, Andalusian, etc. (4) I feel more Basque, Catalan, Andalusian, etc. than Spanish (5) I feel only Spanish. Responses 1 to 3 were recoded as 0, and responses 4 and 5 were recoded as 1.	0.18	0.38
Sociotropic retrospective: How does the country's general situation compare to 10 years ago? (5) much worse, (4) a little worse, (3) the same, (2) a little better, (1) or better.	2.9	1.03
Sociotropic prospective: What will the country's general situation be in 10 years? (5) much worse, (4) a little worse, (3) the same, (2) a little better, (1) or better.	2.7	0.85
Sex: 1 = male 2 = female	1.50	0.50
Age in years	49.6	16.7
Education: What is the last year of education you completed? Incomplete elementary education (1), complete education (2), secondary incomplete (3), secondary complete (4), incomplete professional institute or technical education (5), incomplete professional institute or technical education (6), incomplete university (7), complete university (8), postgraduate (9).	51% only completed primary school, 28% finished college.	

Greece

The Hellenic Voter Study for the Greek Parliamentary elections of January 2015 (Andreadis, Kartsounidou, and Chatzimallis 2015) is a mixed-mode survey conducted by the Laboratory of Applied Political Research at Aristotle University of Thessaloniki. The recruitment process lasted from June 12 until July 16 using RDD (Random Digit Dialing). The respondents were asked to provide their email address in order to participate in a web survey conducted by Aristotle University of Thessaloniki. The 1,008 completed cases were collected either as web-based self-administered questionnaires or using telephone interviews (CATI). The web was the main data collection mode of the survey and the telephone interview was used as an auxiliary method for the respondents who lacked Internet access and/or an email account (Andreadis, Kartsounidou, and Chatzimallis 2015).

Bolivia, 2016

The 2016 Bolivia survey was conducted in June 2016 by Ipsos. The survey was an omnibus survey to which we added questions on populism and government support. The survey was conducted face-to-face with 1,060 respondents in households located in the urban centers of La Paz, El Alto, Cochabamba, and Santa Cruz.

Table 10.A7 Variables and summary statistics, Greece

Variable	*Mean*	*s.d.*
Populist attitudes: Index of six populism items described in the text, averaged.	3.7	0.67
Economic ideology: (index of attitudes on economic policy; recoded so that 1 = left 2 = right)	1.5	0.20
Social ideology (index of attitudes on social policy; recoded so that 1 = left 5 = right)	3.1	0.63
European unification (0 = has already gone too far, 10 = should be pushed further	5.7	3.45
Pocketbook retrospective (How their personal economic situation compares to 10 years ago; Greece: compared to 12 months ago; recoded so that 1=worse and 3=better)	1.4	0.60
Pocketbook prospective (How their personal economic situation will be in 10 years; Greece: in 12 months; recoded so that 1=worse and 3=better)	1.4	0.66
Sex (recoded 1= male 2 = female)	1.48	0.50
Age (years)	46.1	16.29
Education (1 = elementary education incomplete 9 = postgraduate)	44.4% have completed secondary or lower	

The following questions were used in the analysis of government support in 2016. The populism battery is summarized in Table 10.1 in the chapter text. For continuous variables we provide the mean and standard deviations; for the binary and categorical variables we provide the percentage of the sample that fits that category. The sample skews young but is evenly split on gender lines.

Bolivia, 2008

The 2008 survey data from Bolivia came from the 2008 AmericasBarometer survey conducted by the Latin American Public Opinion Project. The survey was conducted in February 2008 using a nationally representative stratified probabilistic sample of 3,000 respondents. For this survey, we are able to use a question that was used on half the sample, with a maximum N of 1,500.

The following questions were used in the analysis of government support in 2008. For continuous variables we provide the mean and standard deviations; for the binary and categorical variables we provide the percentage of the sample that is in that category.

Table 10.A8 Variables and summary statistics, Bolivia 2016

Variable	*Mean*	*sd*
Populist attitudes: index of six populism items described in the text.	16.2	4.3
How would vote if the election were held today: If this week there were presidential elections, what would you do: (2) vote for the candidate or party of the current president, (3) vote for a party or candidate different from the current government, (4) would vote blank or null, (1) would not vote.	Would not vote: 3.49 % Would vote for the president's party: 32.21% Would vote for an opposition party: 40.72% Would cast a null vote: 23.59%	

(continued)

Table 10.A8 (continued)

Variable	*Mean*	*sd*
Presidential approval: In general, would you approve or disapprove of the performance of president Evo Morales (1) Approve or (0) Disapprove	54% approve	
Economy compared to previous year: What do you believe is the situation of the national economy compared to 12 months ago: (0) much worse, (1) a little worse, (2) the same, (3) a little better, (4) much better	2.02	1.06
Personal finances compared to last year: What do you believe is the situation of your personal finances compared to 12 months ago: (0) much worse, (1) a little worse, (2) the same, (3) a little better, (4) much better.	2.12	1.01
Education: What is the highest school grade you achieved? (0) none/illiterate, (1) incomplete primary, (2) complete primary, (3) incomplete secondary, (4) complete secondary, (5) incomplete technical, (6) complete technical, (7) incomplete university, (8) complete university, (9) post graduate	5.93	2.24
Female: (0) Male, (1) Female	49.8% Female	
What is your exact age? A series of 0/1 dummies where the omitted category is 46–55. Dummies for age 16–25, Age 26–35, Age 36–45, Age 56–65, Age 66+	Age 16-25: 33.49% Age 26-35: 28.49% Age 36-45: 17.64% Age 56-65: 8.40% Age 66+: 3.21%	
Wealth: An index generated by IPSOS based on the number of the following items the household owns: a working electric dryer, a working washing machine, a working refrigerator or freezer, a computer. Ranges from 0–2.	0.79	0.65
Ethnicity: A series of dummy variables coded from the question "People sometimes describe themselves as belonging to an ethnic group. What ethnic group do you consider yourself a part of?" The baseline is "Quechua" and then there are 0/1 dummies for Mestizo, Aymara, White, Afro-Bolivian, "Indigenous" coded to combine those who said "indigenous, originiario, or Guaraní), and then "No ethnicity" for those who said "none," did not know, or rejected the question.	Mestizo: 51.41% Quechua: 14.51% Ayamara: 24.63% Indigenous: 2.24% Afro-Bolivian: 2.04% Mulato: 1.07% No Indigenous: 4.09%	

Table 10.A9 Variables and summary statistics, Bolivia 2008

Variable	*Mean*	*s.d.*
Populist attitudes. Additive scale of two questions. Would you agree or disagree with the following statement: In the world today, there is a fight between good and evil and people need to choose between the two? Would you agree or disagree with the following statement: The largest obstacle for our country's progress is the dominant class or oligarchy that takes advantage of the people? (1) strongly disagree, (7) strong agree.	9.17	2.73

Economy compared to previous year: Do you think that the **country**'s current economic situation is better than, the same as or worse than it was 12 months ago? (2) better (1) same (0) worse.	0.87	0.80
Personal finances compared to last year: Do you think that your **personal** economic situation is better than, the same as or worse than it was 12 months ago? (2) better (1) same (0) worse.	1.00	0.72
Ideological self-identification on the right: On this card there is a 1–10 scale that goes from left to right, where 1 means left and 10 means right. Nowadays, when we speak of political leanings, we talk of those who sympathize more with the left and those who sympathize more with the right. According to the meaning that the terms "left" and "right" have for you, and thinking of your own political leanings, where would you place yourself on this scale? Indicate the box that comes closest to your own position.	5.27	2.15
Government should own more businesses: On a scale where 1 means strongly disagree and 7 means strongly agree, to what extent do you agree or disagree with the following statement: The national government, instead of the private sector, should own the most important enterprises and industries of the country. How much do you agree or disagree with this statement? Recoded to range from 0–1.	0.64	0.30
State should reduce inequalities: On a scale where 1 means strongly disagree and 7 means strongly agree, to what extent do you agree or disagree with the following statement: The national government should implement strong policies to reduce inequality between the rich and the poor. Recoded to range from 0–1.	0.76	0.24
Income quintile: Based on a factor analysis of household ownership of various goods, including television, refrigerator, landline, cell phone, car, washing machine, microwave oven, motorcycle, indoor plumbing, indoor bathroom, computer. For more information on the variable, see Córdova, Abby. 2009. "Methodological Note: Measuring Relative Wealth Using Household Asset Indicators." *AmericasBarometer Insights* 6. Vanderbilt University: Latin American Public Opinion Project (LAPOP).	1.94	1.42
Education: What was the last year of education you completed? Primary (1–6), secondary (7–11), 6th form (12–13), university (14–18).	9.94	4.89
Age: What is your current age? 0/1 dummies for falling in the following categories: Age 16–25, age 26–35, age 36–45, age 56–65, age 66+ (baseline is 46–55).	Age 16–25: 29.34% Age 26–35: 24.67% Age 36–45: 17.97% Age 56–65: 9.03% Age 66+: 4.93%	
Female: Male (0), Female (1)	Female:49.6%	
Ethnicity: Do you consider yourself white, mestizo, indigenous, black, mulato, or other? Dummy variables for all categories, with "white" as the baseline	White: 8.73% Mestizo: 71.56% Indigenous: 17.94% Black: 0.52% Mulato: 0.21% Other: 1.04%	
Rural: Urban (0), Rural (1)	Rural: 37.10%	

Appendix 10.3

Conditional models for Spain and Chile

As described in the text, we interact the populism attitudes scores in the two countries where they had a substantial effect with the salient issue cleavages in those countries to test whether populist attitudes can make people support a politician whose policy vision they disagree with. The text contains the marginal effects from those models; the full models are available below. The first two focus on interacting populist ideologies with the dominant cleavage in the country at the time of the election (left-right, Grexit). The third table looks at the three-way interaction described in the text for Greece that looks at social ideology, attitudes about EU integration (Grexit), and populism.

Table 10.A10 Model of party preference in Spain, populism x left-right self-placement

Variable	*PSOE*		*Podemos*		*Ciudadanos*		*IU*	
Populist attitudes	0.22		0.70	***	0.50	**	0.56	
Left-right	−2.98	***	−2.79	***	−0.70	***	−3.33	***
Populist att*left-right	−0.13		−0.14		0.03		−0.33	
Market	0.20		−0.27		0.02		−0.15	
Globalization	0.30		0.55	***	0.05		0.45	*
Peripheral identity	2.08	*	2.83	**	1.77		1.70	
Sociotropic retrospective	0.61	***	0.84	***	0.43	*	0.67	**
Sociotropic prospective	0.01		−0.09		0.03		0.24	
Primary education	0.10		−0.06		−0.65		−0.97	
College education	0.10		0.06		0.34		−0.09	
Age	−0.03	**	−0.05	***	−0.04	***	−0.03	*
Sex	0.21		0.58	*	0.49		−0.31	
Constant	0.12	**	1.92	*	2.08		−2.44	
Variable	*UPyD*		*DiL*		*ERC*		*Abstain*	
Populist attitudes	0.69		0.80		0.39		0.70	***
Left-right	−1.41	**	−0.57		−2.58	***	−1.63	***
Populist att.*left-right	−0.03		−0.38		−0.31		−0.09	
Market	−0.27		0.07		0.09		0.24	
Globalization	−0.09		0.22		0.13		−0.02	
Peripheral identity	1.94		7.30	***	7.20	***	3.17	**
Sociotropic retrospective	0.06		0.98	*	0.47		0.21	
Sociotropic prospective	0.99	*	−0.06		−0.09		0.59	**

Primary education	1.42		−1.32		−0.82		−0.11	
College education	1.22		0.18		0.15		−0.07	
Age	−0.03		0.03		0.00		−0.04	***
Sex	−0.32		−0.34		−0.13		0.17	
Constant	−4.18		−8.84	***	−4.83	**	0.53	
Model type	*Multinomial logit, PP is the baseline*							
N	1,208							
pseudo R2	0.22							

*p<.05 **p<.01 ***p<.001 (two tailed)

Table 10.A11 Model of party preference in Spain, populism x peripheral identity

Variable	*PSOE*		*Podemos*		*Ciudadanos*		*IU*	
Populist attitudes	0.22		0.83	***	0.47	***	0.70	**
Left-right	−2.96	***	−2.76	***	−0.70	***	−3.38	***
Populism* peripheral identity	−0.50		−0.96		0.58		−0.02	
Market	0.19		−0.29		0.03		−0.15	
Globalization	0.30		0.55	***	0.06		0.45	*
Peripheral identity	2.08	*	2.93	**	1.22		1.26	
Sociotropic retrospective	0.60	**	0.83	***	0.43	*	0.67	*
Sociotropic prospective	0.02		−0.09		0.03		0.22	
Primary education	0.11		−0.09		−0.64		−0.95	
College education	0.10		0.06		0.34		−0.09	
Age	−0.03	**	−0.05	***	−0.04	***	−0.03	*
Sex	0.22		0.59	*	0.49		−0.29	
Constant	0.15		−0.96		2.05	**	−2.34	
Variable	*UPyD*		*DiL*		*ERC*		*Abstain*	
Populist attitudes index	0.78	*	−0.09		1.23		0.77	***
Left–right	−1.37	**	−0.68		−2.57	***	−1.60	***
Populism*peripheral identity	−1.17		0.40		−1.34		−0.83	
Market	−0.28		0.05		0.06		0.24	
Globalization	−0.11		0.19		0.13		−0.03	
Peripheral identity	1.93		7.24	***	7.41	***	3.19	**
Sociotropic retrospective	0.08		0.97	*	0.46		0.20	
Sociotropic prospective	0.99	*	−0.07		−0.07		0.59	**
Primary education	1.39		−1.31		−0.80		−0.12	
College education	1.23		0.17		0.16		−0.07	
Age	−0.03		0.03		0.00		−0.04	***
Sex	−0.32		−0.35		−0.12		0.17	
Constant	−1.17		−8.83	***	−5.05	**	0.56	
Model type	*Multinomial logit, PP is the baseline*							
N	1,208							
pseudo R2	0.22							

*p<.05 **p<.01 ***p<.001 (two tailed)

Table 10.A12 Model of party preference in Greece, populism x Grexit

Variable	*SYRIZA*		*GD*		*POTAMI*		*KKE*		*ANEL*	
Populist attitudes index	1.58	**	0.77		−1.28		2.04	*	1.45	*
Social ideology	−1.63	***	2.01	**	−1.18	***	−1.84	***	0.32	
Economic ideology	−6.40	***	−2.74		−0.12		−6.90	***	−5.66	***
European unification	−0.14		−0.56		−0.49		−0.00		−0.15	
Populist attitudes * European unification	0.02		0.10		0.19	*	−0.06		−0.01	
Pocketbook retrospective	0.28		−0.04		0.07		1.38	**	0.53	
Pocketbook prospective	0.53	**	0.06		−0.08		−1.23	*	0.32	
Age	0.00		−0.02		−0.01		−0.04		0.03	
Sex	−0.14		−0.84		0.06		0.30		−0.53	
Education	−0.09		−0.32		0.11		−0.35		−0.20	
Constant	9.68	***	−2.78		6.25	*	10.35	*	1.57	
Variable	*PASOK*		*OTHER*		*NONE*		*MISSING*		*Abstention*	
Populist attitudes index	0.95		2.61	***	0.59		2.32	***	2.70	***
Social ideology	−1.45	***	−1.54	***	0.16		−0.98	***	−1.68	***
Economic ideology	−1.94		−4.15	***	−5.11	**	−3.27	***	−2.12	*
European unification	0.39		0.75	*	−0.49		0.68	**	0.59	
Populist attitudes * European unification	−0.11		−0.21	*	0.12		−0.19	**	−0.17	*
Pocketbook retrospective	0.01		0.00		−0.48		0.06		0.22	
Pocketbook prospective	0.06		−0.82		0.03		−0.26		0.01	
Age	0.02		−0.01		0.01		0.00		−0.04	*
Sex	−0.09		−0.04		−0.87		−0.38		0.12	
Education	−0.18		−0.08		0.00		0.01		0.06	
Constant	2.98		2.53		4.75		0.48		−1.16	
Model type	*Multinomial logit, baseline is New Democracy*									
N	910									
pseudo R2	0.19									

*p<.05 **p<.01 ***p<.001 (two tailed)

Table 10.A13 Model of party preference in Greece with triple interaction results: populism x social ideology x European unification

Variable	*SYRIZA*		*GD*		*POTAMI*		*KKE*		*ANEL*	
Populist attitudes index	2.94		−0.58		3.58		3.39		−6.25	
Social ideology	0.80		1.60		4.32		0.42		−7.90	
Populism*social ideology	−0.52		0.39		−1.71		−0.55		2.25	
European unification	1.04		0.76		0.93		1.74		−4.35	*
Populist attitudes * European unification	−0.20		−0.03		−0.23		−0.51		1.17	*
Social ideology * European unification	−0.48		−0.38		−0.51		−0.70		1.22	*

Populism*social ideology * European unification	0.10		0.04		0.15		0.18		−0.34	*
Pocketbook retrospective	0.32		−0.03		0.09		1.43	***	0.56	
Economic ideology	−6.44	***	−2.62		−0.10		−6.83	***	−5.82	***
Pocketbook prospective	0.49	*	0.08		−0.09		−1.23	*	0.33	
Age	0.00		−0.02		−0.01		−0.04		0.03	
Education	−0.11		−0.36	*	0.10		−0.39	*	−0.19	
Sex	−0.12		−0.93		0.06		0.37		−0.62	
Constant	3.34		−1.43		−9.40		4.67		29.75	*

Variable	*PASOK*		*OTHER*		*NONE*		*MISSING*		*Abstention*	
Populist attitudes index	−5.44		2.88		2.82		−1.41		1.92	
Social ideology	−8.98	*	−0.90		3.34		−5.75		−3.44	
Populism*social ideology	2.15		−0.07		−0.68		1.27		0.29	
European unification	−3.02		0.40		0.44		−1.74		−0.65	
Populist attitudes * European unification	0.91		−0.04		−0.01		0.50		0.09	
Social ideology * European unification	1.16	*	0.12		−0.31		0.82		0.45	
Populism*social ideology * European unification	−0.35	*	−0.06		0.05		−0.23		−0.09	
Pocketbook retrospective	0.00		0.04		−0.47		0.06		0.23	
Economic ideology	−2.04		−4.18	**	−5.24	**	−3.31	***	−1.92	
Pocketbook prospective	0.06		−0.85		0.06		−0.28		0.06	
Age	0.02		−0.01		0.01		0.00		−0.04	*
Education	−0.19		−0.09		−0.01		0.00		0.05	
Sex	−0.13		−0.02		−0.85		−0.41		0.17	
Constant	25.48		0.44		−5.60		14.63		3.12	
Model type	*Multinomial logit, baseline is New Democracy*									
N	910									
Pseudo R2	0.20									

*p<.05 **p<.01 ***p<.001 (two tailed)

Appendix 10.4

Results by populism indicator, Bolivia 2016

In the chapter text we show that there is no correlation between populist attitudes and support for the MAS in 2016. In the analysis below we check whether part of the attitudes scale might have a correlation with political attitudes, but we again find generally null results across the board. The only correlation that approaches statistical significance is a model suggesting that individuals who think politicians talk too much are prone to support opposition candidates, but this variable has no correlation with presidential approval.

Table 10.A14 Elements of the populist attitude scale and presidential support in Bolivia, 2016

	Multinomial logit, vote for President's party is the baseline category			*Logit model: presidential approval*
	Vote for an opposition candidate	*Blank or null vote*	*No vote*	
Differences between people and elite	−0.028 (0.077)	−0.034 (0.086)	−0.050 (0.171)	−0.027 (0.066)
People not politicians	−0.001 (0.079)	−0.028 (0.087)	−0.044 (0.188)	0.015 (0.069)
Ordinary citizen, not experienced politician	−0.043 (0.071)	0.071 (0.081)	−0.011 (0.147)	−0.031 (0.063)
Politicians talk too much	0.130° (0.067)	0.084 (0.074)	−0.118 (0.139)	0.006 (0.059)
Congress follow people	0.047 (0.075)	−0.022 (0.082)	−0.187 (0.150)	−0.014 (0.065)
"Compromise" is just selling out	0.044 (0.069)	0.002 (0.080)	−0.213 (0.150)	−0.051 (0.061)

Each row is from a separate model controlling for one component of the populism index, with the controls from Table 10.5 included. Standard errors in parentheses. ° $p<0.10$, two-tailed

11 Populist success

A qualitative comparative analysis

Bruno Castanho Silva

"Out with them all!":[1] this was the motto of popular revolt in Argentina during the 2001 crisis. These words, and the context in which the slogan emerged, enclose much theory on the definition of populism and explanations for its rise across countries. Conceptually, populism is typically seen as a call for systemic change, to wipe out all traditional politicians and bring politics back into the people's hands (Canovan 1981; Mudde 2004). This sentiment is clear, for example, in Donald Trump's appeals to "drain the swamp" in Washington. As for its causes, intuitively and in general discourse, it is often associated with crisis scenarios.

Often, however, crises in Western democracies have not spurred populist parties and leaders. The European Great Recession since 2008 has led populists to power in Greece and bolstered them in Spain and Italy, but not in Portugal or Ireland. In Latin America, the left-populist "pink-tide" came together with relative economic prosperity and improvement in life conditions (Remmer 2011). These, and other exceptions, beg the question of why populism emerges in some countries and not others.

Several tentative answers have been provided. Those were reviewed in the introduction to this volume. Traditionally, they include major social changes that leave entire groups marginalized (the "losers of globalization" theories), economic crises that lead to general dissatisfaction with the political establishment, and widespread corruption and bad governance. Most of these, however, suffer the major empirical limitation of having been developed and tested within a single region – usually Europe or Latin America. From a theoretical perspective this has led to a dead end. Europeanists highlight the importance of social changes brought about by globalization and the restructuring of political cleavages, which led to a yearning for "good old times" among social groups that lost prestige and jobs – mostly blue collar workers (e.g. Betz 1994; Kitschelt and McGann 1995; Kriesi et al. 2006; Kriesi 2014). Such an explanation, however, hardly applies to Latin America. Populists are historically recognized in the region for mobilizing and incorporating into politics those sectors that had been for a long time, or always, marginalized in society (Conniff 1999; di Tella 1965; Madrid 2008; Stein 1980). Urban workers in the 1940s, or indigenous populations in the 2000s, are not groups that had enjoyed prestige but lost it due to modernization or globalization. On the other hand, explanations devised for Latin America, such as high corruption (Hawkins 2010), are a hard sell in several important, and squeaky clean, European cases. That the populist radical right almost won the 2016 presidential elections in Austria, for example, certainly cannot be explained by egregious levels of corruption and bad governance.

A key theoretical advantage of the ideational definition of populism adopted in this volume is that it provides a way to overcome the tensions across these region-bound literatures without discarding their findings. By emphasizing the ideas behind populist discourse, instead of its ideological associations in different cases, ideational populism proposes that the most immediate cause of support for populists is an absolute loss of citizen trust in political institutions, an individual-level phenomenon that is triggered by contextual factors marking dysfunctional political representation, such as bad governance and elite collusion. In this chapter, I test what combination(s) of macro-level causes lead to the electoral success of populist parties.

This chapter examines this theoretical framework, with evidence from the 27 countries covered by Hawkins and Castanho Silva earlier in this volume (Chapter 1). I test both the ideational theory, that populism is primarily led by factors that trigger lack of confidence in political institutions, and alternative explanations for the success of populist parties. This is the first study to compare the causes of populist-party success in and out of government in both Europe and the Americas.[2] Therefore, it is possible to overcome potential idiosyncrasies present in either region presently taken to be more general causes of populism. Results provide confirmatory evidence that elite collusion and corrupt governments are the most important factors behind the rise of populists. Based on this analysis, the ideational theory of populism is the most successful at explaining the emergence of populism across regions.

The context of populism

The causes of ideational populism are presented at length in the theoretical introduction to this volume. In this section, I briefly review those which can be applied to country-level research and that are tested in this chapter.

The ideational theory argues that the causes of populism must be connected to populist *ideas*. Therefore, any explanation must focus on how the proposed set of causes leads individuals to see politics as a moral opposition between the good people and evil elites. The theory proposes that such a discourse, marked by opposition to the entire political system and preaching a reinvention of political institutions, is expected to resonate with individuals who are the most dissatisfied with such institutions. This dissatisfaction might be driven by different factors in each case. Nevertheless, in essence, the acceptance of populist ideas is associated with a contemptuous view of politics.

The ideational theory argues that populism is most likely to emerge out of failures of democratic representation, which cause the public to lose confidence in representative institutions. It identifies two main contextual triggers of such failures. First, widespread and systematic corruption, together with consistent policy failure, would lead the public to reject the entire political establishment and wish for its complete renewal (Acemoglu, Egorov, and Sonin 2013; Hawkins 2010). Second, a lack of responsiveness by governing parties. Political forces become distant from the electorate – because they converge to a technocratic center or cede sovereignty to global economic forces or institutions – fuelling a broad sense of lack of popular representation or real alternatives (Mouffe 2005). Populist parties break this spiral, politicizing issues that had not been part of public discourse and addressing real concerns from voters ignored by mainstream political parties. The first and second hypotheses tested in this chapter reflect these two contextual settings, and expressly test the ideational theory: a) populists are more successful when governance is poor; and b) populists are more successful when mainstream parties are ideologically closer to one another.

At the same time, alternative theories have been proposed to explain the success of populism. A first set of explanations discusses the role of political institutions. One such theory focuses on institutions that make it easier for newcomers and/or charismatic leaders to emerge (Norris 2005). This is because, both in established and new democracies, populist leaders tend to first appear as outsiders. Therefore, the higher the barrier to entering the political arena, the harder it is for a (populist) challenger to become a relevant political force.

Two kinds of institutions can be identified with such theories: proportionality in the electoral system, and presidentialism. The first eases the establishment of smaller and niche parties. Majoritarian systems notably impose high informal thresholds for entrance into parliaments, following Duverger's Law (see Singer 2013). For example, a new populist party could get 15–20% of votes for several elections without ever making more than a handful of MPs, and this makes its emergence into a relevant position in national politics more difficult (Kitschelt and McGann 1995).

Presidentialism, for its part, also facilitates the election of charismatic leaders with weakly institutionalized party structures (Carreras 2012; Linz 1990). Presidential systems, especially in conjunction with weak party systems, have occasionally observed politicians rise to power who were relatively unknown shortly before the elections, or who created taxi-parties for themselves to run. If charisma is a correlate of populist leadership (Weyland 2001; Pappas 2016) – even if not a definitional part of it – presidential systems should facilitate the emergence of populist actors. Therefore, the analysis below incorporates these two institutional features, proportional representation and presidentialism, into the broader explanation of the success of populists.

A related condition that might foster the rise of populists is the age of democracy in a country. Younger democracies tend to have less institutionalized party systems, leaving more room for populist mobilization (Kriesi 2014). Indeed, despite all the talk about the recent rise of populists in Western Europe, the only countries in the continent ruled by unquestionable populists as of this writing are third- and fourth-wave democracies: Greece, Hungary, and Poland. Moreover, one might expect that in young democracies the public lacks a high attachment to liberal democratic norms, so that an illiberal discourse such as populism is more palatable. Therefore, I also test whether being a young democracy is more conducive to the success of populism.

The second alternative set of arguments is labeled the *Downsian approach* in the introduction. It treats populist voters as rational actors who behave according to their material interests. Support for populism, therefore, comes out of economic hardship. In recent accounts, the theory proposes that globalization, and the transference of industrial jobs overseas, make blue-collar workers in developed nations resent mainstream political parties (Betz 1994; Kriesi et al. 2006; Kriesi 2014). In consequence, these sectors turn to anti-globalization populists who combine protectionist economics with anti-immigrant policies (de Lange 2007), at least in the case of radical right populists in Europe. This explanation also resonates well with popular understandings of populism across the continent.

Face validity notwithstanding, the idea that declining economic status necessarily precipitates populism has been consistently challenged by recent empirical findings. The left-populist wave that swept Latin America in the 2000s followed a period of relative economic prosperity in several countries (Remmer 2011). In Europe, there is a far from perfect overlap between the countries hit hardest by the 2008 crisis and those that saw the rise of populism in this period (Kriesi and Pappas 2015). In any case, this argument is tested again in this chapter.

The third alternative, or the *Cultural* mechanism, suggests that populism is a reaction to great *social* changes brought about by globalization. According to this argument, anxiety over globalization is not caused by economic, but by social transformations. With demographic changes in post-industrial societies, accompanied by the emergence of new cleavages, populists mobilize social groups who have experienced relative loss of prestige (Betz 1994; Elchardus and Spruyt 2016). Moreover, conservative individuals among these groups react against the stream of post-material values (such as secularism and minority rights), and turn to reactionary right-wing populists as the defenders of an old order dominated by traditional ones (Inglehart and Norris 2016; Parker and Barreto 2013). In this chapter, therefore, I also test the competing hypothesis that higher levels of exposure to social globalization are conducive to populist electoral success.

In sum, causal explanations for the success of populism tested in this chapter are: a) bad governance and b) lack of representation, the contextual factors proposed by the ideational theory; c) presidentialism, d) proportionality, and e) age of democracy, in accordance with institutional accounts; f) economic crisis, connected to the rational-choice/Downsian argument, and g) social globalization, testing the cultural approach. The goal is to see how well the ideational explanation fares once alternative explanations are taken into account.

Method and data

I use fuzzy-set qualitative comparative analysis (fsQCA) to test which conditions, or combinations of conditions, are indeed associated with the electoral success of populist parties. This method treats conditions and outcomes as *sets*, to which a case has a degree of *membership* or, conversely, *non-membership*. After classifying all cases in each set, fsQCA uses Boolean algebra to minimize the combinations of conditions that are associated with the presence of the outcome.[3]

The advantages of this methodological approach are two-fold. First, it can accommodate medium-n samples that are too small for statistical inference but too large for in-depth comparative case studies. This is because the interpretation of results neither depends on assumptions regarding the true distribution of the data and estimated parameters, nor on (random) sampling. Inferences are restricted to the sample of cases at hand. Second, it can uncover what combinations of conditions may (alternatively) lead to the same outcome, allowing us to observe more complex causal structures. The following pages present the sets used in this analysis, and how cases are classified in each.

Outcome: success of populism

For this study, the units of analysis are country-elections and the outcome of interest is the electoral success of populism. Data on this outcome comes from the content-analysis study presented in the chapter by Hawkins and Castanho Silva in this volume. They have coded party manifestos of 144 parties in 27 Western European and American countries, and candidate speeches for all parties in 18 of them,[4] on the Hawkins (2009) populism scale with three categories: 0 – not populist at all; 1 – presence of necessary elements of populism, but not strong or consistently used; and 2 – all necessary elements of populism are present and consistent throughout the text. The sample includes all parties that received more than 5% of the national vote and, in some cases, extends to smaller parties that reached more than 1%. To include as much information as possible, I also use speeches' scores when available. To produce a final aggregated party score, the average scores for the leader or candidate speeches are averaged with the party manifesto score.

In fsQCA, cases' membership in sets is continuous and ranges from 0 to 1, denoting the uncertainty around their classification. There are three important cutpoints: at 0 a case is considered fully out; at 1 it is considered fully in, and at 0.5 is the cross-over point where it is considered more in than out. The rules for converting the data from Hawkins and Castanho Silva into country set-membership rates are in Table 11.1, along with which cases fall in each category.

In total, ten cases score above 0.5, which count as successes of populist parties, and 17 below 0.5. At the top, there are no surprises, with Venezuela – 2013, Bolivia – 2014, and Greece – 2015, the victories of Nicolas Maduro, Evo Morales, and SYRIZA. It is hard to imagine a stronger case of populist success than those. This classification takes into account a trade-off between the strength of populism and the electoral success of parties. It considers, for example, that 15% of the votes for a party whose manifesto has the necessary elements of populism (meaning, a grade ≥ 0.75), or at least 10% to a stronger populist (with a score ≥ 1.0) are the minimal requirements for considering that populists were successful in that election. To give examples, Spain and the Netherlands are right above the cross-over, with set-membership scores of 0.6. In the Spanish case, the score is attributed due to Podemos, which has a populism score of 0.78 and received more than 20% of the popular vote, coming in third. In the Netherlands, the successful party had a stronger populist discourse (1.25), but received only 10.8% of the national vote. Right below the line we see Germany. In the 2013 elections, two parties received fairly high scores: Die Linke, with 1.3, and the NPD, with 1.4. Both put together, however, still fell short of a 10% mark in the popular vote – and the NPD did not even make it into parliament. Therefore, while close to being a successful election for populism, according to this classification scheme it falls just short.[5]

Table 11.1 Definition of the "populist electoral success" set

Condition	*Membership*	*Cases*
A party ≥ 1.5 was first or second;	1	Bolivia, Greece, Venezuela
A party ≥ 1.0 was first;	0.9	Ecuador, Switzerland
A party ≥ 1.0 was second, OR ≥ 1.5 received more than 10%;	0.8	–
A party ≥ 0.75 was first or second, OR ≥ 1.0 received more than 15%, OR ≥ 1.5 received more than 10%	0.7	Austria, Mexico, Peru
A party ≥ 1.0 received more than 10%, or ≥ 0.75 received more than 15%	0.6	Netherlands, Spain
A party ≥ 1.0 received more than 5%, OR ≥ 0.75 received more than 10% OR a party ≥ 0.5 was first or second;	0.4	Argentina, Canada, Germany
A party ≥ 0.5 received more than 10%	0.3	Chile, France
The first or second party is ≥ 0.35 and < 0.5	0.2	US, Italy
A party with ≥ 1 received more than 1%	0.1	Brazil
A party with ≥ 0.5 received more than 1%	0.05	Belgium, Colombia, Paraguay, Portugal, UK, Uruguay
No party coded scores above 0.5	0	Ireland, Norway, Sweden

Causal conditions

Explanatory variables in the analysis presented here fall into one of two categories – those meant to operationalize the ideational approach and those that allow us to test alternative theories. I address them each in turn.

Ideational approach

While the ideational approach is basically a psychological, individual-level argument, it can be translated seamlessly to the macro as follows. First, while the ideational argument deals intrinsically with populist *attitudes*, for which we have only few aggregate comparative measures so far (e.g. Akkerman et al. 2014; Andreadis et al. in this volume, Chapter 10), if a root cause of support for populist parties is institutional distrust, then it should be related to the central behavioral outcome, namely electoral support for populists. Since the coding effort in Hawkins and Castanho Silva has evaluated the level of ideational populism in parties' discourse, support for such parties may be seen as a (admittedly imperfect) behavioral proxy for populist attitudes. At the same time, factors contributing to lower institutional trust would translate into populists' success.

Bad governance. This concept is represented by two sets, following the factors suggested in the introduction to this volume: high corruption and ineffective government. For corruption, I use the country score in the Corruption Perceptions Index from Transparency International, from the year prior to the election.[6] Looking at the data distribution, there is a gap between 45 and 60 (where higher numbers mean less corruption), and several countries clustered above or below these marks. Taking advantage of this natural cutpoint, 59 is taken to represent the 0.5 cutpoint in the analysis. Government performance is assessed with one dimension of the World Bank's Worldwide Governance Indicators: Government Effectiveness (Kaufmann, Kraay, and Mastruzzi 2010). It takes into account several indicators of how governments perform their roles, including the quality of infrastructure, public and social services, bureaucracy, and civil service[7] – but not indicators of corruption that would overlap with the TI's index on Corruption Perceptions. It ranges from –2.5 to 2.5, where higher values mean higher effectiveness. In the sample at hand, there is a leap between 0.5 and 1, where the cut for set membership in this set is placed. A case is fully *out* at the upper end, above 1.5, and fully *in* at the bottom end, below –1.

Elite collusion. To assess whether voters might perceive a failure of partisan representation, I create a set of *grand coalition*, informed by whether the government in place before the elections coded included a coalition with both right- and left-of-center parties. In cases of "grand-coalitions," when the two (or more) main parties in a political system are allied in government, voters might consider that voting for one or the other does not make a difference. The calibration is as follows: if the two mainstream center–left and center–right parties are together, the membership is 1. There are three such cases. If a major party has as junior partner a smaller party from the other side, it is 0.6. For example, in Brazil the center–left Workers' Party (PT) headed the government having, among its coalition partners, smaller conservative parties such as the Brazilian Republican Party (PRB) and the Progressive Party (PP), but not the mainstream center–right. This is the case in four countries. If there is a coalition of a centrist and a center-left or center-right party, it is a 0.1 (as in the CDU-CSU-FDP coalition in Angela Merkel's second cabinet). Single-party governments and ideologically coherent coalitions (left–left, or right–right) are fully out, and make the majority of the sample, with 17 cases.

Institutional accounts

Proportional electoral system. This comes from the "housesys" variable of the Database of Political Institutions (DPI, Beck et al. 2001, updated in 2012), which indicates what regime is used to elect the majority of members of the lower house – proportional representation or plurality. Calibration is done as follows: if all seats are allocated with PR, a case is 1. If it is a mixed system with PR defining the majority, 0.75; if the system is mixed with majoritarian rules defining the majority, 0.25; and if all are through majoritarian rules, 0. The majority of cases (20) is a member of this set, by deciding either all or most of their parliamentary seats through PR rules.

Presidentialism. Presidentialism is classified based on the "system" variable of the DPI. The sample comprises 12 presidential, 14 parliamentary, and 1 (France) semi-presidential systems. All presidential countries are coded as 1, and France as 0.6 – this seems the sensible choice given the large powers held by the president in current French politics (see Doyle and Elgie 2016 for a cross-national assessment of presidential powers). Parliamentary systems with a directly elected president – with little power – are a 0.2, and parliamentary systems with presidents that are not directly elected are a 0 (as well as parliamentary systems with no president at all, naturally).

Young democracy. To test whether the age of democracy makes a difference, I create a set of *young democracies*. Data comes from the Polity IV index (Marshall, Gurr, and Jaggers 2016), and a country is considered democratic if it scores 6 or above in it – meaning, democratization is considered to have happened when a country gets a score of 6 for the first time. Membership is assigned based on the decade of democratization: if it is the 2000s, set-membership is 1. For the 1990s, 0.9, for the 1980s, 0.8, and for the 1970s (the earlier third-wave democracies of Greece, Portugal, and Spain), 0.6. France, which got back to >6 in the 1960's, receives a 0.2, and older democracies a 0. Three exceptions to this coding are: a) Germany, given that part of the country democratized in the late 1940s and the other part in 1990, is a 0.4; and b) Ecuador and Venezuela, which have Polity scores below 6 in the electoral year, receive a 1.

Rational choice accounts

Economic crisis. To assess economic crisis I use two sets: *recession*, and *unemployment increase*. They are based, respectively, on the lagged (one year) GDP growth, and the percentage change in unemployment rates estimates in the three years before the election coded.[8] A country is considered to be in the *recession* set if its growth, in the year before the election, was zero or negative, while *unemployment increase* includes countries where the unemployment rate had a net increase during the three years prior to the elections. Twelve countries have set-membership higher than 0.5 in *unemployment increase*, while only four had a zero or negative GDP growth.

Cultural accounts

Social globalization. To address the mass-society argument, globalization is treated as a causal condition. Data comes from the KOF Globalization Index, which incorporates three dimensions: political, social, and economic (Dreher 2006; Dreher et al. 2008).[9] It takes into account how much a country is integrated into the global economy, as well as flows of people and capital, to reach a globalization scale along which countries are classified, ranging from 0 (not at all) to 100 (completely global). I use the second dimension, the social, as a proxy for the idea of great social transformations caused by globalization that are embedded in the mass-society approach.[10] In these data, we see two clusters, one between 35 and 54, and one from 75 to 92. The middle point is therefore set at 60, with cases below 40 being fully out, and above 90 fully in. There are 11 cases below 0.5, and 16 above, reflecting the open and global nature of much of the Western Hemisphere today.

Explaining populism

Analysis of sufficiency

Sufficiency analysis in QCA starts with building a *truth table*, in which each row is a unique combination of presence/absence of all conditions (in case of fsQCA, having a score above or below 0.5), and cases with that combination are assigned to it. If their membership on the outcome is above a certain consistency threshold, the combination of conditions in that row is considered sufficient for the outcome. Table 11.2 shows the resulting truth table of the configuration of populist success and the nine conditions.

The next step is the logical minimization of this truth table. It consists of identifying redundant rows that lead to the same outcome: for example, if both A and B are sufficient for C, and A without B is also sufficient for C, one may simply say that A is sufficient for C. It is indifferent whether B is present or not. Different solution formulas may be obtained depending on how one uses counterfactuals: if none are included, the resulting minimization yields the most conservative solution. Below, however, I present the result of an intermediate solution which includes logical remainders (truth table rows with no cases in them) assuming that all conditions are conducive to the positive outcome, what helps to make solution formulas more parsimonious.[11]

First path: left populism in Latin America

The first path in the solution formula is

$$\text{COR}\star\text{rec}\star\text{gcoal}\star\text{YDEM} \rightarrow \text{POPULISM}$$

which reads "high corruption, lack of recession or of grand coalitions, and being a young democracy is sufficient to populism".[12]

This path explains six cases: Argentina, Bolivia, Ecuador, Mexico, Peru, and Venezuela, with a consistency of 0.77. The one inconsistent case is Argentina, which does not have a successful populist election (close to it, however, with a set-membership of 0.4) but shares all the conditions with others who do.[13] This is the group of left-populism in Latin America, and can be translated as explaining the successes of Evo Morales, Rafael Correa, Andrés Manuel López Obrador, Ollanta Humala, and Nicolás Maduro. The solution is consistent with the ideational approach and previous findings (Doyle 2011; Hawkins 2010), showing that high corruption is an essential element for successful populists in Latin America, added to the fact that these are all countries with new democratic systems.

The path also largely confirms other previous findings about these cases: for example, that populism was successful in a scenario lacking an economic crisis (Remmer 2011), but with corrupt and bad governments that erode public trust in the political class. What they also show is a lack of a cross-ideological coalition prior to the election analyzed. In these cases, the success of populism was not associated with a party system where leading forces had become allies or too close to one another – an explanation that may better apply to

Table 11.2 Truth table for electoral success of populism

PRES	*COR*	*INEF*	*PR*	*REC*	*UNMP*	*GCOAL*	*SGLOB*	*YDEM*	*POPULISM*	*Consistency*	*Cases*
0	1	1	1	0	1	1	1	1	1	1.00	Greece
1	1	1	0	0	0	0	0	1	1	1.00	Bolivia
1	1	1	0	0	1	0	0	1	1	1.00	Mexico
0	0	0	1	0	0	0	1	1	1	0.88	Spain
1	1	1	1	0	0	0	0	1	1	0.84	Argentina, Ecuador, Peru, Venezuela
0	0	0	1	0	0	1	1	0	1	0.79	Austria
0	0	0	1	0	1	1	1	0	1	0.78	Netherlands, Switzerland
0	0	0	0	0	0	0	1	0	0	0.68	Canada
1	0	0	0	0	1	0	1	0	0	0.61	France
0	1	1	1	1	1	1	1	0	0	0.58	Italy
1	0	0	0	0	0	0	1	0	0	0.52	US
1	1	1	1	0	0	0	0	0	0	0.49	Colombia
1	0	1	1	0	1	0	0	1	0	0.47	Uruguay
0	0	0	1	1	1	1	1	0	0	0.47	Belgium
1	0	0	0	0	0	0	0	1	0	0.41	Chile
0	0	0	1	0	0	0	1	0	0	0.40	Germany, Norway
0	0	0	0	1	1	0	1	0	0	0.25	UK
0	0	0	1	0	1	0	1	0	0	0.24	Ireland, Sweden
0	0	0	1	0	1	0	1	1	0	0.23	Portugal
1	1	1	1	0	0	1	0	1	0	0.19	Brazil
1	1	1	1	1	0	0	0	1	0	0.19	Paraguay

Table 11.2 Notes: **PRES:** Presidentialism; **COR:** corruption; **INEF:** inefficient government; **PR:** PR electoral system; **REC:** recession; **UNMP:** unemployment increase; **COAL:** grand coalition; **SGLOB:** social globalization; **YDEM:** young democracy; **POPULISM**: outcome, electoral success of populism; **Consistency:** consistency of outcome, threshold at 0.8.

crises of representation in Europe. Quite the contrary, many of the successes of populism in the region reflected the success of a leading party. Indeed, it is important to note that of the five consistent cases, three had populists in power running for re-election (Bolivia 2014, Ecuador 2013, and Venezuela 2013), while two had populist challengers: Ollanta Humala in Peru 2011, and AMLO in Mexico 2012. The same set of conditions, therefore, contributed both to outsider populism as to the maintenance of power by populists (all three running for re-election did win). This suggests that the perennial structural conditions of corruption which erode trust in politicians – and which usually do not vary too much from one year to the other at the country level – lead to a fertile ground for populist discourse in and out of power. This challenges the notion of populist success solely thanks to a protest vote against corrupt and/or inefficient governing elites, a phenomenon often seen in studies of European opposition populist parties.

Second path: European populism, left and right

The second path in the solution formula is

pres*rec*GCOAL → POPULISM

and applies to Austria, Netherlands, Switzerland, and Greece. For them, it was sufficient to have a lack of presidentialism and of recession, and to feature a grand coalition. This is an essential point, and also fits the expectations from the ideational theory: a failure in political representation, approximated by cross-ideological governing coalitions that give an impression of lack of alternatives, was the sole positive necessary condition that, together with the other two negative ones in this path, led to the success of populism. Their economic situation was irrelevant. In fact, the absence of a recession in the year prior to the election was another necessary condition in this path.[14] Institutional facilitators do not appear greatly important – lack of presidentialism is present as a condition, and PR is not there in any form. Moreover, in a clearly distinctive feature from Latin America, indicators of bad governance are not a part of this formula. Austria, Switzerland, and the Netherlands are not members of either the *corruption* or the *ineffective government* sets. The disconnect between political elites and masses that gives rise to populism comes from another source: failure in accountable political representation.

Third path: Spain

The third path uniquely explains the Spanish case. It is

pres*unmp*YDEM → POPULISM

which simply states the lack of presidentialism and of increase in unemployment, and the presence of being a young democracy leads to populism. Spain does not fit with the other Europeans for the lack of a grand coalition prior to the elections where populists were successful. It is a possibility, however, that the fact that both major parties had been in government after the beginning of the Great Recession, and by and large failed to bring the country back to its pre-2009 prosperity, might have worked as a functional equivalent to the perception of lack of mainstream alternatives (more on the Spanish case on the chapter by Gómez-Reino and Llamazares in this volume). Moreover, Spain is also not a case of a corrupt or inefficient government to a point that would put it together with the Latin American ones. As for institutional facilitators, while not having a presidential system it does use PR for the election of its lower chamber.

Combined solution

The combined solution, including all three paths and fit information, is in Table 11.3, while the XY plot with all cases' membership in the three-path solution formula and the outcome is in Figure 11.1. The solution has a good overall consistency, of 0.8, with coverage of 0.84. In graphical terms, consistency decreases as there are more cases above the line – meaning, they have higher set membership on the outcome than on the solution formula, being deviant or unexplained cases. If all were below, consistency would be 1. Coverage decreases as the cases below the line get more distant from it. Those furthest have much more of the conditions than of the outcome, and are considered negative cases.

As the overall consistency and coverage rates indicate (0.8 and 0.84, respectively), the solution formula does a good job explaining the success of populist parties in this sample. Most cases in Figure 11.1 are close to the diagonal line, meaning their levels of populism are consistent with what we would expect given how much of the causal conditions they display. Two of the prime examples of populism in the world today, Greece and Bolivia, have more of it than would be expected given their membership in the solution formula. Nevertheless, a set membership around 0.7 is fairly high, and suggests they are

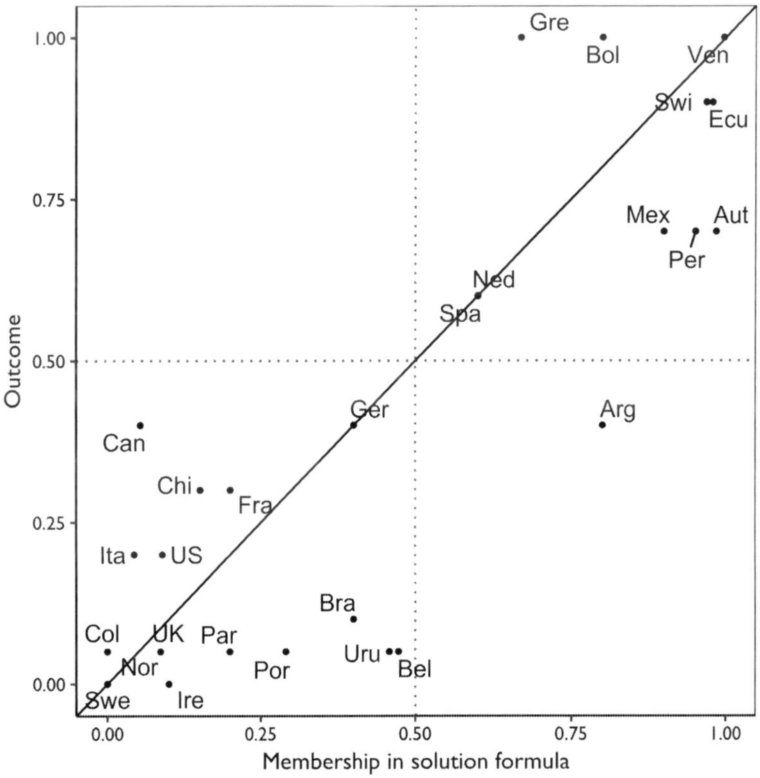

Figure 11.1 Combined solution

well explained. Venezuela, Spain, and the Netherlands are perfect fits, and would be good candidates as typical cases for future case studies, while the very strong cases of Ecuador and Switzerland are even a bit lower on their level of populism in relation to what we would expect given their membership in the solution.

Considering their coverage, the first two paths are the most powerful: they explain all cases of successful populism in Europe (first) and Latin America (second), while the third emerges as an explanation solely for Spain. What the first two paths show is a striking confirmation of the ideational theory's hypotheses regarding the rise of populism: it is the result of contextual conditions expected to elicit a perception of representation failure, and these contextual conditions vary across continents. We may interpret this as saying that countries with successful populists either had high corruption or elite (partisan) collusion right before the elections.

Discussion and conclusion

Findings in this analysis are perfectly in line with the ideational theory of populism, which showed more explanatory power than any of the alternatives. Ideational populism proposes that populist attitudes lay dormant among the public, and through framing can be activated given the right contextual conditions. The theory suggests that these conditions are those leading individuals to completely lose confidence in political institutions, and are connected with failures of political representation. These failures can take different forms, and the ideational theory outlined in the introduction suggests two: such as corruption and general ineffectiveness of the state, and lack of proper political representation by ruling political parties. This chapter confirmed these hypotheses: these factors are found to be the most relevant conditions for the success of populism across Europe and Latin America.

The popular rational-choice approach, once again, fails an empirical test. The only cases under study where populism immediately followed an economic crisis were Greece and Spain. However, as we have seen, the Greek case can be explained by factors other than the crisis – the same ones that cover Austria, the Netherlands, and Switzerland. Spain, for its part, did not have high levels on either of the economic crisis indicators used right before the 2015 elections: it was not in a recession, and unemployment was not increasing (albeit still very high). This suggests that economic failures do not clearly trigger a process leading to institutional trust erosion and from that to populism, as popular beliefs still hold.

Institutional features that have been proposed as facilitators of populist success also do not seem essential. All the Latin American countries are presidential, and not all have

Table 11.3 Intermediate solution formula for presence of populist success

Path	*Cons.*	*R. Cov.*	*U. Cov.*	*Cases*
COR*rec*gcoal*YDEM → POPULISM	0.77	0.50	0.44	Austria, Greece, Netherlands, Switzerland
pres*rec*GCOAL → POPULISM	0.82	0.29	0.26	Argentina, Bolivia, Ecuador, Mexico, Peru, Venezuela
pres*unmp*YDEM → POPULISM	0.91	0.13	0.06	Spain

Table 11.3 Notes: **Cons.** indicates the consistency of individual paths as sufficient for the outcome; **R. Cov.** indicates the raw coverage of the path; **U. Cov**. indicates the unique coverage of the path. For the whole solution formula, consistency is 0.80 and raw coverage 0.84.

populism, while none of the populist European cases are presidential systems. PR electoral systems are almost ubiquitous in this sample, so that PR's explanatory power is limited. Either way, neither of these two institutional factors seemed to matter much for the presence of strong populists. While being a young democracy appeared as relevant in the Spanish case, it was not a discriminating factor between positive and negative cases in other paths of the solution formula.

As for the mass-society approach, which stresses the role of major social transformation, this study has not found supporting evidence for it. Material or status loss among blue collar workers, the "losers of globalization," cannot account for populism, even in Europe (let alone Latin America). It is possible, however, that this theory is limited to right-wing European and North American populism, in which case it is a better explanation of radical right support than of populism.

In the end, after comparing the success of populism across very different contexts in two regions, what emerges as a common ground for its rise are, indeed, the contextual factors outlined by ideational populism. Nevertheless, much research still lies ahead to confirm the ideational theory of populism. First of all, this chapter has only tackled the success of populism at the country level. The ideational theory is framed at the individual level, and as such requires individual level tests (such as those performed with mass surveys and experiments in other chapters in this book) to confirm whether indeed those contextual conditions are instrumentalized by populist actors in the activation of dormant populist attitudes among the public.

A second avenue for future studies is to investigate whether different kinds of contextual conditions give rise to different kinds of populisms. In other words, are failures of governance (such as corruption) more associated with a specific left or right populism? What combinations of conditions could account for the different kinds of populisms seen in Europe today? Would they be different, or is there that much in common between the factors behind the rise of Podemos and Geert Wilders? These questions await further studies to tackle them head-on.

Notes

1 *Que se vayan todos!*, in Spanish.
2 The edited volume by Mudde and Rovira Kaltwasser (2012) features a cross-regional analysis that focuses more on the consequences of populism, and is divided into country-specific chapters. The cross-regional analysis by Hawkins (2010) studies only populists in government.
3 For more technical details, see Ragin 2006, Rihoux and Ragin 2009, Schneider and Wagemann 2012.
4 From the most recent national elections up to March 2015, with three exceptions: Austria 2008, Canada 2006, and Spain December 2015. In total, there are 11 Latin American countries, 14 West European, plus Canada and the United States.
5 Previous QCA studies of populist parties' emergence have followed similar lines. Van Kessel (2015, 76–78) defines an election as a member of the set of populist success when the combined vote-share of populist parties exceeds 10%, and fully member when the combined vote-share exceeds 20%. In Hanley and Sikk (2016), which studies anti-establishment reform parties (some of which are populists), full membership in the set of these parties' electoral success is defined at a combined 30% of votes, and the crossing point into more-in-than-out (0.5) is set at 7%.
6 Available at: www.transparency.org/research/cpi/overview. Only data from after 2012 are used, even for countries where the election coded happened earlier, because the TI changed its methodology for calculating the index in 2012, and results from the two stages should not be compared. Country scores show little variation on the short term, and therefore using data from years after the election should not pose major problems.

7 Data available at http://info.worldbank.org/governance/wgi/index.aspx, accessed on February 5, 2016.
8 Available at: http://data.worldbank.org/. Last accessed on September 25, 2015.
9 Data available at http://globalization.kof.ethz.ch/, accessed on November 14, 2016.
10 Other sources of data for this approach are problematic for lack of coverage. Using the World Values Survey, for example, as in Inglehart and Norris (2016), would mean excluding four of our ten cases of success of populism which have not been part of their two most recent waves.
11 The minimization algorithm produced 14 alternative solutions, which were deemed equally good by it. The one selected for presentation of results is that with highest coverage and consistency above 0.8.
12 Following QCA standards, the presence of a set is denoted with it being written in all caps, while the negation of a set (as in lack of recession) is shown by it being in small letters. The arrow in this direction means "is sufficient for," while the * is a logical AND operator, defining that all conditions must appear together for the outcome to occur.
13 It must be noted that Cristina Fernandez de Kirchner's speeches and electoral manifestos were close to being considered populist by Hawkins and Castanho Silva, and that more generally it is debated whether she is a populist or not. This is captured by Argentina's 0.4 set-membership rate, which indicates that populism was not irrelevant in the country in that election.
14 Given Greece's economic turmoils on the years before, however, it would be a stretch to say it lacked an economic crisis before populists' success simply due to it not being technically in recession in 2014.

References

Acemoglu, Daron, Georgy Egorov, and Konstantin Sonin. (2013). "A Political Theory of Populism". *The Quarterly Journal of Economics* 128(2):771–805.

Akkerman, Agnes, Cas Mudde, and Andrej Zaslove. (2014). "How Populist Are the People? Measuring Populist Attitudes in Voters." *Comparative Political Studies* 47(9): 1324–1353.

Beck, Thorsten, George Clarke, Alberto Groff, Philip Keefer, and Patrick Walsh. (2001). "New Tools in Comparative Political Economy: The Database of Political Institutions". *World Bank Economic Review*, 15(1):165–176.

Betz, Hans-Georg. (1994). *Radical Right-Wing Populism in Western Europe*. New York: Palgrave Macmillan.

Canovan, Margaret. (1981). *Populism*. London: Junction Books

Carreras, Miguel. (2012). "The Rise of Outsiders in Latin America, 1980–2010: An Institutionalist Perspective." *Comparative Political Studies* 45(12):1451–1482.

Conniff, Michael (ed). (1999). *Populism in Latin America*. Tuscaloosa: University of Alabama Press.

de Lange, Sarah L. (2007). "A New Winning Formula? The Programmatic Appeal of the Radical Right". *Party Politics* 13(4):411–435.

Doyle, David. (2011). "The Legitimacy of Political Institutions: Explaining Contemporary Populism in Latin America". *Comparative Political Studies* 44(11):1447–1473.

Doyle, David, and Robert Elgie. (2016). "Maximizing the Reliability of Cross-National Measures of Presidential Power". *British Journal of Political Science* 46(4):731–741.

Dreher, Axel. (2006). "Does Globalization Affect Growth? Evidence from a New Index of Globalization". *Applied Economics* 38(10):1091–1110.

Dreher, Axel, Noel Gaston, and Pim Martens. (2008). *Measuring Globalization – Gauging Its Consequences*. New York: Springer.

Elchardus, Mark, and Bram Spruyt. (2016). "Populism, Persistent Republicanism and Declinism: An Empirical Analysis of Populism as a Thin Ideology." *Government and Opposition* 51(1):111–133.

Hanley, Seán, and Allan Sikk. (2016). "Economy, Corruption or Floating Voters? Explaining the Breakthroughs of Anti-establishment Reform Parties in Eastern Europe". *Party Politics* 22(4):522–533.

Hawkins, Kirk. (2009). "Is Chavez Populist?: Measuring Populist Discourse in Comparative Perspective." *Comparative Political Studies* 42(8):1040–1067.

Hawkins, Kirk. (2010). *Venezuela's Chavismo and Populism in Comparative Perspective.* Cambridge: Cambridge University Press.

Inglehart, Ronald F., and Pippa Norris. (2016). "Trump, Brexit, and the Rise of Populism: Economic Have-Nots and Cultural Backlash", Faculty Research Working Paper Series, RWP16-026. Available at: https://research.hks.harvard.edu/publications/getFile.aspx?Id=1401.

Kaufmann, Daniel, Aart Kraay, and Massimo Mastruzzi. (2010). "The Worldwide Governance Indicators: Methodology and Analytical Issues." World Bank Policy Research Working Paper No. 5430.

Kitschelt, Herbert, and Anthony J. McGann. (1995). *The Radical Right in Western Europe: A Comparative Analysis.* Ann Arbor, MI: The University of Michigan Press.

Kriesi, Hanspeter. (2014). "The Populist Challenge". *West European Politics* 37(2):361–378.

Kriesi, Hanspeter, Edgar Grande, Romain Lachat, Martin Dolezal, Simon Bornschier, and Timotheos Frey, (2006). Globalization and the Transformation of the National Political Space: Six European Countries Compared. *European Journal of Political Research*, 45(6):921–956.

Kriesi, Hanspeter, and Takis S. Pappas. (2015). "Populism in Europe during Crisis: an Introduction." In *European Populism in the Shadow of the Great Recession*, edited by Kriesi, Hanspeter, and Takis S. Pappas, 1–22. Colchester: ECPR Press.

Linz, Juan. J. (1990). "The Perils of Presidentialism". *Journal of Democracy* 1(1):51–69.

Madrid, Raul. (2008). "The Rise of Ethnopopulism in Latin America". *World Politics* 60(3):475–508.

Marshall, Monty. G., Ted R. Gurr, and Keith Jaggers. (2016). *Polity IV Project Dataset Users' Manual.* Vienna, VA: Center for Systemic Peace.

Mouffe, Chantal. (2005). "The 'End of Politics' and the Challenge of Right-Wing Populism". In *Populism and the Mirror of Democracy*, edited by Panizza, Francisco, 32–49. London: Verso.

Mudde, Cas. (2004). "The Populist Zeitgeist". *Government and Opposition* 39(4):542–63.

Mudde, Cas, and Cristóbal Rovira Kaltwasser (eds.). (2012). *Populism in Europe and the Americas: Threat or Corrective to Democracy?*. Cambridge: Cambridge University Press.

Norris, Pippa. (2005). *Radical Right: Voters and Parties in the Electoral Market.* Cambridge: Cambridge University Press.

Pappas, Takis S. (2016). "Are Populist Leaders 'Charismatic'? The Evidence from Europe". *Constellations* 23(3):378–390.

Parker, Christopher S., and Matt A. Barreto. (2013). *Change They Can't Believe In: The Tea Party and Reactionary Politics in America.* Princeton, NJ: Princeton University Press.

Ragin, Charles C. (2006). "Set Relations in Social Research: Evaluating Their Consistency and Coverage". *Political Analysis* 14(3):291–310.

Remmer, Karen L. (2011). "The Rise of Leftist-Populist Governance in Latin America: The Roots of Electoral Change". *Comparative Political Studies* 45(8):947–972.

Rihoux, Benoit, and Charles C. Ragin. (2009). *Configurational Comparative Methods: Qualitative Comparative Analysis (QCA) and Related Techniques.* Thousand Oaks, CA: Sage.

Schneider, Carsten Q., and Ingo Rohlfing. (2016). "Case Studies Nested in Fuzzy-set QCA on Sufficiency: Formalizing Case Selection and Causal Inference". *Sociological Methods & Research* 45(3):526–568.

Schneider, Carsten Q., and Claudius Wagemann. (2012). *Set-Theoretic Methods for the Social Sciences: A Guide to Qualitative Comparative Analysis.* Cambridge: Cambridge University Press.

Singer, Matthew M. (2013). "Was Duverger Correct? Single-Member District Election Outcomes in Fifty-three Countries". *British Journal of Political Science* 43:201–220.

Stein, Steve. (1980). *Populism in Peru: The Emergence of the Masses and the Politics of Social Control.* Madison, WI: University of Wisconsin Press.

di Tella, Torcuato. (1965). "Populismo y Reforma en América Latina". *Desarrollo Económico* 4(16):391.

van Kessel, Stijn. (2015). *Populist Parties in Europe: Agents of Discontent?* New York: Palgrave Macmillan.

Weyland, Kurt. (2001). "Clarifying a Contested Concept: Populism in the Study of Latin American Politics". *Comparative* 34(1): 1–22.

12 Populism in Spain

The role of ideational change in Podemos

Margarita Gómez-Reino and Iván Llamazares

Ideational approaches have identified the necessary presence of three ideas in populist discourse: a morally Manichean cosmic struggle, a virtuous and homogeneous people, and a corrupt and self-serving elite (see Hawkins and Rovira Kaltwasser's introduction to this volume). This set of ideas was conspicuously absent in Spanish party politics over the past 40 years. The outburst of Podemos in 2014, however, introduced a new populist rhetoric exhibiting the key three components of the ideational definition of populism adopted in this volume. The political message of Podemos (We Can) was a cry for rupture and change directed against the economic and political establishment – *la casta*, in the language of the party. Populist ideas moved to center stage as Podemos attained, just two months after its official foundation, 8% of the votes in the 2014 European Parliament Elections. And in the general elections of December 2015 and June 2016, the electoral alliance built around Podemos attained 20.7 and 21.1% of the votes respectively, at very short distance from the Socialist Party.

This chapter addresses the recent emergence of a populist political discourse in the Spanish context. It focuses on the factors that led some political activists to articulate a populist discourse in a country in which such a set of ideas had been missing since the transition to democracy in the 1970s. In this chapter, we seek to explain why, how and when a group of radical left activists came to adopt a populist political discourse to launch a new political party. In line with the theoretical interpretation underlining this volume (see the introduction by Hawkins and Rovira Kaltwasser to this volume), our approach highlights the crucial and autonomous role that populist ideas played in processes of political change. Our objective is to trace the intellectual and ideological developments that took place among radical left social science researchers and activists and that led to the launching of Podemos and the adoption of a populist rhetoric. Background conditions for these developments were the perceived shortcomings of Marxist political theory, the weakness of radical left political groups, and the vitality of populist transformative movements in Latin America. It is in this context that some of the founders of Podemos concluded that Laclau's discourse theory was much more useful for the success of a radical and transformative political project than Marxism. Particularly important in this respect were the learning processes and theoretical reflections of one of the founders of Podemos, Íñigo Errejón, whose scholarly and political texts displayed a transformation in the direction of a populist proposal around the year 2011. This proposal, later labeled the "populist hypothesis," implied a theoretically grounded conjecture about Spanish politics that had to be subjected to empirical test. This chapter explains the processes by which the populist ideas came into existence, how the populist project was pushed to the front in the hands of Errejón for the 2014 European Elections and became afterwards the successful new rhetoric of the party.

Our chapter consists of a process-tracing case study (George and Bennet 2005; Collier 2011; Beach and Pedersen 2013; Bennett and Checkel 2015b) of the jointly sufficient mechanisms that led to the adoption of a populist discourse by Podemos in 2014. Given its case-centered character, our work fits well the main characteristics of explaining-outcome case studies (Beach and Pedersen 2013, 12). However, by showing the crucial role played by ideational transformations, our chapter aims also at improving our theoretical understanding of the processes by virtue of which ideas can act as causal forces (see also Hawkins and Rovira Kaltwasser in the introduction to this volume) and determine processes of change and innovation in party discourses and strategies. As it is claimed in this volume, the effects of these changes can be measured by empirical analyses on both the populist contents of party discourses (Hawkins and Silva in this volume, Chapter 1) and the electoral activation of populist public attitudes (Andreadis et al. in this volume, Chapter 10).

The evidence we found in scholarly and political texts shows with certainty the presence of strong ideational transformations among some of the founders of Podemos in the period preceding party formation. The perception shared by orthodox Marxist and non-Marxist activists that populist discourse theory determined the populist character of the 2014 electoral campaign is also consistent with this causal interpretation. In our view, these combined facts discard the hypothesis that populist discourse was developed and advocated in order to "strategically misrepresent the reasoning underlying" political choices, one of the challenges identified by Jacobs for ideational explanations, since evidence can be biased when actors conceal their true motives (Jacobs 2015, 45).

Our analysis provides us with evidence that is highly certain (the explanatory hypothesis on the role of ideational changes certainly predicts the evidence), and, to a slightly lesser degree, unique (our explanatory hypothesis uniquely predicts the evidence we gathered in political texts and personal interviews). Our work thus approaches the characteristics of doubly decisive evidentiary tests (Van Evera 1997; Bennett 2015, 288). This evidence also falsifies rival hypotheses on the emergence of populist discourse. Populist discourse did not arise out of the preexisting political ideas of radical left activists (who in many cases perceived populist elements with skepticism and mistrust, even within the close group that founded Podemos). And it did not arise either out of the populist orientations of the Spanish public, through a bottom-up deliberative process emerging out of the preceding 15M mobilization. Rather, the introduction of a populist discourse resulted from changes in the ideas held by key political actors and from the political and strategic opportunities that shaped the course of ideational change (Jacobs 2015).

In this respect, our theory follows Popper's interpretation on the crucial role played by *world 3* abstract components: the objective contents of thought (theoretical systems, problems, problem situations, and critical arguments) in social life (Popper 1985, 58–59, 265–256; Popper and Eccles 1985, 38–41). As in the case of Popper's interpretation, ideational and theoretical changes are connected to problem situations (the failure of Marxist political theory, radical left political actors, and social mobilization in this case). In turn, the adoption of a new theoretical framework would lead to the adoption of a new competitive strategy (populist discourse). In this case, changes in theories and ideas cannot be predicted in a mechanistic way based on social, economic or political events. Ideas have an at least partially autonomous character, and they can evolve in initially unimagined directions depending on quite complex combinations of circumstances (such as individual thought-processes, public deliberation, political-institutional settings, exogenous events, and emerging problem situations).[1] In our case, the fact that an articulated and persuasive populist discourse theory was first developed by a political science researcher and activist who ended up becoming the campaign chief for the 2014 European elections campaign also reveals the importance of the sequence of events and contingent developments in this political process of ideational change.

In the first section of this chapter we present the political opportunity structure that preceded the launching of Podemos. In the second section we narrow our focus by analyzing the foundation of Podemos as a result of the confluence of different political groups and activists. Finally, in the third section we analyze political and scholarly texts, published interviews, and oral testimonies in order to trace the purposeful adoption of populist ideas. Our analysis thus moves from the general historical and political context to the ideational processes of innovation that preceded the adoption of a populist discourse.

The political opportunity structure: the great recession and the 15M

On May 12, 2010, the Socialist Spanish government presided over by José Luis Rodríguez Zapatero announced a severe austerity package that reduced public expenditures by 1.5% of the GDP. This package followed the escalation of the debt crisis and the financial rescue of the Greek economy in April–May 2010. It also responded to the rapidly growing pressures exercised by European governments on the Spanish government to adopt severe fiscal consolidation measures, most notoriously, in the 9 May EU meeting of the economics and finance ministers.

Economic reforms aiming at fiscal consolidation would continue under the Rodríguez Zapatero government. These reforms did not bring economic recovery. The Spanish economy grew by 0.2% in 2010 and –0.6% in 2011, and the unemployment rate rose to 20.1% in 2010 and 22.6% in 2011. Among people younger than 25 years old, the unemployment rate in 2010 was higher than 40%.[2]

Poor economic performance and negative economic evaluations had quite negative effects on voting for the Socialist Party in 2011 (Fraile and Lewis-Beck 2014; Torcal 2014).[3] As President Rodríguez Zapatero himself later acknowledged (Rodríguez Zapatero 2014), these reforms implied a strong departure from the policies advocated by Socialist governments from the 1980s onwards and led to a strong sense of alienation among Socialist votes. From 2008 to 2011 the share of vote for the Socialist party in the general elections dropped from 43.9 to 28.7%, and the absolute number of socialist voters fell by more than 4 million.

Almost in a parallel way very important corruption cases came to light. Corruption scandals were connected to the funding of political parties (as in the Gürtel, Púnica, and Bárcenas cases for the Popular Party, and the Palau and ITV cases for the Catalan Democratic Convergence), to the clientelistic allocation of large sums of money (as in the case of the ERE funds that the Andalusian Socialist government provided for businesses in crisis and employees losing their jobs), or to the mismanagement and fraudulent use of regional banking institutions, as in the case of the Bankia. By 2014, the number of individuals subjected to judicial proceedings due to corruption scandals rose to almost 2000.[4] Not surprisingly, public concern with political corruption escalated. The percentage of people who thought that corruption was one of the main problems of the country jumped from less than 5% in the early 2000s to more than 40% in 2013 (Medina 2015, 12).

In this social and economic context, in May 2011, a wave of social protests against unemployment, cuts in social expenditures, and the privileges of the political class erupted

(Mora 2012; Minguijón Pablo and Pac Salas 2013). Protests crystallized in camp-outs all across Spain that would last in some cases until August 2011. Although protesters had a distinctive social and ideological profile (young people with a high overrepresentation of college graduates and leftist activists) (Calvo, Gómez-Pastrana, and Mena 2011; Minguijón Pablo and Pac Salas 2013), this wave of social mobilizations had transversal characteristics and appealed to people with quite diverse previous political sympathies. According to different surveys (Calvo, Gómez-Pastrana and Mena 2011, 5), in 2011 more than 70% percent of Spaniards felt sympathy for the 15M movement and its demands. Given the transversal and catch-all nature of this wave of social mobilization, and the adversarial, anti-elitist, and wide-range nature of its political demands, the 15M movement fitted very well the characteristics of a populist social movement (Errejón 2015, 145–146; Aslanidis 2016, 305–307).

In the November 2011 general elections, the Popular Party attained an absolute majority of seats in parliament. Rajoy's government continued the austerity policies initiated under Rodríguez Zapatero. Economic reforms did not manage to reduce Spanish unemployment rates, which escalated above 25% by the end of 2012 and remained above that threshold level until mid-2014. Public trust in President Rajoy suffered from this performance and from the scandals affecting the Popular Party. In early 2013, the Bárcenas case broke out in the national press. Allegedly, Luis Bárcenas, the treasurer of the Popular Party, had been using money illegally delivered to the Popular Party in order to fund the party and to pay monthly bonuses to party leaders.[5] In June 2013 Bárcenas was sent to prison. By early 2013, surveys conducted by Metroscopia indicated than more than 80% of citizens did not trust President Rajoy.[6] By mid-2013, according to the same polling agency, 60% of the PP voters did not trust the President.[7]

By the end of 2013, the combination of unpopular economic measures, deep economic crisis, and corruption scandals had triggered a strong sense of discontent and political alienation among many Spanish citizens. That feeling was especially acute among former socialist voters, who had witnessed the sharp policy switch made by the Rodríguez Zapatero government, a switch whose economic benefits were very hard to grasp for most Spanish citizens. As shown by different contributions (Roberts 2013 and 2015; Hawkins's and Rovira Kaltwasser's introduction to this volume; Bornschier in this volume, Chapter 9), this type of scenario was highly favorable to both a party system transformation and the emergence of a populist discourse.

Particularly important in this process of acute political change was the 15M movement. The 15M paved the way for the emergence of both new political discourses and new political organizations (Errejón 2015; Medina 2015; Nez 2015; Fernández Albertos 2015; Torreblanca 2015). By articulating a transversal social mobilization process, dichotomizing the political space, and channeling intense grievances against the political and economic establishment, the 15M adopted populist features and prefigured a more elaborate populist discourse (Errejón 2015: 145–146; Aslanidis 2016). The 15M replaced old divides internal to the political system (left–right) by a new, more radical confrontation between those who were up and those who were down (Errejón 2015, 138–139; Cano 2015, 164–165 and 37–38).

The economic, social, and political events that took place from the 2010 Socialist government austerity package to the 2014 European Parliament elections created a context that was favorable to the emergence of new political forces and the articulation of a disruptive and anti-elite populist discourse. However, the creation of a new political organization and the articulation of populist appeals were also made possible by organizational and ideational developments taking place among specific groups of political activists. In the following section, we turn to the processes by virtue of which these activists coalesced in the foundation of Podemos.

From social unrest to the foundation of Podemos

The launching of Podemos was preceded by debates and meetings among social and political activists that went back to at least 2011. In particular, the open political debates organized by Izquierda Anticapitalista – Anticapitalist Left – in its 2013 summer university led leftist activists to examine the organization of a political alternative for the 2014 European Parliament Elections (Rivero 2015a, 125–127). Izquierda Anticapitalista was a small radical left party born in 2008[8] that defined itself as a "revolutionary, anticapitalist, internationalist, feminist and socialist organization."[9] It had run in the 2009 European elections with very poor results and obtaining no representation (0.13% of the vote). The party was, however, very active among the groups and organizations that participated in the 15M movement.

Two very active participants in the debates on the creation of a new party were Pablo Iglesias and Miguel Urbán, the latter an activist of Izquierda Anticapitalista. In December 2013 concrete plans for the launching of a new electoral platform were elaborated by Urbán and Iglesias among other activists. These plans included the electoral platform name and the special role that Iglesias would play in it (Rivero 2015a, 138–139).[10] In addition to Iglesias, Urbán, and Izquierda Anticapitalista, members of other networks of activists joined the project in December (Anon. 2016: 22; Rivero 2015a, 139).

The launching of the party was preceded by the manifesto *Mover Ficha*, released in January 14, 2014. Podemos was officially presented in a press conference in Madrid three days after the Manifest, in January 17, 2014. The manifesto *Mover Ficha* was based on an internal document of Izquierda Anticapitalista. Both documents ended with the same statement:

The signatories of this Manifest are convinced that this is the moment to make a step forward. Indignation and new forms of participation must also reach out to politics. In the streets it is repeated "Yes it can be. We say: We can" (*"Sí se puede. Nosotros decimos: Podemos"*) (our translation).

Thus, *"Sí se puede"* became the motto to organize the party and gather popular support. The list of signatories of the Manifest included members of Izquierda Anticapitalista, activists from social movements, leftist intellectuals, and trade unionists. However, the future main leaders of Podemos – Iglesias, Carolina Bescansa, and Errejón, all of them young social science researchers connected to the Universidad Complutense – were not among the first signatories.[11]

Izquierda Anticapitalista was one of the main actors leading to the foundation of Podemos. The other one was the Complutense group, in which Iglesias played a key role. Political activism and cooperation within this Complutense group had evolved in the context of academic life, political associations, and think tanks.[12] Some researchers had collaborated with the now extinct Foundation CEPS (*Centro de Estudios Políticos y Sociales*), a foundation that defined itself as "a political organization (not a party) dedicated to the production of critical thinking and cultural and intellectual work to build consensus among the left." CEPS had been involved in different types of research and in its 15 years of existence it had carried out different projects in Latin America, including Venezuela. Future founders of Podemos, in particular Juan Carlos Monedero, but also Iglesias, Bescansa, and Errejón participated as advisers and strategic analysts in different projects linked to the Chaves' government.[13]

The confluence between activists of Izquierda Anticapitalista and Complutense members had also crystallized through the media. *La Tuerka* (the Nut), a TV program created in 2010, broadcasted through local TVs and internet, and *Fort Apache*, created in 2012 and broadcasted through HispanTV, the Spanish language emission of the Iranian public TV, served as political talk shows for some of the members of the Complutense team (Giménez 2014b). Iglesias, then an adjunct professor at the Universidad Complutense de Madrid, was the anchor and director of a program of political debate that gathered some of the later key figures of Podemos. Beyond *La Tuerka* and *Fort Apache*, Iglesias was able to access the mass media in several TV private channels as a regular *tertuliano*, a talk show guest representing in this case an alternative political discourse. With his characteristic ponytail, eloquent expression, and gentle manners, Iglesias became an increasingly popular public figure.

Podemos as a new political party was officially registered in March 11, 2014. The first electoral list to the European elections was prepared using the main tools later developed by the organization: the web and the *circles* (the local party branches).[14] Iglesias and his team decided to launch a participatory process both to open up the selection of candidates and elaborate an electoral program for the European elections.

Izquierda Anticapitalista purposefully supported the political project under the banner of *Podemos*, even if it recognized the complex nature of the political confluence between what they considered as two separate souls (*Bulletin 84*, March 5th, 2014). Two months before the European elections, an internal document of Izquierda Anticapitalista stated:

> We are aware that we are launching an initiative with a *populist political culture*, but they have a significant convening power, influence and popularity.
>
> (our translation, emphasis added).

More importantly, between the launching of the Manifest of Podemos in January and the registration of Podemos as a political party in March, just before the 2014 European elections, two key developments took place. First, the party formation process was put in the hands of Iglesias, Bescansa, and Errejón. Second, Iglesias delivered the control of the electoral campaign to Errejón. A small coordinating team organized by Errejón was in charge of an electoral campaign highly personalized around the character of Iglesias.

Iglesias's electoral speeches adopted a strongly populist character. They portrayed a Manichean vision of society that pitted the people (*la gente* or *la gente de este país*) against "the caste" (*la casta*),[15] that is, the political and economic elites that occupy privileged positions and claim to represent the people through the institutional mechanisms created by the 1978 Spanish Constitution. *La casta* was corrupt and narrowly self-interested; while *la gente* represented hard-work, dignity, solidarity, and true patriotism.

Iglesias's speeches also gave voice to a new type of patriotism aimed at overcoming traditional distinctions between the left and right. In this new interpretation, patriotic pride and dignity were not linked to the Spanish language or ethnic particularism, but to solidarity, hard work, and care for the common good. Patriotism stood now in sharp contrast to the values of those who, notwithstanding the intensity of their Spanish (or peripheral) nationalist appeals, evaded taxes, placed their money in tax havens, and cared only about their banking accounts. These dichotomies conveyed intense antagonisms and an initial rejection of conventional and institutionalized politics (negotiations, consensus, agreements based on mutual compromises). They also turned to rhetorical radicalism in pursuit of systemic changes. In Iglesias's words, who paraphrased Marx's famous revolutionary dictum, "heavens are not taken by consensus, they are taken by assault."[16] The use of Hawkins's (2010) holistic grading technique reveals that Iglesias's speeches in 2014 were extremely populist – close to the ideal type of populist discourse (a grade of 2 in Hawkins's populism score).[17]

The electoral success confirmed the extraordinary appeal of this new discourse and consolidated the power positions of Iglesias and Errejón.[18] Their power was institutionally consecrated by the results of the founding party congress in November 2014. This congress witnessed the triumph of the organizational model advocated by Iglesias (80.7% of the votes for his top-down model, against the 12.3% received by the bottom-up model proposed by prominent members of Izquierda Anticapitalista)[19] and the total victory of the candidature of Iglesias and his closer associates to the *Consejo Ciudadano*, the governing body of Podemos (Iglesias received 88.6% of the votes for the position of secretary general, while Izquierda Anticapitalista finally declined to present alternative candidates).[20] In this Assembly, Errejón was appointed as responsible for both the political secretariat and electoral campaigns and strategy. This series of political victories consolidated the adoption of a populist discourse in the 2015 general elections.

This does not mean, however, that more classical radical leftists lost all influence in Podemos. Former members of Izquierda Anticapitalista attained positions of power in important regional branches – like Madrid and Andalusia – and they would exercise strong influence in future political developments in Podemos, both at the regional and national levels.

Learning processes and discursive transformations in the radical left space

The adoption of a populist discourse by Podemos was made possible by ideational and political developments taking place among a few radical left activists and scholars in the first decade of this century. Many of the founders of Podemos were researchers linked to the Universidad Complutense, in particular to the Political Science and Philosophy schools, as well as the CEPS working group. And it was also in the school of Political Science that the anticapitalist student association *Contrapoder* was created by Iglesias in 2006. In 2008, a group of researchers within that same school, including Iglesias, Errejón, Bescansa, Ariel Jerez, and Monedero founded the group *Promotora de Pensamiento Crítico* in order to debate Spanish politics and issues such as the transition to democracy. The political socialization and activism of this group of activists had consistently taken place in the ideological space of the radical left, an environment in which different versions of Marxist social and political theory had prevailed. Sympathy with new Latin American popular movements had made members of this group well acquainted with populist politics, but it was Errejón who focused in depth in the analysis of populist politics and discourse. Within this group, he was also the one who showed a deeper interest in Laclau's theories of populism. In fact, with a few exceptions leftist political activists in the Spanish academia were not well acquainted with Laclau's ideas, and tended to adhere to other streams of Marxist or post-Marxist political thought.

Errejón would play a crucial role within this group of activists in the theoretical diffusion of Laclau's theory on populism. Errejón himself narrates how his theoretical and political views were transformed by his study of popular movements in Latin America (Errejón and Mouffe 2015, 70–71). His first ideological steps were strongly influenced by autonomist Marxism and Gramsci, and his first militant commitments took place in anti-globalization movements (Errejón and Mouffe 2015, 72). However, contact with Latin American politics in 2006 changed his political views and led him to study and interpret popular discourses and movements (Errejón and Mouffe 2015, 73).[21] Such ideological transformation was mostly absent from the texts written by other very prominent founders of Podemos. For instance, Luis Alegre, a lecturer of philosophy at the Universidad Complutense de Madrid, who later became general secretary of the Madrid party branch of Podemos, defended his Ph.D. dissertation in 2008 on the concepts of class and citizenship in Karl Marx. No references to Laclau, Mouffe or the concept of populism were present in that text, a philosophical and theoretical exercise focusing on Marx's *Capital*. Iglesias defended his political science Ph.D. dissertation in 2008. The main theoretical frameworks on which this work was based were Wallerstein's world-systems theory and the Italian based stream of autonomist Marxism (Iglesias 2008, 168). Iglesias referred to Laclau's work on populism only when he pointed out that leaders play a critical role in the development of interpretative frameworks, even in the types of movements his work analyzed (Iglesias 2008, 112–113). Neither did other dissertations written by future members of the governing body of Podemos, the *Consejo Ciudadano* (Gemma Ubasart's 2008 political science dissertation on emergency state responses to disruptive political action in Europe, and Eduardo Maura's 2011 philosophy dissertation on Walter Benjamin, both of these activists future members of Podemos) address or use theoretical frameworks focusing on populist phenomena or discourse.

The absence of a theoretical examination of populism is more striking in works that specifically addressed Latin American political experiences. Even essays praising Chavismo, like Fernández Liria and Alegre Zahonero's *Comprender Venezuela* (2006), avoided the use of Laclau's theoretical framework and the defense of populism in the interpretation of the Bolivarian revolution. Fernández Liria and Alegre linked the Chavista movement to the emancipatory projects of enlightenment and Marxism, and claimed that the Bolivarian revolution was the most successful instance of the state of law in the Kantian tradition. Thus, the political interest and solidarity raised by the Boliviarian revolution among some leftist activists was not followed by interest in theoretically exploring or politically applying the discursive elements of Latin American populist movements nor, arguably, the populist discourse theory of one of its most influential thinkers, Ernesto Laclau.

Quite different in character was Errejón's political science dissertation on the construction of political and discursive hegemony in Bolivia during the first MAS government. Errejón's work dedicated its three main theoretical chapters to the construction of hegemony through political discourse, mostly drawing on Gramscian ideas that he interpreted, with some caveats, through Laclau and Mouffe's lenses (Errejón 2012, 227). Following Laclau and Mouffe, Errejón emphasized the contingent character of the construction of political discourses and identities, but also underscored, to some extent in contrast to Laclau and Mouffe's ideas, the fact that such contingent processes were constrained by both socioeconomic structures and preexisting cultural elements and practices (Errejón 2012, 227–228). Errejón's work paid especial attention to the conditions of possibility for the emergence of the concept of "pueblo" through the constructed equivalence of multiple grievances and demands. Under conditions of state crisis, this political process could crystallize in the antagonistic constitution of a "pueblo," in opposition to both elites and the status quo (Errejón 2012, 233). Errejón's analysis identified several crucial steps in the construction of a hegemonic populist discourse: the characterization of the victims of injustice, the division of the political community into two poles, and the identification between the people and the general interest (Errejón 2012, 440). Populist discourse would involve a mythical and historicist reconstruction of the people, and it would also lead to simple and feasible solutions to national problems (Errejón 2012, 459–460).

As noted above these researchers were also strongly committed to political activism. And some of them produced texts aimed at political intervention in the midst of the economic and social crisis. These texts help identify the timing of incorporation of certain ideas in the emergence of Podemos, and in particularly, the adoption of the "populist hypothesis" as the dominant ideational and strategic framework.

Populism was discussed in connection with the European radical right in an article published by Urbán in *Viento Sur* (a radical left magazine), in 2010. The article focused on the populist radical right and did not transcend the classical frame of Marxist theory. Urbán highlighted the main characteristics of the new populism in Europe and the emphasis on the antagonism between the people and the elite. But it did not consider the potential that populist discourses or ideas might have for transformative and radical politics in Spain. Interestingly, the following year Errejón published two articles in *Viento Sur* on the subject of populism, the first one synthesizing his knowledge from Latin America, the second speculating on the prospects of populism in the Spanish case.[22] Paradoxically, no debate on populism and its combination with left or right wing politics in Europe emerged then. Errejón's interpretation of populist movements would become three years later the intellectual basis of Podemos' alternative political project. In his two 2011 articles Errejón explored the meanings of populism, the limitations of the European left and the possibilities opened in Europe for different types of populist movements. For Errejón, the defining characteristic of populism was the antagonism between the people and the elites (2011a, 82–83). Both terms (the people and the elites) lacked any specific content, and were therefore open to new assignments of meaning by political actors (2011a, 82–83). The weakness of the European left resulted from its adoption of the liberal and pluralist creed and from its renunciation to political antagonism. In his view, emancipatory politics required the reenactment of intense political antagonisms through a morally loaded dichotomization of society. Errejón's analyses from 2011 did not offer a specific guideline for action. They pointed out some of the limitations that a leftist populist discourse would face in Spain. Critical among them was the fact that the multinational character of Spain had made it very difficult to use the concept of "pueblo" in an emancipatory way (2011b, 111). In fact, as Errejón pointed out in his 2015 debate with Mouffe, words and slogans had to be empirically tested and used on the basis of their mobilizing power (Errejón and Mouffe 2015, 126). Given the multinational character of Spanish society, the politicization of peripheral cultures, and the uses Francoism had made of the terms *nación* (nation) and *pueblo*, these words had to be discarded. Instead of them, the term *gente* (also people, but less politically loaded, and with pluralistic connotations), or the expression *gente de este país* (people of this country) had to be used, always in opposition to the privileged or the *casta* (the caste) (Errejón and Mouffe 2015, 126). In his 2015 debate with Mouffe, Errejón noted also the crucial role of passions and emotions, always acknowledging the masterful use that radical right movements made of these crucial elements of political action (Errejón and Mouffe 2015, 58–59, 61). Eventually Errejón's reconstruction of the populist discursive processes by virtue of which MAS had reached hegemony in Bolivia would serve as a map for the articulation of a populist discourse in Spain.

Between 2011 and 2012, Errejón was the main proponent of the "populist hypothesis." Iglesias has also pointed out that the innovative analyses and reflections developed by Errejón gave rise to new political perspectives and stimulated politically committed researchers in the Universidad Complutense to participate in public communication arenas in order to create a new ideological hegemony. In Iglesias's words,

> This is a reflection that Íñigo Errejón started to develop from his experiences in Latin America, which has to do with the hypothesis of the role of the national-popular in order to construct big political aggregations . . . It was a very Gramscian discussion *that we both shared, but Errejón took it much further by applying the work of Enesto Laclau.*
>
> (Rivero 2015b, 96, our translation, emphasis added)[23]

The populist hypothesis was not initially shared by all the members of the core group of activists that became the founders of Podemos and, according to some former members of Izquierda Anticapitalista, it remained in a minority position among the rank and file of the new party.[24] Key figures in the initial founding process such as Monedero (who would abandon the direction of Podemos in April 2015) had also reservations about this project. And certainly, from a more radical perspective, members of Izquierda Anticapitalista also pressed in a different strategic direction since the party foundation.[25]

However, the positions or power conquered by Iglesias and Errejón (as main candidate and electoral campaign chief respectively) allowed them to implement the populist hipothesis in the 2014 European elections. In particular, Errejón would become a key mobile carrier (Jacobs 2015: 51) in the process of adoption of a populist discourse by Podemos.[26] In cooperation with other social science scholars and activists, some of whom had previously participated in *Contrapoder*, they managed to tailor the discourse and slogans in a clearly populist direction. A reduced number of activists sharing a common political diagnosis prepared an electoral campaign aiming at the construction of new antagonistic categories.[27]

From the perspective of this group, the 2014 electoral results confirmed the validity of the populist hypothesis, always against the reservations and even hostility of the left (Giménez 2014a: 105). As Ínigo Errejón explained in a interview,

> in politics we all have opinions . . . The only way to validate opinions is to test them and to see if they work. You can think you are entirely right, but if you do not prove it, you are not. And that is what we did.
>
> (Giménez 2014a, 101; our translation)

The evidence presented above allows us to falsify rival hypotheses about the causes for the adoption of a populist discourse by Podemos. Populist discursive strategies did not arise out of a shared and/or preexisting populist political culture among radical left activists, nor out of the bottom-up demands of the 15M, even if this movement created very favorable conditions for the appeal of populism. Instead, populist elements resulted from the reflections and ideational transformations that took place among some social science political activists who would later be situated in key positions of authority and influence in the new party. Many radical left activists within Podemos continued to view populism with a combination of skepticism and mistrust. However, the roles played by Iglesias and

Errejón in the 2014 European elections, the electoral success of the 2014 populist campaign, and, finally, the fact that Iglesias and Errejón became the two most important party authorities in the November 2014 party congress, decisively contributed to consolidate the prevalence of the propopulist group in Podemos.

Following standard practices in process-tracing studies (Bennett and Checkel 2015b; Waldner 2015), we present in Figure 12.1 a causal map of the main processes that led to the emergence of a populist discourse. In the first place, due to a combination of intellectual and political developments (the crisis of Marxist theory, the strength of Latin American populisms, and the influence of Laclau's discourse theory) some young activists and social science scholars (first and foremost Errejón) adopted a pro-populist interpretation of radical political change. Key elements of this interpretation were developed and refined by Errejón, Iglesias and other close associates in their debates and seminars during the 2010–2013 period, no doubt stimulated by a conjuncture of deep political-economic crisis and widespread bottom-up social mobilization.

The socioeconomic and political crisis stimulated as well radical left political activism challenging and the popularity of Iglesias. Of course, both the substantive political approach Iglesias chose to articulate (a result to a large extent of the ideational transformations experienced by the Complutense group) and his remarkable rhetorical skills contributed to Iglesias's popularity among significant sectors of the Spanish society. It is as a result of this combination of ideational changes, media influence, and radical left political entrepreneurship, that the foundation of Podemos took place. The leadership of Iglesias granted Errejón and a close group of associates a decisive role in the articulation of

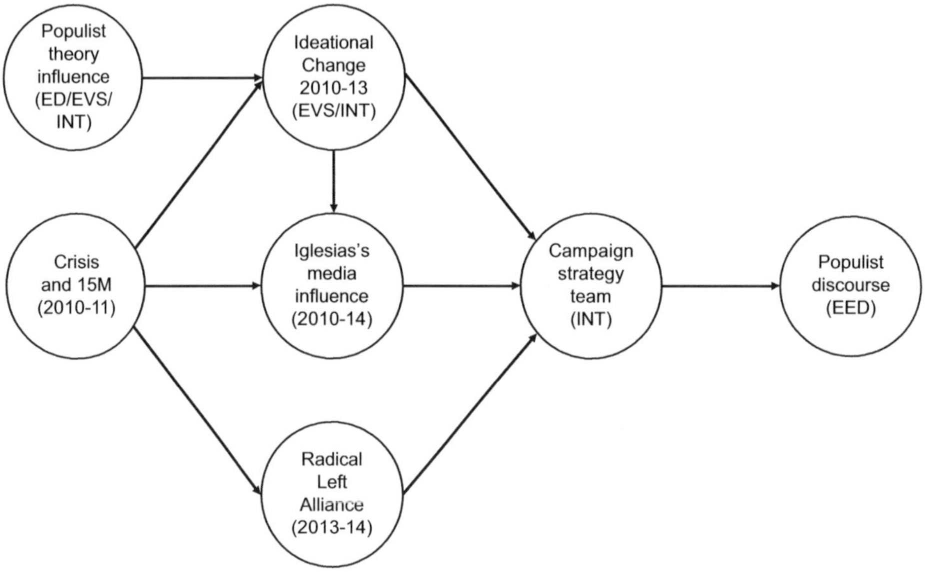

Figure 12.1 Causal graph: ideational and sociopolitical changes in the emergence of a populist discourse (corresponding pieces of evidence are reported in parentheses)

Note: Corresponding pieces of evidence are reported in parentheses, where ED = Errejón's dissertation (2006–2012), EVS=Errejón's articles in Viento Sur (2011); INT = Interviews and testimonies; EED = European elections discourse (2014).

the campaign strategy and, ultimately, in the elaboration of new populist discourse. The success attained in the 2014 elections consolidated the leadership of Iglesias, the influence of Errejón, and, consequently, the power of the populist discourse framework, despite the persistence of political-ideological pluralism within Podemos.

Conclusion

As other pieces in this volume show (see Carlin et al.'s conclusion to this volume), the activation of populist attitudes requires a context of failed democratic representation. In this chapter we have emphasized the importance of the political and economic contexts in the rise of new populist ideas. Ultimately the choice of a populist discourse was favored by a specific political–institutional conjuncture characterized by a Socialist economic policy switch, corruption scandals, and the 15M social mobilization. These circumstances created a context in which populist ideas became particularly appealing for significant sectors of the Spanish electorate. The selection of Iglesias as leading candidate and the appointment of Errejón as campaign chief in the European Parliament Elections granted pro-populist actors a decisive role in the electoral strategy of Podemos.

The understanding that populisms lack a systematic set of ideas still appears in many academic analyses. "They are about emotions and not about convictions," points out Delsol (2015, 66). By contrast, the results of our analysis are more consistent with the ideational and discursive interpretations of populism as a set of ideas (Hawkins 2010; Hawkins and Rovira Kaltwasser in the Introduction to this volume) and as a thin ideology that associates itself to other "host ideologies" (Mudde 2004; Mudde and Rovira Kaltwasser 2013). Furthermore, in the case of Podemos the process by which a group of political entrepreneurs adopted a populist discourse had a strongly deliberate character. What is remarkable about this case is the degree to which abstract thought, theoretical reflections, and comparative political analyses led to the adoption of a populist discourse.[28] The reception and adaptation of Laclau's discourse theory provided a group of political activists with an interpretive framework and a set of ideas ready to radically transform democratic politics. Certainly, the flows of political and personal communication linking Spain and Latin America facilitated the process of reinterpretation and innovative appropriation of Latin American populisms in Spain. But this change was also made possible by the crisis of Marxist social theory and radical left political actors. In the face of this crisis, an alternative program of radical, politically oriented social research, to borrow Lakatos's terminology, became extraordinarily attractive to interpret the political scenario and performatively anticipate a populist situation. Intellectual reflections by Errejón first and by Iglesias and other activists later played a key role in this process. That is, in the case of Podemos, changes in the abstract and objective contents of thought aimed at overcoming a problem situation (Popper 1985, 58–59, 265–266) preceded the adoption of an innovative, populist discursive strategy.

There are interesting parallels between the process of theoretical transformation that led to the adoption of a populist discourse by Podemos and the reinterpretation of Marxism that Georges Sorel proposed at the beginning of the twentieth century – even if the latter led to an even more radical departure from Marxism. In the case of Sorel, the perception of the theoretical failure and political weakness of economicist and determinist Marxism, in combination with the emergence of new ideas in social psychology and other social sciences, led to a new emphasis on the role of emotions and myths in politics. In Sorel's interpretation, the myths of the general strike and violence should lead to the generation of intense social antagonisms and to radical social transformations. As Sternhell points out

(1995, 57), "not the scientific method, but 'social myths' would enable the existing difficulties of socialism to be overcome." In Sorel's theory, even Marx's *Capital* should be interpreted as an "apocalyptic text . . . created for the purpose of molding consciousness" with radical political goals (as quoted in Sternhell 1995, 56). In the case of Podemos, the perception of the crisis of Marxism and the political failure of the radical left led some activists to adopt a new theoretical framework aimed at generating new cultural understandings (myths, emotions, discursive mechanisms), intense social antagonisms, and politically winning coalitions. The electoral and political success of Podemos in 2014 and 2015 seemed to confirm the usefulness of the "populist hypothesis."

The widespread acceptance of populism as a useful mobilizing tool did not imply the demise of radical leftism within Podemos. In fact, for both internal and external, electoral reasons, the combination of left radicalism and populist discourse remained a key characteristic of the party. Despite their organizational and electoral success, populist positions remained just one of the ideological streams within Podemos. Moreover, Podemos faced different dilemmas regarding its ideological and electoral strategy that led to growing internal tensions from 2016 onwards. In the 2016 general elections Podemos built an electoral coalition with IU (Unidos Podemos) as an attempt to surpass the Socialist party, This electoral alliance failed in its objective of making Podemos the second most voted for party, and triggered a conflict between Iglesias, the main proponent of the leftist strategy, and Errejón who disputed the usefulness of the alliance with IU and favoured a populist transversal strategy.[29] Internal conflict reached its highest point in the February 2017 party congress, as Iglesias and Errejón competed for the control of the party by presenting alternative lists to the Consejo Ciudadano Estatal, the governing body of Podemos. This contest was settled by the clear victory of Iglesias and his group while Errejón lost his positions as political secretary and as speaker of Podemos in the Spanish parliament.[30] This outcome confirmed the strength of radical left positions among the activists of Podemos and the difficulties faced by the advocates of a transversal populist strategy. In a parallel way, the heterogeneous and distinctive character of radical left coalitions in several territories created serious strains for Podemos, which faced the challenge of balancing demands for self-determination and a patriotic project for the whole Spanish people.[31] In both ideological and political–territorial respects, the dilemmas faced by Podemos showed that, despite their innovative potential, populist ideas had not managed to escape the constraining power of long term structures of political conflict in Spain.

Notes

1 Ideational contents cannot be understood merely on the basis of objective sociopolitical phenomena, even if such contents aim in the end at interpreting and transforming prevailing political conditions. It has been often shown how strictly social and political analyses, no matter how sophisticate they are, fall short of their goal of interpreting the objective content of intellectual works (see for instance Gordon's reflections on Bourdieu's sociological analysis of Martin Heidegger's ideas) (Gordon 2012, 351–354).

2 See BBVA Research (2011).

3 The voting impact of economic evaluations remained crucial in future electoral contests. Negative sociotropic evaluations punished the PP and favored its main competitors, in particular, Podemos. See Andreadis et al.'s chapter in this volume and Lavezzolo and Ramiro (2017).

4 See www.europapress.es/nacional/noticia-radiografia-corrupcion-espana-mas-1900-imputados-menos-170-condenados-mas-130-causas-20141102111941.html (accessed November 11, 2016).

5 For detailed journalistic reports on the Bárcenas case, see Gallero (2016) and Ekaizer (2013).

6 See http://politica.elpais.com/politica/2013/01/12/actualidad/1358017058_376467.html, accessed July 30, 2016.
7 http://politica.elpais.com/politica/2013/09/14/actualidad/1379177988_228092.html, accessed July 30, 2016.
8 Allegedly, it was included in *Bulletin* n.82 of Anticapitalist Left. See www.eldiario.es/politica/nacimiento-Podemos-candidatura-Pablo-Iglesias_0_220478302.html (accessed August 20, 2016).
9 Its origins go back to the organization of *Espacio Alternativo* (Alternative Space), which was created in 1995 by former members of the Trotskyite *Liga Comunista Revolucionaria* (Communist Revolutionary League).
10 See also interview to Miguel Urbán in Anon. (2016, 22)
11 Allegedly, the content of the Manifest was perceived as "too leftist" and this prevented the signature of the future leaders of the party.
12 The previous connection between some of the members of the Complutense group and the post-communist coalition Izquierda Unida – United Left – (IU) is also very clear. Iglesias was previously a member in the Communist Party youth organization. Iglesias and Errejón worked as advisers for IU in the 2011 electoral campaign (Giménez 2014a, 101; Rivero 2015b, 128–129).
13 The advice provided to Chaves entailed some generous payments by the Venezuelan government to some founders of Podemos. Monedero received more than 400,000 euros in 2013 for a report that has not been made public yet on the prospects of a single currency in Latin America. See http://politica.elpais.com/politica/2015/01/20/actualidad/1421789190_331983.html, accessed on August 5, 2016).
14 The election was organized as a primaries process (a total of 33,165 people participated).
15 The expression "the caste" was popularized in Italy by two journalists, Stella and Rizzo (2007), to refer to the privileged status of professional politicians. Iglesias wrote his Ph.D. dissertation on social movements in Italy and Spain, and was familiar with this term and its political uses (Domínguez and Giménez 2014, 142). Errejón explains some of the reasons for choosing the term caste in Giménez (2014a, 104)
16 *"El cielo no se toma por consenso, el cielo se toma por asalto."* (Opening speech in the 2014 Asamblea Ciudadana).
17 This grading is based on two discourses made by Iglesias in 2014: his closing campaign speech in the European elections and opening speech in the founding congress. This grading was conducted by Hugo Marcos-Marne and Carolina Plaza, two researchers at the Salamanca University. For data on the more recent 2015 election, see Hawkins's and Silva's chapter.
18 Interview with Jaime Pastor.
19 See www.eldiario.es/politica/Pablo-Iglesias-votacion-partido-Podemos_0_318118325.html, accessed August 5, 2016.
20 See www.eldiario.es/politica/personas-Pablo-Iglesias-incontestable-Podemos_0_324767662.html, accessed August 5, 2016. On the strategic implications of the organizational model chosen by Podemos, see Gutiérrez and Llamazares (2016: 11).
21 Errejón's analysis was not influenced by the works by Monedero, senior lecturer at the Universidad Complutense, on the politics of the Chavist revolution. No publication of Monedero's is quoted or referred to in Errejón's more than 600 page long dissertation.
22 The editor of *Viento Sur* pointed out that Errejón's intentions were to follow up these two articles with a special issue on populism, but his proposal was not finally accepted (interview with Jaime Pastor).
23 In his 2015 *New Left Review* article Iglesias stated also that the "populist possibility was theorized most specifically by Errejón, drawing on the work of Ernesto Laclau" (Iglesias 2015, 14).
24 Interviews with Miguel Urbán and Jaime Pastor.
25 Criticisms from the radical left pointed to the excessive importance assigned to discourse vis-à-vis socio-structural conditions (interviews with Miguel Urbán and Germán Cano).
26 Errejón would continue to play a key role in Podemos as campaign chief for the 2015 and 2016 general elections, as responsible for the political secretariat of the party, and as speaker for the Podemos parliamentary group.
27 Interview with Germán Cano. See also Giménez (2014a, 101, 105–106).

28 This point is stressed also by Kioupkiolis (2016).

29 In Errejón's words, "we are moving in a direction that prevents us from building a new majority" (www.errejon.info/ha-habido-un-viraje-ideologico-que-nos-ha-alejado-de-la-idea-inicial-de-podemos/). See also the political proposal of Errejón and his group in the 2017 Congress, which advocated leaving left-right labels behind and transcending the "unity of left" in favor of "the unity of the people" (Recuperar la Ilusión 2017: 17).

30 The candidates endorsed by Iglesias attained almost 59.7% of the seats in the governing body of Podemos. Those favored by Errejón obtained 37.1% of the seats. The anticapitalist group, despite attaining 13.8% of the votes, obtained 3% of the seats. Iglesias obtained 89% of the votes for the position of secretary general. See www.eldiario.es/politica/datos-cocina-votaciones-Podemos_0_612089572.html (accessed on February 15, 2017).

31 The challenges posed by the multinational character of Spain for a populist project were already highlighted by Errejón (2011b). An illustration of the complex position of Podemos can be grasped in the fact that it endorses Catalan self-determination and opposes Catalan independence. The negative public impact of support for self-determination has been emphasized by Bescansa, one of the founders of Podemos. See www.eldiario.es/politica/Bescansa-Podemos-proyecto-politico-Espana_0_700979973.html (accessed on November 4, 2017).

References

Alegre, Luis. 2007. *Ciudadanía y Clase Social en El Capital de Marx: el Reconocimiento de una Distancia Teórica y No Histórica entre Mercado y Capitalismo como Condición Necesaria para Sacar a la Luz la Naturaleza de las Leyes que Constituyen la Sociedad Moderna*. Ph.D. Universidad Complutense de Madrid.

Anon. 2016. *Anticapitalistas en Podemos: Construyendo Poder Popular*. Barcelona: Sylone.

Aslanidis, Paris. 2016. "Populist Social Movements of the Great Recession." *Mobilization* 21(3): 301–321.

BBVA Research. 2011. "Desempleo Juvenil en España. Causas y Soluciones." *Documentos de Trabajo* 11/30. Available at www.bbvaresearch.com/KETD/fbin/mult/WP_1130_tcm346-270043.pdf?ts=2152012 (accessed March 12, 2017).

Beach, D. and Pedersen, R. 2013. *Process Tracing Methods: Foundations and Guidelines*. Michigan: University of Michigan Press.

Bennett, Andrew. 2015. "Disciplining our Conjectures: Systematizing process Tracing with Bayesian Analysis," in *Process Tracing. From Metaphor to Analytic Tool*, edited by Andrew Bennett and Jeffrey Checkel. Cambridge: Cambridge University Press.

Bennett, Andrew and Jeffrey Checkel (eds.). 2015a. *Process Tracing. From Metaphor to Analytic Tool*. Cambridge: Cambridge University Press.

———. 2015b. "Process Tracing: From Philosophical Roots to Best Practices," in Andrew Bennett and Jeffrey Checkel (eds.). 2015. *Process Tracing. From Metaphor to Analytic Tool*. Cambridge University Press.

Calvo, Kerman, Teresa Gómez-Pastrana and Luis Mena. 2011. "Movimiento 15M. ¿Quiénes son y qué Reivindican?" *Zoon Politikon*, 4: 4–17.

Cano, Germán. 2015. *Fuerzas de Flaqueza. Nuevas Gramáticas Políticas*. Madrid: La Catarata.

Collier, David. 2011. "Understanding Process Tracing." *Political Science and Politics* 44 (4): 823–830.

Delsol, Chantal 2015. *Populismos. Una Defensa de lo Indefendible*. Barcelona: Ariel.

Domínguez, Ana and Luis Giménez. 2014. "Nos Encontramos en un Momento de Transición hacia otro Régimen Político. Entrevista a Pablo Iglesias," in *Claro que Podemos*, edited by Ana Domínguez and Luis Giménez. Barcelona: Los Libros del Lince.

Ekaizer, Ernesto. 2013. *El caso Bárcenas*. Madrid: Espasa.

Errejón, Íñigo. 2012. *La Lucha por la Hegemonía durante el Primer Gobierno del MAS en Bolivia (2006–2009)*. Ph.D. Universidad Complutense de Madrid.

———. 2011a. "La Construcción Discursiva de Identidades Populares." *Viento Sur* 114: 75–84.

———. 2011b. "También en Europa: Posibilidades Populistas en España y en Europa". *Viento Sur* 115: 105–114.

———. 2015. "We the People. El 15M: ¿Un Populismo Indignado?." *ACME. An International Journal for Critical Geographies* 14 (1): 124–156.

Errejón, Íñigo and Chantal Mouffe. 2015. *Construir Pueblo. Hegemonía y Radicalización de la Democracia*. Barcelona: Icaria.

Fernández Albertos, José. 2015. *Los Votantes de Podemos: Del Partido de los Indignados al Partido de los Excluidos*. Madrid: Los Libros de la Catarata.

Fernández Liria, Carlos and Luis Alegre Zahonero. 2006. *Comprender Venezuela, Pensar la Democracia: el Colapso Moral de los Intelectuales Occidentales*. Caracas: Fundación Editorial El Perro y la Rana.

Fraile, Marta, and Michael Lewis-Beck. 2014. "Economic Vote Instability: Endogeneity or Restricted Variance? Spanish Panel Evidence from 2008 and 2011." *European Journal of Political Research* 53: 160–179.

Gallero, Marisa. 2016. *Bárcenas: La Caja Fuerte*. Madrid: La Esfera de los Libros.

George, Alexander and Andrew Bennet. 2005. *Case Study and Theory Development in the Social Sciences*. Cambridge, MA: MIT Press.

Giménez, Luis. 2014a. "El Estilo Tuerka a la Campaña de Podemos," in *Claro que Podemos*, edited by Ana Domínguez and Luis Giménez. Barcelona: Los Libros del Lince.

———. 2014b. "La Experiencia Tuerka," in *Claro que Podemos*, edited by Ana Domínguez and Luis Giménez. Barcelona: Los Libros del Lince.

Gordon, Peter E. 2012. *Continental Divide: Heidegger, Cassirer, Davos*. Cambridge, MA: Harvard University Press.

Gutiérrez, José Manuel and Iván Llamazares. 2016. "Collective Members in West European Political Parties." *Revista Internacional de Sociología* 74/2: 1–14, DOI: http://dx.doi.org/10.3989/ris.2016.74.2.030.

Hawkins, Kirk. 2010. *Venezuela's Chavismo and Populism in Comparative Perspective*. Cambridge: Cambridge University Press.

Iglesias, Pablo. 2008. *Multitud y Acción Colectiva Postnacional: un Estudio Comparado de los Desobedientes de Italia a Madrid (2000–2005)*. Ph.D. Universidad Complutense de Madrid.

———. 2015. "Understanding Podemos." *New Left Review* 93: 7–22.

Jacobs, Alan M. 2015. "Process Tracing: the Effects of Ideas," in *Process Tracing. From Metaphor to Analytic Tool*, edited by Andrew Bennett and Jeffrey Checkel. Cambridge: Cambridge University Press.

Kioupkiolis, Alexandros. 2016. "Podemos: the Ambiguous Promises of Left Wing Populism in Contemporary Spain." *Journal of Political Ideologies* 21(2): 99–120, http://dx.doi.org/10.1080/13569317.2016.1150136.

Lavezzolo, Sebastián and Luis Ramiro. 2017. Stealth Democracy and the Support for New and Challenger Parties. European Political Science. Online first. https://doi.org/10.1017/S1755773917000108.

Medina, Lucía. 2015. "From Recession to Long Lasting Political Crisis? Continuities and Changes in Spanish Politics in Times of Crisis and Austerity." ICPS. *Working Paper* 334.

Minguijón Pablo, Jaime and David Pac Salas. 2013. "La Primavera Española del Movimiento 15M." *Política y Gobierno* 20 (2): 359–389.

Mora Rodríguez, Fernando. 2012. "Organización y participación en el 15M." *Praxis Sociológica*. 16: 99–124.

Mudde, Cas. 2004. "The Populist Zeitgeist." *Government and Opposition* 39(4): 542–563.

Mudde, Cas and Cristóbal Rovira Kaltwasser. 2013. "Populism." In *Oxford Handbook of Political Ideologies*, edited by Michael Freeden, Lyman Tower Sargent, and Marc Stears. Oxford: Oxford University Press.

Nez, Héloïse. 2015. *Podemos: De l'Indignation aux Élections*. Paris: Les Petits Matins.

Popper, Karl R. 1985. *Selections*. Princeton, NJ: Princeton University Press.

Popper, Karl R. and John C. Eccles. 1985. *The Self and its Brain*. Berlin, New Yorm and London: Springer.

Recuperar la Ilusión. 2017. *Documento Político*. Available at https://recuperarlailusion.info/documentos/ (accessed on February 14, 2017).

Rodríguez Zapatero, José Luis. 2014. *El Dilema: 600 Días de Vértigo*. Barcelona: Planeta.

Rivero, Jacobo. 2015a. *Podemos. Objetivo: Asaltar los Cielos*. Barcelona: Planeta.

———. 2015b. *Conversación con Pablo Iglesias*. Madrid: Turpial.

Rizzo, Sergio and Gian Antonio Stella. 2007. *La Casta*. Milan: Rizzoli.

Roberts, Kenneth M. 2013. "Market Reform, Programmatic (De)alignment, and Party System Stability in Latin America." *Comparative Political Studies* 46(11): 1422–1452

———. 2015. *Changing Course in Latin America: Party Systems in the Neoliberal Era*. Cambridge: Cambridge University Press.

Sternhell, Zeev. 1995. *The Birth of the Fascist Ideology*. Princeton, NJ: Princeton University Press.

Torcal, Mariano. 2014. "The Incumbent Electoral Defeat in the 2011 Spanish National Elections: The Effect of the Economic Crisis in an ideological Polarized Party System." *Journal of Elections, Public Opinion & Parties* 24(2): 203–221.

Torreblanca, José Ignacio. 2015. *Asaltar los Cielos: Podemos o la Política después de la Crisis*. Barcelona: Debate.

Urbán, Miguel. 2010. "Una Europa en Crisis, una Extrema Derecha en Ascenso," *Viento Sur* 111: 33–42.

Van Evera, Stephen. 1997. *Guide to Methods for Students of Political Science*. Ithaca, NY: Cornell University Press.

Waldner, David. 2015. What Makes Process Tracing Good? Causal Mechanisms, Causal Inference, and the Completeness Standard in Comparative Politics," in *Process Tracing. From Metaphor to Analytic Tool*, edited by Andrew Bennett and Jeffrey Checkel. Cambridge: Cambridge University Press

13 Populism in Venezuela

The role of the opposition

Sahar Abi-Hassan

Since the turn of the millennium, Venezuela has experienced a steady progression towards a highly polarized political system and society in general. This has been mainly attributed to the leadership style and populist discourse of the late president Hugo Chávez. A landslide victory in 1998 allowed Chávez ample space to set in motion a radical political project that began with the 1999 constitutional reform. Capitalizing on the crisis of representative institutions and his soaring popularity, Chávez redrafted the political space intent on making it more inclusionary, specifically, to promote the participation and inclusion of the most neglected and disenfranchised sectors of the population (Roberts 2012).

Chávez's political style has been widely characterized by an antagonistic discourse, an anti-status-quo mode of governance bent on reforming all political institutions. Moreover, the late president was the central figure of a new inclusive nation-project, with a strong emphasis on turning the country into a participatory democracy (Brading 2013; De la Torre 2013; Ellner 2010; Hawkins 2010; Roberts 2012). Although ideas are the "central feature of populist forces," populism does have real implications for the behavior of political actors, public policies and the institutions of democracy (see Hawkins and Rovira Kaltwasser's introductory chapter in this volume).

The literature on populism has mainly focused on the holders or active generators of populist ideas, and those who sympathize with these ideas. However, while Chávez's populist style and rhetoric was a major driver for radical political reform in Venezuela, it did not occur in a vacuum. Creating a political space open to everyone and constructing an alternative form of participatory democracy was accompanied by the displacement of the political establishment known as the *Punto Fijo* system.[1] This set in motion a reactionary movement driven by groups affiliated with the old establishment and new political actors that viewed Chávez's policies as a threat to democracy, which led to the emergence and consolidation of two distinct political camps: *Chavismo* and *la oposición* (opposition), umbrella terms for those supporting and those against the late Hugo Chávez, respectively.

As argued in the introductory chapter of this volume, an ideational approach to populism focuses on the impact of ideas on politicians' behavior, as well as the factors motivating people to support those forces; but what about those who reject those forces? If populism is a set of ideas that inundate the political space, the reaction of those constructed as the "other" within this space should necessarily play a role in reinforcing and legitimizing these ideas, or otherwise. This points to an active role for those that fall into the category of the "other" or "corrupt elite" as much as those that are considered the "pure people." Using the case of Venezuela, this chapter investigates the role of the political opposition in radicalizing Chávez's populist discourse and consolidating populist policies in Venezuela. It contends that the deepening of Chávez's populist policies was greatly mediated by the responses of the political opposition.

In order to understand the extent to which populist ideas have become embedded into the political space in Venezuela, first we need to have a clear understanding of the concept of populism. For this, the first section builds on the conceptualization of populism used in this edited volume to analyze the emergence of, and responses to populism within different contexts. Following an outline of the methodology for data gathering and analysis, the next section presents the historic-institutional context in which a populist logic emerged in Venezuela, the rise of political opposition and its evolution until the 2012 presidential elections. This is used to frame the analysis of ideas and actions of the opposition in support of the main arguments. As a way of concluding, the chapter discusses the potential harms for liberal democracy that come from the style and timing of reactions to populist politics. The analysis of this case opens the way for future research into how responses to populism might play a role in exacerbating political and social polarization, and creating a toxic political environment that is detrimental to democracy.

In response to populism: for better or worse?

The recent emergence of populist leaders in Latin America and Europe has proven that populism is not a thing of the past, but a recurrent phenomenon compatible with multiple economic models, social bases, and political ideologies (Panizza 2008; Weyland 1999). According to Panizza and Miorelli (2009, 42), "the appeal of populism in the region (Latin America) has to be understood with reference to past and present political dislocations. Unmet social needs and heightened economic insecurities, for instance, provide raw material for the articulation of political grievances." So far, Chávez's regime, among others in Latin America, stands as one of the most influential cases.

Socioeconomic factors have been cited as the primary explanation for the rise of populist leaders in Latin America (Brading 2013; De la Torre 2013; Hawkins 2010; Laclau 2005b; Panizza and Miorelli 2009). Decades of exclusionary policies led to the accumulation of disenfranchised groups looking for greater representation in the political system. Chávez himself was shaped within these sectors of the population, and his political project was oriented towards changing what was considered a pervasive status quo. So what makes Chávez and his government populist?

An ideational approach characterizes populism as a Manichaean discourse or thin-centered ideology, which divides society into an "us" versus "them" through a struggle between a symbolic will of the people and a corrupt elite, and where the populist content is relative to the socio-political context in which it takes place (Mudde and Rovira Kaltwasser 2011; see also Hawkins and Rovira Kaltwasser's introductory chapter). Hence, populism operates as a logic that constitutes "the people" in an antagonistic relationship to dominant institutions and actors (Laclau 2005b; Panizza 2008).

Moreover, with an ideational normative framework, the category of "the people" is not necessarily automatic or uniform. Laclau (2005b, 39) argues that "the construction of an enemy" or opposition to the status-quo requires the identification of an anchor or "empty signifier" to embody or unify these disparate demands; a concept or name that without losing its own specificity, stands as a universal representation for various social demands to which it is seen as equivalent (Laclau 2005a; 2005b; Panizza 2005).

Following an ideational approach to populism provides three critical thresholds against which to undertake empirical research, and make the causal connections necessary under an ideational theoretical framework. First, consistent with this moral discourse, populists reject the political establishment, constructing the political elites as the enemy. In Venezuela, populism is manifested through Chávez's rejection of the *Punto Fijo* system, and redrafting the political space to promote the participation and inclusion of the most neglected and disenfranchised sectors of the population (Roberts 2012).

Second, this definition presupposes that ideas do not operate in a vacuum; they are greatly mediated by their context. As argued by Hawkins and Rovira Kaltwasser in the introductory chapter "the interpretation of the context is not automatic, political leaders (in this case Chávez) have to articulate the populist message . . ." as well as "provide the organizational framework for (populist) political mobilization." Chávez capitalized on the weakening of the *Punto Fijo* system to articulate his populist discourse and undertake major institutional reforms.

Finally, by weakening and overriding the country's political institutions, a special relation of representation is established between the leader and his followers; therefore, people identify directly with the leader (Panizza 2005). Although this is not a necessary component of populism, in Venezuela the legitimacy of Chávez as "the one who speaks for the people" is drawn from this dynamic. These theoretical thresholds direct our attention to the content of ideas and discourse of populist leaders and the institutional context in which they operate (Gidron and Bonikowski 2013; Mudde 2007; Rooduijn, de Lange, and Van Der Brug 2012).

Beyond Venezuela, the rise of populism has become all too evident, from the emergence of radical-right parties such as the National Front in France or FIDEZ in Hungary, to leftist governments in countries like Bolivia and Ecuador. While consumers of the ideational definition of populism have been highly cognizant of contextual factors, their studies have mainly focused on the leaders/parties themselves or the content of populist forces. Yet, is not the "other" also part of the context?

When it comes to the role of the opposition, Rovira Kaltwasser and Taggart (2016, 206) argue that "the reaction of those against populism matters, . . . whether they adopt a tolerant or punitive reaction." We know from several studies of the European radical-right that the strategies of mainstream parties in response to radical parties determine their electoral success (Art 2011; Meguid 2005). Moreover, the electoral success of European "niche parties" is closely associated not just with the actions, but also timing of the mainstream parties' response (Meguid 2005).

In Latin America, the recent work of Laura Gamboa (2017) highlights the role of the opposition in furthering or hindering a leader's ability to undermine checks and balances and centralize powers in the executive. Using the first years of the governments of Hugo Chávez in Venezuela (1999–2013) and Alvaro Uribe in Colombia (2000–2010), she (Gamboa 2017) argues that the opposition's choice between using institutional or extra-institutional strategies combined with moderate or radical goals, shapes the ability of the government to implement a more or less radical agenda, potentially eroding democracy.

Both opposition factions, in Venezuela and Colombia had similar levels of political leverage. However, the Venezuelan opposition chose to use extra-institutional strategies, such as strikes, coups, protests and boycotts, in response to Chávez's policies. This delegitimized the opposition, decreasing the cost of and increasing the incentives for repression. In contrast, the Colombian opposition's focus on institutional strategies or extra-institutional strategies with moderate goals, helped weaken Uribe's ability to weaken checks and balances from other branches (Gamboa 2017).

This points our attention towards the actors, timing, and strategies of those who oppose populism as much as populists themselves (Rovira Kaltwasser and Taggart 2016), if we are to better understand the factors driving the emergence and consolidation of populism. In its most basic form, the type of opposition and its ability to maneuver will greatly dependent on the type of ruling regime: liberal or authoritarian. For instance, an indicator of opposition strength is its ability to operate as a cohesive unit. This is less likely to be the case in a regime with authoritarian tendencies (Blondel 1997). While populist politics cannot be automatically qualified as authoritarian, its authoritarian tendencies mixed with a semblance of democratic procedures means that we are dealing with a hybrid type of opposition.

In the particular case of the opposition in Venezuela during the tenure of Hugo Chávez, some studies have favored institutionalist and structural explanations, either as it emphasizes Chávez's weakening of traditional democratic institutions (Corrales and Penfold 2007) or the opposition's undemocratic practices (Domínguez 2011). Others have focused on the social realm, particularly the role of civil society in driving political and ideological polarization (García-Guadilla 2005).

All these inquires point to the multivariate nature of the opposition in Venezuela (Cannon 2014), which requires a more flexible approach that studies political opposition from a parliamentary as well as extra-parliamentary view (Rovira Kaltwasser and Taggart 2016). This presupposes the inclusion of formal as well as informal institutions, structures and political actors as part of the analysis, as well as its wider ideological and social manifestations (Cannon 2014, 53).

Taking into consideration the multivariate nature of the opposition in Venezuela allows us to not only understand the ideological and sociopolitical forces that shaped it, but more importantly the impact of its reactions on the type and depth of populism in the country.

Framing an equally radical response: data and methods

To measure the progression of the opposition's reaction to populism in Venezuela and how it shaped the institutional environment, this research undertakes a qualitative approach of process tracing. Process tracing is particularly useful for studying deviant cases and learning the factors that led them to diverge from what would be an expected trend (Collier 2011). While populism is a worldwide phenomenon, the deep level of social and political radicalization in Venezuela makes it a unique case study.

The outcome of interest is populism, and the independent variable is the discourse and actions of the opposition. The process tracing mechanisms being applied here focus on the independent variable. As such, this contribution investigates the evolution of the opposition's discourse and how it converges into a series of conditions that further radicalize and deepen populism in Venezuela. It contends that the discourse of the opposition contributed to the radicalization of Chávez's populist discourse. Moreover, the opposition's course of action in a wide range of situations fostered a political institutional environment, which severely strained any liberal political alternatives.

Consistent with the ideational framework proposed in the volume, I identify the ideas of the opposition and test their effect on the political landscape throughout Chávez's government. For this, I constructed a diagnostic temporal sequence of the discourse of the opposition between 2000 and 2012. This is used to show how the opposition's discourse manifests in a set of empirical regularities, which reinforced a populist logic in Venezuela.

The discursive temporal sequence is based on a qualitative content analysis of 240 online news articles from a variety of national and international sources. The criteria for selecting the news articles were based on both content and availability. Through a systematic search of the archives of various news outlets (see Appendix A Sources), I identified and collected any articles that contained quotes by Venezuelan opposition leaders.[2] As a secondary criterion, any articles that referenced statements made by opposition leaders or course of action taken by the opposition were also collected and analyzed.

Considering that we are not interested in generalizing to a broader population, and because we are interested in how specific political elites representing the opposition shaped the deepening (or not) of populist politics, I use non-probability sampling to select the opposition leader's names used for the analysis. As argued by Tansey (2007, 15), "the goal when applying the process tracing method, . . . [will be] to obtain the testimony of individuals who were most closely involved in the process of interest." The decision of who is a relevant opposition actor is made by virtue of their membership in combination to position and reputational traits within the opposition movement.

Thereafter, based on the statements contained in the articles, each article was coded into one or more of these three categories: 1) reinforcing the "us" versus "them," 2) fighting the status-quo with emotional appeals, and 3) creating a direct connection between the leader and the "people." The coding categories map onto the definition of populism outlined in this chapter and the edited volume (see Appendix B Samples of coding mechanism).

The first category includes any statements that compel individuals to think about their political allegiance in dualistic terms. For instance, any articles that contained statements by opposition leaders such as: "we are the majority," "Chavistas are the other," and/or "the opposition is the people," were coded under category 1.

The second category contains all ideas and discourse that frame the opposition's disagreement with Chávez's political project in emotional terms. This category is intended to capture instances where the opposition formulated its political platform mainly on its desire to remove Chávez from power or their assessment of the erosion of democracy in Venezuela, and not based on actual programmatic policies. For instance, articles that mentioned that "Chávez's regime was eroding democracy," "Chávez is turning Venezuela into another Cuba" or that "removing Chávez from power would solve all problems," were put under the second category.

The third category captures instances where the opposition emphasizes the need for a unity leader to solve what they consider an ongoing crisis of governability. While the "leader–people" relationship is something characteristic of Chávez's populist style, articles placed under category 3 capture the extent to which the opposition remained trapped in its own populist logic as it sought to unify the opposition behind one representative leader. This also includes any discourse by opposition leaders that seeks to reconcile their antagonistic stance with an attempt to achieve greater political legitimacy.

All news articles were individually read and analyzed by the author. Any phrases that were considered to fall within one or more of these categories were coded as such using the numbers assigned to each category (Appendix C Summary table for Figure 13.1). Thereafter, this was compiled into frequencies for each category and graphed under a normalized scale to address the variation in the number of articles found for each period.

In the second part of the analysis, the chapter examines the unfolding of events in Venezuela between 1999 and 2012, broken into a two-stage periodization built upon existing literature about the emergence and evolution of political opposition in the country (Cannon 2014; Hawkins 2016). According to Cannon (2014), the opposition as a political body went through an important transformation after 2005.[3] This first phase, mainly driven by civil-society based actors, is characterized by protest and insurrectionary practices (Hawkins 2016). Thereafter, the opposition transformed into a more party-based entity, shifting its focus towards electoral contestation (Hawkins 2016).[4] Evidently, breaking the evolution of the opposition into these two periods does not mean the absence of protest in the second phase or electoral contestation in the first. These phases are mainly an analytical tool based on the predominant factions, major shifts in strategy, and the timing and overall direction taken by the opposition. By analyzing both the evolution of discourse and the actions of the opposition during Chávez's tenure, this chapter provides a comprehensive picture of how the response of the "other" played an important role in shaping the emergence and consolidation of populism in Venezuela.

The "other": consolidating a populist discourse in Venezuela

After winning the 1998 presidential election with 56.2% (CNE 1998), Chávez had a strong mandate to implement his main campaign promise: to lead the country towards a more inclusionary and participatory political system. However, making this promise materialize required the dismantling of institutional structures and sidelining political actors that had prevailed in Venezuela for the past 40 years. *Punto Fijo* loyalists still controlled key institutions such as the legislative, state and local governments, trade unions, business organizations, and the oil industry. Chávez turned to the voters in order to overcome this challenge.

Starting with the constitutional reform, Chávez initiated a process to dismantle the country's political institutions, which he considered to be exclusionary and elitist. As eloquently put by Roberts (2012, 147), "participation, then, was both an end and a means for *Chavismo* . . . it helped Chávez refound the constitutional order, sideline the political establishment, and deliver social and economic benefits to a broad range of political supporters." In line with the latter, Chávez implemented innovative social programs or "*misiones*,"[5] which provided a sense of inclusion and empowerment by extending state access to segments of the population that were previously neglected.

Nevertheless, despite the tangible outcomes generated by these massive redistribution efforts (Ellner 2010), the political discussion about policies or programmatic plans inevitably spilled over into a moral struggle. Chávez's political project was presented as a "worldview or discourse about the nature of politics, one revolving around the struggle between 'good,' and 'evil'; where good encompasses the «will of the people», and evil the 'elite attempting to subvert the common interest of the people'" (Hawkins 2010, 5).

Moreover, following the participatory model enshrined in the 1999 constitution, Chávez encouraged the formation of grass roots movements for the promotion of revolutionary processes, such as the Bolivarian Circles, the Urban Land Committees, and communal councils (De la Torre 2013). While this was considered a step towards greater citizenship and social responsibility (Machado, 2008 cited in De la Torre 2013, 32), because they were created and regulated by Chávez himself, they greatly served to consolidate the president's populist discourse. Also, it has been argued that this moved the country closer to authoritarianism. Corrales and Penfold (2011) and Brewer-Carías (2010) – a former official in the pre-Chávez era – argue that the same bold political and economic reforms that supported Chávez's inclusionary project also facilitated the consolidation of crony and clientelist practices. This has been accompanied by the centralization of government functions and providing the president with substantial advantage over his political challengers (Brewer-Carías 2010; Corrales and Penfold 2011). Despite mixed results, when it comes to the achievements and shortcomings of the Chávez regime, undoubtedly, for the past 18 years the political space in Venezuela has been dominated by a populist logic. This evidently presents major challenges for the survival of democracy, and hence the viability of the opposition.

First, the deep political polarization that pervades Venezuela's institutions has made it impossible for the government or the opposition to serve the needs of the country, beyond what suits their political agenda. Second, adopting an anti-status quo mode of governance designed to override all institutions associated with the old elites also removed the mechanisms of checks and balances embedded within the political system. Finally, moving the country towards a participatory democracy and a nation-project centered in the figure of the leader eliminated the protection to minorities afforded by a representative system. The ability of populism to weaken democracy from within makes it imperative that not only we better understand populist forces, but the reactions against, as it shapes the evolution of democratic political regimes.

A diagnostic temporal sequence: from insurrection to electoralism

Tracing the evolution of the meaning–context that shaped political opposition demonstrates how its discourse contributed to the radicalization of Chávez's populism, and his ability to present it as a legitimate political project. As shown in Figure 13.1, the analysis registers any claims by opposition leaders that fell under either one or more of the following categories: 1) reinforcing the "us" versus "them," 2) fighting the status-quo with emotional appeals, and 3) creating a direct connection between the leader and the "people." At first glance, between 2000–2002 and 2006–2007 there is greater emphasis on antagonistic rhetoric framed in an "us" versus "them" discourse (Category 1) and emotional appeals (Category 2). Starting in 2006 this kind of discourse begins to give way to greater focus on electoral strategies and the selection of a unity candidate.

During the initial period of Chávez's tenure, the opposition's discourse was consistently framed within antagonistic and emotional appeals. For instance, opposition leaders repeatedly used language like "we are the majority" and "the people are with the opposition." Under this kind of discourse it is argued that individuals are compelled to think about their political allegiance in dualistic terms, deepening the notion of "us" versus "them." Moreover, disagreement with Chávez's political project contains highly emotional rhetoric, mainly "remove Chávez from power through any means necessary, including a coup" (opposition leaders quoted in *Financial Times* 2002), "Mr. Chávez is trying to create a Cuban-style authoritarian regime" (e.g. Moffett and Lifsher 2002), and "Chávez must be substituted by capable leaders if we are to reach an understanding" (Córdova 2000), or asserting that Chávez is a "dictator aiming for totalitarian control" (The Christian Monitor 2003).

Starting in 2006 the opposition places greater emphasis on electoral strategies, as the main solution to what they consider an ongoing crisis of governability in Venezuela. For instance,

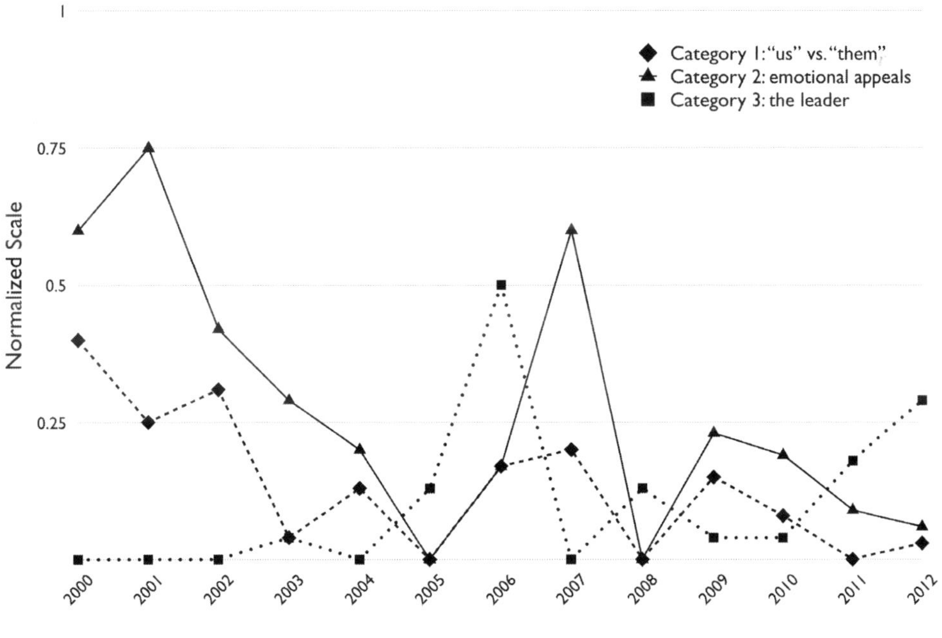

Figure 13.1 Temporal sequence of opposition discourse

in response to campaign attacks from Chávez's administration, Henrique Capriles Radonski, the oppositions's unity candidate in the 2012 election, vows to want to be

> the President of all Venezuelans. I won't let them down. I am not the enemy of anyone, I am the enemy of the problems, of the violence, I am the enemy of a country whose government prevents us from going forward.
>
> (RTT News 2012)

Although this strategy did have some payoff for the opposition, it also signaled the extent to which a populist logic had permeated political life in Venezuela.

Over time, the opposition transformed into a formal political base that transcended its anti-Chávez origins; it rejected populist politics through moderation and a more conciliatory discursive strategy. Yet, the meaning context and institutional setting in which it operates remains populist. Its emphasis on unity and the selection of a single candidate is evidence that it remains trapped within a populist logic. As such, while the opposition's ideas and discourses helped reinforce a populist logic in its early stages, later on, its programmatic approach is constrained by a set of institutions that operate within populist politics.

The opposition's initial reaction was a natural response to the reforms and policies adopted by Chávez's administration, as it began to displace the old establishment. Over time, the choice and timing of its responses greatly contributed to the deepening of Chávez's populist discourse. As it is evidenced in Figure 13.1, in its infancy, the opposition adopted a discourse, sometimes more radical and polarizing than Chávez himself. This created a polarized political environment where these two opposing forces did not differ much in terms of the content of their ideas. Later on, even when the opposition began to tone down its polarizing discourse, it is observed that the meaning context had been entirely transformed, leaving no room for other possible political logics besides populism.

Although it is possible to analytically break the opposition's strategies into two phases, in reality it is much more diverse. The predominant strategies depended mainly, on which faction won the argument of the day. The range of actors operating within the opposition can be grouped under the title of old political elites, labor and business leaders, new political leaders, the student movement and to an extent some *Chavismo* detractors. The old political elites and labor and business leaders were the main drivers of insurrectionary strategies during the first phase. New political leaders and for a short period the student movement were predominantly more supportive of electoral strategies.

Opposition through insurrection and protest, 2000–2005

Fighting established institutions and breaking with the status quo was instrumental for the constitution of a *Chavista* identity. However, the analysis shows that in the first few years of the Chávez administration, the anti-Chávez movement greatly contributed to the crystallization of these divisions. Starting with inoffensive protests and condemnation of Chávez's policies, followed by the failed coup of 2002 and the general strike of 2002–2003, the opposition created a crisis environment where people were compelled to think about their political allegiance in dualistic terms.

The first serious point of contention between the new government and the old establishment came after Chávez's party took control of the National Assembly (AN), allowing him to obtain a special constitutional power to rule by decree on matters of economic and social policy.[6] The most vociferous opposition actors at the time were the *Venezuelan*

Confederation of Workers (CTV) and the *Venezuelan Federation of Chambers of Commerce* (FEDECAMARAS), which immediately condemned this as government overreaches. Under a "unified protest strategy," the two organizations, along with traditional political parties (AD and COPEI) began encouraging protests and strikes across the country.

In a climate of growing discontent, the opposition called for a national strike in April of 2002, which culminated in clashes with Chávez supporters. While the circumstances remain unclear, the protests ended with several people dead and many more wounded, leading to Chávez's short-lived resignation on April 11, followed by his return to office two days later. While both sides attempted some form of conciliation after the failed coup,[7] the opposition continued along the insurrectionary road by calling for a strike of the national oil company (PDVSA) (EFE 2002). This was intended to weaken Chávez's base and force him to resign.

Instead it served to strengthen his political project. First by handing him full control of the oil company and its massive amounts of revenues, and second by further consolidating the government's antagonistic discourse (Brading 2013, 74–75). The opposition was left waiting for the presidential mid-term to request a recall referendum. After a failed first attempt and several subsequent delays, it lost to a 58% vote for the *NO* option (*Wall Street Journal* 2004). Despite verification by the Organization of American States and the Carter Center, the opposition rejected these results and continued to call for protests, and even civil disobedience during the 2004 regional elections (Noticias Financieras 2004; Notimex 2004).

In the aftermath of the referendum, the opposition's discourse turns to disqualifying the electoral system in an attempt to delegitimize the government, especially in the eyes of the international community. The logic was that as Chávez's position was consistently reassured through the rule of the majority, if the opposition could show that the system was fraudulent, the government would lose its legitimacy. Citing lack of freedom and fairness in the electoral process, opposition parties withdrew from the legislative elections of 2005 (LANS 2005). In the end, this gave Chávez's coalition of parties a two-thirds majority (supermajority) in the AN.

In addition to the detrimental consequences of these events (failed coup, strikes, protests, referendum and electoral boycott) for the economy and the general stability of the country, they created an environment that required people to take a position. For instance, during the national strike in December 2002, the opposition's discursive strategies politicized individual decisions on whether to go to work or to keep businesses open (Córdova 2000). Moreover, although the massive rallies were intended as protest against Chávez's policies, they also served to reinforce social divisions. Venezuelans, knowingly or not, were compelled to think about their place in the political arena, either for or against Chávez and his policies.

The dichotomous nature of the opposition's discourse did not allow for a third alternative. Perhaps, this was the only possible strategy in a divided and non-cohesive political movement. During this phase, the opposition had a weak discourse when it came to any specific policies or programmatic agenda for the future. As such, its discursive strategy was suspended in a philosophical level of generality, only capable of arguing that the measures being implemented by the government were not consistent with their worldview of a democratic system (Coordinadora Democratica De Venezuela 2002).

From its beginnings in 2000 until the legislative elections of 2005, all factions of the opposition consistently communicated that the only viable solution was for Chávez and his loyalists to be removed from power, both with words and actions (Brading 2013, 67–75; Cannon 2004; Coordinadora Democratica De Venezuela 2002).

Regardless of which faction predominated, the opposition's discourse was mainly framed in normative terms. Consequently, a public debate about the county's political institutions was necessarily pushed into the moral terrain. Political discussion was no longer about what was best for the country considering the current political or economic conditions. It became about what the different opposition leaders or the government considered it best, based on their respective position within the current institutional framework.

Towards a more programmatic approach, 2006–2012

By mid-2006 the opposition reverted back to constitutional solutions, this time in preparation for the presidential election at the end of the year. Despite the opposition's best organizational efforts (through *Sumate*[8]) to select a unity candidate, Chávez won again with 63% of the popular vote. Backing a unity candidate (Manuel Rosales) was considered the best strategy to run against a president that reinforced a personalistic style and remained quite popular. However, it also reinforced the notion that the course set by Chávez could only be reverted by changing the president. In any other political scenario this would have been inconsequential. In a country where a populist logic pervades every aspect of society, the representation of the opposition in a single figure further reinforces the idea that politics is about the leader.

Following the 2006 presidential election, the opposition lost much of its momentum, which opened the space for new movements to emerge. The student movement, sparked by the government's announcement to discontinue Radio Caracas Television's[9] (RCTV) broadcasting license, filled the void. This was the first time a group not associated with a political party or the old establishment became the face of the anti-Chávez movement. This also represented a shift from the anti-Chávez discourse to one in support of freedom of expression, at least momentarily.

Not long after, the student movement combined efforts with opposition parties to campaign against the 2007 constitutional amendment and the 2008 regional elections. On one hand, the increasing salience of the student movement provided the opposition with an alternative to show its discontent with government policies (Brading 2013, 81–82). On the other hand, the movements' association with the political elites meant a return to the same anti-Chávez rhetoric.

In this phase, the opposition's discourse continued to reinforce the "us" versus "them" and the validity of emotional appeals. However, greater cohesion allowed it to formulate a cohesive programmatic platform. While to an extent this is a mild shift away from populism, the emphasis placed on being represented by a single leader keeps it operating within a populist logic.

The opposition's participation and acknowledgment of the results of the 2009 constitutional amendments demonstrates greater willingness to play by the government's rules and to legitimize the country's electoral system. By mid-2009, the opposition had already organized around the MUD[10] as the main representative of its political and electoral platform in the upcoming 2010 legislative elections (La Verdad 2009).

While the opposition united under one platform, the MUD was composed of a number of actors ranging from extremist parties that wanted to remove Chávez by any means necessary to the more moderate players that took center-stage during the upcoming presidential elections. Following the lead of the moderate faction and within this new institutional framework, a more formal opposition entered what the 2012/2013 presidential candidate Henrique Capriles Radonski called "a new era of hope, without fights with Chávez's government, [. . .] working towards the objective of providing people a better living standard" (El Pais 2008).

Leading up to the legislative elections of 2010, the opposition was in a better position due to the declining state of the economy and internal struggles within Chávez's coalition. But more importantly, it had reoriented its efforts towards crafting a programmatic platform that the people could understand and vote for. While its purpose had not changed, it still opposed Chávez and everything he stood for, its discourse became more conciliatory and inclusive. Evidence of this can be found in the words of former Caracas mayor Leopoldo Lopez: "Chávez, king of the poor versus the rich opposition is an old story to me. Law and order, infrastructure and development, and respect for human rights, these are the main plank of the new opposition" (Morales 2009). Or as put by Julio Borges, leader of *Primero Justicia* party: "portraying the fight for Venezuela as a personalized battle to stop Chávez instead of offering a vision for a better country has been our biggest mistake" (Asia News Monitor 2010).

Within this newfound political consensus, in 2011 the opposition began formulating its plans for the selection of a unity candidate for the 2012 presidential election. All the extremist unconstitutional methods, the personality-based conflicts within opposition parties, and the aggressive anti-Chávez rhetoric seemed to have become a thing of the past. The new platform promoted by the MUD was intent on reconnecting with voters and presenting an alternative solution to the country's most pressing problems such as crime, inflation and a diminishing quality of life. Leading up to the elections of 2012, the opposition focused on promoting its new vision for the country through its unity presidential candidate (Mesa de Unidad Democratica 2012).

A new programmatic-based approach allowed the opposition to target not only Chávez the leader, but also the institutions he had helped create and the government he commanded. By then, the ideological affiliation of political institutions such as the legislative, the judicial, and the electoral board had clearly become partisan and mostly in favor of the president. While this presented an institutional disadvantage for the opposition, it did create a more predictable institutional framework within which the opposition could clearly present its party program.

Nevertheless, the leading strategy of the opposition remained focused on elevating an opposition figure to the presidency. Through emphasis on the idea that change would only be possible through a new leader, the opposition reinforced the representational space attributed to the leader and its claim to embody "the people" in populist terms (Laclau 2005a; Panizza 2008). Hence, the opposition continued to reinforce the validity of a populist logic as a viable political project.

Discussion

An inquiry into the active role of the "other" is crucial, not only for understanding how populism is radicalized, but also its implication for the survival of democracy. Through an analysis of the discourse of the anti-Chávez movement in Venezuela, this chapter shows that the opposition was instrumental for the consolidation of a populist logic in the earlier stages of the Chávez regime. Although the analysis is limited to Chávez's presidential tenure, it is a good approximation of the extent to which the reactions to populism can either constrain or shape it ability to survive and translate into tangible public policies.

A populist logic emerged in Venezuela with Chávez's antagonistic discourse, which framed all things associated with the old regime as the "other." However, the opposition reinforced this antagonistic relation not only through its discourse, but also through coordinated actions (insurrection). Through protests, strikes, a coup and the revocatory referendum the opposition created a crisis environment, which compelled people to think in dualistic terms when choosing their political allegiance.

Moreover, through the formulation of a rather emotional appeal, the opposition communicated that the problems of the county could be reduced to Chávez's presidency. Mainly, because the one thing the opposition could agree on was the desire to remove Chávez from power. While in another political context this would be inconsequential, in this case it reduces the discussion to a moral dichotomy of "Chávez equals bad", "opposition equals good." At this point, the potential for a discussion about the appropriateness of current policies or why the opposition's program serves the country's interests better was lost in a personality struggle devoid of any real contribution or possibility of change.

Thereafter, the new cohesive opposition was instrumental in making important political gains. Yet, its unification behind a single candidate, in this case, makes it about the leader and not the institutions. Once more, telling the people that the faith of the country depends on a single individual (the leader) falls within a populist framework, highlighting the importance of an agent or empty signifier. It is important to note that this does not make the opposition populist per se. Nevertheless, its emphasis on the significance of projecting unity and support behind one candidate reinforces the validity of a populist logic as a sustainable political project.

Following Chávez's death, his successor Nicolas Maduro has remained on a populist course. Although the opposition has been able to remain a partially united front, for both the 2013 special presidential election and the 2015 legislative election, its radical faction has continuously carried a message of insurrection. For example, during the February 2014 student led protests, the opposition leader Leopoldo López called for peaceful protests pressing for the resignation of President Maduro (Nagel 2015). The moderate camp of the opposition mainly represented by former presidential candidate Henrique Capriles Radonski followed a more conciliatory approach. While they did support the idea of peaceful protest, their requests were oriented towards restituting peace and order, and their discourse put great emphasis on remaining within the rule of law (El Universal 2014).

To date, the government of President Maduro has remained committed to the ideas of the late Hugo Chávez, despite the severity of the socioeconomic crisis facing the country. Since April 2017 dozens of citizens have been killed amidst anti-government protests, following a series of announcements by Maduro's government (BBC News 2017). As the current president has been unable to inspire the same tame response that recruited supporters during Hugo Chávez's tenure, Maduro has made a series of proposals to further erode the separation of powers (*The Guardian* 2017). The ability of the opposition to hinder Maduro's power grabs has continued to be severely limited by divisions within the opposition itself. But more importantly, its capacity to steer the country in a different direction through institutional mechanisms (such as the National Assembly) is drastically hindered by the populism that has pervaded the political system and the empirical regularities that this generated for almost two decades; in short the timing of the opposition's moderate reaction is approximately 15 years too late.

The set of findings in this chapter highlight a broader debate about the kind and timing of reactions to populism, and its role in promoting change and/or continuity within a populist logic. This points the way to further research into the relationship between the "other" and populist parties/leaders in other contexts, e.g. Europe and the United States. In the U.S., the election of Donald J. Trump as president marks a departure from traditional political transitions. A businessman and outsider to the Washington establishment, President Trump carried a campaign that promised to return the country to the "people," and "drain the swamp," which in his discourse includes political elites from both parties and the media. This has generated a wide range of reactionary movements, including protests, fundraising efforts and counterattacks by some media outlets. Whether President Trump can be categorized as populist is still out for debate, but undoubtedly he espouses the same Manichean ideas that pit the "people" against a "corrupt elite" necessary for populism.

In Germany there is a growing divide between the populist radical-right within and outside the country and the government of Chancellor Angela Merkel. As she ventures onto her fourth campaign, the Chancellor is being challenged not only by her political opponents running for the post, but also by Marine Le Pen (France's National Front) and Geert Wilders (The Dutch Freedom Party). The "polarization and populism" pervading Europe, as Merkel has called it, stems from her stance on the refugee crisis (Donahue 2017).

As both advanced industrialized countries and the developing world grapple with the rise of populist politics, it is crucial that we put as much emphasis in understanding reactionary forces, as we do in studying populism itself. Whether populists are in power or within the opposition, the reactions of the mainstream are likely to play an important role in (de)legitimizing their appeal. In sum, this work makes an important call to further inquiry into the effects of reactionary forces to populism's proliferation and survival.

Notes

1 This was a formal pact or political project, following the fall of Marcos Pérez Jiménez's dictatorship, between Venezuela's three main parties, Acción Democrática, COPEI and Union Republicana Democrática to accept the result of the 1958 elections and to safeguard the democratic regime being inaugurated with it.

2 This includes, but is not limited to names such as: Pedro Carmona Estanga, Arias Cardenas, Manuel Rosales, Leolpoldo Lopez, Maria Corina Machado, Henrique Caprlies Radonski, Julio Borges.

3 This period contained important events such as: the 1999 constitutional reform, the failed coup of 2002, the general strike of 2003, the presidential referendum of 2004, the boycott of the legislative elections in 2005.

4 As evidenced by these events the presidential election of 2006, the failed constitutional amendment of 2007, the successful constitutional amendment of 2009, the legislative elections of 2010, and the presidential election of 2012.

5 Venezuela's social programs in areas of food, health, education, and housing.

6 Making use of this parliamentary authorization, in 2000 Chávez introduced a package containing 49 laws that covered six critical areas: economy, transport, service, infrastructure, science and technology, crime, and reorganization of his cabinet.

7 Mediated by the Carter Center and the Organization of American States (OAS), the Forum for Negotiation and Agreement was established in 2002 to attempt an agreement between the government of Venezuela and its supporters, and the *Coordinadora Democrática* and civil society. The parties agreed in May 2003 to call for a revocatory referendum.

8 *Sumate* is a non-profit civic organization created in 2002, which works to facilitate citizen's participation, mainly in electoral processes. *Sumate* played a major role in collecting signatures for the referendum in 2004, and continued to organize, and participate electoral processes for the opposition until the present (Sumate, n.d.).

9 One of Venezuela's leading television network and a longstanding critic of President Chávez.

10 The MUD was instrumental in selecting single candidates for the upcoming legislative elections, as well as the organization of primary elections in preparation for the 2012 presidential elections.

References

Art, David. 2011. *Inside the Radical Right. The Development of Anti-Immigrant Parties in Western Europe*. New York, NY: Cambridge University Press.

Asia News Monitor. 2010. "Venezuela: Venezuelan Opposition Parties Aim to Break Cycle of Failure," September 8, 2010.

BBC News. 2017. "Venezuela Crisis: What Is behind the Turmoil?," May 4, 2017.

Blondel, Jean. 1997. "Political Opposition in Contemporary World." *Government and Opposition* 32 (4):462–86.
Brading, Ryan. 2013. *Populism in Venezuela*. New York, NY: Routledge.
Brewer-Carías, Allan R. 2010. *Dismanteling Democracy in Venezuela*. New York, NY: Cambridge University Press.
Cannon, Barry. 2004. "Venezuela, April 2002: Coup or Popular Rebellion? The Myth of a United Venezuela." *Bulletin of Latin American Research* 23 (3):285–302.
———. 2014. "As Clear as MUD: Characteristics, Objectives, and Strategies of the Opposition in Bolivarian Venezuela." *Latin American Politics and Society* 56 (4):49–70.
CNE. 1998. "Elecciones Presidenciales, 6 de Diciembre de 1998." Caracas, Venezuela: Consejo Nacional Electoral. www.cne.gov.ve/web/documentos/estadisticas/e98_01.pdf.
Collier, David. 2011. "Understanding Process Tracing." *The Teacher*.
Coordinadora Democratica De Venezuela. 2002. "Pacto Democrático Por La Unidad y Reconstrucción Nacional."
Córdova, Luis. 2000. "VENEZUELA: Oposición a Chávez Comienza a Salir Del Letargo." *Inter Press Service*, February 22, 2000. www.ipsnoticias.net/2000/02/venezuela-oposicion-a-chavez-comienza-a-salir-del-letargo/.
Corrales, Javier, and Michael Penfold. 2007. "Venezuela: Crowding Out the Opposition." *Journal of Democracy* 18 (2):100–113.
———. 2011. *Dragon in the Tropics: Hugo Chavez and the Political Economy of Revolution in Venezuela*. Washington, DC: The Brookings Institution.
De la Torre, Carlos. 2013. "In the Name of the People: Democratization, Popular Organizations, and Populism in Venezuela, Bolivia, and Ecuador." *European Review of Latin American and Caribbean Studies* 95:27–48.
Domínguez, Francisco. 2011. "Venezuela's Opposition: Desperately Seeking to Overthrow Chávez." In *Right-Wing Politics in the New Latin America: Reaction and Revolt*, edited by Geraldine Lievesley Domínguez and Steve Ledlum, 113–30. London: Zed.
Donahue, Patrick. 2017. "Merkel Hits Back at Populists in Defense of Refugee Stance." *Bloomberg Politics*, January 24, 2017.
EFE. 2002. "El Gobierno y La Oposición a Chávez Se Sientan Hoy En La 'Mesa de Diálogo' de La OEA." *El Mundo*, November 8, 2002.
El Pais. 2008. "El Partido de Chávez Gana En La Mayoría de Estados, Pero Pierde Los Más Poblados y Caracas," November 24, 2008.
El Universal. 2014. "Protestas En Venezuela: Capriles Llama a Movilización Contra La Violencia y El Paramilitarismo." *El Universal*, February 16, 2014.
Ellner, Steve. 2010. "Hugo Chávez's First Decade in Office: Breakthroughs and Shortcomings." *Latin American Perspectives* 37 (1):77.
Financial Times. 2002. "Paranoia and Hate Stalk the Streets of Caracas: Venezuela's Opposition Groups Argue That a Military Coup Is the Only Solution to the Civil 'Problems' Embodied in President Hugo Chávez," June 20, 2002.
Gamboa, Laura. 2017. "Opposition at the Margins: Strategies against the Erosion of Democracy in Colombia and Venezuela." *Comparative Politics* 49 (4):457–77.
García-Guadilla, María Pilar. 2005. "The Democratization of Democracy and Social Organi-Zations of the Opposition: Theoretical Certainties, Myths, and Praxis." *Latin American Perspectives* 32 (2):109–23.
Gidron, Noam, and Bart Bonikowski. 2013. "Varieties of Populism: Literature Review and Research Agenda." In *Working Papers Series*. Vol. 13–0004. Weatherhead Center for International Affairs.
Hawkins, Kirk A. 2010. *Venezuela's Chavismo and Populism in Comparative Perspective*. New York, NY: Cambridge University Press.
———. 2016. "Responding to Radical Populism: Chavismo in Venezuela." *Democratization* 23 (2):242–262.

La Verdad. 2009. "Oposición Escoge Dos Métodos: Primero El Consenso y Segundo Las Primarias." *Informe 21*, October 19, 2009.

Laclau, Ernesto. 2005a. *On Populist Reason*. London and New York: Verso.

———. 2005b. "Populism: What's in a Name." In *Populism and the Mirror of Democracy*, edited by Francisco Panizza. London and New York: Verso.

LANS. 2005. "Opposition Party in Venezuela Withdraws from Congressional Elections." *Noticias Financieras*, December 2, 2005.

Meguid, Bonnie M. 2005. "Competition between Unequals: The Role of Mainstream Party Strategy in Niche Party Success." *American Journal of Political Science* 99 (3):347–359.

Mesa de Unidad Democratica. 2012. "Lineamientos Para El Programa de Gobierno de Unidad Nacional (2013–2019)." www.unidadvenezuela.org/wp-content/uploads/2012/01/lineamientos2012.pdf.

Moffett, Matt, and Matt Lifsher. 2002. "Venezuela's New Radicals: Long Strike Is Forcing People from All Walks of Life to Take a Stand." *The Wall Street Journal*, December 27, 2002.

Morales, Pablo. 2009. "Venezuela's Opposition: Back into the Frying Pan." *NACLA Report on the Americas*, June 2009.

Mudde, Cas. 2007. *Populist Radical Right Parties in Europe*. New York, NY: Cambridge University Press.

Mudde, Cas, and Cristobal Rovira Kaltwasser. 2011. "Voice of the Peoples: Populism in Europe and Latin America Compared." *The Helen Kellogg Institute for International Studies* Working Paper #378:1–47.

Nagel, Juan Cristobal. 2015. "Venezuela's Most Famous Dissident Gets 13 Years." *Foreign Policy*, September 11, 2015.

Noticias Financieras. 2004. "Week's Top Story – Opposition Rejects Results of Fecall Referendum," August 20, 2004. http://search.proquest.com.ezproxy.bu.edu/docview/468287593?accountid=9676.

Notimex. 2004. "Venezuela: Opposition Predicts Street Protests next Week." *BBC Monitoring Americas*, August 21, 2004. http://search.proquest.com.ezproxy.bu.edu/docview/460235056?accountid=9676.

Panizza, Francisco. 2005. "Introduction: Populism and the Mirror of Democracy." In *Populism and the Mirror of Democracy*. London and New York: Verso.

———. 2008. "Fisuras Entre Populismo y Democracia En America Latina." *Stockholm Review of Latin American Studies* 3: 81–93.

Panizza, Francisco, and Romina Miorelli. 2009. "Populism and Democracy in Latin America." *Carnegie Council for Ethics and International Affairs*, 2009.

Roberts, Kenneth. 2012. "Populism and Democracy in Venezuela under Hugo Chavez." In *Populism in Europe and the Americas: Threat or Corrective for Democracy*, edited by Cas Mudde and Cristobal Rovira Kaltwasser, 136–159. New York, NY: Cambridge University Press.

Rooduijn, Matthijs, Sara L. de Lange, and Wouter Van Der Brug. 2012. "A Populist Zeitgeist? Programmatic Contagion by Populist Parties in Western Europe." *Party Politics* 20 (4):563–75.

Rovira Kaltwasser, Cristobal, and Paul Taggart. 2016. "Dealing with Populists in Government: A Framework for Analysis." *Democratization* 23 (2):201–220.

RTT News. 2012. "Capriles Registers As Candidate for Venezuela Presidential Elections," 2012.

Sumate. n.d. "Quienes Somos?" www.sumate.org/nosotros.html.

Tansey, Oisín. 2007. "Process Tracing and Elite Interviewing: A Case for Non-Probability Sampling." *Political Science and Politics* 40 (4): 765–772.

The Christian Monitor. 2003. "Venezuela's Opposition Ignores the Constitution," 2003.

The Guardian. 2017. "The Observer View on the Crisis in Venezuela," August 5, 2017.

Wall Street Journal. 2004. "Venezuela's Chavez Vows to Fight Recall Effort," June 7, 2004.

Weyland, Kurt. 1999. "Populism in the Age of Neoliberalism." In *Populism in Latin America*, edited by Michael Conniff. Tuscaloosa, Alabama: The University of Alabama Press.

Appendix A

Sources

- InterPress Services
- The Wall Street Journal
- The New York Times
- El Pais
- Los Angeles Times
- Oxford Analytica Daily Briefs
- Defense and Foreign Affairs Strategic Policy
- The Guardian
- The Financial Times
- Oil Daily
- The Economist
- El Mundo España
- The Christian Monitor
- National Post
- BBC Monitoring America
- NACLA Report
- Energy Compass
- Hoy Digital
- World Sources Online
- Noticias Financieras
- Foreign Policy
- Informe 21
- El Universal
- La Verdad
- Noticias 24

The selection process was somewhat hindered by the availability of news articles in online archives. For the period between 2000–2002 and 2005–2007, I was able to collect a smaller number of articles for analysis, due to this restriction. While this creates some concern for bias, I address this in two ways. First, the number of statements in each category is normalized to account for this difference in the number of articles. Second, I ensure that articles in the early years of the opposition are collected from a wide range of sources, to account for content bias.

Appendix B

Samples of coding mechanism

Table 13.A1 Category 1 examples: "us" versus "them"

Article Title:	La oposición prolonga un día más el paro y advierte que no cejará hasta sacar a Chávez del poder
Author:	No author mentioned
Source:	El Mundo España via Reuters
Date:	December 13, 2002
Statement:	El presidente de la Confederación de Trabajadores de Venezuela (CTV), Carlos Ortega, calificó la medida de fuerza como de "resistencia combativa" al señalar que llamará al pueblo a declararse en desobediencia civil hasta alcanzar el objetivo deseado.

Article Title:	Venezuelan opposition calls street protests to stress fraud allegations
Author:	Patrick J. O'Donoghue
Source:	BBC Monitoring via VENews
Date:	September 12, 2004
Statement:	Pablo Medina, opposition leader, "A cavalcade will set off from Parque del Este and make its way around Caracas . . . [ellipsis as published] we want people to know who is the majority."

Table 13.A2 Category 2 examples: emotional appeals

Article Title:	Francisco Arias Cardenas: A former coup partner takes on Venezuela's populist President
Author:	Sandra Hernandez
Source:	Los Angeles Time
Date:	July 23, 2000
Statement:	"Venezuelans will vote to assert democracy and eliminate the risk of an authoritarian government, which is what we are living through." (Arias Cardenas)

Article Title:	Doubts cloud prospects for referendum on Chavez rule: Venezuela's opposition is focusing efforts on a mid-term vote on the president, but it is easier said than done.
Author:	Anonymous
Source:	Financial Times

(continued)

Table 13.A2 (continued)

Date:	July 1, 2003
Statement:	His fiercest opponents see the bombastic Mr Chavez as a dictator in waiting, bent on holding on to power. "Chavez is going to do everything possible to ensure a referendum doesn't take place," says Pastor Heydra, an opposition legislator in the national assembly. "At some point Chavez is simply going to kick over the table and enforce his militaristic brand of autocracy."

Table 13.A3 Category 3 examples: the leader

Article Title:	The Americas: Damned whatever they do. Venezuela's opposition
Author:	No author mentioned
Source:	The Economist
Date:	July 22, 2006
Statement:	All three agree that the opposition's only hope is to unite behind a single candidate. But they disagree about how that person should be chosen. On August 13 most of the hopefuls will take part in a primary organized by Sumate, the opposition's main electoral pressure group.

Article Title:	Maria Corina Machada: La oposición Venezolana debe definer el perfil del candidato de unidad.
Author:	No author mentioned
Source:	Editor DJ
Date:	April 13, 2011
Statement:	"Creo que en este momento es mas important el perfil . . . consider que necesitamos una persona con autoridad moral, con capacidad para resolver los problemas y garantice a todos los sectores que no habra sectarismo, privilegios, no divisions" declare la Congresista independiente (Maria Corina Machado) a periodistas en Miami, FL.

Appendix C

Table 13.A4 Summary table for Figure 13.1

	2000	*2001*	*2002*	*2003*	*2004*	*2005*	*2006*	*2007*	*2008*	*2009*	*2010*	*2011*	*2012*	*Totals*
Category 1: "us" vs. "them"	0.4 (2)	0.25 (1)	0.31 (8)	0.04 (1)	0.13 (4)	0	0.17 (1)	0.2 (1)	0	0.15 (4)	0.08 (2)	0	0.03 (1)	**25**
Category 2: emotional appeals	0.6 (3)	0.75 (3)	0.42 (11)	0.29 (8)	0.2 (6)	0	0.17 (1)	0.6 (3)	0	0.23 (6)	0.19 (5)	0.09 (3)	0.06 (2)	**51**
Category 3: the leader	0	0	0	0.04 (1)	0	0.5 (1)	0.5 (3)	0	0.13 (1)	0.04 (1)	0.04 (2)	0.18 (6)	0.29 (10)	**25**
Total Articles	**5**	**4**	**26**	**28**	**30**	**8**	**6**	**5**	**8**	**26**	**26**	**33**	**34**	

Note: numbers in parenthesis are the raw count of statements coded under each category

14 Populism in Belgium

The mobilization of the body anti-politic

Koen Abts, Thierry Kochuyt, and Stijn van Kessel

Belgium was among the first European countries to witness the breakthrough of a populist radical right (PRR) party: Flemish Interest (*Vlaams Belang*, VB), until 2004 named Flemish Bloc (*Vlaams Blok*). The success of PRR parties like the VB reveals a growing unease: discontented voters raise their voice and reclaim popular sovereignty. They stand up against political elites neglecting the demos, and against migrants threatening the ethnos. Surveys show that PRR voters combine political cynicism and ethnocentrism (Abts 2012; Betz 1994; Billiet and De Witte 1995; Decker 2004; Mayer 1999; Mudde 2007; Van Hauwaert and van Kessel 2018). Yet, they do not illustrate how both come together, and are activated into a populist vote.

Using in-depth interviews with voters from the VB in the city of Antwerp, the party's traditional stronghold, this article retraces the process through which a variety of people became alienated from the multiethnic city, drifted away from traditional politics, and gradually sympathized with a PRR party. While our study focuses on VB voters in particular, the proposed framework has wider relevance: our contribution develops an analytical model to assess how discontented citizens develop populist attitudes, which are subsequently cultivated and strengthened by the frames and cues of political parties. We argue that, on the one hand, populist attitudes loomed as a result of broad social changes: people in Antwerp felt threatened by the multicultural city, and drifted away from traditional parties that were no longer deemed to represent and protect them. On the other hand, we need to consider the role of a populist party politicizing these problems whilst pitting "the people" against the "elites" and non-native "outsiders," thereby reinforcing its supporters' populist interpretation of social reality. In line with the ideational approach to populism, we thus show how in the Flemish case both contextual and agential factors were key to the activation of latent populist dispositions, translating into the support for a PRR party. The diffuse protest of isolated voters aligned itself with the VB as the only party opposing migrants and elites for the sake of "our own kind of people." The VB could monopolize the PRR territory and maintain the forged electoral coalition as long as internal conflicts were contained and political opponents failed to address salient issues, related to immigration in particular.

The chapter proceeds as follows. After a brief introduction to the VB, the methodology of our qualitative study is outlined. Subsequent sections analyze, first, the social and political context provoking populist resentment among our respondents. Second, we demonstrate how VB voters, diverse as they were, found an ally in this populist party, whose discourse matched their ideas. Third, our study illustrates how the bond between the party and its supporters strengthened, and how the latter perceived the VB as the only party that represented their interests in a polarized political space, in which the "demos/ethnos" was mobilized against the political establishment who were perceived to privilege the immigrant "outsiders." For as long as this antagonism remained in place, the VB could consolidate its prominent position in Belgian politics.

The VB's life cycle

Founded in 1978, the VB was initially a marginal separatist faction calling for an independent Flemish state. Expanding its agenda, it gradually transformed into a successful ethno-populist party portraying threatening immigrants and corrupt political elites as enemies of the common people. Hence the VB transformed itself into a typical PRR party characterized by nativism, authoritarianism and populism (Mudde 2007).

Alarmed by its electoral success and xenophobic discourse, the other parties decided to exclude the dissident from governance, erecting a so-called *cordon sanitaire*. This brought Flemish politics into a stalemate during two decades, since the *cordon* failed to stop the electoral rise of the VB. From 1985 until 2004, its vote share rose steadily, and with more than 24 percent in 2004, the anti-establishment party even became the largest in Flemish parliament.[1] In that year the party changed its name from Flemish Bloc to Flemish Interest, after a Supreme Court ruling indicted the party for violating the racism and xenophobia law. It was the beginning of a string of internal problems and electoral setbacks. The disappointing local elections of 2006, in which the party lost its status as the largest party in its traditional stronghold Antwerp, confirmed the loss of momentum. The VB faced increasing competition from the conservative and Flemish-nationalist party New-Flemish Alliance (*Nieuw-Vlaamse Alliantie*, N-VA), and saw the defection or resignation of prominent members. In the Flemish parliamentary election of 2014 the party obtained a mere 5.9 per cent of the votes.

While the party's recent misfortunes provide scope for research (see e.g. Abts, Van Kessel and Swyngedouw 2016; Pauwels 2011), our study focuses on how populist sentiments were activated and translated into support for the VB. We therefore interviewed VB voters during a period in which the party was in its electoral prime.

A qualitative study

This qualitative study is based on in-depth interviews conducted in 2004. Using a stratified sample, a total of 37 VB voters were selected through a random walk in five contrasting neighborhoods within the city of Antwerp. On the one hand, interviews were conducted in the inner-city, i.e. the highly disadvantaged and multiethnic neighborhood Seefhoek; the working class district Moretusburg; and the middle-class area Deurne-East. On the other hand, respondents were interviewed in the affluent and "white" suburbs of Brasschaat and Schoten. The interviews lasted between one and two hours and, once transcribed, resulted in almost 900 pages. Although our sample is not statistically representative, the geographical, social and economic variety nevertheless reflects the urban diversity and the wide reach of the party. Without claiming external validity, we achieve internal validity, allowing us to explain why and how a populist electoral coalition materialized. We reconstruct the subsequent political polarization step-by-step as a generative process. While results of larger-N surveys tend to provide a snapshot of a particular point in time, our inductive analysis of the in-depth interviews helps to reconstruct the origins and build-up of citizens' cultural and political resentment. Our semi-structured interviews asked the respondents to discuss their neighborhood, migrants, integration, the welfare state and politics in general (see Kochuyt and Abts 2017). People answered using their own words, developing their own narrative. In this chapter, the selected quotes will voice the logics of their discontent.

Defending common but neglected people, the VB initially called itself a "bloc" that stood united and undivided (Abts and Rummens 2007; Mudde 2007; Schedler 1996). Nevertheless, our sample is very heterogeneous in terms of gender, education, residential setting and social class (see Appendix). Economic backgrounds range from business owners, civil servants, small entrepreneurs, working class people and long-term unemployed. Some respondents lacked schooling, others were higher educated. Ideologically, the VB recruits from various walks of life: our sample includes atheists and church-going Catholics, right-wing minds and old leftists, Flemish nationalists and Belgian royalists. One respondent collaborated during WWII, another joined the resistance. Not all supporters are Flemish natives: one had Francophone origins; another was born in the Netherlands.

In our sample diversity prevails, yet all 37 respondents aligned and voted for the same party. This is revealing since it shows that the so-called bloc did not stand for a genuine *body politic* substantiated by a common language, culture or history; there was no consistent community of interest or a deep ideological core. The populist electoral coalition has instead been socially and discursively constructed by integrating different discontented voters from various backgrounds.

Populist resentment: scapegoating ethnic minorities and political establishment

Concerns about immigration and multiculturalism

The issue of immigration is cardinal in the worldview of our VB supporters, since they define themselves in opposition to the non-native outsiders. Biological and ethno-cultural differences are not main concerns, yet migrants are seen to disturb the social order and to threaten the balance of power to the detriment of the native population.

> This migrant issue is an endless story: for the past 30 years they talked and bullshitted but failed to do anything. (. . .) The VB has some credit since they were the first to have the guts and shout out loud: "Hey, we have a problem with those migrants!"
>
> (Student, 26 years, Schoten)

> Why I voted for the VB? Yes, migrants and that sort of stuff. That's the main point. In the end you feel as if they get more from the government – more than we Belgians.
>
> (Cashier, 43 years, Brasschaat)

When migrants concentrate in certain neighborhoods, social cohesion is threatened and people gradually feel like strangers in their own country (compare Gregory 1998; Haegel 2000; Hartigan 1999). The public space is perceived to be unsafe, lower educated natives feel sidelined on the labor market. Respondents are concerned about the viability of the welfare state, as unemployed migrants are perceived to live at the expense of the native population. Instead of assimilating, the outsiders cling to their own customs and traditions, language and religion; some even demand more political power. These accumulated transformations afflict the social order of society, and thus the alienated VB-voters define themselves as victims of changes for which, time and again, the outsiders are to blame. Immigration is considered a zero-sum game, where migrants' gains result in relative deprivation among natives, and that feels unfair.

> An invasion of illegal migrants, an invasion of outsiders, an invasion of shops where you ask yourself: "For God's sake, how can they survive?" Our people disappear; this means the city becomes deserted. People are chased away here, shops are closed. (. . .) This did not happen overnight but slowly. . . It is like a cancer growing (. . .) and the good cells are eaten.
>
> (Retired man, 72 years, Seefhoek)

Social change creates a whirlpool centering around the sole figure of the migrant. The perception of our respondents becomes constricted in a tunnel-vision focusing on the ethnic outsider as the source of all evil. Once the scapegoat is found, the larger picture disappears from sight. In reality, social change has multiple causes and implications, including the restructuring of the economy and the welfare state, the shrinking of local employment and industry, suburbanization and the unraveling of traditional community ties and networks of social and cultural organizations. People ignore these structural changes and so their tunnel-vision de-contextualizes social transformations; moral blame is placed on others, and a 'them vs. us' polarization is generated.[2]

Inner-city inhabitants have first-hand experience, since the entry of migrants coincided with radical transformations that affected their everyday life and the local balance of power (compare Elias and Scotson 1965; Karrer 2002; Kefalas 2003). Surprisingly, however, the tunnel-vision is shared by the richer suburbanites who did not experience an influx of migrants in their neighborhoods. In their perception, the threats associated with immigration are nevertheless looming, and minor incidents – a burglary or the opening of a new refugee center nearby – are magnified, justifying the fear that the suburban periphery will follow the precedent of inner-city decline.

> Quite some people contact me and say: "They are advancing". As if migrants are banging on the gates of Deurne. Strange to say but that is what they make of it: "They are advancing."
>
> (VB- parliamentary assistant, 30 years, Deurne)

Fear of "what is next" largely replaces the sense of local reality: affluent suburbanites tend to disregard their satisfaction with the governance of their municipalities. What prevails is a fear-laden prognosis in which the multicultural metropolis – as a center of alienation – spreads and affects their suburban well-being. Hence preemptive action is needed to counter the anticipated multicultural danger. Indeed, for the VB's electoral base, the tunnel-vision is instrumental in bridging the gap between supporters from the poor inner-city and rich suburbia. The "desperate racism" of the lower positions, who are permanently confronted with intercultural issues, meets the "distinctive racism" of the higher positions, who try to hold "the others" at bay (Kesteloot and De Decker 1992). As a scapegoat the migrant is a unifying figure: natives from different walks of life are united in the fear that their status is threatened, or will be threatened soon, by greedy outsiders. Xenophobia blurs and blends different classes: populism is not just appealing the losers of modernization. Even the better-off can feel relatively deprived when anticipating adversity.

Discontented by unresponsive politics

Resentment is not only directed towards immigrants. A similar estrangement takes place in the political realm: our respondents do not recognize themselves any longer in the present party system. The bonds between parties and the people have weakened. On the one hand, traditional parties are no longer part of everyday life since the historical pillars based on class, religion and ideology disintegrated, while political patronage largely disappeared. Civil society lost its mediating function. On the other hand, former distinctions between the parties have faded, resulting in weaker electoral ties. Working-class voters feel that the socialist party neglects the common people. Defending equality of opportunity and multiculturalism, the party is blamed for disregarding the interests of older adherents. Meanwhile, the affluent middle-classes accuse the liberals and Christian democrats of betrayal and abandoning their core principles: the political right became leftish and progressive, the center too indistinctive.

> The only party for which I feel some affinity – apart from the VB – are the socialists. Just after the war they did far more for the ordinary people than the others. But now I think that is fading. (. . .) The socialists now look as a party made for migrants, not for us.
>
> (Retired municipal worker, 66 years, Seefhoek)

> Before I would have thought: the liberals . . . but they became too leftist. That is not a good match. And the Christian democrats? That party has too much, too many interest-groups.
>
> (Former entrepreneur, 76 years, Schoten)

Where the tunnel-vision connected suburbia with the inner-city through fear, political disaffiliation brokers a second alliance that bridges all former political cleavages from right to left (compare Bihr 1998, 1999; Castel 2003; Fitoussi and Rosanvallon 1996; Krouwel and Abts 2006). People no longer identify with traditional parties, and, they feel that, ever since migrants entered society these parties no longer address and understand the problems people are facing. The recurrent complaint is that authorities fail to act; institutional indifference prevails and people feel abandoned. Hence the traditional political parties are no longer seen to represent the citizens or defend their cause.

> How to say, I feel bad, I feel discarded by them.
>
> (Cleaning lady, 43 years, Moretusburg)

> They promise you everything: to help the Seefhoek and to improve things – whatever. But I have not seen much. (. . .) Do you think that they listen to the people here? Nothing, not a word.
>
> (Unemployed man, 43 years, Seefhoek)

The complaints about unresponsive politicians mainly come from the inner-city; in the richer suburbs respondents are rather satisfied with local governance. This does not, however, ease their fear for an imminent take-over. Respondents feel that the problems related to the entry of migrants have been (deliberately) ignored for too long: they lament the lack of solutions and feel that the politically correct elites turned a blind eye to pressing problems.

> The other parties I ran away from have never addressed the migrant problem. Now they raise the issue, but according to me, 15 years too late.
>
> (Retired sailor, 72 years, Brasschaat)

> The major problem is migrants, and they avoid the topic. They try to cover up and dismiss the issue. (. . .) Face that problem and do something about it, but no . . . like an ostrich, they bury their heads in sand.
>
> (Salesman, 46 years, Deurne)

The activated populist discontent not only targets the political elites, but also the police and judges are blamed for a lack of security. Those who should impose law and order fail to act, giving offenders *carte blanche* to commit crimes, whilst leaving victims defenseless.

When authorities do not respond, people find themselves deprived, isolated and powerless. At the end of the tunnel there is no light, just political misapprehension and arrogance.

> I see a couple of things where I think: how is this possible for God's sake? Because politicians live in an ivory tower. High up they have a view, but without knowing what is happening on the ground.
>
> (Clerk, 41 years, Deurne)

Passionate as they are, the complaints indicate a double frustration: politicians do not only neglect the real problems, but also ignore the subjects who complain and ask for solutions. It is not merely a matter of incompetence; our respondents suspect that politicians obstinately refuse to recognize discontented citizens as credible speaking partners. They feel discredited as racists and pushed aside as "deficient beings" (Laclau 2005, 86).

> Politicians have the obligation to listen to the people and to hear what bothers them. And they should take that into account, rather than using the simplistic labels "racist" or "not-racist."
>
> (Clerk, 43 years, Brasschaat)

> They don't want to listen; the parties don't want to hear. Why are most people voting for the VB? Because of one major issue: migration, and they just don't want to listen. Just listen to the people, to their voice.
>
> (Dockworker, 32 years, Deurne)

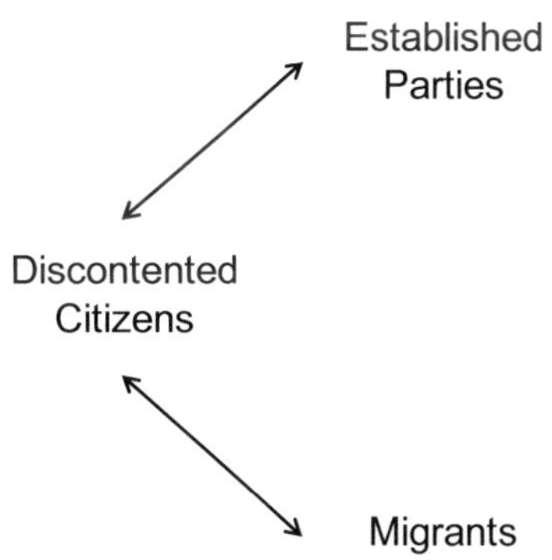

Figure 14.1 Contextual threats

Figure 14.1 visualizes the cultural and political alienation that unites a growing number of discontented citizens who all find themselves at odds with migrants and established politics. The arrows stand for rejection or threat; double arrows for a reciprocal antagonism that is gradually shared by a growing number of aggrieved individuals who feel threatened by established parties as well as immigrants. It remains to be seen how this figuration will link up with the populist party and become politicized by the framing of perceptions.

Populist resentment turning political

The construction of a dichotomy

Our respondents find no support among the governing parties, who disqualify the discontented voices. Without other credible alternatives during the 1990s, they lend their vote to the only contender left: the VB. To the extent that the VB opposes the multicultural society and profiles itself as the antipode of the political establishment, protest voters arrive at a point where they consider the party as an option. Ideological orthodoxy is only decisive for some; most respondents seek to make a statement and regain recognition. From the moment they take sides, however, the political field is reshuffled into a clarifying contrast: there are those parties where no salvation can be found, and there is an outsider listening to the people and their problems (Schedler 1996).

> I have seen things deteriorating in this part of Antwerp. The City Council did nothing, so automatically you end up with a protest party. (. . .) One of the reasons why I vote for the VB is precisely because people, ordinary people, simple citizens, can rely on the VB when there is a problem.
>
> (Self-employed woman, 49 years, Seefhoek)

> The VB is candid, and they surely are genuinely committed to their own people. Among the other parties I can't find a politician who is defending the cause of the people . . .
>
> (Retired entrepreneur, 77 years, Deurne)

Our disaffiliated respondents view all traditional parties as lookalikes. As Laclau (2005) argues, a chain of equivalence arises which makes an amalgam of all political families, leaving the VB as sole alternative. The agonistic space where the opposition counterbalances the government transforms into an antagonistic space where "we fight all others" (Mouffe 2005). This populist polarization mirrors the rigid perspective of the tunnel-vision: the focus is on the same problems and recognizes people's agony. The definition of the situation is restated, while the defining subjects are re-accredited as full-fledged citizens. In this sense, a vote for the VB entails empowerment. What was lacking before is regained: voice and access to the political forum to address problems in society. Hence, the party promises to make up for the democratic deficit of unresponsive policy-makers.

> A good politician is able to listen, and ready to transmit what people think. It is not about imposing one's opinion – we have had enough of those.
>
> (Professional soldier, 44 years, Moretusburg)

For any populist movement this is a defining moment to position itself as an equal among equals; at the same level as those neglected citizens it seeks to defend. Yet, to extend the momentum of contestation it should also organize and invigorate the discontented. The paradox is to take the lead without taking a superior position. The latter might be seen as betrayal since it brings the contender too close to those in power, which is detrimental to the needed credibility (Van Kessel 2015). Because of this hurdle some protests either fade out, remaining weak and disorganized, or get encapsulated by the establishment since they aspire too much power and therefore lose their popular integrity (Kochuyt 2015).[3] The VB remarkably avoided this obstacle through its immensely popular slogan "We say what you think." As a result, the VB was not simply representing voters, but it incarnated them. Following Arditi (2003, 22), one could speak about a "joint presence without representation." As Figure 14.2 shows, the populist party does not profile itself as yet another conventional party. On the contrary, by opposing the same antagonists the populist challenger succeeds to position itself at the same level as the people it seeks to reach out to. Their concerns are being recognized and recycled into a populist frame that claims to speak in the name of the people. Notice as well in this figure the void: no other party is able to position itself at the same level as the discontented, hence the populist party gains a huge potential to recruit protest votes.

The construction of an electoral coalition

The antagonists central to the tunnel-vision – migrants and politicians – are constitutive of the creation of a populist electoral coalition, yet it remains a fragile one. There are socio-economic and socio-cultural divisions among the electorate, and not all VB supporters are convinced and loyal to the same extent. Victorious polling-results and the following polarization are, however, helpful in strengthening the alliance. Thanks to the party and its electoral success, the isolated subjects discover they are not alone in their discontent. In the mirror of the media the rising successes reveal to different individuals that they are part of a growing political entity that can conceive itself as a "silent majority." A collective sense of reality emerges, proving that the tunnel-vision is justified since it is shared by many. This experience validates the democratic claims of the VB and enhances its electoral appeal. Political convictions are rarely pre-existent: they grow gradually. Aggrieved voters find each other thanks to a party that legitimizes their individual frustration. They can thus set aside their hesitation, and share a sense of injustice with other like-minded individuals. Electoral victories make and consolidate the *body anti-politic* like a self-fulfilling prophecy.

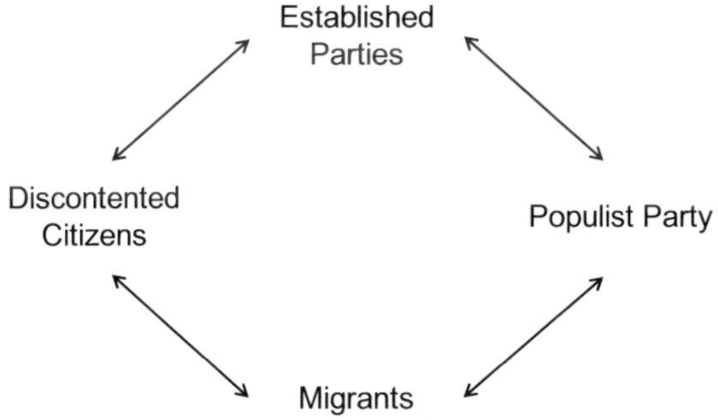

Figure 14.2 Political framing

> Apparently you are not alone with this opinion. When you see: 25 per cent of the Flemish people are voting for the VB, then you are not alone I think. A lot of people probably think the same way as me.
>
> (Salesman, 46 years, Deurne)

> According to me they represent the public opinion of a lot of Flemish people who don't dare to speak up. For a long time they did not dare to say that they are in favor, but now you see. . .
>
> (Retired sailor, 72 years, Brasschaat)

On "judgment day" the polling results constitute a discharging and emotional moment where hitherto isolated voters and the party cheerfully join and make themselves a political player impossible to ignore. The VB unites so-called like-minded citizens and amplifies their protest. Acting as a mouthpiece, the party not only transmits people's discontent, it also prompts official propaganda. Many voters repeat the slogans cued by the VB, subscribing to a discursive frame through which the party and its following come to strike the same chord. Echoes resonate, and the fact that these voices become ever louder is considered as evidence for the accuracy of the analysis. By 2004, the VB set the tone and gained hegemony in addressing problems such as migration and crime.

> If many vote for the VB, there must be something good about it.
>
> (Student, 18 years, Seefhoek)

At first sight it seems that party and voters speak with one voice, but listening carefully to the interviews reveals there is also blur and distortion. Despite numerous echoes, the discursive framing is not conclusive: citizens vote for the party, but that does not always imply that all wholeheartedly agree. Many respondents remain skeptic, and object to the extremist and xenophobic nature of the party and the harsh style of its leadership.

> I never voted for Dewinter. I hate it when I hear "our people first." (. . .) That is wrong, I despise that slogan. I think when the most competent is to be selected for a job, it should actually be the most competent – irrespective of the person being a Belgian or a foreigner.
>
> (Retired executive, 61 years, Brasschaat)

> That is in fact my biggest fear if the VB gains power: I want it, but at the same time I don't want it. I'm afraid that it would turn out too extreme (. . .) I'm always hesitating but seeing the things as they are, then . . ..
>
> (Unemployed woman, 49 years, Deurne)

> Sometimes they are too blunt, way too tough I think. (. . .) Statements like "all black people out": that's bullshit; you should treat a human being as a human.
>
> (Retired municipal worker, 66 years, Seefhoek)

This criticism regarding the party is often neglected by bystanders who just see an alarming surge of the radical right. Growing polarization leaves no place for ambivalence or any deeper understanding of the reasons that triggered the divide. Ethno-populists and the defenders of political correctness become engaged in a dangerous *pas de deux* where each finds a partner in the other's miscomprehension.

Brothers in arms: shared antagonistic positions and the appeal to the ethnos/demos

The cordon sanitaire

The VB heralds itself as radically antagonistic, stirring resistance in the political and social arenas. Traditional parties, trade unions, media, and public opinion see the future of democracy endangered. They point out that the founding members of the party collaborated during WWII, and condemn its racism as a threat to human rights. Yet, our respondents do not perceive these arguments as legitimate, but rather understand them as maneuvers to sideline and isolate the party. Instead of having a serious discussion, opponents avoid debate by tarnishing and stigmatizing the populist party (Abts 2015).

> They consider them as pariahs . . . they are spit out by the established politics.
>
> (Retired man, 72 years, Seefhoek)

> They want to demonize the VB.
>
> (Former entrepreneur, 76 years, Schoten)

The arguments supporting the *cordon sanitaire* fall on deaf ears, and do little to sway even skeptical VB supporters. They do not feel invited for discussion but misapprehended and rejected. There is much irritation regarding the way opponents portray the VB-electorate as frustrated, retarded and racist. Respondents feel disallowed to have their say and so they are – once again – excluded from political participation.

> It's like you cannot criticize things that bother you, and it feels like no longer having any freedom of speech. (. . .) Should I call a black person white from now onwards?
>
> (Retired municipal worker, 66 years, Seefhoek)

> Time and again the party is depicted as a party of the marginal, the frustrated, the underclass . . ..
>
> (Student, 26 years, Schoten)

To counter the advance of the VB, the stigma expands and becomes institutionalized. In 1989 the ruling parties installed a *cordon sanitaire* to quarantine the VB (Rummens and Abts 2010; Abts 2015). None of them is willing to enter a coalition with the party; the VB thus remains effectively blocked from all executive power. Notwithstanding its electoral victories, the dissident party is condemned to dwell in opposition, effectively disqualifying the votes of our respondents.[4] In their eyes the *cordon* is a litmus test that finally proves the obstinate unwillingness of the established parties, and their perverse tactics to cling to power. VB supporters are silenced, and so they cry out in indignation, take an even tougher stance, and prepare for the trenches. The *cordon* constitutes an extra motivation to vote for the VB. In 2004 the party even became the largest in Flanders.

> As long as they don't get a fair chance because of this sabotage from the other parties, I think: "Yes, I'll back them." (. . .) They thought: "Look, that is the way to break the VB. People will start to realize that they are excluded from power." (. . .) But the more they curse and damn the VB, the more votes they will get.
>
> (Clerk, 43 years, Schoten)

> A major reason – and you'll see that it is true for many – is this hostility towards one specific party. And then there is something in me that pops up and says: "Oh no, I don't take that." Nobody can say what I should or shouldn't think. I become a bit rebellious.
>
> (Retired nurse, VB-mandatary, 64 years, Brasschaat)

The unintended consequences of the cordon

Why does a disqualified voice reinforce the vote for the VB? Reminiscence explains a lot: the exclusion of the political underdog reenacts, in a way, the deprivation the voters felt themselves. So they set aside their skepticism and finally sympathize. Again, a chain of equivalence develops between voter and party. Because both are damned, the culprits find each other and start to perceive themselves as brothers in arms. Sharing the same stigma, voters and party can identify and nurture their political cynicism.

> They are the biggest party now, but people still can't say much because they are suffocated from all sides. . . . I think that this is a crime: it is our voice that is being silenced!
>
> (Retired worker, 85 years, Hoboken)

Since the established parties ignore their complaints and votes, our respondents argue that the existing regime loses legitimacy: there is a breach of contract. Who can recognize authority when the freedom of speech and equal representation are impaired? The *cordon sanitaire* contradicts core democratic principles, leading to a decline of faith in established political institutions.

> In a democracy there is freedom of speech, and when you neglect one million people, is that democratic?
>
> (Doctor, 37 years, Brasschaat)

> But for the time being they don't get into power, and that is in my opinion the biggest flaw of democracy. That you say to a certain group: "You don't play along." I think that's unfair and undemocratic.
>
> (Retired sailor, 72 years, Brasschaat)

Racism or a violation of human rights are dismissed as legitimate motives for ostracizing the VB. The political cynicism of our respondents sees the quarantine as a dubious strategy to exclude political adversaries and thus the *cordon* perverts democracy. Although the VB is well-represented in legislative bodies across different tiers of government, this is deemed irrelevant by both party and supporters. The real goal is executive power: the winner should take it all. Since this aim is not reached, they think representative democracy functions in a repressive way and acts against the will of the people.

Elaborating the analytical figure, we add – because of the *cordon* – two arrows which stand for the rejection by the established parties, reinforcing the already existing reciprocal antagonisms. Consequently, these shared and reaffirmed oppositions result in a firmer alliance between the revolting protagonists – which is visualized as an equation (=) between the discontented and the populist party. Hence, a "chain of equivalence" develops via the imaginary community of "we, the people."

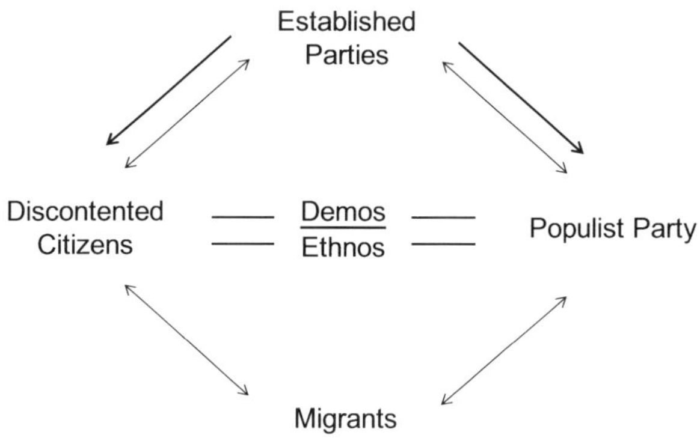

Figure 14.3 Populist axis

Ethno-populist framing: the VB electorate as the demos/ethnos

When faith in existing democratic institutions fades, respondents are in search of an alternative. To structure their worldview, the notion of "we, the people" proves pivotal. Seen as a homogenous and virtuous body, it gives leverage to the lonesome voter and the isolated party. This demos is sizeable and sovereign, which makes its cause justified, and as other parties mismanage the country, it has to find shelter with the VB. "We, the native people" indeed becomes the new denominator connecting people and party by giving substance to their coalition. Speaking on behalf of the demos/ethnos and rating high in the polls, the voters and party can counter the *cordon* and give their political aspirations an authoritative tone. Based on an ethno-populist framing, the "*vox populi*" appeals to the demos/ethnos and rejects, with one voice, the majority of the established parties and their murky politics based on compromise.

> They neglect, in fact, the voice of the people with this cordon sanitaire. They simply say: they are stupid because they vote for the VB. No, we are not stupid; we're wise and are with more people. They have to listen to us!
>
> (Unemployed man, 24 years, Moretusburg)

> Those who say out loud that they are democrats, they should examine the word and its meaning. Democracy is the will of the people. So if the people have a certain idea, a certain inclination, then policy has to follow. (. . .) Yet we are dictated here from all sides, we have to swallow all this, and that has to stop.
>
> (Self-employed woman, 49 years, Seefhoek)

Populism is at odds with the idea of a plural society in which a multitude of opinions and interests exist. It opposes a democracy that functions through concessions between multiple parties. The voice of the people is united and undivided, therefore compromises are unnecessary. In addition, the demos is reluctant to grant rights to minorities, as majority rule should naturally prevail (see Abts and Rummens 2007). Hence, we have a new political benchmark that delegitimizes the Belgian tradition of coalition governments. By invoking their conception of democracy populists strongly oppose brokered majorities; the winner of an election should not have to share power. These high expectations are not realistic, yet they do allow the VB to stay on the sideline of the political arena without making concessions. Populism can thus gain strength without having to share the unpopular responsibilities of governance. Hence the *cordon* paradoxically turns into an incubator.

Invoking the sovereignty of the people, populists prove single-minded democrats. Yet, democracy is a coin with two sides: it institutionalizes not only people's voice but also the rule of law (Abts and Rummens 2007; Canovan 1999; Urbinati 1998). The constitution of the liberal state protects human rights and minorities: it builds in "checks and balances" to protect citizens against the abuse of power. Based on past experiences this legal framework acts as a collective conscience to avoid today's opinion from relapsing into former mistakes that could endanger the future of democracy. Following populist reasoning, however, this historical balance of powers subdues the sovereignty of the demos, cherished by the populist party and its following.

A polarized political space: the populist axis vs. the axis of evil

In 2004 the VB becomes the largest party in Antwerp, yet because of the *cordon* it remains excluded from office. This "*coup d'état*" reveals the true nature of the antagonists. On the one hand we have the governing parties that are blind to the real problems, and deaf to those who complain. Hence the establishment no longer represents the population but places itself above the demos, while indulging in the privileges of officialdom. The political establishment is indeed seen as a superior scapegoat that has stolen the power of the people. On the other hand, there is the imaginary ethnos that opposes immigrants, and represents the native heartland and the neglected popular values of the VB voters. Disqualified as they are, they can only express their concerns through a party that is excluded in similar ways. Discontented citizens identify with the populist party because the enemy (VB) of their enemies (both scapegoats) turns out to be an ally. That makes three in a row: the misapprehended voice; the party-as-embodiment; and the demos/ethnos as nexus forging the horizontal, populist axis.

Deprived, powerless and bewildered, our respondents develop conspiracy theories trying to come to grips with a complex reality. By blaming superior and inferior scapegoats they can explain "why bad things happen to good people" (Groh 1987; Taguieff 2005). Thus, the populist imagination knows what is really happening – a complot – and people regain the sense that something can be done. Revealing as it is, the conspiracy theory can again unite and mobilize different voters. They indeed suspect that all the enemies of their ally – the VB – must be mutual friends who constitute "the axis of evil" that is orthogonally constructed to the populist axis of good. Hence, the horizontal populist axis is complemented with a vertical chain of equivalence where the political establishment and migrants plot together against the people. This presumed alliance is visualized through the vertical equation in Figure 14.4 that overrules the interests of "we, the people" and crosses their interests. This cross-shaped configuration brings the populist perceptions to a dramatic climax: the mobilization is massive and the electorate proves determined. Clearly, the power base of the populist party is consolidated.

According to the VB and its electorate, migrants constitute multiple threats. Yet the authorities do not react, neglect the problem, and therefore become accessory to the hardship people have to endure. People speak of complicity, treason and a breach of contract. They get the impression that migrants receive a preferential treatment while

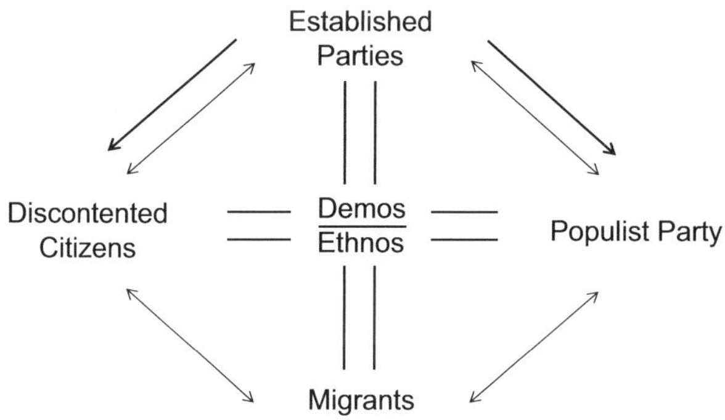

Figure 14.4 Axis of evil

native Belgians are sidelined. Politicians are not only lenient; they back and protect those undeserving outsiders.

> Migrants are spoiled and pampered. Yes, it goes without saying that they take advantage. But that is not because of those strangers, but because of the policy-makers.
>
> (Former entrepreneur, 76 years, Schoten)

> I'm disgusted, disgusted by these (immigrant-)hugging politicians. I intend to paint myself black and get curly hair . . . then I can do whatever. I think the hugging of migrants by our local authorities is sad and revolting. And what problems do they create? All sorts of problems!
>
> (Retired entrepreneur, 77 years, Deurne)

The positions of migrants and policy-makers are far apart, but both harm the people, and hence there must be some complicity. The migrant (*the inferior scapegoat*) threatens the settled positions of the in-group, while the unresponsive establishment (*the superior scapegoat*) favors the sake of these outsiders (Girard 1961). In this dual opposition, both scapegoats connect through a chain of equivalence that suspects a plot against the demos/ethnos. This is what we call "the axis of evil," where elites look for support and find mercenaries to reinforce their grip on power (compare Mudde 2007, 64–88). For this reason migrants are easily granted Belgian nationality, and even allowed to vote.

> Why do you think they protected those people so much; tolerating them and handing out entitlements? Because they were hoping that they would vote for them afterwards. And so they watered down our democracy (. . .) To get the votes, their only concern. Not for the public good, just to attract more votes.
>
> (Retired executive, 61 years, Brasschaat)

In this conspiracy we find politicians and migrants, yet also the media and the judicial system are involved. The press is considered far too critical towards the VB, and determined to stigmatize the party. Media neglect the opinion of the people since they have a hidden interest to please political elites. Judges are also part of the plot because in 2004 they convicted NGOs linked to the VB for racism.

> He who pays the piper, calls the tune. So, they are no longer honest, I have to say it as it is. That applies to all the press: they serve the government, they repeat their words.
>
> (Former entrepreneur, 76 years, Schoten)

> They are hand and glove. Who still believes the courts? There is no separation of powers, they are all politicized appointments, all judges are political appointments. And all say: the judicial system is independent; they say so on TV. . . But people know this – people are not stupid.
>
> (Retired executive, 61 years, Brasschaat)

By discrediting the court ruling as politically motivated and undemocratic, the VB and its supporters show again how little appreciation they have for the rule of law that institutes "checks and balances." The *vox populi* ought to supersede the legal jurisdiction of the state instead (Abts and Rummens 2007).

> When a million people think like that and share the same opinion, how can, for heaven's sake, a court say that this is against the law? In my opinion, there is something fundamentally wrong.
>
> (VB-mandatary, 30 years, Deurne)

Misapprehended and excluded, the discontent citizen retaliates by discrediting politicians as incompetent and corrupt. The establishment only stays in power because of abuses and plots, excluding the people they should represent. Equality and political participation are betrayed ideals; and so resentment is expressed – again, and this time with great indignation – by voting for the VB. Anger does not wane, and, up until 2004, it made the party's electorate quite loyal.

> They disregard democracy, and they think that this can be done without punishment.
>
> (Retired executive, 61 years, Brasschaat)

> The more they sideline the VB, the more votes they will get. They will be astonished.
>
> (Retired housewife, 64 years, Deurne)

However, since 2006 – after judiciary convictions, internal dissent and external competition – the VB lost much of its appeal. The alliance of both skeptical and convinced VB supporters (Abts 2012), forged during 20 years, largely fell apart since it was mainly based on circumstantial and therefore temporary alliances. Without a deep ideological core, and lacking a consistent community of interests, the VB always relied on a heterogenous electorate. The *cordon* long ensured that the VB could monopolize all protest votes, yet the rise of the New-Flemish Alliance (N-VA) as a nationalist substitute on the right put an end to the hegemony.

This decline does not invalidate our analysis; it actually confirms the importance of the political configuration. A new contender entered the field, the political opportunity structure changed, and the VB lost its dominant position because the N-VA rebranded the VB's ethno-populist message into a more civic and acceptable version. Yet, by opposing the dictates of the Belgian establishment and the usurping demands of the French-speaking parts of Belgium, the N-VA re-introduces new superior and inferior scapegoats. This frame formally reproduces the previous political configuration (Abts, Dalle-Mulle and Laermans 2016). Parties may come and go, but populism seems to be a sign of late modernity where political representation turns into an audience democracy – in Belgium and elsewhere. In a political realm no longer tightly structured by class alignments and ideological divides, populist mobilizations are a powerful alternative for people and parties to come together and join forces. Scapegoating will help them to find common ground and forge an identity.

Conclusion

In this chapter we showed how the populist radical right VB built up support through tapping into existing concerns and anxieties among the people of Antwerp. Growing resentment regarding the multicultural society and people's alienation from the traditional parties fed into discontent and populist attitudes. That these exist at the individual level has been shown already by several quantitative studies (see e.g. Hawkins, Riding and Mudde 2012; Akkerman, Mudde and Zaslove 2014; Van Hauwaert and Van Kessel 2018). Yet, populist attitudes are not given, nor can they be taken for granted. Our qualitative study provided a unique in-depth appraisal on how populist attitudes can contextually develop among "the people" themselves. Addressing the multicultural concerns and blaming the political elites for their unresponsiveness, the VB introduced a frame that subsequently strengthened and lent credence to these attitudes by successfully referring to the notion of "we, the common people." Populism is indeed an engaging idea that mobilizes lonely crowds and reconnects people and politics.

Yet, this powerful notion is not the authentic and genuine reality it pretends to be. The figures of our model demonstrate that it is rather a social construct that is gradually built by scapegoating migrants and politicians in an effort to give democracy back to the authentic ethnos/demos. As the introduction of the ideational approach central to this volume already stated, "the people" as an imaginary community are seen as homogenous and virtuous, and set against the unresponsive, self-serving and corrupt elite. This idea connects the voters and the frames of the populist party, which reinforce one another by opposing the contextual threats of both inferior and superior scapegoats. Hence "the people" as thin-centered signifier gives birth to an anti-political alliance through shared antagonistic perceptions that restructure the political configuration.

The apotheosis of this is a Manichean cosmology juxtaposing good and evil. Voters and party come together within a populist axis since they have to fight the axis of evil in which the political elite and the usurping outsiders plot against the discontented voters and the party by using a *cordon sanitaire*. "We, the people" is a uniting idea that results in a chain of equivalence, yet it is primarily based on a confrontational reconfiguration of the political arena. Inferior and superior scapegoats are the contextual threats through which, in the case of radical right-wing populism, ethnocentrism and political cynicism become the two sides of the same coin that constitutes the ethnos/demos as sole alternative. Looking at the interactions in which respondents position themselves and address others, it is clear to see that populist unity is based on division.

Future studies should clarify whether this model is also applicable in other countries, preferably by engaging in similar in-depth interviews with populist party supporters elsewhere. Listening to populist voters is essential, because their voice articulates a change of politics. Democracy proves to be a malleable idea indeed.

Notes

1 Wallonia and Flanders have their own party systems, and Walloon and Flemish parties also compete separately in federal elections.
2 Human perception is always selective. Making sense of the world, we filter information and according to the position, interests and cultural background, one and the same reality can be understood differently. Labeling the view of our respondents as a tunnel-vision (Rassin 2007) does not suggest that they are blind or retarded. They face reality but their focus is such that the surrounding, structural conditions – central to the sociological understanding – tend to disappear.
3 In the Netherlands the PRR Freedom Party gave parliamentary support to the centre-right government of Mark Rutte between 2010 and 2012. The party faced a loss in the subsequent election. The Austrian Freedom party entered a coalition government with the conservatives in 2000, but lost massively in the 2002 elections. Like moths, populist parties are attracted to power but they get easily burned by it. Both parties, however, recovered from their losses in the longer run.
4 A similar obstruction occurred in 2002 during the French presidential elections. Having beaten the socialists in the first round, Jean-Marie Le Pen, leader of the PRR *Front National* (FN), lost against the contender of the center-right (Jacques Chirac) in the second. Many votes for Chirac could be interpreted primarily as anti-Le Pen votes. Emmanuel Macron's victory in the presidential election of 2017 was also partly based on voters opposing the subsequent FN leader, Marine Le Pen.

References

Abts, Koen. 2012. "Maatschappelijk onbehagen en etnopopulisme: laatmoderniteit, burgers, ressentiment, migranten, politiek en Vlaams Belang stemgedrag." PhD diss., KULeuven.

Abts, Koen. 2015. "The cordon sanitaire vis-à-vis radical right: between pragmatic, affective and ideological positions." *Ethical Perspectives* 22(4): 667–698.

Abts, Koen, and Stefan Rummens. 2007. "Populism versus democracy." *Political Studies* 55(2): 405–424.

Abts, Koen, Stijn van Kessel, and Marc Swyngedouw. 2016. "A giant with feet of clay. A dynamic life cycle approach to the rise and fall of the Vlaams Belang." Paper presented at the ECPR General Conference, Prague, September 7–10.

Abts, Koen, Emmanuel Dalle-Mulle, and Rudi Laermans. 2016. "The multilayered appeal of N-VA's nationalism: the communitarization of economic, political and cultural cleavages." Paper presented at the International Political Science Association Conference, Poznan, July 23–28.

Akkerman, Agnes, Case Mudde, and Andrej Zaslove. 2014. "How Populist Are the People? Measuring Populist Attitudes in Voters." *Comparative Political Studies* 47(9): 1324–1353.

Arditi, Benjamin. 2003. "Populism, or politics at the edges of democracy." *Contemporary Politics* 9(1): 17–31.

Betz, Hans-Georg. 1994. *Radical right-wing populism in Western Europe*. New York: St. Martin's Press.

Bihr, Alain. 1998. *Le spectre de l'extrême droite: Les Français dans le miroir du Front National*. Paris: Les Éditions de l'Atelier.

Bihr, Alain. 1999. *L'actualité d'un archaïsme: La pensée d'extrême droite et la crise de la modernité*. Lausanne: Éditions Page Deux.

Billiet, Jaak, and Hans De Witte. 1995. "Attitudinal dispositions to vote for a 'new' extreme right-wing party: The case of 'Vlaams Blok'." *European Journal of Political Research* 27(2): 181–202.

Canovan, Margaret. 1999. "Trust the people! Populism and the two faces of democracy." *Political Studies* 47(1): 2–16.

Castel, Robert. 2003. *From manual workers to wage laborers: Transformation of the social question.* London: Transaction Publishers.

Decker, Frank. 2004. *Der neue Rechtspopulismus.* Opladen: Leske+Budrich.

Elias, Norbert, and John Scotson. 1965. *De gevestigden en de buitenstaanders: Een studie van de spanningen en machtsverhoudingen tussen twee arbeidersbuurten.* Utrecht: Het Spectrum.

Fitoussi, Jean-Paul, and Pierre Rosanvallon. 1996. *Le nouvel âge des inégalités.* Paris: Seuil.

Girard, René. 1961. *Mensonge romantique et vérité romanesque.* Paris: Bernard Grasset.

Gregory, Steven. 1998. *Black Corona: Race and the politics of place in an urban community.* New Jersey: Princeton University Press.

Groh, Dieter. 1987. "The temptation of conspiracy theory." In *Changing conceptions of conspiracy*, edited by Carl Graumann and Serge Moscovici, 1–38, New York: Springer Verlag.

Haegel, Florence. 2000. "L'expression xénophobe dans une cité de banlieue: le modèle de l'hospitalité dévoyé." In *La xénophobie en banlieue: Effets et expressions*, edited by Florence Haegel, Henri Rey and Yves Sintomer, 73–89, Paris: L'Harmattan.

Hartigan, John. 1999. *Racial situations: Class predicaments of whiteness in Detroit.* Princeton, NJ: Princeton University Press.

Hawkins, Kirk, Scott Riding, and Cas Mudde. 2012. "Measuring populist attitudes." Political Concepts Committee on Concepts and Methods Working Paper Series, 55: 1–35.

Karrer, Dieter. 2002. *Der Kampf um Integration: Zur Logik ethnischer Beziehungen in einem sozial benachteiligten Stadtteil.* Wiesbaden: Westdeutscher Verlag.

Kefalas, Maria. 2003. *Working-class heroes: Protecting home, community, and nation in a Chicago neighborhood.* Los Angeles, CA: University of California Press.

Kesteloot, Chris, and Pacal De Decker. 1992. "Territoria en migraties als geografische factoren van racisme." In *Gezichten van het hedendaags racisme*, edited by Els Deslé and Albert Martens, 69–108, Brussel: VUBPress.

Kochuyt, Thierry. 2015. "Force et faiblesse des médias sociaux dans le processus politique." In *La Rue et l'E-rue. Nouvelles contestations citoyennes*, edited by Petia Gueorguieva and Anna Krasteva, 45–58, Paris: L'Harmattan.

Kochuyt, Thierry and Koen Abts. 2017. *Ongehoord populisme: Gesprekken met Vlaams Belangkiezers over stad, migranten, welvaartsstaat, integratie en politiek.* Brussels: Academic and Scientific Publishers.

Krouwel, André, and Koen Abts. 2006. "Politiek cynisme: Voedingsbodem of creatuur van populisten?" In *Politiek cynisme*, edited by Paul Dekker, 99–118, Driebergen: Stichting Synthesis.

Laclau, Ernesto. 2005. *On populist reason.* London: Verso.

Mayer, Nonna. 1999. *Ces Français qui votent FN.* Paris: Flammarion.

Mouffe, Chantal. 2005. *On the political.* London: Routledge.

Mudde, Cas. 2007. *Populist radical right parties in Europe.* Cambridge: Cambridge University Press.

Pauwels, Teun. 2011. "Explaining the strange decline of the populist radical right Vlaams Belang in Belgium: the impact of permanent opposition." *Acta Politica* 46(1): 60–82.

Rassin, Eric. 2007. *Waarom ik altijd gelijk heb: over tunnelvisie.* Schiedam: Scriptum.

Rummens, Stefan, and Koen Abts. 2010. "Defending democracy: the concentric containment of political extremism." *Political Studies* 58(4): 649–65.

Schedler, Andreas. 1996. "Anti-political-establishment parties." *Party Politics* 2(3): 291–312.

Taguieff, Pierre-André. 2005. *La foire aux illuminés: Ésotérisme, théorie du complot, extrémisme.* Paris: Mille et une nuits.

Urbinati, Nadia. 1998. "Democracy and populism." *Constellations* 5(1): 110–24.

Van Hauwaert, Steven, and Stijn van Kessel. 2018. "Beyond protest and discontent. A cross-national analysis of the effect of populist attitudes and issue positions on populist party support." *European Journal of Political Research* 57(1): 68–92.

Van Kessel, Stijn. 2015. *Populist parties in Europe: Agents of discontent?* London: Palgrave Macmillan

Appendix

Description of respondents

Seefhoek

Female, aged 49, self-employed, university degree, married.

Female, aged 64, retired cleaner, primary school, single.

Male, aged 18, student, vocational secondary education (BSO), living with parents.

Male, aged 43, unemployed, lower technical secondary education (TSO), married.

Male, aged 46, unemployed, general secondary education (ASO), cohabiting.

Male, aged 66, retired municipal worker, primary school, married.

Male, aged 72, retired, general secondary education (ASO), married.

Moretusburg

Female, aged 41, worker, lower technical secondary education (TSO), cohabiting.

Female, aged 43, cleaner for the city of Antwerp, lower technical secondary education (TSO), married.

Male, aged 24, unemployed, technical secondary education (TSO), single.

Male, aged 44, professional soldier, general secondary education (ASO), cohabiting.

Male, aged 46, truck-driver, lower general secondary education (ASO), married.

Male, aged 85, retired worker, primary school, widower.

Deurne-East

Female, aged 49, unemployed, lower general secondary education (ASO), divorced.

Female, aged 64, retired housewife, primary school, married.

Male, aged 30, VB-parliamentary assistant, higher education (non-university), married.

Male, aged 32, dockworker, vocational secondary education (BSO), married.

Male, aged 41, clerk, university degree, married.

Male, aged 46, salesman, higher education (non-university), married.

Male, aged 77, retired entrepreneur, primary school, married.

Brasschaat

Female, aged 39, industrial worker, lower technical secondary education (TSO), single.

Female, aged 43, supermarket cashier, vocational secondary education (BSO), married.

Female, aged 46, housewife, university degree, married.

Female, aged 61, retired entrepreneur, lower general secondary education (ASO), married.

Female, aged 63, retired, general secondary education (ASO), married.

Female, aged 64, retired nurse + VB mandatary, higher education (non-university), widow.

Female, aged 67, retired nurse, higher education (non-university), married.

Male, aged 20, student, technical secondary education (TSO), living with parents.

Male, aged 37, doctor, university degree, divorced.

Male, aged 39, parliamentary assistant, university degree, married.

Male, aged 61, retired executive, university degree, married.

Male, aged 72, retired sailor, primary school, married.

Schoten

Male, aged 21, student, university, single.

Male, aged 26, student, university degree, cohabiting.

Male, aged 27, clerk, general secondary education (ASO), single.

Male, aged 43, clerk in harbor, lower general secondary education (ASO), married.

Male, aged 76, retired entrepreneur, lower technical secondary education (TSO), married.

15 Populism in the US

The evolution of the Trump constituency

Wendy Rahn

The development of ideational theory has brought conceptual rigor to the study of the populist ideas and the leaders who purport to speak in the name of "the people." As a consequence, analysts have made considerable empirical progress in charting the ebbs and flows of populist discourse in a given context. In the US case, for example, Bonikowski and Gidron (2016), drawing on ideational theory and using computer-assisted text analysis, code the degree of populism expressed by the presidential nominees of the two major political parties in the elections of 1952 through 1996. They find that the language of challengers, political outsiders, and Republicans was more likely to be populist than that of incumbents, political careerists and Democrats.

Ideational theory has also contributed to measuring the demand side of populism. Surveys in a variety of national contexts indicate that large proportions of the mass public subscribe to the tenets of populism, and that these attitudes can be activated by the political context and affect electoral choices. However, unlike temporal studies of populist supply like those of Bonkowski and Gidron (2016) or Deegan-Krause and Haughton's (2009) in Slovakian case, the work on populist attitudes largely has been cross-sectional in nature. Despite clear theoretical expectations that representational crises provoke widespread populist sentiment, it is not at all clear that populist demand responds to such system-level variables in the ways that theory predicts (but see chapters by Andreadis et al. and Bornschier in this volume) or that the success of populist forces can be attributed to such representational failures as mediated through populist attitudes.

Using the improbable triumph of Donald J. Trump's presidential bid as its focus, this chapter adopts a more dynamic approach to populist demand using a variety of survey data sources. I first document that, by 2014, a large "Representation Gap" had emerged in the American electorate, a gap that appears closely related to high levels of post-9/11 partisan conflict in the US Congress. I then, in the words Ross Perot, another populist politician, "look under the hood" to show that the basis for this upsurge in political discontent had shifted in ways that prefigured Trump's ultimately winning coalition of white, working-class voters. Not only was his constituency in place months before he began to shake up the political establishment, so too were their concerns about economic opportunity in America and their unease with immigration and the changing face of American society. Trump articulated these grievances, to be sure, but populist attitudes already implicated them before his emergence. As I demonstrate, these populist sentiments in turn were strongly correlated with preferences for Trump during the Republican nominating process. These preferences, abetted by the inability of Republican Party elites to come together around an acceptable alternative, likely were responsible for Trump's capture of the nomination. Finally, I use the 2016 American National Election Studies to show that

Trump indeed got more support than his rival, Democrat Hillary Clinton, from people who believed that the political system was unresponsive to their needs. I conclude, therefore, that the perfect storm that is a populist moment — "the right rhetoric spoken by the right person to the right audience at the right time" (Oliver and Rahn 2016) – did indeed rain down on the American polity in 2016.

Why populism now?

Historical accounts of populism in the United States naturally gravitate toward the leaders who talk in populist ways. Vintage populists, such as "Pitchfork Ben" Tillman, Ignatius Donnelly, Mary Lease, William Jennings Bryan, and Tom Watson, denounced bankers, railroads, English capitalists, and corrupt politicians as enemies of the people. Their fiery discourse drew on the Jeffersonian ethic of producerism, a notion vague and capacious enough to submerge regional and economic differences among farmers, wage earners, artisans, and small merchants (Kazin 1995). A unifying vocabulary of evangelical Protestantism (Kazin 1995; Williams and Alexander 1994) and popular nationalism (Gerteis and Goolsby 2005) provided additional rhetorical tools to construct a homogenous moral community, a "people" engaged in a righteous battle against its oppressors.

The People's Party failed as a political movement, but its distinctive discursive strategy remains intact. At various times in American political history, others have drawn on its rich legacy to pursue their own political ambitions. Depicting themselves as "outsiders" who can take on the ruling class in the name of the people, and thereby restore the rightful democratic order, a number of political aspirants in US politics have reached into the populist repertoire to fuel their own desires for public office. Colorful personas, plain talk, and unusual political pedigrees frequently accompanied their deployment of the populist patois, further bolstering their claims to be the people's champion.

Given the idiosyncratic and often fleeting appearance of populism in US political history, scholars have struggled with understanding its timing. Why was 2016 in the United States such a ripe time for a populist appeal? Although there is plenty of speculation as to what motivates popular populist movements (economic conditions, class stratification, new media technologies, etc.), according to ideational theory, populism often originates in a political source, namely, when democratic institutions, and, especially, the elites who wield power in them, fail to meet citizens' expectations for responsiveness (editors' Introduction). The more voters who came to believe that existing political arrangements betray their interests, the larger the gap between democratic hopes and the disappointments of reality becomes; accordingly, the political opportunity for would-be populist entrepreneurs expands under such conditions (Oliver and Rahn 2016). In the language of economics, when the demand curve for populism shifts to the right, populist leaders should receive a better "price" for their messages at given level of supply.[1]

Eric Oliver and I have developed a measure of the demand for populism in the US public that we have formalized as the concept of the Representation Gap (Oliver and Rahn 2016). The Representation Gap can be thought of as the system-level manifestation of the "anti-elite" dimension of populist attitudes measured in individual-level surveys (see Chapters 6 and 7 by Castanho Silva et al. and Van Hauwaert, Schimpf, and Azevedo, this volume). It takes into account that, while populist attitudes may be present to some degree across all democratic political systems, *within* an individual country over time it is possible that populist attitudes will be more or less widespread depending on the responsiveness of the political system. As Marty Gilens (2012) has shown in the US context, the American public's policy preferences have been better reflected in political outcomes during certain periods more so than in others. Larry Bartels (2016a) also has shown that partisan control of government affects which groups of people in the US receive representation. Each of these works implies that political responsiveness is dynamic; as such, we should expect that the Representation Gap moves with changes in political context.

Our measure takes advantage of the dyad-ratios algorithm developed by political scientist James Stimson to track, using different survey questions, macro "policy mood," the public's relative preference for liberal or conservative government policy across time (Stimson 1991). Figure 15.1 displays the Representation Gap as measured in this way using a variety of differently worded survey questions about government responsiveness (see Oliver and Rahn, 2016, for details of its construction).

The Representation Gap has two obvious peaks, one at the end of the series and the other, in the middle 1990s, a time path that does not correspond with any economic indicator as far as we could tell, and we examined many. There are, however, several striking social and political parallels in these two periods (see Oliver and Rahn 2016), the most important of which, for this purpose of this chapter, is the sizable correlation (r = .72) between levels of party polarization in Congress (as measured by the percentage of party unity votes, those votes where a majority of Republicans oppose a majority of Democrats) and the size of the Representation Gap. No other variable even comes close to matching the trajectory in Figure 15.1.

The strong correspondence between party polarization and the size of the Representation Gap is consistent with the ideational argument that, in developed countries, populist demand is more likely to emerge when political "parties became ideologically distinct from their voters (see Introduction)." In the case of the United States, however, it is party

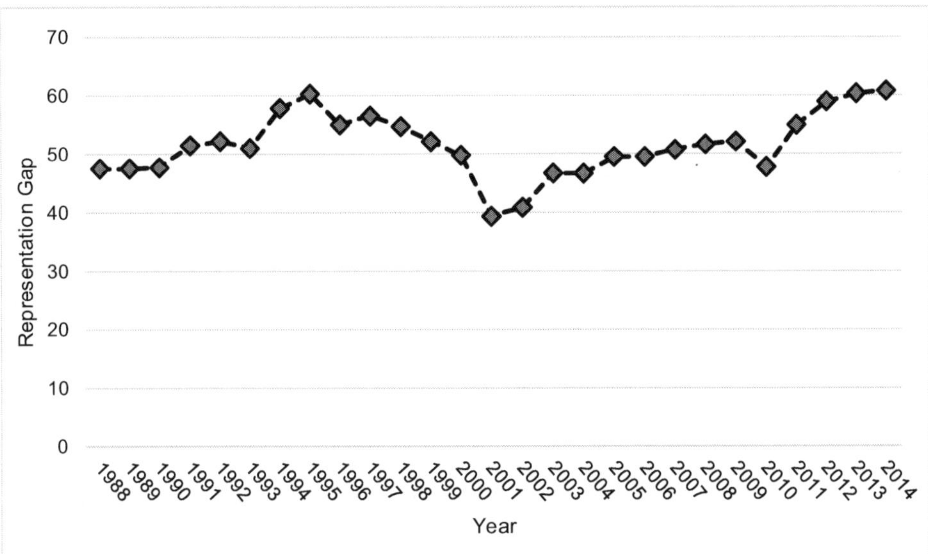

Figure 15.1 The Representation Gap, 1988–2014

Source: Oliver and Rahn (2016)

divergence rather than party convergence that is constraining the ability of political actors to be responsive to the "average American" who is largely a centrist. A variety of scholars in recent years have demonstrated that partisan polarization in the US skews the behavior of political elites in ways that reduce electoral accountability (e.g. Ansolabehere, Snyder, and Stewart 2001; Bartels 2016b; Bafumi and Herron 2010; Egan 2013; Rogers 2017) and lowers voter turnout (Rogowksi 2014). The analysis here complements that work by demonstrating that failures in democratic representation provoke a response in citizens in ways that could open the door to populist politicians.

Populist attitudes on the eve of Trump: evidence from the General Social Survey

As a macro concept, the Representation Gap tells us something about how the level of populist demand is changing in the American public, but it cannot tell us *who* comprises the potential constituency for populist appeals. We know from Figure 15.1 that this constituency in the US, circa 2015, was bigger than in previous twenty-first-century presidential elections. Can we learn something about the sorts of people who might have been receptive to populist messages as the 2016 presidential hopefuls began to hit the campaign trail?

An affirmative answer is possible, courtesy of the General Social Survey (GSS), a probability sample, in-person interview that has been conducted annually or biennially for over four decades by the National Opinion Research Center. The typical GSS survey consists of a common core of demographic, behavioral, and attitudinal variables as well as special topic modules on a variety of different subjects. Many of such topic modules stem from the GSS's participation in the International Social Survey Programme (ISSP). The ISSP has developed a rotating list of topical modules on such subjects as religion, the environment, and social inequality, modules administered as part of national surveys in dozens of countries. For the purposes of this chapter, I make use of the ISSP module on "Citizenship" that was included as part of the GSS in 2004 and 2014. These years mark the beginning of the rise in the Representation Gap post 9/11, as registered in Figure 15.1, and its peak at the end of the series. The citizenship module contains several questions suitable for measuring the anti-elitism aspect of populist attitudes, and they are like the questions comprising the measure of the Representation Gap. The citizenship module was administered to approximately half of the GSS samples in each of the two years (ns = 1472 and 1242, respectively).

After inspecting item distributions and inter-item correlations on several potential questions in the ISSP citizenship module, I selected the following five questions in the two GSS survey years to construct the dependent variable of interest.

- **Serve the people** Thinking of government administrators in America, how committed are they to serve the people? Very committed, somewhat committed, not very committed or not at all committed?
- **Government doesn't care** To what extent do you agree or disagree with the following statements? I don't think the government cares much what people like me think. Strongly agree, agree, neither agree nor disagree, disagree, strongly disagree.
- **Trust people in government** To what extent do you agree or disagree with the following statements? Most of the time we can trust people in the government to do what is right. Strongly agree, agree, neither agree nor disagree, disagree, strongly disagree.

- **Self-interested politicians.** To what extent do you agree or disagree with the following statements? Most politicians are in politics only for what they can get out of it personally. Strongly agree, agree, neither agree nor disagree, disagree, strongly disagree.
- **Government corruption** How widespread do you think corruption is in the public service in America? Hardly anyone is involved, a small number of people are involved, a moderate number of people are involved, a lot of people are involved, or almost everyone is involved.

The GSS questions have as their focus governmental elites. Given their specificity, I will refer to the attitude scale resulting from their combination as anti-elitism (AE). While these items did not cover all of the conceptual terrain of populist attitudes as identified by Castanho Silva and colleagues in Chapter 7 of this volume (see also Schulz et al. 2017), the fact that they are repeated allows me to assess at the individual level whether beliefs about the quality of political representation in the US deteriorated over time and for which groups of voters they did so. The latter is especially attractive, as it helps to identify the constituency with the most populist potential. Later in the chapter, I make use of other surveys whose questions are a bit more diverse and capture additional aspects of populist ideas. I will call scales built from them populist attitudes (PA).

I recoded the GSS items to have a 0–1 range with higher values indicating more negative assessments of government and public officials. The reliability of the AE scale (Cronbach's alpha) was virtually identical in 2004 and 2014, .74 and .75 respectively, with a standard deviation of .18 and .19. However, American attitudes at the individual level became more hostile toward the political establishment in the decade that separated survey administrations, as we would expect from the marco-level dynamics of the Representation Gap in Figure 15.1. In 2004, for example, three out of every four people thought government administrators were committed to serving the American people. Between 2004 and 2014, such positive sentiments declined by nearly 15 points. The AE scale mean rose from .51 to .58, not quite half a standard deviation, between 2004 and 2014.

Who are the anti-elitists?

As repeated cross-sections, the two GSS surveys allow me to explore whether the demographic correlates of anti-establishment attitudes were stable or changing. Did the same groups simply become more populist, or, did the change in politico-economic context between 2004 and 2014, such as the party controlling the White House or the fallout from the Great Recession, reshuffle the basis for anti-elite sentiments? To find out, I regressed AE in each year on the same set of demographic characteristics: age, sex, race, education, community type, and social class self-identification.[2] I also included individuals' party identification, as it is well established in the American politics literature that people tend to think more highly of government and politicians when their party controls the presidency. In fact, in recent years, partisan identity even more sharply demarcates public opinion about government owing to the increased polarization of party elites (Hetherington and Rudolph 2015).

Table 15.1 reports the results of regression models run on AE using these variables.[3] The third column in the table presents the difference in the size of the coefficients across years (2014–2004) and whether or not the difference is statistically significant.

Table 15.1 Anti-elitism in the American public, 2004 and 2014

	2004	*2014*	*Difference (2014–2004)*
Republican	−0.081**	0.025	0.106**
	(0.015)	(0.017)	
Democrat	−0.027	−0.021	0.006
	(0.015)	(0.016)	
Age	0.0005	−0.0002	−0.001
	(0.0003)	(0.0003)	
Male	−0.009	0.017	0.026
	(0.010)	(0.012)	
White	0.024	0.065**	0.041
	(0.023)	(0.020)	
Black	0.073**	0.006	−0.067**
	(0.025)	(0.023)	
Less than high school	0.122**	0.077**	−0.045
	(0.024)	(0.023)	
High school grad	0.094**	0.043**	−0.051
	(0.019)	(0.018)	
Junior college	0.027	0.040	0.013
	(0.024)	(0.027)	
College degree	0.023	0.015	−0.008
	(0.019)	(0.021)	
Lower class	0.068**	0.111**	0.043
	(0.022)	(0.023)	
Working class	0.010	0.056*	0.046**
	(0.012)	(0.013)	
Smaller metro area	0.026	0.007	−0.019
	(0.026)	(0.020)	
Larger suburbs	−0.004	0.020	0.016
	(0.023)	(0.021)	
Smaller suburbs	−0.027	0.002	0.029
	(0.022)	(0.020)	
Other urban	−0.002	0.015	0.017
	(0.020)	(0.019)	
Rural	0.025	0.046*	0.021
	(0.025)	(0.022)	
Constant	0.441**	0.456**	
	(0.030)	(0.031)	
R^2	0.147	0.097	
N	1400	1234	

*p ≤ .05 **p ≤ .01, two-tailed

I begin with a comparison of the effects of party identification. In 2004, an election year, the American public had become deeply divided in its evaluations of the sitting President, George Bush, as well as over issues such as the right of gay couples to marry. The Republican Party had picked up House and Senate seats in the 2002 midterms and controlled both branches of Congress. Not surprisingly, Republicans had less negative assessments of government elites than those without a partisan leaning or

Democrats. Interestingly, AE attitudes of Democrats did not significantly improve in 2014 even when one of their own, Barack Obama, occupied the Oval Office, perhaps because of a divided government. After losing control of the House of Representatives in 2006, the Republicans retook it after the 2010 midterms and the Democrats lacked a filibuster-proof majority in the Senate (and would lose the Senate in the 2014 election cycle). Consequently, Congressional Republicans were able to thwart most of President Obama's second-term agenda. On the other hand, having a Democrat occupy the White House made a huge difference to Republican identifiers in the mass public. AE levels rose 16% among GOP supporters, almost a full standard deviation. Independents, who were more dissatisfied than partisans of either strip in 2004, were indistinguishable from Republicans or Democrats a decade later. The steep increase in political disaffection among Republicans and the lack of change among Democrats rendered partisanship a non-factor in explaining AE in 2014. The high levels of AE and its partisan agnosticism in 2014 suggests that there was political room for populist entrepreneurs to emerge anywhere along the ideological spectrum; that is, the "host ideology" for populism was up for grabs.

Turning to the demographic variables in Table 15.1, a comparison of the effects of race in the two periods indicates that the first African-American president brought about a reversal in the relative positions of Blacks and whites in the electorate in levels of AE. Between 2004 and 2014, African-Americans experienced a significant decline in levels of AE whereas levels among whites had increased enough that, by 2014, their levels of AE exceed those of people of color, one clue, perhaps, that a racialized construction of a populist people had some potential. As noted by Michael Tesler and others (Schaffner, MacWilliams, and Nteta 2016; Tesler 2016; Tesler and Sides 2016), racial resentment among whites played an outsize role in shaping support for Trump during the campaign.

Exits polls revealed additional demographic bases for his winning coalition; in particular, his voters tended to hail from rural areas and to be less well-educated, the latter often characterized as "working class." It is therefore interesting to note that type of community was unrelated to AE in 2004. By 2014, however, rural residents were significantly more disgruntled than were their urban cousins. Although the difference between the magnitudes of the rural coefficient is not significant, its larger size in the last survey may indicate that rural consciousness (Cramer 2016) was feeding into greater displeasure with governing elites leading into the 2016 election.

On the other hand, and seemingly inconsistent with the popular accounts of Trump's victory, we see in Table 15.1 that the influence of education in 2014 is muted in comparison to 2004. Although people with no college experience (compared to post-college graduates) are more likely to hold populist attitudes at both times, the magnitudes of most of the education coefficients in 2014 are about half their 2004 size. Social class, on the other hand, becomes more important in shaping AE. In 2004, distinctions between the middle and the working class are blurred – the coefficient for the working class (compared to the middle class), while positive, is small and clearly insignificant. In 2014, however, people who identified as working class had become significantly more attracted to populist ideas than their middle-class counterparts had. The impact of membership in the working class, in fact, is five times what it was in 2004, and the coefficient on the lower-class category almost doubles.

A shift in the proportion of people claiming working-class status accompanied the larger imprint of social class on AE. In 2004, a near majority of Americans (49%) declared a middle class identity; by 2014, more people (47%) saw themselves as working class rather than middle class (42%). Moreover, a cross-tabulation of education by social-class identity reveals not only that more people identified as working class in the later survey, but, among those with less than a college degree, more saw themselves as belonging to the working class in 2014 than in 2004. For example, among people with some college experience, but not a degree, about half saw themselves as working class in 2004. In 2014, the proportion had risen to 62%. Thus, while education level is a handy journalistic shortcut for talking about class in American, equating the two may obscure interesting processes in the dynamics of class consciousness (Gest 2016).

What do anti-elitists want?

Thus far, I have demonstrated that dissatisfaction with America's governing class not only grew between 2004 and 2014, but its demographic patterning foreshadows the electoral forces that propelled Donald Trump into the Oval Office. In this section, I delve more deeply into the specific grievances that animated his ultimately winning coalition of rural, white, working-class voters.

My finding that class identification, even controlling for educational levels, is an independent predictor of AE in 2014 runs against commonly held ideas about the (ir)relevance of class consciousness in American public opinion. Class stratification in the US is thought to be much weaker than in other industrialized democracies for myriad reasons: the absence of a feudal past, weaker unions, a fragmented political system, and the stubborn persistence of belief in social mobility and the American Dream (Abramowitz and Teixeira 2009; Lipset 1996; Manza and Brooks 2014; Rank, Hirschl, and Foster 2014).

In the aftermath of the Great Recession, however, a number of economists began documenting that the conditions that made the American Dream possible for many were eroding: the American economy was no longer a ship that floated all boats. A leading explanation for Trump's appeal to the white working class points to these structural changes. One such development was the spectacular rise in income inequality over the last three decades, a trend the Great Recession only accelerated. Income growth rates by income group also showed remarkable disparity. The average income of the bottom half barely budged and that of the middle class rose only 42%, whereas for the top 10% it increased 121%, and for the top 1%, it tripled (Piketty, Saez, and Zucman 2016).

While not the only explanation for rising income inequality in the US and in other developed economies, global trade is certainly a suspect. According to the "globalization losers" thesis, the gains from an increasingly globalized economy accrued to a growing middle class in the developing world, especially China, and to the very rich in developed countries. "The 'losers' were predominantly the people who in their [developed] countries belong to the lower halves of national income distributions" (Milanovic 2016).

The publication in 2014 of Thomas Piketty's *Capital in the Twenty-First Century* catapulted the subject of economic inequality to center stage worldwide, but beneath the headline were several other unsettling trends in the United States regarding the prospects for people in "the other 99%." Raj Chetty and colleagues (2017) finds that rates of absolute income mobility – the fraction of children who earn more than their parents did – have fallen sharply since the 1940s, especially in the industrial Midwest. The "earnings gap" between full-time workers with and without college degrees doubled between 1979 and 2012, due largely to the increased premium placed on cognitive skills (Autor 2014). Disconcertingly, these economic changes occurred over the same period that average life expectancy of middle-aged whites was declining. The higher mortality rate in this group appears to result from the increased incidence of "diseases of despair," such as drug addiction, chronic pain or alcoholism (Case and Deaton 2015). On the other hand, during the same time, mortality rates among African-Americans declined sharply (Case and Deaton 2017).

There is evidence in the GSS that awareness about these trends had diffused beyond academic circles. The GSS asks a question that captures well the national narrative about hard work, success, and upward mobility: *The way things are in America, people like me and my family have a good chance of improving our standard of living. Do you agree or disagree?* Figure 15.2 displays the proportion, in each survey year, agreeing or disagreeing with the statement. In both years, considerably more people were optimistic than were pessimistic about their prospects. Nevertheless, there is an obvious decline in Figure 15.2 in positive beliefs about economic mobility and a smaller uptick in the number of respondents who were more downbeat. The American Dream, apparently, had lost a little bit of its luster.

A subsample of the 2014 GSS survey received both the American Dream and the AE items on the same ballot. Unfortunately, in the 2004 GSS there is no overlap between the two sets of questions, so no overtime comparison is possible. It seems worthwhile, nonetheless, to look at the relationship between populist sentiment and expectations regarding economic mobility in the most recent survey. Several studies of candidate preference in 2016 indicate that Trump supporters, while not currently hard pressed economically, were more anxious about their and the nation's economic prospects than were supporters of his Republican rivals or his general election opponent (Gest 2016; Oliver and Rahn 2016; Schaffner, MacWilliams, and Nteta 2016), and, as already noted, exit polls indicated greater Trump allegiance among more economically marginalized whites.

I regressed the AE scale on the GSS standard-of-living question (recoded to have a 0–1 range with higher values indicating more disillusion), along with all the independent variables in Table 15.1. Table 15.2 displays the results. We see there that lack of confidence

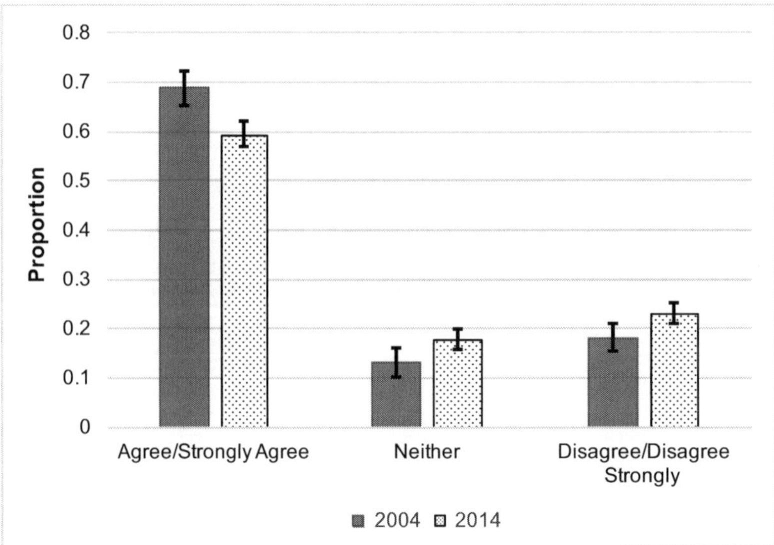

Figure 15.2 Belief in the American Dream, 2004 and 2014 GSS

Source: 2004 and 2014 General Social Survey

in the American Dream is powerfully associated with feelings of political disaffection. People with more pessimistic (optimistic) views are substantially more (less) likely to express negative sentiment about politicians and the government. The most optimistic differ from the most pessimistic by more than one standard deviation of the AE scale.

Table 15.2 Anti-elitism and belief in the American Dream, 2014 GSS

	Anti-elitism, 2014
American Dream	0.215**
	(0.030)
Republican	0.005
	(0.020)
Democrat	–0.023
	(0.019)
Age	–0.0008
	(0.0004)
Male	0.025
	(0.014)
White	0.029
	(0.024)
Black	–0.028
	(0.029)
Less than high school	0.074**
	(0.028)
High school grad	0.043*
	(0.022)
Some college	0.029
	(0.032)
College degree	0.038
	(0.026)
Lower class	0.063
	(0.029)
Working class	0.045*
	(0.018)
Smaller metro areas	–0.012
	(0.025)
Larger suburbs	–0.003
	(0.024)
Smaller suburbs	0.002
	(0.024)
Other urban	0.005
	(0.023)
Rural	0.021
	(0.028)
Constant	0.661**
	(0.052)
R^2	0.168
N	816

*p ≤ .05 **p ≤.01, two-tailed

Moreover, beliefs about the American dream mediate some of the impact of the important demographic variables (e.g., being white or rural residence) shaping AE in the first place, although people at the lower end of the status hierarchy are still significantly more populist even controlling for their views on economic advancement.[4]

In summary, working-class Americans' loss of faith in the American Dream had ample justification. Analyses of 2016 election returns, in fact, shows communities of hard-pressed Americans were more attracted to Trump, perhaps because of his populist messaging. Autor and co-authors (2017) show that in areas hard hit by Chinese import competition, Trump did especially well. His trade protectionist platform, therefore, aligned with these voters' lived experience. Jed Kolko (2016) finds that Trump improved on Mitt Romney's performance in the 2012 presidential election in counties "where unemployment was higher, job growth was slower and earnings were lower." Ben Casselman (2017) notes other economic correlates of Trump's vote share at the county-level: lower credits scores, lower labor-force participation rates among men, more subprime loans, and more residents receiving disability payments. For many Americans, their reality and those of their neighbors no longer matches the uplifting rhetoric of the national imaginary. No wonder Trump's slogan, "Make America Great Again," proved resonant. With trust in the governing class at low ebb and with nothing much to lose, less well-off Americans may have been ready to take a political risk.

Another leading explanation for Trump's strong showing among the white working class downplays the significance of economic grievances, instead stressing cultural backlash against the growing presence of immigrants in American society (e.g., Tesler 2015; Inglehart and Norris 2016), much as nativism has been integral to the appeal of the populist right in Europe (Mudde 2010; Rooduijn 2014).[5] Hostility toward immigrants, however, is nothing new in the annals of American populism. Throughout its history, various constructions of "the people" were built on the edifice of the nation; "the people" were imagined as belonging to a territorially bounded community and to share a common way of life that transcended their differences. Although not remembered as such, even the original Populists were nativists (Gerteis and Goolsby 2005: Kazin 1995; Postel 2007): The Omaha Platform of 1892, for example, contained a resolution calling for a ban on Chinese contract workers, along with progressive planks advocating for the nationalization of the railroads, the establishment of postal savings banks, and an eight-hour workday, among other things.

Although many Americans share a foundational myth that the US is a "nation of immigrants," there are many reasons to think that unhappiness with US immigration policy could have been a factor in the rising political discontent documented in the GSS analysis. Efforts by congressional leaders in both political parties to pass comprehensive immigration reform failed repeatedly between 2006 and 2013, prompting several states and localities to take matters into their own hands and the President to issue an executive order in 2012 to create the Deferred Action for Childhood Arrivals (DACA) program. In the summer of 2014, as the GSS was in the field, the US experienced an immigration crisis at the US–Mexico border when thousands of children fleeing violence in Central America, many of whom were unaccompanied by adults, were detained. The crisis stirred several demonstrations and counter-demonstrations across the country with polls indicating that a majority of Americans disapproved of the President's handling of the situation.

A year later, Trump notoriously claimed in his announcement speech that Mexico was "killing us economically," and, sounding just like the Populists of yore,[6] he further averred that when it "sends its people, they're not sending their best . . .They're sending people that have a lot of problems, and they're bringing those with them. They're bringing drugs. They're bringing crime. They're rapists" (*Time* 2015). Trump combined his anti-immigrant rhetoric with an equally ferocious attack on political elites, claiming that they were stupid, morally corrupt, controlled by lobbyists, and were "selling [the] country down the drain." In an immigration policy speech in Phoenix, AZ, in September 2016, Trump blamed "wealthy donors, political activists, and powerful, powerful politicians" (*New York Times* 2016) for the problems in the country's immigration system. Failure to secure the borders meant lower wages for the "forgotten working people," and cost "innocent Americans" their lives. Only the wholesale replacement of the Washington establishment and the building of an "impenetrable, physical, tall, power [sic], beautiful southern border wall" (ibid.) could bring an end to the "quagmire." In the end, Trump won 64% of the voters who told exit pollsters that immigration was the most important issue facing the country and fully 86% of those who supported building a wall.

The GSS contains a core question asking respondents whether they think the number of immigrants to the country should be increased, decreased, or kept the same. Therefore, I can examine whether the public also combined hostility toward immigrants with its critique of the political status quo. Figure 15.3 plots mean values of AE by these responses in each survey year. Among those who favor an increase in immigration, sentiments were unchanged. However, both those who opted for continuity and those who wished to see levels cut back expressed more AE in 2014 compared to 2004.

I regressed levels of AE in each year on the independent variables in Table 15.1 and the immigration question. Table 15.3 presents their coefficients and compares their magnitude. In each year, immigration restrictionists are also more populist. However, in 2014, the coefficient is twice its 2004 size and the difference is statistically significantly. Trump's evocative imagery of an unassailable wall between the US and Mexico merely rendered concrete, so to speak, a connection between nativism and populist attitudes forged already in public's mind.

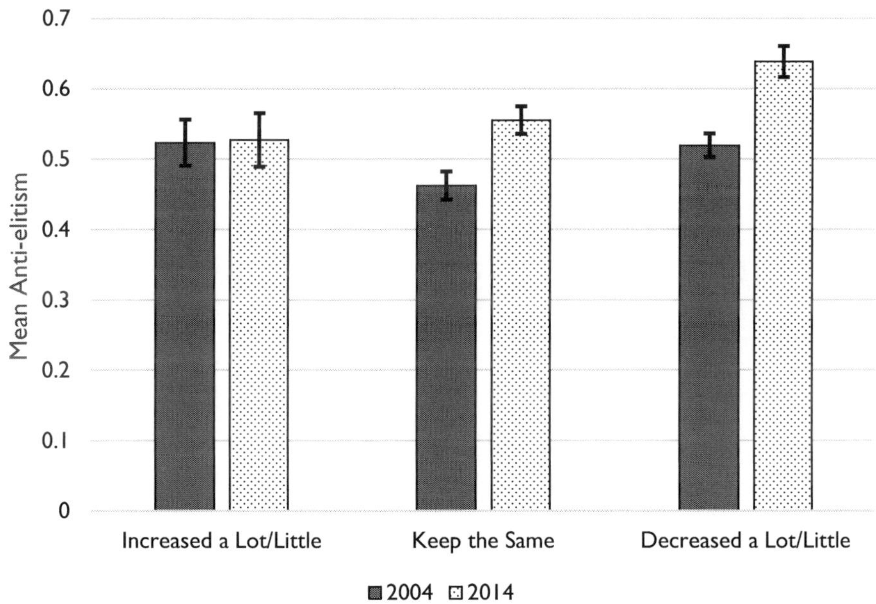

Figure 15.3 Anti-elitism by immigration attitudes, 2004 and 2014 GSS

Source: 2004 and 2014 General Social Survey

Table 15.3 Anti-elitism and immigration, 2004 and 2014

	2004	*2014*	*Difference*
Immigration levels	0.075**	0.153**	.078*
	(0.024)	(0.027)	
R^2	.154	.133	
N	1063	813	

Note: Models include the variables in Table 15.1
* p ≤ .05 ** p ≤.01, two-tailed

Table 15.4 Immigration, the American Dream, and anti-elitism in the 2014 GSS

	Anti-elitism
Immigration levels	0.132**
	(0.027)
American Dream	0.220**
	(0.036)
R^2	0.133
N	411

Note: Model contains variables in Table 15.1
*p ≤ .05 **p ≤ .01, two-tailed

Finally, before leaving 2014 behind for a more contemporary analysis, in Table 15.4, I examine the joint impact of economic disillusion and immigration on anti-elitism while including all the variables in Table 15.1. Only partial overlap among the key variables reduces the number of cases available for analysis by half; nonetheless, I find that both variables are strongly and significantly related to levels of AE, and their coefficients are little changed by the inclusion of the other variable. A focus on populist attitudes, therefore, reconciles the two contending master narratives (Hochschild 2016) about Trump's eventual victory. It is not a question of whether his support came from voters motivated primarily by economic dislocation *or* by cultural grievances. Each contributed independently to the sense that political elites were only interested in themselves rather than the fates of ordinary Americans.[7]

Populist attitudes and the 2016 Republican primaries

As discussed by Andreadis et al. in Chapter 10 of this volume, the ideational account specifies three necessary conditions for the electoral expression of populist attitudes. First, the context must be such that many people perceive breakdowns in the process of democratic representation. This renders populist claims of elite failure credible and makes people receptive to calls for political change. We saw in the previous sections that at both the macro- and micro-levels, Americans were unhappy with existing political arrangements. The timing appears to have been "right" for a populist moment.

Second, the populist has to be the "right person," someone not entrenched in the governing class. Features of the aspiring candidate's biography typically support the assertion of non-elite status. For example, despite their enormous wealth, the two most successful presidential populists in recent memory, Texas billionaire Ross Perot, whose third-party candidacy in 1992 received 20% of the popular vote, and real-estate mogul and 2016 victor, Donald Trump, earned their "outsider" pedigrees in part by claiming that their vast fortunes insulated them from the influence of special interests.

Finally, a populist's appeals must be embedded within a larger political project, a "host ideology" that provides the vessel for carrying the populist's water. As a flexible discourse, populism grafts easily onto different policy platforms, typically described as either left wing or right wing.[8] As the political parties engaged in selecting their standard-bearers for the 2016 presidential race, two candidates, one Republican, the other, nominally a Democrat, emerged as having the right rhetoric (Oliver and Rahn 2016; Hawkins 2016), the requisite qualifications as political outsiders, and a distinct political program, Donald Trump and Bernie Sanders, respectively. Political observers judged them both as having little chance to secure their party nominations. *Politico*, for example, described Trump's quest as "quixotic," and the *New York Times* called Sanders a "longshot."

These two men, so markedly different in their political visions, epitomize the ambidexterity of the populist idiom. Senator Bernie Sanders, a self-declared Socialist, spliced his populist message unto a progressive economic and cultural agenda, and challenged the Democratic heir-apparent, Hillary Clinton, to her left. His forces, known as "Berners," ultimately lost their fight with the Democratic Party establishment, not unlike other insurgents before him – Estes Kefauver in 1952, Pat Buchanan in 1996, and Howard Dean in 2004, for example – whose ambitions were stymied because party insiders coalesced around a more acceptable (to the party) candidate.

> Clinton may not have been the most charismatic or the most in tune with every voter's aspirations, but the support of regular party players was, as the Sanders faction loudly complained, critical to her ability to notch a win anyway.
>
> (Cohen, Karol, Noel, Zaller 2016: 703)

On the other hand, Donald Trump's populism appeared not to have a host ideology if defined by the conventional left-right economic axis. Spurned by virtually the entire Republican establishment for his unorthodox (for a Republican) platform (Noel 2016; Bycoffe 2016), the political scientists Doug Ahler and David Broockman (2015) declared Trump to be a "textbook example of an ideological moderate." From his heretical promise to protect from budget cuts the popular old-age entitlement programs, Medicare and Social Security, to his failure to sign a pledge saying he would not raise taxes, and his tough talk on international trade, Trump was a conservative apostate. That he went on to win the nomination anyway "is one of the most remarkable developments in the history of American politics. No politician has come as close to the presidency with as little elite support as Trump had" (Cohen, Karol, Noel, Zaller 2016: 705).

If classic, small-government conservatism did not accommodate Trump's populism, what did? As Eric Oliver and I (2016) documented, he frequently comingled his anti-elitism with a large dose of aggrieved nationalism. According to Trump, the country was in "serious trouble," in danger of "becoming a third world country." Political elites were "stupid" because they let other countries, like China and Mexico, take advantage of the American people. Controlled by "special interests," politicians, he said, were "all talk and no action." Their incompetence had allowed America's enemies to steal her jobs and left the country vulnerable to Islamic terrorists. Trump repeatedly reinforced his role as representative of the national people by liberal use of the collective pronoun, "we," in marked contrast to Hillary Clinton's frequent iteration of particularistic social groups when characterizing the American people (Oliver and Rahn 2016).

In part to gauge the role of populist attitudes during the nomination campaign, we designed a survey, the details of which are discussed elsewhere (Oliver and Rahn 2016), that was fielded the week before the "Super Tuesday" contests of March 1. In developing our measure of PA, we drew on the works of other scholars working in the ideational tradition, including Akkerman, Mudde and Zaslove (2014) and Spruyt, Keppens, and Van Droogenbroeck (2016), while devising some of our own items. The following six items load on a single factor and the resulting scale has a mean of .66, a standard deviation of .15, and a Cronbach's alpha of .64.[9]

- **No say**: People like me don't have much say in what government does
- **People vs. powerful**: Politics usually boils down to a struggle between the people and the powerful
- **System stacked**: The system is stacked against people like me
- **Rich control parties**: It doesn't really matter who you vote for because the rich control both political parties
- **New party**: We need a new party to represent ordinary Americans
- **Congress:** Congress is no longer an institution that speaks for the American people.

In a preliminary analysis (results not shown), I regressed the PA scale on a measure of immigrant threat[10] and an item that tapped pessimism about the economic mobility of future generations,[11] along with several control variables. The PA scale had similar associations with these variables as anti-elitism did in the 2014 GSS survey, providing assurance that, despite the somewhat different mix of items in our survey, the grievances driving populist demand in 2014 were still operative in 2016.

Confident of the continuity in public opinion between 2014 and 2016, I now turn to an analysis of the relationship between PA and candidate preference. In keeping with this chapter's focus on Trump's candidacy, I limit my attention to explaining people's preferences for a Republican nominee. All respondents, not just Democrats, were asked the question: "If you were going to vote (or did already vote) in the Republican primary, which candidate would you (or did you) support?" and provided the options of Donald Trump, Jeb Bush, Ted Cruz, Marco Rubio John Kasich, and Other. I estimated a logit model of Trump preference (compared to the alternatives) using the PA scale, attitudes about immigration and economic mobility, and a variety of control variables. In addition, I included the strength of national identity as an additional independent variable to see whether Trump's nationalism was an important contributor to his appeal.[12]

Table 15.5 displays the results. To aid in interpretation of the logit coefficients, I include a column reporting the change in predicted probabilities of Trump preference associated with moving across the full range of the significant predictor variables, holding the other variables at their means. The evidence in the table is quite clear. Populist demanders were strongly attracted to Donald Trump. So were American nationalists, indicating that his host ideology also served to mobilize support. Even though immigration was itself related to populism, it emerges as an independent predictor of Trump preferences. The effects of skepticism about the American Dream, however, appear to be mediated fully through populist attitudes.

Table 15.5 Trump preferences during the 2016 primaries

	Trump preferences	*Δ Probability*
Populist attitudes	2.68**	36.6%
	(0.62)	
National identity	1.40**	18.8%
	(0.38)	
Immigrants burden	0.72**	12.7%
	(0.18)	
American Dream	0.11	
	(0.23)	
Republican	0.72**	13.3%
	(0.21)	
Democrat	–0.56**	–9.1%
	(0.23)	
Constant	–5.53**	
	(0.69)	
Pseudo R^2	.14	
N	1043	

Note: Model also contains age, sex, race, education, and conservative Protestant.
* p ≤.05 ** p ≤.01, two-tailed

Populist attitudes and support for Trump in the general election

To the dismay of many Republican leaders, Trump proved unstoppable. Last-ditch efforts by Ted Cruz and John Kasich to deny him a majority of delegates and force a brokered convention failed spectacularly, and both suspended their campaigns in early May. In accepting his party's nomination in July, Trump sounded the same populist, nationalist, and nativist themes from the campaign trail. Declaring that he was the voice of "the forgotten men and women of our country," he promised to put the American people first, prevent American companies from moving to other countries, build a border wall, and restore law and order. Ever the populist, Trump continued to target the stupidity and cupidity of America's political class at his campaign rallies and in his speeches during the general election while reiterating his policy platform. Telling Americans that it was "time to drain the swamp," he proposed a series of ethics reforms to "make our government honest once again." Although heavily outspent (Allison, Rojanasakul, Harris and Sam 2016) and out-advertised by his opponent (Fowler, Ridout, and Franz 2016), he nonetheless eked out enough votes in key states to secure an Electoral College victory.

The 2016 American National Election Studies (ANES), a pre- and post-election survey, allows me to assess the degree to which the collision of "the right words" with "the right people" at "the right time" contributed to his November triumph. The ANES is ideally suited to this task because of its extensive inventory of questions, including not only PA, but also other elements of the package that was candidate Trump: his nationalism, his trade protectionism, and his promises to do away with Obama-era "job-destroying" regulations on the environment and to repeal and replace Obamacare with something "terrific."

The 2016 ANES featured an unusually rich set of questions about people's attitudes toward politicians and government because of its participation in the Comparative Study of Electoral Systems (CSES), an arrangement like that of the GSS with the ISPP. Based on some initial exploratory factor analyses, I selected the following to measure PA. All but the last one are Likert format with responses ranging from strongly disagree to strongly agree.

- **Don't care 1**: Public officials don't care much what people like me think.
- **People decide:** The people, not politicians, should make our most important policy decisions.
- **Don't care 2:** Most politicians do not care about the people.
- **Rich and powerful:** Most politicians care only about the interests of the rich and powerful.
- **Trustworthy (reversed):** Most politicians are trustworthy.
- **Main problem:** Politicians are the main problem in this country.
- **Corruption:** How widespread do you think corruption such as bribe taking is among politicians in the United States? (very widespread, quite widespread, not very widespread, or it hardly happens at all).

I recoded the questions to unit range and averaged them. The resulting scale ranges from 0 to 1 and has a reliability coefficient of .76. The scale mean is .62 and has a standard deviation .17. As a preliminary step (results not shown), I estimated the associations between the ANES scale and variables akin to the ones I used with the GSS and our 2016 primary survey,[13] finding that populist attitudes in the fall of 2016 were rooted in both economic and cultural grievances. Skepticism about the American Dream and preferences for reduced immigration independently were associated with populist attitudes. The consistency of this pattern across three different surveys is noteworthy.

Did populist demanders find their champion in one Donald Trump? To answer this question, I constructed a candidate preference variable using respondents' stated vote intention in the pre-election survey so that their choices would be unaffected by the actual election outcome. I restricted the dependent variable to those people who indicated a preference for Trump or for Clinton, putting supporters of Jill Klein, Gary Johnson, or other candidates aside.[14] I then estimated a logit model of candidate choice using the populist attitudes scale, preferences for reduced immigration, and beliefs about the American Dream, as well as a dummy variable indicating whether respondents considered themselves to be conservative Protestants or not,[15] in addition to controls for demographics and partisanship. Results from this specification are displayed in Table 15.6 under the column heading, Populism. Because I will be presenting results from two additional models of candidate choice, to reduce table size, I report only the coefficients for immigration, American Dream, and partisanship.

An initial answer to my query appears to be yes. Populist attitudes significantly increased the probability that people preferred Trump to Clinton. Like the results obtained for our February survey, unhappiness with the political establishment mediates fully American's bleak views about economic mobility, but immigration remains as an independent source of candidate choice. Unlike for primary preferences, however, immigration is the more consequential. Based on marginal predicted probabilities (with other variables at their means), compared to people fully content with the political status quo, ardent populists were about 24% more likely to support Trump. Immigrant restrictionists, on the other

Table 15.6 Preferences for Trump vs. Clinton, 2016 ANES

	Populism	*+ Nationalism*	*+ Issues*
Populist attitudes	1.16*	1.27*	0.74
	(0.49)	(0.51)	(0.69)
National superiority		1.63**	1.24**
		(0.33)	(0.41)
National identity		1.09*	1.44**
		(0.40)	(0.52)
Oppose free trade			0.77**
			(0.35)
Oppose ACA			2.96**
			(0.29)
Oppose business regulations on environment			1.91**
			(0.38)
American Dream	0.12	0.29	0.03
	(5.10)	(0.41)	(0.54)
Immigration levels	3.87**	3.64**	2.99**
	(0.36)	(0.37)	(0.48)
Republican	2.04**	1.88**	1.37**
	(0.21)	(0.21)	(0.28)
Democrat	–2.49**	–2.59**	–2.47**
	(0.20)	(0.21)	(0.29)
Constant	–4.38**	–5.25**	–7.11**
	(0.55)	(0.61)	(0.81)
Pseudo R^2	0.60	0.62	0.72
N	2461	2439	2096

Note: Model also includes age, sex, race, education, and conservative Protestant.
*p ≤ .05 **p ≤ .01, two-tailed

hand, were over 60% more likely to prefer him to his Democrat opponent than those with the most welcoming attitudes.

In the next model, I add two indicators of nationalism, one for the strength of national identity,[16] and the other, a belief in national superiority.[17] As discussed earlier, Trump's nationalism, succinctly summed up by his phrase, "Make America Great Again," was the context in which his critique of the political class was set. It allowed him to draw strong boundaries around the people's membership while also placing responsibility for the people's plight on its current leaders. The table shows that these two measures of national orientation significantly contribute to explaining candidate choice, and, when taking nationalism into account, the coefficient on PA strengths a bit. Trump's supporters apparently were attracted both by his populism and by his "America-First" promises. Interestingly, the inclusion of nationalism does little to mitigate the force of nativism. People who wished to decrease current levels of immigration favored Trump regardless of their identity with the nation or their desire to remake the world in America's image.

The final model includes opinions on three issues that Trump emphasized throughout his campaign, the repeal and replacement of the Affordable Care Act,[18] his promises to renegotiate NAFTA and other unfair trade agreements,[19] and his pledge to rollback Obama-era regulations protecting the environment,[20] the latter of which he moved on aggressively very early in his new administration. In this last model, inclusion of specific policy positions renders the PA scale insignificant. The impact of opposition to Obamacare, on the other hand, is notable and about on par with that of opposition to immigration. This may reflect, in part, that views on health care reform became significantly racialized during the Obama Administration (Maxwell and Shields 2014; Tesler 2012). The extra psychological freight carried by this particular policy opinion may have enhanced its role in voter decision making in 2016.

Given the findings of the last model, it may be tempting to conclude that individuals' policy positions eclipsed populist attitudes as determinants of Trump support in the general election. This result is not necessarily inconsistent with ideational theory; populist attitudes are not thought to displace other, more conventional determinants of vote choice. This is especially likely in political systems in which the major political parties are well-institutionalized (editors' introduction). Moreover, the interpretation that voters' policy preferences matter more than populist attitudes depends on the dubious assumption that views on political issues are exogenous to candidate choice. Plenty of studies have demonstrated that voters adopt the issue stances of their preferred candidates (Lenz 2012). While it is impossible to sort out the direction of causality in a cross-sectional analysis such as mine, they are reasons to believe that endogeneity could be a factor in the results. Trump dominated news coverage from his announcement on (Patterson 2016), and very few voters changed their minds over the course of the campaign (Hopkins 2016). Both candidates were well known even before their epic clash; there was little left to learn about them during the fall campaign. Even if some policy learning did occur as a result of their advertising or their debate encounters, any new evidence was likely overwhelmed by voters' prior attitudes, resulting in little, in any, updating. Ordinary citizens (and experts, for that matter) are far more likely to be rationalizers than rational actors (Rahn, Krosnick, and Breuning 1994; Lodge and Taber 2013).

Only multi-wave panel data that started collection before the candidates announced their intentions and that continued through the nomination and general election phases of the campaign can truly sort out how much the apparent evidence of policy voting is truly causal. However, the fact that I established in this chapter that political disaffection had significantly increased before Trump became a candidate, that it reflected at that time the demographic coalition that Trump ultimately put together, and that it already incorporated certain themes that would emerge later in his rhetoric gives me some confidence that populist demand existed before its supply was provided.

Discussion

As this volume attests, social scientists have made great strides in defining, measuring, and theorizing populism. This chapters builds on this progress, finding that the 2016 American election adheres closely to what ideational theory would lead us to expect: a deepening sense among members of the public that existing political arrangements failed to meet their needs made for a favorable climate in which the anti-establishment rhetoric of outsider candidates could gain traction. In the case of the Republican Party, this discursive opportunity could be effectively exploited because of the disarray among party stalwarts. Both of these conditions were unanticipated by leading theories of American electoral politics, theories that now stand in need of revision in light of the developments of 2016. As scholars undertake this work, they would be well served by deeper engagement with the rich body of research that has emerged on comparative populism, using the ideational approach to populism to develop new, conceptually driven measures that map the multiple dimensions of populist attitudes

The US case, on the other hand, suggests that ideational theory could also be amended. Populist demand figures largely in its account, but its engine, failures of democratic representation, lacks specificity and rigorous empirical testing. In part this reflects the fact that survey analysis of populist attitudes is of more recent vintage than textual and other kinds of analyses of populist supply. The new CSES module will enable researchers to conduct multi-level studies to model more explicitly the linkages between system-level factors, voter attitudes, and party choice, thereby clarifying the necessary and sufficient conditions for populist success.

Notes

1 The supply curve also can shift even in the absence of a shift in demand. For example, technological innovation may make it "cheaper" to "produce" populism.

2 Given the small numbers of respondents who self-identified as upper class, to simplify presentation, I collapsed them into the middle class category.

3 All tabulations and regressions based on the GSS surveys use NORC's recommended weight variable, wtssall. The excluded categories in the regression are female (compared to male), large metropolitan areas (in comparison to other places of residence), Hispanics and other races (compared to whites and Blacks), lower and working class (compared to middle or upper class), and post-graduates (compared to the less-well educated categories).

4 I regressed the American Dream variable in 2014 on the independent variables in Table 15.2. Self-identification as working class significantly depressed belief in the American Dream. Thus social class shaped anti-elitism in 2014 both indirectly, through more skeptical beliefs about the American Dream, and directly. The total effects of social class on AE in 2014, therefore, are quite substantial.

5 Although ideational theory is careful not to conflate nativism with the populist "core" (Mudde and Rovira Kaltwasser 2017), they are such frequent co-travelers in developed democracies to suggest some natural affinity between them. As Bernard Yack (2001) has argued, the doctrine of popular sovereignty, so central to the claims of populists, is itself inextricably tied to images of the nation as both an egalitarian body of citizens and as a cultural community with unique historical characteristics.

6 From the 1892 Populist platform: *Resolved, [t]hat we condemn the fallacy of protecting American labor under the present system, which opens our ports to the pauper and criminal classes of the world and crowds out of wage-earners; and we denounce the present ineffective laws against contract labor, and demand the further restriction of undesirable emigration.*

7 The most ambitious and wide-ranging effort to pit an economic insecurity explanation of support for populist parties against a cultural backlash thesis can be found in Inglehart and Norris (2016). However, their analysis does not contain an independent measure of populist attitudes, nor do their measures of economic insecurity appropriately capture the sociotropic dimension of beliefs about the American Dream. People may sense that economic opportunity is limited without necessarily being in desperate situations themselves. Inglehart and Norris, instead, regard economic insecurity as a current, egocentric state, despite evidence from many countries that voters' choices about chief executives are driven by sociotropic considerations of national welfare (e.g., Duch and Stevenson 2008). Moreover, Inglehart and Norris (2016) use attitudinal questions to gauge cultural backlash whereas economic orientations are indexed only by demographic variables. Is it any wonder that they find that attitudes predict vote choices better than demographic categories? In their choice of independent variables, they stacked the deck in favor of their cultural explanation.

8 In characterizing the content of populists' policy views, those ideological labels are more analytically convenient than illuminating. The original Populists combined progressive economic ideas with what many present-day observers would regard as culturally conservative views on race,

immigration and religion (Postel 2007). In fact, William McKinley's defeat of Williams Jennings Bryan in the 1896 election – the "Populist Waterloo" (Postel 2007) – involved a significant shift of Catholics into the Republican column because they regarded him as less hostile to their faith than the evangelical Bryan (Mayhew 2015). And several "right-wing" populist parties in Europe combine their criticism of the mainstream parties with "welfare chauvism," a belief that simultaneously supports an extensive welfare state and redistribution from rich to poor with the desire to restrict welfare state entitlements to the native born (Elchardus and Spruyt 2012; Koster, Achterberg, and van der Waal 2013; Schumacher and van Kersbergen 2016). Such a combination positions these parties as "off diagonal" to the main axis of left-right conflict in two-dimensional (economic and cultural) ideological space.

9 The somewhat lower reliability of the PA scale compared to the AE scale may result from the breadth of targets in the items comprising the former.

10 Respondents were asked choose between whether they believed that immigrants were "more of a burden on our country, taking jobs, housing, and health care" or "strengthened our country with their hard work and talents."

11 The question, "When your children are your age, do you think their standard of living will be worse than yours, about the same as yours, or better than yours?" gauged belief in the American Dream.

12 In regression results not show, American identity itself was weakly, but *negatively*, associated with populist attitudes ($b = -0.04, p < .06$). The model included all variables in Table 15.5.

13 The ANES contains the exact question about immigration levels as the GSS, and I combined two items. to measure people's beliefs about economic mobility: How much opportunity is there in America today for the average person to get ahead? When it comes to people trying to improve their financial well-being, do you think it now easier, harder, or about the same as it was 20 years ago?

14 Results are no different if these candidates are included.

15 Conservative Protestants were those who identified as either born-again, evangelical, fundamentalist, or Pentecostal Christians.

16 How important is being American to your identity?

17 The world would be a better place if people from other countries were more like Americans.

18 Do you favor, oppose, or neither favor nor oppose the health care reform law passed in 2010? How strongly do you [favor/oppose] it?

19 Do you favor, oppose, or neither favor nor oppose the US making free trade agreements with other countries? How strongly do you [favor/oppose] it?

20 Where would you place yourself on this scale? Regulate business to protect the environment and create jobs or No regulation because it will not work and will cost jobs.

References

Abramowitz, Alan, and Ruy Teixeira. 2009. "The Decline of the White Working Class and the Rise of a Mass Upper-Middle Class." *Political Science Quarterly* 124(3): 391–422.

Ahler, Doug, and David Broockman. 2015. "Donald Trump is a Textbook Example of an Ideological Moderate." The *Monkey Cage, Washington Post*. December 16. www.washingtonpost.com/news/monkey-cage/wp/2015/12/16/donald-trump-is-a-textbook-example-of-an-ideological-moderate/?utm_term=.88cd7b4abfa0. Accessed December 14, 2016.

Akkerman, A., C. Mudde, and A. Zaslove. 2014. "How Populist Are the People? Measuring Populist Attitudes in Voters." *Comparative Political Studies* 47(9): 1324–53.

Allison, Bill, Mira Rojanasakul, Brittany Harris, and Cedric Sam. 2016. "Tracking the 2016 Presidential Money Race." *Bloomberg Businessweek*, Dec. 9. www.bloomberg.com/politics/graphics/2016-presidential-campaign-fundraising/. Accessed May 30, 2017

Ansolabehere, Stephen, James M. Snyder, Jr. and Charles Stewart III. 2001. "Candidate Positioning in U.S. House Elections." *American Journal of Political Science* 45(1): 136–159.

Autor, D. H. 2014. "Skills, Education, and the Rise of Earnings Inequality among the 'Other 99 Percent.'" *Science* 344(6186): 843–851.

Autor, David, David Dorn, Gordon Hanson, and Kaveh Majlesi. 2017. "A Note on the Effect of Rising Trade Exposure on the 2016 Election." www.ddorn.net/papers/ADHM-President2016.pdf

Bartels, Larry M. 2016a. *Unequal Democracy: The Political Economy of the New Gilded Age*. Second edition. New York: Russell Sage Foundation.

Bartels, L. M. 2016b. "Failure to Converge: Presidential Candidates, Core Partisans, and the Missing Middle in American Electoral Politics." *The ANNALS of the American Academy of Political and Social Science* 667(1): 143–165.

Bafumi, Joseph and Michael C. Herron (2010). "Leapfrog Representation and Extremism: A Study of Voters and Their Members in Congress." *American Political Science Review* 104(3): 519–542.

Bonikowski, Bart, and Noam Gidron. 2016. "The Populist Style in American Politics: Presidential Campaign Discourse, 1952–1996." *Social Forces* 94(4): 1593–1621.

Bycoffe, Aaron. 2016. The Endorsement Primary. *FiveThirtyEight*. http://projects.fivethirtyeight.com/2016-endorsement-primary/ Accessed May 17, 2017.

Case, Anne, and Angus Deaton. 2015. "Rising Morbidity and Mortality in Midlife among white non-Hispanic Americas in the 21st Century." *PNAS* 112(49): 15078–15083.

Case, Anne, and Angus Deaton. 2017. "Mortality and Morbidity in the 21st Century." *Brookings Papers on Economic Activity* 2017(1): 397–476.

Casselman, Ben. 2017. "Stop Saying Trump's Win had Nothing to do with Economics." FiveThirtyEight, Jan. 9, 2017. http://fivethirtyeight.com/features/stop-saying-trumps-win-had-nothing-to-do-with-economics. Accessed Jan. 13, 2017.

Chetty, Raj, David Grusky, Maximilian Hell, Nathaniel Henderen, Robert Muanduca, and Jimmy Narang. 2017. "The Fading American Dream: Trends in Absolute Income Mobility since 1940." *Science* 356(6336): 398–406.

Cohen, Marty, David Karol, Hans Noel, and John Zaller. 2016. "Party Versus Faction in the Reformed Presidential Nominating System." *PS: Political Science & Politics* 49(04): 701–8.

Cramer, Katherine J. 2016. *The Politics of Resentment: Rural Consciousness in Wisconsin and the Rise of Scott Walker*. Chicago Studies in American Politics. Chicago; London: University of Chicago Press.

Deegan-Krause, Kevin, and Tim Haughton. 2009. "Toward a More Useful Conceptualization of Populism: Types and Degrees of Populist Appeals in the Case of Slovakia." *Politics & Policy* 37(4): 821–841.

Duch, Raymond M., and Randolph T. Stevenson. 2008. *The Economic Vote: How Political and Economic Institutions Condition Election Results*. New York: Cambridge University Press.

Egan, Patrick J. 2013. *Partisan Priorities: How Issue Ownership Drives and Distorts American Politics*. Cambridge: Cambridge University Press.

Elchardus, Mark, and Bram Spruyt. 2012. "The Contemporary Contradictions of Egalitarianism: An Empirical Analysis of the Relationship between the Old and New Left/Right Alignments." *European Political Science Review* 4(2): 217–39.

Franklin Fowler, Erika, Travis N. Ridout, and Michael M. Franz. 2016. "Political Advertising in 2016: The Presidential Election as Outlier?" *The Forum* 14(4). doi:10.1515/for-2016-0040.

Gerteis, Joseph, and Alyssa Goolsby. 2005. "Nationalism in America: The Case of the Populist Movement." *Theory and Society* 34(2): 197–225. doi:10.1007/s11186-005-0342-y.

Gilens, Martin. 2012. *Influence and Affluence: Economic Inequality and Political Power in the United States*. New York and Princeton, NJ: Russell Sage Foundation and Princeton University Press.

Gest, Justin. 2016. *The New Minority: White Working Class Politics in an Age of Immigration and Inequality*. New York, NY: Oxford University Press.

Hawkins, Kirk. 2016. "Populism and the 2016 U.S. Presidential Election in Comparative Perspective." *Comparative Politics Newsletter* 26(2):91–96. http://comparativenewsletter.com/files/archived_newsletters/fall_2016.pdf

Hetherington, Marc J. and Thomas J. Rudolph. 2015. *Why Washington Won't Work: Polarization, Political Trust, and the Governing Crisis*. Chicago, IL: University of Chicago Press.

Hochschild, Jennifer L. 2016. "What Happened on November 8, and What Happens Next? A Tour of Social Scientists' Answers." (December 10). SSRN: https://ssrn.com/abstract=2884365. Accessed December 12, 2016.

Hopkins, Dan. 2016. Most Voters Haven't Changed Their Minds All Year." FiveThirtyEight. Nov. 2. http://fivethirtyeight.com/features/most-voters-havent-changed-their-minds-all-year/. Accessed December 12, 2016.

Inglehart, R. F., and Norris, P. (2016). "Trump, Brexit, and the Rise of Populism: Economic Have-Nots and Cultural Backlash", *Faculty Research Working Paper Series*, RWP16-026. https://research.hks.harvard.edu/publications/getFile.aspx?Id=1401. Accessed May 5, 2017.

Kazin, Michael. 1995. *The Populist Persuasion: An American History*. New York, NY: BasicBooks.

Kolko, Jed. 2016. "Trump Was Stronger Where the Economy is Weaker." FiveThirtyEight, Nov. 20, 2016. http://fivethirtyeight.com/features/trump-was-stronger-where-the-economy-is-weaker/. Accessed November 21, 2016.

Koster, Willem de, Peter Achterberg, and Jeroen van der Waal. 2013. "The New Right and the Welfare State: The Electoral Relevance of Welfare Chauvinism and Welfare Populism in the Netherlands." *International Political Science Review* 34(1): 3–20.

Lenz, Gabriel S. 2012. *Follow the Leader?: How Voters Respond to Politicians' Policies and Performance*. Chicago Studies in American Politics. Chicago; London: The University of Chicago Press.

Lipset, Seymour Martin. 1996. *American Exceptionalism: A Double-Edged Sword*. New York: W.W. Norton.

Lodge, Milton, and Charles S. Taber. 2013. *The Rationalizing Voter*. Cambridge Studies in Public Opinion and Political Psychology. Cambridge; New York: Cambridge University Press.

Manza, Jeff, and Clem Brooks. 2014. "Prisoners of the American Dream." https://as.nyu.edu/content/dam/nyu-as/faculty/documents/PrisonersoftheAmericanDream.pdf. Accessed November 6, 2014.

Maxwell, Angie, and Todd Shields. 2014. "The Fate of Obamacare: Racial Resentment, Ethnocentrism and Attitudes about Healthcare Reform." *Race and Social Problems* 6(4): 293–304.

Mayhew, David R. 2015. "What Does McKinley's Election in 1896Teach Us about Today?" *Washington Post*, December 9. www.washingtonpost.com/opinions/what-does-mckinleys-election-in-1896-teach-us-about-today/2015/12/08/640ee8a6-7ce0-11e5-beba-927fd8634498_story.html. Accessed May 29, 2017.

Milanovic, Branko. 2016. "Winners and Losers of Globalization: The Rich and the Chinese Middle Class. Losers: The American Middle Class." www.huffingtonpost.com/branko-milanovic/winners-of-globalization-_b_4603454.html. Accessed May 8, 2017.

Mudde, Cas. 2010. "The Populist Radical Right: A Pathological Normalcy." *West European Politics* 33(6): 1167–86.

Mudde, Cas, and Cristóbal Rovira Kaltwasser. 2017. *Populism: A Very Short Introduction*. Very Short Introductions. Oxford; New York, NY: Oxford University Press.

New York Times. 2016. Transcript of Donald Trump's Immigration Speech. *New York Times*, Sept. 1, 2016. www.nytimes.com/2016/09/02/us/politics/transcript-trump-immigration-speech.html. Accessed Sept. 2, 2016

Noel, Hans. 2016. Ideological Factions in the Republican and Democratic Parties. *The Annals of the American Academy of Political and Social Science* 667(1):166–188.

Oliver, J. E., and W. M. Rahn. 2016. "Rise of the Trumpenvolk: Populism in the 2016 Election." *The ANNALS of the American Academy of Political and Social Science* 667(1): 189–206.

Patterson, Thomas E. 2016. "News Coverage of the 2016 General Election: How the Press Failed Voters." Harvard Kennedy School Shorenstein Center on Media, Politics, and Public Policy. https://shorensteincenter.org/news-coverage-2016-general-election/. Accessed May 29, 2017.

Piketty, Thomas. 2014. *Capital in the Twenty-First Century*. Cambridge, MA: Belknap Press.

Piketty, Thomas, Emmanuel Saez, and Gabriel Zucman. 2016. "Distributional National Accounts: Methods and Estimates for the United States." *National Bureau of Economic Research* Working Paper No. 22945. www.nber.org/papers/w22945. Accessed December 29, 2016.

Postel, Charles. 2007. *The Populist Vision*. New York: Oxford University Press.

Rahn, Wendy M., Jon A. Krosnick, and Marijke Breuning. 1994. "Rationalization and Derivation Processes in Survey Studies of Political Candidate Evaluation." *American Journal of Political Science* 38(3):582–600.

Rank, Mark R., Thomas A. Hirschl, and Kirk A. Foster. 2014. *Chasing the American Dream: Understanding What Shapes Our Fortunes*. Oxford; New York: Oxford University Press.

Rogers, Steven. 2017. "Electoral Accountability for State Legislative Roll Calls and Ideological Representation." *American Political Science Review* 111 (03):555–571.

Rogowksi, Jon C. 2014. "Electoral Choice, Ideological Conflict, and Political Participation." *American Journal of Political Science* 58(2):479–494.

Rooduijn, Matthijs. 2014. "Vox Populismus: A Populist Radical Right Attitude among the Public?" *Nations and Nationalism* 20(1): 80–92.

Schaffner, Brian F., Matthew MacWilliams, and Tatishe Nteta. 2016. "Explaining White Polarization in the 2016 Vote for President: The Sobering Role of Racism and Sexism." Manuscript available at http://people.umass.edu/schaffne/schaffner_et_al_IDC_conference.pdf. Accessed January 3, 2017.

Schulz, A., P. Müller, C. Schemer, D. S. Wirz, M. Wettstein, and W. Wirth. (2017). "Measuring Populist Attitudes on Three Dimensions." *International Journal of Public Opinion Research*. Online first. doi: https://doi.org/10.1093/ijpor/edw037

Spruyt, Bram, Gil Keppens, and Filip Van Droogenbroeck. 2016. "*Who* Supports Populism and *What* Attracts People to It?" *Political Research Quarterly* 69(2): 335–346.

Stimson, James A. 1991. *Public Opinion in America: Moods, Cycles, and Swings*. Boulder, CO: Westview.

Schumacher, Gijs, and Kees van Kersbergen. 2016. "Do Mainstream Parties Adapt to the Welfare Chauvinism of Populist Parties?" *Party Politics* 22(3): 300–312.

Tesler, Michael. 2012. "The Spillover of Racialization into Health Care: How President Obama Polarized Public Opinion by Racial Attitudes and Race." *American Journal of Political Science* 56(3): 690–704.

Tesler, Michael. 2015. "How Anti-immigrant Attitudes are Fueling Support for Donald Trump." *Monkey Cage, Washington Post*, Nov. 24, 2015. www.washingtonpost.com/news/monkey-cage/wp/2015/11/24/how-anti-immigrant-attitudes-are-fueling-support-for-donald-trump. Accessed March 17, 2016.

Tesler, Michael. 2016. "Views about Race Mattered more in Electing Trump than in Electing Obama." *Monkey Cage, Washington Post*. Nov. 22. www.washingtonpost.com/news/monkey-cage/wp/2016/11/22/peoples-views-about-race-mattered-more-in-electing-trump-than-in-electing-obama/?utm_term=.9495b64beac3. Accessed March 17, 2017.

Tesler, Michael and John Sides. 2016. "How political science helps explain the rise of Trump: the Role of White Identity and Grievances." *Monkey Cage, Washington Post*, March 3, 2016. www.washingtonpost.com/news/monkey-cage/wp/2016/03/03/how-political-science-helps-explain-the-rise-of-trump-the-role-of-white-identity-and-grievances/. Accessed March 17, 2017.

Time. 2015. "Here's Donald Trump's Presidential Announcement Speech." *Time*, June 16, 2015. http://time.com/3923128/donald-trump-announcement-speech/. Accessed April 4, 2016

Williams, Rhys H. and Susan M. Alexander. 1994. "Religious Rhetoric in American Populism: Civil Religion and Movement Ideology." *Journal for the Scientific Study of Religion* 33(1): 1–15.

Yack, Bernard. 2001. "Popular Sovereignty and Nationalism." *Political Theory* 29(4): 517–536.

16 Activating populist attitudes

The role of corruption

Ethan C. Busby, David Doyle, Kirk A. Hawkins, and Nina Wiesehomeier

In recent years, scholars have improved our understanding of populism not only from an aggregate perspective (de la Torre 2010; Hawkins 2010; Kriesi 2014), but from an individual-level one. Survey research shows that populist attitudes are widespread among citizens in many different countries (Akkerman, Mudde, and Zaslove 2014; Hawkins, Riding, and Mudde 2012; Spruyt, Keppens, and Droogenbroek 2016; see also chapter by Andreadis et al. in this volume, Chapter 10). Likewise, experimental research increasingly demonstrates that politicians' framing of the social and political world is essential for activating and directing those attitudes (Bos, Van Der Brug, and De Vreese 2013; Hameleers, Bos, and de Vreese 2017; Hawkins et al. 2014a). The ideational argument in this volume builds on these findings, combining them into a nuanced argument about how populist attitudes are activated by the combination of context and framing.

In this chapter we explore a piece of the ideational argument that has not been tested at the individual level, namely, what it is about policy failure that induces populist behavior. The ideational argument suggests that widespread violations of democratic norms, in terms of corruption and elite collusion, are necessary conditions for populist forces to successfully contest elections. This argument is confirmed by aggregate-level studies, such as the chapter by Castanho Silva in this volume (see also Hawkins 2010). However, because these are aggregate level studies, they fail to show what it is about the political context that actually prompts a populist response from voters. Perhaps voters are not responding to corruption or elite collusion per se, but to its consequences for economic or other policy performance.

To clarify and test this argument, we introduce the concept of *normative democratic threat*. This concept situates the ideational argument more carefully in current theories of political psychology and lets us spell out a set of hypotheses. We then test these hypotheses with two laboratory-based experiments: one on a student sample at Northwestern University in the United States, the other on a mixed student/resident sample at Oxford University in the United Kingdom. In both studies, we ask subjects to give their reactions to a problem with local infrastructure. While in the comparison group, subjects are presented with information that suggests the problem results from unavoidable shortfalls in the government budget, in two different treatment conditions the evidence shows that this shortfall is caused by the systematic abuse of government funds.

The use of a lab is an important innovation for populism experiments. We take advantage of this not only by introducing new treatment designs, but by introducing a new outcome measure. In addition to a few standard gauges of attitudes and rhetoric, we include a measure of social interaction by asking subjects to select a partner in the lab for a problem-solving exercise. This better captures actual populist mobilization, which as the ideational approach emphasizes, involves cooperation with like-minded citizens to win power and enact a political agenda. The results of our experiments are ultimately mixed: among Northwestern students, those receiving the treatment are much more likely to respond to the problem with populist language and to collaborate with populist partners, but among Oxford participants the effects are muted and confined primarily to non-students in the sample. This raises questions about student samples and heterogeneous treatment effects that are likely to afflict other populism experiments. We discuss these implications in the conclusion.[1]

Theory

The starting point for theorizing about our causal mechanism is recent micro-level explanations for populism, which have emphasized the framing effect of populist discourse in triggering latent populist attitudes (Bos, Van Der Brug, and De Vreese 2013; Hawkins et al. 2014a). To this, the ideational approach adds the understanding that the activation of attitudes also requires contextual triggers, which activate existing latent dispositions (e.g., Chanley 1994; Cesario et al. 2010; Tett and Guterman 2000). Attitudes must be made salient by some context or life experience. Theories of political psychology help us better understand this context.

According to the ideational theory of populism, the context most likely to activate populist attitudes is one of widespread policy failure that could be interpreted as a symptom of systematic elite malfeasance. One way of theorizing about this type of failure is in terms of threat. Threat here is meant as anything, such as a person, condition, or event that could harm oneself or one's group. Threat has long had a prominent place in political, psychological, and sociological studies of human behavior. It plays a role in the study of personality characteristics (e.g., Feldman and Stenner 1997), conservatism (Jost et al. 2007), political tolerance (Gibson 2006), race (Craig and Richeson 2014; Enos 2016), and more.

Here we focus on one particular kind of threat that is important for activating populist attitudes: normative threat. A normative threat is "a generalized anxiety and sense of threat to society, the country as a whole, or the region where one lives" (Davis and Silver 2004, 34). At its heart, a normative threat is anything that targets a group's basic shared values, rather than their physical existence. An example would be immigrants from different cultural backgrounds threatening the perceived cultural homogeneity of a community. Research on politically important traits (like authoritarianism) has theorized and found that these kinds of threats serve as important situational triggers (Feldman 2003; Hetherington and Weiler 2009; Stenner 2005).

The concept of normative threat is also useful because it refers to one's group, or the collective, and not just a threat to oneself. In general, collective concerns – about terrorism, the economy, etc. – are more potent predictors of individual political attitudes than individualistic anxieties.[2] The best demonstration of this comes from research on retrospective voting and economic evaluations, which finds that evaluations of the nation as a whole are more predictive for attitudes of trade preferences or party support than evaluations of an individual's personal experience (Kinder and Kiewiet 1981; Kiewiet 1983; Mansfield and Mutz 2009). The same relationship exists between collective threats and political tolerance (Gibson 2006).

Populist discourse points a finger at a particular type of normative threat, one that challenges the basic norms of citizenship and democracy. We call this a *normative democratic threat*. Here, the threat is enemies who are in a position of trust – the elite – who are using the institutions of democracy to protect and empower themselves. These actions are not isolated, but widespread and coordinated. And because these foes are internal, they are more sinister, less honorable and less deserving of legal protections or respect for their personhood. In other words, the political elite as a class is working against the interests of the people, threatening democratic norms not by openly challenging them, as an enemy does in wartime, but by subverting them. Because these elite efforts are coordinated, they are more likely to harm the entire community, thus reinforcing the collective side of the threat. The implication is that the entire democratic system is at risk, requiring wholesale institutional change and political mobilization.

In the context of the ideational approach to populism, this means that other types of normative threat such as those posed by immigrants are not by themselves enough to activate populist attitudes, because these groups do not occupy a position of power and trust in the democratic order. In order to be a normative democratic threat, the threat must be connected to intentional action by political or economic elites. Hence, we consider evidence of widespread, intentional action by elites to be a *necessary condition* for the activation of populist attitudes.

> H1: Policy failures that result from intentional elite misbehavior are more likely to trigger a populist response than failures resulting from elite negligence or external causes.
>
> H2: Intentional elite misbehavior is more like to trigger a populist response when it is widespread.

Experimental design

In order to test our two hypotheses, we conducted two laboratory experiments: one at Northwestern University in the United States, the other at Oxford University in the United Kingdom. In these 1 × 3 experiments, subjects were told that they would be interacting with another subject in a problem-solving exercise dealing with the budgetary problems of a small community far from their university. The problems concerned sidewalk damage and a lack of funds to pay for repairs. Subjects in the comparison condition learned that the budget shortfall was the result of bad weather. But subjects in the first treatment condition learned that this shortfall resulted from expensive and ethically questionable team-building trips by the government agency in charge of sidewalk repair (testing H1), while subjects in the second treatment condition learned that the agency's misbehavior was widespread in the local government (testing H2)

The experiment had several important features for testing our hypotheses. First, we selected a place most, if not all, of our subjects would be unfamiliar with and a topic most would have little knowledge of (sidewalk repair and local government). This simplified the experiment and reduced treatment effect heterogeneity due to individuals' pre-existing opinions. It also established a most-difficult case for testing our hypotheses: a problem with sidewalk repair is by itself unlikely to represent any kind of threat, let alone a threat to the values of the subjects' own communities.

Second, we took advantage of the lab environment to introduce a novel outcome measure for what we deem a populist response. Previous experiments in populism have all been online and tend to explore outcomes that are attitudinal and self-oriented, such as vote preference or approval of issue positions; we include two such measures described below. A lab environment, however, creates opportunities for more innovative outcomes gauging behavior. Building off the ideational theory's focus on the collective action problems underlying populist mobilization, we are interested in the effects of populism to overcome such problems and focus on populism-induced partner selection for the problem-solving exercise.

Study 1: Northwestern University

The first of these two studies, at Northwestern University, was conducted in May 2016. In total, 153 undergraduates participated in the experiment as part of a political science course.

Procedure

Subjects came to the lab in small groups and completed the experiment at isolated computer terminals. Figure 16.1 lays out the general structure of the experiment, which consisted of three parts. Part I began upon arrival to the lab, when participants were told that they would participate in a task about problem solving in a group setting and that this would involve completing several tasks. Importantly, subjects were told that they would be interacting with another student in a problem-solving exercise. This setup made the other parts of the experiment more credible; subjects did not actually interact with one another and were fully debriefed at the end of the experiment. Following this brief overview, subjects completed an introductory survey instrument measuring relevant individual-level characteristics, such as demographic variables. While not representative in many respects (overwhelmingly liberal, for example), the sample contains significant variation on a number of demographic traits. Table 16.1 displays the characteristics of the sample.

Part II of the experiment consisted of the actual manipulations. Students were randomly assigned to one of three different scenarios, each of which dealt with a small, rural town over 500 miles from the university where the experiment took place (Seward, Nebraska). Each scenario began with the same description of the problem, as indicated by the materials in the Appendix. This description stated that the town of Seward was unable to repair badly damaged sidewalks, and then identified two different reasons for this failure. The first, given to all three groups, attributed the problem to residents' reluctance to report damage; this reference was included to make the partner selection stage in Part III more believable (see next paragraph). The second reason for the problem served as our randomized treatment. For our comparison group, the lack of repairs was blamed on especially bad winter weather, which resulted in reduced

Table 16.1 Sample characteristics, Study 1

	Percentage of sample
White	50.7
Female	51.6
Liberal	76.5
Moderate	8.5
Conservative	13.7
Fairly or very interested in politics	76.5
First or second year students	81.1
	Sample median
Age	19
Family income	More than $150,000 USD
N	153

government funds. While this is not a pure control group, the condition allows us to compare subjects' responses to a problem without corruption or normative threat.[3] In contrast, for treatment group 1, the lack of funds was traced to mismanagement and expensive team-building trips by the Public Works department, thus embodying a more localized normative threat. For the second treatment group, we further suggested that the misconduct was systematic; in addition to the report of inappropriate team-building trips by the Public Works department, we included a report of mismanagement throughout the city government.

Part III immediately followed the scenarios and incorporated three outcome measures. We first asked participants to rate on a scale from not at all concerned (1) to very concerned (10) how they felt about the situation just described. While this variable may reflect more than populist sentiments, it captures the perception of threat in our treatments. Next, we presented a brief task asking the subjects to discuss in a few words "what group or individual is responsible" for the problem described and "what should be done about them." This procedure prompted subjects to frame the threat in a populist way and made our claims about their interaction partner more credible. This elaboration task served as a second outcome measure, allowing us to gauge subjects' expressions of populist ideas as a result of the treatment.[4]

After the vignette and text-response items, for the purposes of experimental realism, subjects were instructed to "wait a moment" while other students in the lab completed the two free response items with relation to the problem description (in reality, subjects viewed pre-programmed responses and waited a set amount of time). What followed was our third and most innovative outcome measure. Participants were presented with responses of two other (fictitious) students in the lab and asked to choose one as their partner for the problem-solving exercise. One partner presented a pluralist perspective, noting the importance of working together to solve the problems faced by Seward and advocating greater responsiveness by residents; the other partner advocated a populist position, suggesting that the solution required the removal of the elite who had acted against the interests of the people of Seward.

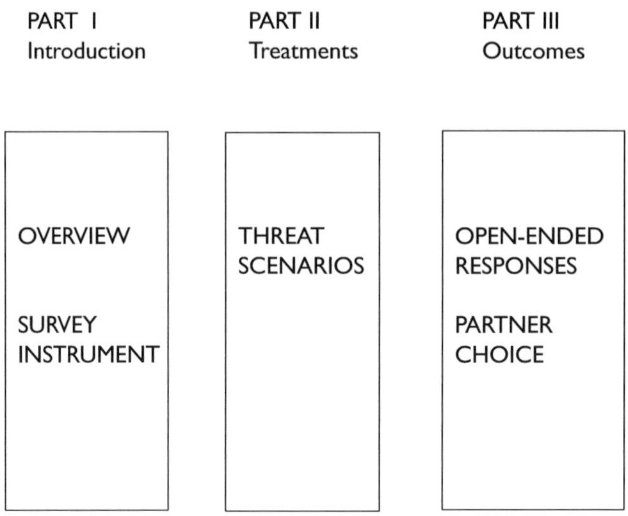

Figure 16.1 Structure of the experiment

These responses were written in a concise, colloquial way and presented in the format required by the earlier open-ended questions (see the Appendix for the appearance of these responses). This mild deception was designed to encourage subjects to take the experiment seriously.

After completing these tasks, subjects were informed about the deceptions involved in the study (fully debriefed) and then allowed to leave the lab. At this point, their participation in the experiment was complete.

Results

To test our hypotheses, our outcome of interest is populism-induced partner choice, i.e. if individuals selected the populist partner over the pluralist option. This choice is a binary one, and is coded as 1 if individuals selected the populist partner and 0 if they selected the pluralist. However, to determine whether our treatment conditions worked as intended, we start by examining subjects' responses to two additional tasks.

First, we examine responses to the item that asked subjects to rate how concerned they were by the scenario they were presented with. This item ranged from 1 (not at all concerned) to 10 (very concerned). We compare this item across scenarios to determine if the treatments created a larger sense of worry (as compared to each other and the comparison group).

Second, we examine subjects' responses to the open-ended questions indicating what groups they felt were responsible for the scenario they read and what should be done about these groups. Two research assistants coded the text of these responses for three elements that correspond to the definition of populism: (1) if the subjects attributed blame to a specific actor, (2) if they identified this actor as an elite, and (3) if they referenced the people in some positive way. If participants included both the second and third elements, they were coded as providing a populist response, which was represented by a value of one; otherwise, they received a zero. Inter-coder reliability on these items was high.[5] Details of this coding process can be found in the replication files in the online appendix. We use these coded responses as the expression of populist ideas. If the treatment scenarios are provoking the normative concerns and populist attitudes that our theories predict, the amount of concern and expressed populism should be higher in the treatment conditions than in the comparison condition.

Figures 16.2 and 16.3 show the level of concern and expressed populism for the treatment and comparison groups. In general, the findings in these figures support H1. Subjects receiving either treatment 1 or treatment 2 display stronger feelings of concern than subjects in the comparison group (p-values approximately equal to 0.000). Substantively, these changes represent an increase of around 33 percent. Likewise, subjects receiving either treatment 1 or treatment 2 express populism more frequently than the comparison group ($p = 0.001$ and $p = 0.073$ respectively)

However, the results in these figures fail to support H2. In terms of expressed concern, subjects in treatment 1 and treatment 2 are statistically indistinguishable from one another ($p = 0.898$). And in terms of expressed populism, the magnitude of the increase differs significantly across the two treatments and points in the wrong direction. Treatment 1 more than quadruples the likelihood of expressing populism, whereas treatment 2 only about doubles it ($p = 0.079$).

In a final step we consider the outcome tailored to the lab setting: the choice of a populist partner. Figure 16.4 shows the probability of selecting the populist partner. As with the concern and expression items, the difference between the comparison and

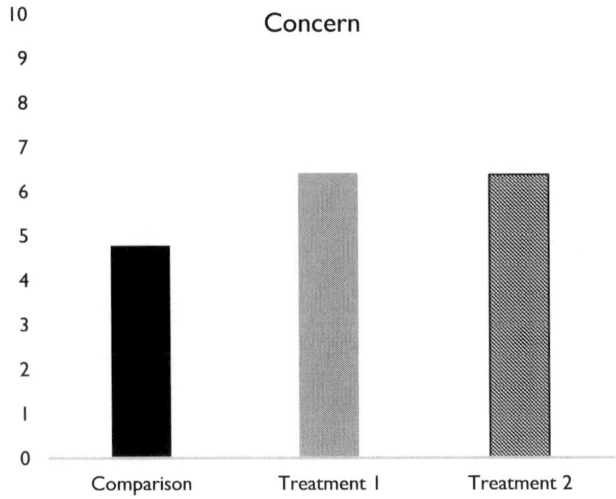

Figure 16.2 Concern, Study 1

Note: The two-tailed *p*-value on the difference between treatment 1 and comparison group is 0.000. For treatment 2 and the comparison group, it is 0.000. The two-tailed *p*-value of the difference between treatment 1 and treatment 2 is 0.898

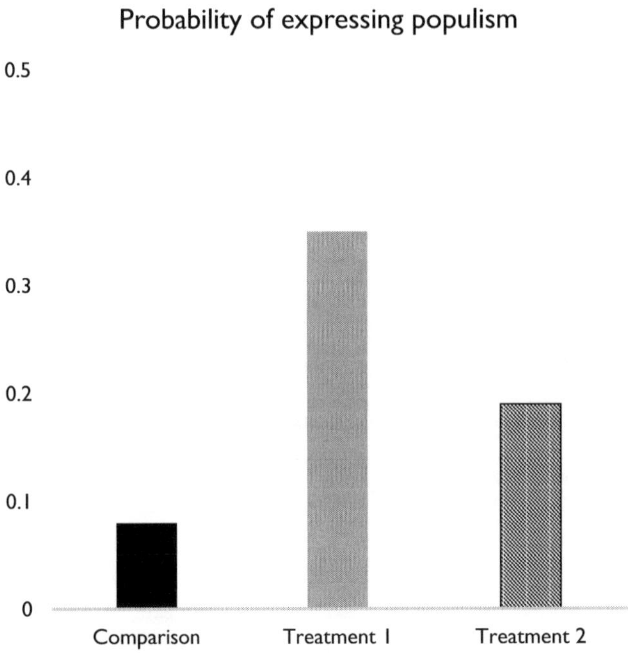

Figure 16.3 Expressed populism, Study 1

Note: The two-tailed *p*-value on the difference between treatment 1 and comparison group is 0.001. For treatment 2 and the comparison group, it is 0.073. The two-tailed *p*-value of the difference between treatment 1 and treatment 2 is 0.079

treatment groups is statistically significant ($p = 0.009$ for treatment 1 and 0.058 for treatment 2) and substantively large (representing a more than 100 percent increase in both treatments). These findings suggest that the corruption treatments prompt individuals to prefer a populist collaborator over a pluralist one.

Yet, just as with the measure of concern or the likelihood of expressing populism, we again observe a stronger effect from treatment 1 as compared to treatment 2, albeit this difference is not statistically significant ($p = 0.402$). Given that our second hypothesis suggested that we should see stronger effects in treatment 2, this null finding is substantively important: on none of our variables (concern, expressed populism, or the choice of populist partner) did we observe a stronger effect for treatment 2, which involved a more systemic normative threat. As discussed in the following section, this leads us to find support for only our first hypothesis.

Discussion

In general, we find that failures of government that are attributed to intentional elite misbehavior provoke more concern, a clearer populist response, and a preference for a populist partner in resolving political and social problems. This is true even given the low-stakes of the political problem (sidewalk and spending problems) and the distance between the subjects and problem. However, we do not find support for our second hypothesis, that these effects should be more pronounced when the normative threat was more pervasive.

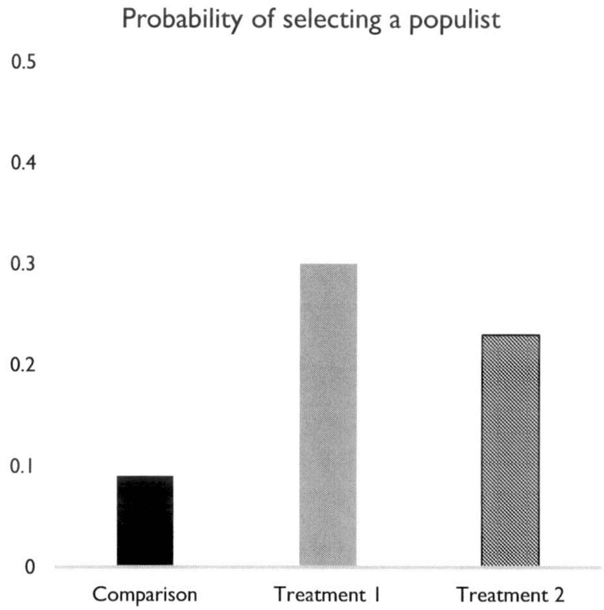

Figure 16.4 Probability of selecting a populist, Study 1

Note: The two-tailed p-value on the difference between treatment 1 and comparison group is 0.009. For treatment 2 and the comparison group, it is 0.058. The two-tailed p-value of the difference between treatment 1 and treatment 2 is 0.402

As a result, we are left with a number of questions. First, why did subjects react as they did to the two corruption treatments? Informal focus groups conducted after the experiment suggest that perhaps the mention of corruption was all that subjects remembered from the treatments and that other considerations may have been less important. That said, we still know little about why subjects reacted to the different treatment groups in a way that runs counter to our expectations. Our findings may be contextually bound and may not replicate in another political climate, a different institutional environment, or with nonstudents. Some scholars have concerns about the use of undergraduates as subjects (e.g. Sears 1986) as student samples may differ from the general population. As pointed out in our theory section, attitudes must be made salient by some context or life experience and, particularly regarding a topic such as government failure as perceived of here, students may have limited exposure when it comes to dealing with problems of this kind. To address these concerns, we implemented a second study in a different environment with a mixed sample of students and nonstudents.

Study 2: the UK context

In order to address the degree to which we could generalize from our first study, we replicated the experiment in a different context with a mixed sample. We conducted our second study in December 2016 at the Centre for Experimental Social Science (CESS) at the University of Oxford in the United Kingdom.

Procedure

To replicate our study as much as possible, the general structure of the experiment remained the same as that depicted in Figure 16.1 above, with some minor contextual or linguistic variations. Here, subjects came to the lab within one of several two-hour sessions. Subjects completed the experiment in isolated computer terminals and once finished were free to leave. Providing that there was still time in a particular session, their seat was then taken by the next subject. Just as in Study 1, Part I began upon arrival at the lab, when participants were told that they would participate in a task about problem solving in a group setting and that this would involve completing several tasks.

Importantly, however, the CESS lab does not allow deception of any sort in its experiments. Because of this we diverged from Study 1 and told subjects that they had to choose a *hypothetical* partner to work with in a problem-solving exercise. Of course, we realize that this may have rendered Study 2 less credible, thereby undermining the strength of the results; we discuss this concern later. As in Study 1, subjects then completed the introductory survey instrument with the battery of political and demographic questions.

Table 16.2 displays the characteristics of the Study 2 sample, which involved 175 individuals, comprising current students and general townspeople, who participated in the experiment in return for a small monetary reward. As in Study 1, while not representative in many respects, the sample contains significant variation on a number of demographic traits.

Part II of the experiment consisted of the manipulations. Our subjects were again randomly assigned to one of three different scenarios, each of which dealt with the budgetary problems of a UK town called Kirkville. Given the prohibition on deception at the CESS lab, we were unable to use a real location and made it explicit to all subjects that both the town, and the partner that they had to choose to work with, were hypothetical. Again, each scenario began with the same description of the problem, as indicated by the

Table 16.2 Sample characteristics, Study 2

	Percentage of sample		
	Whole sample	*Students*	*Non-students*
Female	54.3	52.8	54.4
Left[1]	55.4	60.8	45.7
Centrist[2]	24	22.4	30.4
Right[3]	13.1	10.4	15.2
Fairly or very interested in politics	73	73.6	71.7
Students in the sample	73.1	–	–
	Sample median		
Age	25	24	41
Monthly family income	Between £2,201 and £2,700	Between £2,201 and £2,700	Between £1,601 and £1,800
N	175	125	46

1 This was operationalized as responses falling between (and including) 1–4 on the 10-point ideology scale.
2 This was operationalized as responses falling between (and including) 5 and 6 on the same ideology scale.
3 This included responses between and including 7–10 on the 10-point ideology measure. The three ideology items do not sum to 100 because they do not include individuals who gave the "don't know" response.

materials in the Appendix. This description described the extent of pavement damage (or sidewalks in US parlance) in Kirkville as a consequence of heavy rainfall and flooding over the last number of years – a more widespread problem across the UK, but analogous to heavy snowfall. The description stated the Kirkville County Council had failed to repair the pavements as they had exceeded their annual budget for such repairs.

As before, all three scenarios suggested that the failure of the County Council to repair these pavements and footpaths was due to a hesitance of residents to report damage, plus one additional reason. The first of these was for our comparison group and indicated that the budgetary shortfall was due to the fact that the Council had largely spent their budget on sandbags to hold back floodwaters. As in Study 1, the second reason was our treatment, which we subdivided into two different scenarios; in treatment 1 it was suggested that the lack of funds was traced to mismanagement and expensive team-building trips by the Council's Highway Authority; in treatment 2 the same team-building trips were highlighted, but also included reports of systemic mismanagement throughout the Council, all the way to the City Councilors themselves.

In line with Study 1, immediately after the scenarios we asked participants to rate on a scale from not at all concerned (1) to very concerned (10) how they felt about the situation just described. And as before, subjects were subsequently asked to discuss in a few words "what group or individual is responsible" for the problem described and "what should be done about them."

Once this was completed, participants were presented with the responses of the two hypothetical partners. Based on these responses, subjects were again asked to select the person they would like to work with to come up with a solution to the problem discussed. As in Study 1, this served as our primary dependent variable of interest. We then thanked subjects and asked them for one final clarification question: whether they were currently students or not. All subjects were then free to leave the lab.

Results

As in Study 1, our novel outcome of interest is the binary partner choice of all subjects, coded as 1 if individuals selected the populist partner and a 0 if they selected the pluralist one. We also measure the level of concern for all subjects, ranging from 1 (not at all concerned) to 10 (very concerned), and we code the subjects' responses to the open-ended questions concerning the causes of the pavement problem. Most importantly, our subject pool comprises students and residents of the town of Oxford and we include this distinction in some of our analyses that follow.

As in Study 1, we begin by examining our two preliminary items, the level of concern raised by each scenario and the probability of expressing populism as captured in the responses to the open-ended item.[6] Figure 16.5 illustrates the amount of concern reported by subjects in each of the three experimental groups. Unlike in Study 1, we see no significant differences between the three groups. Furthermore, the level of concern for the comparison group is significantly higher in our Oxford experiment than at Northwestern (6.19 at Oxford versus 4.78 at Northwestern). While we cannot definitively say why respondents reported being more concerned at Oxford, that difference may drive the non-finding in Figure 16.5.

When we consider the differences between students and non-students (two groups with very different experiences in dealing with municipal problems of this kind), we find that non-students are significantly more concerned than students (see Figure 16.6).[7] This may explain some of the difference in the comparison group between Oxford and Northwestern, but examining only students in the comparison group still reveals an elevated level of concern in comparison with the Northwestern sample (5.79 out of 10 for Oxford students). Note that when we explore the different experimental groups using only students or only non-students, we still do not find a reliable difference among the three groups.

We observe, however, an interesting difference when we examine the measure of self-expressed populism (see Figure 16.7). The pattern is similar to Study 1: individuals who received treatment 1 or treatment 2 were significantly more likely to express populism

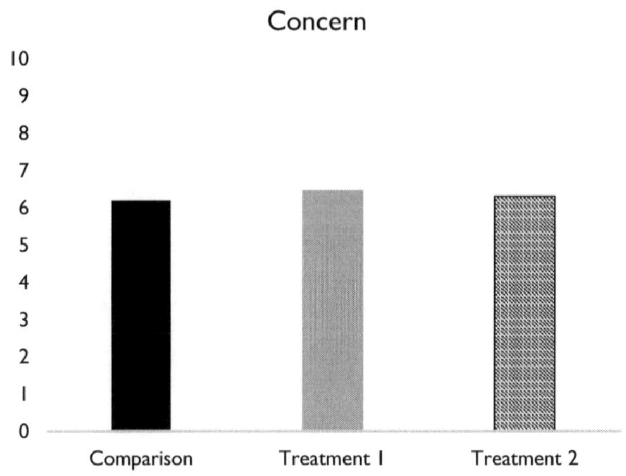

Figure 16.5 Concern, Study 2

Note: None of the differences between the comparison group, treatment 1, and treatment 2 are statistically significant.

in their response to the situation in Kirkville.[8] The pattern is slightly different than at Northwestern, in that we see no statistically significant difference between treatment 1 and treatment 2; if anything, the trend seems to suggest that treatment 2 may prompt more populism (but note that the *p*-value on the difference is 0.446). However, both treatments prompt more expressions of populism.

When we examine the differences between students and non-students, we find that students are more than twice as likely to give a populist response as non-students (*p*-value = 0.074). This again runs counter to the findings on the concern variable, as non-students seemed more concerned about the situation than students. When we break down our treatment group analyses among students and non-students, we see the same pattern of effects in Figure 16.7 for students, but fail to find significant effects among non-students (perhaps due to the sample size of 46).

These findings suggest that the treatments may prompt populism without changing underlying levels of concern. To examine this possibility further, we turn to the analysis of our main outcome of interest: the probability of choosing a populist partner (see Figure 16.9). Although in this case we do observe the expected pattern, none of the differences between the comparison group and the treatment groups are statistically significant ($p>0.40$). This may be because of a reduced willingness to choose a populist partner overall – even in the treatment groups, the probability of choosing a populist partner is not higher than about 0.15, as compared to 0.25 in study 1.

Once again, however, there appears to be a difference between students and residents of the town, as Figure 16.10 illustrates. The pattern suggests that with a larger sample, there might be an effect as predicted among non-students. The number of subjects is relatively small here, but non-students that received either treatment 1 or treatment 2 had a probability of choosing a populist partner of 24 and 27 percent (respectively). Non-students in the comparison group, by contrast, had a probability of only 14 percent. These results are more in line with those observed at Northwestern, where the comparison group had a 9 percent probability of choosing a populist partner, subjects in treatment 1 a 30 percent probability, and subjects in treatment 2 a 23 percent probability.

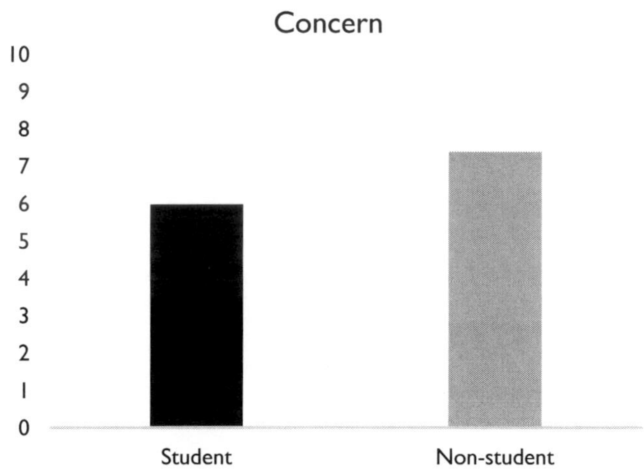

Figure 16.6 Concern among subgroups, Study 2

Note: The difference between the students and non-students is statistically significant ($p = 0.000$).

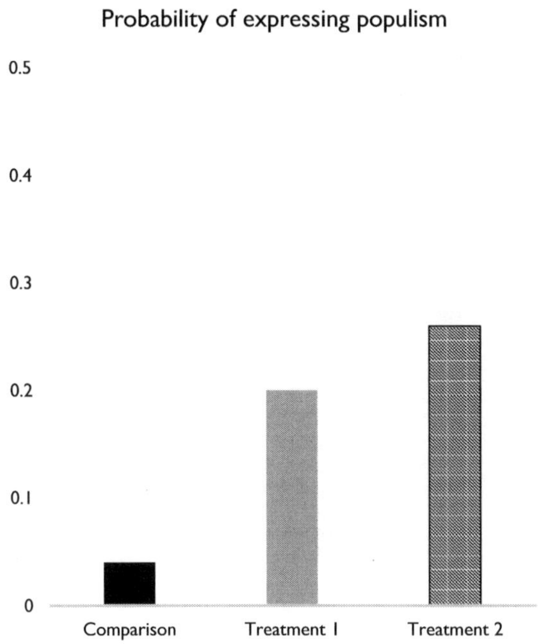

Figure 16.7 Expressed populism, Study 2

Note: The two-tailed *p*-value on the difference between treatment 1 and comparison group is ≈ 0.000. For treatment 2 and the comparison group, it is 0.001. The two-tailed *p*-value of the difference between treatment 1 and treatment 2 is 0.446

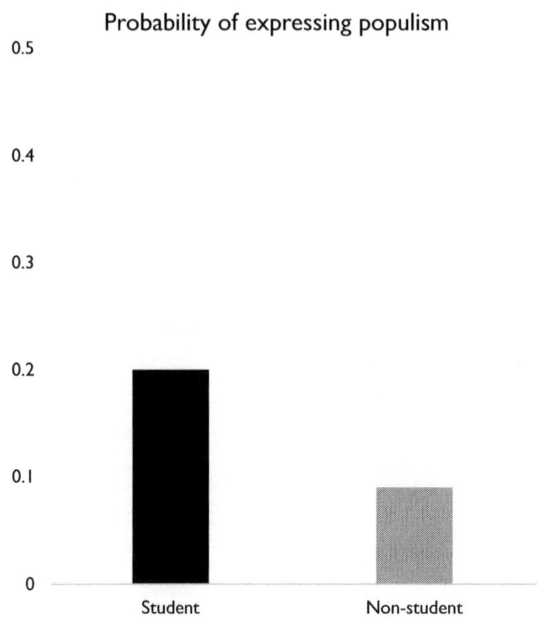

Figure 16.8 Expressed populism among subgroups, Study 2

Note: The two-tailed *p*-value on the difference between students and non-students is 0.074

Discussion

We see some interesting similarities and differences between Study 1 and Study 2. In this study we find only weak support for H1, observing that the treatments produce expressions of populism, but not preferences for a populist partner. Our results also suggest the possibility that H2 is correct, but we only observe these trends among the non-students in the sample, and the treatment effect here is not statistically significant because of low power. We see at least two reasons for the difference. First, given that we were unable to use deception in the CESS lab in Oxford, we were forced to state that both the scenarios and partners were hypothetical. Although the problem of flooding and the thorny issue of paying for flood defenses and flood repair are real and widespread in the UK, the hypothetical nature of our experiment may have undermined its realism and the strength of its effects – especially in choosing a partner to interact with. Second, while in Study 1 all of our participants were students, in Study 2, our subjects were a mix of students and townspeople. As we discussed above, there appears to be a notable difference in populist behavior between the students and non-students.

Nonetheless, Study 2 raises a number of interesting possibilities that should be explored in future research. The first is that a normative democratic threat may prompt populist expressions while failing to motivate populist action. This further emphasizes the need to explore populist behaviors alongside populist attitudes. Second, it is possible that normative democratic threats face ceiling effects when creating concerns among citizens; as observed in Study 2, some issues may have high baseline levels of concerns that limit the ability of elite messages to create further alarm. While we cannot empirically establish these possibilities, they will likely prove fruitful in future research.

General discussion and conclusion

In this chapter, we set out to advance the ideational theory by testing its implications at the individual level. We expected that policy failures resulting from widespread, intentional elite misconduct would be more likely to trigger a populist response than those resulting

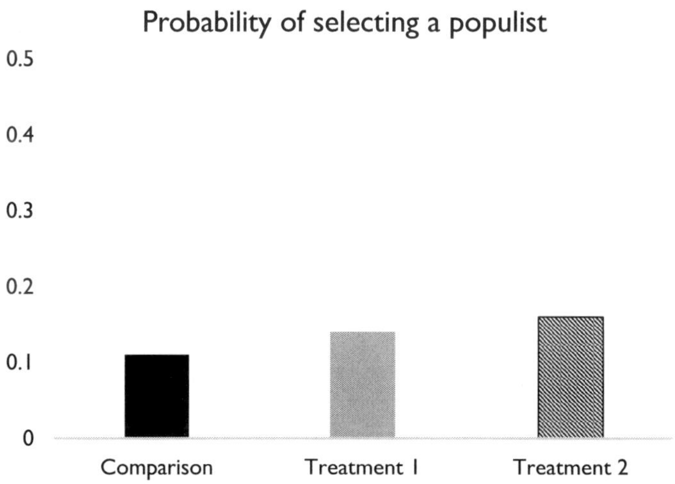

Figure 16.9 Probability of selecting a populist, Study 2

Note: None of the two-tailed *p*-value on the difference between the treatment and comparison groups is not significant; $p>0.40$ in all cases.

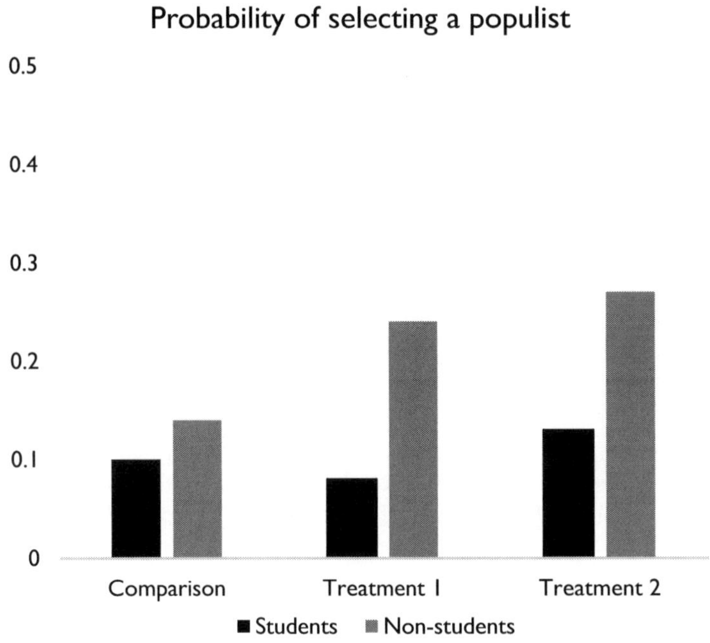

Figure 16.10 Treatment effects by subject group, Study 2

Note: None of the two-tailed *p*-values on the difference between the treatment and comparison groups for either students or non-students is significant; $p>0.40$ in all cases. However, when collapsed across treatments, the difference between students and non-students is significant at the $p = 0.054$ level.

from negligence or external causes, and that this response would be greater when the misconduct was endemic. In the experiments that we ran at Northwestern and Oxford, our empirical support for our assertions proved weaker than we hoped; our second hypothesis (misconduct should be widespread) was not generally supported, and our first hypothesis (the importance of intentional misconduct) was supported inconsistently. Nonetheless, we still believe that our study has some important implications for future work.

First, we should emphasize that in a general, if not a statistical sense, we found evidence across both our experiments that policy failures do induce populist behavior when framed in the context of a normative democratic threat. Where policy failures were attributed to elite corruption and collusion, as opposed to exogenous events beyond anyone's control, our subjects were more likely to feel concern, to voice the elements of populist rhetoric, and to choose a populist partner to work with. Although at Oxford the general hypothesized relationship was noisy and fell short of statistical significance, we saw promising results among Oxford townspeople and clearer results at Northwestern. Across two very different contexts, we think these results provide limited evidence for a key causal mechanism of the ideational approach: intentional, selfish betrayal by elites prompted concern and encouraged populist thinking. According to our theory, individuals reacted with populism to protect and defend democratic norms and values for the larger community – in other words, in protection of the good people. While this mechanism should be tested through further experimental research, we are encouraged by these findings. Given the importance of *intentionality* in the ideational argument, future experiments could more carefully test whether the effect of elite misconduct differs from that of mere incompetence.

Second, our results suggest that the extent of corruption among politicians does not seem to matter all that much. At both Northwestern and Oxford, there was no discernible difference between our two different treatments, which attempted to capture different degrees of corruption among local officials. It may be that in describing the misconduct of an entire department of local government we already made the misconduct appear widespread; this could be tested in future experiments by making the misconduct more localized (for example, attributing it to a rogue official). But it may also be that any information about corruption, regardless of whether it is widespread or more localized, is enough to trigger a populist response. Mentions of corruption may trigger a powerful affective response that connects to populist attitudes, as in other instances of affective cognition (Hameleers, Bos, and de Vreese 2017). While our results are therefore an intriguing first application of the concept of democratic normative threat, we invite researchers to further test the degree of violation of democratic norms related to populist responses and to further scrutinize the role of emotions in this context.

Third, we think that our experiments also raise some potentially serious concerns about the use of student samples. Why do we see lower populist mobilization among students than non-students at Oxford? After all, students and young adults in other countries sometimes provide crucial support for populists (attested by the movement supporting Bernie Sanders in the 2016 US presidential primaries). This is largely speculation as we have no way of confirming this post-hoc, but we think part of the reason may lie in the fact that the policy failure – pavement damage and flooding – was simply too far removed from the students' daily concerns. Some tentative evidence for this can be found in Figure 16.6. When asked how concerned they were about this issue, there was no observable difference at all amongst students regardless of whether they received the treatment or comparison conditions and in general, students reported far lower levels of concern than local residents. Of course, the fact that Northwestern students were still affected by our treatment, even in the context of a similar minor local policy failure, partly undermines this explanation. But there is one further difference. The no-deception rule at the CESS lab at Oxford meant both the policy failure and the potential partners were presented to our subjects as purely hypothetical. This may have further undermined its realism for our subjects, particularly the students, leading them to say more populist things without translating them into populist behavior.

If true, our experience at Oxford suggests that we need to be careful when selecting our samples for future lab-based experiments related to populism. Clearly, labor market position, life experience, and education are all important conditioning factors for populist behavior, and they can interact with the context to produce different results. Experimental psychologists have long debated the issue of student samples, but recent work from the CESS laboratory in particular has highlighted that students and non-students behave differently in the lab (indeed, in this particular lab). Students are more likely to exhibit different social preferences and to behave as rational and selfish agents (Belot, Duch, and Miller 2015). This is a problem if populism truly reflects normative concerns or draws heavily from emotional reasoning.

Finally, we believe that our approach to measurement opens new avenues of thinking about populist behavior in experimental settings. Lab-based experiments offer a number of possibilities, including more sophisticated treatments but also outcome measures, such as eye-motion tracking for gauging attention and preference, skin-conductivity tests for measuring emotion, and fMRI for identifying portions of the brain activated by the treatment. They also allow for interactions of subjects with each other and with the experiment moderators. In our case, we used the lab setting (at least at Northwestern) to gauge something akin to populist mobilization.

The possibility of measuring other social interactions is ripe with potential. As the ideational theory argues, collective action is both necessary for populism to become electorally successful and problematic. Potential participants in populist parties and movements may take strategic considerations into account when they decide to participate. All of this can be gauged through lab experiments, for example, through behavioral games. Future studies should build upon the experiments presented here to continue testing the propositions of the ideational approach.

Notes

1 We are grateful to the Political Science Research Laboratory at Northwestern University for providing the student subjects for the Northwestern portion of the experiments, and to Ray Duch and the CESS laboratory at Nuffield College, for their help with the running of the experiment at Oxford.
2 Even recent work that challenges some of these findings concludes that collective concerns are as important as individualist perspectives (see Healy, Persson, and Snowberg 2017).
3 In our design, a pure control (where the subjects see no problem or scenario) makes our dependent variables nonsensical. As a result, we elected for this comparison group approach.
4 In other studies, we have used these questions successfully to frame normative threats in a populist way (Hawkins et al. 2014b; 2014c).
5 For the mention of a bad elite, the two coders had a raw percentage agreement of 89.5% and a Cohen's kappa of 0.78. For the second indicator, the mention of a good people, the two coders had a raw percentage agreement of 95.4% and a Cohen's kappa of 0.84.
6 Coding procedures were the same here as in Study 1. For the mention of a bad elite, the two coders had a raw percentage agreement of 89% and a Cohen's kappa of 0.78. For the second indicator, the mention of a good people, the two coders had a raw percentage agreement of 96% and a Cohen's kappa of 0.86.
7 Note that in total, there are 46 non-students in our sample.
8 Note that the overall tendency to express populism is lower in Study 2 than Study 1.

References

Akkerman, Agnes, Cas Mudde, and Andrej Zaslove. 2014. "How Populist Are the People? Measuring Populist Attitudes in Voters." *Comparative Political Studies* 47 (9): 1324–1353.

Belot, Michele, Raymond Duch, and Luis Miller. 2015. "A Comprehensive Comparison of Students and Non-Students in Classic Experimental Games." *Journal of Economic Behavior & Organization* 113: 26–33.

Bos, Linda, Wouter Van Der Brug, and Claes H. De Vreese. 2013. "An Experimental Test of the Impact of Style and Rhetoric on the Perception of Right-Wing Populist and Mainstream Party Leaders." *Acta Politica* 48 (2): 192–208.

Cesario, Joseph, Jason E. Plaks, Nao Hagiwara, Carlos David Navarrete, and E. Tory Higgins. 2010. "The Ecology of Automaticity How Situational Contingencies Shape Action Semantics and Social Behavior." *Psychological Science* 21 (9): 1311–1317.

Chanley, Virginia. 1994. "Commitment to Political Tolerance: Situational and Activity-Based Differences." *Political Behavior* 16 (3): 343–363.

Craig, Maureen A., and Jennifer A. Richeson. 2014. "On the Precipice of a 'Majority-Minority' America Perceived Status Threat From the Racial Demographic Shift Affects White Americans' Political Ideology." *Psychological Science* 25 (6): 1189–1197.

Davis, Darren W., and Brian D. Silver. 2004. "Civil Liberties vs. Security: Public Opinion in the Context of the Terrorist Attacks on America." *American Journal of Political Science* 48 (1): 28–46.

Enos, Ryan D. 2016. "What the Demolition of Public Housing Teaches Us about the Impact of Racial Threat on Political Behavior." *American Journal of Political Science* 60 (1): 123–142.

Feldman, Stanley. 2003. "Enforcing Social Conformity: A Theory of Authoritarianism." *Political Psychology* 24 (1): 41–74.

Feldman, Stanley, and Karen Stenner. 1997. "Perceived Threat and Authoritarianism." *Political Psychology* 18 (4): 741–770.

Gibson, James L. 2006. "Enigmas of Intolerance: Fifty Years after Stouffer's Communism, Conformity, and Civil Liberties." *Perspectives on Politics* 4 (1): 21–34.

Hameleers, Michael, Linda Bos, and Claes H. de Vreese. 2017. "'They Did It' The Effects of Emotionalized Blame Attribution in Populist Communication." *Communication Research* 44 (6): 870–900.

Hawkins, Kirk A. 2010. *Venezuela's Chavismo and Populism in Comparative Perspective*. Cambridge: Cambridge University Press.

Hawkins, Kirk A., Joshua R. Gubler, Ethan C. Busby, and Christian Carter. 2014a. "Why Individuals Support Populist Candidates." In *Annual Meeting of the Midwest Political Science Association*. Chicago, IL.

——. 2014b. "Solving the Puzzle of Populism." In General Conference of the European Consortium for Political Research. Glasgow, UK.

Hawkins, Kirk A., Scott Riding, and Cas Mudde. 2012. "Measuring Populist Attitudes." *Working Paper Series on Political Concepts, ECPR Committee on Concepts and Methods.*

Healy, Andrew J., Mark Persson, and Erik Snowberg. 2017. "Digging into the Pocketbook: Evidence on Economic Voting from Income Registry Data Matched to a Voter Survey." *American Political Science Review* 111 (4): 771–785.

Hetherington, Marc J., and Jonathan D. Weiler. 2009. *Authoritarianism and Polarization in American Politics*. Cambridge: Cambridge University Press.

Jost, John T., Jaime L. Napier, Hulda Thorisdottir, Samuel D. Gosling, Tibor P. Palfai, and Brian Ostafin. 2007. "Are Needs to Manage Uncertainty and Threat Associated with Political Conservatism or Ideological Extremity?" *Personality and Social Psychology Bulletin* 33 (7): 989–1007.

Kiewiet, D. Roderick. 1983. *Macroeconomics and Micropolitics: The Electoral Effects of Economic Issues*. Chicago, IL: University of Chicago Press.

Kinder, Donald R., and D. Roderick Kiewiet. 1981. "Sociotropic Politics: The American Case." *British Journal of Political Science* 11 (2): 129–161.

Kriesi, Hanspeter. 2014. "The Populist Challenge." *West European Politics* 37 (2): 361–378.

Mansfield, Edward D., and Diana C. Mutz. 2009. "Support for Free Trade: Self-Interest, Sociotropic Politics, and Out-Group Anxiety." *International Organization* 63 (3): 425–457.

Sears, David O. 1986. "College Sophomores in the Laboratory: Influences of a Narrow Data Base on Social Psychology's View of Human Nature." *Journal of Personality and Social Psychology* 51 (3): 515.

Spruyt, Bram, Gil Keppens, and Filip Van Droogenbroek. 2016. "Who Supports Populism and What Attracts People to It?" *Political Research Quarterly* 69 (2): 335–346.

Stenner, Karen. 2005. *The Authoritarian Dynamic*. Cambridge: Cambridge University Press.

Tett, Robert P., and Hal A. Guterman. 2000. "Situation Trait Relevance, Trait Expression, and Cross-Situational Consistency: Testing a Principle of Trait Activation." *Journal of Research in Personality* 34 (4): 397–423.

Torre, Carlos de la. 2010. *Populist Seduction in Latin America, Second Edition*. 2nd ed. Athens: Ohio University Press.

Appendix

Populist attitudes index

Next, we would like to know some of your political views. To what extent do you agree or disagree with the following statements?

	Strongly disagree	*Disagree*	*Somewhat disagree*	*Neither agree nor disagree*	*Somewhat agree*	*Agree*	*Strongly agree*
The politicians in Congress need to follow the will of the people. (1)	❍	❍	❍	❍	❍	❍	❍
The people, not the politicians, should make our most important policy decisions. (2)	❍	❍	❍	❍	❍	❍	❍
The political differences between the people and the elite are larger than the differences among the people. (3)	❍	❍	❍	❍	❍	❍	❍
What people call "compromise" in politics is really just selling out on one's principles. (4)	❍	❍	❍	❍	❍	❍	❍

To what extent do you agree or disagree with the following statements?

	Strongly disagree	*Disagree*	*Somewhat disagree*	*Neither agree nor disagree*	*Somewhat agree*	*Agree*	*Strongly agree*
It is important to listen to groups with different opinions. (1)	❍	❍	❍	❍	❍	❍	❍
Diversity limits my freedom. (2)	❍	❍	❍	❍	❍	❍	❍
Politicians should lead the people, not follow them. (3)	❍	❍	❍	❍	❍	❍	❍
Our country would run better if decisions were left up to non-elected, independent experts. (4)	❍	❍	❍	❍	❍	❍	❍
Politics is ultimately a struggle between good and evil. (5)	❍	❍	❍	❍	❍	❍	❍
Democracy is about achieving compromise among differing viewpoints. (6)	❍	❍	❍	❍	❍	❍	❍

To what extent do you agree or disagree with the following statements?

	Strongly disagree	*Disagree*	*Somewhat disagree*	*Neither agree nor disagree*	*Somewhat agree*	*Agree*	*Strongly agree*
I'd rather be represented by an ordinary citizen than an experienced politician. (1)	❍	❍	❍	❍	❍	❍	❍
Politicians talk too much and take too little action. (2)	❍	❍	❍	❍	❍	❍	❍
The power of a few special interests prevents our country from making progress. (3)	❍	❍	❍	❍	❍	❍	❍
Our country would run better if decisions were left up to successful business people. (4)	❍	❍	❍	❍	❍	❍	❍

Treatments

The bolded text was varied across treatment conditions.

Thank you for your responses. Next, you will be participating in a study that will help us understand how individuals approach problem-solving in a team setting. You will be given information on a current problem and then asked to work with a partner from here in the lab to come up with a solution.

We will first have you read a description of the problem and answer a few questions about what you think is causing it. We will then ask you to choose your partner from among two other people who are currently in the lab. To help you with your partner selection, we will provide you with their answers to the same questions that you answered about the problem. Once we have collected everyone's choice of partners, we will make the final assignment and let you meet each other. Whenever possible, we will respect your choice of partners.

Please read the scenario below and answer the questions that follow.

The amount of sidewalk damage in Seward, Nebraska, has increased in recent years. Although the walkways are not old, winter weather conditions have been unusually severe and resulted in extensive cracking and pitting. Most of the sidewalks in the city are now in need of repair, and many residents are bothered by the cracked, uneven concrete.

The city government has a program to maintain these walkways, but the number of damaged areas has exhausted the annual $25,000 set aside for repairs. As of 2016, contractors estimate that repairs throughout the city will cost over $50,000. However, the city budget is tight across the board, and funds cannot be moved over to these repairs.

The Seward County Independent, a local newspaper, points to two additional reasons for the shortfall besides the bad weather. First, the city relies on residents to report problem areas, but few residents or businesses are willing to report problems in their neighborhoods as it sometimes results in charges to home and business owners.

Second, the city's Public Works Department has overspent its budget on salt and sand to deal with the unusually high snowfall; this deficit costs thousands of dollars each year and is paid for by funds originally set aside for sidewalks. Internal city auditors have said that there is some room for improvement in how these funds are managed, and they recommend cutbacks in the department's personnel costs and a restructuring of its budget. City managers said they are taking immediate steps to address the concerns in the auditor's report. (*Comparison Group*) / Second, the city's Public Works Department has overspent its budget on team-building trips to resorts in California; these trips cost thousands of dollars each year and are paid for by funds originally set aside for sidewalks. Internal city auditors have said there is a culture of mismanagement in the department and recommend sweeping changes in its accounting procedures. City managers said they are taking immediate steps to address the concerns in the auditor's report. (*Treatment 1*) / Second, the city's Public Works Department has overspent its budget on team-building trips to resorts in California; these trips cost thousands of dollars each year and are paid for by funds originally set aside for sidewalks. Internal city auditors have said there is a culture of mismanagement, not only in the department but at all levels of city government, and they recommend sweeping changes in accounting procedures. City managers declined to comment on this issue. (*Treatment 2*)

These items followed the treatments and were the same for all subjects:

On a scale from not at all concerned (1) to very concerned (10), how do you feel about the situation just described to you?

1 Not at all concerned (1)
2 (2)
3 (3)
4 (4)
5 (5)
6 (6)
7 (7)
8 (8)
9 (9)
10 Very concerned (10)

What groups or individuals do you think are most responsible for the situation regarding sidewalks in Seward? (Please limit your response to a few words)

In at least a few sentences, explain why you think these groups or individuals are responsible and what should be done about them.

Partner descriptions:

The following responses from fictitious partners were presented to subjects. The order (that is, which came first) was fully randomized.

Pluralist partner:

In at least a few sentences, explain why you think these groups or individuals are responsible and what should be done about them.

Residents and the city government need to work together or they won't solve this issue. Residents and businesses need to report when things break, but that's not enough. City officials should address concerns raised in the auditing report and should be accountable for budget shortfalls. The public works department has to make changes so that this doesn't happen again.

Populist partner:

In at least a few sentences, explain why you think these groups or individuals are responsible and what should be done about them.

This is just another sign that city officials can't be trusted. These politicians don't care about the people. No matter how much citizens report sidewalk problems or a department changes, things won't improve until the people in Seward vote those politicians out. We need to replace them with people who will make the city work for the citizens of Seward.

---

17 Populist voters

The role of voter authoritarianism and ideology

Rosario Aguilar and Ryan E. Carlin

The electoral success of Donald Trump in 2016 sent scholars and pundits of American politics scrambling. How could Trump have gained such broad appeal? To answer these questions, observers invoked familiar, if complex, concepts of populism and authoritarianism (*inter alia*, Baggini 2016; Federico, Johnston and Lavine 2016; Hawkins 2016; MacWilliams 2016; Mudde 2015; Norris 2016; Postel 2016; Taub 2016; Yglesias 2015). Evidence that Trump voters exhibit greater authoritarian predispositions than other voters (Rahn and Oliver 2016) dovetails nicely with Hetherington and Weiler's (2009) argument that the Republican Party's shift to a traditional values and law-and-order message swelled its ranks with authoritarian individuals. Trump's campaign rhetoric was, indeed, populist according to the ideational definition guiding this volume (Hawkins 2016). An uncanny match between this body of evidence and findings that authoritarians tend to support far-right populist parties in Europe (Dunn 2015; Stubager 2013; Inglehart and Norris 2016) has led some to declare that the "populist *Zeitgeist*" (Mudde 2004), and its attitudinal antecedents, extend to the United States and beyond (Mudde 2015; Norris 2016).

Taken together, these studies provide a warrant to investigate whether authoritarian dispositions lay the groundwork at the individual level for ideational populism. Their diversity implies this general proposition could hold under distinct governance structures, such as the supra-national European Union, longstanding democracies like the United States, or new democracies. It also holds irrespective of democratic model (presidentialism, parliamentarism, semi-presidentialism), and apparently does not hinge on whether candidates or parties are the main agents of populism. So far so good. But other scope conditions remain unclear. Namely, is the authoritarianism-populist connection proper to right-wing parties and candidates, or can left-wing parties and candidates make the same connection? Answering this question will shed light on the psychological and ideological correlates of ideational populism.

Based on prior research it is unclear whether left-wing populists can reliably drum up support by activating authoritarian predispositions. On the one hand, left-wing authoritarianism is largely confined to former Communist countries in Eastern Europe (de Regt, Mortelmans, and Smits 2011). Their tendency to vote for populist parties is unknown. Yet in Western Europe, left-wing authoritarians are scarce, and what little evidence we have suggests they support extremist, but not populist parties (Van Heil, Duriez, and Kossowska 2008). In the United States, primary voters of left-wing populist Bernie Sanders (Hawkins 2016) score lower on authoritarian traits than voters of all other candidates studied, i.e. Donald Trump, Ted Cruz, Marco Rubio, John Kasich, and Hillary Clinton (Rahn and Oliver 2016). And although several recent Latin American populists are ideologically leftist, Latin Americans with authoritarian predispositions tend to vote for rightist, not leftist, candidates (Cohen and Smith 2016). Hence the authoritarianism-populist connection may well be confined to right-wing candidates and parties. That expectation guides our analysis.

To gain more purchase on this question, we conduct a survey experiment featuring a left-wing populist candidate who ran for president in Chile in 2013, Roxana Miranda. We find no evidence that authoritarianism conditions the effects of populist messages on *vote intentions* for Miranda. And when it comes to *leadership ratings* – which consistently predict willingness to vote for Miranda – individuals with strong authoritarian predispositions exposed to Miranda's populist rhetoric give her *worse*, not better marks. Though contrary to the conventional wisdom on right-wing populism, voters did not support a populist option in a time of dire political crisis in Chile. Such crisis, brought on by the established elites, could have worked as a threat to the status quo and mobilized authoritarian voters in favor of a populist alternative. This conclusion therefore serves as a call to probe more fully the proposition that the authoritarianism is orthogonal to, or cuts against, support for left-wing populists or populist parties. As such, this case study should guide future research on the psychological microfoundations of ideational populism.

This chapter proceeds as follows. First, it maps the concept of individual-level authoritarianism and identifies which definition the current study uses. Next, a theoretical section describes the assumed mechanisms underlying the linkages between authoritarian predispositions and political support for populists. Then, the discussion moves to case selection in order to acquaint the reader with Roxana Miranda, the candidate in our experiment. From there, we transition into a discussion of the experimental design and, then, the results. A concluding section focuses on the potential theoretical implications of this negative case study for our understanding of ideational populism across the ideological spectrum.

The authoritarian predisposition

The concept of authoritarianism has morphed substantially since Adorno and colleagues (1950) introduced us to the authoritarian personality almost seven decades ago. To them, the authoritarian personality exhibits a high degree of cultural conformity, a need for situational structure, and a yen for passionate leadership. These characteristics presumably provide fertile ground in which to sow the seeds of fascism. The authors measure individuals' authoritarian personality with the F Scale, which taps conventionalism, propensity of submission, superstition, propensity of stereotyping, authoritarian aggression, cynicism, among other traits that the authors argued predicted authoritarianism.[1] So conceived, authoritarianism is posited to undergird a conservative ideology that predicts voting for right-wing candidates (Higgins 1965).

Later work on the authoritarian personality largely maintains this conceptual and theoretical framework but seeks to develop refined measures and predictions. For example, Altemeyer (1996) conceptualizes right-wing authoritarianism as a personality trait, and those who exhibit high levels of this trait need little pressure to submit to authority and to attack others. Accordingly, his Right Wing Authoritarianism Scale (RWA) is based on three attitudinal clusters: orientations to authoritarian submission; levels of authoritarian aggression; and conventionalism.[2] Critics claim these items are not unidimensional, a critique that fits more recent incarnations of the scale as well (Duckitt and Bizumic 2013).

More recently, Stanley Feldman and Karen Stenner have begun to view authoritarianism as a predisposition to favor obedience and conformity, which represent oneness and sameness, over freedom and difference. A predisposition is "any preexisting and relatively stable tendency to respond in a particular way to certain objects or events or events"

(Stenner 2005, 14). As such, they identify an authoritarian predisposition by gauging childrearing values. Those people who believe *good manners* and *obedience* are the most important values to teach children score high on the authoritarian predisposition, while those who choose *imagination* and *independence* score at the libertarian end of the scale (Feldman 2003; Feldman and Stenner 1997; Stenner 2005, 2009). By breaking with measurement approaches that employ ideology-laden questions, their approach allows authoritarians to locate ideologically on the left *or* the right. It also is at odds with Altemeyer's (1996) contention that authoritarianism is a generally salient trait. Although Stenner (2005, 2009) finds authoritarian attitudes are key drivers of intolerant attitudes across domains and cultures, since it is a predisposition, highly authoritarian individuals do not always act in an authoritarian way: a normative threat is required to trigger the authoritarian predisposition. Normative threats include "beliefs, values, and behavior that are inconsistent with perceptions of social conventions—but also behavior that is a challenge to the government's ability to enforce compliance with social rules and regulations" (Feldman 2003: 50). The most effective normative threat is one that endangers the feeling of oneness and sameness. Threats to culture (e.g., Stenner 2005), economic wellbeing (Rickert 1998), or physical safety (Merolla and Zechmeister 2009; Hetherington and Suhay 2011) can be effective as can, we submit, the moral threat posed by a widespread corruption of the political establishment where corruption is abnormal (see also Busby et al. in this volume, Chapter 16).

More recent work thinks of authoritarianism as a worldview – "beliefs and ideals that a person uses as a guide to interpret the world" – by which authoritarians emphasize the need for order, quick responses to threats to order, and support for authorities who can maintain order (Hetherington and Weiler 2009, 36.) In line with Altemeyer's conceptualization, under this view, authoritarians typically behave in an authoritarian manner and, thus, a normative threat is not needed to trigger authoritarian behavior. Authoritarians might therefore oppose expanding civil rights, such as same-sex marriage, simply because they view such policies as contrary to the social order. Building on that assumption, Hetherington and Weiler (2009) interpret current levels of ideological polarization in American politics as the joint product of the Republican Party moving to the right, thereby motivating Republican authoritarians to engage more in politics, and the Democratic Party moving to the left, thus provoking political disengagement in Democrat authoritarians. Recent research shows that individuals who score high in authoritarian attitudes tend to support authoritarian policy measures, while those who do not score high in these attitudes only support authoritarian policies when facing a physical threat (Hetherington and Suhay 2011). In short, threat is not necessary to induce authoritarians to behave as such, but it is sufficient to induce non-authoritarians to do so.

We follow Feldman and Stenner in defining authoritarianism as a predisposition that varies across individuals and that, when interacted with normatively threatening environments, triggers actual attitudes. This definition is appealing for at least two reasons. First, since it is based on child-rearing principles rather than politics, it helps us avoid endogeneity problems we might otherwise run up against in exploring the political consequences of authoritarian attitudes. Second, taking authoritarianism as a predisposition gives us license to theorize about the political conditions that can turn it on and off. Populist rhetoric could very well be such a condition.

Authoritarianism and support for populists, right and left

How might authoritarian predispositions influence support for populist candidates? By populism we mean a Manichaean discourse that views politics as a struggle between a reified general will of the people and a conspiring elite (Hawkins, Riding, and Mudde 2012;

Hawkins 2010; Mudde 2004). As such, populism can be viewed as a latent ideational phenomenon. Though it lacks the conscious and programmatic articulation of an ideology, populism may contain programmatic content (e.g., popular sovereignty) and latch onto "host" ideologies across the political spectrum. Thus, populism can help justify a broad array of policy positions (Hawkins and Rovira Kaltwasser forthcoming).

From this perspective, the basic story of the rise of a populist candidate is as follows. A challenger campaigns with rhetoric that frames mainstream, establishment politicians as so corrupt and unresponsive to the people that they make a mockery of the democratic process. The populist charges that ignoring the general will of the people indicts the entire political class and, thus, the people deserve a candidate who will be their mouthpiece in government. Convinced that only the populist candidate can be the conduit to the sorts of commonsense policies that will serve the people's interest, and that mainstream politicians have sold the people out, voters support the populist as the antidote to the corrupt establishment.

This stylized story ignores powerful authoritarian predispositions that voters may hold. How should we expect authoritarian individuals to react to such a populist campaign? By our definitions of populism and authoritarianism, a populist's anti-elite/pro-people political messaging is expected to incite a normative threat that triggers individuals who are predisposed to authoritarian attitudes to support the populist who pledges to reunify society by casting out the agents of division – the political establishment. That is, by linking the political class to a general corruption of authority, and a menace to common values, populist rhetoric should spur authoritarians to vote for (populist) leaders who promise to restore a more harmonious status quo ante.

This expectation is in line with Adorno et al.'s (1950) seminal theorizing on the political implications of an authoritarian personality. And, crucially, it is consistent with most of the research linking authoritarian attitudes to support for populists who have latched on right-wing host ideologies. But should we expect authoritarians to support candidates espousing populist rhetoric but who have, instead, affixed themselves to left-wing host ideologies? If ideology is totally irrelevant the answer is an unequivocal yes. But reality may not be so cut and dried. Authoritarians may react quite differently to left-wing and right-wing solutions to a corrupt political establishment.

The key distinction, we propose, is that right-wing host ideologies permit populists to credibly commit to *reactionary* solutions – restoring some real or imagined status quo ante – whereas left-wing host ideologies are inextricably linked to *radical* changes, making large-scale changes to the status quo. In the eyes of an authoritarian this makes a world of difference. Their penchant for obedience and conformity over freedom and difference should more reliably predispose authoritarians to support right-wing populists who promise to restore a more harmonious status quo ante. By the same token, this attitudinal predisposition should make authoritarians reject left-wing populist candidates who propose radical new policies to address the corrupt status quo. Authoritarians may classify a left-wing populist calling for radical change as yet another agent of polarization threatening the social oneness and sameness authoritarians crave. Averse to the dangers of aggravating social division *a fortiori*, authoritarians might be expected to react negatively towards a left-wing populist. If this is true, then the authoritarian–populism connection that has received great scholarly and journalistic attention hinges on ideology.

Case selection

We explore authoritarians' reactions to a left-wing populist candidate in the context of Chile's 2013 presidential campaign: Roxana Miranda. Self-identified with the extreme political left, Miranda and her party regularly espoused radical populism. When on message, Miranda railed against the failed policies of entrenched political elites whom she claimed had long governed in their own self-interest rather than in the interest of the working class. For example, as president, Miranda proposed to change the rules of the game to benefit "the people" who, at present, are "slaves" to an oppressive, elite-captured system. The system, according to her, has entrenched unchecked capitalism which has deepened social inequalities. In 2013, the slogan adopted by Miranda and her party, *Partido Igualdad*, was, "Let the people command!" (*¡Que el pueblo mande!*). And as of this writing, the phrase "Nobody has ever asked permission to change history" (*Nunca se ha pedido permiso para cambiar la historia*) appears three times on *Partido Igualdad's* homepage. Thus, her political messaging is characterized by left-wing radical ideational populism.

Our labeling of Roxana Miranda as populist is validated by Hawkins and Castanho Silva's (this volume, Chapter 1) study of populist rhetoric across party leaders, presidential candidates, and party manifestos in Western Europe and the Americas (2010–2013). The two Miranda speeches they sampled rate *more populist than of any other candidate* in the sample, and *Partido Igualad*'s party manifesto rated as the most populist manifesto in the sample. In sum, we are confident that both Roxana Miranda and the party backing her in 2013 employed a political communication style that qualifies as ideational populist.

To claim external validity from our sample of the electorate, Chilean voters must have heard her populist messages. Here we note that Miranda participated in the *franja política*, the state-sponsored television advertising slots allocated equally to all candidates in the final 28 days of the presidential campaign. In 2013 *franja* ad spots lasted about 2 minutes and 10 seconds. Additionally, Miranda participated in all major televised presidential candidate debates and was a guest on the most popular television and radio political talk shows. Thus, we can safely assume the Chilean electorate had been exposed to Roxana Miranda's left-wing populist rhetoric.

Though Miranda successfully painted establishment elites as a normative threat to society's "oneness" and/or the political system, she failed to convince many voters that she could solve the problem, receiving just 1.24% of valid votes. Indeed, despite the flagging popularity of incumbent president, Sebastián Piñera, voters had not cast off the political elite entirely. Two establishment female candidates – Michelle Bachelet (left-wing coalition) and Evelyn Matthei (right-wing coalition) – garnered a large majority of first round votes. Bachelet, who served a term as president from 2006 to 2010, resoundingly won the second round election. Therefore, one could argue that, as Singer et al. do in this volume, the contextual conditions for authoritarians to feel persuaded by populist discourse were lacking in the 2013 Chilean election (which may explain Miranda's poor showing).

The political conditions in which we fielded our study, however, were riper for populism. Chilean political elites of all ideological stripes, including those in government, were implicated in a slew of campaign finance and influence trafficking scandals beginning in January 2015. To argue that this crisis of representation provided enough normative threat to trigger authoritarian attitudes and, thus, support for a populist leadership, we must substantiate the claim that these scandals damaged elites' public image. To that end, let us consider public opinion evidence surrounding this period.

Chile's highest quality public opinion surveys are the Centro de Estudios Públicos's (CEP) semi-annual polls. Their impact on elite behavior and mass political consciousness is unrivaled. Here we analyze polls straddling the rash of scandals – November 2014 and April 2015 (margin of error: +/– 3%, 95% c.i.) – the latter conveniently overlapping with the period in which we fielded our survey experiment.

Figure 17.1 displays striking differences in political trust, perceptions of corruption, and overall public mood between the two surveys presumed to reflect the scandals. From

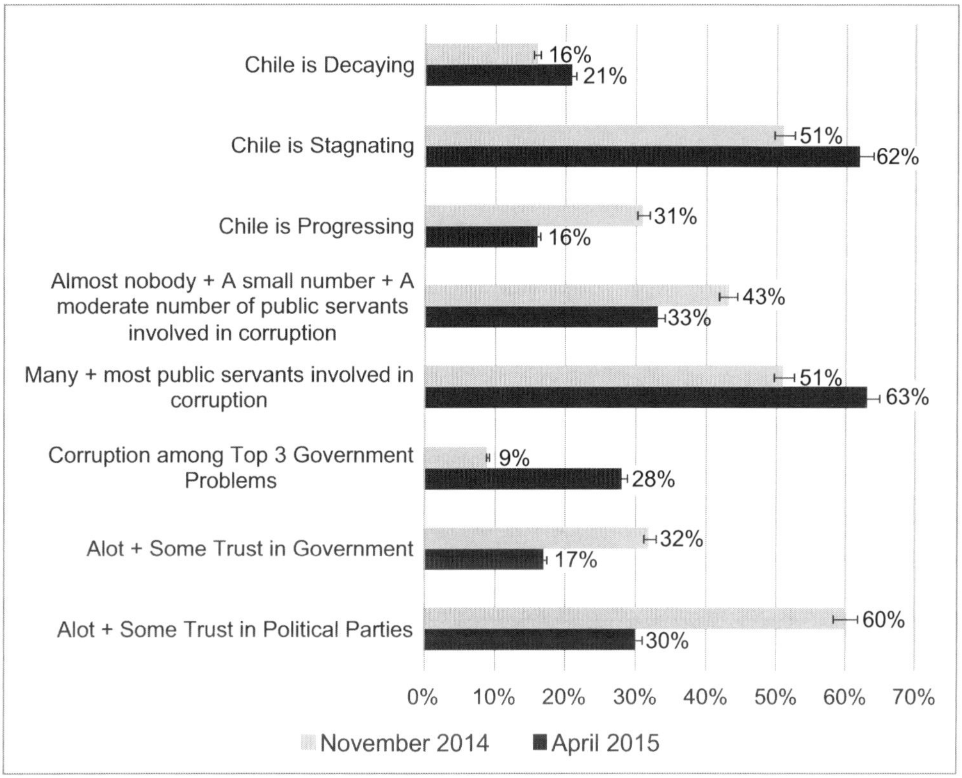

Figure 17.1 Corruption and public opinion in Chile

Source: Centro de Estudios Públicos

November to April, trust in government dropped 15 percentage points, and trust in political parties – already near rock bottom – was halved. The proportion of Chileans putting corruption among the top three problems the government should address more than tripled in this six-month span.[3] In a related way, Chileans' opinions of the magnitude of corruption changed substantially.[4] Before the scandal, the gap between those who felt corruption was widespread as opposed to fairly localized went from +9 in November to +30 in April. Public mood also tanked.[5] The percentage who saw Chile progressing fell from 31% to 16%, while views that stagnation and decay had sunken in rose by 11 and 5 points, respectively.

All differences reported here save one ("Chile is decaying") are statistically significant at the 95% confidence level. While just two time points are used for brevity, a look at the longer time series does not reveal any obvious secular trends that could account for these shifts. Yet, the conduct of science warrants skepticism in the absence of a larger, more rigorous model. While that is beyond the scope of this paper, we feel obligated to support more soundly our claim that these trends owe to a context of scandal about which the Chilean public was aware.

This evidence bolsters our claim that by April 2015, when we conducted our study, Chile had more of the conditions theorized to nurture populism among authoritarians – establishment politicians in a crisis of representation presenting a normative threat. To much of the public, a systematically corrupted ruling class had violated laws meant to shield politicians from moneyed interests and, in so doing, made democratic representation look like sham. Presumably, only the pervasiveness of the scandal, through parties, the presidency, and both legislative chambers, forestalled calls for impeachment of Michelle Bachelet, despite calls for her to step down. Not implicated herself, Roxana Miranda kept a low profile during the crisis, confining herself largely to tweeting criticism of big business, and banks.

By way of summary, a corruption scandal whose breadth and gravity are without precedent in Chile's post-authoritarian era preceded our study by a few months thereby substantiating our claim that voters with authoritarian predispositions who are exposed to Miranda's populist message may, indeed, view the political establishment as a normative threat to Chile's hard-won democracy and, in turn, support Miranda. That is, our study features a real populist, conveying a populist message, and in a context more ripe for populism than two years earlier (Rovira Kaltwasser 2015; Rovira Kaltwasser and Hawkins 2016). How will the authoritarians react: by embracing Miranda and her radical left-wing message as a potential solution, or rejecting her as just another threat to the status quo they cherish?

Experimental design

We recruited 605 Chilean subjects from an invitation-only online panel managed by Netquest, a Spanish marketing firm, to form a quota sample representative of Chile's voting-age population in terms of gender, age, and region. In order to achieve a sample size with sufficient statistical power to find significant results if there were any to be found, we conducted a power analysis. Since the only experimental work manipulating populism we could find is Bos et al. (2013), we reviewed effect sizes in the following studies of candidate traits looking at interaction effects in addition to Bos et al. (2013): Aguilar (2009) and Aguilar et al. (2015a, 2015b). To compute the necessary number of cases, we relied on the statistical tool, *G Power* (Faul et al. 2007). Our calculations, revealed that we would need 351 subjects in the overall sample to recover the average effect size across these studies (d = 0.30) (Cohen 1988).[6] Thus, setting the number of subjects per condition to 302 is warranted on the following grounds. First, since Roxana Miranda fared so poorly in the 2013 election, the effect of the discourse on vote intentions might be far weaker than those observed in previous studies. Second, we needed additional statistical power to test the interaction effect between authoritarian predisposition and populism.

Subjects were randomly assigned to view a one-minute video clip of Roxana Miranda delivering either a populist or a non-populist message during a televised candidate debate hosted by the National Press Association. Sampling both video clips from this debate allows us to limit variation on context-specific elements – location, camera angles, dress, interlocutors, audience, etc. For our purposes, we refer to the subjects (n = 303) who viewed the populist message as the treatment group and those (n = 302) who view the non-populist message as the reference group. Spanish transcriptions of the videos are provided in the Appendix, English translations are provided below.

Non-populist message frame (167 words, 51 seconds)

> It is super simple to fix this. Look, I have here a tool [plastic pipe] that I brought to demonstrate this disposable system. This disposable system is plastic, disposable, it breaks. This contaminates. This [copper pipe] is what we need. This is ours. By

recovering copper we are going to have free education, housing, health, and all the rights that have been privatized. Only with this. And this is what they are selling today. We have to buy, on top of all that, this pipe from abroad. It is simple what we are proposing. To recover our strategic resources is key. And not only in economics. We need to recover the communications media in order to educate our people. Today our people are disinformed and that is why we have the reality of the regions, the impoverished regions. Look at Calama, I just travelled to Calama, where they extract the income of Chile, one of the most impoverished regions, the water contaminated for 40 years with arsenic.

Populist message frame (177 words, 60 seconds)

I want to address my people. If God left us, or gifted us, the land, the cordillera, the fields, the fish and the fruits, the rivers, who gave authorization to five families to do or undo what they want with our rights? Who gave them permission to leave my unborn grandchildren nothing to eat? We are the ones who work. We are the ones who clean their toilets. We are the ones who are working in the mines. We are the ones who work for this country. How long will they trample us? For the first time in Chile we have risen up from below, from all the public policies without common sense. For the first time a popular candidacy of the poor people, of the nobodies, of the landless, of the homeless, of the toothless, of my neighbors who clean toilets, of the thousands of Chileans who are trampled underfoot. And do you think that I'm going to believe today that they are going to change my life? If they have never done it in history?

Both messages clearly communicate a left-wing agenda. The non-populist one proposes nationalizing the mining sector and links privatization to inequality and poverty in the northern regions of Chile. The populist message also harps on deep structural inequalities and class cleavages. But, additionally, the populist message draws a Manichean distinction between a corrupt, immoral elite and a pure, hardworking people. Drawing attention to this otherness should, in the wake of the most extensive corruption scandal in post-authoritarian Chile, invoke a moral threat to our Chilean subjects.

Before going forward, let us consider two essential aspects of the analysis. First, a manipulation check at the end of the questionnaire found that subjects who viewed the populist frame video rated Roxana Miranda's message significantly more critical of Chile's political elites than those who viewed the non-populist message ($\mu_{treatment} - \mu_{control} = 0.81$; $t = 6.34$, $p = 0.00$). This strongly suggests the populist message activated populist sentiments, as the ideational theory predicts. Second, the random assignment of subjects appears to have worked. As Table 17.1 below shows, randomizations produced excellent balance across the non-populist and populist conditions. After regressing the treatment assignment on all covariates in Appendix Table 17.A1, a joint F-test suggests we can reject the hypothesis that they jointly predict treatment assignment (F (32, 542) 0.81, Prob > F 0.77). Satisfying these two conditions gives us greater confidence in our experimental set-up.

Variables and measurement

We present a post-test only control group test. The treatment and randomization to treatment and control groups are described above. Prior to administering the treatment and control videos, subjects in both conditions answer questions tapping authoritarian predispositions. We craft these responses into an authoritarianism index which we will interact with the treatment in a regression model to test our hypotheses. Now let us discuss the measurement and construction of this index.

Following Feldman and Stenner (Feldman 2003; Feldman and Stenner 1997; Stenner 2005, 2009), we asked respondents to order seven traits based on their perceived importance for children to learn at home based on the following question:[7]

> Thinking about the qualities that children can be encouraged to learn at home, if you had to choose, which do you consider the five most desirable that children should have? And of these desirable qualities please number them in order of importance where 1 is the least important and 5 is the most important.
>
> Good manners
>
> Independence
>
> Feeling of responsibility
>
> Imagination
>
> Obedience
>
> Being clean and tidy
>
> Curiosity

Of these, obedience and good manners are the two traits Stenner theorized, and found, to map onto an authoritarian predisposition across countries. Two other measures – imagination and independence – account for libertarian predispositions.[8] Thus, we created an authoritarian predisposition scale by averaging responses that mentioned good manners and obedience as important values that children should learn at home; as well as independence and imagination (reverse coded).[9] Therefore, following Stenner's methodology (2005), the authoritarian and libertarian items have opposite signs, cancelling each other out in the case that a respondent mentioned all of them. The measure takes on four values; the highest corresponds to the highest level of authoritarian predisposition, and the lowest corresponds to the highest value of libertarian predisposition. Figure 17.2 shows the distribution of the data. Most respondents fall into the middle categories; a small minority (<5%), fall into the very libertarian or very authoritarian categories.

Post-treatment, we gauged subject responses to two related dependent variables. The first and most central gauges the probability of voting for Miranda in a hypothetical election held this week.[10] Answers were arrayed on a 7-point Likert scale on which higher values indicate a greater likelihood of support Miranda if an election were held next week. The second dependent variable reflects evaluations of Roxana Miranda as a leader. Subjects were asked, "How much do you agree or disagree with the following statement: Roxana Miranda is a good leader."[11] Responses, gauged on a 7-point Likert scale, are recoded so that increasing values on indicate increasing agreement.

Results

We first explore the descriptive relationship the populist discourse, an authoritarian predisposition, and intentions to vote for Miranda. Figure 17.3 shows no direct treatment effects of populism on vote intentions. The small difference (0.10 on a 7-point scale) is not statistically significant. In terms of the relationship between subjects' authoritarian

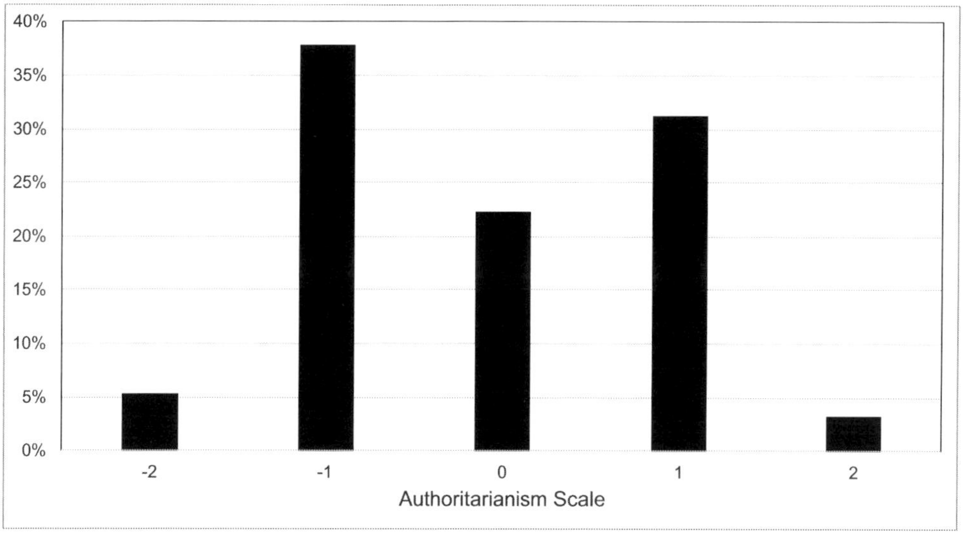

Figure 17.2 Sample distribution of authoritarian predispositions

predisposition and the likelihood of voting for Miranda, the results are convoluted. In the non-populist condition, a negative linear relationship between authoritarianism and willingness to vote for Miranda appears. No such linear relationship is found in the populist condition. While High Authoritarians are more willing to vote for Miranda in the populist condition than in the non-populist condition, subjects at any other level of authoritarianism are equally willing. To test with more confidence the notion that, indeed, authoritarian predispositions make voters more attracted to populist messaging, we turn to interactive regression analysis.

A possible reason for the lack of significant results might be the sample size, even if such sample is larger than the one calculated by the power analysis. Thus, we tested whether there were meaningful effects that could support our hypothesis (Rainey 2014). We simulated the difference on voting preferences among subjects in the treatment and control conditions under a 90% confidence interval to find out whether there were absolute differences at least of 1-point, which would mean that the treatment moved subjects one point on the voting scale for Miranda, either in a positive or negative direction. We used Clarify (Tomz et al. 2003) to calculate such differences and none of them reached an integer. Such evidence makes us confident that our experiment is not masking any meaningful effects that would have otherwise been observed with a larger sample size.

We model the effects of our populist treatment and authoritarian predispositions on vote intentions for Miranda. Results are presented in Table 17.1. First, and in line with the descriptive results, we note that Model 1 finds no direct treatment effects of populist discourse on vote intentions for Miranda. Simply receiving this populist message did not woo voters, thus corroborating the descriptive statistics in Figure 17.1. Adding our index of authoritarianism to the equation, Model 2 indicates no direct effect of authoritarianism on vote intention for Miranda.

Of course, we did not seek to test a direct relationship but rather a conditional one common in the literature: whether individuals with authoritarian predispositions are more

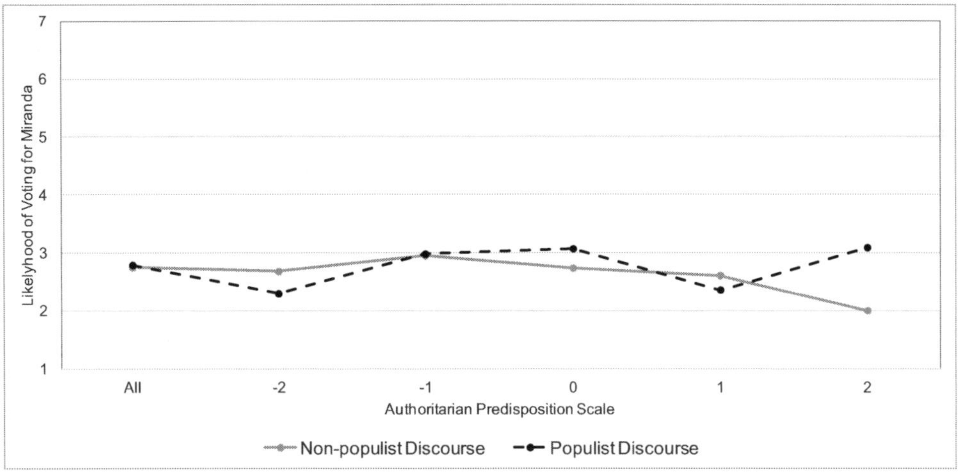

Figure 17.3 Distribution of authoritarian predisposition scale

or less likely to respond positively to populist rhetoric. According to the insignificant coefficient on the interaction term of authoritarianism and the treatment condition in Model 3, the difference in voting likelihood for Miranda among High Authoritarians in the populist and reference conditions is not statistically significant. The marginal effects of populism and authoritarianism are not significant at any value of the authoritarianism scale. Hence this analysis casts doubt on the proposition that populism works by candidates employing populist rhetoric to activate authoritarian predispositions to attract voters. However, it is not the sort of evidence that allows us to establish the alternative hypothesis, i.e. populist messaging and populists themselves represent normative threat that authoritarians are likely to reject. Neither possibility is supported by the evidence.

What accounts for this disjuncture between theory and empirics? Are authoritarianism and support for ideational populists orthogonal? We believe such a conclusion would be hasty for context-specific reasons. Making authoritarians – or Chilean voters in general – more or less willing to support Miranda in an election may simply be too much to ask of our stimulus. Unlike much of Latin America, competition in presidential and legislative elections in Chile is extremely stable (Mainwaring forthcoming). In other words, new entrants capture very little support, and vote shares for the main coalitions barely fluctuate from one election to the next. At the same time, new generations of voters are increasingly unlikely to vote at all, systematically lowering turnout as a percentage of the voting-age population (Navia 2004; Carlin 2006; Došek and Freidenberg 2014). Therefore much of the Chilean electorate appears to hold what Key (1955) calls a "standing decision" either to vote for their coalition's candidate or not to vote at all.

Assuming the above true, we should be more likely to observe authoritarianism's conditioning effects on factors that vary more than Chileans' past voting behavior. For example, candidate character traits, such as leadership, are known to vary over campaigns and to be strong predictors of vote choice (Alvarez 2010; Funk1999; Kinder 1986; Pierce 1993). We do not claim that populism influences authoritarians' voting behavior indirectly, via perceptions of candidate character traits (in this case leadership perceptions). This is certainly a hypothesis others could test with more appropriate designs. Rather, we

Table 17.1 Effects of populism and authoritarianism on vote intention

	Model 1	*Model 2*	*Model 3*
Populist discourse	0.051	0.064	0.062
	(0.252)	(0.248)	(0.247)
Authoritarian predisposition		–0.137	–0.129
		(0.093)	(0.124)
Populist discourse × authoritarian predisposition			–0.016
			(0.099)
Constant	2.753*	2.732*	2.733*
	(0.122)	(0.116)	(0.118)
N	605	605	605
R^2	0.00	0.006	0.006

Note: Entries are OLS regression coefficients with robust standard errors in parentheses.
*p <0.05 (two-tailed)

simply posit that our stimulus may work better on character evaluations, which are more subject to change in the Chilean context, than hypothetical vote intentions. We find in our sample a positive relationship between subjects' positive evaluations of Miranda and their electoral support to the candidate by regressing the latter on the former ($\beta = 0.085$, $t(603) = 2.04$, $p < 0.05$; $R^2 = 0.01$; $F(1,603) = 4.15$, $p < 0.05$).

To that end, we test whether populist discourse interacts with authoritarianism to affect voters' evaluations of Miranda as a leader. Figure 17.4 reveals two patterns. First, Miranda receives slightly better evaluations in the non-populist reference condition than in the populist one. Second, there is almost a linear and positive relationship between the level of authoritarianism and Miranda's evaluation for those exposed to the non-populist rhetoric. The opposite happens in the populist condition: as subjects' authoritarian predispositions increase they tend to evaluate the candidate's leadership more harshly. Consequently, the largest (conditional) treatment effect is among the High Authoritarians. Judging by these

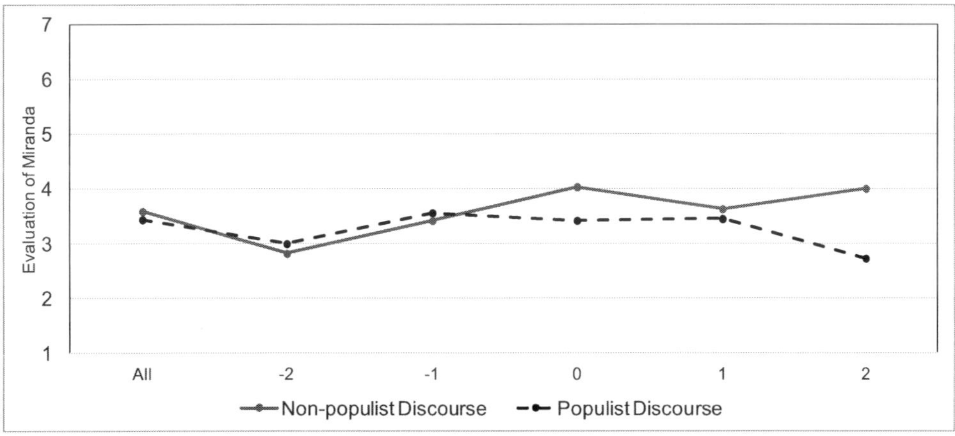

Figure 17.4 Likelihood of voting for Miranda, authoritarian predisposition scale, and populist discourse

purely descriptive results, then, authoritarian predispositions may (negatively) condition the effects of populist discourse on how individuals rate candidates' leadership traits. Let us turn to regression analysis to get a sense of how large and reliable these effects are.

We model the effects of populist discourse and authoritarian predispositions on the evaluation of Miranda as a good leader (Table 17.2 and Figure 17.5). Again, we observe neither direct treatment effects – leadership evaluations are unaltered by populist discourse (Model 1) – nor any direct effects of authoritarianism on leadership evaluations – the extent to which one displays authoritarian predispositions is not independently associated with one's ratings of Miranda as a leader (Model 2). However, as in the descriptive statistics for candidate leadership evaluations, there are conditional effects. Populism affects candidate evaluations differently depending on one's level of authoritarian predisposition.

To tease this out a bit more, Figure 17.5 illustrates the interactive results. At the highest level of authoritarian predisposition, voters in the populist condition tend to evaluate

Table 17.2 Effects of populism and authoritarianism on candidate leadership evaluation

	Model 1	*Model 2*	*Model 3*
Populist discourse	–0.131	–0.139	–0.167
	(0.179)	(0.183)	(0.181)
Authoritarian predisposition		0.077	0.207+
		(0.073)	(0.101)
Populist discourse × authoritarian predisposition			–0.274*
			(0.129)
Constant	3.592*	3.603*	3.623*
	(0.144)	(0.151)	(0.151)
N	605	605	605
R^2	0.001	0.003	0.009

Note: Entries are OLS regression coefficients with robust standard errors in parentheses.
*p < 0.05 (two-tailed);
+p < 0.10 (two-tailed)

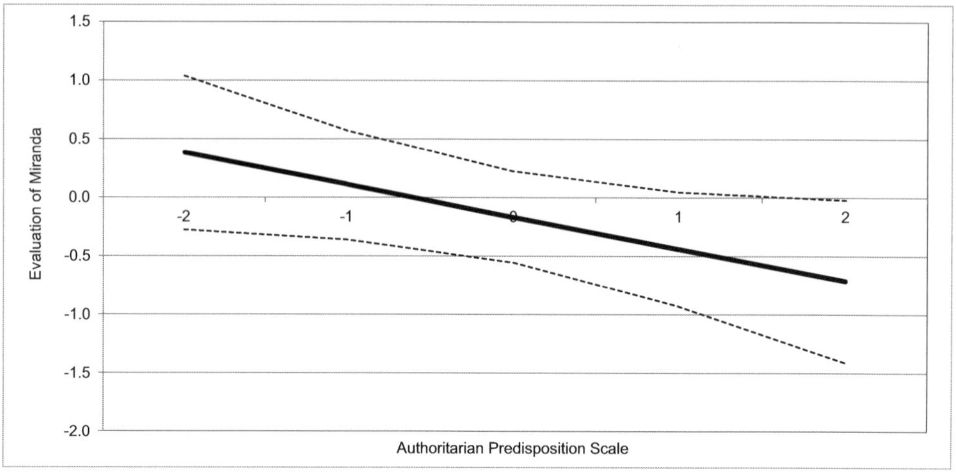

Figure 17.5 Evaluation of Miranda, authoritarian predisposition scale, and populist discourse

Miranda's leadership more poorly than in the non-populist condition (dy/dx = –0.71, p = 0.05). This is consistent with the notion that authoritarians might feel normatively threatened by a populist message and, in turn, reject a candidate who espouses such views. Yet, the effect is visible at low levels of authoritarian predisposition under a one-tail test (dy/dx = –0.44, p = 0.08). Thus we submit that, despite her best efforts to paint the corrupt political establishment as a normative threat, Miranda herself may have embodied such a threat – and authoritarians reacted with disdain.

Discussion

Populism and authoritarianism have long histories in political discourse in the United States, Europe, and Latin America. This volume makes a strong case for populism as a set of ideas that resonate with voters when populist rhetoric is pitched in a context of corruption or representation crisis allows. For their part, the identification and measurement of the traits that make individuals receptive to, if not demand, authoritarian leadership has evolved mightily since Adorno and his colleagues (1950) began their classic work on the authoritarian personality in the wake of World War II without consensus emerging. Rigorous research on these concepts, and their relationship to voting behavior, may be out of its infancy but it still suffers from growing pains.

Against this backdrop, the current study can only hope to make incremental progress towards answering the research question that motivates it: Does authoritarianism condition the translation of populist messages into political support differently for populist candidates of the left and right? By locating our study in the context of a Chilean election featuring a left-wing populist candidate, Roxana Miranda, we probed the scope conditions of theories linking authoritarianism to support for – mostly right-wing – populists grounded in evidence largely gathered from Europe and, most recently, the United States. Contrary to this received wisdom, we proposed the alternative hypothesis that left-wing populists would be less likely to generate support among individuals with authoritarian predispositions. This logic drew on the crucial distinction between the sorts of change these two populists champion: right-wing populists call for a *reactionary* return to some real or imagined *status quo ante* – a move that fits the authoritarian worldview – and left-wing populists call for *radical* transformations away from the *status quo* – moves that rankle authoritarians. Our evidence allows us to weigh in on these competing hypotheses with a case study.

Our case-study design sought to balance the realism of an actual populist candidate communicating an actual populist message in the midst of an ongoing crisis of representation against experimenter control. When it comes to voting intention, we found no proof that authoritarianism produces a wholesale embrace of left-wing populists. Indeed, the results show that the basic link between authoritarianism and voting intentions for the left-wing populist, Roxana Miranda, is broken. If this is true more broadly, then authoritarianism and populism may be simply orthogonal for left-wing populists. Yet evidence with respect to a more malleable consideration augurs against this interpretation. Namely, we find as levels of authoritarian predisposition increases, individuals more heavily downgrade Miranda's leadership qualities when exposed to her radical left-wing populist message. This is in keeping with our expectation that authoritarian-populism nexus functions oppositely for leftists. While this evidence constitutes but a single datum, viewed in relation to the relative strengths of case studies such as ours – to generate new hypotheses and to identity potential scope conditions (e.g. Gerring 2004) – it may indeed contribute to our understanding of the psychological foundations of populism.

Drawing on both the strengths and weaknesses of our approach, let us conclude by discussing the hypotheses emerging from our analysis that could, in future, prove to be theory-generative. First, the foregoing analysis implies an ideological asymmetry in the psychological foundations of populism. We obtain null results for the interaction of authoritarian predispositions with populist messaging when it comes to predicting vote intentions for Miranda; we also observe a negative interactive effect between populist messaging and authoritarian predispositions on Miranda's leadership traits. Both findings stand in direct opposition to evidence of an affinity between authoritarianism and right-wing populist support. In an ideal world, the election under scrutiny would have also contained a right-wing populist against which we could balance this inference. However, evidence from the U.S. case that primary voters for Bernie Sanders are far less authoritarian than voters for Donald Trump (Rahn and Oliver 2016) bolsters the notion that the authoritarian–populist connection is ideologically asymmetric. Evidence from Latin America associating authoritarianism with support for right-wing authoritarian politicians, but not left-wing authoritarian populists (Cohen and Smith 2016), also resonates with our findings. So, while our case study cannot *test* a theory of ideological asymmetry vis-à-vis the authoritarian–populist link, taken in concert with evidence elsewhere, the proposition deserves broader scrutiny on new data. The proliferation of populists of all ideological stripes provides an additional warrant for research in this vein.

Second, the results above are ambivalent with respect to how authoritarians should be expected to behave under threat. If Feldman and Stenner are right, normative threat is crucial to activating authoritarian attitudes and connecting them to political and social policy preferences and actors. The neat interaction by which populist treatment (the threat) and authoritarian predispositions influence evaluations of Miranda as a leader supports this model. But if Hetherington and Suhay (2011) are correct, then a normative social threat could incline both authoritarians and nonauthoritarians to support authoritarian policies and actors. Neither of our analyses fit this model exactly. The willingness to vote for Miranda is certainly not a linear function of the interaction between authoritarianism and populist messaging (Table 17.2). There could, however, be a non-linear relationship at work. Descriptive analysis in Figure 17.1 reveals that both low and high authoritarians, but not moderate authoritarians, exhibit a slightly greater willingness to vote for Miranda after hearing the populist message compared to the non-populist message. Though this finding does not reach statistical significance, in the context of a case study it is suggestive. Altogether, then, our analyses imply that authoritarianism and populism may not always interact in a linear way to influence political behavior and attitudes; it may be domain specific. Future studies with more statistical power and a tailor-made design may wish to test this proposition more explicitly.

A secondary goal of our analysis is to probe the scope conditions of the link between authoritarianism and support for populists. Per the discussion above, however, our strong hunch is that ideology – not country, region, or election-specific characteristics – is the key scope condition. Namely, we find it intuitive that authoritarians (who strongly value conformity, convention, and unity) should prefer the reactionary appeals most commonly associated with right-wing actors, as opposed to radical proposals which are the *modus operandi* of the extreme left. Nevertheless, a single case study cannot rule out alternative interpretations. Here, we lay out three of them.

First, historical context could alter how authoritarians perceive populists across the political spectrum. More specifically, the authoritarianism–populism thesis may work with leftist populists, but not where left–populism has become a major political division. If so, then Chileans might be particularly sensitive to radical left-wing populists given the bloody history of Salvador Allende – one of the most populist presidents in Latin America history

(Hawkins and Rovira Kaltwasser forthcoming) – and the political learning that followed (Roberts 1998). Therefore, recent histories of failed left-wing populism may shape the scope conditions under which our inferences apply. While the Chilean case may be *sui generis*, tests that could incorporate the legacies of Perú's Juan Velasco Alvarado or, perhaps at some point, Greece's SYRIZA and *chavismo* in Venezuela, could provide leverage on the question.

Second, our results and, therefore, the scope conditions of the authoritarianism–populism connection, could be determined by specific conditions of Miranda's candidacy. Had her chances of victory been greater, would we have found evidence of populist rhetoric driving authoritarians to support her? Such an objection cannot be easily dismissed in light of ample evidence of strategic voting. So as not to waste votes, the theory goes, voters will strategically support whomever they perceive to be the least-worst candidate over their preferred candidate if the latter has little chance of winning. However, our design mitigates such a facile conclusion. If this were the dominant strategy governing our subjects' responses, it could not explain why authoritarians would judge Miranda's leadership qualities so much more poorly after hearing her populist message than after hearing a non-populist appeal. Moreover, the Chilean case features two rounds of presidential voting, which allows voters to be sincere in the first round and strategic in the second. Thus, we doubt this factor heavily conditions our results or delimits the theory's scope.

Third, gender may be factor. Is there something about women populist leaders that repels authoritarians? To the extent that authoritarianism overlaps with attitudes concerning traditional gender roles, this is a distinct possibility (but see Mudde and Rovira Kaltwasser 2015). A partial, but straightforward test of this hypothesis would have been possible. Speeches by another candidate in the 2013 presidential race, Marco Enríquez Ominami, register moderate levels of populist rhetoric (Hawkins and Castanho Silva 2016). Thus we could have compared the authoritarianism–populism link across the two candidates who differ chiefly in gender. Though a leftist in his 2009 bid for the presidency (Bunker and Navia 2013), Enríquez Ominami's increasingly centrist positions may have confounded such an analysis by 2013. Moreover, his subsequent indictment for violating campaign finance laws would clearly preclude such an analysis now. Replicating the analysis in additional case studies of female populist candidates, or cross-case comparisons matching other female populist candidates with male populist candidates who are alike on all other relevant traits represent fruitful ways to explore this hypothesis.

Notes

1 The F Scale has been critiqued on several grounds. Namely, that it measures old-fashioned Victorian values rather that authoritarian ones; that because the direction of the questions always aim at what the authors consider to be authoritarianism there is a bias towards over-representing the authoritarian personality of the respondents; and that some respondents can guess the concepts the scale measures and lie when answering it (see Brown 1965; Christie 1954; Gul and Ray 1989; Hyman and Sheatsley 1954).

2 Altemeyer's instrument taps these attitudinal clusters with items worded in different directions, for some agreement with the question depicts an authoritarian attitude for others disagreement connotes an authoritarian attitude.

3 "*¿Cuáles son los tres problemas a los que debería dedicar el mayor esfuerzo en solucionar el Gobierno? Corrupción.*"

4 "*¿Qué tan extendida piensa usted que está la corrupción en el servicio público de Chile? Casi nadie está involucrado; un pequeño número de personas están involucradas; un número moderado de personas están involucradas; mucha gente está involucrada; casi todas las personas están involucradas.*"

5 "*¿Ud. cree que en el momento actual Chile está: Progresando, Estancado o En decadencia?*"

6 This *a priori* power analysis to calculate the sample size we would need to find a minimal statistically significant main effect based on the expected average effect and standard deviation based on the aforementioned research under a two-tailed test. We also conducted a *post-hoc* power analysis to test the minimal effect size that would produce a statistically significant (under a two-tailed test) result from an interaction term, taking into account the sample size, power, and variance of the residuals from the data. The results from both analyses are in Figure 17.A1 and Figure 17.A2, respectively.

7 "*Pensando en las cualidades que se pueden fomentar en los niños en el hogar, si tuviera que escoger ¿cuáles considera usted que son las 5 cualidades más deseables que deberían de tener los niños? Y de esas cualidades que son deseables por favor enumérelas en orden de importancia donde 1 es la menos importante y 5 es la más importante. Buenos modales, independencia, sentido de responsabilidad, imaginación, obediencia, que sean limpios y ordenados, curiosidad.*"

8 The questionnaire did not include tolerance as a trait.

9 Cronbach's α for the scale is reasonable, 0.46. Both authoritarian items are negatively correlated to both libertarian items. Surprisingly, obedience and good manners are uncorrelated ($\rho = -0.006$, $p = 0.89$ as are independence and imagination ($\rho = -0.02$, $p = 0.66$).

10 "*Si esta semana fueran las próximas elecciones presidenciales y Roxana Miranda estuviera compitiendo para la presidencia ¿qué tan probable sería que votara por ella?*"

11 "*¿Qué tan acuerdo o en desacuerdo está con la siguiente afirmación: Roxana Miranda es una buena líder?*"

References

Adorno, Theodor, Else Frenkel-Brunswik, Daneil Levinson, and R. Nevitt Sanford. 1950. *The Authoritarian Personality*. New York: Harpers.

Aguilar, Rosario. 2009. *The Political Consequences of Prejudice among Mexicans and Mexican Americans*. Ph.D. Dissertation, Department of Political Science, The University of Michigan, Ann Arbor.

Aguilar, Rosario, Saul Cunow, and Scott Desposato. 2015a. "Choice Sets, Gender, and Candidate Choice in Brazil." *Electoral Studies* 39(1): 230–242.

Aguilar, Rosario, Saul Cunow, Scott Desposato, and Leonardo Sangali Barone. 2015b. "Ballot Structure, Candidate Race, and Vote Choice in Brazil." *Latin American Research Review* 50(3): 175–202.

Altemeyer, Bob. 1996. *The Authoritarian Specter*. Cambridge, MA: Harvard University Press.

Alvarez, Michael. 2010. "Predicting Election Outcomes from Positive and Negative Trait Assessments of Candidate Images." *Political Psychology* 31(1): 41–58.

Baggini, Julian. 2016. "How Rising Trump and Sanders Parallel Rising Populism in Europe." *New Perspectives Quarterly* 33(2): 22–25.

Bos, Linda, Wouter van der Brug and Claes H. de Vreese. 2013. "An Experimental Test of the Impact of Style and Rhetoric on the Perception of Right-wing Populist and Mainstream Party Leaders." *Acta Politica* 48(2): 192–208.

Brown, Roger. 1965. *Social Psychology*. New York: Free Press.

Bunker, Kenneth, and Patricio D. Navia. 2013. "Latin American Political Outsiders, Revisited: The Case of Marco Enríquez Ominami in Chile, 2009." *Journal of Politics in Latin America* 5(2): 3–35.

Carlin, Ryan E. 2006. "The Decline of Citizen Participation in Electoral Politics in Post-authoritarian Chile." *Democratization* 13(4): 632–651.

Centro de Estudios Públicos. 2015. "Estudio Nacional de Opinión Pública N° 73." www.cepchile.cl/cep/site/artic/20160304/asocfile/20160304101227/EncuestaCEP_Abril2015.pdf.

Centro de Estudios Públicos. 2014. "Estudio Nacional de Opinión Pública N° 72." www.cepchile.cl/cep/site/artic/20160304/asocfile/20160304100954/EncuestaCEP_Noviembre2014.pdf.

Christie, Richard. 1954. "Authoritarianism Re-examined." In *Studies in the Scope and Method of "The Authoritarian Personality,"* edited by Richard Christie and Marie Jahoda, 123–196. Glencoe, IL: Free Press.

Cohen, Mollie, and Amy Erica Smith. 2016. "Do Authoritarians Vote for Authoritarians? Evidence from Latin America." *Research & Politics* 3(4): 1–8.

De Regt, Sabrina, Dimitri Mortelmans, and Tim Smits. 2011. "Left-wing Authoritarianism Is Not a Myth, but a Worrisome Reality. Evidence from 13 Eastern European Countries." *Communist and Post-Communist Studies* 44(4): 299–308.

Došek, Tomáš, and Flavia Freidenberg. 2014. "Voto hacia nuevos candidatos en sistemas de partidos (des)institucionalizados: el caso de Marco Enríquez-Ominami en Chile 2009." *Revista SAAP* 8(1): 11–42.

Duckitt, John, and Boris Bizumic. 2013. "Multidimensionality of Right-Wing Authoritarian Attitudes: Authoritarianism-Conservatism-Traditionalism." *Political Psychology* 34(6): 841–862.

Dunn, Kris. 2015. "Preference for Radical Right-Wing Populist Parties among Exclusive-Nationalists and Authoritarians." *Party Politics* 21(3): 367–380.

Faul, Franz, Edgar Erdfelder, Albert-Georg Lang, and Axel Buchner. 2007. "G*Power 3: A Flexible Statistical Power Analysis Program for the Social, Behavioral, and Biomedical Sciences." *Behavior Research Methods* (2)39: 175–191.

Federico, Christopher, Christopher Johnston, and Howard Lavine. 2016. "Here's Why Trump's Supporters Tolerate his 'Liberal' Economic Positions." *The Monkey Cage, Washington Post*, March 8, www.washingtonpost.com/news/monkey-cage/wp/2016/03/08/heres-why-trumps-supporters-tolerate-his-liberal-economic-positions/.

Feldman, Stanley. 2003. "Enforcing Social Conformity: A Theory of Authoritarianism." *Political Psychology* 24 (1): 41–74.

Feldman, Stanley, and Karen Stenner. 1997. "Perceived Threat and Authoritarianism." *Political Psychology* 18(4): 741–770.

Funk, Carolyn L. 1999. "Bringing the Candidate into Models of Candidate Evaluation." *Journal of Politics* 61(3): 700–720.

Gerring, John. 2004. "What is a Case Study and What is It Good for?" *American Political Science Review* 98(02): 341–354.

Gul, Ferdinand A., and John J. Ray. 1989. "Pitfalls in Using the F Scale to Measure Authoritarianism in Accounting Research." *Behavioral Research in Accounting* 1(1): 182–192.

Hawkins, Kirk A. 2010. Venezuela's Chavismo and Populism in Comparative Perspective. New York: Cambridge University Press.

Hawkins, Kirk A. 2016. Populism and the 2016 US Presidential Election in Comparative Perspective. *APSA Comparative Politics Section Newsletter* (Fall).

Hawkins, Kirk A., and Bruno Castanho Silva. 2016. "Mapping Populist Parties in Europe and the Americas." Paper prepared for presentation at Explaining Populism: Team Populism Conference, Provo-UT, January 28–30, 2016.

Hawkins, Kirk A., Scott Riding, and Cas Mudde. 2012. "Measuring Populist Attitudes." *The Committee on Concepts and Methods Working Paper Series No. 55.*

Hawkins, Kirk A., and Cristóbal Rovira Kaltwasser. forthcoming. "The Ideational Approach to Populism." *Latin American Research Review.*

Hetherington, Mark J., and Jonathan D. Weiler. 2009. *Authoritarianism and Polarization in American Politics.* New York: Cambridge University Press.

Hetherington, Mark J., and Elizabeth Suhay. 2011. "Authoritarianism, Threat, and Americans' Support for the War on Terror." *American Journal of Political Science* 55(3): 546–560.

Higgins, Jerry. 1965. "Authoritarianism and Candidate Preference." *Psychological reports* 16(2): 603–604.

Hyman, Herbert H., and Paul B. Sheatsley. 1954. "The Authoritarian Personality': A Methodological Critique." In *Studies in the Scope and Method of "The Authoritarian Personality*, edited by Richard Christie and Marie Jahoda, 50–122. Glencoe, IL: Free Press.

Key, Vladimir. O., Jr. 1955. "A Theory of Critical Elections." *Journal of Politics* 17 (1): 3–18.

Inglehart, Ronald and Pippa. Norris. 2016. "Trump, Brexit, and the Rise of Populism: Economic Have-Nots and Cultural Backlash." *HKS Working Paper No. RWP16-026.*

Kinder, Donald R. 1986. "Presidential Character Revisited." In *Political Cognition: The Nineteenth Annual Carnegie Symposium on Cognition*, edited by Richard. R. Lau and D. O. Sears, 233–255. New Jersey: Erlabum.

MacWilliams, Matthew. 2016. "The Best Predictor of Trump Support Isn't Income, Education, or Age. It's Authoritarianism." *Vox*, February 23, www.vox.com/2016/2/23/11099644/trump-support-authoritarianism.

Mainwaring, Scott, ed. forthcoming. *Party Systems in Latin America: Institutionalization, Decay, and Collapse*. New York: Cambridge University Press.

Merolla, Jennifer, and Elizabeth J. Zechmeister. 2009. *Democracy at Risk: How Terrorist Threats Affect the Public*. Chicago, IL: University of Chicago Press.

Mudde, Cas. 2004. "The Populist Zeitgeist." *Government & Opposition* 39(3): 541–563.

Mudde, Cas. 2015. "The Trump Phenomenon and the European Populist Radical Right." *The Monkey Cage, Washington Post*, August 26, www.washingtonpost.com/blogs/monkey-cage/wp/2015/08/26/the-trump-phenomenon-and-the-european-populist-radical-right/.

Mudde, Cas, and Cristóbal Rovira Kaltwasser. 2015. "Vox Populi or Vox Masculini? Populism and Gender in Northern Europe and South America." *Patterns of Prejudice* 49(1–2): 16–36.

Navia, Patricio D. 2004. "Participación Electoral en Chile, 1988–2001." *Revista de Ciencia Política* 24(1): 81–103.

Norris, Pippa. 2016. "It's not just Trump. Authoritarian Populism Is Rising across the West. Here's why." *The Monkey Cage, Washington Post*, March 11 www.washingtonpost.com/news/monkey-cage/wp/2016/03/11/its-not-just-trump-authoritarian-populism-is-rising-across-the-west-heres-why/.

Pierce, Patrick A. 1993. "Political Sophistication and the Use of Candidate Traits in Candidate Evaluation." *Political Psychology* 14(1): 21–35.

Postel, Charles. 2016. "If Trump and Sanders Are Both Populists, What Does Populist Mean?" *The American Historian*, February http://tah.oah.org/february-2016/if-trump-and-sanders-are-both-populists-what-does-populist-mean/.

Rahn, Wendy and Eric Oliver. 2016. "Trump's Voters Aren't Authoritarians, New Research Says. So What Are They?" Blog. *The Washington Post: Monkey Cage*. March 9. www.washingtonpost.com/news/monkey-cage/wp/2016/03/09/trumps-voters-arent-authoritarians-new-research-says-so-what-are-they/.

Rainey, Carlisle. 2014. "Arguing for a Negligible Effect." *American Journal of Political Science* 58(4): 1083–1091.

Rickert, Edward J. 1998. "Authoritarianism and Economic Threat: Implications for Political Behavior." *Political Psychology* 19(4): 707–720.

Roberts, Kenneth M. 1998. Deepening Democracy?: The Modern Left and Social Movements in Chile and Peru. Palo Alto, CA: Stanford University Press.

Rovira Kaltwasser, Cristóbal. 2015. "La ceguera de la elite chilena." *El País*, January 30, 2015.

Rovira Kaltwasser, Cristóbal, and Kirk A Hawkins. 2016. "Chile ¿un país inmune al populismo?" *Qué Pasa*, September, www.quepasa.cl/articulo/politica/2016/09/chile-un-pais-inmune-al-populismo.shtml/.

Stenner, Karen. 2005. *The Authoritarian Dynamic*. New York: Cambridge University Press.

Stenner, Karen. 2009. "Three Kinds of 'Conservatism'." *Psychological Inquiry* 20(2–3): 142–159.

Stubager, Rune. 2013. "The Changing Basis of Party Competition: Education, Authoritarian–Libertarian Values and Voting." *Government & Opposition* 48(3): 372–397.

Taub, Amanda. 2016. "The Rise of American Authoritarianism." *Vox*, March 1, www.vox.com/2016/3/1/11127424/trump-authoritarianism.

Tomz, Michael, Jason Whittenberg, and Gary King. 2003. "Clarify: Software for Interpreting and Presenting Statistical Results." American Statistical Association.

Van Hiel, Alain, Bart Duriez, and Malgorzata Kossowska. 2006. "The Presence of Left-wing Authoritarianism in Western Europe and its Relationship with Conservative Ideology." *Political Psychology* 27(5): 769–793.

Yglesias, Matthew. 2015. "If You want to Understand Donald Trump, Look to the Success of the European Far-Right." *Vox*, August 25 www.vox.com/2015/8/25/9203405/trump-european-far-right.

Appendix

Table 17.A1 Balance table for randomization between non-populist and populist conditions

	Non populist	*Populist*	*Test*
Woman	155	155	$\chi^2(1) = 0.002$
Man	147	148	$p = 0.967$
Age	39.41	38.46	Diff: 0.95; $t = 0.860$ H_a: diff > 0, $p = 0.195$
Education	2.87	2.79	Diff: 0.08; $t = 0.811$ H_a: diff > 0, $p = 0.209$
Number of children	1.41	1.28	Diff: 0.13; $t = 1.084$ H_a: diff > 0, $p = 0.139$
I Región de Tarapacá	6	5	$\chi^2(14) = 17.601$
II Región de Antofagasta	9	9	$p = 0.226$
III Región de Atacama	5	3	
IV Región de Coquimbo	15	10	
V Región de Valparaíso	36	27	
VI Región de O'Higgins	14	19	
VII Región del Maule	21	13	
VIII Región del Bío Bío	36	38	
IX Región de La Araucanía	14	21	
X Región de los Lagos	10	20	
XI Región de Aysén	1	4	
XII Región de Maganalles y la Antártica Chilena	3	3	
XIII Región Metropolitana	122	121	
XIV Región Los Ríos	4	9	
XV Región Aria y Parinacota	6	1	
Mining Regions: I–VI; XIII	302	303	Diff: 0.05; $t = 1.174$ H_a: diff > 0, $p = 0.120$
Miranda vote intention	2.75	2.79	Diff: –0.04; $t = -0.243$ H_a: diff < 0, $p = 0.404$
Miranda feeling thermometer	3.16	3.20	Diff: –0.04; $t = -0.273$ H_a: diff < 0, $p = 0.393$

(continued)

Table 17.A1 (continued)

	Non populist	*Populist*	*Test*
Miranda leadership evaluation	4.41	4.56	Diff: –0.15; t = –1.015 H_a: diff < 0, p = 0.155
New ideas better than old ideas	4.58	4.64	Diff: –0.05; t = –0.421 H_a: diff < 0, p = 0.337
Individuals not government responsible for assuring a living	3.59	3.54	Diff: 0.05; t = 0.323 H_a: diff > 0, p = 0.374
Need inequality to incentivize individual effort	2.39	2.45	Diff: –0.06; t = –0.437 H_a: diff < 0, p = 0.331
Others are trustworthy	5.54	5.49	Diff: 0.04; t = 0.401 H_a: diff > 0, p = 0.344
Others are fair	5.24	5.13	Diff: 0.11; t = 0.830 H_a: diff > 0, p = 0.203
Others are helpful			Diff: –0.11; t = –0.751 H_a: diff < 0, p = 0.227
Reciprocate a favor	6.00	6.08	Diff: –0.07; t = –0.650 H_a: diff < 0, p = 0.258
Reciprocate a bad turn	1.97	2.08	Diff: –0.11; t = –1.017 H_a: diff < 0, p = 0.155
Reciprocate a difficult position	2.22	2.24	Diff: –0.02; t = –0.193 H_a: diff < 0, p = 0.424
Reciprocate kindness	6.50	6.52	Diff: –0.03; t = –0.415 H_a: diff < 0, p = 0.339
Reciprocate an insult	2.79	2.67	Diff: 0.12; t = 0.836 H_a: diff > 0, p = 0.202
Reciprocate help	5.81	5.99	Diff: –0.17; t = –1.791 H_a: diff < 0, p = 0.037 H_a: diff = 0, p = 0.074

Transcripts of the videos in Spanish

Non-populist message frame

Es súper simple resolver esto. Mire yo tengo aquí una herramienta que traje para demostrar este sistema desechable. Este sistema desechable, es plástico, desechable, se rompe. Esto es contaminante. Esto es lo que nosotros necesitamos. Esto es nuestro. Recuperando el cobre vamos a tener educación gratuita, vivienda, salud y todos los derechos que han sido privatizados. Sólo con esto. Y esto hoy en día lo están vendiendo. Tenemos que comprar, más encima, esta cañería en el extranjero. Es simple lo que nosotros estamos planteando. Recuperar los recursos estratégicos es clave. Y no solamente es lo económico.

Necesitamos recuperar los medios de comunicación para educar a nuestro pueblo. Hoy en día nuestro pueblo está desinformado y por eso es que tenemos la realidad de las regiones, las regiones empobrecidas. Mira Calama, yo acabo de viajar a Calama, donde se saca el sueldo de Chile, una de las regiones más empobrecidas, el agua contaminada hace 40 años con arsénico.

Populist message frame

Quiero dirigirme a mi pueblo: Si Dios nos dejó o nos donó la tierra, la cordillera, los campos, los peces y las frutas, los ríos ¿Quién les dio autorización a cinco familias para que hicieran y deshicieran con nuestro derecho? ¿Quién les dio permiso para dejar a mis nietos no nacidos sin comida? Somos nosotros los que trabajamos. Somos nosotras las que les hacemos el aseo. Somos nosotros los que estamos en la minera. Somos nosotros los que trabajamos por este país. ¿Hasta cuándo nos pisotean? Por primera vez en Chile nos hemos levantado desde abajo, desde todas sus políticas públicas sin sentido común. Por primera vez, una candidatura popular del pueblo pobre, de los nunca, de los nadie, de los sin tierra, de los sin casa, de los sin diente, de mis vecinas que hacen aseo, de los miles de chilenos que estamos pisoteados. Y ¿ustedes creen que yo les voy a creer hoy día que van a cambiar la vida mía? Si no lo han hecho por historia.

Power Analysis

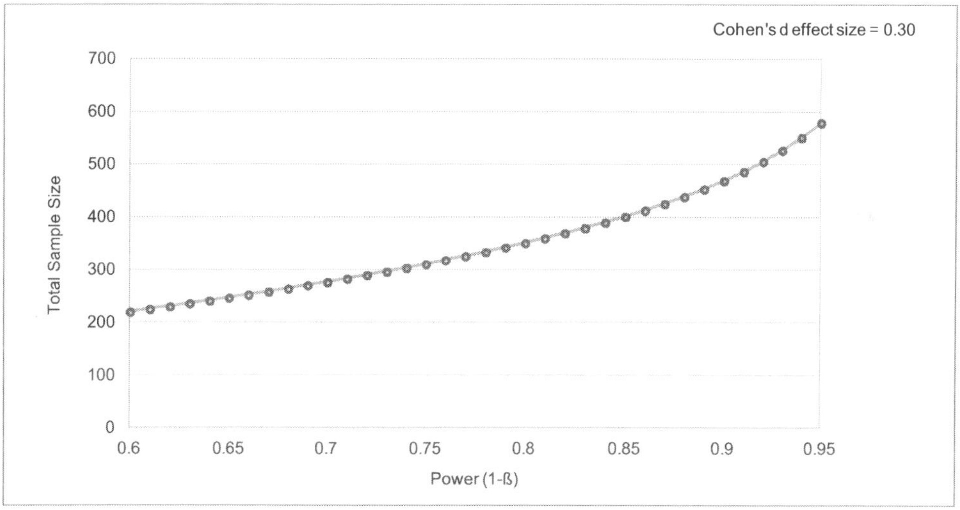

Figure 17.A1 Power analysis: ratio of sample size to power by effect size

Note: The graph shows the sample sizes required to acquire different levels of power by the expected size effect. The test used is a difference of means (t-test) on two independent samples under a two-tailed significance text.

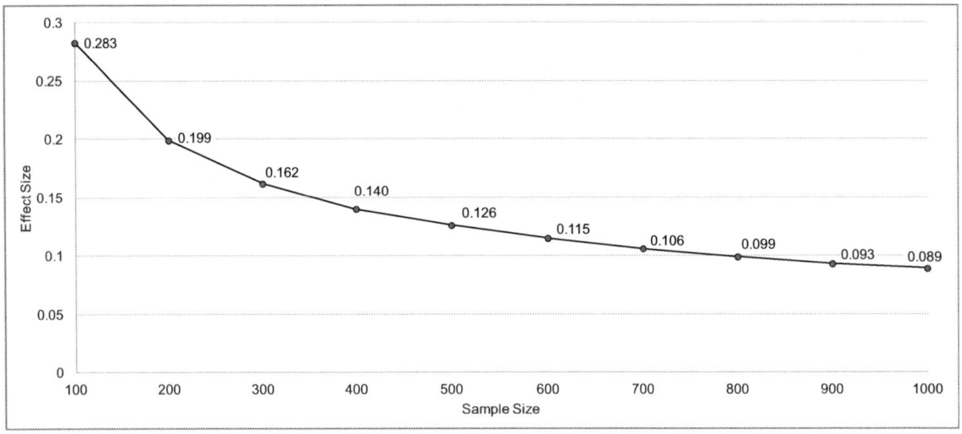

Figure 17.A2 Power analysis: ratio of sample size to effect size by power

Note: Graph shows the smallest effect that yields a statistically significant result of an interaction term for different sample sizes at a power level of 0.8. The parameters used are:$\alpha = 0.05$, $1 - ß = 0.8$, $Nc = 2$; $Nr = 5$ $\sigma_e^2 = 0.35$

Conclusion

Ryan E. Carlin, Kirk A. Hawkins, Levente Littvay, Jennifer McCoy, and Cristóbal Rovira Kaltwasser

This book is not the first attempt to explain the causes of populism, nor will it be the last. But unlike previous attempts, our approach is broadly collaborative in the best sense of the word. Contributors hail from three continents and over a dozen countries; the theoretical framework that they invoke combines insights from work in political science, psychology, communication, and political sociology; and their methods highlight numerous approaches in the social scientist's toolkit. We believe this eclecticism allows us to move beyond the limitations of previous studies and make the conceptual, theoretical, and methodological advances around which a systematic comparative research program can emerge.

At the core of this research program is a clear conceptualization of populism and a theoretical framework built around the ideational definition. Although previous works laid the foundation for this concept and theory, the Introduction presents a definitive statement on what ideational populism is, and is not, and why voters find it so attractive. Subsequent chapters measure populist ideas and test some of the ideational theory's implications. The book's contribution should not be estimated by any single result or a cherry-picked selection of results. Rather, it should be judged by the convergence of the diverse bits of evidence brought to bear on its descriptive and causal inferences, as well as the breadth of contexts from which they are drawn. Let us review these in turn.

Contributions to this book measure populist ideas at several units of analysis and with multiple techniques. Chapters by Hawkins and Silva, March, and Grbeša and Šalaj score the text of campaign speeches, party manifestos, and/or news interviews, each using different methodological approaches. Wiesehomeier asks experts to rate parties and leaders on dimensions of ideational populism. Andreadis and Ruth-Lovell extract populist attitudes from surveys of parliamentary elites themselves. And chapters by van Hauwaert, Schimpf, and Acevedo, and by Castanho Silva et al. share the goal of assessing the validity of mass populist attitude measurements.

Likewise, the hypotheses derived from the ideational theory of populism are tested with case study, large- and small-n observational, longitudinal, and experimental research designs. Within these broad design families, the contributors adopt a wide range of methodological techniques to test their hypotheses. These include process tracing (Betz; Llamazares and Gómez-Reino; Abi-Hassan; Rahn), qualitative comparative analysis (Castanho Silva), in-depth interviews (Abts, Kochuyt, and van Kessel,), cross-country survey data analysis (Singer et al.), congruence analysis (Bornschier), framing experiments (Aguilar and Carlin), and behavioral experiments (Busby et al.). Results appear robust to these types of research design.

Finally, both the descriptive and causal analyses are conducted across multiple subtypes of populism and contexts. Each of the techniques used to measure populism in Part I is applied to parties and voters of varying ideological stripes, and while some (expert surveys) are implemented only in Latin America, all of the others are applied to parties and citizens in the Americas and Europe. In Part 2, the case studies include parties of the left (Spain) and right (Belgium and the US), and developed democracies as well as less-developed ones. This same diversity characterizes the comparative analyses by Castanho Silva, Andreadis et al., Bornschier, and Betz. Only the experiments are limited in their geographical and ideological scope.

The convergence of these diverse research designs lends validity to the conceptual and theoretical framework of the ideational approach. These findings cannot be easily dismissed as artifacts of a particular method, nor can they be explained away as idiosyncratic to a specific case, region, or time period. Cross-regional and over-time analysis in several chapters suggest the inferences drawn from the ideational approach are generalizable. Hence the research program that this book promotes is already on a strong footing.

However, our main reason for presenting the ideational approach in this volume is not to bring it to closure, but to provide a path for future scholarship. A strong research program suggests new observable implications and gives instructions and examples of how these can be tested. Along the way, it encounters anomalies that have to be resolved. And the tentative answers it provides have policy implications that need to be clearly rendered. The task of this Conclusion is to lay out this path.

Conceptual lessons

By defining populism as a set of ideas that understands politics as a Manichean struggle between a reified will of the people and a conspiring elite, we have advanced a conceptual umbrella capable of analyzing instances and subtypes of populism across time and space. To use the language of Giovanni Sartori, the conceptualization works as a minimal definition that "travels" well to study different realities. Although it is true that the authors of this volume use the notions of "discourse," "(thin-centered) ideology" and "worldview" somewhat interchangeably, all these terms share an understanding of populism as a specific set of ideas. This set has three key components: a) a Manichean and moral cosmology; b) the proclamation of 'the people' as a homogenous and virtuous community; and c) the depiction of 'the elite' as a corrupt and self-serving entity. Many of the contributions in this book (including most of those in Part I) reveal that fully populist expression – spoken, written, or revealed via surveys – requires all three of these components. (Although again, we do not argue that populism is an either-or affair, especially considering texts, individuals, or groups in the aggregate.) Elaborating an anti-establishment stance or speaking in favor of popular sovereignty alone is not enough for something to be considered populist. This is an important lesson, since pundits and academics alike sometimes use the notion of populism without paying enough attention to whether all the elements of a populist set of ideas are present.

What is the relationship between this conceptualization of populism and others? Our impression is that other conceptualizations point out certain elements that should not be definitional; however, this does not mean that other conceptualizations should be forgotten, since they draw attention to issues that scholars of populism can examine. As we have argued elsewhere in more detail (Hawkins and Rovira Kaltwasser 2017a), alternative definitions help us think more broadly about populism's causes and consequences.

First of all, economic conceptualizations of populism emphasize the potential irrationality of democratic citizens. While economists prefer to highlight the impact of this irrationality on macroeconomic policy (e.g., Dornbusch and Edwards 1991), the fact that populism seems to lead citizens to ignore or misperceive the long-term consequences of policy change and institutional reforms is deeply troubling. It calls into question the foundational assumptions of liberal democratic theory, and it calls for more systematic research into the cognition of citizens and politicians who come under the sway of populist rhetoric. In addition, structuralist conceptualizations point out that the rise of populism is usually related to changes in the social fabric: socioeconomic and sociocultural transformations can lead to the formation of segments of the population that do not feel part of the community, which in turn can be easily mobilized by populist actors who will claim that 'the establishment' is not taking into account the ideas and interests of 'the people' (e.g., Oxhorn 1998; Rydgren 2007). In this volume, we have presented a model that specifies these kinds of structural changes and the causal mechanisms by which they operate. Last but not least, political–strategic definitions highlight that the populist set of ideas more often than not is employed with great success by personalist leaders, who thanks to their outsider status, have enough credibility to present themselves as clean actors and the political skills to establish a direct and unmediated link with 'the people' in a larger movement (Levitsky and Loxton 2013; Weyland 2001). While we do not think this type of leadership or organization should be definitional, we do think it is essential for scholars to study the conditions under which different types emerge and see this as one of the frontiers of populism research (Hawkins and Rovira Kaltwasser 2017b).

Theoretical lessons

Causal theorizing – including creating a theoretical framework and providing preliminary tests – is one of the main contributions of this volume. The ideational theory builds from individual-level assumptions to aggregate-level consequences, arguing that populism exists as a set of latent attitudes in the minds of most citizens, and that these attitudes are activated by a combination of context, framing, and specific organizations. Chapters in the second half of this volume provide important tests of each part of this framework, but key aspects remain to be tested.

The role of attitudes

Historically, populism was a concept studied on the level of the elites, such as parties or politicians, and research focused on little more than populism's rhetorical aspects, or a populist communication style. Over the past decade, however, populism has been successfully conceptualized as an attitude, allowing both the continued study of elites through a new lens, as well as a shift in the level of analysis to the masses. Comparative assessment of both mass and elite attitudes with the same tool set, together with new techniques for studying voting behavior, has opened new horizons for understanding populism.

Initial studies of populist attitudes were limited, focusing on single countries using survey inventories that, as highlighted by van Hauwaert et al. in their chapter (Chapter 6), suffered from limitations. In this volume, Castanho Silva et al. (Chapter 7) not only provide a new inventory that overcomes some of these shortcomings but show persuasively that, when measured appropriately, populist attitudes remain common and comparable across a broad sampling of countries. Furthermore, the four-country analysis by Andreadis et al.

(Chapter 10) reaffirms that these attitudes (albeit using the older inventory from Akkerman et al.) are strong predictors of vote choice for populist parties, especially in interaction with traditional ideologies (see also Van Hauwaert and van Kessel 2018).

While these results are encouraging and provide a robust tool for future cross-country research, they raise additional questions. Some of the most policy-relevant ones include where populist attitudes come from and how to mitigate their negative societal consequences (like polarization) without affecting the positive ones (such as increased interest or participation in politics). While some survey research implies that these attitudes are the product of long-term forces of socialization (such as their correlation with education; see Hawkins, Riding, and Mudde 2012), other results (the correlation with age) as well as competing arguments such as those of the Essex school (Laclau 2005) suggest that these attitudes derive from short-term experiences, including the framing used by populist politicians. This question is more than academic. It has implications for how policymakers mitigate the potentially negative impact of populist attitudes through civic education. Answering this question requires additional survey research across countries, but also across time, possibly through long-term panel studies.

The role of context

In order to become activated, populist attitudes require a context of failed democratic representation. Traditional issue positions explain the attractiveness of particular flavors of populism, such as left and right, but the demand for populism itself requires a deeper and more normatively significant failure of representation. This aspect of the ideational argument is one of the most thoroughly tested in this volume, with contributions providing tests at multiple levels of analysis and across different types of populism. Castanho Silva's (Chapter 11) cross-regional, country-level analysis demonstrates that corruption and weak political representation are the only necessary contextual factors for populist electoral success, and that they may be sufficient. In his historical analysis, Betz finds that widespread anger towards democratic politics, or resentment, characterizes all five of his cases. A small-N comparative study by Bornschier shows that recent patterns of populist success correlate with the level of unresponsiveness of the political system, although the gaps in representation are specific to class-based interests. In her case study of the 2016 US presidential election, Rahn shows that measures of a "representation gap" coincide with and seem to explain the emergence of recent populist forces, including Trump. The multi-country vote-choice analysis by Andreadis et al. demonstrates the interaction between populist attitudes and traditional ideologies that define populist subtypes. Finally, the experiment by Busby, Doyle, Hawkins, and Wiesehomeier indicates that evidence of corruption can prompt populist reactions to even the smallest policy failures. Overall, we think it is impressive that the ideational argument about context withstands a wide variety of methods across various regions and historical periods.

However, portions of this argument are not yet fully substantiated. Busby et al.'s experiment provides a strong result at their first site (Northwestern University) but doesn't replicate as well at their second site (Oxford), and it would be reassuring to see it confirmed in the context of more serious political issues such as immigration or mistrust of national/supranational government. While an impressive first, Castanho Silva's country-level findings will need to be confirmed across more countries from additional regions, such as Central and Eastern Europe or the democracies of Africa, and East and Southeast Asia.[1] Finally, while the study of Andreadis et al. highlights the fundamental importance of populist attitudes, it would be reassuring to use this kind of survey-based data to test the impact of context at the individual level. Thus, we might test the *mediating impact* of corruption and weak representation on populist voting. In summary, while we think the overall results of these contextual studies are persuasive, we see potential for additional experimental, survey-based, and comparative research across a more systematic selection of countries and regions.

The role of framing

Beyond the context in which populist attitudes gain traction, this book makes limited strides towards identifying the interpretative lenses that populists foist on the public so that they view a crisis of representation as an elite conspiracy against the people. In our theory we refer to this as "framing." Aguilar and Carlin's chapter (Chapter 17) comes closest to a traditional framing experiment. Their evidence that populist rhetoric activates authoritarian logics that can, in some contexts, support the status quo is suggestive of the insights these tools can reveal. The book does not, however, present evidence either for or against the other theoretically powerful frames that invoke, for example, in-group/out-group discrimination, blame attribution, or emotional triggers. Although some initial work suggests these factors are at play (Hameleers, Bos, and de Vreese 2016; Busby et al. forthcoming), studies of populist communication present additional opportunities through which to build out the ideational framework (c.f. Aalberg et al. 2016). For instance, Rico et al. (2017) show for the case of Spain that anger and not fear is positively associated with support for populist attitudes and the leftist populist party Podemos, while Meléndez and Rovira Kaltwasser (2017) rely on survey data from contemporary Chile to demonstrate that levels of positive and negative partisan identification help explain support for and rejection of populist attitudes.

The role of supply/organization

The ideational theory sees the supply of populists – in terms of various modes of organization – as essential for coordinating the actions of would-be populist supporters. Furthermore, it argues that the choice of organizational mode, and thus electoral success, is connected to available resources and prevailing forms of political representation.

However, other than categorizing some of the movements and parties in individual chapters, none of our contributors test this argument at any level of analysis. For example, although recent scholarship outside this volume shows a strong aggregate-level correlation between charismatic leadership and populist success, at least in Europe (Pappas 2016), there are no experiments or case studies testing whether charismatic or personalistic leadership changes activists' calculations. Likewise, there are few country-level studies demonstrating that the mode of populist organization is connected to country-level factors such as historical patterns of clientelism or a high demand for radical populism (Kenny 2017). Nor are there interview data or surveys showing that individual voters and politicians in these party systems are really aware of or constrained by these patterns. Indeed, there are no experiments that we are aware of demonstrating that individuals even behave strategically, rather than emotionally, once their populist attitudes are activated. As already mentioned, we see this as another important frontier of populism studies.

Ultimately, in order to better understand populism, we need to learn more about the agency of populist voters. This is an important area of study in terms of policy implications, because populist and non-populist politicians will both want to know if would-be supporters are swayed largely by emotion or are open to careful reasoning and persuasion, in other words, where the boundaries of populist rationality lie.

The role of formal institutions and the media

Another area that needs more attention is the role institutions play in fomenting or constraining the emergence and consolidation of populist forces. Traditionally, the study of formal institutions and populism has focused on electoral rules and their capacity to restrict the emergence of populist forces. Particularly in the European context, scholars have argued that high electoral thresholds and first-past-the-post systems prevent the emergence of populist radical right parties (Carter 2005; Golder 2003; Norris 2005; van Kessel 2015). At the same time, other studies show that these types of institutional factors lack the power to impede the rise of populist actors if the demand for populism is especially strong (de la Torre and Ortíz 2016; Hawkins 2016).

While this is an important debate that we reference in our discussion of policy implications, it is also relevant to consider how much institutional variables impact populist actors' room for maneuver once in government (Cristóbal Rovira Kaltwasser and Taggart 2016). For instance, the Latin American experience reveals that once populist leaders control the government, they usually undertake major institutional reforms with controversial legacies and effects on the democratic regime. The last wave of populism in this region is characterized by the emergence of radical leftist leaders who changed the constitution by convoking constituent assemblies; these constitutions often incorporated measures for direct democracy, but were also used as tools to restrict civil liberties, undermine the separation of powers, and create an unlevel playing field in elections (Hawkins and Ruth 2015; Houle and Kenny 2018; Huber and Schimpf 2016a). It is unclear whether domestic and international institutions were able to check any of this illiberal behavior.

The recent rise of Trump in the US is another case in point. Did institutions curb or foster populist rule? As is well known, American democracy is distinguished by strong checks and balances. This means that the president should not be seen as an almighty figure, but as an actor constrained by multiple institutions. Given that not only the Congress but also the judiciary and various governmental agencies limit the president's room for maneuver, it will be important to monitor whether the US institutional setting is strong enough to limit Trump's agenda. If so, one could expect that the Trump administration might be forced to moderate its populist tone in order to reach agreements and generate governability. If not, the US could witness similar erosions of democratic norms and liberal institutions as other cases of populism have suffered.

Another source of constraint that needs closer inspection is the media. In the last few years several studies have examined the relationship between populism and the media (Krämer 2014; Mazzoleni 2008; Mazzoleni, Stewart, and Horsfield 2003; Waisbord 2013). Many of these scholars argue that media outlets play an important role in diffusing populist ideas, because they promote populist messages and give more visibility to populist actors, thereby helping spread a populist Zeitgeist (Rooduijn 2014). However, it is not clear whether tabloid-style coverage is merely a precondition for the diffusion of the populist message or actually plays an independent role; other studies of party manifestos and news media content in Western Europe fail to find evidence for a populist Zeitgeist in the media (Manucci and Weber 2017; Rooduijn, Lange, and van der Brug 2012). To what extent can the ideational framework illuminate this debate? We believe the ideational concept offers the possibility of measuring not only the presence of populist ideas but who the actors are that promote these ideas. This means that the ideational framework can be employed to assess the extent to which media outlets produce populist ideas, as well as whether political actors who rely on the populist set of ideas are prone to develop specific media logics. As Manucci (2017) has recently indicated, the best way to advance this type of empirically oriented research program consists in establishing a dialogue between media studies and the ideational approach.

Methodology

The third main goal of this volume consisted in bolstering the ideational approach in terms of method. Whether we understand "method" as measurement or theory testing, the ideational approach has implications for both. Concerning measurement, it points to the need for techniques that can measure populist ideas at the level of citizens and politicians, ideally in ways that are continuous rather than dichotomous. While endorsing the most common choices of scholars today—textual analysis for politicians, and surveys for citizens—this volume suggests repurposing these techniques to study other levels of analysis: surveys for politicians, for example, or textual analysis for citizens. As regards theory testing, our findings call distinctly for multi- and mixed-method research rather than any one technique. The ideational theory has causal mechanisms reaching up to the systemic and down to the individual levels, and different methods will be suitable for each.

Measuring populism at the elite level

When it comes to measuring populist ideas at the level of political elites—the supply of populists—we reaffirm the utility of textual analysis. In particular, we find the holistic approach developed originally by Hawkins (2009) is still useful for measuring populist ideas across multiple countries, and that it can be applied to party manifestos as well as political speeches. This makes holistic grading a tool for cataloging larger numbers of parties and whole party systems. Importantly, we also find promise in computer assisted text analysis techniques. The allure of automated techniques is obviously great, given their potential to provide large amounts of data with high reliability. Hawkins and Castanho Silva show in their chapter (Chapter 1) that some algorithms provide reasonably accurate, if rougher estimates within narrow genres such as manifestos. More work needs to be done to see if the technique can travel to other textual genres, which will be crucial for rendering not just a reliable but a valid, representative depiction of parties' populist discourse.

In contrast, we are more cautious about using dictionary-based approaches for generating large datasets across countries or time. These tools seem to work best in single-country or small-N studies, where they allow us to analyze discourse more deeply. While we do not directly compare these to holistic grading or the fully automated approaches, semi-automated dictionary analyses are used in the chapters by March (Chapter 2) and Šalaj and Grbeša (Chapter 3). Each study uses the approach to break political discourse down into its components. The results are illuminating, providing persuasive and detailed estimates for parties and candidates, showing for example that notions of a good people (demotism or "thin populism") are relatively common and do not always coincide with anti-establishment talk. However, both analyses require modifying or constructing entirely new dictionaries reflecting not just the unique languages but the contemporary *political* languages of their countries. Even then, some kind of human intervention is needed in both cases not only to prepare texts, but to double-check ambiguous or misleading codes. This is similar to the challenges encountered by others who have used dictionary-based approaches in other countries (Bonikowski and Gidron 2016; Rooduijn and Pauwels 2011). Thus, we feel that analytical approaches have an important place, even though they may be less suited for cross-country studies.

Measuring populism at the citizen level

When survey based measures of populist attitudes were first introduced (Hawkins, Riding, and Mudde 2012), the field of populism studies was already miles ahead of the discipline. Political scientists are often content to write a single survey question that they believe measures their construct of interest. Measures of populist attitudes were always multi-item, where reliability and validity were further assessed by factor analytic approaches, putting it well ahead of the disciplinary standards. Fortunately, whenever new measures were introduced, they followed the lead of the pioneers in this area. Van Hauwaert et al. in this volume (Chapter 6) provide an extensive overview of the various measures proposed. The most popular of these measures by Akkerman et al. (2014) turns out to perform quite well, which was good news for our volume where multiple studies rely on these items. But work in scientific refinement is never done, and to achieve truly comparable and objective measures we need to move further and test measurement invariance. It will never be possible to develop a survey measure that works everywhere the same way (or test a measure everywhere across both time and space), but through broad sampling from multiple regions and multiple continents with both left, right wing, and even absent populist forces, and by following cutting edge approaches from psychometrics of measurement invariance, Castanho Silva et al. provide a standard of comparative attitudinal research largely unseen in political science to date. Armed with broadly comparable attitudinal measures, we can compare countries on the level (and variation) in populist attitudes, and we can develop truly comparative studies assessing both the causes and consequences of populist attitudes. While the ability of these measures to travel across mass and elite levels of analyses remains untested, the new measures certainly help us move away from proxies of populism that are little more than regionally acceptable measures of extreme right wing policies or ideologies, including anti-immigration sentiments, racial prejudice, social dominance orientation, or authoritarianism. As the ideational approach presented in this book establishes, populism is distinct from these concepts that are, unfortunately, still confused and confounded with populism, often for no other gain than a search for a catchy and timely study title.

Repurposing old measures: surveys and social media

Taking an ideational approach means that any technique for measuring ideas can be applied to populism. Thus, we should be looking for ways to repurpose frequently used measures to see if they can be fruitfully applied to other objects of analysis. The clearest examples of this at the elite level come from the chapter by Andreadis and Ruth-Lovell (Chapter 5) and the chapter by Wiesehomeier (Chapter 4). Andreadis and Ruth-Lovell adapt the Akkerman et al. (2014) inventory to elite surveys—specifically, surveys of members of parliament or parliamentary candidates. Such surveys are regularly conducted in certain regions such as Latin America and could be a convenient vehicle for measuring populist attitudes. They offer the advantage not only of identifying attitudes of politicians below the party leader, but of gauging precisely how different attitudes correlate with each other, and of seeing how those attitudes correlate with those of the parties' constituents. Thus, we can examine how populism correlates with traditional political ideologies and issues positions. Andreadis and Ruth-Lovell's own exploration is limited—they look only at the reliability of the inventory—but it reminds us that elite attitudes can differ from those of voters, especially when it comes to attitudes that politicians have about themselves. Not only do we need to change item wording to reflect the politicians' unique position (Andreadis and Ruth-Lovell offer sensible suggestions) but we should anticipate that politicians see themselves more favorably than voters do.

In contrast, Wiesehomeier offers a more complete exploration of her own measures of elite attitudes, based on expert surveys. Although collected using very different instruments from mass and elite surveys, expert surveys offer some of the same possibilities for analysis, such as comparisons of populist attitudes with other ideologies and issue stances. In her analysis of Latin American parties and presidents, Wiesehomeier confirms a strong leftist cast to populism in this region and is able to address the specific issues that qualify these parties and leaders as leftist—mostly economic issues, rather than social ones. She also offers an important critique of other expert survey-based measures (the Chapel Hill Expert Survey) and efforts to aggregate different definitions. She shows that different definitions of populism (ideational, stylistic, political–institutional) do not always go together, and that highly aggregated measures can yield false positives. That said, taking populist elements in isolation (such as antiestablishment rhetoric) can also produce measurement error. The best approach is probably to use disaggregated measures and let the researcher aggregate based on definition.

In terms of mass-level measures, chapters in this volume do not really attempt any serious, quantitative textual analysis. Abi Hassan's chapter on Venezuela comes close with a content analysis of opposition quotes in print media, but technically this is still an elite-level measure. Probably the closest examples are the chapter by Abts, Kochuyt, and van Kessel (Chapter 14), which uses a qualitative analysis of semi-structured interviews of Vlaams Belang supporters; and the chapter by Busby et al. (Chapter 16), which performs a content analysis of open-ended responses by experimental subjects. Both show indirectly that populist discourse is present at the mass level just as it is at the elite level. But further studies are needed to demonstrate this across more countries and for larger, more representative samples.

The main challenge for this type of mass-level study is identifying a comparable source of texts. One obvious possibility is social media. In today's world of big data, where tweets, social media contributions and even social networks can be gathered and analyzed automatically (even real time), the potential for understanding the populist phenomenon seems endless. While our book primarily revolves around the ideational conceptualization of populism and explanation of its causes, many of us are already looking to understand the consequences of populism, an effort that suggests analysis of social media. One such consequence is political polarization. Automated analyses of online political discourse, medial consumption, and social networks of voters show great potential in understanding at least this one impact of populism.

Ethnographic approaches

While we claim the book validates the ideational approach from many levels of analysis and from a multi-method perspective, the coverage is hardly comprehensive. Something that this book does not emphasize is the use of ethnographic techniques. Although these

democratic contestation merely by relying on rational-choice accounts of politicians and voters as scheming, vote- or revenue-maximizing decision-makers. We must also take into account people's normative ideas, including those captured in the populist message. This argument highlights the paradox of populism, which uses a democratic argument to undermine key features of democracy, or at least liberal versions of it. Theoretical studies making these arguments abound (Abts and Rummens 2007; Canovan 1999; Urbinati 1998; Rovira Kaltwasser 2014), but there is very little large-N work testing these causal mechanisms.

A related set of consequences concerns democratic participation. Ideational scholars are among the few to suggest that populism can potentially have beneficial effects on this aspect of democracy (Canovan 1999; Mudde and Rovira Kaltwasser 2012). The argument is that populism reaches out to politically excluded sectors and enhances their representation, not only by dignifying their members and their concerns but by creating institutions that mobilize and facilitate their involvement. These tendencies will be more manifest among left-populists than right-populists. While both sets of populists reach out to sectors that feel unrepresented, left-populists appeal to ethnic minorities and the poor that are typically less likely to have any form of involvement, while right-populists reach out to sectors of formal, blue-collar workers and the middle class that are more likely to have a history of voting or other kinds of civic participation. Thus, increased participation is not simply a result of populism's tendency to raise the stakes of democratic competition and force both sides into the streets (a somewhat more questionable type of democratic participation anyway), but of the other ideas that combine with the populist message.

In contrast, the ideational approach does not see populism having a consistent effect on most other policy areas, especially economic policy. Of course, we argue that populism should not be defined in economic terms. This is not because we want to include pet cases of right-populism in our datasets, but because evidence shows that populist ideas are not limited to any policy position except perhaps a dim view of liberal democratic institutions. In other words, the effects of populism on most policy areas should be conditional, or indirect. For example, in recent work Roberts (2017) argues that left-wing populism is common in Latin America because of the legacy of low labor incorporation across the region, a legacy that leaves workers in the informal sector and makes them more willing to tolerate redistributive policies. We think these kinds of conditionality deserve further analysis. While there are recent empirical studies on the impact of populism on policies besides democratic reform, such as macroeconomic policy and economic outcomes (Houle and Kenny 2018), none of these use fully ideational measures of populism.

At a lower level of analysis, we should consider the impact of populism on the party system or on the attitudes of individual citizens, especially the propensity to polarize. By this we mean the tendency of populism to harden and sharpen the attitudes of politicians and voters in ways that make them not only more ideologically distant, but less willing to cooperate or even coexist. At the level of party systems, the ideational approach treats populism as an additional dimension on which parties begin to compete. Party leaders and their voters neglect differences over other policy issues in order to create and compete through new coalitions or alliances that celebrate their support or rejection of the establishment and their embrace of the populist message. Ideational scholars do not argue that politicians always do this consciously, although some politicians may (see Gómez-Reino and Llamazares in this volume, Chapter 12); populists and anti-populists may simply react to rhetorics that target them and which they reject. The point is that not all programmatic party competition revolves around manifest issue positions, but around discursive positions as well (Rovira Kaltwasser 2017). This argument can be tested with ordinary techniques of spatial analysis, by measuring the populist discourse of electorally relevant parties alongside their traditional ideology or issue positions. But it would also benefit from elite level interviews to determine whether politicians are shifting their competitive focus and reacting to populist discourse consciously.

Among citizens, the question is not so much whether polarization happens and how to measure it, but what aspects of populism do the work. Here the emphasis is largely on framing studies, to see what components of populist rhetoric are responsible for changing citizens' tolerance for opposition or their support for other liberal democratic principles, and whether any of this polarization can be reversed through alternative rhetorics. But here we begin to shift to our final area of concern, namely, what lessons our research can provide to concerned citizens and policy elites.

Policy implications

While one measure of a research program's effectiveness is its ability to generate new testable implications, another is its ability to answer questions with policy relevance. A research program that speaks only to academics is likely to provide powerful answers to small questions – at the very least, a lost opportunity. In our view, the marginal benefits of spelling out the policy implications of research findings nearly always outweigh the costs. Furthermore, we have choices about what aspects of populism to study and which pieces of our theory to test; if we take into account the likely policy implications of the answers, we can design our research with higher value added from the start.

What are the policy implications of our findings? To be clear, our view of populism as a set of ideas is relatively ambivalent about its normative merits with regard to democracy. A populist agenda privileging the views and interests of "the people" can alert mainstream political parties and leaders to their failures to represent new or significant sectors of the population, and it may bring a redistribution of resources to marginalized sectors of the population. It may be a response to an elitist form of politics that denigrates mass preferences and identity, or to a technocratic, consensual form that offers little choice to voters.

Nevertheless, our concern here is to consider what the research can tell us about strategies to mitigate the negative consequences of populism. Most policymakers' concerns derive from the destabilizing and conflictive nature of populist appeals and the solutions they offer that often divide societies, creating or magnifying societal polarization. Populist politics privilege popular sovereignty and demonize the conspiring elite, and thus threaten the protection of minority rights and the accountability mechanisms of checks and balances. The consequences of the polarizing electoral strategy of populist leaders and parties can impede effective governance by undermining the willingness of political actors to negotiate and compromise. Such strategies at a minimum tend to paralyze government decision-making, but in more extreme forms will concentrate power in the hands of the executive and undermine liberal democracy (Mudde and Rovira Kaltwasser 2012; Rovira Kaltwasser 2014; Rovira Kaltwasser and Taggart 2016).

Institutional engineering

For policymakers interested in mitigating populism's negative effects, our first piece of advice is *not to focus on formal institutions as a tool for blocking populists*. The more negative consequences of populist politics for liberal democracy tend to occur when charismatic, personalist leaders can activate populist attitudes *and* mobilize these voters to achieve electoral majorities. As discussed in the Introduction to this volume, this mode of organization is most common in countries with clientelist party systems and deeper crises of governance. In such contexts, voters are more willing to give leaders carte blanche to override the checks and balances of liberal democracy in order to deliver on their promises to address material grievances or economic and security crises. In contrast, where party systems are more programmatic, the populist parties that emerge are more likely to be smaller, niche-based parties with ideological and policy content addressing gaps in the mainstream party offerings.

The options for institutional engineering around electoral rules and party competition to address the supply of populism must be based on these considerations. They are not encouraging for the most high-risk populist contexts. As mentioned already, many studies of populism emphasize electoral rules and how these shape the competitive space of the party system. According to this argument, majoritarian electoral rules (for example, single member districts) discourage the electoral breakthrough of populist parties by setting high vote thresholds for winning seats, while consensual rules lower the barriers to entry. While we are sympathetic to this argument, the ideational approach suggests that electoral rules and spatial dynamics are more important constraints when populist forces are small and when ideologies or issue positions are highly relevant dimensions of competition, as they are in countries with programmatic linkages and well-functioning states. Thus, electoral rules and other formal institutions matter most where the demand for populism is relatively low.

Once the demand for radical populist solutions grows to cover the bulk of the population, as it does in clientelist systems plagued with corruption and weak states, electoral rules and other formal institutions may cease to be constraints (Hawkins 2016; Rovira Kaltwasser and Taggart 2016). Instead, populist leaders tend to use institutional engineering to augment their power base, building on electoral majorities and rewriting constitutions to create over-representation in parliaments and enhancing presidential authority relative to courts and parliaments. Leaders in Turkey, Hungary and Venezuela, for example, each spearheaded constitutional rewrites that included electoral rule changes and enhanced executive authority while weakening independence of the courts (McCoy, Rahman, and Somer 2018). In this way, populist leaders are often able to take advantage of existing democratic procedural rules and then use them to further concentrate power and weaken accountability mechanisms. In this context, institutional fixes may end up doing more harm than good.

Validating populist demands

This brings us back to root causes on the demand side arising from intentional failures of democratic representation. These failures often take the form of widespread and systematic corruption, when political and private elites are perceived to use state resources to benefit their personal or partisan interests at the expense of the public. Policy responses to this source of populist demand thus require addressing the conditions for corruption, usually involving strengthening judiciaries and enforcement and accountability mechanisms, as well as longer-term educational efforts.

A second pattern of failed democratic representation involves political leaders' lack of responsiveness to citizen demands. That is, parties may be acting in what they consider to be responsible ways to address economic or social problems, but these may tend toward technocratic solutions that exclude some sets of voters or miss issues that are important to these voters. Policy responses to this source of populist demand lie in greater transparency and inclusiveness in decision-making.

In poorer countries or post-communist countries, the first pattern of systemic corruption is common in the emergence of populism, whereas the second pattern of lack of responsiveness is prevalent in richer countries, as well as poorer or post-communist ones. *In both contexts, educating party leaders about the link between these failures of democratic representation, and their roles in them, may help them formulate strategies and practices in a proactive way to become more responsive and accountable to voters.*

Not only political parties, but also international development organizations can play a role in addressing the anxieties and resentments that are commonly activated by populist leaders. Many grievances underlying contemporary populism arise from the differential impact of globalization and market economies, which create winners and losers in each society. Commonly identified scapegoats include immigrants, corporate out-sourcing or trade policies that are perceived to steal jobs and lower wages. *Acknowledging the differential impacts and articulating policies to compensate the losers can go a long way to respond to the populist allegation of intentional harm.*

Challenges of polarization

A common outcome of populism is polarization not only at the political level but societally. The divisive framing of polarizing leaders relies on scapegoating and the identification of enemies to rally against. In populism, the division is between the conspiring elite and the virtuous people. The framing attempts to create bonds within the 'in-group,' while creating distance from and antipathy towards the 'out-group.' As the research in this volume demonstrates, a populist leader is not creating such attitudes out of thin air, but activating latent attitudes that are commonly shared across populations. Voters become more receptive to such framing in contexts of failures of democratic representation. But the content of the messaging can vary, depending on the context and the underlying social cleavages. The 'out-group' may be immigrants, the political establishment, a religious group, rich bankers, or foreigners, but they are blamed for the problems of the supporters of the populist leader.

The consequences of the polarizing electoral strategy that populists so artfully use can be quite negative for democratic governance. When the opposition unites in an anti-populist incumbent coalition and follows similar tactics, then a dangerous logic of polarization sets in (McCoy 2017). This logic entails several characteristics. *First, polarization rewards extreme positions and weakens centrist moderates.* The extremists on either side of the divide then label moderates willing to compromise as "traitors colluding with the enemy" or "sell-outs." In this way, the center disappears and radical positions dominate, resulting in political gridlock or even violent conflict.

Second, polarization affects individual perceptions and is hard to reverse once in place. Once a polarized way of thinking seeps in and voters feel deeply divided psychologically and spatially, it's very hard to reverse. The psychological concept of motivated reasoning helps us understand this problem (Flynn, Nyhan, and Reifler 2017; Taber and Lodge 2006). Emotions influence the way we interpret information, especially if we feel threatened. Voters are motivated to eliminate cognitive dissonance by rejecting facts that challenge their worldviews or self-concepts. Populist leaders learn that exploiting supporters' fears and anxieties will win elections – and they encourage that motivated reasoning. As a result, when leaders resort to conspiracy theories to explain the nation's dire problems, their hard-core supporters tend to believe them without question, rather than holding the leaders accountable or demanding effective policy-making to address their country's problems.

Third, opposing and demonizing a personality, rather than constructing an attractive alternative message, rarely succeeds. Opponents to populist leaders often coalesce against the incumbent, and become united in a desire to defeat or remove them. Polarization occurs when opponents form a camp counter to the populist camp. However, this can backfire for several reasons (Rovira Kaltwasser 2017). What unites the opposition is often simply the dislike of the incumbent. This makes it particularly difficult to fashion an alternative message and program that is convincing to supporters of the populist leader, even after they have lost faith in him or her. Demonizing a populist leader also implies discrediting his or her supporters as either villains or dupes. This becomes particularly dangerous when democratic norms themselves are threatened by a populist leader. Opponents may find it difficult to enlist allies and broaden the coalition against the populist leader if they have been purely obstructionist or personalized their opposition from the start (McCoy 2017). Witness the attempted coups against Chávez in Venezuela or Erdogan in Turkey. Opposition leaders tried to demonize these leaders, and factions in the military attempted to remove them from office through coups. That discredited the opponents, and the public rallied around the leaders. When these presidents then used illiberal measures to repress dissent and boost presidential powers – for instance, closing media outlets and removing presidential term limits – the opponents were isolated and divided and couldn't build the coalitions needed to resist (McCoy, Rahman, and Somer 2018).

Can mainstream parties effectively compete against populist parties? Yes, but through crafting strong alternative messages, not imitating the populists. Although the psychological research and that presented in this volume indicate that emotions play a large role in political decision-making, simply mimicking the populist appeal to resentment and anxiety is not a long-term governance strategy. Instead, parties should strive to be responsive to the needs and anxieties of voters and address the issues they are concerned about, while explaining the bases of the policies the political parties are adopting.

Political parties and elected officials should defend the protections of liberal democracy – checks and balances, due process, free speech, minority rights – against the populist temptation to privilege popular sovereignty (majority rule) over such restraints on government power and protections of individual rights. Political parties should also be aware of the opposite Achilles heel – the temptation to resort to technocratic, exclusionary policy-making. As discussed in the Introduction to this volume, this type of decision-making contributes to the perception of out-of-touch elites making decisions that do not necessarily respond to the interests and needs of their constituents. Finally, internal party democracy – that is, transparency and inclusiveness in choosing candidates and positions, can help increase credibility of the party to voters as well.

Transnational and domestic organizations working in conflict resolution, reconciliation and peace-building also have an important role to play. Once divided, societies are not easily reconciled. The research from experiments in political psychology in this volume and more broadly has indicated the role of emotions and framing. *Responses to these problems may include creating spaces in which groups can identify shared interests and identities that surpass their divisions, such as a shared concern about their children's future or their own patriotism.*

Timing also plays an important role. Once a populist party is in power for any length of time, it becomes the establishment, responsible for the decisions it makes and their outcomes. If that party is unable to sustain the policies and satisfy the demands of voters, such as when resources diminish, it will lose popular support. Likewise, if the party has relied on a charismatic leader, it is difficult to sustain its popularity after that leader has passed from the scene.

In the end, democracy is a slow and messy affair, full of compromise and concessions. It comprises a tension between majority rule and the rights of the minority. Unfortunately, incentives in our systems impede our ability to create citizens fully informed about the nature and limits of democracy. Our education systems often fail us, as civics is dropped from curricula or left to the end of the textbook. The media's role in informing voters and holding politicians accountable through investigative reporting has been severely hampered by the profit-driven motive, 24-hour news cycles, and the internet explosion creating echo chambers and opinion passing as "news."

A long-term civic education plan to educate citizens about the nature of collective goods and government's role in providing them, as well as the procedures of democratic politics, can help create more tempered expectations of politics and political leaders. Transparency in politics – fighting corruption, disclosing campaign finance – can help rebuild credibility and confidence in public institutions and politicians that anti-establishment populists love to attack. And depoliticizing the media, while guaranteeing pluralist sources of information, can help combat the conspiracy theories populists rely on to rally mobilize their supporters.

Note

1 Indeed, the study of populism in these other regions is an important frontier for many other aspects of the ideational approach, including survey research and framing studies.

References

Aalberg, Toril, Frank Esser, Carsten Reinemann, Jesper Stromback, and Claes De Vreese, eds. 2016. *Populist Political Communication in Europe*. New York: Routledge.

Abts, Koen, and Stefan Rummens. 2007. "Populism versus Democracy." *Political Studies* 55 (2):405–424.

Aguilar, Rosario, and Ryan E. Carlin. 2017. "Ideational Populism in Chile? A Case Study." *Swiss Political Science Review* 23 (4):404–422.

Akkerman, Agnes, Cas Mudde, and Andrej Zaslove. 2014. 'How Populist Are the People? Measuring Populist Attitudes in Voters'. *Comparative Political Studies* 47 (9):1324–1353.

Bonikowski, Bart, and Noam Gidron. 2016. "The Populist Style in American Politics: Presidential Campaign Discourse, 1952–1996." *Social Forces* 94 (4):1593–1621.

Bos, Linda, Wouter van der Brug, and Claes H. de Vreese. 2013. "An Experimental Test of the Impact of Style and Rhetoric on the Perception of Right-wing Populist and Mainstream Party Leaders." *Acta Politica* 48 (2):192–208.

Busby, Ethan C., Kirk A. Hawkins, and Joshua Gubler. Forthcoming. "Framing and Blame Attribution in Populist Rhetoric." *Journal of Politics*.

Canovan, Margaret. 1999. "Trust the People! Populism and the Two Faces of Democracy." *Political Studies* 47 (1):2–16.

Carter, Elisabeth. 2005. *The Extreme Right in Western Europe*. Manchester: Manchester University Press.

Cramer, Katherine J. 2016. *The Politics of Resentment: Rural Consciousness in Wisconsin and the Rise of Scott Walker*. Chicago, IL: University of Chicago Press.

de la Torre, Carlos, and Ortíz Lemos, Andrés. 2016. 'Populist Polarization and the Slow Death of Democracy in Ecuador'. *Democratization* 23 (2):221–241.

Dornbusch, Rudiger, and Sebastian Edwards, eds. 1991. *The Macroeconomics of Populism in Latin America.* Chicago, IL: University of Chicago Press.

Fernandes, Sujatha. 2010. *Who Can Stop the Drums?: Urban Social Movements in Chávez's Venezuela.* Durham, NC: Duke University Press.

Flynn, D. J., Brendan Nyhan, and Jason Reifler. 2017. "The Nature and Origins of Misperceptions: Understanding False and Unsupported Beliefs about Politics." *Political Psychology* 38 (S1):127–150.

Golder, Matt. 2003. "Explaining Variation in the Success of Extreme Right Parties in Western Europe." *Comparative Political Studies* 36 (4):432–466.

Hameleers, Michael, Linda Bos, and Claes H. de Vreese. 2016. "'They Did It' The Effects of Emotionalized Blame Attribution in Populist Communication." *Communication Research* 44 (6):870–900.

Hawkins, Kirk A. 2009. "Is Chávez Populist? Measuring Populist Discourse in Comparative Perspective." *Comparative Political Studies* 42 (8):1040–1067.

Hawkins, Kirk A. 2016. "Responding to Radical Populism: Chavismo in Venezuela." *Democratization* 23 (2):242–262.

Hawkins, Kirk A., Scott Riding, and Cas Mudde. 2012. "Measuring Populist Attitudes." *Working Paper Series on Political Concepts, ECPR Committee on Concepts and Methods.*

Hawkins, Kirk A., and Saskia Ruth. 2015. "The Impact of Populism on Liberal Democracy." Conference paper at "8o Congreso de La Asociación Latinoamericana de Ciencia Política." Lima, Peru.

Hawkins, Kirk A., and Cristóbal Rovira Kaltwasser. 2017a. "The Ideational Approach to Populism." *Latin American Research Review* 52 (3):513–528.

———. 2017b. "What the (Ideational) Study of Populism Can Teach Us, and What It Can't." *Swiss Political Science Review* 23 (4):526–542.

Houle, Christian, and Paul Kenny. 2018. "The Political and Economic Consequences of Populist Rule in Latin America." *Government and Opposition* 53 (2):256–287.

Huber, Robert A., and Christian H. Schimpf 2016a. "Friend or Foe? Testing the Influence of Populism on Democratic Quality in Latin America." *Political Studies* 64 (4):872–889.

———. 2016b. "A Drunken Guest in Europe? The Influence of Populist Radical Right Parties on Democratic Quality." *Zeitschrift Für Vergleichende Politikwissenschaft*, July, 1–27. https://doi.org/10.1007/s12286-016-0302-0.

Kenny, Paul. 2017. *Populism and Patronage: Why Populists Win Elections in India, Asia, and Beyond.* Oxford: Oxford University Press.

Kessel, Stijn van. 2015. *Populist Parties in Europe: Agents of Discontent?* New York: Palgrave Macmillan.

Krämer, Benjamin. 2014. "Media Populism: A Conceptual Clarification and Some Theses on Its Effects." *Communication Theory* 24 (1):42–60.

Laclau, Ernesto. 2005. *On Populist Reason.* London: Verso Books.

Levitsky, Steven, and James Loxton. 2013. "Populism and Competitive Authoritarianism in the Andes." *Democratization* 20 (1):107–136.

Manucci, Luca. 2017. "Populism and the Media." In *The Oxford Handbook of Populism*, edited by Cristobal Rovira Kaltwasser, Paul A. Taggart, Paulina Ochoa Espejo, and Pierre Ostiguy, 467–88. Oxford: Oxford University Press.

Manucci, Luca, and Edward Weber. 2017. "Why the Big Picture Matters: Political and Media Populism in Western Europe since the 1970s." *Swiss Political Science Review* 23 (4):313–334.

Mazzoleni, Gianpietro. 2008. "Populism and the Media." In *Twenty-First Century Populism. The Spectre of Western European Democracy*, edited by Daniele Albertazzi and Duncan McDonnell, 49–64. Basingstoke: Palgrave Macmillan.

Mazzoleni, Gianpietro, Julianne Stewart, and Bruce Horsfield. 2003. *The Media and Neo-Populism: A Contemporary Comparative Analysis.* Westport, CT: Greenwood Publishing Group.

McCoy, Jennifer. 2017. "Before Going Nuclear, Republicans and Democrats Might Consider These Four Lessons from Polarized Democracies." *Washington Post: Monkey Cage* (blog). April 3, 2017.

McCoy, Jennifer, Tahmina Rahman, and Murat Somer. 2018. "Polarization and the Global Crisis of Democracy: Common Patterns, Dynamics and Pernicious Consequences for Democratic Polities." in Special Issue on Polarization and Democracy: A Janus-faced Relationship with Pernicious Consequences, American Behavioral Scientist 62 (1):16–42.

Meléndez, Carlos, and Cristóbal Rovira Kaltwasser. 2017. "Political Identities: The Missing Link in the Study of Populism." *Party Politics* online first (November). https://doi.org/10.1177/1354068817741287.

Mudde, Cas, and Cristobal Rovira Kaltwasser, eds. 2012. *Populism in Europe and the Americas: Threat or Corrective to Democracy?* Cambridge: Cambridge University Press.

Norris, Pippa. 2005. *Radical Right: Voters and Parties in the Electoral Market.* Cambridge: Cambridge University Press.

Oxhorn, Philip. 1998. "The Social Foundations of Latin America's Recurrent Populism: Problems of Popular Sector Class Formation and Collective Action." *Journal of Historical Sociology* 11 (2): 212–46.

Pappas, Takis S. 2016. "Are Populist Leaders 'Charismatic'? The Evidence from Europe." *Constellations* 23 (3):378–90.

Rico, Guillem, Marc Guinjoan, and Eva Anduiza. 2017. "The Emotional Underpinnings of Populism: How Anger and Fear Affect Populist Attitudes." *Swiss Political Science Review* 23 (4): 444–461.

Roberts, Kenneth M. 2017. "Bipolar Disorders: Varieties of Capitalism and Populist Out-Flanking on the Left and Right." Conference paper at "Global Populisms: A Threat to Democracy?" *Stanford University, CA.* https://fsi.stanford.edu/global-populisms/docs/global-populisms-conference-memos

Rooduijn, Matthijs. 2014. "The Mesmerising Message: The Diffusion of Populism in Public Debates in Western European Media." *Political Studies* 62 (4): 726–744.

Rooduijn, Matthijs, and Teun Pauwels. 2011. "Measuring Populism: Comparing Two Methods of Content Analysis." *West European Politics* 34 (6):1272–1283.

Rooduijn, Matthijs, Sarah L. de Lange, and Wouter van der Brug. 2012. "A Populist Zeitgeist? Programmatic Contagion by Populist Parties in Western Europe." *Party Politics*, April.

Rovira Kaltwasser, Cristóbal. 2014. "The Responses of Populism to Dahl's Democratic Dilemmas." *Political Studies* 62 (3):470–487.

———. "Populism and the Question of How to Respond to It." In *The Oxford Handbook of Populism*, edited by Cristobal Rovira Kaltwasser, Paul A. Taggart, Paulina Ochoa Espejo, and Pierre Ostiguy, 489–507. Oxford: Oxford University Press.

Rovira Kaltwasser, Cristóbal, and Paul Taggart. 2016. "Dealing with Populists in Government: A Framework for Analysis." *Democratization* 23 (2):201–220.

Ruth, Saskia Pauline. 2017. "Populism and the Erosion of Horizontal Accountability in Latin America." *Political Studies* online first (September):1–20. https://doi.org/10.1177/0032321717723511.

Rydgren, Jens. 2007. "The Sociology of the Radical Right." *Annual Review of Sociology* 33:241–262.

Taber, Charles S., and Milton Lodge. 2006. "Motivated Skepticism in the Evaluation of Political Beliefs." *American Journal of Political Science* 50 (3):755–769.

Urbinati, Nadia. 1998. "Democracy and Populism." *Constellations* 5 (1):110–24.

Van Hauwaert, Steven, and Stijn van Kessel. 2018. "Beyond Protest and Discontent: A Cross-National Analysis of the Effect of Populist Attitudes and Issue Positions on Populist Party Support." *European Journal of Political Research* 57 (1):68–92.

Waisbord, Silvio. 2013. "Democracy, Journalism, and Latin American Populism." *Journalism* 14 (4): 504–21.

Weyland, Kurt. 2001. "Clarifying a Contested Concept: Populism in the Study of Latin American Politics." *Comparative Politics* 34 (1):1–22.

Index